398.20942
B854d
v.4

D0871315

A DICTIONARY OF
BRITISH FOLK-TALES

A DICTIONARY OF
BRITISH
FOLK=TALES

IN THE
ENGLISH LANGUAGE

INCORPORATING THE
F. J. NORTON COLLECTION

———————

KATHARINE M. BRIGGS

———————

PART B
FOLK LEGENDS
VOLUME 2

LONDON
ROUTLEDGE & KEGAN PAUL
1971

First published 1971
by Routledge & Kegan Paul Ltd
Broadway House, 68–74 Carter Lane
London, E.C. 4
Printed in Great Britain
at the University Printing House, Cambridge
(Brooke Crutchley, University Printer)
© K. M. Briggs 1971
No part of this book may be reproduced
in any form without permission from
the publisher, except for the quotation
of brief passages in criticism
ISBN 0 7100 6364 4

CONTENTS
VOLUME 2

21266

VIII HISTORICAL TRADITIONS

HISTORICAL TRADITIONS

Historical traditions are of various types, and so numerous that only representative specimens of them can be given.

I. The Migratory Legend, Type ML 8000 (Legends of wars and warriors), is one great subdivision of historical traditions. In the English-speaking part of these islands the wars that are most constantly remembered are, the Roman Conquest, the Danish invasions, the Norman Conquest, the wars between England and Scotland and the Border affrays that followed them, the great Civil War, the Monmouth Rebellion, and the 'Forty-five. The Monmouth Rebellion, because of the horrors that followed it, made a deep and lasting impression in the West Country, as the 'Forty-five did in Scotland. All over the country, as is natural, the great Civil War was most lastingly remembered. The Wars of the Roses, which was a nobles' war, made less impression, but some popular memories of it remain, as of the Peasants' Rising and the Chartist times. In the North, particularly, the suppression of the monasteries made a deep impression.

II. Legends of famous people are allied to these memories of wars, some of them apparently rather erratically chosen. King Alfred is rightly dear to Englishmen, but William Rufus is more remembered than one would expect, and Richard Cœur de Lion, Bonnie Prince Charlie, and Cromwell are specially conspicuous. There are some outstanding men to whom a legend of wizardry was attached, some of them men of learning, such as Roger Bacon, but others, men of outstanding brilliance, such as Sir Francis Drake.

III. Allied to the local traditions are those memories of comparatively obscure happenings which illustrate social history and show how actual events are reshaped in popular thought. These often have supernatural beliefs attached to them. With these, too, we have links with the past—long-lived individuals who have bridged generations, and fascinating instances of folk-memory, such as the tradition of Chaucer at Ewelme.

IV. A fourth type of historical tradition is that tale—often an international tale-type—which is told, circumstantially and with full belief, as having happened at various places and to various people. It is often difficult to decide whether the event has ever actually occurred, and, if so, to whom. Sometimes it is possible to find some circumstance which has given rise to the tale, sometimes again, it seems probable that it is in the main true, though details may have been attached to it to bring it in line with the archetypal tale. Examples of this kind are Tale-type 990 (The apparently dead revives), and the Oxford Student, often loosely connected with the Robber Bridegroom tales, some of which are to be found among the Novelle.

The line dividing Local Legends from Historical Traditions is a narrow one, and the distinction between them is not easy to make. If a particular tale is not to be found in one division it may well turn up in another. Many favourites may, however, be searched for in vain.

BECKET'S PARENTS [summary]

Hartland, *English Fairy and Folk-Tales*, p. 60.

It is said that Gilbert, the father of the great Thomas Becket, as a young man had gone with the Crusaders to the Holy Land, where he became the prisoner of a Saracen lord, who confined him within his castle. But the Saracen's daughter, a fair and gentle girl, fell in love with the young prisoner, and pitied him. At last she rescued him, and helped him to escape, and in gratitude he promised to return and marry her, as soon as he had a settled home in his own land to offer her.

But after years had passed, and no word of him ever came, the faithful girl determined to follow her lover to England. The only words of English she knew were "Gilbert" and "Cheapside", which was the part of London where he lived. Yet she accomplished her journey, and her lover was found to be ready to marry her when she had first been baptized into the Christian faith. Six bishops came to their wedding in St Paul's Cathedral, and in due time their son was born. His devotion to his Church in later life was a fitting reflection of his mother's in seeking out her lover and winning him to fulfil his promise.

This is a rationalized form of Type 313.
MOTIFS: R.162 [*Rescue by captor's daughter*]; T.91.6.4.1 [*Sultan's daughter in love with captured knight*]; H.1385.5 [*Quest for vanished lover*].
¶ Ballads founded on this legend are "Young Bekie", which introduces a supernatural element, and "Lord Bateman", which is nearer to the story, though the name Bekie is nearer to Becket.

THE BISHOP'S MOTHER

Denham Tracts, I, p. 47.
"Ye're like the Bishop's mother, ye're nivver content, nowther full nor fasting."

Upon the elevation of Robert de Insula to the See of Durham, A.D. MCCLXXIV, he gave to his aged mother, who was still living a life of poverty and privation in her island home of Lindisfarne, now Holy Island, what he conceived an ample provision and honourable establishment. He surrounded her with menservants and maidservants, suitable to her income. But the poor old widow, instead of being elated with at least her own good fortune, became so much the more wretched and unhappy in proportion as the number of her household servants increased and her means enlarged. The Bishop shortly afterwards went to pay his parent a visit at the place of his nativity; when, to his great grief, he found the ancient lady, his mother, in not only a very sorrowful mood, but also in a very ill-humour to boot. He asked, "And how fares my sweite mother?" "Never worse!" quoth she. "And what ails thee or troubles thee? Hast thou not men and women and attendants sufficient?" "Yea," quoth she, "and more than enow. I say to one 'go,' and he runs; to another, 'Come hither, fellow,' and the varlet falls down on his knees; and in short all things go on so abominably smooth that my heart is bursting within me for something to spite me, and pick a quarrel withal." This unhappiness still increasing, she ere long begged to be restored to her solitary life with a moderate competency.

This is all consistent with reason and daily experience. Her habits had too long been formed, and she was too far advanced in years, to lay them aside and begin to ape the manners of a gentlewoman.

MOTIF: J.1085.1 [*The happy friar becomes unhappier as he receives ever more and more money: gets rid of money and is as happy as before*].

¶ The song of King Gama in Gilbert's *Princess Ida*, "Oh, don't the days seem lank and long, When all goes right and nothing goes wrong..." might have been sung by this old lady.

THE BLACK DOUGLAS

H. Bett, *English Myths and Traditions*, p. 102.

The Black Douglas died in 1330. He was Sir James Douglas, the best lieutenant Bruce had in his long struggle with the English for the independence of Scotland....

Sir Walter Scott tells in the *Tales of a Grandfather*...that Roxburgh Castle was held by the English, and the Scots, led by the Black Douglas, determined to make an attempt to capture it, on the night of Shrovetide, when the men of the English garrison were carousing. The wife of one of the English officers was sitting on the battlements, nursing her baby, and she saw in the gloaming a number of black objects approaching the castle. She called the attention of one of the sentinels to this, but he said it was only the cattle of some neighbouring farmer, who had neglected to fold his bullocks in the farmyard, and, said the sentry, "If the Douglas come across them before morning, he is likely to rue his negligence." The black objects were Douglas's men, who had put black cloaks over their armour, and finally had crept near enough to the castle to set up scaling ladders. The Englishwoman, knowing nothing of this, of course, sat on the wall and began to sing to her baby. The name of Douglas had become so terrible to the English that the women used to frighten their children with it, and the soldier's wife was singing to her child:

> "Hush ye, hush ye, little pet ye.
> Hush ye, hush ye, do not fret ye.
> The Black Douglas shall not get ye!"

"You are not so sure of that!" said a voice beside her, and at the same moment a heavy hand in a steel gauntlet was laid on her shoulder. A tall, swarthy man was standing close to her, the Black Douglas himself! It is pleasant to read that Douglas protected the woman and her child.

TYPE ML.8000.

¶ No appropriate motif.

THE BLIND BEGGAR OF BETHNAL GREEN

W. Carew Hazlitt, *National Tales and Legends*, p. 395.

I

In former days when the rose of England eclipsed the lilies of France, and true English valour made that nation bow to us, among other brave gallants that went over to try their fortune was one Montfort, a person well descended, and who was not to be turned from his purpose either by the entreaties of friends or the tears of a kind and beautiful wife; so naturally was he inclined to war and so greedy of fame.

So, taking his lady, who would by no means stay behind, and who accompanied him in man's attire, he, with many hundreds more, crossed to Calais, and engaged in all the battles and skirmishes that arose between the French and English, and was more than once saved from capture by the courage of his wife, till it chanced in a great fight that Montfort fell, and was left for dead among the slain.

But his wife, since he returned not in the evening to their home, sought him out on the field of battle, and there found him by the aid of the moon's light almost at the last gasp. Whom this noble lady raised gently up, and bore to a shepherd's cottage, where she dressed his wounds, and by administering cordials, and by carefully tending him, she brought him back to life, to his great amazement and her unspeakable joy.

Unhappily, through a blow which he had received, his eyesight was lost, and he was condemned to endure blindness during the whole remainder of his days. With such money as she had left, however, his wife took him back to England, where, after a perilous voyage, they arrived, and settled at Bethnal Green, which is beside London.

While Montfort was abroad in the wars of France his parents died, and his kindred had taken and wasted much of his patrimony; and because they deemed, as indeed they hoped, him dead, they looked coldly and shrewdly upon him, when he sought alms at their hands. Whereupon Montfort, because he was blind, and could follow no craft, resolved to live by begging of charitable people, while his goodwife plied her spinning-wheel; and he awakened in the breasts of many well-disposed passengers a lively interest in the strange and stirring scenes that he had witnessed in France, and gat much money thereby. Yet none wist who he was, nor whence descended; and he was commonly called " The Blind Beggar of Bethnal Green ".

II

This Montfort, in his rambles, shortly contracted acquaintance with others who pursued a like industry, and one day he came home, seeking his way with his staff, as he was wont, and told his wife that he had been bidden as a guest to a certain house in White-chapel, which was a beggars' hospital, or home; and when he went there, accompanied by the faithful partner of all his joys and sorrows, they were something at first abashed, for that all those present wore such gay clothes, and made so merry. He, however, that of all the rest had specially bidden them stood forward, and made them both welcome, and prayed them to share their good cheer, which they were accustomed to make on that their yearly meeting; and at their departure they chose Montfort to be one of them, and presented him with a dog and a bell, which he found ever after, so long as he exercised that calling, very serviceable to him in his travels.

His success in the begging trade waxed so great by reason of the greater curiosity that people entertained about his strange fortune, that he no longer remained content with frequenting Bethnal Green and White-chapel, but went up to London, where he never returned without plenty of coin in his pouch, till he and his good wife exchanged a bed of straw for one of down, and began to live more freely; and in due time it happened that God blessed them with a daughter, whom they baptized under the name of Elizabeth.

Montfort resolved, his employment as a beggar notwithstanding, that their child should be educated in all arts and accomplishments becoming her birth, of which none yet knew the secret; and pretty Bessy, for so she grew to be called, by virtue of her beauty, gradually excelled in music, singing, dancing, and all other matters all the virgins of that neighbourhood, of what degree soever. Whose envy was there-by moved toward her, that they mocked her in the street, and asked what a beggar's child should do with so much learning. But Bessy bore their cruel taunts meekly, and only reproved them by saying that, if they had been born as she was, they would not have wished to be so evil intreated.

7

Albeit Montfort thus caused his daughter to be instructed in all the sciences befitting a woman to know, he did not refuse her suit one day when she fell on her knees and begged his blessing and leave to seek her fortune. Yet she had gone no farther than Romford in Essex, when, frequenting an inn there to get refreshment, the mistress looked kindly upon her, and hearing her history, and that she was of honest parents, persuaded her to abide with her, and take service, telling her that she should be to her as a daughter rather than a servant.

III

This accident brought unlooked for fruit, for a great multitude of persons resorted to that house, where Bessy the beggar's daughter lay, and certain courted her in the way of marriage. To all of whom she pleaded the meanness of her birth and the inequality of fortune. But in especial she was sought by four, to wit, her master's son, a London merchant, a gentleman of fair estate, and a knight; and they offered her rich jewels to prevail upon her, which she refused, praying them of their courtesy to spare the blushes of an innocent maid.

This backwardness still further inflamed their desire to possess and enjoy her: and then she resolved, in order to make trial of their constancy, to enter upon a further discovery of her parentage.

So, when she had on a certain day, asked those four to be present together, to enable her to choose truly which she would have to her spouse, she spake as follows: "My parents, worthy sirs, live at Bethnal Green. My father is a beggar, who is led, for that he is blind, by a dog and a bell; and my mother plies her spinning-wheel. Without their consent cannot I wed no man."

These words struck the inn-keeper's son, the merchant, and the gentleman dumb; and they found cause to excuse themselves, leaving the maid alone with the knight. Who showed her how the others had courted her for her beauty and youth, yet when they heard her low birth eschewed her, and proved untrue; while he, being possessed of a good fortune, loved her for her excellent qualities, and was ready straightway to make her the mistress of all that he owned.

Nevertheless, Bessy refused to accept his hand until such time as he had seen her parents, and obtained their agreement to the marriage. But she acquainted him with her favourable feeling toward him, whom from the beginning she had secretly preferred to all the rest.

IV

It was accordingly agreed that Bessy should ride behind the knight to Bethnal Green; but they had scarcely started on their way when the knight's uncle, with many of his friends, came to the inn to inquire for him, and finding that he had departed with the beggar's daughter, pursued and overtook them hard by Montfort's little house on the green.

The knight's uncle was loth that he should marry below his degree, and some of those that were with him coveted the hand of Bessy for themselves; so that there was a sharp skirmish outside the house, which Montfort hearing, came to learn what it signified.

Then, when he understood that pretty Bessy was without, and that a knight had brought her hither to gain his consent to their marriage, he waxed wroth at the tumult which they raised at his door, and advancing toward the knight's uncle said to him so: "Sir, I cannot see you, for I am blind; but I hear more than is customary among civil people, nor is my daughter so mean that she should be thus accosted and affronted on my own threshold. Wherefore, I pray you, sir, desist from your brawling, or I may seek you out with my staff. I have known the day when a taller fellow than you durst not rouse me. If your kinsmen or you do not hold my child a fit match for you, even let her alone. In beauty and good breeding she is not much wanting: and, as for money, her father is ready to drop angels with any man for her. So mark me, sir."

The old beggar's speech confounded the knight's uncle, who nevertheless sent for his bag of gold, that he had with him by his servant; and when he gat it, out from under rags and old shoes, fetched Montfort two coney-skins crammed with coins. Then they began to drop their money, angel for angel; but the knight's uncle shortly yielded the palm to the beggar, for his store was spent, and Montfort had plenty left.

"I think you have the philosopher's stone, good sir," quoth the other, "or keep a familiar to bring you treasure from the Golden Mountains. But I withdraw my objection to the marriage of my nephew, and the sooner they go to church, the better."

The knight's uncle was in truth afeard lest the knowledge of the beggar's riches should rob his kinsman of so great a prize, and the other suitors were mad enough to miss Bessy, as soon as they understood that she was to be wedded to the knight.

The old beggar spared no cost to make the ceremony sumptuous and becoming the dignity of the husband of his pretty Bessy; and a rich feast was appointed with music and dancing, and all kinds of merriment; and the bride was dressed in the choicest stuffs, and wore the most splendid jewels that could be bought against gold.

At the banquet, the guests drank to the health of the knight and his lady; and while they were all assembled there, and merry over their cups, the old beggar rose from his seat, and craved the attention of as many as were present to what he had to tell them. Whereupon, amid a deep silence, he described to them his illustrious descent from that Simon de Montfort who had been one of the most powerful barons in England, his own exploits in the wars of France, his wonderful rescue from death on the field of battle, and his resort, when he came back to his own country, to a beggar's life at Bethnal Green.

When he sat down, after he had recounted these things, the company loudly applauded all that had fallen from him; and the knight and his friends were overjoyed to find that Bessy, as she had Simon de Montfort to her grandsire, not only surpassed her husband in fortune, but at least equalled him in birth.

MOTIFS: L.419.2 [*Prince becomes beggar*]; T.91 [*Unequals in love*].

¶ Carew Hazlitt has followed the prose pamphlet, but Percy's "Beggar's Daughter of Bethnal Green" (*Reliques*, I, pp. 361 *sqq.*) contains what Hazlitt himself considers a more reasonable explanation of Henry de Montfort's disguise as a beggar. According to this, he was blinded and left for dead at the Battle of Evesham, and found and nursed in secret by the lady who loved him and afterwards married him.

A literary treatment is given to this tale by Charlotte Yonge in *The Prince and the Page*.

See "The Dorsetshire Garland" (A, IV).

BRUNANBURH [shortened]

J. R. W. Coxhead, *Legends of Devon*, p. 114.

Through the centuries a story has been handed down in the district of a great battle, fought near Axminster, between King Athelstan and the Danes, in which five kings and seven earls were killed.

A further local legend, almost certainly connected with the battle, relates that a stream called War-lake, which flows into the River Axe just north of the road between Musbury and Whitford, ran with blood on the occasion of a great slaughter many hundreds of years ago.

Tradition also states that the bodies of seven earls slain in the battle were buried at Axminster, and that Athelstan founded a college of priests to pray for their souls by an endowment which remains to this day.

Many authorities consider this battle to have been the famous and almost legendary fight of Brunanburh, which took place in the year 937 between King Athelstan, together with the Ethelings, Edmund, Elwin and Ethelwin on the one side, and Anlaf, the Dane, with Constantine, King of Scotland, on the other....

William of Malmesbury gives a romantic story about the Danish Chieftain:

Anlaf, wishing to discover something about the strength of King Athelstan's force, entered the King's camp disguised as a minstrel, carrying a harp. He entertained the King and his nobles so well, that when he took his departure, largesse was given him.....

A sharp-eyed sentry noticed that as soon as Anlaf was clear of the camp he dug a small hole and buried the money, because, being of noble blood, it was beneath his dignity to retain what in these days would be called a "tip". The sentry then recognized him as Anlaf the Dane, and at once went and told the King. Athelstan was furious, and said: "Why did you not arrest him and deliver him to me?"

The sentry replied: "I once served with Anlaf and have sworn an oath of fealty to him; therefore, if I had betrayed him to you, would you have ever trusted me again? My advice to you, O King, is to move your camp before nightfall!"

Athelstan took the sentry's advice, and moved his camp.

Shortly after the move, Werstan, Bishop of Sherborne, arrived with his men, and pitched his camp on the spot vacated by the King. During the night Anlaf made a surprise attack, fell on the camp, slew the Bishop and massacred most of his men before they could stand to their arms.

The noise caused by the surprise attack was heard by the King in his new camp, so, calling his men to arms, he made a great onslaught upon his enemies, and the furious conflict which followed lasted throughout the night and the following day, resulting in a decisive victory for the English.

William of Malmesbury relates in his *Chronicle* that early in the battle King Athelstan lost his sword, whereupon the King prayed earnestly to God and St Ealdhelm for aid. After his prayer Athelstan put his hand down to his scabbard, and found there another sword, with which he created great havoc among his enemies.

In those far-off days there was a fine estuary at the mouth of the Axe, and Axmouth was a port of some importance. The Danes probably sailed their ships right into the estuary, in order to land their troops, and pitched their camp on one of the hills.

TYPE ML.8000 (Legends about wars). MOTIF K.2357.1 [*Disguise as musician to enter the enemy's camp*].

¶ The legend of the disguised harper is most commonly told about Alfred himself. In that form it is given literary treatment in Chesterton's "Ballad of the White Horse".

See "St David's Flood".

BURKE AND HARE

School of Scottish Studies, John Elliott, *Notebooks*.

In the old days [in] which doctors and students needed dead bodies for science, in their medical research, doctor Knox in the Cannongate of Edinburgh, offered ten pound, and sometimes more, for a corpse, at that time in Scotland. A lot of Irish harvesters came over from Ireland to harvest, and two of these harvesters settled down in Tanners' Close, in the Grass Market of Edinburgh. Their names were Burke, and the other Hare. They were men of no human feeling, and would do anything for money. Burke was married, and his wife stopped with them in their two dark and dirty hovels.

I

A young country woman, who had a bairn to a young farmer in the country, was driven from home by her parents, sought refuge in Edinburgh, and was stopping with some people not far from Tanners' Close. Her name was Mary Paterson, and she got into bad company, and soon learned to drink. Of course her heart was fair broken, and she drank to drown her sorrows.

As Burke and Hare had learnt that Dr Knox would buy dead bodies, they went to him, and made inquiries, and was told he would give ten pound, so they met in with Mary Paterson in a pub, and Mrs Burke invited Mary to Tanners' Close for a drink.

They got her in, and sent out for drink, and kept Mary drinking till she was drunk, then they threw her into bed, and put another tyke on top of her, and smothered her.

They took her down to Dr Knox, and got the ten pound. Not long after, a little woman from the country, who had comed in to do some shopping, but was very fond of drink, was invited into Tanners' Close. She was a little bright and high-spirited woman, and sang them songs, and drank along with them. They carried her on till they got her stupid with the drink, and was not long before they were doing a roaring trade in the body-snatching.

About that time, a boy called [him] daft Jimmy roamed about the streets in search of a crust of bread, or anything he could get to make a scanty living. He was well kenned in the town, and was always ready to help anyone he thought he could get a penny from. Burke and Hare had been away lifting a dead body that had been buried the day before. They had hired a cuddy and cart, and was bringing the body up a street in the middle of the night, when the old cuddy dropped down dead. They were so feared they would be caught, that they unyoked the dead cuddy out of the cart, and got into the trams themselves, and pulled it home.

Not long after they had disposed of the body, they began to look around for another victim, and they thought of trying daft Jamie. The boy was hungry, and they told him to come in and have some tea. Jimmy sat down at the so-called table to get his tea. They slipped whiskey into his tea, but Jimmy told them he did not like the whiskey, but said, "I will take as much tea as ye like." But he did not want the whiskey, but they tried him just to take a wee drop, but he would not. Burke was not for taking Jimmy, as he kenned he would be missed off the streets, but Hare threw

Jimmy into a bed, and put another tyke on him, but Jimmy was strong, and Hare could not hold him down, and he called to Burke, if he did not come and help him, he would kill him too. Burke had to go to his assistance, and poor daft Jimmy was murdered too, but Jimmy was soon missed off the streets, and he was traced to Tanners' Close. [and] They were both apprehended, and tried in Edinburgh, but Hare turned King's evidence, and was set free, but the police had to give him protection, or he got out of Edinburgh, as the crowds would have torn him to pieces. He made for Ireland, and he was not long in Ireland till one night a young student went into his house and murdered him. It was said after that the young man that murdered Hare was his own son, and did not know him. At that time kirk yards had to be watched for some time after a burial, and in a little house a man watched at night, as body-snatchers were always on the look-out for fresh dead bodies.

II

One dark night, at a wayside inn, a pony and trap drove up, and stopped. There was two men and a woman. The woman was sitting between the two men, with a hood on her head, and her face was covered with a veil. The men jumped out, and left the woman setting. They went into the pub for a drink. The ostler was busy in the stable, and one looked out, and when he saw the woman settin [by] herself, he went up to the trap, and said to the woman, "It's a cauld night the night!" But he got no answer. He spoke again, but still no answer. He had a close look at her, and he saw it was a corpse. He got up and got hold of her, and carried her into the stable, and took off her disguise, and put it on himself. Then he got into the trap in the woman's place, and was setting bolt upright and just like the woman when the men came out, and jumped in, one at either side. They just thought it was the dead woman.

After travelling some distance along the road, one of the men said to the other, "D'ye ken that body's getting warm?" The other said, "I was just thinking the same." Then the ostler spoke up and said, "If ye had been as lang in Hell as me, ye'd be warm too!" That was enough. The men jumped out and ran for their life. The ostler saw no more of them; he just turned the pony and trap, and took it back to the inn.

It was now his property, as he knew they dare not come back to claim it.

III

A school in a mining village...the schoolmaster was busy with the classes...a big boy was getting punished. Not long after the children got out for dinner, the boy who had got punished went home, and told his mother he would not go to school in the afternoon. His mother told him he would catch it from his father when he came home for not going to school. But the mother told him to go down to the grocer for half a stone of self-raising flour, as she had to bake. Away went the boy, and got the flour. By this time the school was in again, and the boy had to pass not far off the school door. He was carrying the flour. He heard the schoolmaster laying the law off inside. He noticed the door was not right shut, and he stepped up and keeked in. The schoolmaster's back was to him; he gently eased the door open, and hurled the flour at him, and nearly blinded the schoolmaster with the flour, and then he dare not go home, as he knew what he would get. So he hid in the kirk-yard under a flat headstone. He lay there till nearly midnight, when a grand trap drove into the kirk yard. Two men got out to lift a body, but they had some trouble with the horse as it would not stand.

At last the boy crawled out from below the flat tombstone, and said, "I'll haud the horse." The men bolted, and the boy kept holding the horse till daylight. The minister eyed the trap from his window, and went to see what the horse and trap were doing there. The boy told the minister that the two men ran away, and left him holding the horse.

"Well," said the minister, "the men will not come back for their horse and trap, so it is now yours. So you can drive it home to your father." So that put things right with his father and mother.

TYPE 1318A. MOTIFS: S.113.2 [*Murder by suffocation*]; Q.211 [*Murder punished*]; J.1499.6* [*Corpse-robber feels the warm corpse, etc.*] (Baughman); J.1782.1 [*Robber or dog in churchyard thought to be ghost*]; J.1782.6 [*Person in white thought to be ghost*].

¶ This account of the fifteen murders committed by Burke and Hare is, on the whole, correct, though the discovery of the crimes was finally due to an old woman, Margaret Docherty, wife of Silly Jimmy, who had been killed earlier. Burke was executed in 1829. The crimes made an immense impression on the popular imagination, and a whole series of tales about the "Burkers" has been collected from the travelling people of Scotland.

A black coach driven by a gang of medical students in "lum hats" features in many of them, and is a kind of successor of the death-coach (see "Lady Howard's Coach", B, VI).

In England there are tales of the "Resurrection Men", "The Corpse in the Cab", one of the tales told here, is to be found among the Jocular Tales (A, III).

It will be remembered that Jerry Cruncher, in *The Tale of Two Cities*, was a Resurrection Man. The Burke and Hare story is dramatized by James Bridie in *The Anatomist*.

A BURKER TALE: I

School of Scottish Studies, Hamish Henderson, from Davie Stewart.

There was once a tinker had a wife and two wee children, and they were so poor that they had only a wee donkey with a sack on each side of it, and no cart.

One awful bad night as they were tramping along, the man sent his wife to get a dish of tea from a keeper's lodge they passed, to give the bairns a drink. She did that, and then he said, "Where'll we sleep this awful night?" For they had no tent.

"Away back, and ask at the lodge if we'll get a welcome at the big farm up by." "Oh, ay," said the keeper's wife. "Ye'll get a welcome right enough. There's many an old tramping man I've seen going up that road. I can't say I've ever seen one coming back, but maybe there's another way out." The tinker wife didn't like the sound of that, but her man said, "I'll sleep there, if it's the last sleep I have."

So they went in, and they had a grand welcome.

"Come away in," said the farmer's wife, "and have a dish of tea. I'll find you a bed in the barn."

They came into the warm kitchen, and she gave them big bowls of tea. The man drank up his, but the wife poured hers and the bairns' into their can, for they had just had some. They sat and talked, and the man fell sound asleep. At last the wife said, "Where are we to lie?" and the farmer's wife took her out to the barn. She took a look round it, and she did not fancy it at all. The bairns were asleep by now, so she set them down in a corner, and went to waken her man. She shook him, and cried at him, but he never wakened. Then she took the skewer that held her shawl, and ran it into him, but he never stirred. "Leave him alone," said the farmer's wife.

"What have you done to him?" said the woman. "You've poisoned him."

"I have not," said the farmer's wife. "He's fallen asleep with the hot fire, and the hot drink after the cold." So the wife went back to the barn, and picked up the two bairns, and set them on the donkey's back, and she knocked up the keeper's cottage, and told them how she could not wake her man. And she said that she had taken a scunner at the barn, for there were stains of blood in one corner, and in another there were bits of sticks that had been tent-poles, and piles of rags and old boots.

"What did you do with the tea?" said the keeper's wife.

"I have it here in my can," said the woman.

"Well, keep it, and don't drink it, whatever you do."

"I'm thinking that," said the tinker's wife. "But, for God's sake, will you not get my man back to me alive?"

"I'll do what I can," said the keeper. He loaded his gun, and sat at the open door, and before the dawn they heard a rumbling and a clattering down the road from the farm, and here a black hearse comes down, drawn by four black horses, and there were four men sitting on it, in black coats and bowler hats, and with white shirts and black ties.

"Stop," said the keeper, "or I'll fire at you." But it came on.

"Speak," said the keeper, "whether ye be alive or dead, or I'll fire." But they neither spoke nor stopped.

"This is the last time, I warn you," said the keeper. "Stop and speak, or I'll fire." They neither stopped nor spoke, so he fired at one of the horses, and shot its leg, so that it could not move, and the other horses stopped. Then the two women opened the back of the hearse, and there was the body of the man, stark naked, with the score of the skewer still on him. They fetched the police, and the tinker woman was kept in the lock-up in the police station while the trial was on, and the two bairns were sent to a home, but the farmer and his wife were hanged.

TYPE 955B*. MOTIFS: K.2294 [*The treacherous host*]; S.113.2 [*Murder by suffocation*]; Q.211 [*Murder punished*].

¶ See notes on "Burke and Hare".

A BURKER TALE: II

THE RED-HEADED FAMILY

Kenneth S. Goldstein, School of Scottish Studies.

This is a story that I've heard from some of the...when was been a child, about a reid-heidit family.

Once on a day there is no beggars would go near a house where there's a reid-heidit father, a reid-heidit mother, a reid-heidit sister, and a brother. That was in the olden days, of course. So, because I'll tell ye, in that time the college used to give a lot of money for bodies.

And this reid-heidit father and mother and sister and brother used to be the ones that used to take the people in, murder 'em, then sell the bodies.

So, at one time or another, there was a man and a woman were beggars, and they had a little boy, so they were comin' on the road one night,.... it was getting very late, but it happent to be a moonlight night, so the boy was getting tired, and he was getting sleepy, so he was asking his father and mother to get them in somewhere, intill a barn to sleep.

"Ah, well now," they says. "Well, the first farm we come to, we'll ask in."

So they came til a farm. And this time it'll be about, eh, nine or ten o'clock. So they chappit at the door.

"Oh," they says, "we are on the road—we are beggars on the road—could they get into the barn to sleep?"

"Oh, yes, certainly," they says, "you come inside, and we'll give ye a good feed before ye go to the barn."

So they set them down and gave them a good feed. But the father and mother was a bittie timorous, because they saw that the farmer was reid-heidit. So—oh, well, they couldnae back oot now ye see—they had tae go intae the barn.

So after about ten o'clock at night they put them into the barn, gave them strae and that, and lockit aa the doors. So the man and the woman and boy, they makes down a bed, but the father he says, "Look here," he says, "we'll have to be on our road." He says, "I don't like the reid-heidit father and reid-heidit mother and sister and brother. So," he says, "the quicker we get out of here the better," he says. "I didnae like them lockin' ae the doors."

So now—he says—"We'll hae to see if we can get out of here."

But when they tried to get out, they couldnae get oot. They were trapped in—they couldnae get oot. And it was gettin' very near time for this students comin' liftin' bodies. The only [?] snag wis now wis a little window, and the woman wis a stoot kinna lady, this beggar-woman, so they pushes the boy through this skylight—gets the boy through, and the father gets through, but the woman couldnae get through.

But hooiver, with great force and that, they did get the mother through, and then they dout across a plewed field, right on. But they're no jist aafie faur awa from this fairm-house, when they saw a dark coach with two horses, and two men sittin' wi' tile-hats, comin' in aboot by the farm. By this time they're away a-back of a dyke, a good bit from the house, and here this coach draws up to the farm.

The next thing was this men cam' out, and the farmer and his wife and that, lookit aa the barn, lookit aa the field, but this folk wis hidden, well-hidden, and that. They carried on like that till about two or three o'clock in the mornin', this—students, but couldn't find them.

So next day this beggar and his wife and boy went in a house—a cottar's it'd be—told them what had happent.

He says, "Well, ye're lucky to be alive," he says, "because this farm-people," he says, "had got a lot of bodies the same way, by takin' them into the barn, givin' them a good feed and that, and gettin' the students out, murder 'em, and sellin' the bodies for ten pound apiece."

Told by Jean Stewart, Fetterangus, 1960.

TYPE 956A. MOTIFS: K.2294 [*The treacherous host*]; R.116 [*Rescue from robbers' den*]; C.863 [*Tabu: following three red men to certain place*].

¶ There is some idea of danger about red-headed people, as in the bad luck of a red-headed first-footer on New Year's Day. Danish and pixy blood are both supposed to produce red-heads, and are sometimes confused. See "The Red-Heads" (B, V). Judas Iscariot was traditionally a red-head. For other notes see "Burke and Hare".

A BURKER TALE: III

THE TIME I RAN AWAY WITH MY BROTHERS

Maurice Fleming, School of Scottish Studies.

This was a time when my brothers were going to pipe in Glasgow, but I couldn't go with them, because I had a few days yet at the school.

So when they'd set out, I slipped away from the school, and ran after them, along the road from Blairgowrie to Bankfoot. And when I was up on them, they said maybe I'd be useful, so they let me go along with them.

So we went on and went on, till we got to Edinburgh, and we went to a lodging. My brothers sent me out to get a can of milk. It was a far road, and the mist came down, and I lost my road on the way back, so I started to greet. And an old lady came along, and asked me what I was greeting for, and I told her, and she said it was too far to get to my brothers that night, and she would take me to a lodging. We went up along a long drive, and into a house, and she took me to a wee room at the top, and told me to take off my clothes, and hang them over the edge of the bed when I got in. So I did that, and the bed swung round, and I was dropped down into a great drain. But I was not killed, so I crept along the drain till it came out at the sea, and there I was, mother-naked. So I took some tangle and wrapped it round me, and I peeked about, and I saw a young lady, and I told her what had happened to me. And she was real kind, and gave me some clothes that had belonged to her son, and something to eat, and set me on the road to Edinburgh.

And I went to the lodging, and found my brothers gone. So I set out after them, and on the road I met a herd driving cattle, and asked him if he had met two pipers on the road. He said he had, but they were ahead, and I would not get to Glasgow that night. "But if you go on so far," he said, "you will come to a house, and if you tell them I sent you, they will put you up for the night." I went on till I was getting near to Glasgow, and I saw the house, and I asked the wife if I might bide there the night.

"No, you'll not get biding here," she said, but when I told her about the drover I got leave to bide, for the drover was her son. And we were to sleep three in the bed, and I was to sleep on the outside. So we sat and sat, and the one son went to bed, and then I went up, and I heard the old man say to the old wife, "You take the pail, and I'll take the knife, and we'll let him bleed till morning." And then the drover came in, and I heard the old wife say, "Mind and take the middle place in bed."

Then the drover came and climbed over me, and took the middle place.

I waited and waited till he was sound asleep, and then I climbed over him and pushed him to the side of the bed. The old man and old woman came up, and they cut their son's throat, and said: "We'll just leave him to bleed till morning."

Then they went down, and I took the first coat I could find, and away with me out. But I had not gone very far when they found what they had done, and here they were after me, and the dog with them. I ran till I came to a wee cottage, and I knocked and kicked, and asked them for the mercy of God to let me in. There was an old woman who bided there alone, and she said: "I doubt I can't hide you, laddie, if the dog's after you, but climb up to the top of the tent-bed, and maybe you'll find something there that'll be useful to you."

So they were at the door, and the old woman says: "Who's there?"
And they say: "Did a laddie come in here?" And she says: "No."
And they say: "Aye, but he did, for the doggie trails him."

So they came in, and I felt about at the top of the bed, and I found one of they double-headed axes. So when the first man came for me, I cutted off his head, and I did the same by the second, and the old wife ran away. So the old woman and I buried the bodies, and I set out on the road. And as I was walking, I felt something bump-bumping against my side. I looked down, and here I had put on the carter's coat, and there was a purse of gold in the pocket, and a wad of notes in the breast-pocket. So there I was, rich. And I came to a grand hotel, and I went in, and got myself a meal, and took a room for a week. And they asked me did I play cards, and I said yes, I loved playing cards. So they said there was a house down there I could go and play at. So I went and played and I lost ten pounds. And when I went back to the inn, the chambermaid said, "Dinna go there again, for they'll take all your money from you." But I didn't want to leave ten pounds behind me, so I went back and back, and still I lost, till I had no money left. And an old man in a ragged coat came up to me, and offered to play me for my good clothes. So I played, and I lost to him, and here I had nothing but his ragged clothes, and I set out on the road again, for I was ashamed to go to the Hotel.

And I came up with an old travelling man, and asked him if he had seen two pipers. "Aye, they passed me an hour ago," he says. "Augh, you'll hear the skirl of the pipes." We listened, but we heard a kind of rumbling and clattering behind us.

"It is the Burkers' coach," said the old man, and we made for the nearest ditch, and the Burkers' coach came rumbling up like a black hearse, and the fellows on it were in black coats with black hats, and white dickies with black ties. And they'd spied us, for they stopped the coach, and they caught us both in the ditch, and put the old man into the hearse, but it was overfull to take me, so they put me up to ride between, and we went on till we were near the outskirts of Glasgow, and they came to a pub, and they said, "We must have our breakfast, but who'll hold the horses?"

"Oh, this fellow will hold the horses," says one.

"Oh, yes, I'll hold the horses," I says. So when they went into the pub, I got down, and I opened the back door of the hearse, and I gave the horses a whack, and off they set towards Glasgow, with the corpses tumbling out on the road. And I ran down by a side lane, and came to a little house, and said to a woman, "Have you seen two pipers on the road?"

"That's a queer thing," she says, "there's two pipers tenting down in the field there, with an old man and an old woman."

So I heard the pipes, and I went down, and there were my two brothers with my father and mother.

From John Higgins, Lower Mill Street, Blairgowrie.

TYPES 955B* and 963*. MOTIFS: K.735.4 [*Capture in trap-bed*]; K.1611 [*Beds exchanged with ogre's children*].

¶   This is an embroidering on the Burker tale which hardly claims to be historically true. The basic belief is the same, but other motifs have been woven into it.

For other motifs see "Burke and Hare".

THE BURLY STRANGER

J. R. W. Coxhead, *The Devil in Devon*, pp. 35-7.

For over two hundred and fifty years a cottage called Beira stood on the left-hand side of the road, half-way between Woolley and the ancient market-town of Bovey Tracey, until it was destroyed by fire about the year 1897.

According to a very interesting local tradition, this cottage was occupied by a man named Coniam, at the beginning of the year 1646, and one cold winter's evening he heard a knock at his door. When he went to see who it was, he found a burly-looking man standing outside in the gathering darkness. The stranger, who looked rather like an itinerant preacher, inquired whether there was a Presbyterian meeting-house in Bovey Tracey, and, if so, at what hours the services were held. Coniam told the man that part of the old monastery was being used as a Presbyterian meeting-house, and that he would be very willing to conduct him to the place, as he thought that if they went straight away they would be in time for the evening service.

On their way into Bovey, the unsuspecting Coniam told the stranger that the people of the neighbourhood were expecting fierce fighting to take place before long, as a strong detachment of Lord Wentworth's brigade held the town, and it was reported that Cromwell himself was coming to drive them out.

The broad-shouldered, soberly dressed man listened to his companion's conversation with the greatest interest, and for a very good reason—

because he was no less a person than Cromwell himself, skilfully disguised as a preacher and out to gain all the information he could get about the disposition of the Royalist troops in Bovey.

Having acquired a considerable amount of news about the strength of the enemy forces, the stranger obtained permission from the minister of the meeting-house to address the congregation, and, after giving them a rousing discourse, he bade them good night, climbed over the steep hillside, and rejoined his men at Canonteign.

It is said that the next morning Cromwell, with some of his men stopped to have breakfast at a farm-house in Hennock, and a family tradition there relates that he was a stern and fierce warrior, who threatened that, unless a golden guinea was placed on each man's plate with the food, dire punishment would follow.

Later in the day, most of the royalist officers were drinking and playing cards for large sums of money in a private house in Bovey Tracey. They would appear to have neglected to place outposts around the town to protect themselves against surprise attack, and their absolute lack of preparedness led to a disaster, as the majority of their men were entrenched in positions on a heath just outside the town.

Cromwell, who had issued orders that every horse was to carry a footsoldier behind each trooper, came down the steep lane from Hennock, and arrived at the house in question without opposition. His unexpected appearance put a sudden stop to the game of cards, and as the Roundheads were about to break into the building one of the Cavaliers had the presence of mind to gather up all the money on the tables, and throw it out of the window into the midst of the invading troops in the street outside.

The temptation proved too strong for Cromwell's soldiers, and a general scramble for the money took place—giving the royalist officers time to escape through the back door of the house, and away across the brook.

It is said that some of them were caught by the Roundheads, others rejoined their comrades on the heath, and a third party seem to have made their way to Ilsington, where they appear to have quartered for the night in the church before eventually reaching Lord Wentworth at Totnes.

The royalist soldiers entrenched on the heath close to Bovey, by the side of the Newton Abbot road, deserted by many of their officers, were taken by surprise and fared badly.

From *Transactions of the Devonshire Association*, XXXIX, pp. 341–5.

TYPE ML.8000. MOTIF: K.2357.0.1 [*Disguise to spy on enemy*].

¶ This is one of the many Civil War traditions about Oliver Cromwell. Any general of the Parliamentary party was likely to be remembered as Oliver Cromwell. A case in point is the tradition at Whittington in Gloucestershire that King Charles and Cromwell fought in single combat on the drawbridge.

See "Cromwell in Yorkshire", "Cromwell in Glasgow", "Grey Goose Feathers".

CHARLES I AND THE SOUTHWELL SHOEMAKER

J. P. Briscoe, *The Book of Nottinghamshire Anecdote*, p. 13.

Walking about the town, as it was his practice to do, Charles the First entered the shop of a fanatical shoemaker, named James Lee. Finding that his person was unknown to the "knight of the awl and lapstone", the King entered into conversation with him, and in the end, wished to be measured for a pair of shoes. Lee had no sooner taken His Majesty's foot in his hand to measure it, than, eyeing him very attentively, he was suddenly seized with a panic, and would not go on. The King, surprised at his behaviour, pressed him to proceed, but this disciple of St Crispin absolutely refused, informing the King that he was the customer himself whom he had been warned of in his sleep the preceding night; that the King was doomed to destruction, and those who performed any work for him would never thrive. The forlorn monarch, whose misfortunes had opened his mind to the impressions of superstition, uttered an ejaculation expressive of his resignation to the will of Providence, and retired.

TYPE ML.8000. MOTIFS: M.340.6 [*Prophecy: great misfortune*]; N.119.3 [*Ill-omened face of king: harbinger of evil*].

CHRISTIE'S WILL

Scott, *Minstrelsy of the Scottish Border*, IV, pp. 61–3.

I

In the reign of Charles I, when the moss-trooping practices were not entirely discontinued, the tower of Gilnockie, in the parish of Cannoby, was occupied by William Armstrong, called, for distinction's sake, *Christie's Will*, a lineal descendant of the famous John Armstrong, of Gilnockie, executed by James V. The hereditary love of plunder had descended to this person with the family mansion; and, upon some marauding party, he was seized, and imprisoned in the Tolbooth of Jedburgh. The Earl of Traquair, Lord High Treasurer, happening to visit Jedburgh, and knowing Christie's Will, inquired the cause of his confinement. Will replied, he was imprisoned for stealing two *tethers* [halters], but, upon being more closely interrogated, acknowledged that there were two *delicate colts* at the end of them. The joke, such as it was, amused the Earl, who exerted his interest, and succeeded in releasing Christie's Will from bondage. Some time afterwards, a lawsuit, of importance to Lord Traquair, was to be decided in the Court of Session; and there was every reason to believe that the judgment would turn upon the voice of the presiding judge, who has a casting vote, in case of an equal division among his brethren. The opinion of the President was unfavourable to Lord Traquair; and the point was, therefore, to keep him out of the way when the question should be tried. In this dilemma, the Earl had recourse to Christie's Will; who, at once, offered his services to kidnap the President. Upon due scrutiny, he found it was the judge's practice frequently to take the air, on horseback, on the sands of Leith, without an attendant. In one of these excursions, Christie's Will, who had long watched his opportunity, ventured to accost the President, and engage him in conversation. His address and language were so amusing, that he decoyed the President into an unfrequented and furzy common, called the Frigate Whins, where, riding suddenly up to him, he pulled him from his horse, muffled him in a large cloak, which he had provided, and rode off, with the luckless judge trussed up behind him. Will crossed the country with great expedition, by paths only known to persons of his description, and deposited his weary and terrified burden in an old castle, in Annandale, called the Tower of Graham. The judge's horse being found, it was concluded he had thrown his rider into the sea; his friends went into mourning, and a successor was appointed to his office. Meanwhile, the poor President spent a heavy time in the vault of the castle. He was imprisoned, and solitary; receiving his food through an aperture in the wall, and never hearing the sound of a human voice, save when a shepherd called his dog, by the name of *Batty*, and when a female domestic called upon *Maudge*, the cat. These, he concluded, were invocations of spirits; for he held himself to be in the dungeon of a sorcerer. At length, after three months had elapsed, the lawsuit was decided in favour of Lord Traquair; and Will was directed to set the President at liberty. Accordingly, he entered the vault, at dead of night, seized the President, muffled him once more in the cloak, without speaking a single word, and, using the same mode of transportation, conveyed him to Leith Sands, and set down the astonished judge on the very spot where he had taken him up. The joy of his friends, and the less agreeable surprise of his successor, may be easily conceived, when he appeared in court to reclaim his office and honours. All embraced his own persuasion, that he had been spirited away by witchcraft; nor could he be convinced of the contrary, until, many years afterwards, happening to travel in Annandale, his ears were saluted, once more, with the sounds of *Maudge* and *Batty*—the only notes which had solaced his long confinement. This led to a discovery of the whole story, but, in these disorderly times, it was only laughed at as a fair *ruse de guerre*.

II

Tradition ascribes to Christie's Will another memorable feat, which seems worthy of being recorded. It is well known, that, during the troubles of Charles I, the Earl of Traquair continued unalterably fixed in his attachment to his unfortunate master, in whose service he hazarded his person, and impoverished his estate. It was of consequence, it is said, to the King's service, that a certain packet, containing papers of importance, should be transmitted to him from Scotland. But the task was a difficult one, as the Parliamentary leaders used their utmost endeavours to prevent any communication betwixt the King and his Scottish friends. Traquair, in this strait, again had recourse to the services of Christie's Will; who undertook the commission, conveyed the papers safely to His Majesty, and received an answer, to be delivered to Lord Traquair. But, in the meantime, his embassy had taken air, and Cromwell had despatched orders to intercept him at Carlisle. Christie's Will, unconscious of his danger, halted in the town to refresh his horse, and then pursued his journey. But, as soon as he began to pass the long, high, and narrow bridge, which crosses the Eden at Carlisle, either end of the pass was occupied by a party of Parliamentary soldiers, who were lying in wait for him. The Borderer disdained to resign his enterprise, even in these desperate circumstances; and at once forming his resolution, spurred his horse over the parapet. The river was in high flood. Will sunk—the soldiers shouted—he emerged again, and guiding his horse to a steep bank, called the Stanners, or Stanhouse, endeavoured to land, but ineffectually, owing to his heavy horseman's cloak, now drenched in water. Will cut the loop, and the horse, feeling himself disembarrassed, made a desperate exertion, and succeeded in gaining the bank. Our hero set off, at full speed, pursued by the troopers, who had, for a time, stood motionless in astonishment at his temerity. Will, however, was well mounted; and, having got the start, he kept it, menacing with his pistols any pursuer who seemed likely to gain on him—an artifice which succeeded, although the arms were wet and useless. He was chased to the River Esk, which he swam without hesitation; and, finding himself on Scottish ground, and in the neighbourhood of friends, he turned on the northern bank, and, in the true spirit of a Border rider, invited his followers to come through and drink with him. After this taunt, he proceeded on his journey, and faithfully accomplished his mission. Such were the exploits of the very last Border freebooter of any note.

Ibid. pp. 64–6.

I. MOTIFS: J.1160 [*Clever pleading*]; J.1786 [*Man thought to be devil*]; R.4 [*Surprise capture*]; R.41.3 [*Captivity in dungeon*].

II. TYPE ML.8000. MOTIF: R.200 [*Escapes and pursuits*].

THE COURT CAVE [abbreviated]

Wilkie, *Bygone Fife*, p. 133.

Legend explains the designation of the Court Cave, not content with the historical fact that the Colvilles of Ochiltree, who acquired Easter Wemyss in 1530, held their Baron Court within it. Their castle was that which was abandoned and fell into decay when the lands of Easter and Wester Wemyss were reunited in possession of the old family, and which goes by the name of the Thane of Fife. The tradition runs that the father of that Gudeman o' Ballangeich who figures in the story of the Setons once held a court there, unique even for the romantic Stewarts. Like his son, he was for ever wandering about "the Kingdom" in disguise, seeking adventure and incidentally acquiring that knowledge of his humbler subjects which made him "King o' the Commons". On such an expedition he fell in with a band of gypsies.... A comradeship was struck up at once, and he went with them to the cave at Wemyss, which was their headquarters at the time. There was no need to smuggle in Stewart Scotland; wine came to the little havens from oversea, and the gypsies had their share. So there they sat, "birling" it as gaily as the king in the ballad . . . till they became

> very, very merry
> For all our men were drinking.

James tried to make peace. They would have none of his efforts. At last he threw off his homespun disguise, drew himself up to his full height, and stood revealed as their sovereign lord. All the gypsies and broken men of Fife, like the peasantry, held him in great affection and respect. The tumult ceased at once; his fellow revellers in the cave drank to his health and escorted him on his way; they left him with every demonstration of loyalty and regard, and ever after the cavern has borne its proud title in memory of the boisterous court the good and chivalrous king held in its dark recesses.

MOTIF: P.14.19 [*King goes in disguise at night to observe his subjects*].
¶ See "The Guidman of Ballengeich", "King Alfred and the Cakes", "The Origin of Littleport" (B, IX), "Edward IV and the Tanner of Tamworth" (A, IV).

CROMWELL IN GLASGOW

Scott, *Minstrelsy of the Scottish Border*, II, pp. 232–3.

The following tradition, concerning Cromwell, is preserved by an uncommonly direct line of traditional evidence; being narrated (as I am informed) by the grandson of an eyewitness. When Cromwell, in 1650, entered Glasgow, he attended divine service in the High Church; but the Presbyterian divine who officiated, poured forth, with more zeal than prudence, his indignation against the person, principles, and cause, of the Independent General. One of Cromwell's officers rose, and whispered his commander; who seemed to give him a short and stern answer, and the sermon was concluded without interruption. Among the crowd, assembled to gaze at the General, as he came out of the Church, was a shoe-maker, the son of one of James the Sixth's Scottish footmen. This man had been born and bred in England, but, after his father's death, had settled in Glasgow. Cromwell eyed him among the crowd, and immediately called him by his name—the man fled, but, at Cromwell's command, one of his retinue followed him, and brought him to the General's lodgings. A number of the inhabitants remained at the door, waiting the end of this extraordinary scene. The shoemaker soon came out in high spirits, and showing some gold, declared he was going to drink Cromwell's health. Many attended him, to hear the particulars of his interview; among others, the grandfather of the narrator. The shoemaker said that he had been a playfellow of Cromwell, when they were both boys, their parents residing in the same street; that he had fled, when the General had first called to him, thinking he might owe him some ill-will, on account of his father being in the service of the Royal Family. He added that Cromwell had been so very kind and familiar with him, that he ventured to ask him what the officer had said to him in the church. "He proposed," said Cromwell, "to pull forth the minister by the ears; and I answered, that the preacher was one fool, and he was another." In the course of the day, Cromwell held an interview with the minister, and contrived to satisfy his scruples so effectually, that the evening discourse, by the same man, was tuned to the praise and glory of the victor of Naseby.

TYPE ML.8000. MOTIF: J.215.1.2 [*King refuses to banish gossipers*].
¶ This anecdote has probably a good deal of truth in it, for it shows the character-istic tolerance of Cromwell, and also his concern to ingratiate himself with people who disliked him. Among the Cromwell anecdotes, see "Cromwell in Yorkshire", "The Burly Stranger", "The Grey Goose Feathers".

CROMWELL IN YORKSHIRE

Parkinson, *Yorkshire Legends and Traditions*, 1st series, pp. 187–98.

In the garden of a cottage at Long Marston...is a well still known as "Cromwell's Well", from which the village girls took water in their milk-pails to quench the thirst of soldiers encamped on the hill-tops. In Moor Lane close by, belated travellers still hear, it is said, the ghosts of horsemen galloping past, headless and blood-stained, as if in the heat of battle.

On Cromwell's Gap, between three fences, is a bare space where no bushes will grow, though repeatedly they have been planted to try to fill it up.

Sir Richard Graham, of Norton Conyers, rode from the field, when the battle was irretrievably lost, with twenty-six wounds, and had been no more than an hour at his home before he died of exhaustion. Cromwell was his implacable enemy, and pursued him with a troop of horse. Even on hearing of his death he was not satisfied, but is said to have ridden his horse up the wide staircase, where the marks of its hoofs are still to be seen, and, finding that his enemy was indeed dead, he gave leave to his men to pillage the house. They utterly despoiled it, and destroyed all that they could not carry away.

That same night Cromwell rode on to Ripley, and sent an officer to announce his intention to spend the night at the castle, which belonged to a loyal Royalist, Sir William Ingleby. The master being away, the lady of the castle received the officer, and told him that no traitor should be sheltered there. But at last persuaded that they had no power to resist, she received Cromwell herself, standing at the gate with a pair of pistols stuck in her apron-strings, and demanded his promise that he and his men would behave decorously while under her roof. She then led him to the hall, pointed to a sofa, where he might sit, and herself sat down on another facing him. Thus they passed the night, jealously watching each other, and in the morning she remarked that "it was well for him that he had behaved so peaceably; had it been otherwise, he could not have left the house alive".

A gentler story is that of Mary, daughter of Sir Francis Trapper, whose husband, Charles Townley, was killed at Marston Moor. On hearing of his death, she came next morning to seek his dead body on the battlefield. An officer to whom she told her errand heard her with great courtesy, but earnestly begged her to leave the field, for, besides the distressing scenes she would witness, she ran the risk of being insulted.

She complied, and on her way home she inquired the name of the officer who had treated her so kindly, and was told it was Lieutenant-General Cromwell.

TYPE ML.8000.

¶ The first of these anecdotes illustrates the ruthless side of Cromwell's character, the third the gentler, the second shows him dominated by a determined woman. See "Cromwell in Glasgow".

CURWEN'S CARD: THE KNAVE OF CLUBS

Denham Tracts, I, p. 217.

Curwen was a native of Westmorland and Archbishop of Dublin. In Queen Mary's reign, a commission was sent over to Ireland, to persecute the Protestants with fire and faggot. The bearer of these unchristian-like orders stopt one night at Chester, and his host, a true Protestant, having got an inkling of the nature of his journey, stole his commission, and in place thereof inserted the *knave of clubs*. Some short time after he arrived in Dublin and lost no time in laying his orders before the Archbishop and the Privy Council; when lo! on opening the packet, nothing presented itself but a dirty and worthless old card! He returned with all speed to England for a renewal of the orders, but although he made all haste on his second visit to Ireland, the Queen's death took place before his arrival, and the poor Protestant people were preserved!

MOTIF: K.978.2 [*Message of death lost*].
¶ Curwen was a fit agent for persecution. He was a notorious "Vicar of Bray" and seems to have advocated persecution in whatever party he was engaged. In his old age he was made Bishop of Oxford and made his palace at Swinbrook, where he died in 1568. He was buried at Burford.

DANIEL BRYAN

Hone's *Table Book*, III, p. 631.

During the siege of Acre, Daniel Bryan, an old seaman, and captain of the foretop, who had been turned over from the *Blanche* into Sir Sidney Smith's ship *Le Tigre*, repeatedly applied to be employed on shore; but being an elderly man and rather deaf, his request was not acceded to. At the first storming of the breach by the French, one of their generals fell among the multitude of the slain, and the Turks, in triumph, struck off his head, and, after mangling the body with their sabres, left it a prey to the dogs, which in that country are of great ferocity, and rove in herds. In a few days it became a shocking spectacle, and when any of the sailors who had been on shore returned to their ship, inquiries were constantly made respecting the state of the French general. To Dan's frequent demands of his messmates why they had not buried him, the only answer he received was, "Go and do it yourself." One morning, having obtained leave to go and see the town, he dressed himself as though for an excursion of pleasure, and went ashore with the surgeon in the jolly-boat. About an hour or two after, while the surgeon was dressing the wounded Turks in the hospital, in came honest Dan, who, in his rough, good-natured manner, exclaimed, "I've been burying the general, sir, and now I'm come to see the sick." Not particularly attending to the tar's salute, but fearing that he might catch the plague, which was making great ravages among the wounded Turks, the surgeon immediately ordered him out. Returning on board, the cockswain asked the surgeon if he had seen old Dan? It was then that Dan's words in the hospital first occurred, and on further inquiry of the boat's crew, they related the following circumstances:

The old man procured a pick-axe, a shovel, and a rope, and insisted on being let down out of a port-hole, close to the breach. Some of his more juvenile companions offered to attend him. "No!" he replied. "You are too young to be shot yet; as for me, I am old and deaf, and *my* loss would be no great matter." Persisting in his adventure, in the midst of the firing, Dan was slung and lowered down, with his instruments of action on his shoulder. His first difficulty was to beat away the dogs. The French levelled their pieces—they were on the instant of firing at the hero!—but an officer, perceiving the friendly intentions of the sailor, was seen to throw himself across the file: instantaneously the din of military thunder ceased, a dead, solemn silence prevailed, and the worthy fellow consigned the corpse to its parent earth. He covered it with mould and stones, placing a large stone at its head, and another at its feet. The unostentatious grave was formed, but no inscription recorded the fate or character of its possessor. Dan, with the peculiar air of a British sailor, took a piece of chalk from his pocket, and attempted to write

"HERE YOU LIE, OLD CROP!"

He was then, with his pick-axe and shovel, hoisted into the town, and the hostile firing immediately recommenced.

A few days afterwards, Sir Sidney, having been informed of the circumstance, ordered old Dan to be called into the cabin—"Well, Dan, I hear you have buried the French general."—"Yes, your honour."—"Had you any body with you?"—"Yes, your honour."—"Why, Mr ——— says you had not."—"But I had, your honour."—"Ah! Who had you?"—"God Almighty, sir."—"A very good assistant indeed. Give old Dan a glass of grog."—"Thank your honour." Dan drank the grog, and left the cabin highly gratified. He was for several years a pensioner in the Royal Hospital at Greenwich.

MOTIF: G.303.9.4.7.1, in which the Devil, tempting a girl, asks if she is lonely, and the girl replies, "No, Devil, with God and the Angels", is the nearest to old Daniel's reply.

¶ There is no express motif for "Acts of Piety", of which burying the dead is one of the chief.

Sir Sidney Smith succeeded in raising the Siege of Acre, besieged by Napoleon, in 1799. Old Daniel was risking his life to bury the body of an enemy, killed and mangled by his allies.

THE DEATH OF KING ELLA [summary]

Parkinson, *Yorkshire Legends and Traditions*, 1st series, p. 14.

When York fell to the Danes, about A.D. 867, King Ella was absent from the city on a hunting expedition. As he sat at dinner one day, a blind man, ringing a little bell which he carried in his hand, came and asked to speak with the King. He was first given food, and then, at the end of dinner, he said to the King that, though they had had such good success with their hunting, the Danes had done better, for they had taken York, and slain many barons, as well as King Ella's ally, Osbert, the King of Deira. "How do you know all this?" asked Ella. "My sense has shown it to me," said the blind man, and went on to say that Ella's nephew, Orrum, would be the first to be killed in the battle there. "If you believe me," he continued, "you will not go forward. And, nevertheless, it cannot be otherwise; a king must lose his head." And he added, "If this is not the truth, kill me."

The King, enraged, put the blind man under strict guard; shut up his nephew in a high tower; summoned his guard and his followers, and set out for York. As they went, they met many wounded and others who had escaped from the city, and found that everything was as the blind man had related.

But in the meantime, Orrum, infuriated by his confinement, found two shields in his tower and, fitting them to his arms as wings, leapt from the window to the ground. Miraculously, he escaped unhurt; he saw a knight standing nearby, and seized his horse, and three javelins which he held in his hand, and rode off towards York, determined to be the first to strike a blow there. With his first and second darts he slew two knights in the enemy's front rank; but before he could shoot the third, an archer pierced him through the heart, and he fell dead.

King Ella was beside himself with grief, but in his frenzy he penetrated two ranks of the Danes, not knowing what he did. Then, with Danes all around him he too was slain, and few of his men escaped. The place where he was wounded became known as Elle-croft. The English call it Elle-cross.

TYPE 934*. MOTIFS: M.370.1 [*Prophecy of death fulfilled*]; M.341.2.18 [*Prophecy: death in battle*].

¶ O'Suilleabhain cites a number of Irish versions of this legend, of which that given in Kennedy's *Fireside Stories of Ireland* is the nearest.

THE DEATH OF RALPH CHEINDUIT
[slightly shortened]

Matthew Paris, *English History*, I, p. 460.

On the same day [1 December 1243] breathed forth his spirit Radulph Cheinduit, the inexorable and unwearied persecutor of the Church of St Alban's, and the impudent usurper of its liberties, for the space of three years. This I say, that all Christ's faithful followers may see the evidence of the miracle, and the just vengeance which Alban, the protomartyr of England, inflicted upon him. In fact, having been for three years lying under a sentence, and having insolently despised the keys of the Church, he, in the palace of Westminster, tossing up his head, said to many there assembled: "Ha! What do you say about the monks of St Alban's? Eh! What do you say about them? They have excommunicated me so long a time, so often, and so effectually, that I am much the better for it—fat and well—and so stout, that I can hardly get into my saddle, when I ride on horseback." Scarcely had he finished, when he was suddenly struck with infirmity, and lack of strength, and in a desperate state, scarcely breathing, he was carried home. He was just about to draw his last breath, and the hiccough which precedes death was manifesting itself, when the most benignant martyr St Alban, interposed, by the will of the Lord, who wishes that no one should perish, but rather that he should be converted. Then Ralph, uttering a deep sigh, caused to be called, in great haste, some of the monks, whom he knew better than the others, to submit himself to their will, and offer them full satisfaction for the transgressions he had been guilty of towards them; which they benevolently accepted. In order that, if he died, he might not fall into the abyss of despair,...they granted him the benefit of absolution, when he had promised to make reparation for the injuries and wickednesses committed by him.

MOTIFS: Q.220 [*Impiety punished*]; Q.551.6 [*Magic sickness as punishment*]; Q.572 [*Magic sickness as punishment remitted*].

THE DEATH OF SINGING JAMIE

School of Scottish Studies, John Elliot, *Notebooks*.

Before Macpherson died, he played his fiddle on the gallows, and sung "A Lovesong for Mary Gordon"—then he submitted to execution. Immediately after, his reprieve arrived.

The day Jamie Macpherson was to die, was bleak with snow and a searing wind that swept down from the Highlands. By noon the streets of Banff between the Tolbooth and the cross-roads where the gallows stood, were solid with people, and rumours rippled among [them] that Braco Buff, guarding against a reprieve, had put the town clock on by half an hour.

Macpherson's whole life had been of the stuff of legend, and his walk to the gallows, on November 16th, 1700, was in keeping with his strong character. He led the Sheriff's procession, playing his violin, and the music and the words he had written especially for the occasion:

> "But dauntingly and wantonly
> And rantingly I'll gae.
> I'll play a tune, and dance it roon,
> Below the gallows-tree."

Because of the poignant love story behind it, "Macpherson Rant", as it came to be known, was to stir ballad-makers for decades. Robert Burns used it to make one of his loveliest poems.

Jamie Macpherson was the natural son of a Highland chieftain by a gypsy mother. He spent his boyhood at Invereshie, where his doting father gave his wild nature all the freedom it craved; but the family priest saw a gentle streak in the lad, and fostered his love for music and poetry by teaching him the violin. Soon the fiddle became as constant a companion as his sword—twin symbols of the opposed sides of his nature. When he was fifteen, his father died, and because of Jamie's illegitimate birth, a distant cousin became the new Laird of Invereshie. The boy felt it keenly. Even before the drinking bout following the old Laird's funeral was half over, Jamie had disappeared. Taking his sword and fiddle, he went into the mountains to join his mother's people. His mother had never married, preferring to remain faithful to the memory of Jamie's father. She now transferred her adoration to his son, and under her guidance he became the gypsies' leader.

They wandered the Highlands, buying horses, which they sold to the farmers of the Northern Lowlands. Only on two small counts were they law-breakers—[as] *Sorners*—an offence in Scots laws, which vagabonds committed when they took up winter-quarters in farmers' empty barns and outhouses. It was a trivial offence; there wasn't a farmer in the Highlands who would refuse Jamie his shelter, for he paid a handsome rent, and he made the winter gay with his music and dancing. But *sorning* was to cost Jamie Macpherson dear, after he had run foul of the vindictive Alexander Duff, Laird of Braco.

A Girl Screamed

Jamie came one night to a farmhouse near the Balloch, the long hill dividing Banffshire from Aberdeenshire. Horses were tethered at the door, and all looked peaceful enough; but as he dismounted, a girl's scream ripped the silence. Jamie kicked open the door, his sword at the ready. A strange sight met his gaze. By the light of the peat fire in the open hearth he saw a girl cowering in the corner. The bodice of her gown had been torn from her shoulder, and her eyes were wide with terror.

Standing over her was Braco, swaying tipsily. He turned with a snarl as Jamie entered, and giving a bellow that brought his henchmen running from the kitchen, he hurled himself upon him. In a moment Jamie's men had joined in, and a desperate brawl began. But Braco's men were no match for the tough mountain gypsies; they were glad to throw themselves on their horses, and gallop away. Braco, badly mauled by Jamie, rode off, beside himself with fury and humiliation. The girl, Mary Gordon, overwhelmed Jamie with gratitude. She had long gone in fear of Braco, and some creature of his must have told him her father was away from the farm that night.

As they talked, they knew they were in love. Mary Gordon had great beauty, and she was defenceless. Before he left that night, Jamie vowed to protect Mary from the loutish attentions of Braco Duff.

Next day, Braco in his fury, went to Nicholas Dunbar, the hereditary Sheriff of Banffshire, and got him to issue a warrant for Macpherson's arrest, on the charge of *sorning*. Jamie, hearing what was afoot, waylaid the messenger, and, robbing him of the warrant, he escaped to the mountains. Dunbar promptly declared him an outlaw in the county of Banff.

Jamie made for Inverness, to the district of Badenoch, where he was born, taking refuge with his cousin, the Laird of Invereshie. Convivial Donald Macpherson was delighted. Jamie's music brought a gaiety back to Invereshie it had lacked since he left.

Donald was fond of a midnight raid upon the cattle of neighbours with whom he had quarrelled. This was common practice in the Highlands, and was not thought a crime, since retaliation always followed. One night Jamie foolishly joined in such a raid. He was caught and imprisoned.

Escape was easy, but the Sheriff of Inverness followed the example of Banff, and declared him an outlaw. The forces arrayed against Jamie were now becoming formidable, he was only safe when sheltering in lonely mountain sheilings. Yet Mary Gordon saw much of him. He would come down from the mountains, eluding every trap Braco Duff set for him. Then one winter Jamie moved into quarters at Kincardine O'Neill, a few miles from Aberdeen. The magistrates, hearing the notorious outlaw was *sorning* at their very gates, ordered the farmers to drive him away, but the farmers refused. Jamie, with equal recklessness, announced he would parade openly in the streets of Aberdeen the following day.

In spite of his friends' appeal, he set off early next morning in his kilt, carrying his great two-handed sword over his shoulder as a further touch of defiance. His piper, Jamie Brown, led the way. His approach, heralded by Brown piping, brought a cheering mob on his heels, while the magistrates sat in the Guildhall, biting their nails at this affront. At last they ordered the town guard to arrest him. They did, but only after a bitter fight, in which the townspeople sided with the fight Jamie had made. Even then, James Brown escaped. Macpherson was shut in the Tolbooth, and a courier was sent to warn Braco Duff that his enemy was at last in captivity. Braco returned with a posse of men to carry Macpherson back to Banff, but when he arrived the magistrates had grown cautious. After all, there was no warrant against Jamie in Aberdeenshire. They refused to hand him over, without the [consent] of their Sheriff, who was in Edinburgh, attending the high court of justiciary.

Tremendous Ride

Meanwhile, Jamie's mother ordered Brown to ride to Invereshie with the news. "If Donald Macpherson has one drop of the old Laird's blood," she cried, "he'll come back with you like the wild cat to his mate."

It was a tremendous ride when the uplands were deep in snow, but Brown did not hesitate. He roughened the pony's shoes, and set off up Deeside, and across the forbidding mountains. Beyond three stops at remote sheilings, where friendly shepherds gave him food and rest, he did not draw rein until his pony stood exhausted before the door of Invereshie Castle.

In four hours, Brown was on his way back with Donald Macpherson at his side. They reached Aberdeen on the night of the fifth day after Jamie's arrest, to find the Sheriff had returned, and had authorized Braco to carry Jamie into Banff on the following day.

Invereshie laid his plans, and long before daylight, he and Jamie Brown were making for the Tolbooth. Brown's first task was to break into the council chambers and collect Jamie's great sword, which was on show there as a trophy. Hiding it under his plaid, he hurried to overtake Donald.

The first streaks of dawn were in the sky as they came to the prison. Already there were two or three stragglers in the castle gates, and two guards were pacing outside the court-house adjoining the Tolbooth. At the foot of the steps leading to Jamie's cell, a huge turnkey slept over a peat fire. Silently, Invereshie threw his plaid over the sleeper's head, Before the man was properly awake, his hands were tied, and Brown had robbed him of his keys. By now the turnkey was roaring the alarm, and the guards came at the double. But Brown had opened the cell, and Jamie leaped out, wielding his sword. The three men fought their way down the steps, and the enemy fell back. Soon the way was clear, and they were running for Broad Street. Here horses awaited them.

Shortly after the escape, Jamie's mother died, and with her passed much of his love for wild life. He now craved the peace of a home with Mary Gordon, yet, when he had decided to emigrate to America with her, he recklessly took his band on a last trip into the Banffshire town of Keith, during the fair of St Rufus.

No Escape

The town was crowded, and friends warned him Braco and his henchmen were there, but Jamie heeded none, until he faced his enemy in the Square. They fought their way into a narrow street, where Braco, calling three of his men, dashed into a house. He appeared shortly afterwards in an upper window, throwing plaids and blankets down upon the heads of the Macphersons. The trick worked. Jamie's men got their weapons entangled, and they were overpowered.

There was no escape this time. After a hasty trial, Jamie Macpherson, for his crimes of *sorning*, was condemned to death. In the last days before the execution, while his cousin, the Laird of Invereshie, was fighting hard for his reprieve, Jamie was strangely occupied with his fiddle, and the last time Mary Gordon visited him in his last cell, he handed her a manuscript, the words and music of the famous "Rant".

When the procession reached the gallows, Jamie ran up the steps on to the platform, and with infinite grace, began playing his "Rant" for the last time:

> But Braco Duff, in rage enough,
>   He first laid hands on me.
> If death did not arrest my course,
>   Avenged should I be.
>
> But dauntingly and wantonly
>   And vauntingly I'll gae,
> I'll play a tune, and dance it roon,
>   Below the gallows-tree.

In the silence after the wild music had finished, Jamie stepped forward, and offered his violin to anyone in the vast crowd who would take it. But he had so moved them with his playing, that nobody could speak. With a shrug, Jamie broke his beloved instrument over his knee, and threw it into the waiting grave.

When all was over, a horseman rode over the Brig o' Banff with the reprieve that Jamie's cousin had been fighting for, and Mary Gordon, hearing of this, became half crazed. She wandered the countryside for years afterwards, always clutching to her heart the manuscript of "Macpherson's Rant".

MOTIF: P.515 [*Pardon of criminal comes too late*].

¶ James Macpherson is one of the many outlaws endeared to the popular imagination, but a much pleasanter and more attractive character than Gilderoy or Dick Turpin. See "Christie's Will", "Dicky of Kingswood".

THE DEVIL'S CLOAK

Wilkie, *Bygone Fife*, p. 13.

Though it was not till 1627 that the "wast o' fife, specially Dunfermlin and Torryburn, began to be infested be witches and warlocks", there was already a tradition there which Dr Robert Chambers heard two centuries later. It seems to show that even while the Scottish Solomon was in residence in the royal palace of his ancestors above the brawling burn, Satan was wont to stroll through the corridors.

The story is too familiar to need repetition in detail. Briefly, it runs that, when the King and Queen and all the court had retired, Their Majesties were awakened by the scream of the nurse who watched over the recently born infant, afterwards Charles the First. James rushed into the chamber, in none the best of humour at being aroused, and gathered from the agitated dame that "there was ane like an auld man came into the room and threw his cloak owre the Prince's cradle; and sune drew it till him again, as if he had ta'en cradle, bairn an' a' awa' wi' him".

The King, deeply versed in demonology, concurred in the nurse's suspicions as to the identity of the visitor, and augured the worst for his unfortunate son.

"The deil has cussen his cloak ower him already."

MOTIFS: N.101 [*Inexorable fate*]; N.112 [*Bad luck personified*].
See "Charles I and the Southwell Shoemaker".

DICKY OF KINGSWOOD

Denham Tracts, I, p. 246.
"'By my faith, but ye're welcome,' quoth Dicky of Kingswood".

Dicky of Kingswood, or Cunning Dick, as he was more generally called (who lived in Staward Peel), was a noted Northumbrian riever, and entertained an opinion that taking life was unnecessary in plundering, except to those unacquainted with their art. Many tales are told of Dick's prowess in this department. The following exploit gave birth to the above saying: Happening one evening to call at a country inn, he found a number of farmers enjoying themselves over their cups. Their horses, a dozen in number, were in the stable at the back part of the house; this Dicky had previously ascertained, and he placed his own brood mare along with them. After continuing some short time at the inn, he mounted his own grey mare, Meggy, left the stable door open, and had not proceeded far on his homeward journey ere he discovered the whole of the horses in full gallop after him—"By my faith, but ye're welcome," cried Dicky—and the lucky thief got off clear with his booty.

To make the story more clear, it may be necessary to note that the farmers' horses were what in common parlance we term "stallions", and this happening in the "spring time of the year", there was small need of a helping hand to unloose them.

TYPE 1525B (variant).

¶ It is not uncommon for a proverbial phrase to arise out of a story.
  See "The Case is Altered" (A, III).

DONIBRISTLE [abbreviated]

Wilkie, *Bygone Fife*, p. 58.

From St David's to Aberdour, the highway dividing them from Fordell and Otterston, extend the fair lands of Donibristle, with the Firth stretching away to the south and beyond it the Pentlands and the ridge that slopes gently down from Edinburgh Castle to Holyrood....

Donibristle will always keep its memories of the bonnie Earl of Moray.

> He was a braw gallant
> And he played at the glove,
> And the bonnie Earl of Moray
> He was the Queen's love.

So at least James is alleged to have thought; but, in truth, Queen Anne, married to him two years earlier, seems to have given him little real cause for jealousy. They were neighbours, the court at Dunfermline and the Morays at Donibristle, and doubtless the young Queen may sometimes have been tempted to compare the tall, handsome and accomplished noble with her shabbily-dressed, "shauchly", intemperate and oath-addicted spouse. For whatever reason, Huntly's trial for the murder was half-hearted, and he was allowed to escape.

James Stewart, son of Lord Doune, had married Elizabeth, Countess of Moray in her own right, in 1580. He was two years younger than the King, from whom he had a pension of £500 a year. He had quarrelled with Huntly, his hereditary enemy, or Huntly with him, and had retired from court. His foe obtained a commission for his capture. His sympathy with that strange and reckless adventurer, Francis Stewart, Earl of Bothwell, was the ground alleged. A promise of pardon had, however, been sent to Moray through Lord Ochiltree, and it was in reliance on that being implemented that he came to Donibristle. Upon the castle on a dark February night in 1591–2, when it was occupied only by Moray himself, the Sheriff of Moray, and a few retainers, Huntly descended with overwhelming force. The red cock crew, and from Aberdour to Spencerfield, from Otterston to Balbougie, the cry went up that Donibristle was in flames. Yet no man, in an age when each had need to keep his own head with his hand, seems to have rushed to the rescue.

Exit from the doomed stronghold appeared impossible. It was beset by Huntly's clansmen, who watched each door and gateway. The Sheriff made a dash for life, and was instantly slain. Perhaps his object was to distract the attention of the besiegers, for, as in the case of most castles, there was a concealed subterranean way that opened in a secret place upon the shore. Through it Moray stole. He emerged under the stars, and, exhausted with the struggle and the smoke, sat down upon a rock. The sea breeze fanned into a glow a smouldering tassel on his cap and betrayed his presence to a prowling band of his enemies. They caught him ere he could flee, and in a hand-to-hand combat with Huntly himself and Gordon of Buckie, he fell, his head slashed by the sword of the ferocious northern chief. He had but time to accuse Huntly of spoiling a better face than his own when Buckie struck the mortal blow....

Donibristle has accomplished its destiny. The first destruction was that in which Huntly smoked out his hereditary foe. The second followed in due time, by accident. Then once more, in the end of the eighteenth century, the castle was rebuilt. It endured this time for sixty years. It was in 1858 in the days of the 12th Earl that, for the last time, the dark woodland was reddened by the glare of the burning pile. The portraits of the family perished, and with them that of Prince Charlie. All went, with the exception of a few pieces of ancient furniture and some priceless books.

MOTIFS: P.515 [*Pardoning of criminal comes too late*]; S.112.0.2 [*House burned with all inside*]; U.34 [*Nobleman unpunished for murder*].

¶ The ballad on the tale, "The Bonnie Earl of Moray", is Child, No. 181. This is a specimen of many tales of feuds between the nobles of Scotland.

DRAKE AS A WIZARD

Mrs Bray, *A Description of the Parts of Devonshire Bordering on the Tamar and Tavy* (1836), 3 vols, II, pp. 170–3.

I. DRAKE AND THE ARMADA

The day as Sir Francis Drake was playing at kales on Plymouth Hoe he had news that a foreign fleet was sailing into the harbour. He finished his game and then took a hatchet and ordered a large block of wood to be brought to him. He chopped this up into small pieces and threw them into the sea with magic words. As they touched the water each one became a fire-ship and sailed against the foreign fleet so that it was utterly destroyed.

II. DRAKE AND HIS LADY

When Drake sailed away to circumnavigate the world, and "shot the gulf", he was away so long that his lady despaired of ever seeing him again. After seven years she decided to re-marry; the bridal day came, and the bridal party were in the church.

At that moment one of the spirits who served Sir Francis brought him news, as he sailed in the Antipodes, of what was happening in England. At once he took a cannon and fired right down into the sea. So powerful was the shot and so true was his aim that the ball sped straight through the earth and landed with a loud explosion between the bride and bridegroom just as they reached the altar.

"That is Drake's shot," said his lady. "I am still a wife." And she went home and waited patiently for his return.

III. DRAKE AND THE RIVER

In Drake's days there was no fresh water at Plymouth, so that the housewives had to go all the way to Plympton to wash their clothes. Sir Francis Drake resolved to cure this, so one day he called for his horse and rode off to Dartmoor, where he hunted about until he found a fine spring that suited his notions. He pronounced a magic word and turned his horse's head for home. Off he went as fast as he could gallop, and the spring followed his horse's heels all the way back. So the good wives of Plymouth were never without fresh water again.

IV. DRAKE'S CANNON BALL

Ruth L. Tongue, *Folktales of England*, p. 94.

There were one o' the Sydenham maids, and 'er got 'erself betrothed to Sir Francis Drake. But afore they could be married, 'e 'ad to go away on a voyage, and 'ow long it'd be afore 'e could come back, no one knew, and 'e didn't trust 'er father. So they took their troth-plight, the two of 'en, afore Drake sailed away. Well, 'e sailed away, for three long years, and Sir George Sydenham, 'e found another suitor for 'is daughter, a much richer one. Well, no matter what the maid do say, marriage were announced, and she were half afraid o' Sir Francis Drake, but she were more afraid of 'er father. So she gave in.

Well now, Sir Francis Drake, 'e did do some very strange things—'e did sit on Plymouth 'oe, a-whittling of a stick, and all the chips that fell into the sea, they did turn into ships, to go fight the Spanish Armada. Now, although 'e'd been gone three years, 'e knew what was 'appening, so at the very door o' the church, 'e dropped a red-'ot cannon ball in front o' the bridal party. Oh! give 'en a fright, did—and when 'e come 'ome at last, 'twas to find 'is bride and 'er dear father a-waiting for 'en with smiles. As for t'other bridegroom, 'e'd a-taken 'isself across the length and breadth of England. But I expect Sir Francis Drake knew where 'e was tew!

From a member of Watchet W.I., 1950. Also heard at Chipstable in 1960.
I. MOTIF: G.295*(g) [*Wizard produces gunboats from pieces of wood in water*] (Baughman).
II and IV. MOTIF: G.295(k*) [*Wizard throws cannon-ball several thousand miles to prevent second marriage of his wife, who thought him dead*] (Baughman).
III. MOTIF: D.2151.2 [*Magic control of rivers*].
IV. MOTIF: N.681 [*Husband arrives home just as wife is to marry another*].
¶ Sir Francis Drake was believed to be a wizard by the Spaniards, and even in his own country he shared with other outstanding men, such as Roger Bacon, Cardinal Wolsey, Sir Walter Raleigh, Owen Glendower and Oliver Cromwell, a reputation for wizardry. The people round Combe Sydenham still believe that Drake's cannon ball rolls up and down in time of national danger, and his drum was said to sound during the Second World War. Newbolt's "Drake's Drum" is written on a variation of these traditions, by which it is said that if the drum is beaten, Drake will return. In the modern version of Drake and his Lady, Drake was merely betrothed to the Sydenham girl, as he was in Noyes' long poem on Drake, which, however, does not introduce the supernatural element.
See "Sir Francis Drake and the Devil" (B, III).

DREAM PORTENDING THE DEATH OF WILLIAM RUFUS

Roger of Wendover, *Chronicle*, I, p. 443.

A.D. 1100, King William Rufus held his court at Christmas with much magnificence in Gloucester, at Easter in Winchester and at Whitsuntide in London. On the morrow of St Peter's ad vincula* he went to shoot in the New Forest, where Walter Tyrrel, shooting at a stag, unintentionally struck the king, who fell pierced to the heart, without uttering a word, and thus by a miserable death ended his cruel life. Many signs presignified his departure; for the day before his death, he dreamed that he was bled by a physician, and that the stream of his blood reached to heaven, and obscured the sky. Upon this, he sprang up from sleep, invoking the name of St Mary, and calling for a light, kept his chamberlains with him for the remainder of the night. In the morning, a foreign monk, who was at court on some business connected with his church, related to Robert Fitz-Hamon, a powerful nobleman, intimate with the king, a wonderful dream which he had seen the preceding night; he saw the king enter a church, and cast his usual haughty look on the congregation round him, after which he took the crucifix between his teeth, and almost bit off its arms and legs; the crucifix was at first passive, but afterwards kicked the

* August 2nd.

40

king with its right foot, so that he fell upon the pavement, and emitted such a large flame from its mouth that the smoke of it rose in a cloud even to the stars. Robert told this dream to the king, who said with a laugh, "He is a monk, and, like all monks, dreamed this to get something by it; give him a hundred shillings, that he may not say he has dreamed in vain." The king's wretched death was also foretold...by the blood which oozed out from the ground, though there was no want of other tokens, presignifying the same event. For Anselm, archbishop of Canterbury, when he was in exile for three years, through his tyranny, went from Rome to Marcenniac, about the first of August, to enjoy the conversation of Hugh, abbat of Cluny; there a conversation arose between them, concerning King William, and the abbat affirmed with the most solemn protestation of truth, that in the past night he had seen the king summoned before the throne of God, accused of his crimes, and sentenced by the just Judge to damnation; but he did not explain how he was informed of it, neither did the archbishop or any other of those who were present, ask him, out of respect to his great holiness. The following day also, the archbishop went to Lyons, and the same night, when the monks who had accompanied him had chanted the matin-service, behold, a young man, simply dressed, and of a mild countenance, stood by one of the clerks of the archbishop, who had his eyes shut; and calling him by name, "Adam," said he, "are you asleep?" The clerk answered, "No," and the young man continued, "Do you wish to hear some news?" "Most willingly," said Adam. "Then," said the young man, "be informed for certain that the quarrel between the archbishop and king William is now put an end to." The clerk, roused by these words, looked up, and opened his eyes, but saw no one. The next night also, one of the monks of the same archbishop was standing at his post, and chanting matins, when someone held out to him a small paper to read, on which the monk read the words, "King William is dead." He immediately opened his eyes, but saw no one except his companions. A short time after, two of his monks came to him, and telling him of the king's death, earnestly advised him immediately to return to his see.

MOTIFS: M.302.7 [*Prophecy through dreams*]; H.617 [*Symbolic interpretations of dreams*]; V.515 [*Allegorical visions*].

¶ The number of prophetic dreams and visions heralding the death of Rufus, the way in which the rumours spread beforehand among the common people, and the weeping crowd which followed his body, have been utilized by Dr Margaret Murray as a proof that William Rufus was a sacred king who submitted himself as a pre-arranged sacrifice. In her book on the Divine King Charles II is cited as the last example of a sacrificed king, and à Becket, Joan of Arc, and Gilles de Rais are supposed to have been willing substitutes for the monarch.

The bias of the Church against William Rufus is clear in the form these dreams took. See "The Death Fetch of William Rufus" (B, XII).

THE EAGLE AND CHILD

Harland and Wilkinson, *Legends and Traditions of Lancashire*, p. 259.

When the war was 'twixt the Englishmen and the Irishmen, the power of the English so sore assaulted the Irishmen, that the king of them, being of Ireland, was constrained to take succour, by flight, into other parts for his safeguard; and the queen, being pregnant, and great with child, right near the time of deliverance, for dread of the rudeness of the commonalty, took her flight into the wilderness, where her chance was to suffer travail of child; bringing forth two children, the one a son, the other a daughter; when after by natural compulsion, she and such gentlewomen as were with her was constrained to sleep, insomuch that the two children were ravished from the mother; and the daughter, as it is said, is kept in Ireland with the fairies. Insomuch that against the time of death of any of that blood of Stanleys, she maketh a certain noise in one quarter of Ireland, where she useth [to stay].

The son was taken and borne away with an eagle, and brought into Lancashire, into a park called Lathom Park, whereat did dwell a certain Lord named the Lord Lathom; the which Lord Lathom walking in his park, heard a child lament and cry, and perceived the skirts of the mantle lying over the nest side, and made his servants to bring down the child unto him.

And whereas both he and his wife being in far age, and she past conceiving of child; considering they never could have issue; reckoning that God had sent this child by miracle, they condescended to make this child their heir, and so did. At length this Lord Lathom and his wife deceased, and this young man, which was named Oskell of Lathom, reigned and ruled this land as right heir, and he had to issue a daughter, which was his heir and child by the Lady Lathom.

It chanced so that one Stanley, being a younger brother of the house of Wolton in Cheshire, was servant to the Abbot of West Chester; this young man Stanley was carver to the Abbot, and he would not break his fast on the Sunday till he had heard the High Mass. Insomuch that it chanced one Sunday when the meat was served on the table, he had so great hunger he carved the pig's head, and conveyed one of the ears of the pig and did eat it.

When the Abbot sat down, and perchance missed this pig's ear, he was miscontent, and in a great fume, and reviled so extremely and so heinously this young Stanley, that he threw the napkin at his head, and said he would do him no more service and departed. And he came to the king's court, and obtained his service, and proved so active a fellow that the renown sprang and inflamed upon him, insomuch that the fame and bruit descended from him around this realm.

And when, as the use then was, that noble adventurers would seek their fortune and chance into divers and strange nations, one renowned gallant came into England, and he called as challenger for death and life, come who list. Insomuch that the king commanded this Stanley to cope with him; and, to make short protestation, his chance was to overthrow the challenger and obtain the victory.

Then the king made him knight, and gave him certain lands to live on.

After this foresaid Stanley came for marriage to the daughter of Oskell of Lathom, which was found in the eagle's nest, and obtained her favour, and espoused her. And then after the death of Oskell he was Lord Lathom, and enjoyed it many years. And for such service as he did afterwards the king made him Lord Stanley; and he was the first lord of the name; and so by that reason the Stanleys descended of Lathom give the eagle and child in their arms.

From Hare's MSS. *Journal of The British Archaeological Association*, Vol. VII.
MOTIFS: R.131 [*Abandoned child rescued*]; S.354.3 [*Prince adopts exposed child*]; P.14.15 [*King has champion to enforce respect*]; Q.113.0.1 [*High honours as reward*].
¶ The legend does not explain how the origin of the child in the eagle's nest was discovered, nor the connection with his twin sister, who had disappeared in an equally mysterious way.

THE EARL OF TRAQUAIR

Scott, *Minstrelsy of the Scottish Border*, II, p. 220.

A tradition...bears, that the Earl of Traquair, on the day of the battle [of Philiphaugh, 1643], was advancing with a large sum of money, for the payment of Montrose's forces, attended by a blacksmith, one of his retainers. As they crossed Minchmoor, they were alarmed by firing, which the Earl conceived to be Montrose exercising his forces, but which his attendant, from the constancy and irregularity of the noise, affirmed to be the tumult of an engagement. As they came below Broadmeadows, upon Yarrow, they met their fugitive friends, hotly pursued by the Parliamentary troopers. The Earl, of course, turned, and fled also: but his horse, jaded by the weight of dollars which he carried, refused to take the hill; so that the Earl was fain to exchange with his attendant, leaving him with the breathless horse, and bag of silver, to shift for himself, which he is supposed to have done very effectually. Some of the dragoons, attracted by the appearance of the horse and trappings, gave chase to the smith, who fled up the Yarrow; but finding himself, as he said, encumbered with the treasure, and unwilling that it should be taken, he flung it into a well, or pond, near the Tinnies, above Hangingshaw. Many wells were afterwards searched in vain; but it is the general belief, that the smith, if he ever hid the money, knew too well how to anticipate the scrutiny. There is, however, a pond, which some peasants began to drain, not long ago, in hopes of finding the golden prize, but were prevented, as they pretended, by supernatural interference.

1803.

The story must be mere fiction. A troop of horse, which Traquair had sent under Lord Linton, to join Montrose, was withdrawn by him on the night before the battle, on which account Traquair was denounced as a traitor, both by Wishart and Guthrie.

TYPES ML.8000 ML.8010

¶   The persistence of the legend of the treasure guardian is shown by its appearance in this tale of accidentally lost treasure.

THE EARL OF TYRONE

J. Roby, *Lancashire Traditions*, I, p. 274.

At the end of the Irish Rebellion in 1603, a number of dispossessed chieftains fled to England. Among them was Hugh O'Neale, whom Elizabeth had created Earl of Tyrone; in spite of this favour, he had intrigued with Spain, in the hope of driving the English out of Ireland altogether. He took refuge in the woods surrounding Rochdale, venturing out only at night, and lay there concealed, until a rumour of a "wild man of the woods" sprang up, for the natives of the place took him for a ghost.

An ancient manor-house, Grislehurst, stood near these woods; the seat of Sir Francis Holt, whose wife Constance had borne him one son, Francis, and a daughter named liked her mother, Constance. The son was abroad on foreign travel, and the mother had died some years before. The daughter, now aged nineteen, was mistress of the house, but her old nurse still tended and cherished her, and accompanied her on all her walks.

One night they had gone out to watch the sunset, and to catch its last rays. Constance climbed a steep cliff, overhanging the river. The nurse could not climb so far, but anxiously watched from below. To her horror, she suddenly saw a great piece of the cliff on which the girl was standing, break away and plunge her into the water far below. It was impossible to reach her, the swift current bore her along, and she seemed beyond all aid, when a figure bounding out of the woods leapt into the water, plunged in, and rescued the drowning girl. It was Tyrone, and though he vanished into the woods without a word, the nurse had taken in his strange garb and appearance, and her account confirmed the general belief that some supernatural being haunted the woods. The girl's father, however, was deeply concerned by the tale of the strange rescuer; and his dismay increased when in the evening, the tall stranger suddenly appeared in his room, and confessed that he had watched the lovely Constance from his hiding-place, and now that he had actually held her in his arms, his love for her was such that he could no longer remain in hiding. He begged her father to give her to him as his wife, then, not pausing for a reply, glided from the room.

The strange incident had been almost forgotten in the following weeks, except that Constance lost much of her former radiance, until, late one night, the mysterious stranger again appeared in the house, and begged for shelter. His enemies had got word of his hiding-place, and for Ireland's sake, he could not let himself be taken. Constance hid him in a secret room, and tended him there for some time, but one moonlight night, as she walked by the pond, before her bed-time, Tyrone suddenly appeared at her side, and confessing his love, bade her an agonized farewell. But as he spoke, footsteps sounded, and he knew he must be discovered. Once again Constance saved his life, hiding him this time in her own room. The soldiers knocked, and despite Holt's angry insistence that his house was unshakably loyal, they demanded to enter, and searched every room, even that of the lady of the house. In a minute his hiding-place behind the arras was revealed, and the officer burst into it. So long a silence followed, that at last Holt himself entered the place, to find, not the captive Tyrone, but the officer himself, gagged and bound, while Tyrone's abandoned mantle showed that he had made good his escape. He did in fact make his way to London, where his great influence and charm prevailed on Queen Elizabeth to give him a free pardon.

His strong love for Constance forced him to return to Grislehurst. He found her on her death-bed, wasted with feverish longing for her lover. Her father and the old nurse stood by her, praying and weeping. Tyrone burst into the room unannounced, and Constance's eyes fell upon him. He took her in his arms, but it was too late to save her life. She died a victim to the doom that overtook all women beloved by Tyrone.

MOTIFS: T.80 [*Tragic love*]; T.15 [*Love at first sight*]; T.97 [*Father opposed to daughter's marriage*]; R.162 [*Rescue by captor's daughter*]; T.81 [*Death from love*].

¶ This legend seems to have had little historical foundation. It seems unlikely that O'Neale was in England after his defeat in 1603, as he was in Ulster, negotiating his submission and pardon when Elizabeth died. He was possibly in a position to marry Constance Holt, as his third wife had died in 1594 and he had probably not yet married his fourth.

He was ardent in his love affairs, and attractive to women, but did not seem capable of retaining their affection. If Constance had seen more of him, her love in all likelihood would have been cured.

ELA OF SALISBURY

H. Bett, *English Legends*, p. 28.

There is a tradition, curiously parallel to that about Blondel and his search for Richard Cœur-de-Lion, relating to Ela, Countess of Salisbury, the wife of William Longspée, who was the natural son of Henry the Second by Fair Rosamund. It is said that at a very early age, after the death of her father, Ela was taken into Normandy, and there brought up in close custody. An English knight, William Talbot, went to Normandy disguised, and sought the Lady Ela for two years. At last, in the guise of a harper, he found the rich heiress and brought her to King Richard, who gave her hand in marriage to his brother, the Earl of Salisbury, she being then only ten years old. The Earl was in the entourage of King John, and was present at the signing of Magna Charta. After the death of the King, the Earl returned to his castle at Salisbury, and assisted in founding the Cathedral. He died in 1226. Six years after his widow founded in his memory the monastery at Laycock, in Wiltshire, and in 1238 took the veil, and became Abbess of the establishment. She died in 1261, and was buried in the choir. It is said that her second son perished in battle in the Holy Land, and the legend related that his mother, seated in her stall at Laycock, saw at the very moment his mailed form admitted into Heaven in a cloud of glory.

MOTIFS: R.111 [*Rescue of captive maiden*]; T.122 [*Marriage by royal order*]; V.511.1 [*Vision of Heaven*].
¶ See "Fair Rosamund".

THE ENCHANTED STEED [summary]

J. R. W. Coxhead, *Devon Traditions and Fairy Tales*, pp. 26–8.

The famous West Country highwayman, Tom Faggus, known to all readers of *Lorna Doone*, is said to have owed his success in great part to his strawberry roan, said to have been possessed of magical powers, which rescued him from many a tight corner.

He was a blacksmith, a native of South Molton, but, being ruined by a lawsuit, he took to the road, sometimes in company with a certain Penn, but more often alone.

To avoid meeting him, a company of farmers once, riding home together for greater safety, met Tom, nevertheless, on the top of Bratton Down, with the reins lying loose on his horse's neck, and a cocked pistol in each hand. At his command they all laid down their money-bags at his feet, and Tom rode off with the booty. Again the horse saved him when he was once arrested in an ale-house at Simonsbath, for, at his whistle, the horse broke down the stable-door, rushed into the house, mauled the constables with hooves and teeth, and bore off his master in triumph.

Another time, on Barnstaple Bridge, finding his escape barred at either end, Tom set his horse at the parapet, it jumped clear, and swam off down the river to safety.

One of his most daring exploits was to disguise himself, and riding up to a party of men who were waiting to capture him, ask why they were assembled there. On being told, he said he knew Tom Faggus well for a great rogue, and would be glad to stay and help them. Presently he advised them to discharge their firearms to be sure that the early morning damp had not injured the powder and priming. As soon as this was done, he produced his pistols, and, declaring his name, robbed all the party, and rode away.

In Porlock, while he was hiding in a certain house, a company armed with guns, pitchforks, scythes, and other country implements, surrounded the house, shouting "Faggus is taken!" But he leapt on his horse, dashed through the crowd, and, heedless of the blows they aimed at him, disappeared.

At last, however, he was taken. A constable, disguised as an old woman, entered the ale-house where Tom sat, and when Tom, always kindly disposed to the old and poor, had ordered him a drink, the constable gave a prearranged sign, and his companions entered, caught Tom, and bound him hand and foot. Even then he managed to give the shrill whistle which always brought his horse to his aid, but it was in vain; the horse had been shot dead in its stable, for all believed that while it lived Tom would never be captured.

Tom was hanged at Taunton at the next Assizes. But it was said that he had never been cruel to the poor, the sick, or those in distress. Like Robin Hood, what he took from the rich he conferred on the poor.

TYPE 1527A (variant). MOTIFS: B.301.4.8 [*Faithful horse fights together with its master*]; B.520 [*Animal saves person's life*]; B.335 [*Helpful animal killed by hero's enemy*].

¶ Tom Faggus is another of the sympathetic robbers. He is a secondary hero in Blackmore's *Lorna Doone*.

See "The Death of Singing Jamie".

FAIR ELLEN OF RADCLIFFE [summary]

J. Roby, *Traditions of Lancashire*, I, p. 134.

Fair Ellen was the daughter of Richard Radcliffe, whose second wife, her stepmother, regarded her with secret hatred and jealousy, for her father loved her very dearly.

The stepmother, pretending to be on her way to church, met Ellen, and bade her take a message to the master-cook. He was, on receiving the message, to dress at once for dinner the fairest white doe in the park. This message was a secret sign to the cook, contrived beforehand, that he should kill the lady Ellen herself, and make her flesh into a pie. But as the cook was about to plunge his ready-sharpened knife into the girl's heart, the scullion cried out to him to spare her, and make a pie of him instead. But the cook paid no heed, but threatened to slay the boy as well, if he dared betray him to Sir Richard.

At night Sir Richard came home, and sitting down to table, called for his daughter to serve him, as his custom was. His wife said that he must forget her, for she had gone away into a convent. But her father refused to eat until she came to him. Then the scullery-boy could keep silent no longer, and cried out, "If you will see your daughter, my lord, cut up that pie!" At this Sir Richard ordered the wicked wife to be burnt at the stake, and the cook to be stewed in boiling lead. The scullery-boy became his heir, and, as Radcliffe, Baron Fitzwalter, succeeded to all his estates.

MOTIFS: S.31 [Cruel stepmother]; S.115 [Murder by stabbing]; G.61 [Relative's flesh eaten unwittingly]; Q.414.1 [Punishment: boiling in lead].

¶ This is a naturalized version of "The Juniper Tree", without the reincarnation or the ghost. The story is attached to the tomb of one of the Radcliffes of Radcliffe Hall and his daughter. There appears to be not the slightest foundation for it, though in Roby's time the bloodstain on the floor was still shown. No heiress daughter was lost prematurely, and Radcliffe, Lord Fitzwalter, on whom the estate was settled on the failure of heirs, was certainly not a scullery-boy. The ballad in Percy's Reliques, which Roby quoted, is called "Fair Isabella".

See "Rosy", etc. (A, II).

FAIR ROSAMUND

H. Bett, English Legends, p. 27.

One of the most famous of the English traditions which are tragedies of love and jealousy, is the story of Fair Rosamund and her Bower. Nearly a century after her time, there is a description of "Rosamund's Chamber" in Woodstock Palace, but the usual belief about the Bower is that it was a sylvan lodge approached by a maze in the park. Holinshed records as a tradition among the people in his day the story of the discovery by the Queen of her husband's paramour. He writes that "the Queen found hir out by a silken thriddle, which the King had drawne after him out of hir chamber with his foote, and dealt with her in such sharpe and cruell wise that she lived not long after".

The angry Queen was supposed to have stabbed or poisoned her rival.

The tradition is that Rosamund was buried "in a house of nunnes, beside Oxford", with the famous verse upon her tomb:

> Hic jacet in tumba, Rosa mundi, non Rosa munda;
> Non redolet, sed olet, quae redolere solet.

There is a sixteenth-century ballad, entitled "Fair Rosamund", in Percy's *Reliques*. It tells us that the King had the bower made, and gave the charge of it to a faithful knight:

> Most curiously that bower was built
>   Of stone and timber strong,
> A hundered and fifty doors
>   Did to this bower belong.
>
> And they so cunninglye contriv'd
>   With turnings round about
> That none but with a clue of thread
>   Could enter in or out.
>
> And for his love and ladyes sake,
>   That was so fair and brighte,
> The keeping of this bower he gave
>   Unto a valiant knight.

The ballad goes on to relate that, during the King's absence in France, the Queen had the knight attacked and wounded. She secured the "clue of twined thread" which was in his keeping, and so found her way to Rosamund, and made her drink a cup of poison.

The facts appear to be, briefly, that Rosamund was the daughter of Walter de Clifford, and was born about 1140; that she became the mistress of Henry the Second; that she lived at Woodstock; that her connection with the King was a matter of common knowledge after he had imprisoned his wife, Eleanor; that Rosamund died not long after this, probably about 1176; and that she was buried in the chapter-house at Godstow. The story of the Queen's vengeance appears first of all in the fourteenth-century *French Chronicle of London*. The detail of the silken clue occurs first in Fabyan's *Chronicle*. The poison seems to be a later addition; the maze is a somewhat earlier detail. There is no historic warrant for the more dramatic element in the legend, which has found so memorable an expression in our poetry:

> Would I had been some maiden coarse and poor!
>   O me, that I should ever see the light!
> Those dragon eyes of anger'd Eleanor
>   Do hunt me day and night.

MOTIFS: T.230 [*Faithlessness in marriage*]; F.781.1 [*Labyrinth*]; T.257 [*Jealous wife*]; S.111 [*Murder by poisoning*].

¶ According to a common tradition not recorded in this ballad, Queen Eleanor offered Fair Rosamund the choice of dying by poison or a dagger. "The dagger or the bowl" was an almost proverbial expression.

See "Ela of Salisbury".

THE FATE OF A REBEL

J. R. W. Coxhead, *Legends of Devon*, p. 112.

After the Battle of Sedgemoor, in the year 1685, the survivors from the Duke of Monmouth's defeated army, and also people who had favoured his cause, were subjected to the most inhuman reprisals. Brutal troopers from the King's forces scoured the countryside throughout the western counties in search of their hapless victims.

Most of the poor fugitives, when captured, were at least given a mockery of a trial by the cruel Judge Jeffreys, before he condemned them to a dreadful death, but there are records of a few cases where bloodthirsty troopers took the law into their own hands and executed a victim on the spot with the greatest brutality.

One of these horrible cases is said to have occurred in the small town of Colyton, about four miles from Axminster. According to a local tradition, a fugitive from the battle, who lived in the lower part of the town at a place known as Bull's Court, had managed to reach his home safely. He was with his family when soldiers searching for him entered the house.

Slipping out of the back door into his garden, he concealed himself among some cabbages. The soldiers asked his children where their father was, and the children, apparently being too young to realize the gravity of the situation and the consequences to their father if he were caught, told them he was in the garden.

The bloodthirsty ruffians rushed out and soon discovered the unfortunate man among the cabbages. There, in his own vegetable patch, they executed him on their own authority.

Having killed him, they quartered his body, and put one of the pieces into a wheelbarrow.

As they wheeled their ghastly burden along the street, a shoemaker, who was also implicated in the rebellion, called out to the soldiers: "Ho! Ho! Then you've caught one of the rascals!"

The soldiers, not knowing that the shoemaker was also a fugitive from the battle, did him no harm, but, nevertheless they compelled him to perform the horrid task of wheeling the bloodstained portion of his late neighbour round the town as a warning to the rest of the inhabitants.

From this terrible tale, it can well be understood why the people of the West Country, even to this day, speak of the "Bloody Assizes"—or "Duking Days", as they were also called—with such aversion.

TYPE ML.8000. MOTIFS: S.100 [*Revolting murders and mutilations*]; S.139.2 [*Slain person dismembered*].

¶ This is one of the many "Duking Days" stories.

See "The Legend of the Sword", "The Puppy under the Table", "The Rebel's Dog" (B, VI).

THE FEARLESS BOY

Short Stories, Chambers, p. 12.

A little boy, five years of age, was on a visit to his grandmother. One day he was missed, and could nowhere be found. At last, after hours of anxiety on the part of the old lady, the little truant was found standing— but without the slightest sign of alarm—by the side of a deep and rapid river, which he was unable to cross. When brought into her presence, his grandmother reproved him for going out without a guide. She then told him of the dangers which he had escaped, and said: "I wonder that fear did not drive you home."

"Fear, Grandmamma!" replied the child. "I never saw fear."

This boy was little Horatio Nelson, who afterwards became the great naval hero of England.

¶ There are various motifs of fearlessness, but generally attached to some supernatural episode or test.

This story is to be found on p. 2 of Southey's *Life of Nelson*, which is admirably written, but not historically critical. The story has passed into tradition.

FLOOD LAW IN THE FENS [extract]

W. H. Barrett, *Tales from the Fens*, pp. 114–5.

[During a great flood]...in a few days' time the fen looked the same as it was before it was drained; all the wild water-fowl came back, and so did some of the people living on the edge of it. They came at night, trying to loot the houses, but they didn't have any luck because we were out in boats, keeping guard. They ran a big risk because, as soon as the waters came, the old fen flood law began to work. This law said that anything found floating about had to be brought to Stack's Hill at Southery, and if it wasn't claimed after a time, then the finder could have it. If anybody was found robbing a house, then he had his boat smashed in and he himself was left in the house. And he had to stay there starving for a week if he couldn't swim his way out, till a boat went to pick him up—if he was still alive, that is. This law was kept so well that a man could leave his watch on the mantelshelf and know it would still be there when he went back for it. Old Lawyer Archer of Feltwell was a very old man when he told me that this law, though it wasn't in any of his books, had been kept since long before Ely Cathedral was built.

There was another one, too, and this was that no man should go out in his boat alone. This one goes back a couple of hundred years to the time when a chap, after being flooded out, rowed back to his house to fetch some things. When he got there he found two gypsies robbing the place; they'd rowed out from Hockwold in a stolen boat. Well, the man's boat was found next day tied to the door-latch, while he was sitting on his bedroom floor with an axe stuck in his skull. Those gypsies had loaded their boat with his stuff, but they weren't looking where they were going as they made off for higher ground, because they rammed a gate-post, and ripped the bottom out of the boat. They couldn't swim, but they stood on the boat, as it lay under five foot of water, and by clinging to the gate-post they managed to keep their heads above water.

Next day a chap rowed past, towing the dead man's body in another boat, and he heard the gypsies shrieking for help. He guessed who they were, so he rowed over, staked the boat with the body in it to the post, saying they could have company, as they looked a bit lonely. Then he rowed off and left them. He came back next day, just to see how they were getting on, and the next day, but by then they'd gone, so the dead man was taken home and buried.

That's a cruel tale, I know, but everything was cruel when the waters poured in.

Told by Chafer Legge.
MOTIF: C.923 [*Drowning as punishment for breaking tabu*].
¶ This was the flood of 1861 between Brandon Creek and Southery. The whole chapter is worth reading for the account it gives of the precautions taken to prevent the river walls being broken by people who wanted to save the upper fens from flooding. This they often did without warning, so that the fen-dwellers were exposed to terrible risks.

Jean Ingelow's *High Tide on the Coast of Lincolnshire* tells of a similar catastrophe.

FOLK MEMORIES OF CROMWELL

H. Bett, *English Myths and Traditions*, p. 104.

I

The Church of Burton Bassett in Warwickshire is rather a remarkable building. It stands on the slope of a hill, so that the western end is much lower than the chancel, and you climb up the nave by a number of steps.

The church tower commands a view of the plain below where the important Battle of Edgehill was fought on the twenty-third of October, 1642—the first battle of the Civil War. There is a local tradition to the effect that Cromwell climbed the tower of the church to see how the battle was going, and, observing some movement that presented either a danger or an opportunity, slid down one of the bellropes in his haste to regain the battlefield. Cromwell was a captain of horse at the time.

II

At Winceby, near Horncastle in Lincolnshire, there is a by-road called Slash Lane, where after a fight many of the fleeing Royalists were cut down by Cromwell's troopers. A house near, where Cromwell spent the night before the skirmish, is still pointed out, or was within living memory, and in that house a man sat up all that night casting bullets for the approaching fray. So an old man said, who had known a much older man, whose father remembered seeing the soldier who cast the bullets !

That is the way that tradition bridges the centuries.

III

Sir Archibald Geikie, the eminent geologist, stated that he heard this from an aged lady in the Lammermuirs: Cromwell found, before the Battle of Dunbar, that his retreat was blocked by General Leslie, and as the English fleet was delayed by storms, he tried to communicate with his base by land. The Lammermuir tradition was that two soldiers were disguised as natives and sent on this dangerous errand. They got as far as the valley of the Whiteadder, and there they were detected and shot.

The local tradition said that they were buried where some old whin-bushes grew at the opening of the clough. At the instigation of the lady who related the tradition to Sir Archibald, the ground was dug up, and some mouldering bones, a few decayed buttons, and a coin of Charles I were found. The popular mind had retained the memories of the exact place of the burial.

TYPE ML.8000.
¶ See "The Burly Stranger", "Cromwell in Yorkshire". See also "A Link with the Past", "Old Parr".

FOLK-MEMORY OF CHAUCER

H. Bett, *English Myths and Traditions*, p. 106.

An old gardener in Oxfordshire said to Mr Cecil Roberts in reference to a local road: "I've 'eard my granddad say as 'is granddad said that Mr Chaucer, the king's poet, used to walk this way."

"I suppose," said Mr Roberts, "Mr Chaucer was on his way to Oxford when he went past here?" "Not at all, sir. He was going to visit his son at Ewelme.... It's about ten miles from here, sir, just off the Oxford road. Mr Chaucer's son's buried there, where old Henry the Eighth 'ad 'is 'oneymoon—one of 'em. My granddad said the poet was very fond of the country. He wrote a lot about it."* Now Thomas Chaucer, the son of the poet, married Matilda, the daughter of Sir John Burgersh, who brought him large estates, amongst them the Manor of Ewelme, in Oxfordshire, where he is buried. There is an altar-tomb, with brasses, of Thomas Chaucer and his lady in the church, and also another magnificent altar-tomb, one of the finest in England, of the Duchess of Suffolk, the widow of William de la Pole, and the granddaughter of the poet. She founded the ancient almshouse in the village. The manor-house, or palace, of Ewelme was a splendid building, where Margaret of Anjou was confined for several years. It is a fact, by the way, that Henry VIII did spend a honeymoon there with Jane Seymour.

¶ See "A Link with the Past", "Old Parr".

FRENCH PRISONERS IN THE FENS

W. F. Barrett, *Tales from the Fens*, p. 73.

... When Father was a young man he was a smart sort of chap, washing himself in winter the same as he did in summer, and never going out anywhere unless he was all dressed up. He wore a rosette in his otter-skin cap to show he was Cock of the Walk and could do nearly as he liked, without anyone stopping him. He was rather on the quiet side when he was sober; it was when he was drunk that the devil in him came out. He was like that one day, at Ely Fair, when he saw two gypsies giving a young woman a fright by trying to get hold of her purse. Father started in to help, and he wouldn't have done so badly if the two gypsies hadn't turned into six; so, when they'd finished with him he was in a pretty bad state.

As soon as she saw how things were going, the young woman, who belonged to the fair, ran off and brought a lot of the fair people, and they weren't long in showing those gypsies that, though it was some way to the hospital in Cambridge, the sooner they got there might save them from being buried in Ely. Then the fair people carried father into one of their vans and when the girl's mother had given him something to drink and cleaned him up, he said he was all right. But the girl's mother said he wasn't, he was going to stop where he was and when the fair closed down

* Cecil Roberts, *Gone Rustic*, pp. 166–8.

they were going to drive him home in a horse and cart, because what he'd done for them would take a long time to pay back.

Father soon found that the girl he had helped was pretty well off, because her father did well with his stalls. She told him she liked travelling about with the fair, but more often than not she was in London. She had a friend who travelled about with her and who was staying at the best pub in Ely, and, if Father felt he was able to walk, she'd take him along to see her. So presently they set off for the Lamb, the girl wearing Father's otter-skin cap, because she said she liked it so much. When they got to the hotel and the girl told the other young woman what Father had done to stop her purse from being stolen, she grabbed hold of him and started kissing him. Then she said he was to stay at the Lamb that night and next morning they'd both drive him home, which they did.

They pulled up at the Ship in Brandon Creek and, after the horse had had a rest and feed, the young woman who'd been at the Lamb said she was going to stay on at the Ship for a bit, and she wanted Father to stay there, too, and show her over the Fens. So, after the fair girl had driven off, things were settled with the landlord and Father went off across the Fen to fetch his claying* tools. The young woman and Father stayed at the Ship for quite a while; she paid for everything and bought a pony and cart and father spent a lot of time driving her about. Then one day she went off to Cambridge and bought a sailing-boat with two cabins and the two of them went in it all over the place.

One day they staked the boat down the Little Ouse close to Shrub Hill, where a farmhouse stood. The girl asked Father if he knew the people living in it and he said he did, but they were very poor, as the land was so waterlogged. So she went over and saw the people and looked over the house; she liked it so much that she asked if she could come and lodge there and she offered to pay as much in one week as the farmer and his wife made in a month. She soon moved in and, in no time at all, was like a daughter to the old couple.

The house was three miles from the nearest neighbours and the girl said that was what she liked about it. Father stayed on the boat and took her out in it now and then, but he didn't have much to do except eat his head off, and she paid him well to do that. Then one day she asked him if he could take her to Peterborough. Father said he could, by going round Salter's Lode up to Wisbech and then down the Nene. They were gone for a fortnight and Father used to say, he noticed the girl made such a fuss of any bargemen they met that they wanted to come back with her.

For three days after they got to Peterborough Father didn't see anything of the girl, and when she did come aboard he could see she'd been crying, and he wondered what had happened to upset her. But he didn't like to

* Claying tools: tools for cleaning and maintaining the dykes.

ask and she didn't say anything. All the way home she was very quiet and was writing most of the time. Then, not long after they'd got home, some of the bargemen began finding their way down to Shrub Hill and there was a lot of coming and going when they were there.

One night Father was asleep in his cabin when he was woken up by hearing some barges pull in. He got up and saw two chaps jump off the first barge on to the bank, and who should be waiting for them there but the young girl, and she kissed them and took them up to the farmhouse. Father was a bit upset at seeing this so, next morning, when she came down to the boat, he was a bit on the quiet side. The girl asked him what the matter was and he told her there was a lot the matter, and asked her what game she was playing at. She went a bit white when she heard that, and said:

"Why, what have you seen to make you say a thing like that?"

"Only two men and girl kissing on a lonely bank at two o'clock in the morning," said father.

"One of those was my brother," said the girl, "and the other one was the man I hope to marry."

"Well," said Father. "That's nice; to have a best man as well as a bridegroom. And I suppose I get up tonight and meet the two brides-maids and do some kissing myself on that old bank."

The girl told Father not to be silly; there was a lot she wanted to know about but she wasn't going to get him into any bother if she could help it. He'd helped her a lot already, and it wasn't fair to run him into risks he didn't know anything about. So Father let her know that he wanted to know what sort of risks he was running, and if she'd only put all her dominoes face up on the table then he could tell her what risks he was willing to take.

When she heard that, the girl took a gold cross that was round her neck and told father to swear on it that anything she told him he must keep to himself. When he'd done that she made him kiss the cross. Then she told him that her young man and her brother had been fighting for France, which was her country too, and they'd been taken prisoners. They'd been sent first to a place called Dartmoor,* and then to Norman Cross, on the other side of Peterborough. The war had been over some time but the prisoners weren't allowed to go home because France had to pay a lot of money to England as she'd lost the war, and until it was paid the prisoners were being kept in gaol. She'd come over here and seen her sweetheart and it looked as if it would be years before they could get married. She'd met those fair people she was friends with at Peterborough Goose Fair and told them all about it, and they'd promised to do everything they

---

* Dartmoor Prison was opened in May 1809 for the reception of prisoners captured in the French wars. It became a convict prison in 1850.

could to help her. So then she'd gone back to London with them and then over to France and collected all the gold money she could get hold of, which was a lot. Those people had changed it for her into English gold and, so no one could steal the lot, the fair girl had said she would carry half of it about with her. That's why she was so grateful to Father for the way he'd taken a hiding from those gypsies when they tried to steal the money.

She told Father, too, that she was really grateful to those thieves because it was through them that she'd met him. If he hadn't turned up then, she'd been going to stay in Ely, because she'd heard it called a Haven of Refuge; but after seeing Father and what he could do, she'd thought her prayers had been answered and that a man in a thousand had been sent to help her. She said she'd told the old couple at the farm what she was telling him and the wife had kissed her and said she'd do everything she could to help, but her old man must answer for himself. Then the farmer had got up and fetched a goose quill and cut it down the middle and given her one piece of it. He'd put his bit down on the table and told her to put her piece next to it; when she'd done this he said that, until there were no more adders in Hockwold Fen he'd be her man, and if he didn't do all he could to help her then he hoped his body would be split like that feather.

Then she showed Father her piece of goose quill and told him he'd once said that no man asking for help and shelter, unless he'd done murder, was ever turned away, and that was Fen law, which had been running for hundreds of years. So Father promised her that, until geese stopped grow-ing feathers, he'd be her brother, and then she shook his hand and kissed him to seal the bargain. After that he went with her to see the two men, who were in a bad way; but they said there were hundreds worse off than they were where they came from, rotting away in prison with no hope. But they'd been lucky to get away and now the path was opened, they hoped a lot more would be able to find their way along it.

That night two more prisoners came. Father was there when they jumped off the barge and he took them to the farmhouse. They were in such a state, he said, that if it hadn't been for their clothes keeping them together they'd have fallen to pieces. It upset him so much that he told the girl he was going to that Norman Cross himself, to have a look at things. She didn't want him to go as it was too risky, but he touched the cross round her neck and said it was risky to wear that, as anyone might try to steal it. He was going to get into Norman Cross and anyone stop-ping him would get the same treatment that they'd get if they tried to pinch her cross. So she laughed and said she wouldn't stop him going, but he'd better take some money with him in case he had to buy himself out. But Father told her he was going to take a lot of split goose feathers, for if they didn't work the trick then nothing would.

He went on to the hailing side of the river and when the barges came along he told the chap who was driving the towing horse that he'd take on his job for him, all the way to Peterborough. The chap was glad of that, as the crew of the barge had to take turns driving the horse, and none of them liked the job. When they pulled in for the night at the Creek, everyone wanted to know if Father had lost his job as skipper on a boat, but he said he was on holiday and he wanted all the goose wing feathers they could lay hands on. So he was brought a big bundle and he went all the night splitting them down with his razor.

He enjoyed that trip with the bargemen and when they got to Stanground, which was as far as they went, he left them and went off to Norman Cross and, before long he'd got a job, cooking grub for the soldiers who were guarding the prisoners. And it wasn't long before a lot of Frenchmen knew that, if they took the half of a feather they were given, and could get a few miles away, then they'd be looked after all the way to Hockwold Fen. A lot of the old Fen folk soon got used to going to the door and seeing a chap outside with a split feather in his hand, but not able to speak a word they could understand. He'd be taken in and fed and sent on his way after he'd stuttered out "Hockwold Fen".

So many turned up at Shrub Hill that the young girl wondered if Father had killed all the soldiers and set all the prisoners free. Then, one day, when a chap handed in his feather he told her that the man who'd given it to him was in gaol in Peterborough. At least, that was where he'd been expecting to go because a soldier had given him a ding on the ear because the grub wasn't cooked right and Father had forgotten what he was there for and, by the time he remembered, there were four soldiers who'd be getting their discharges. But she wasn't to worry, as he was born to die in the Fens, he'd said, and not in prison. But she did worry about him and told the farmer and his wife that she was going to sail the boat to where father was and try to help him. But the farmer said she mustn't go alone; he'd sail the boat for her.

So away they went and got as far as Wisbech, where the young woman went to get some grub in. Suddenly she heard someone call out "*Parlez-vous*", and when she looked round there was Father, who said he was trying to get home as quick as he could. He told her what had happened and how the magistrate had ordered twenty lashes and how, when Father gave him a quick look at the goose feather, he called him back and gave him a month instead. And when he was taken to gaol he showed the warder the feather and his cell door was left unlocked; so he'd walked out and got as far as Wisbech.

Father and the girl sailed back with the farmer as far as Salter's Lode,* but they were so full of the wine the young woman had bought that they

* Lodes are artificial waterways leading from the chalk-edge to the Rivers Cam and Ouse.

didn't notice that the sluice doors were shut and drove full pelt into them, knocking the stern back a bit, but not letting the water in. So they had to stay for a couple of days at Denver Sluice where the boat-builder knocked it back again. Father took the girl to Lynn while they were waiting for the boat to be mended; they went to the Mart and then down to where the ships were unloading. Father took her to see a couple of fishermen who lived on their smacks and a lot of gold changed hands. Then the two fishermen sailed them back to Denver, just to show what their boat could do, but not before they found out that a lot of ships were always leaving Lynn empty, after bringing a cargo of wine from France. Back in Denver they picked up the farmer and the boat, said goodbye to the fishermen, and set off home.

A few days after this Father saw a couple of soldiers walking along the river bank and, as his boat was only a short way from the farmhouse, he wondered what he was going to do. One of the soldiers asked if there was a chance of a drink, as they were thirsty after walking from the Staunch. Father had a drop of beer by him, so he gave them a drink and they told him they were looking for Froggies, because a lot had got out of the prison at Norman Cross, and they asked if he'd seen any. He said that where they were was no place for frogs, as it was smothered with snakes and vipers; they ought to go up to the Creek.

As soon as they'd gone, Father slipped across to the farmhouse and told them that search parties were out in the fen. The young woman wanted to move on somewhere else, but father said, if they weren't safe there, he didn't know of any other hiding-place as good. If she left things to him, he reckoned his fen training was as good as the soldiers'. Then he had a long talk with the farmer and they both went to have a good look at the duck decoy,* which wasn't far away. They cut a lot of reeds to make great big frames of osiers, and thatched them, and it wasn't long before they had a fair-sized shed which was a good shelter from the fen wind. And every morning the Frenchmen moved into it and stayed there all day till the sun was gone.

A few days later a lot of soldiers were seen coming across the fen. So Father slipped over to the decoy, fetched all the Frenchmen out and made them get into the water and walk along the pipe right to the end, which was in a great clump of reeds and osiers. Then he told them that, when they heard a duck quack three times, they were to get down so their heads were only just above water; then he went into the shed and waited for the soldiers to come.

---

* Tame duck were kept on a central pool to entice the wild birds down the "pipes", or fifty-yard-long, curved approaches from the pool to the reed beds. They were fenced in with reed screens, and a trained dog, the "piper", drove the wild duck up them to the pool.

When they came they wanted to know if there were any Froggies about. Father told them his job was with ducks and, with the row they were making, he'd soon be out of a job, as the ducks wouldn't come when there were people about. The soldiers had a good look round and even went right up to the pipe, wanting to know what was up there.

"Frenchmen," said Father.

The officer gave one look at the water and another at Father, then told his men he wasn't stopping there to be made a fool of, and cleared off, leaving father laughing fit to bust himself. Then he lit a big fire with old osier stumps and the Frenchmen came out of the water and dried their clothes.

Next morning, when Father looked out of his cabin, he saw the fishing smack which they'd sailed in from Lynn staked a little way off, so he went along and told the two fishermen he'd come to breakfast with them. Then the young woman came down to the river and all of them went back to the farmhouse, each of them carrying a big bundle of clothes for the Frenchmen. Everybody was very excited that day and, just as it was getting dark, the dozen prisoners were packed into the smack, Father and the young woman with them, and, with a good wind behind them and a running tide, they were soon at Denver, just in time to shoot the eye [go down the doors of the sluice] before the doors closed. As the tide was so strong they had to pull in and stake just after they left Stowbridge; so the Frenchmen got out and lay under a hedge. Then, just before dark, they went back, one by one, to the smack and down into the hold, where they were covered up with a sail.

It was past midnight when the smack, with her sails down, drifted through Lynn and into the Cut and soon, with a lot of other smacks, out to sea. Two lanterns were hung on each side of the smack and another one run up to the top of the mast. When they were some miles away from the shore they saw a ship anchored, with three lights on her mast, and they knew she was the one they were looking for. When they'd tied up alongside, they all went aboard and had a real old do, because there were barrels and barrels of wine and brandy on that ship, though Father said he didn't care much for the wine, but the brandy was damn good. They gave him some to take home.

When all the Frenchmen had got on to the ship, the smack was loaded up with tubs and bundles and a start was made for home, though they stopped at one place to cover up everything in the hold with a lot of mussels and whelks. It was daylight when they got to Lynn. A customs chap came aboard, looked in the cabins and then at the mussels and said they hadn't done a bad night's fishing; seeing there was no customs stuff aboard, he hoped the passengers would have a good trip and thanked the young woman when she pushed a bit of gold in his hand.

Well, believe it or not, it was only a couple of miles this side of Lynn that the smack pulled into the bank and, over on the other side, were two carts and horses. All the tubs were taken out of the boats and put on to the carts, and the horses trotted off down the high road, while the smack sailed on to the Little Ouse to the farmhouse. Father told the farmer all about the trip, and the tubs and bundles they'd brought back, and where they'd been unloaded. "And do you know, bor," Father said, "those horses and carts belong to the biggest chap there is between Downham and Lynn and those fishermen say they've been working for him a long time. They were caught, once, by a new customs man, but nothing was ever done about it because, after he'd seen what was in the hold, he was never seen again till he was found floating upstream, beyond Denver. They say all the other smacksmen know he didn't get there on his own."

Father took home some of the stuff he'd been given because his Father liked a good drink. The old chap thought it wasn't any stronger than beer, so he put it back like cow's milk, and if he hadn't been put to bed he'd have pulled the place down. When he woke up he found his hands and feet were roped to the bedposts and when they untied him he rushed straight for the bottle, said there wasn't a Frenchman in France who was going to beat him, and drank the lot. Then he put on his water-boots, walked into the fen and threw twelve clay holes, where eight would have been a good day's work for any men. When he got home after that, he found the bottle empty, so he walked the six miles to Father's boat, wanting to know where the other bottles were.

Father was talking to the young woman when he came and she was laughing like billy-ho as he told her how grandfather got on with French brandy. So she gave the old chap two bottles to take home, but he didn't get there till three days later, and he wouldn't have got there then if a gang of lighters hadn't found him lying on a bank, and taken him back.

It wasn't long before there was another lot of Frenchmen ready for the Lynn Deeps run, so the smacksmen came again and loaded up and sailed away, and when they came back who should jump out of the boat but the young woman's brother and her sweetheart and another chap, who was a priest. And next day Father was sent for to go up to the house, and there he found the young woman dressed all in white, and the priest had his robes on and there were a lot of candles on the table which had been pushed up against the wall. Before Father knew what all the jabbering was about he was being told to kiss the bride; and they all said, if this was his first French wedding they hoped it wouldn't be his last, as they'd like him to be there when the brother was married.

Well, the young woman and her husband and her brother stayed down in the fen and time after time the smack came down and it always went back with the sail spread over the hold. So much brandy was passed round that Grandfather got quite used to it and could carry it like he did his beer. Then the time came for the last trip to be made and, as there were only a few Frenchmen to go on it, the young woman and her husband and her brother went too. But before they left she went round the fen, leaving a bit of gold wherever she called; and she gave a party at the farmhouse and went round and kissed everybody; so did the men, as that's the way Frenchmen say goodbye. Father was left with a rattling good boat, and the farmer and his wife were so well off that they took a farm in a better part of the fen and did so well that they were able to go to market in Ely every week.

Told by Chafer Legge, an old Fenman. The depot for French prisoners of war at Norman Cross, Huntingdonshire, with provision for 2,000 inmates, existed from 1797 to 1814.

MOTIFS: R.100 [*Rescues*]; R.121 [*Means of rescue from prison*]; R.152 [*Wife rescues husband*].

¶ W. H. Barrett received some confirmation of this story by hearing of a French Count at Cambridge who said that his father and grandfather had lived in the Fens, and knew about the split goose feathers.

See "The Grey Goose feathers".

FULKE FITZWARIN [summary]

W. C. Hazlitt, *National Tales and Legends*, pp. 196—222.

Warin de Metz, the father of Fulke, was one of the most powerful barons under Henry I, and his son was brought up and educated with those of the king. When they grew up, King Richard made Fulke Lord of the Marches of Wales. But King John bore him an old grudge over a game of chess, and gave his office and lands to Fulke's enemy, Morris Fitz-Roger.

Fulke and his four brothers were outlawed, and fled to the court of their kinsman, the Duke of Brittany. But later they made a secret return, and lay in wait for Fitz-Roger in the woods near Fulke's former castle of Whittington. Though their presence was betrayed to the king, by a treacherous valet who had recognized Fulke, they evaded capture for many months, plundering none but the king and his friends.

At length, they waylaid a train of ten merchants, guarded by fourteen men-at-arms, and finding that the merchandise they carried was the king's, they seized it, and sent the men away with a message of thanks to the king for his goods.

For this a heavy price was set on Fulke's head, and he was forced to move into Kent. Here again he was betrayed more than once, but escaped by cunning and courage, and won such favour among the king's enemies that the Archbishop of Canterbury himself, Hubert le Botiler, sent for him secretly, and persuaded him to marry the Lady Maud de Caus, his brother's widow, whom the king wanted for his mistress. They were privately wedded in his palace by the Archbishop, but two days later Fulke was urgently summoned back to the North, where a certain Peter de Bruvile, a recreant knight, was assuming and dishonouring Fulke's name, by oppressing the people, and breaking violently into the houses of his friends.

Fulke and his band overtook the usurper in the house of Robert Fitz-Sampson, whom he had bound, and was holding prisoner. Fulke so intimidated him, that he unbound his captives, and at Fulke's word, beheaded his own followers; after which Fulke cut off Peter's own head. Soon after this, his old longing for revenge upon Morris Fitz-Roger grew so strong, that he sent one of his own men, John de Raunpaygne, disguised as a minstrel, to Whittington, to find out what hope there was of surprising the castle. He discovered that Sir Morris was about to travel to Shrewsbury; and on the road Fulke overtook and slew him. He now regained his patrimony, but one of his knights, Sir Audulf de Bracy, had been captured in a secret skirmish with the king's men, and was under sentence of hanging.

John de Raunpaygne, therefore disguised himself as an Ethiopian minstrel, and gained access to the king. He sang, in the prisoner's hearing, a song that Sir Audulf himself had been accustomed to sing, and was thus recognized by Sir Audulf. He put sleeping powder into the wine of the king's knights, and so contrived to rescue Sir Audulf, and they made their way back to Whittington in safety.

Prince Owen of Wales had till now been a champion and protector of Fulke, but King John, who feared Fulke's growing power, now tried to bribe Owen to betray Fulke, promising to make over to him all Fulke's lands, if he did so. Owen's wife, who had seen the king's letters, warned Fulke in time, so he bade farewell to Owen, without showing his suspicions, sent his wife and children back to Canterbury to the charge of her brother-in-law, the Archbishop, and with his brothers and companions he made his way to the French King's court. He adopted a French name, Sir Amis du Bois, but was soon discovered, not only for his prowess in jousting, but because King John sent letters to King Philip, demanding Fulke's return.

King Philip offered him rich rewards and estates if he would remain with him in France, but Fulke excused himself, and took ship with a bold Russian captain, whose name was Mador. Mador told him that his father and forefathers, as far back as he could tell, had all died at sea; but when Fulke remarked that he wondered that that did not make him afraid to follow their calling, Mador replied that, since all Fulke's ancestors had died in their beds, Fulke must be afraid to go to bed. So they took ship together, and sank a ship off the coast of England, that was seeking for Fulke as a traitor; but first they secured all her treasure, and sailed on to Scotland, sinking the king's ships, but no others, as they went.

In Scotland a shepherd-boy led them to a magic cave, where Fulke slew six fierce clowns, and then, by blowing a horn, broke the enchantment laid by seven sons of the old woman who lived in the cave, upon seven noble maidens. He took the maidens away in his ship, rid the land of all its thieves, then sailed with Mador to many lands, where he met with many more strange adventures. But at last he returned to Windsor Forest, where, disguised as a charcoal-burner, he encountered the king himself, and, having him in his power, extorted his promise to restore him his heritage in full. But the king broke his oath, and in a later encounter Sir Fulke was gravely wounded, and one of his brothers, William, was taken prisoner. Only after many months had passed did he manage to secure the king's person, by descending on him in force, during a hunt in the New Forest. They carried him and six attendant knights out to sea, and at last secured his promise of full pardon; the six attendant knights being held as hostages until the pardon was sealed.

The news of the pardon soon spread, and gave great joy to all Fulke's friends. At last he came home to Whittington, where he lived in high honour with his wife and children. When they grew up, his daughter Eva married the Prince of Wales.

Fulke built the New Abbey, near Alderbury, in a wood on the Severn, to the glory of Our Lady, and in expiation of his sins; and here he and the lady Maud were buried, leaving their son, Fulke, a worthy heir to their lands, and a valiant knight in the king's service.

MOTIFS: R.110 [*Rescue of captives*]; K.1817.3 [*Disguise as minstrel*]; G.334.1 [*Ogress keeps princess in cave*]; F.757 [*Extraordinary cave*]; R.112.1 [*Three blasts on horn to rescue prisoners from mound*].

THE GHOST'S 'EVIDENCE'

T. F. Thistleton Dyer, *The Ghost World*, p. 83.

In "Ackerman's Repository" for November 1820, there is an account of a person being tried on the pretended evidence of a ghost. A farmer on his return from market at Southam, co. Warwick, was murdered. The next morning a man called upon the farmer's wife, and related how on the previous night her husband's ghost had appeared to him, and after showing him several stabs on his body, had told him that he was murdered by a certain person, and his corpse thrown into a marl-pit. A search was instituted, the body found in the pit, and the wounds on the body were exactly in the parts described by the pretended dreamer; the person who was mentioned was committed for trial on the charge of murder, and the trial came on at Warwick before Lord Chief Justice Raymond. The jury would have convicted the prisoner as rashly as the magistrate had committed him, but for the interposition of the judge, who told them he did not put any credence in the pretended ghost story, since the prisoner was a man of unblemished reputation, and no ill-feeling had ever existed between himself and the deceased. He added that he knew of no law which admitted of the evidence of a ghost, and, if any did, the ghost had not appeared.

The crier was then ordered to summon the ghost, which he did three times, and the judge then acquitted the prisoner, and caused the accuser to be detained, and his house searched, when such strong proofs of guilt were discovered that the man confessed the crime, and was executed for murder at the following Assizes.

MOTIFS: K.2116.4 [*Murderer makes outcry so that innocent person is accused of murder*]; J.1130 [*Cleverness in law court*]; J.1140 [*Cleverness in detection of truth*].

THE GOLDEN GUINEA

J. R. W. Coxhead, *The Devil in Devon*, p. 25.

About the year 1870 a Miss Dunning died at Winkleigh, in North Devon, and, according to local tradition, the last duel in Devon was fought over this lady at a spot near the present Haldon race course.

In 1964, the Rev. H. Fulford Williams of Exeter told the writer of this book the following very interesting story about Miss Dunning:

Just before her death she decided to make a new will, so she sent her groom to North Tawton to demand her lawyer's immediate attendance. But the lawyer, Mr Robert Fulford, who was also the Coroner for the district, had just left his office for Princetown. . . . The journey involved a drive of thirty miles each way, and would take at least two days, so, in view of the old lady's failing health, and the fact that the summons was urgent, the lawyer's son, known to everyone in North Tawton as "young Mr Bob", went to Winkleigh on his father's behalf.

As soon as "young Mr Bob" arrived at Miss Dunning's house he was ushered into her presence without delay. Surprised at his youthful appearance, she said to him, "You are a very young man. Do you really think you can make my will for me?" "Madam," he replied, "I have only been qualified for three days, and yours will be the first will I have ever tried to make, but I will do my best."

When the business was successfully completed, the old lady said, "I shall pay you now and then the matter will be finished. Would you prefer

5   65   BAD

to have an ordinary sovereign and a shilling, or, as this document is the first will you have ever made, a real golden guinea to bring you luck?" The young man answered, "I would very much like to have a golden guinea, please."

Miss Dunning rang for her maid, and told her to fetch her old purse from the writing desk downstairs. When it was brought to her it proved to be an old-fashioned Georgian purse opened by two rings. Taking from it a guinea, almost in mint condition, bearing the date 1792, together with a pair of black silk mittens, she turned to the young man and said, "These have been in this purse since the Duke of Richmond's Ball at Brussels on the eve of the Battle of Waterloo. The gold coin was in my purse, and I was wearing the mittens when I danced with the Duke of Wellington on that great occasion. I now give you the guinea, and I hope it may bring you good fortune."

When he returned home, "young Mr Bob" gave the guinea to his mother as his first earnings, and, in 1901, she left it to her grandson, the Rev. H. Fulford Williams, who treasured it to the day of his death on 23 October 1966.

MOTIF: N.135.2 [*Possession of money brings luck*].

¶ This is another of the "links with the past" tales. See "Old Parr", "A Link with the Past", "Folk Memory of Chaucer".

THE GOODMAN OF BALLENGIECH

Sir Walter Scott, *Tales of a Grandfather*, 1st series, XXVII, p. 287.

When James V travelled in disguise, he used a name which was known only to some of his principal nobility and attendants. He was called the Goodman (the tenant, that is) of Ballengiech. Ballengiech is a steep pass which leads down behind the Castle of Stirling. Once upon a time, when the court was feasting in Stirling, the King sent for some venison from the neighbouring hills. The deer were killed, and put on horses' backs to be transported to Stirling. Unluckily, they had to pass the castle gates of Arnpryor, belonging to a chief of the Buchanans, who chanced to have a considerable number of guests with him. It was late, and the company were rather short of victuals, though they had more than enough of liquor. The chief, seeing so much fat venison passing his very door, seized on it; and to the expostulations of the keepers, who told him it belonged to King James, he answered insolently that if James was King in Scotland, he, Buchanan, was King in Kippen; being the name of the district in which the castle of Arnpryor lay. On hearing what had happened, the King got on horseback, and rode instantly from Stirling to Buchanan's house, where he found a strong, fierce-looking Highlander, with an axe on his shoulder, standing sentinel at the door. This grim warder refused the King admittance, saying that the Laird of Arnpryor was at dinner, and would not be disturbed. "Yet go up to the company, my good friend," said the King, "and tell him that the Goodman of Ballengiech is come to feast with the King of Kippen." The porter went grumbling into the house, and told his master that there was a fellow with a red beard at the gate, who called himself the Goodman of Ballengiech, who said he was come to dine with the King of Kippen. As soon as Buchanan heard these words, he knew that the King was come in person, and hastened down to kneel at James's feet, and to ask forgiveness for his insolent behaviour. But the King, who only meant to give him a fright, forgave him freely, and, going into the castle, feasted on his own venison, which Buchanan had intercepted. Buchanan of Arnpryor was ever afterwards called the King of Kippen.

Upon another occasion, King James, being alone and in disguise, fell into a quarrel with some gipsies, or other vagrants, and was assaulted by four or five of them. This chanced to be very near the Bridge of Cramond; so the King got on the Bridge, which, as it was high and narrow, enabled him to defend himself with his sword against the number of persons by whom he was attacked. There was a poor man thrashing corn in a barn nearby, who came out on hearing the noise of the scuffle, and seeing one man defending himself against numbers, gallantly took the King's part with his flail, to such good purpose, that the gipsies were obliged to fly. The husbandman then took the King into the barn, brought him a towel and water to wash the blood from his face and hands, and finally walked with him a little way towards Edinburgh, in case he should be again attacked. On the way, the King asked his companion who and what he was. The labourer answered, that his name was John Howieson, and that he was a bondsman on the farm of Braehead, near Cramond, which belonged to the King of Scotland. James then asked the poor man if there was any wish in the world which he would particularly desire should be gratified; and honest John confessed, he should think himself the happiest man in Scotland were he but proprietor of the farm on which he wrought as a labourer. He then asked the King, in turn, who *he* was, and James replied, as usual, that he was the Goodman of Ballengiech, a poor man, who had a small appointment about the palace; but he added that if John Howieson would come to see him on the next Sunday, he would endeavour to repay his manful assistance, and, at least, give him the pleasure of seeing the royal apartments.

John put on his best clothes, as you may suppose, and appearing at a postern gate of the palace, inquired for the Goodman of Ballengiech. The King had given orders that he should be admitted; and John found his friend, the Goodman, in the same disguise which he had formerly worn. The King, still preserving the character of an inferior officer of the household, conducted John Howieson from one apartment of the palace to another, and was amused with his wonder and his remarks. At last James asked his visitor if he would like to see the King; to which John replied, nothing would delight him so much, if he could do so without giving offence. The Goodman of Ballengiech, of course, undertook that the King would not be angry. "But," said John, "how am I to know his grace from the nobles who will be all about him?" "Easily," replied his companion; "all the others will be uncovered—the King alone will wear his hat or bonnet."

So speaking, King James introduced the countryman into a great hall, which was filled by the nobility and officers of the crown. John was a little frightened, and drew close to his attendant; but was still unable to distinguish the King. "I told you you should know him by his wearing his hat," said the conductor. "Then," said John, after he had again looked around the room, "it must be either you or me, for all but us two are bareheaded."

The King laughed at John's fancy; and, that the good yeoman might have occasion for mirth also, he made him a present of the farm at Braehead, which he had wished so much to possess, on condition that John Howieson, or his successors, should be ready to present an ewer and basin for the King to wash his hands, when his Majesty should come to Holyrood Palace, or should pass the Bridge of Cramond. Accordingly, in the year 1822, when George IV came to Scotland, the descendant of John Howieson of Braehead, who still possesses the estate which was given to his ancestor, appeared at a solemn festival, that he might perform the service by which he held his lands.

MOTIFS: K.1812 [*King in disguise*]; K.1812.1 [*Incognito king helped by humble man: gives reward*].

¶ Tales of the disguised king are common and widely spread from Haroun al-Raschid downwards. The episode of the uncovered courtiers is a French tradition as well as a Scots one.

See "King Alfred and the Cakes", "Edward IV and the Tanner of Tamworth", "The King and the Northern Man", (A, IV).

THE GREY GOOSE FEATHERS

The Folktales of England, pp. 84–6.

Thousands and thousands of years ago, the Fenmen, living in their desolate wastes, bonded themselves into a secret society. This society was called "The Brotherhood of the Grey Goose Feathers", and anyone who was initiated into that brotherhood, and possessed a grey goose feather, was sure that whenever they were in trouble or distress, help would immediately be given by the whole Fenmen. When King Charles the First escaped from Oxford, he made his way into the uplands of Norfolk and stayed at a place called Snow Hall, just outside of Downham Market. And in passing, I may remark that I saw the chamber where, in case Cromwell's men came to look for him, he did hide. This chamber was aside of a great big chimney; it was hidden by old panelling.

Well, after Charles had consulted with his advisers, he decided to rejoin his troops just outside Oxford. The safest route in those days, for a fugitive, was through the desolate, trackless Fens. There was one man, named Porter, who kept an inn at Southery. He used to guide travellers across the trackless waste. So he was sent for, and asked if he would take a very important personage to Huntingdon, and he said, "Yes. I will." So they brought the important personage to see what sort of a man the old Fenman was, and some of the king's advisers didn't think it was safe for him to go that long journey with only one man. But Porter said if that was worrying them, he would initiate the important personage into the Brotherhood of the Grey Goose Feathers. So they brought a feather, and Porter severed it down the centre, and gave half to the important personage, and retained half himself. As he did so, he said, "Whilst fishes have scales, and birds have feathers, I will do all I can for you, and so will every other man who belongs to the Brotherhood of the Grey Goose Feathers."

Well, the King's advisers seemed quite satisfied to let Porter take him across the Fens alone. When they arrived at St Ives, they had to cross the river by a ford. Guarding this ford were two of Cromwell's soldiers. But when Porter produced the grey feather, they said, "Pass, all is well." They were Fenmen. So eventually King Charles arrived at the "Bell" Tavern, in Huntingdon, and he gave a reward to Porter for taking of him over, but he retained the grey goose feather. Some time afterwards, the King was taken prisoner, but before that happened, one of the officers in charge of the troops in Cromwell's army, heard about how the sentry let them through, and he brought them along to Cromwell. But Cromwell was a Fenman too; so he said to the officer, "It is better for a king to escape than for the Fenman to go back on a man who carries the split goose feather."

So he let the men go, and not long after that King Charles was caught, and they brought him up to London and tried him, and he was sentenced to death. But the night before the execution, when Cromwell was sitting down to supper with his staff, a messenger came from the King, and Cromwell told his servant to let him in.

The messenger said: "His Majesty does not beg for mercy, but he demands as a right the help you must give to every man who carries this token."

And he flung down a grey goose quill on the table in front of Cromwell. Cromwell told everyone to go out, and he sat looking at the grey goose feather. And in the morning when the servants came in he was still looking at it.

Well, the King was beheaded, but Cromwell was never the same man again. He brooded and brooded, and what made things worse, all the Fenmen, who had served him well up to that time, sent back their goose feathers, all broken and bent, and they said they were going back to the Fens, where there were still men who kept their word. And as he'd been false to the old custom of the feathers, none of the promises that went with it would ever be made to him or any of his family again.

Recorded from W. H. Barrett, 11 October 1963. Mr Barrett heard this tradition from Chafer Legge in 1900. His written version is in *Tales from the Fens*, pp. 148–9.

MOTIFS: K.1812 [*King in disguise*]; M.202.0.1 [*Bargain or promise to be fulfilled at all hazards*]; M.205 [*Breaking of promises or bargains*]; C.871 [*Tabu: refusing a request*].

¶ Snow Hall, Snore, or Snowre Hall is in the parish of Fordham, Norfolk, three miles south of Downham Market. Charles I was received here on 30 April 1646 by Mr Skipworth, who was aiding his escape from Oxford before his surrender at Newark on 5 May 1646.

Tales of the Fens gives further particulars of the goose-feather customs. See " French Prisoners in the Fens".

THE GUIDMAN OF BALLANGEICH
AT ANSTRUTHER

Wilkie, *Bygone Fife*, p. 302.

...A visit paid by the Guidman of Ballangeich (James V of Scotland) to Anstruther: On one of his Haroun-al-Raschid-like wanderings he took the character of a strolling piper. When he came to the ford on the Dreel Burn, which was then unspanned by any bridge, he found he could not cross without a wetting, and stood hesitant till a buxom gaberlunzie woman marched up. The piper explained his reluctance. She caught him up and carried him on her back to the other side. It was an experience after James's own heart, and when he reached the bank dry-shod, he concluded an affable conversation with his benefactress by handing her his purse. The legend leaves the listener to discover for himself whether the identity of the generous musician was revealed.

MOTIFS: K.1817.3 [*Disguise as minstrel*]; K.1812.1 [*Incognito king helped by humble man: gives reward*].

HEATHER ALE or THE LAST OF THE PICTS

County Folk-Lore, III, *Orkney and Shetland*, 1901, p. 221.

The first folks that ever were in our island were called Picts.... They brewed a kind of spirit from the heather flowers and this spirit was so much liked that many nations tried to make it, but the Picts kept the secret of how to do it themselves. By and by the Norsemen came unexpectedly and killed all the peace-loving Picts except one man and his son. They were spared that the conquerors might be instructed in the art of brewing spirits from heather-tops. At first both the Picts refused to tell, but after torture was applied, the father said, "Kill the lad, and then I'll tell you." The Sea-Kings did as the father desired. "Now," said he triumphantly, "you can kill me, slow or fast; it is all one. You shall never learn the secrets of our race from the last of the Picts. My son might have been tempted to reveal them, but there is no fear of that now:

> "Kill slow or kill fast,
> Death man come at last."

And that was the end of the Picts in Shetland.

From Edmonston and Saxby, *The Home of a Naturalist*, 1888, p. 222 Cf. Montgomerie, *The Well at the World's End*, p. 43.

TYPE 2412E. MOTIF: C.420 [*Tabu: uttering secrets*].

¶ This type was added to the Aarne-Thompson Index by O'Suilbeahhain and Christiansen in *Types of the Irish Folk-tale*. Van Sydow wrote about the original of this type in *Festschrift till Prof. E. A. Knock*, Lund, 1934, p. 377.

Robert Louis Stevenson wrote a poem on the legend.

See "The Pechs".

HEREWARD THE SAXON [summary]

W. Carew Hazlitt, *National Tales and Legends*, pp. 177-195.

Hereward was the son of Leofric, Earl of Chester and Mercia, and Lord of Coventry, and his wife, Godiva; and from his earliest boyhood he showed himself so fearless and strong that he gathered round him a band of dauntless companions. They would collect by force his father's rents and tolls, and so provide money for their own ends, until at last, when Hereward was eighteen years old, his father, weary of his lawless escapades, persuaded King Edward to outlaw him. Only one of his companions chose to go with him, Martin Lightfoot, a serf of his father.

They went first to Scotland, to the court of Gisebert of Ghent, Hereward's godfather, but when Hereward slew a huge Norwegian bear, he drew on himself the envy of the noble youths at his godfather's court, where he had thought to find shelter; he therefore left the country, and took service with Alef, a Cornish chieftain. Alef's daughter was betrothed by her father to a Cornish lord, whom she did not love. She was secretly in love with the son of the King of Ireland, and confided her secret to Hereward, who undertook to help her. But the Cornish lord set an ambush for him, and Hereward slew him, which stirred up such enmity against him, that he was again forced to take flight. He carried letters from Alef's daughter to her lover in Ireland, who took Hereward into his service. Alef now promised his daughter in marriage to another Cornish chieftain, and she found means to inform her lover of this. On the day of the wedding-feast the bride, with her maidens, and a minstrel in attendance, carried the wine-cup round to each guest in turn, and all joyfully took it from the hands of one of them and drank. But one dark stranger, seated at the lowest table, turned discourteously away. The minstrel was angry and protested, but the stranger seized his harp from him and played it with so masterly a hand that all were amazed. The princess, however, had recognized Hereward in disguise.

He refused to take the cup from any hand but her own, for this was a vow he had made, and she threw a ring into his bosom, unobserved by the others. But Alef the chieftain was advised by some of his followers that perhaps the stranger was an enemy, and he had the doors of his hall guarded to prevent surprise. The wedding procession now set forth, but on the road it was waylaid by Hereward's men, who were lying in ambush. They slew the Cornishmen, and freed the princess and certain messengers from the prince of Ireland, whom Alef had thrown into prison.

At last the princess and her lover were united, with Hereward's aid; but he soon left their service, for his father had died, and the Normans, under their new king, William, had seized his castle, and were ravaging his lands.

A storm drove Hereward's ship off its course, and he landed in Flanders, where he fought, and won high renown, under the standard of the Earl of Flanders, and there he met the lady Torfrida, who became his wife.

At last, with a small band of supporters, he landed on the Lincolnshire coast, on his way home. Torfrida, at her earnest request, accompanied them. They sought shelter for the night with a Saxon and his wife, who told them that, the day before, the young son of Earl Leofric, Hereward's brother, had slain two Normans who had tried to offer violence to his mother; for this they had killed him, and set up his head over the gateway of the castle.

A sudden burst of music, and the noise of revelry from the castle itself nearby, roused Hereward; and taking only Martin with him, he hastened to the place, where he took down his brother's head, kissed it reverently, and wrapped it in a cloth. Then the two took their places, concealed in long black cloaks, within the porch, from which they could see all that went on. The Normans were celebrating their acquisition of the castle, and a minstrel was singing songs in contempt of the Saxons. One of the women reminded them all that Hereward, the boy's brother, was yet alive; but the new Norman lord praised the minstrel for his words, at which he sang more insolently than ever, till a figure leaped out of the darkness, and struck him down with a Saxon sword. Utterly surprised, the Normans fled from Hereward's charge, and those who escaped his sword were cut down by Martin Lightfoot at the door. The next morning there were fourteen Norman heads above the castle gate.

As soon as his coming became known, the Saxons flocked to join Hereward. But they were far outnumbered by the Normans, and withdrew to the Isle of Ely. William had made a Norman, Thorold, abbot of the place, therefore the Saxons raided the Abbey-church, and carried away all its treasures, helped by a band of Danes, with whom they shared the spoil. The Danes returned to their own country, but the Saxons under Hereward now found themselves besieged in Ely by the King's forces. William himself would have made a friend of Hereward, if he might, but the jealousy of Earl Warren, and other Norman nobles, prevented it.

Many Norman knights with their horses were drowned in the marshes around the town; a causeway which they constructed to make it possible to invest the city broke midway as they were crossing it; and a dyke of earth and timber was burnt down at night by Hereward himself, who in disguise, had taken part in its construction, and had lingered beside it when all the other workers had gone home. Besiegers and besieged soon ran short of food, and Hereward again disguised himself, and mounted his mare, Swallow, to spy on the King's court at Brandon, and find out their plans. On the way he met a potter, and forced him to change garments with him; and in this guise he entered the court.

He soon learnt that, since no human means had prevailed to drive the Saxons out of Ely, the king had employed a wise woman of Brandon, and her associate, and the next day a great scaffold was to be set up before the island, from which the two might exercise their spells. The next morning Hereward, still in the part of a potter, entered the Norman court, and hearing talk of Hereward and his doings, and being asked if he knew him, he replied that Hereward had lately robbed him of a cow and his four sheep, which, except his old mare, and his few pots, were all he had in the world to support his wife and two children. But in the evening a Norman in jest, offered to shave the potter's crown, and make him a monk. Hereward's proud temper flamed, and he felled the knight, cut his way out of the crowd who sprang up to try to hold him, and fled away on Swallow before any could prevent him.

A great throng gathered outside the city next day, to hear the wise women pronounce curses against the Saxons. But before they could complete their spells the third time, the grass and thickets around them burst into flame, the witch leapt from her high seat, and was killed, and Hereward and his men fell on the crowd, with bows and swords, working havoc, and piercing the armour of the king himself, before they returned to the safety of their island city.

At last, however, in the year 1072, the monks of Ely, growing weary of the long siege and privation, admitted the king and his men secretly into the city. But Hereward had warning of their treachery, and escaped, with six companions, to Brunnerwold. Here the Saxons again gathered to his support, and he soon had a force of seven hundred men, who laid waste the Norman lands on every side, till at length the king proclaimed that the entire forces of the six Fenland shires were to take service under the Abbot of Peterborough, and Ivo Taillebois, Lord of Spalding, to put the Saxons down. But the Saxons, from their better knowledge of the country, continually evaded open engagements, and at last in a sharp skirmish in a wood, they took prisoner the Abbot Thorold himself, and many Norman nobles, and slew many of their common soldiers. They exacted a ransom of thirty thousand silver marks for the Abbot, and because he had offered the treasures of his church itself to any who would help him, Hereward now advanced against Peterborough, burned the town, and plundered the church. These sacred treasures, however, he was warned in a dream to restore, on pain of the displeasure of God and the Holy Virgin. He therefore carried them back; in this, and on other occasions, he showed himself a generous enemy; even to Ivo Taillebois, his implacable enemy, he gave free pardon, as to all men of Stamford, when the town fell into his hands.

King William, now more than ever anxious to make a friend of Hereward, offered him a proud and noble lady, Elfrida, to be his wife; and in an evil hour Hereward put away the faithful Torfrida, and married the wealthy Norman widow. But so far from bringing him peace and quiet, the marriage involved him in such intrigue and jealousy, that he was thrown, under suspicion of treason, into Bedford castle, to be guarded by Robert de Herepole. Robert treated him kindly, and this inflamed the hatred of his enemies, and it was planned that he should be transferred to Buckingham to the charge of Ivo de Taillebois himself. Hereward's Saxons heard word of this, and rescued him on the way; at his command, they spared the life of the good Robert, and sent him to the king to tell him the truth about Hereward. The result was that Hereward was restored to William's favour, and his lands were given back to him. But his foes still watched for a chance to destroy him, and at last, through the treachery of a chaplain, whom he had set to keep watch while he was at meat, a combined Breton and Norman force surrounded his house, broke in, and fell upon Hereward unaware. He defended himself, as ever, and slew fifteen of them, before his lance and sword were broken and useless. He flung his shield in the face of the next who advanced to destroy him, Ralph de Dol, and brought him also lifeless to the ground, but as he did so, four knights came behind him, and drove their spears into his back. If there had been four such men as Hereward, it is said, the Norman power would have been destroyed.

TYPE ML.8000

¶ Hereward the Saxon was undoubtedly an historical character. Mentions of him are to be found in the Domesday Book and the *Anglo-Saxon Chronicle*, and Florence of Worcester gives an account of his defence of Ely. The legendary tales of his exploits were written down within eighty years of his death. These are Geoffrey Gaimar's *Estorie des Engles* and *Gesta Herewardii Saxonis*.

On these Carew Hazlitt's account is founded, and on these Charles Kingsley built up his story, *Hereward the Wake*. In the thirteenth century a wooden castle in the Fenland was known as "Hereward's Castle" (*The Dictionary of National Biography*), but, curiously enough, W. H. Barrett has not been able to discover any traditions about Hereward in the Fen country round Ely.

See "Fulke Fitzwarin", "Robin Hood" (A, IV).

THE HORN OF ULPHUS [summary]

Parkinson, *Yorkshire Legends and Traditions*, 1st series, p. 96.

Ulphus, son of Thoraldi, was king of the western portion of Deira, when the Danes were in power. The eldest of his four sons, Adelbert, was slain in battle, and the rest, even in their father's lifetime, were for ever quarrelling over their succession to his estates. In his old age, therefore, he determined to put an end to their disputes by giving up his whole dominion to the Church.

He rode to York, carrying with him his largest drinking-horn, made of a portion of an elephant's tusk, about three feet long, beautifully engraved with strange figures, and richly mounted in gold. He knelt down before the High Altar, and drank off the whole contents of the horn, which he had first filled with wine, then placed the horn upon the altar, to be held by the Church as title to all his wealth.

MOTIFS: Q.272 [*Avarice punished*]; Q.300 [*Contentiousness punished*].
¶ The tenure by the gift of a horn is interesting. Crathes was held by the Burnetts by a gift of Robert the Bruce's hunting-horn, which is still displayed in the Castle.

HOW STILTS CAME INTO THE FENS
[shortened]

W. H. Barrett, *Tales from the Fens*, p. 174.

Long ago the Fen was all under water through the whole of the winter. In summer the water drained away and a green grass grew quickly over the black mud it left behind. Queen Boudicca's horses used to graze on it, and what they didn't eat was made into hay, carried up to high ground, and stacked there ready for the winter.

The Romans came, and overran the Fens, though the Queen and the Fenmen put up a great resistance. The Roman vengeance was fierce in proportion; they killed Queen Boudicca and they set the women of the Fen to make a road from Denver, right across the Fens to Peterborough. Roman horses now grazed on the Fens, but many of them sank and were lost in the boggy peat.

Infantrymen who were sent to watch the horses either got lost and were set upon by the surviving Fenmen, and their weapons stolen; or, like the horses, they missed their footing, and fell into the bog. So many men were eventually missing, that their general was recalled for negligence and his successor, who had been reared in the marshes outside Rome itself, provided his men with stilts, which the Fenmen had never seen, and which greatly mystified them, until one of them came on a pair abandoned by its owner. Then, it is said, a man named Thoughtful, armed with a captured Roman sword, cut one of the stilt-poles in half, and showed the others how it could be used to dislodge the men striding about high in the air; especially when they were sitting back to rest with a third pole propping them up at the back. But if the Fenmen who thus ventured out, were caught, their bodies would be found next day strung up and dangling from a tripod made of three of the strange long poles. However, Thoughtful saw to it that the same thing happened to any of the Romans who went straggling.

A Saxon who had set up a shop for trading in captured Roman swords and other weapons now established at the back of it a wine-shop, which he named the Temple of Bacchus, where six pretty girls sat round a table, and he invited the Roman soldiers to visit it every night, telling the Fenmen that, when their would-be conquerors were sunk in sleep it would be easy to steal their swords and armour; which they could bring to him, and he would re-sell them second-hand to the Romans. At the same time, this Saxon's brother set up not far away as a horse-dealer, and the wine-shop girls, who called themselves Vestal virgins, persuaded their Roman visitors first to steal from the Fenmen, and then sell to the Saxon dealer. By these tricks they even entrapped four of the Roman officers one night, robbed them, stripped them, and carried them back to their own camp, where they roused the guard by their noise, so that the gates were opened and the four men fell in, still in their drunken stupor.

The Romans now attempted to round up their stolen horses, but the total of those recovered fell far short of what there should have been, even when they included those whose hooves or heads could be seen sticking up out of the bog. This led to a parley between Thoughtful and the Roman cavalry officer, and Thoughtful pointed out that by cutting apart the fore and hind legs of the dead horses, they could make each horse count as two, if they set the legs in different places in the bog; by severing the heads also, they could make up the total to even more than expected. This device so pleased the Roman, that he promised to withdraw his men altogether; in fact, he said, if they did any more grazing it would be on the marshes outside Rome, where people walked on stilts. This was because thousands and thousands of barbarians, far worse than the Fenmen, were threatening Rome. The Romans left little behind in the Fens, except their stilts, but those lasted the Fenmen for hundreds of years, though they are never seen using them now.

TYPE ML.8000.MOTIFS: A.1459 [*Acquisition of crafts*]; K.300 [*Thefts and cheats*]; K.258 [*Stolen property sold to owner*].

¶ This is an example of the long and circumstantial tales told in the Fens about events far back in history. It is doubtful whether these were traditions handed down from the earliest times, or whether they were embroideries of stories told to the Fenmen by Cambridge scholars who went fishing or shooting in the Fen country.

INA THE KING

Ruth L. Tongue

The Princess of Hunder was so proud and beautiful that men said she would find no husband good enough for her but Ina the Wise, the King of Wessex, whose palace of Gladerhaf stood at Somerton. But the Princess did not think him good enough either, for he had been a ploughman in his youth. So when his messengers came she sent them back again, and so she did with all the kings who courted her, until no more came, and the Princess was left alone with her pride.

After a time, however, King Ina sent another messenger, and the Princess thought she had never seen so fine a man. "I am not for your master," she said, "but there is no need to go and tell him so. Stay here and serve me, instead of him." The messenger stayed, and the Princess's liking turned to love, and then to longing, until she told him her mind, and asked him to marry her. So they were married, and after the wedding he took a crown and cloak from his baggage, and she found that she had married Ina the King, whom she had scorned. So her pride was humbled, and she went home with him, and many tales are told of his great doings, and in the end, they say, it was he who became proud, and his Queen who taught him to be humble. However that may be, they were fit mates for each other, and lived together happily until they died.

From local traditions. Somerton, Somerset.

TYPE 900 (variant). MOTIFS: T.75.0.1 [*Suitor ill-treated*]; K.1816.0.3 [*Menial disguise of princess's lover*].

¶ King Ina's life was well documented, with references in the *Anglo-Saxon Chronicle*, Florence of Worcester, Henry of Huntingdon, etc. According to a tenth-century tradition, he was a ceorl who was taken from his father's ox-plough at Somerton in Somerset, and was made King of all England south of the Humber. He married Adelburh, the heiress of Northern England, at Wells. (See the *Somersetshire Archaeological Journal*, XVIII, ii, pp. 17–21, for an examination of this legend.) He was chosen King of the West Saxons in 688, and subsequently enlarged the kingdom considerably. His laws are the earliest extant specimens of West Saxon legislation. He finally abdicated, and he and his wife made pilgrimage to Rome, where they eventually died. After death they were supposed to perform miracles. King Ina was a kinsman of St Aldhelm.

JACK OTTER

S. O. Addy, *Household Tales*, p. 10.

In Lincolnshire there once lived a man, called Jack Otter, who had been married nine times, and had murdered all his wives one after another. One day he was angry with the woman that he was courting, and whom he intended to take for his tenth wife. So he asked her to go for a walk with him, and when they had got into a lonely place he stabbed her and buried her on the spot. But his crime was found out, and he was gibbeted on a post in the lane. Now a bird, called the willow-biter, built her nest in the dead man's mouth, as he hung on the gallows-tree, and brought up her fledglings in it. And hence this riddle is asked:

> There were ten tongues within one head,
> And one went out to fetch some bread
> To feed the living in the dead.

MOTIFS: S.62.1 [*Bluebeard*]; H.793 [*Seven tongues in a head*].

¶ This brief tale is allied to two different types, "Mr Fox", "The Oxford Student", etc., Type 312, and "Outriddling the Judge", Type 927.

For rather insufficient reasons, Addy identifies Jack Otter with Odin.

JACK WHITE'S GIBBET

Briggs and Tongue, *Folktales of England*, pp. 96–8.

Jack White were a ostler, 'e weren't a very good one neither—a bit too fond o' cards 'e was; and 'e took to dipping 'is fingers into other people's pockets to find the cash to pay back 'is debts. Well now, there come a traveller to the inn, and 'e got over-full o' zider, and 'e wasn't very wise about things, and 'e let on that 'e'd got a lot o' gold about 'en. Well, next morning, when 'e do leave the inn, and go on 'is way, Jack White, 'e up and followed 'im, and when 'e'd gotten up by the crossroads, 'e murdered 'im, dead. Some say that 'e knifed 'im with 'is own knife. 'Twere a case-knife, and the man were a sailor. Anyways, Jackie White, 'e took the gold, and 'e run back to inn.

Well, someone came along, and they found that man all dead and murdered in 'is gore, and they bring corpse down to town, and they put 'en out, so's everyone should see 'en—see if they recognize 'en; and the crowds did come from Wincanton and Castle Carey, all round like, to see if they recognise dead man; and Jack White, 'e just daresn't stay away. Well, when the crowd began to press round like, to 'ave a look at the dead corpse, Jack White, 'e got pushed to the front, and so soon as 'e got pushed to the front, that there corpus's nose began to bleed, a little bit, just a little trickle, but someone spied 'en, and they said, "'Tis a-bleeding! 'Ere!" And they looked round, and there were Jack White, so white as— oh! like a bit o' snow. And they pushed 'en a bit further near corpse and— well! blood came gushing out like, and they laid 'ands on Jack White, and they said, "'Ere be murderer!"

And they took 'en, and they 'anged 'en, up by cross-roads. And there 'e do 'aunt. Ah! They do say, some on 'em, as the man killed were 'is own dear brother, come 'ome from the seas, and Jack 'e never recognized 'e, and the brother never let on. And that's why Jack do 'aunt.

Recorded from Ruth L. Tongue, 9 September, 1963. This version was heard in a composite discussion at Wincanton in 1948, but Miss Tongue had been familiar with the story from 1906 onwards.

MOTIFS: E.274 [*Gallows ghost*]; D.1318.5.2 [*Corpse bleeds when murderer touches it*].

¶ Jack White was hanged and ultimately gibbeted on the scene of his crime in 1790. An article on the actual event and the traditional accretions of the story was contributed by H. B. Irving to the *Somerset Year Book* for 1922 (p. 60). The murdered man was killed chiefly from motives of greed, aroused ironically enough by a gilded Nuremberg token which Jack White mistook for a guinea. It was through this that he was traced. After his execution rumour got to work, and characteristic folk-motifs were introduced into the tale. A rumour that Jack White had unwittingly killed his own brother even brought the tale into the orbit of the widespread Type 939A, that of the returning son killed for gain by his parents (see "The Penryn

Tragedy", (B, IX)). Such incidents as this were only too common. An unfortunate stranger was followed and murdered for his watch and chain at the end of the last century at Leafield, but the murderers were never brought to book. A similar incident is told in Laurie Lee's *Cider with Rosie*.

The interest of this tale is not in the incident, but in the characteristic haze of rumours that soon surrounded it.

KING ALFRED AND THE CAKES

Asser's Life of Alfred, Six Old English Chronicles, edited by J. A. Giles, p. 60.

At the same time the above-mentioned Alfred, king of the West Saxons, with a few of his nobles, and certain soldiers and vassals, used to lead an unquiet life among the woodlands of the county of Somerset, in great tribulation; for he had none of the necessaries of life, except what he could forage, openly or stealthily, by frequent sallies from the pagans, or even from the Christians who had submitted to the pagans, and as we read in the Life of St Neot, at the house of one of his cowherds.

But it happened on a certain day, that the countrywoman, wife of the cowherd, was preparing some loaves to bake, and the king, sitting in the hearth, made ready his bow and arrows and other warlike instruments. The unlucky woman espying the cakes burning at the fire, ran up to remove them, and rebuking the brave king, exclaimed:

"Ca'sn thee mind the ke-aks, man, an doossen zee 'em burn?
I'm boun thee's eat 'em vast enough az zoon az 'tiz the turn."

The blundering woman little thought that it was King Alfred, who had fought so many battles against the pagans, and gained so many victories over them.

MOTIF: P.15.1 [*Disguised king punished by peasant*].

¶ There is little doubt that in the main *Asser's Life of Alfred* is a genuine contemporary document, but the manuscript contains many twelfth-century additions, of which this is one. Roger of Hovendon's *Chronicle* gives a brief account of the same story (I, p. 211), but it is not certain how early the tradition arose.

Literary use of it is made by Chesterton in "The Ballad of the White Horse".

THE KING OF THE PEAK [summary]

A. Cunningham, *Traditional Tales of the English and Scottish Peasantry*, p. 213.

"The King of the Peak" was the nickname of Sir George Vernon, who, about the year 1560, held a great hunting festival at Haddon Hall. He was renowned for his wealth, his hospitality, his prowess in every kind of sport, but most of all for the beauty of his two daughters, Margaret and

Dorothy. He himself, for the beauty of his person, and his courtly manners, was something of a favourite of Queen Elizabeth. His festival, therefore, was eagerly attended by all whom he invited, and at the end a great banquet was prepared, and many toasts were drunk, and ballads sung, to the lovely Dora or Dorothy Vernon. So hot was the contest for her favour that her father's anger rose, and he bade her leave the hall, and go to her chamber, attended by only one of her women, a comely but staid maiden of thirty or so years of age. Some time after midnight this young woman came to her mistress and begged her leave to go for half an hour to meet her lover, who had come seven miles in the hope of seeing her. Dora agreed, and the maid left her.

Meantime one of the keepers, whose duty to guard the chase had kept him from joining in the revels, saw two cloaked figures approaching, the taller of whom called to him by name, "Jasper Jugg, is that you?" and told him that Nan Malkin, Mistress Dora's maid, had left her mistress unguarded, and was even then whispering with her lover under the terrace. The keeper, fuddled with wine, made after them, for he was himself in love with the pretty Nan, and as soon as he was out of sight the taller of the two cloaked figures blew a silver whistle. At once several armed men appeared, leading horses. The two, who were now revealed as Dora Vernon herself and her lover, Lord John Manners, mounted, and rode swiftly away to a distant land to escape the wrath of her father.

MOTIFS: T.97 [*Father opposed to daughter's marriage*]; T.46 [*Suitor outwits watchman to meet lady*]; R.225 [*Elopement*].

KING RICHARD AND THE
PENITENT KNIGHT [abbreviated]

Roger of Wendover, *Chronicle*, II, p. 547.

(A.D. 1232.) A certain English knight, living in the New Forest, who had long made a practice of clandestinely hunting the king's deer, was on one occasion caught with some stolen venison, and by a decree of the court of the king was condemned to exile. This merciful king had mitigated the law in reference to stolen venison...he...considered it quite a sufficient punishment for any, who was caught committing that offence, either to be banished from England, or to undergo imprisonment saving his life and limbs. The above-mentioned knight then was sent into exile, and he, who had formerly enjoyed all the dainties of life, was, with his wife and children, obliged to beg his bread among foreigners. The knight, after some reflection, at length determined to implore the king for mercy, and for his estate to be restored to him, and he accordingly went to the king in

Normandy, where he found him early in the morning in a church, about to hear Mass. The knight tremblingly entered the church, and did not dare to raise his eyes to the king, for although he was the most handsome of men to look upon, there was still something dreadful in his look; he therefore went to an image of Christ on the Cross, and, weeping incessantly, he humbly on his knees besought the Crucified One through his unspeakable grace, compassionately to make his peace with the king, by which means he might recover his lost inheritance. The king, seeing the knight thus earnestly and with unfeigned devotion praying and weeping, witnessed an occurrence wonderful and worthy of narration; for whenever the knight, who he knew was not of his retinue, bent his knees to worship the image, the image, in all humility, bowed its head and shoulders as it were in answer to the knight, and the king was struck with wonder and astonishment to see this repeated frequently. As soon as the service of Mass was ended, he sent for the knight to speak with him, and inquired of him who he was and whence he came. The knight replied with fear said, "My lord, I am your liege subject, as my ancestors also have been"; and then, beginning his history, he told the king how he had been deprived of his inheritance and banished together with his family, having been caught with some stolen venison. The king then said to the knight, "Have you ever in your life done any good act in respect, and to the honour, of the holy Cross?" The knight then, after carefully thinking over the events of his past life, related to the king the following deed, which he had done in his reverence for Christ:

"My father," said he, "and another knight divided between them a town which belonged to them by hereditary right; and whilst my father abounded in all kinds of wealth, the other knight, on the contrary, was always poor and needy, and, becoming envious of my father, he treacherously murdered him. I was then a boy, but when I arrived at manhood, and was installed in my paternal inheritance, I made a resolute determination to slay that knight in revenge for my father's death; he was, however, forewarned of my purpose, and for several years by his cunning escaped the snares I had laid for him. At length...as I was going to church, to hear Mass, I saw my enemy before me, also on his way to church. I hastened on behind him, and drew my sword to kill him, when by some chance he looked round, and, seeing me rushing upon him, fled to a cross which stood near the road, being worn down by age, and unable to defend himself. And when I endeavoured with upraised sword to slay him and dash out his brains, he encircled the cross with his arms, and adjured me in the name of that Christ, who on that day was suspended on the Cross for the salvation of the whole world, not to slay him, but faithfully promised and vowed, that he would appoint a chaplain to perform a Mass every day from that time for the soul of my father whom he had killed. When I saw the old man weeping I was moved to pity, and thus in my love and reverence for Him who, for my salvation and that of all, ascended the Cross, and consecrated it by His most holy blood, I forgave the knight for my father's murder." The king then said to the knight, "You acted wisely, for now that Crucified One has repaid one good turn by another." He then summoned the bishops and barons who were there with him, and, in the hearing of all, related the vision he had seen, how at each genuflection made by the knight, the image of Christ had humbly bowed its head and shoulders. He then summoned his chancellor to him, and commanded him by his letters patent, to order the sheriff whom the knight should name to him, at sight of the warrant, to restore to the knight the whole of his property in the same condition as he received it at the time of his banishment.

MOTIFS: Q.431 [*Punishment: banishment*]; V.410 [*Charity rewarded*]; V.441 [*Forgiveness*].

¶ Later historians have been unfavourable to Richard I, but he was revered in his own age, as various traditions show. Among them is his pardon of the young archer from whose arrow-shot he died, and the well-known, though rather late, story of Blondel. This tale of Roger of Wendover is less known, but particularly charming.

LADY RESTORED TO LIFE

County Folk-Lore, Vol. I, Part 1, *Gloucestershire*, etc., p. 27.

I have met with the following statement: "Eliza, the wife of Sir W. Fanshawe of Woodley Hall, in Gloucestershire, was interred, having, at her own request, a valuable locket, which was her husband's gift, hung upon her breast. The sexton, proceeding to the vault at night, stole the jewel, and by the admission of fresh air restored the body, who had been only in a trance, and who, with great difficulty, reached Woodley Hall in the dead of night, to the general alarm of the servants. Sir William, being roused by their cries, found his lady, with bleeding feet and clothed in the winding-sheet, stretched upon the hall. She was put into a warm bed, and gave birth to several children after her recovery." On what authority, let me ask, has this statement been made? and, if true, when did the occurrence take place? Change the scene to the town of Drogheda, in Ireland, the lady's name to Harman, and the locket to a ring, and you have a tolerably accurate account of what occurred in the last century, and with the tradition of which I have been familiar from my childhood.

Gloucestershire Notes and Queries I, 1881, pp. 2, 3.

II. LADY SOPHIA MOUNT EDGCUMBE

Augustus Hare, *In My Solitary Life*, p. 58.

The late Lord Mount Edgcumbe lived here* for many years.... It was his mother† who was buried alive and lived for many years afterwards. It was known that she had been put into her coffin with a very valuable ring upon her finger, and the sexton went in after the funeral, when the coffin was put into the vault, to get it off. He opened the coffin, but the ring was hard to move, and he had to rub the dead finger up and down. This brought Lady Mount Edgcumbe to life, and she sat up. The sexton fled, leaving the doors of the vault and church open. Lady Mount Edgcumbe walked home in her shroud, and appeared in front of the windows. Those within thought it was a ghost. Then she walked in at the front door. When she saw her husband, she fainted in his arms. This gave her family time to decide what should be done, and they settled to persuade her it had been a terrible delirium. When she recovered from her faint, she was in her own bed, and she ever believed it had been a dream.

* Stone Hall, Plymouth.
† Sophia, daughter of the 2nd Earl of Buckinghamshire.

III. THE LINDSAY VERSION [summary]

The Land of the Lindsays, Jernis and Ganimark, 1882, pp. 15, 16.

It happened to one of the Lindsays of Edzell. The sexton went down to the vault to rob her and began to cut off her fingers. Startled by her movement, he fainted. The lady took up his candle, raised him and led him out into the open air. She promised him a reward if he took her home, but he begged to be allowed to escape. She gave him her jewels and struggled home alone. Date unknown. The Lindsays were subject to catalepsy.

IV. MISTRESS ERSKINE OF CHIRNSIDE

Communicated by Captain the Chevalier J. H. Macpherson.

Chirnside is a village in the south-east corner of Berwickshire. The Minister in 1672 was Henry Erskine, who married an Orkney woman named Margaret Halcrow—his second marriage. She died within a few months of the marriage and was buried with a valuable ring on her finger. The sexton covered her up lightly and, by night, dug her up again to steal the ring. It stuck on her finger, and he tried to cut it off. She sat up in the coffin, shouted, and ran home to the Manse, where she is said to have aroused her husband by calling, "See's hame! I'm fair clammed!"

She later had two sons, Ralph and Ebenezar, who were founders of the original Secession Kirk.

V. MRS KILLIGREW

Norton Collection, III, p. 37.

Many years ago a Mrs Killigrew was supposed to have been dead about a week. When she was to be put into her coffin, her body was so swelled that it was found impossible to get her diamond hoop-ring off without cutting the finger; this her husband would not consent to; accordingly she was buried with the ring.

The sexton, who had observed this, determined to steal the ring that night. Having forced open the coffin, he proceeded to cut off the finger, but the first gash of the knife brought Mrs Killigrew to life again. The sexton, frightened, ran away, leaving his lantern, which she immediately took, and walked to her own house. There, her appearance, of course, created great consternation among the servants; no one would venture to open the door. Fortunately, the rumour reached the ears of her disconsolate husband, who went directly to receive her. After this event, she lived ten years, and in the course of that time had ten children. A maid who belonged to Mrs Killigrew, after her death lived with Mrs Walter, grandmother to the Grimstones: from her they had this story.

W. E. A. Axon. *Reliquary,* January 1868, p. 150, quoting *Diaries of a Lady of Quality,* Miss Wynne, p. 1.

VI. THE THIEVISH SEXTON

Briggs and Tongue, *The Folktales of England,* p. 88.

Young Mistress Florence Wyndham, 'er were took ill, and in spite of all they could do for she, 'er died, and 'er dear 'usband, 'e were 'eart-broken. They took she from Kentsford Farm, where 'er lived, up to St Decuman's Church, and they buried 'er in the family vault. And then, 'er poor 'usband were took back to Kentsford.

Well, that night, the sexton 'e came creeping back to church, and 'e opened the vault again. You see, she 'ad some lovely jewels, and 'e 'ad a mind to they. 'E crep' in with a little lantern, and 'e took 'old of 'er cold 'and, and 'e wrenched off one ring and another, but there were one 'e couldn't move. So 'e took out 'is knife to cut off the vinger o' she, and it bled! Well, 'e were so terrified, 'e just stood there, quaking, and the vigger of the lady, all in 'er shroud, sat up. Well, 'e turned around, and 'e kick over the lantern, and there 'e stood in the dark, while something rustled past 'e and out. Well, 'e were that terrified, 'e come out o' the church, and 'e run, and 'e run, and 'e run. And in 'is terror, 'e run over the edge of Old Cleeve cliffs, and 'e dropped down ninety feet into the sea, and no one ever saw anything of 'im again.

Well, the volks down to Snailholt Farm, they found themselves awaked by a voice, and it were the voice o' Mistress Florence Wyndham! Oh!

They shook and they shivered, in their beds, and at last, young Missis, she says, "Well, Mistress Wyndham, she never did no 'arm to I. I'll go and see what ghost want."

So 'er took and 'er looked out o' chimmer window, and there were the young mistress alive, with 'er 'and bleeding. Oh! They took the poor soul in, put a cloak round she, and took 'er back to Kentsford, and what's more, 'er was alive and well for years arterwards, and give 'er 'usband two more lusty sons.

Recorded by Ruth L. Tongue, 29th September 1963. Heard by her in Watchet.

VII. THE THIEVISH SEXTON

County Folk-Lore, II, pp. 386–7.

An old gentleman in the village [Rudby] related a curious story of the ghoul-like deeds of a certain parish-clerk, who also officiated as sexton, some years ago. It would appear that a married woman of the village having been given up for dead, was at length removed to the usual place of interment. Whether from some implied wish on her part, or difficulty in releasing it, the wedding-ring was allowed to remain on the finger. This circumstance awakened the cupidity of the parish-clerk, who at the lone hour of midnight, crept cautiously to the new-made grave. Having removed the earth, and unscrewed the coffin, he proceeded to take off the ring, but from the contracted state of the fingers was unable to effect his purpose. Accordingly with his pocket-knife he set about amputating the finger; but he had scarcely reached the bone, when, O horror! the corpse bolted nearly upright in its coffin, at the same time uttering a loud and dismal scream. The parish-clerk, who, by the by, was a tailor, immediately darted homeward with the utmost speed, his hair bristling on end. Meantime the poor woman, who had been unconsciously buried in a trance, alarmed at her strange and peculiar situation, directed her steps to her husband's residence, and knocked at the door. What was her husband's amazement and consternation to behold his buried wife, in her shroud and grave-clothes, standing at the door, calling for admittance! His first alarm having somewhat abated, he proceeded to make further inquiry, and was at length convinced that his true wife, in flesh and blood, had in reality returned from the tomb. Afterwards, the injured finger and the state of the grave, pointed suspicion to the parish-clerk; but the husband, instead of punishing him for allowing his wife to return from her last resting-place, actually presented him annually with a web of the finest linen (he being a linen manufacturer).

Ord, *The History and Antiquity of Cleveland*, p. 470.
TYPE 990. MOTIF: K.426 [*Apparently dead woman revives when thief tries to steal from her grave*].

¶ Scattered instances of this tale are known through Europe, and seventy-seven are recorded in the Irish archives. Baughman records five American versions, of which one is reproduced in R. M. Dorson's *Buying the Wind*. A German version was used in Zangerle's Puppet Theatre in Cologne. The motif and type are common to all versions. They vary in detail and in the degree of substantiation.

I. There seems to be no confirmation of this story in Gloucestershire. Lady Fanshawe's mother, Mrs Harrison, was once in a state of suspended animation, which may have caused the story to be attached to the family.

II. This is still supposed locally to be true, and has a recent date.

III. The only ascertainable corroboration to this version is that one of the Lindsay Lairds fell into a cataleptic state, and was supposed to be dead, but he recovered quite speedily.

IV. This appears to be the best authenticated version of the tale. Mrs Forbes, formerly Evelyn Erskine Hill, has the ring which was on Margaret Erskine's hand when she was buried, with an account of the matter.

V. The line of tradition in this story is fairly convincing, but it is possible that some details may have been added to bring it into conformity with the traditional type.

VI. This version is generally credited, and is told by Cresswell, *The Quantocks*, by Page, *Exploration of Dartmoor*, and twice in the *Somerset Year Book*, 1953, p. 102, and 1935, p. 67. It is so like the other tales, that it is difficult to believe that it has not been forced into the same mould.

THE LASS 'AT SEED HER AWN GRAAVE DUG

M. Peacock, *Tales and Rhymes in the Lindsey Folk-speech*, p. 72.

Did I niver tell ye aboot oor Bessie gran'muther, 'at seed her awn graave dug, poor lass? It's a queer taale that, an' ivry wo'd on it's trew. She was a real pretty lass, wi' flaxen hair, an' blew ees, an' ther' was a man, call'd Fox, 'at was straange an' fond on her. Well, he maade a deäl on her, an' when he'd gotten his awn work dun, he'd tidy hissen up a bit, an' then he'd walk ower to her feyther's hoose, an' help her to milk coos, sarve pigs, an' such-like. Foäks reckon'd he was clear soft aboot lass, bud gell's feyther, 'at haated to sea him loongin' aboot plaace, alus said, "He's ower kean by hairf, an' ye knaw, 'When luve's ower strong it niver lasts long'." Awiver, noabody bud the owd wimmin took noa noatice on him. Ivrybody knawed 'at he thowt 'at lass could ha' gotten her wark dun wi'oot ony o' Fox's help, an' gotten thrif it a deal sharper an' all, an' soa foäks nobbud laughed when he carried on. Well, won daay, when her feyther was oot a singlin' tu'nups, Fox cums an' says, "I've gotten to goa to markit to-morrer. If te can, cum to th' big esh i' Galley-daales, an' then I can seä yer hoam, an' we'll sattle aboot gettin' married." "That's a long waay to walk," says lass, "an' it's a straange loänly road, an' I should be fine an' scarr'd if I met owt." Bud at last Fox gets her talk'd ower an' she says she'll be under th' esh a bit efter seven, an' then off he goäs. Well, that neet th' lass hed a straange queer dreäm, an' she says to hersen next daay, "I hedn't that theare dreäm fer nowt. I'll be i' Galley-dales afoor he tell'd me, I reckon; then I shall get to knaw what he's up to." Soä she gets her wark dun, an' then she shuts off to Galley-daales wi'oot sayin' nowt to noäbody. An' when she gets to big esh-tree, she climbs up, an' hides hersen i' th' beughs, an' sits as still as a beä. An' efter a bit Fox cums, an' pulls a spaade oot'n hedge-bottom, an' begins to dig a graave aneän th' esh. He was that throng wi' it, he niver looked uop an' seed th' lass. An' efter he'd gotten it dun, he walks up an' doon, smookin' an' lookin' at graave, an' talkin' to hissen. Well, he waaited, an' waaited fer lass till he was stalled, bud she niver cum'd, an' at last he shuvels mouds i'to graave agään, an' goäs awaay, chunterin'. Then lass slips doon, an' runs hoäm, as quick as if a boggard was efter her. An' next daay, when Fox cums an' axes why she'd bauk'd him i' that how, she says, "I'll tell th' if te can mak this here oot:

> 'Riddle me, riddle me righ,
>   Up i' th' boughs so high;
>   Th' wind it blew,
>   Th' cocks thaay crew,
>   Th' leäves did shaake,
>   My heart did ache
>   To seä th' hoale
>   Th' fox did maake;
>   Riddle me, riddle me righ.'"

An' when Fox hears this he was fer makkin' off; bud in cums lass's fey-ther, wi' five or six uther men, an' teks him stright awaay to prison. An' if it hedn't been fer that theare dreäm, 'at was sent her, lass wo'd ha' been mo'dered, as trew as I stan' here.

TYPE 955C (Baughman). MOTIFS: C.168 [*Tabu: disregarding dream-warning against marriage*]; H.565 [*Riddle propounded from chance experience*].

¶ Baughman cites a number of versions from America.

See "The Oxford Student", "The Girl Who got up a Tree", "Mr Fox's Courtship" (A, IV).

THE LEE PENNY [summary]

Douglas, *Scottish Fairy and Folk-Tales*, p. 92.

The Lee Penny is an amulet made of a deep red stone, set triangularly in a silver coin, and it is said to have been brought from the Holy Land by Sir Simon Lockhart. In a battle against the Saracens, he captured a wealthy Emir, whose mother came into the Christian camp to offer a ransom for him.

While she was counting out of her purse the money fixed by Lockhart, this amulet fell out, and so captured his imagination, that he insisted it should be included in the ransom. The woman agreed, and told him that it possessed powers of healing when dipped in water. Sir Simon took it home to his family seat of Lee, where it is said to have worked many cures, being handed down in the family in every generation.

Those who drank the water in which the stone had been dipped, and at the same time washed the affected part of the body, whether men or animals, were cured of their diseases, so that the fame of the amulet before long was drawing people from all parts of Scotland, who carried away the precious water to give to those who were sick.

From William Andrews in the *Border Counties' Magazine*.
MOTIFS: D.859.8 [*Magic object as ransom of captive*]; D.1500.1.8 [*Magic amulet cures disease*].
¶ A similar amulet was owned by the village of Fortingal in Perthshire, though it conferred immunity in battle (D.1392.1). It is said that the small band who went out to join Prince Charlie in the '45 all drank of water in which the magic stone had been dipped, except one man, who scoffed at the superstition. He was killed, but all the rest returned safely.

THE LEGEND OF THE SWORD
[Monmouth Rebellion]

Ruth L. Tongue, *Somerset Folklore*, p. 195.

Turrible times the war was! Ah! turrible doings. They d'zay from yur to Burgewalter was all a-ztink with the dead corpuses hanging every step of the way. But there was brave deeds tew, oh yes. Have 'ee ever heard tell how Squire were tew Bristol and they blood-thirsty sojers do come up to Hall? Proper wicked drunk they was, and they offered disrespect to Madam, poor dear zoul, and her near her time. Well then, Miss Mary, and her but a maid in her twelves, she outs the villain's zword and runs he droo the heart so clean's a whistle. No one never blamed her. Proper brave maid her was.

Collected from fragments round Bridgwater and the lower Quantocks, 1912–30s.

Note: I was told the actual sword was in Taunton Museum. The incident is quite true. "The war" may mean any battle from Roman days on. Usually the very old call the Monmouth Rebellion "The Duking Days" in memory of Monmouth.

TYPE 956B (variant). MOTIF: K.912 [*Robbers' heads cut off as they enter house*].

A LINK WITH THE PAST

Augustus Hare, *In My Solitary Life*, p. 73.

"I have frequently seen lately, at the Lefevres', old Lord Redesdale,* with whom we have some distant cousinship, through my Mitford great-grandmother. He is very kind, clever, old-fashioned, and always wears a tail-coat. He took us into the far-away, by telling us of having heard his father, Speaker Mitford, describe having known a man in Swaledale named Rievely, whose earliest recollection was of being carried across the Swale by Henry Jenkyns (who lived to 160), who recollected having gone as a boy, with a sheaf of arrows and his elder brother on a pony, from Ellerton in Swaledale, to Northallerton, to join the army before the Battle of Flodden. He would tell all about the battle in a familiar way—'the King was not there, but the Duke of Suffolk was there', etc."

See "A Folk-memory of Chaucer".

"LITTLE JACK HORNER"

H. Bett, *English Myths and Traditions*, p. 103.

The rhyme about "Little Jack Horner" has unquestionably a historic basis. The tradition was that John Horner was the steward of the last Abbot of Glastonbury, and that he was sent up to London with a Christmas pie as a present to Henry VIII. The pie contained a casket, and the casket contained the title-deeds of twelve manors in the county of Somerset. On the way Horner opened the pie and the casket, abstracted the title-deeds of the Manor of Mells, and kept these for himself. The tradition seemed to be supported by the detail that the Horner family is still seated at Mells. But the facts, which have thus been made into a picturesque story, are these: John Horner and his brother Thomas were concerned in the business of the suppression of the Abbey, then the largest and richest in England, and the last monastery to be sequestrated. Thomas Horner was on the jury that condemned the last Abbot to death. John Horner bought some of the Abbey lands, including the manor of Mells, and founded a county family—a feat which was accomplished by the ancestors of many such families at that time. As the local folk-rhyme has it:

> Wyndham, Horner, Popham, and Thynne,
> When the Abbot went out, they came in!

* John Thomas Freeman-Mitford, 1st Earl of Redesdale, 1805–86. He and his father were strong opponents of Catholic Emancipation, and in the year of this note he carried on a Press controversy with Cardinal Manning that became notorious.

90

The nursery rhyme is a quaint record of the fact that John Horner had a finger in the pie when the Abbey of Glastonbury was suppressed, and that he did very well for himself out of it—he "pulled out a plum".

¶ Glastonbury was the last of the abbeys to be suppressed, and had been promised immunity. The tradition about the pie was first printed in the nineteenth century, but the last Abbot, Sir Richard Whiting, was in the habit of sending rich Christmas gifts to King Henry VIII, pies among them, and the story may have been orally current from the sixteenth century. The whole matter is fully set out in *The Oxford Dictionary of Nursery Rhymes*, Iona and Peter Opie.

LORD DACRE'S DAUGHTER

Parkinson, *Yorkshire Legends and Traditions*, 1st series, p. 225.

A youth named de Lacy was betrothed against his will to the daughter of Lord Dacre, whom he had never seen. One morning, as he was wandering in Haverah Park, he met a shepherdess, whose flocks were grazing on the dew-wet grass.

She was so lovely that he fell instantly in love with her, and swore to make her his bride, and the lady of all his lands. But she bade him ride on and think no more of her, for no shepherdess could be a fit bride for him; besides, Lord Dacre was a terrible man to anger. He, however, boldly caught her up, placed her on his horse, and, walking beside her like a page, he led her to a hermit's cell, where they were married.

Only then, as he caught her in his arms, did he learn that he had been trapped. The shepherdess was indeed herself Lord Dacre's daughter, and she led him, speechless with amazement, to meet her dreaded father.

MOTIFS: T.69.2 [*Parents affiance children without their knowledge (consent)*]; T.15 [*Love at first sight*]; T.55.11 [*Princess transforms self to woo*].
¶ Goldsmith uses the same theme in *She Stoops to Conquer*.

THE LOST BRIDE

Briggs and Tongue, *The Folktales of England*, p. 88.

'Tis a turble zad tale, zo 'tis, but it do go thisaway. Parson had a darter, a purty young thing her was, and her was a-gettin' wed to her true love. There was a fine junketings, and there they all was playing old games and merriment. And her went to hidey in a gurt big chest, in attic 'twas, and lid come down crackey on poor maid's head and her fell in a swound inzide chest, and chest did lock itself. They did go lookin' up and down for the bride and no one could find she—and her true love's heart did break so they buried the poor young man—but her never come back no more. Nobody could tell where her was to; then one day they come into the attic for something or another and opened the chest—And there her lay in her wedding gown, and her was just a skeleton.

Recorded from Ruth L. Tongue, 21 September 1963, who heard the story from "Annie's Granny" in her old age when she was in an almshouse at Chard or Yeovil about 1920.

¶ This version is about Shapwick, where a stone in the chancel of the church tells of the "daughter and heiress of the family honour and estates, who died June 14th, 1681. Taken away by a sudden and untimely fate at the very time of the marriage celebrations". This alone would be enough to attach the "Mistletoe Bough" story to this place (R.L.T.).

There is no known European version of this story, which is not given a number in the Type Index, but it is fairly widely known in Britain and the United States, mainly because of Thomas Haynes Bayley's song, "The Mistletoe Bough", which was very popular at village concerts in the Victorian and Edwardian eras.

In the States the song was spread orally, and rather more altered than in England; for the bride often became a "Princess".

In England the tale is applied to the Yorkshire Lovels of Skelton, to the Lovells of Minster Lovell in Oxfordshire, and to the Copes of Bramshill in Hampshire.

MACCULLOCH'S COURTSHIP [shortened]

Hugh Miller, *Scenes and Legends*, pp. 67–70.

The Maccullochs of the parish of Cromarty, a family now extinct, were for about two centuries substantial respectable farmers. The first of them, says tradition, was a Highlander, Alaster Macculloch. When still a boy, he quitted the Highland home of his widowed mother, and at length procured employment in the parish of Cromarty, on the farm of an old wealthy tacksman. For the first few weeks he seemed gloomy and unsociable, but soon recovered his spirits; and though pride in his Highland birth made him always wear his tartan suit when he attended chapel, with his father's dirk hanging at his side, he became in every other respect a true Lowland Scot, who excelled in sly humour and practical joking.

His master, a widower, had a daughter of nineteen, a laughing, warmhearted girl. She had more lovers than half the girls of the parish put together, but none commanded her love in return, though she thanked them kindly for their tenders of affection. The little shepherd-lad, Alaster, was the last of these, and he and his cattle shared her kindness to everything and everyone connected with her father and his farm. He never spoke of his love, and found it added to his natural happiness, and the pleasantness of his day-dreams, but his courtesy to the girl Lillias made her wonder where the Highland boy had learnt such manners.

But he was five years younger than she, and her father's herd-boy, so she gave the matter little thought.

Late in October of the year 1560, Alaster overheard his young mistress talking with the daughter of a neighbouring farmer about the rites of the appoaching Hallowe'en. The other girl said, "Will you really venture on throwing the clue in the kiln? It is dark and lonely, and there's mony a story no true, if folk havena often been frightened there." "Oh, surely," replied Lillias. "Who would think it worth while to harm the like o' me? And, besides, you can bide for me just a wee bittie aff. One would like, somehow, to know the name of one's gudeman, or whether one is to get a gudeman at all."

After hearing this, Alaster gained permission from her father, with whom he was a firm favourite, to spend his Hallowe'en at a neighbouring cottage, where several young people were to meet; and when the evening came he set out as if to go there, but in fact crept back to the kiln, climbed like a wild-cat up its circular gable, entered by the chimney, and in a few minutes was snugly seated amid the ashes of the furnace. He waited a full hour, but at length heard a light footstep approaching; the door was unlocked, and as it opened, a square patch of moonlight fell on the rude wall of the kiln. A tall figure stepped forward, and stood in the stream of faint light. She looked fearfully round, and then producing a small clue of yarn, she threw it towards Alaster, and immediately began to wind. He suffered it to turn round and round among the ashes, and then cautiously laid hold of it. "Wha hauds?" said his mistress in a low startled whisper, looking over her shoulder as she spoke. "Alaster Macculloch," was the reply; and in a moment she had vanished like a spectre. Soon afterwards the tread of two persons was heard approaching the kiln. It was now Alaster's turn to tremble. "I shall be discovered," he thought, "and my strategem come to worse than nothing." "And did ye hear onything when ye came out yon gate?" said one of the persons without. "Oh, naething, lass, naething," replied the voice of Lillias. "Steek to the door an' lock it;—it's a foolish conceit." The door was locked, and Alaster found his way out in the same way as he had entered.

Next day, when he saw his mistress, she was cold and distant, and had evidently had a quarrel with Destiny. But the years passed, and she rejected one suitor after another, until in her twenty-fourth year, Alaster, now a tall, handsome young man of nineteen, formally paid her his addresses. He was active and faithful, and had by now been entrusted by his master with the whole management of the farm.

A belief in Destiny often becomes a destiny of itself; and it became such to Alaster's mistress. In a few weeks they were married, and when the old man was gathered to his fathers, Alaster succeeded to the well-stocked farm.

TYPE 1476A (variant). MOTIFS: D.1825.1.2 [*Magic view of future lover*]; D.1825.1.2 (*g*) [*Mother of marriageable girl goes to kiln to wind her clew in klu-pot*] (Baughman); K.1971 [*Man behind statue speaks and pretends to be spirit*].

¶ There is an Irish–Californian example of this tale, in which the same method is used by the girl's mother, not by the girl herself.

See "Nowt but a Tailor" (A, III), "St Agnes's Well".

MARSHALL'S ELM

Briggs and Tongue, *The Folktales of England*, p. 96.

There were a varmer o' Walton near Street. 'E 'ad a only son, and 'e were tremenjus proud of 'e. Well, the lad, like so many more lads, 'e went to fight for Duke o' Monmouth down to Sedgemoor battle, and 'e were taken a prisoner. Well, 'is vather 'e were frantic, and 'e try and 'e try to get the lad's life saved. 'E spent all 'is savings, and 'e sold 'is 'arvest, and 'e took 'en to Judge Jefferies. And then, 'aving took all 'e 'ad to offer, the Bloody Judge gave orders the lad should be 'anged right afore 'is 'ome. Well, they did so, and the vather 'e stood by, and when 'twas all over, 'e turned round wi'out a word, and 'e go down to stables, and 'e kill 'is best bullock. And then 'e pull out the girt 'ot bleeding 'eart o' 'im, and 'e drove nail arter nail through 'en, till it looked like a red urchin. Then not saying a word, 'e go back to kitchen, and 'e carry the 'eart there, and 'e nail it up in chimney, where 'twas smoked and scorched for years.

And arter that day, the Bloody Judge, 'e were taken wi' choking coughs, and scorching burning pains all round 'is 'eart, which pierced 'en right through. And whenever 'e got an attack like that, there come a sight afore 'is eyes, no matter whether 'e closed 'em or no—the sight of a 'anging lad.

Recorded from Ruth L. Tongue, 28 September 1963, as she heard the account in 1940, while on a riding-tour in Somerset, from a Glastonbury farmer. She had heard previous mentions in the 1930s from Street.

MOTIF: G.271.4.1(*a*) [*Exorcism by burning or boiling animal-heart stuck with pins. Usually this process brings the witch on the scene, because of the burning it sets up in the heart*] (Baughman).

¶ "Marshall's Elm" is the name of the tree on which the boy was hanged. It was still standing in 1946.

MASTER JOHN SCOT

Roger of Wendover, *Chronicle*, I, p. 215.

The same year [883] there came into England Master John, a Scot by nation, a man of an apprehensive mind, and of singular eloquence. Quitting his country early in life he passed over to Gaul, where he was very honourably entertained by Charles the Bald, who made him the companion both of his meals and of his retirement. Instances of the vastness of his understanding, his knowledge, and of his wit, remain to this day. He was once sitting at table opposite the king, when, at the end of the repast, the cups having passed frequently, Charles became unusually merry, and observing Master John do something which was offensive to Gallic good breeding, he pleasantly rebuked him, and said, "John, what is there between a Scot and a sot?" "Only a table," replied Master Scot; thus turning back the reproach on its author. What can be more facetious than such a reply? For the question had been put with reference to the difference of manners, and John's reply had reference to the difference of place; nor was the king offended at the speech, but rather moved to laughter, in which all present joined. At another time, as the king was at table, one of the servants presented him a dish in which were two very large fishes, and one very small one; the king gave it to Master John, bidding him share it with two clerks who were sitting at meat with him. Now the fishes were of immense size, and Master John was small in person. Ever devising something pleasant for the entertainment of the company, John kept the two large fishes for himself and gave the little one to the two clerks; whereat the king found fault, that he had made an unfair division of the fishes. "Nay," said Master John, "I have made a good and equal division; for here is a small one," alluding to himself; "and here are two great ones," pointing to the fishes. Then turning to the clerks, "Here," said he, "are two great ones," meaning the clerks, "and here is a little one," meaning the fish.

TYPE 1533. MOTIFS: J.1250 [*Clever verbal retorts*]; J.1241 [*Clever division favourable to divider*].
¶ It is interesting to see the anecdote "sot" and "Scot" being revived after several centuries, and told about George Buchanan, another learned Scot. Type 1533 has a fairly wide distribution, principally in Eastern Europe and India.
See "George Buchanan" (A, III).

THE MERRY MONARCH AND
'BLYTHE COCKPEN'

Hone's *Table Book*, III, p. 411.

While Charles II was sojourning in Scotland, before the Battle of Worcester, his chief confidant and associate was the laird of Cockpen, called by the nicknaming fashion of the times, "Blythe Cockpen". He followed Charles to The Hague, and by his skill in playing Scottish tunes, and his sagacity and wit, much delighted the merry monarch. Charles's favourite air was "Brose and Butter"; it was played for him when he went to bed, and he was awakened by it. At the Restoration, however, Blythe Cockpen shared the fate of many other of the royal adherents: he was forgotten, and wandered upon the lands he once owned in Scotland, poor and unfriended. His letters to the Court were unpresented, or disregarded, till, wearied and incensed, he travelled to London; but his mean garb not suiting the rich doublets of court, he was not allowed to approach the royal presence. At length, he ingratiated himself with the king's organist, who was so enraptured with Cockpen's wit and powers of music, that he requested him to play on the organ before the king at divine service. His exquisite skill did not attract his majesty's notice, till, at the close of the service, instead of the usual tune, he struck up "Brose and Butter", with all its energetic merriment. In a moment the royal organist was ordered into the king's presence. "My liege, it was not me!" he cried, and dropped upon his knees. "You!" cried his majesty, in a rapture. "You could never play it in your life—Where's the man? Let me see him." Cockpen presented himself upon his knee. "Ah, Cockpen, is that you?—Lord, man, I was like to dance coming out of the church!" "I once danced too," said Cockpen, "but that was when I had land of my own to dance on." "Come with me," said Charles, taking him by the hand, "you shall dance to 'Brose and Butter' again on your own land to the nineteenth generation"; and as far as he could, the king kept his promise.

MOTIFS: H.12 [*Recognition by song*]; N.130 [*Changing of luck or fate*].

METHWOLD SEVERALS

W. H. Barrett, *More Tales from the Fens*, p. 88.

Folks say that there's always been a Mucky Porter living in the Fens ever since they were made. Anyway, right back in the time when Charles the First was King there was a tavern in Southery kept by a Mucky Porter who, besides being an innkeeper, used to show travellers the way across the Fens. So a lot of people used to call in at the Fleece, which was the name of the tavern, whenever they wanted help on their way.

Well, one day a servant, all dressed up in a fine livery, came to the Fleece and said he'd been sent by his master, Sir Ralph Skipwith of Snowre Hall,* because he wanted Mucky to help him. So Mucky rode back with the servant and when they got to the Hall Sir Ralph asked him: "Are you on old Noll's side?"

"What do you take me for?" asked Mucky. "Do you think I'd be on

---

* Snowre Hall: in Fordham, Norfolk. Charles I was sheltered there on 30 April 1646, during his escape to Oxford, which ended in his surrender at Newark on 5 May 1646.

the side of a chap who's taken all my best customers away to fight for him and only left the old 'uns who're too weak to swallow my best brew?"

"If that's so," said Sir Ralph, "I take it you're willing to help the King?"

"I'm willing to help any king—or queen, too, come to that," said Mucky, "if it means I get a bit of money to buy malt with so I can brew."

So he was made to kiss Sir Ralph's sword and swear that he would do everything he could to help the King, and they promised him a good reward if he did. While Mucky was doing this the door opened and the King came in.

"This is the man, your majesty," said Sir Ralph, "who's going to take you across the Fens to Huntingdon, where you'll find some friends waiting for you." The King had brought a servant into the room with him and this chap kept staring at Mucky so hard that at last he said:

"Well, will you know me next time you see me?" But Sir Ralph told him the chap wasn't being rude, he only wanted to see how Mucky was dressed so that the King could wear the same sort of clothes.

So they rigged the King up to look like Mucky and the two of them got ready to start. Some of the gentlemen at the Hall were a bit doubtful of letting the King ride off alone with Mucky, but the King said that he'd seen so many rogues in his life that he knew an honest face when he saw one. So off they went, with the King riding in front, but when they got to the turnpike he told Mucky to ride alongside of him.

Mucky noticed that, as they went through Hilgay, several people looked a bit surprised to see such poorly dressed men riding such fine horses, so when they got to Southery he told the King that he'd better call in at the Fleece and change his mount for a springhocked creature from the tavern stables. While the King was having a rest and a drink at the inn, Mucky went round to the Rector and borrowed a spavin-kneed horse off him to ride himself. When he got back to the Fleece he found his swarm of children all round the King, who asked the eldest boy what his name was.

"Wart, that's what my father calls me," said the boy. Mucky explained that, as the lad was a bit weak up top, he was no more use to him than the wart on old Noll's nose, but, if the King didn't mind, he'd rather like to change the name to Charles.

"That's all right," said the King, "and then everybody can call him Wag, like they do me behind my back."

Presently they set off again and when they got to the River Ouse and were being ferried across, the ferryman told them to look out when they were crossing Crouchmoor, as he'd heard that there was a band of old

Noll's deserters out there, though he didn't think they'd worry two beggars riding such poor, broken-down horses.

The King and Mucky rode on all day and well into the night till they got to the Manor at Wentworth.* The chap who owned it was away fighting, but his wife saw to it that the King had the best she could give him, and as for Mucky, well, he slept in a feather-bed and between linen sheets for the first time in his life. Next day they set off early and rode across the Fens by the old trackway that the Romans used. They were just getting towards Histon when Mucky saw a troop of Cromwell's soldiers riding in the distance. Luckily, there was a thick hedge alongside the track, so he and the King forced their horses through. On the other side was an osier bed, so the pair of them lay snugly hidden up in this till the soldiers had gone by; that's why the place has always been called the King's Hedges since then. When it was safe to get back on to the track again, they did so and rode on until, just before midnight, they came to the Bell tavern in Huntingdon.

One of the King's friends was waiting for them there and he gave Mucky a bag of money as his reward. Then the King, who'd gone off to change his clothes, came back with his crown and robes on and told Mucky that, as they'd been company for each other across the Fens they'd better spend another hour together enjoying what the tavern could give them in the way of food and drink. So they had a good time enjoying everything that the landlord set in front of them and then, next morning, Mucky set off home again with the spare horse laden with sacks of malt.

It was months after this that a traveller called at the Fleece and told Mucky that Cromwell had chopped off the King's head, which was sad news for Mucky. Then, as time went on, crowds and crowds of men came into the Fens and Mucky found that he had to work day and night brewing ale because all these chaps were working away at draining the Fens, and it was a thirsty job. Suddenly, though, the drainers left as suddenly as they'd come, and so trade became really bad. One day Mucky was sitting in the tavern wondering what to do to get a living when two gentlemen came in asking if a chap called Mucky, who had a son nicknamed Wag, lived there. Mucky told them he did, so then the two gents said that the dead King had written down in a book how Mucky had helped him. So his son, the new King, who was called Charles the Second, had put it down in writing that Mucky was to be taken into Methwold Fen, which had just been drained and where the King had a big share, and he was to choose as much land as would make him a fair-sized farm for himself and his eldest son and *his* sons for ever and ever. Well, after Mucky had chosen a bit of land that looked as if it would suit him nicely, he asked the two gentlemen how many acres there were in the bit he'd

chosen.   * Wentworth: 4½ miles west of Ely.

"I can't really say," said one of them, "but several I should think."

"Well, then," said Mucky, "this land that the King's given me will always be called the Methwold Severals."

And if you look at a map you'll see that the name is still used, and if you go down that way, and meet the chap who lives there and ask his name, he'll tell you he's called Mucky Porter.

TYPE ML.8000. MOTIFS: K.521.4.3 [*Escape in humble disguise*]; K.1812 [*King in disguise*]; K.1812.1 [*Incognito king helped by humble man: gives reward*].

¶ There seems some confusion in this tale between the characters of Charles I and Charles II. It is unlikely that Charles I was ever called "The Wag".
See "The Grey Goose Feathers".

THE MILLER OF DOUNE

The Book of Scottish Story, pp. 321–34.

In the reign of James V, the mill on the Teath near Doune, was occupied by a family named Marshall, a bold, strong race of men. The miller at that time had such strength, that in his prime it was said of him, "Better a kick from a nag's foot, than a kick from John Marshall." His eldest son James grew up as strong as his father, and the second son, William, though slighter in build, so that he could not put the stone, nor throw the hammer, as far as his brother, could jump higher, and run faster than anyone in the country round. They had a sister, Jeanie, sensible, spirited, and the darling of her family.

They were a God-fearing family, kind to man and beast. One day, as the miller was returning from watering his horse, he found a robin being chased by a weasel. He kicked the weasel over the hedge and, picking up the robin, noticed that its feathers were stuck together with bird-lime and full of straws. His horse was impatient, so, instead of stopping to free the bird on the spot, the miller put it into his pouch, and made for home.

A watcher behind the hedge, unknown to Marshall, had his gun cocked to shoot the weasel; but he was so much struck by the miller's care for the robin that he followed him at a distance, to see what manner of man this was. When the miller had stabled his horse, and entered the house, this man stole up to the window and looked in, saw them all at family prayers; for this was a custom never omitted in that house. The miller put his hand in his pouch to find his spectacles for the Bible reading, and out came the robin as well, and pecked at his hand. The miller said it was not to blame, and went on with his reading. When all was done, the stranger knocked at the door, and, announcing himself as John Murdoch, begged shelter for the night. He was made welcome, and first he cleaned the robin's feathers with great skill, then impressed the whole family by his conversation; for, whatever subject they spoke of, the stranger seemed able to outmatch them in knowledge of it—even in country matters, he knew more than they did themselves; and his comic tales kept them entranced, so that Jeanie put two handfuls of salt into the porridge, instead of meal. But the stranger made light of it, and they washed the salt down with so much ale, that it was eleven o'clock before they knew it, and made for their beds.

Next morning the guest was the last down, and the men had been three hours at work when he came into the kitchen. He had already become such a friend of the family that they had confided to him their greatest trouble, which was, that the owner of the mill had just doubled their rent; so that they were to be forced to leave it. It was therefore a shock to Jeanie, when the kindly stranger, after helping her to clean out the kirn, begged for a kiss as his reward, and had helped himself to more than one before she could throw him off. She flung the porridge pot at him, but he dodged it, except that some of the scalding porridge splashed from the wall on to his good coat. Then she began to loose the great house-dog, and John Murdoch, seeing her determined, reached for his gun, which he had hidden the previous night before entering the house. Jeanie, still holding the dog, bade him be off, but he did not move, believing that she would never loose the dog at him. But she did, and the dog seized his coat, and held on, though Murdoch hit him hard on the nose. At last there was no help for it, he fired and the dog fell dead. The noise of the shot brought William and then James home, and they gave chase to Murdoch, who was now in full flight, overtook him, and were only prevented from overpowering him when the stranger tripped William with his foot and flung him aside so roughly that he was stunned, and James, thinking his brother had been killed, gave up the pursuit. They went sorrowfully home, wondering how to tell all to their father when he came home for his breakfast.

Soon afterwards the sports were to be held at Stirling, and the miller and his family drove in to take part in them. James won the prize for throwing; then came the call for the runners; and William, to the surprise of all, was outrun by a red-headed stranger, by a distance of four yards. Never had such a race been seen, and as Jeanie was attempting to console her brother, a man came up, with a red wig in his hand, wiping his face and long yellow hair with a napkin.

It was John Murdoch! The Marshalls had not forgiven him for the death of their dog, and they set on him all at once; but the Earl of Lennox sprang between them, crying, "What, do you dare to strike your sovereign?" Then all came to light; the stranger was indeed King James in disguise. He had been so deeply impressed by the character of the miller and his family, that he had secretly arranged for them to remain in the mill at the old rent; and the runner's prize went to William after all, for the King said it was to be given to the best runner amongst his subjects; so the King himself could not have it. He made amends to all the family, for Geordie Wilson, Jeanie's suitor, whose family had suffered a grievous loss through a fire, on returning from the Stirling games, found six fine cows and two horses grazing in his field, and a letter from his landlord giving him a long lease of his farm at the old rent.

Soon after this, James and William married, and Jeanie, with her father's blessing, left home, to make room for the new wives, and marry her Geordie and they blessed the robin who had been the source of all their recent good fortune, and the generous King, who had so honoured them; James, in due time succeeded his father in the mill, and his sons after him, for many years.

MOTIFS: K.1812 [*King in disguise*]; P.14.19 [*King goes in disguise at night to observe his subjects*]; Q.40 [*Kindness rewarded*]; K.1812.13 [*Incognito king rewards strangers who treat him as companion*].

¶ See "The Goodman of Ballangiech", "King Alfred and the Cakes".

THE MURDER OF CAERLAVEROC

Scott, *Minstrelsy of the Scottish Border*, IV, p. 308.

In the year 1304[6], Bruce abruptly left the Court of England, and held an interview, in the Dominical Church of Dumfries, with John, surnamed, from the colour of his hair, the Red Cuming, a powerful chieftain, who had formerly held the regency of Scotland. It is said, by the Scottish historians, that he upbraided Cuming with having betrayed to the English monarch, a scheme, formed betwixt them, for asserting the independence of Scotland. The English writers maintain, that Bruce proposed such a plan to Cuming, which he rejected with scorn, as inconsistent with the fealty he had sworn to Edward. The dispute, however it began, soon waxed high betwixt two fierce and independent barons. At length, standing before the high altar of the church, Cuming gave Bruce the lie, and Bruce retaliated by a stroke of his poniard. Full of confusion and remorse, for a homicide committed in a sanctuary, the future monarch of Scotland rushed out of the church, with the bloody poniard in his hand. Kirkpatrick and Lindsay, two barons who faithfully adhered to him, were waiting at the gate.

To their earnest and anxious inquiries into the cause of his emotion, Bruce answered, "I doubt I have slain the Red Cuming." "Doubtest thou!" exclaimed Kirkpatrick. "I make sure!"* Accordingly, with

---

* Hence the crest of Kirkpatrick is a hand, grasping a dagger, distilling gouts of blood, proper; motto, "I mack sicker".

Lindsay and a few followers, he rushed into the church, and despatched the wounded Cuming.

A homicide in such a place, and such an age, could hardly escape embellishment from the fertile genius of the churchmen, whose interest was so closely connected with the inviolability of a divine sanctuary. Accordingly...the body of the slaughtered baron was watched, during the night, by the Dominicans, with the usual rites of the Church. But, at midnight, the whole assistants fell into a dead sleep, with the exception of one aged father, who heard, with terror and surprise, a voice, like that of a wailing infant, exclaim, "How long, O Lord, shall vengeance be deferred?"

It was answered in an awful tone, "Endure with patience, until the anniversary of this day shall return for the fifty-second time." In the year 1357, fifty-two years after Cuming's death, James of Lindsay was hospitably feasted in the castle of Caerlaveroc, in Dumfriesshire, belonging to Roger Kirkpatrick. They were the sons of the murderers of the Regent. In the dead of night, for some unknown cause, Lindsay arose, and poniarded in his bed his unsuspecting host. He then mounted his horse to fly; but guilt and fear had so bewildered his senses, that, after riding all night, he was taken at break of day, not three miles from the castle, and was afterwards executed by order of King David II.

TYPE ML.8000. MOTIFS: C.51.1 [*Tabu: profaning shrine*]; S.115 [*Murder by stabbing*]; M.302.7 [*Prophecy through dreams*]; Q.211.0.1 [*God revenges murder after thirty years*].

¶ There are conflicting accounts of Comyn's death. That given by Walter of Westminster is contemporary and appears reliable, but it is, of course, English.

There is no contemporary Scottish account. That by Fordoun (1363) is the earliest.

It seems most likely that Bruce and Comyn quarrelled in the cloisters of the Franciscan Church at Dumfries. Comyn, who was unarmed, was wounded there, and fled for sanctuary to the church. Bruce's followers pursued, and he and his uncle were murdered on the altar steps. The news of the crime excited general horror.

OLD PARR

Norton Collection, II, p. 208.

When I was a boy the following story was current in the neighbourhood of Old Parr's home concerning his summons by Charles I to London, as referred to by your correspondent:

When the Earl of Arundel's messengers were conducted to the cottage, on entering they found the old man, as they supposed, sitting doubled up in an armchair by the fireplace.

"You've got to come along with us, Mr Parr; the King wants to see you." To which a trembling old voice replied: "I reckon it inna [is not] me he wants, but father. Ye'll find un up i' the cherry tree. He be gatherin' the cherries."

The Times, 15 November, 1935, p. 12. "Points from Letters". From the Rev. W. V. Vickers, Bovey Tracey.

TYPE 726. MOTIF: F.571.2 [*Sending to the older*].

¶ See "The Oldest on the Farm", "Painswick Ancients", etc. (A, III), "A Link with the Past".

THE OXFORD STUDENT [shortened]

Halliwell, *Nursery Rhymes and Tales*, p. 166. Oxford.

There was once an Oxford student, who made love to the daughter of a brewer in the town, and got her with child. She pressed him to marry her, and he always put her off, but at last he said that if she would meet him at Divinity Walk the next moonlight night, he would arrange it. So early on the night of the next full moon, she set out for the open orchard land that bordered Divinity Walk in those days. She was very early, so for safety she climbed one of the apple trees and hid there. Presently she heard a heavy step, and saw her lover plodding up the hill with a spade across his shoulders. He came up to the very tree where she was hiding, and began to dig—a long, narrow, deep hole, a grave. Then he stood and waited with his dagger in his hand. But the girl, lying along the branch above him, never stirred, and at length he went away, and she ran, as fast as her feet could carry her, back to her father's house. Next day, as she was going down Brewer's Lane, the student saw her, and greeted her lovingly.

But the girl said:

> "One moonshiny night, as I sat high,
> Waiting for one to come by,
> The boughs did bend; my heart did break,
> To see what hole the fox did make."

As she spoke, the student whipped out his dagger, and stabbed her to the heart. Then there was the greatest fight between Town and Gown that ever was known, and Brewer's Lane ran with blood. The cruel student was killed, but nothing would bring the poor girl back to life, and they say she was buried in the very grave that was dug for her by her false lover.

TYPE 955C (Baughman).

¶ This tale is an offshoot of "The Robber Bridegroom" (Type 955) which is more exactly represented in England by "Mr Fox" and "The Cellar of Blood" (A, IV). In more or less its present form, as a *cante fable*, it is common in England, and is represented in the United States. This version was collected in Oxford by

J. O. Halliwell. On p. 2 of his *Nursery Rhymes and Nursery Tales of England,* he refers to Matthew Paris as giving an account of the matter. Nothing is given in Matthew Paris's successor's account of the genesis of the 1259 riot of the Town against the Gown, except the statement that the students had possibly released one of their number convicted of murder, which looks as if it might relate to this tale, as Halliwell suggested.

Baughman cites several examples from the United States, as well as a number from all parts of England.

See "The Lonton Lass", "Mr Fox's Courtship", "The Open Grave", "The Girl who got up a Tree" (A, IV).

THE PARISH CHEST

Ruth L. Tongue.

Somewhere in mid-Somerset a fugitive Squire, badly wounded, crawled home, leaving his horse dead in the coppice. The soldiers were hot on his track, so his wife and the sexton hastily carried him into the church which adjoined the Manor, and thrust him into the ancient Parish Chest, where they were standing, discussing parish charities, when the troopers arrived. Having searched the Manor, they clattered into the church, and bullied the sexton while the Lady of the Manor stood by. To her horror, she saw a trickle of blood seeping through the worm-eaten bottom of the chest, and, promptly covering it with her skirt, sat on the lid, pretending to be ill. They left her there while they searched, and then rode away, cursing that their bird had flown in spite of his wounds.

In agonizing fear the sexton and the lady waited until it seemed safe to open the chest. They found that the Squire had not been suffocated, nor had he bled to death. The cobwebby old parchments had stayed the worst of the bleeding. He lived to tell the tale in later life, and they say that the brown bloodstain can still be seen on the parish chest.

From a local tradition heard in Taunton, 1907–12.
TYPE ML.8000. MOTIF: K.515 [*Escape by hiding*].
¶ See "The Puppy under the Table".

PAUL JONES AT KIRKCALDY

Wilkie, *Bygone Fife,* p. 250.

It is with Kirkcaldy...that the visit of John Paul of Arbigland, better known as Paul Jones, to the Firth is usually associated. The American Admiral appears to have had some hesitation as to whether or not he should make a descent on Pittenweem....

The tradition goes that when Sir John Anstruther learned that three large vessels had come to anchor off the harbour he jumped to the conclusion that they were those expected to return from a voyage of exploration to the African coast. He sent off a boat with vegetables and with newspapers (a rare product at that time).

With the boat went John Chalmers, Bailie of Anstruther, and two Elie skippers.

To their surprise, they found the decks veiled by a smoke-screen. The presents were accepted from the vessels and the baskets lowered. When they returned they were found to be filled with gunpowder. This gift in acknowledgment was accompanied by a message to Sir John to utilise it in defence of his house.

Andrew Paton, the Pittenweem pilot who had gone out with his crew when the ships arrived, under the impression that they were British, and that his services were needed, had been received on board. There he found to his amazement that he was on a hostile fleet under a commander whose exploits were ringing in the ears of the people, but who was not known to be near the Firth of Forth. The names of the craft were famous —*The Pallas, Le Bon Homme Richard*, and *The Ranger*. The last alone, after the capture of the fort of Whitehaven and the plunder of St Mary's Isle, would have sufficed to perturb the dwellers in the coast towns.

Pittenweem, however, was not to be raided. The pilot and his men were treated courteously, and the latter allowed ashore again at once. Andrew Paton had to remain with the squadron till it reached Holland. He witnessed the defeat of the English fleet off Flamborough Head, and the capture of the Baltic merchantmen under its convoy. When he returned once more to Pittenweem his welcome was as warm and the surprise as great as when Alexander Selcraig* reappeared in Largo an officer of the British Navy.

TYPE ML.8000.

¶   Paul Jones was born at Kirkbean on the Solway, and became a notable privateer and a very able sailor. He joined the American Navy to fight against Britain, and later served in the French and Russian navies. He was a man of great ability, but singularly vain and ambitious. He died in 1792.

THE PECHS

Douglas, *Scottish Fairy and Folk-Tales*, p. 75.

Long ago there were people in this country called the Pechs; short wee men they were, wi' red hair, and long arms, and feet sae braid, that when it rained they could turn them up owre their heads, and then they served for umbrellas.

* Better known as Alexander Selkirk.

The Pechs were great builders; they built a' the auld castles in the kintry; and do you ken the way they built them?—I'll tell ye. They stood all in a row from the quarry to the place where they were building, and ilk ane handed forward the stanes to his neebor, till the hale was biggit. The Pechs were also a great people for ale, which they brewed frae heather; sae, ye ken, it bood to be an extraornar cheap kind of drink; for heather, I'se warrant, was as plenty then as it's now. This art o' theirs was muckle sought after by the other folk that lived in the kintry; but they never would let out the secret, but handed it down frae father to son among themselves, wi' strict injunctions frae ane to another never to let onybody ken about it.

At last the Pechs had great wars, and mony o' them were killed, and indeed they soon came to be a mere handfu' o' people, and were like to perish aff the face o' the earth. Still they held fast by their secret of the heather yill, determined that their enemies should never wring it frae them. Weel, it came at last to a great battle between them and the Scots, in which they clean lost the day, and were killed a' to tway, a father and a son. And sae the king o' the Scots had these men brought before him, that he might try to frighten them into telling him the secret. He plainly told them that, if they would not disclose it peaceably, he must torture them till they should confess, and therefore it would be better for them to yield in time.

"Weel," says the auld man to the king, "I see it is of no use to resist. But there is ae condition ye maun agree to before ye learn the secret." "And what is that?" said the king. "Will ye promise to fulfil it, if it be na onything against your ain interests?" said the man. "Yes," said the king, "I will and do promise so." Then said the Pech, "You must know that I wish for my son's death, though I dinna like to take his life myself.

> "My son ye maun kill,
> Before I will tell
> How we brew the yill
> Frae the heather bell!"

The king was dootless greatly astonished at sic a request; but, as he had promised, he caused the lad to be immediately put to death. When the auld man saw his son was dead, he started up wi' a great stend, and cried, "Now do wi' me as you like. My son ye might have forced, for he was but a weak youth, but me you never can force.

> "And though you may me kill,
> I will not you tell
> How we brew the yill
> From the heather bell!"

The king was now mair astonished than before, but it was at his being sae far outwitted by a mere wild man. Hooever, he saw it was needless to kill the Pech, and that his greatest punishment might now be his being allowed to live. So he was taken away as a prisoner, and he lived for mony a year after that, till he become a very, very auld man, baith bedrid and blind. Maist folk had forgotten there was sic a man in life; but ae night, some young men being in the house where he was, and making great boasts about their feats o' strength, he leaned owre the bed and said he would like to feel ane o' their wrists, that he might compare it wi' the arms of men wha had lived in former times. And they, for sport, held out a thick gaud o' ern to him to feel. He just snappit it in tway wi' his fingers as ye wad do a pipe stapple. "It's a bit gey gristle," he said; "But naething to the shackle-banes o' my days." That was the last o' the Pechs.

TYPES 2412E (O'Suilleabhain); ML.5010. MOTIF: Z.356 [*The last survivor*].
¶ Notes on the first part of the story are to be found in "Heather Ale".
   The second half is to be found in Scandinavian legends and in Celtic legends of Ossian, as in "Ossian after the Feinne" (School of Scottish Studies, Hamish Henderson, from Alexander Stewart) and "The Old Age of Oisin", (Kennedy's *Legendary Fictions of the Irish Celts*).

THE PERPETUAL ALMANACK or GENTLEMAN SOLDIER'S PRAYER BOOK

Norton Collection, v, p. 141.

Showing how one, Richard Middleton was taken before the Mayor of the city he was in for using cards in church during Divine Service: being a droll, merry and humorous account of an odd affair that happened to a private soldier in the 60th Regiment of Foot.

The serjeant commanded his party to the church, and when the parson had ended his prayer, he took his text, and all of them that had a Bible, pulled it out to find the text; but this soldier had neither Bible, Almanack, nor Common Prayer Book, but he put his hand in his pocket and pulled out a pack of cards, and spread them before him as he sat, and while the parson was preaching, he first kept looking at one card and then at another. The serjeant of the company saw him, and said, "Richard, put up your cards, for this is no place for them." "Never mind that," said the soldier, "you have no business with me here."

Now the parson had ended his sermon, and all was over; the soldiers repaired to the churchyard, and the commanding officer gave the word of command to fall in, which they did. The serjeant of the city came and took the man prisoner.—"Man, you are my prisoner," said he.—"Sir," said the soldier, "what have I done that I am your prisoner?"—"You have

107

played a game of cards in the church."—"No," said the soldier. "I have not play'd a game, for I only looked at a pack."—"No matter for that; you are my prisoner."—"Where must we go?" said the soldier. "You must go before the Mayor," said the serjeant. So he took him before the Mayor; and when they came to the Mayor's house, he was at dinner.

When he had dined, he came down to them, and said, "Well, serjeant, what do you want with me?"—"I have brought a soldier before you for playing at cards in the church."—"What? That soldier?"—"Yes."—"Well, soldier, what have you to say for yourself?" "Much, sir, I hope." "Well and good; but if you have not, you shall be punished the worst that ever man was."—"Sir," said the soldier, "I have been five weeks upon the march, and have but little to subsist on; and am without either Bible, Almanack, or Common-Prayer Book, or anything but a pack of cards: I hope to satisfy your Honour of the purity of my intentions."

Then the soldier pulled out of his pocket the pack of cards, which he spread before the Mayor; he then began with the Ace. "When I see the Ace," he said, "it puts me in mind that there is one God only; when I see the Deuce, it puts me in mind of the Father and the Son; when I see the Tray, it puts me in mind of the Father, Son, and Holy Ghost; when I see the Four, it puts me in mind of the four Evangelists, that penned the Gospel, viz. Matthew, Mark, Luke and John; when I see the Five, it puts me in mind of the five wise virgins who trimmed their lamps; there were ten, but five were foolish, who were shut out. When I see the Six, it puts me in mind that in six days the Lord made Heaven and Earth; when I see the Seven, it puts me in mind that on the seventh day God rested from all the works which he had created and made, wherefore the Lord blessed the seventh day and hallowed it. When I see the Eight, it puts me in mind of the eight righteous persons that were saved when God drowned the world, viz. Noah, his wife, three sons and their wives; when I see the Nine, it puts me in mind of nine lepers that were cleansed by our Saviour; there were ten, but nine never returned God thanks; when I see the Ten, it puts me in mind of the Ten Commandments that God gave Moses on Mount Sinai on the two tables of stone." He took the Knave and laid it aside. "When I see the Queen, it puts me in mind of the Queen of Sheba, who came from the furthermost part of the world to hear the wisdom of King Solomon, for she was as wise a woman as he was a man; for she brought fifty boys and fifty girls all clothed in boys' apparel to show before King Solomon, for him to tell which were boys and which were girls; but he could not, until he called for water for them to wash themselves; the girls washed up to their elbows, and the boys only up to their wrists; so King Solomon told by that. And when I see the King, it puts me in mind of the great King of Heaven and Earth, which is God Almighty, and likewise his Majesty King George, to pray for him."

"Well," said the Mayor, "you have a very good description of all the cards, except one, which is lacking"—"Which is that?" said the soldier. —"The Knave," said the Mayor.—"Oh, I can give your Honour a good description of that, if your Honour won't be angry."—"No, I will not," said the Mayor, "if you will not term me to be the Knave."—"Well," said the soldier, "the greatest that I know is the serjeant that brought me here."—"I don't know," said the Mayor, "that he is the greatest knave, but I am sure that he is the greatest fool."—"When I count how many spots there are in a pack of cards, I find there are three hundred and sixty-five; there are so many days in a year. When I count how many cards there are in a pack, I find there are fifty-two; there are so many weeks in a year. When I count how many tricks in a pack, I find there are thirteen; there are so many months in a year. You see, sir, that this pack of cards is a Bible, Almanack, Common-Prayer Book, and pack of cards to me."

Then the Mayor called for a loaf of bread, a piece of good cheese, and a pot of good beer, and gave the soldier a piece of money, bidding him to go about his business, saying he was the cleverest man he had ever seen.

TYPE 1613. MOTIF: H.603 [*Symbolic interpretation of playing cards*].
¶ A widespread tale, to be found in Scandinavia, Finland, France, Spain, Germany, America, etc.

The Elliot notebooks contain a concise account of the same tale, agreeing in almost every detail, under the title of "The Soldier's Bible". Another version is "The Religious Card-player".

PETER CAREW OF MOHUN'S OTTERY
[slightly abridged]

J. R. W. Coxhead, *The Devil in Devon*, pp. 59–63.

On a spur of the Blackdown Hills, known as Hartridge, in East Devon, stand the buildings of a large farmstead [named] Mohun's Ottery.... The structure is of worked stone, the spandrels of the first arch of the gateway being decorated with the arms of the ancient families of the Mohun and Carew—an arm vested in an ermine maunch, the hand grasping a golden fleur-de-lis for Mohun, and three lions *passant* for Carew.

The front doorway is framed in a fine, pointed arch, also decorated, and this, together with an enormous stone fireplace with a span of over sixteen feet, is all that now remains of the original fortified manor house of Mohun's Ottery. About the year 1868 this historic residence of the Carews...was destroyed by fire, and had to be almost entirely rebuilt.

Early in the reign of Henry VIII, Sir William Carew who had married Joan, daughter of Sir William Courtenay of Powderham, was living at

Mohun's Ottery. He had three sons, and the youngest, named Peter, was born about the year 1512. The boy grew up to become one of the most celebrated Devonians of Tudor times, receiving the honour of knighthood, and led a very adventurous and romantic life during an exceptionally colourful period in English history....

He was a bright and intelligent boy, and his father, observing the youngster's quickness to learn, decided to send him to school in Exeter, with the idea of making him the scholar of the family.

When Peter was twelve years of age, he set out on horseback for Exeter under the charge of one of his faithful retainers. The servant took the boy to the house of Thomas Hunt, draper and Alderman of Exeter, who was to look after him during the time he attended the Grammar School.

"I am commanded by Sir William Carew of Mohun's Ottery," said the servant, "to ask you to keep a close eye upon my young master. You are to stand in the place of his father. The boy must have no rude companions; he must go straight from your house to school, and from the school to your house. If he plays truant, flog him!"

Peter was bright and intelligent, but he preferred to use these qualities in other directions than learning grammar and studying books. Passionately fond of sports and the pleasures of the chase, he felt his education should take the form of knightly exercises rather than a study of the classics. To make matters worse, the Headmaster of Exeter Grammar School at that time was a man named Freer, who was noted for his extreme cruelty. Peter's love of adventure...resulted in the lad continually failing to attend school. According to John Hooker, he threatened one day to throw himself from one of the turrets of the city wall, and his guardian, Mr Hunt, had great difficulty in coaxing him down from his perilous position.

Sir William Carew, hearing of his son's unruly behaviour, hastened to Exeter in a furious temper. Calling his high-spirited son before him, he said, "If you behave like a mischievous puppy, you shall be treated as one." He then fastened a large dog-collar round Peter's neck, tied his hands securely, and gave the chain to a servant to hold, and after being taken through the streets in this abject state the boy was led back to Mohun's Ottery like a dog....

On reaching home the wrathful knight had the boy coupled to one of the hounds for a time. Probably this humiliating treatment only served to set Peter's mind more strongly against a scholarly life.

Sir William Carew made one more effort to have his son educated. He took the boy up to London to study at St Paul's School, which had not long been founded by Dean Colet.

After his experiences in Exeter, however, Peter had decided to have nothing further to do with schools. The schoolmaster found him a hope-less case, so he advised Sir William to employ his son in some way more suitable to his vivacious character.

While father and son were walking by St Paul's Cathedral, the knight met a Frenchman, who was an old acquaintance. The latter asked the name of the bright young lad, and upon being informed, he expressed a desire to take the youngster to the French Court as his page, saying he would care for him as though he were his own son. Sir William let him go.

All went splendidly for a time, but gradually, as the boy's fine clothes began to show signs of wear, the shameless courtier, too mean to buy him new clothes, degraded him to the lowly position of stable lad. His victim bore the disgrace in silence, because of the freedom his new life afforded.

One day, Sir John Carew, of Haccombe in Devon, a distant cousin, arrived in France with letters of introduction to the French King from Henry VIII. As he was riding towards the French Court, he heard a youth call out, "Carew Anglois! Carew Anglois!" Stopping, he asked for the boy they called "Carew Anglois" to be brought to him. After questioning the lad, he was amazed to discover that the shabby stable boy was none other than the young son of Sir William Carew of Mohun's Ottery. Seething with anger, he sought out the treacherous Frenchman. Having sternly reproved him for the shameful way he had treated his page, he quickly obtained the boy's freedom. Sir John Carew furnished his young relative with new clothes befitting his rank, and kept the youngster with him at the French Court. At last Peter received the sort of education he most desired. He learnt to ride high-spirited steeds, and was taught all the many things one in his position was expected to know, including skill with sword and lance. The wayward schoolboy, who without doubt had often dreamed of military glory, was about to start along the path to fame.

In 1526, Francis I, King of France, was making elaborate preparations to send a powerful army into Italy in order to liberate Pope Clement VII, who had been imprisoned in the Castle of St Angelo by the Emperor Charles V. Henry VIII of England was assisting the French King by sending a token force of one hundred horsemen to join this army. Sir John Carew had arrived at the French Court to lead the English contingent in the campaign.

The general in command of the army was Monsieur Lautrac, and when all the preparations were completed, a magnificent fighting force had been gathered together. The army set out for Italy in 1527, and to Peter's great joy, his cousin and protector, Sir John Carew, took him along as his page.

At first the campaign was successful, and the Pope was set at liberty, but later the army met with a series of reverses, and in 1528 Sir John Carew died at Pavia. The loss of his kind guardian must have been a severe blow to Peter, who was still only fifteen years of age, but he came of a tough stock—he was brave and resourceful—and realizing the French army was doomed, he decided to become a very youthful soldier of fortune, so he offered his services to Philibert de Chalons, Prince of Orange. The boy's manly bearing and courtly ways gained him friends wherever he went. When the Prince died in the Siege of Florence in 1530, Peter continued in the service of his sister, the Princess Claudia.

At length a yearning to see his home once more caused the young exile to beg the Princess to allow him to return to his native land. The Princess tried hard to persuade him to stay, but visions of the grey weather-beaten walls of his father's house in East Devon were too strong. His kind mistress ordered two of her gentlemen to attend Peter on his journey, and when he set forth she filled his purse with gold and placed a chain of gold about his neck. She also gave him letters of introduction to Henry VIII, and to his father, Sir William Carew.

The boy who, by the sudden death of his guardian, had been left to fend for himself in a foreign land was now a strong broad-shouldered youth of about eighteen, and already a soldier of considerable experience.

Peter hastened to Greenwich, where he presented to Henry VIII the letter of introduction from the Princess of Orange. The King was greatly struck with Peter's gallant bearing and handsome appearance, and after questioning him about his adventures abroad, gladly gave him a position at his own Court.

As soon as he had received permission from the King, Peter set out on the long journey to his home in the West Country. His last return had been a very humiliating one. This time, richly dressed, and mounted on a fine horse, he arrived at his father's house attended by two gentlemen, and wearing about his neck a chain of gold.

John Hooker gives this touching description of the lad's meeting with his parents:

"Being come to the house, and understanding his father and mother to be within, he went into the house without further delay, and, finding them sitting together in parlour, forthwith without any words, in most humble manner, kneeled down before them and asked their blessing, and therewith presented unto him the Princess of Orange's letters. The said Sir William and his lady at this sudden sight were astonished, much musing what it should mean that a young gentleman so well apparelled, and so well accompanied, should thus prostrate himself before them."

When Sir William and his wife realized that the stranger was their youngest son, of whom they had heard nothing for six years, they were overjoyed. Peter stayed with his parents at Mohun's Ottery for a few days, and then returned to the Court, where, owing to his charm of manner, and skill as a soldier, he was very soon in high favour with the King.

From W. H. H. Rogers, "Memorials of the West", 1888, *Transactions of the Devon-shire Association*, XXXII, p. 481. John Hooker, (1525–1601), biographer of Sir Peter Carew.

MOTIFS: Q.325 [*Disobedience punished*]; Q.430 [*Abridgement of freedom as punishment*]; L.101 [*Unpromising hero: youngest son*]; L.10 [*Victorious youngest son*].

¶ This tradition has a slight resemblance to the Child Ballad 271, "The Lord of Lorne and the False Steward", which was known in the reign of Henry VIII. The cruel punishment of coupling the boy with the hound is rather after the ballad style too.

PRINCE GEORGE OF DENMARK

Hone's *Table Book*, III (2nd part), p. 243.

Prince George of Denmark, the nominal consort to Queen Anne, in passing through Bristol, appeared on the Exchange, attended by only one gentleman, a military officer, and remained there till the merchants had pretty generally withdrawn, not one of them having sufficient resolution to speak to him, as perhaps they might not be prepared to ask such a guest to their houses. But this was not the case with all who saw him, for a person, whose name was John Duddlestone, a bodice-maker, in Corn-Street, went up and asked the prince if he was not the husband of the queen, who informed him he was. John Duddlestone then told the prince, that he had observed, with a great deal of concern, that none of the merchants had invited him home to dinner, adding, it was not for want of love to the queen, or to him, but because they did not consider themselves prepared to entertain so great a man; but John said, he was ashamed to think of his dining at an inn, and requested him to go and dine with him, and bring the gentleman along with him, informing him that he had a piece of good beef, and a plum pudding, and ale of his dame's own brewing. The prince admired the loyalty of the man, and though he had bespoke a dinner at the White Lion, went with him; and when they got to the house, Duddlestone called his wife, who was upstairs, desiring her to put on a clean apron and come down, for the queen's husband and another gentleman were come to dine with them: she accordingly came down with her clean blue apron, and was immediately saluted by the prince. In the course of the dinner the prince asked him, if he ever went to London? He said, that since the ladies had worn stays instead of bodices, he sometimes went to buy whalebone: whereupon the prince desired him to take his wife when he went again, at the same time giving him a card, to facilitate his introduction to him at court.

In the course of a little time, John Duddlestone took his wife behind him to London, and with the assistance of the card, found easy admittance to the prince, who introduced them to the queen, who invited them to an approaching dinner, informing them that they must have new clothes for the occasion, allowing them to choose for themselves. Each, therefore, chose *purple velvet*, such as the prince had then on, which was accordingly provided for them, and in that dress they were introduced by the queen herself, as the most loyal persons in the city of Bristol, and the only ones in that city who had invited the prince, her husband, to their house; and after the entertainment, the queen, desiring *him* to kneel down, laid a sword on his head, and (to use Lady Duddlestone's own words) said to him, "*Ston up, sir Jan.*"

Sir "Jan" was offered money, or a place under government, but he did not choose to accept of either, informing the queen that he had "*fifty pounds* out at use", and he apprehended that the number of people he saw about her must be very expensive. The queen, however, made Lady Duddlestone a present of her gold watch from her side, which "my lady" considered as no small ornament, when she went to market, suspended over a *blue apron*.

From Corry's *History of Bristol*.
MOTIFS: P.320 [*Hospitality*]; Q.45 [*Hospitality rewarded*].
¶ In most tales of this kind the King is incognito or unrecognized. There are many tales of a King accepting a poor man's hospitality and entertaining him in turn, but it is surprising to find Prince George of Denmark figuring as one of the heroes. He is chiefly known to tradition as *Monsieur Est-il Possible*.

See "The Goodman of Ballengiech", "The Miller of Doune", "How Littleport Began" (B, IX).

THE PROPHECY OF MERLIN

Roger of Wendover, *Chronicle*, I, p. 15.

While king Vortigern was sitting by the bank of the pool that had been drained, the two dragons came forth; one of them was white, the other red. As soon as they approached each other, they commenced a dreadful combat, breathing forth flames. The white dragon had the better of the contest, and pursued the red one unto the margin of the pool, when the latter, indignant at the repulse, turned on the white dragon and forced him to retire. While they were thus fighting, the king commanded Merlin Ambrosius to say what the battle between the two dragons meant. Whereupon, bursting into tears, and full of the spirit of prophecy, he thus began:—"Woe to the red dragon, for his banishment approaches! The white dragon, which signifies the Saxons, whom thou hast invited over, shall possess his caverns; whereas the red dragon signifies the British people, which shall be oppressed by the white dragon. His mountains shall be brought low as the valleys, and the rivers of the valleys shall flow with blood; his religious worship shall be destroyed, and his churches lie in ruins; when at length the oppressed shall prevail, and shall resist the cruelty of the strangers; for the boar of Cornwall shall afford succour, and shall tread their necks under his feet; the isles of the ocean shall be subdued by his might, and he shall possess the forests of the Gauls; the house of Romulus shall tremble at his rage, and his end shall be doubtful; his praise shall be sounded among the nations, and many shall obtain their bread by relating his exploits", etc., etc. (The rest of this long prophecy is to be found in Geoffrey of Monmouth, *Bohn's Ant. Lib.*, pp. 196–206.)

MOTIFS: D.1812.3.3.5.1 [*Allegorical dream*]; Z.140 [*Colour symbolism*].
¶ See notes on "The Youth without a Father" (B, III).

PUDSAY THE COINER

From Mildred E. Bosanquet, Wrotham, Kent. (Bolton Hall, Bolton-by-Rowland, Clitheroe.)

The Pudsay family were at Bolton Hall from the reign of Edward the Third. One of them, whose tomb is in the church, sheltered Henry VI after the Battle of Wrexham. His descendant in Elizabeth's reign was William Pudsay, and this is the legend about him.

At Rimington on his land lead-mines were discovered. Pudsay started making coins and the Queen's officers came to take him. His life was in danger.

Now Pudsay had the power of seeing fairies, and some time back the local elves, Lob and Michil, were outside Aithura Hoile, and he came upon them, and by his art he made them stay. They gave him a magical bit, which they said he was to keep carefully against the day when he would be in danger, for it would nourish a drooping horse from evening red to morning grey.

When the word came to Pudsay, by what faithful messenger we do not know, he went to the stable, saddled his horse, Wanton Grey, with that fairy bit, and away he went, up over Rainsbut Scaur, for his pursuers were hot on his trail. There was no other way. He looked over the river. It is ninety foot high (known as Pudsay's Leap to this day). And the brave man took his courage and his life in his hands. "I would rather die here than lose my life as a prisoner," and he leaped. And the horse bore him safely to land. And they rode on through the night, and when morning came, the horse was still fresh, and he rode into London. And when he arrived at the Queen's house he went up and asked for her. And they said she was away on her barge on the Thames. Then he set off again, and the good Wanton Grey swam out to the barge, and we hear no more of Wanton Grey. But the mudstained Pudsay clambered on to the barge, and the courtiers stared at this plain, unselfconscious Yorkshireman. But he thrust himself into the presence of her Majesty, and fell on his knees, and reminded her that she had held him at the Font, and was his kinsman, and craved her mercy.

And the royal lady said, "Whatever ails you, Cousin Pudsay?" And she asked him if he had committed murder, for, said she, she would pardon no one who had shed any of her subjects' blood. And Pudsay said, "No, not murder, it was nothing but coining." And he told his story.

And they that stood round spoke for him, saying that he had fought right well at the battle of Zutphen, and had been the Earl of Leicester's Master of the Horse, and no one had been braver than he that day.

And so Queen Elizabeth gave him her pardon, but, said she, there must be no more of the Pudsay shillings. And there wasn't!

MOTIFS: F.989.1.1 [*Horse's tremendous leap*]; D.1209.1 [*Magic bridle*].
¶ The journey to the King to ask directly for pardon occurs in several ballads, such as "Adam Bell, Clym of the Clough and William of Cloudesley" (B, IV).

Yorkshire Version of End of Story

"An a fell upov his knees, an a sed, 'Pardon! Pardon!'
An shu sed, 'Wat ivver hast bin abeouet, Poodsa?'
An a sed, 'Pardon! Pardon!'
An thir wir a deal spak for him, an sed a wir a reet gentlemon, an it didn't look laike at a sud do eouet wrang.
An shu sed, 'Weel, then, eouet, coozn Poodsa, but moordir.'
An a sed it wir nobbut coinin.
So shu sed, 'Waugh.'
But shu told him at a moodn't mak ony moar o' thir Poodsa Shillings.
An a dudn't."

William Pudsay, Esq., Lord of Bolton from 1577 to 1629, who is the hero of this legend, was Queen Elizabeth's godson, and Master of the Horse to the Earl of Leicester. The Pudsay Shillings, handed down in the family and still existing, are the shillings of Elizabeth 1562, having a mullet of six points for a mint mark; Pudsay's arms being *vert*, a chevron between three mullets pierced *or*. This is too early for William Pudsay, but his father, Thomas, Vice-President of the Council of the North, may have introduced the new Elizabethan currency into the country, so that they became Pudsay Shillings. William Pudsay got into trouble for working the "Mine Royal", which may have given rise to the legend, which was current forty years after William Pudsay's death. Webster (Johannes Hyphantes), 1671, mentions it. Michil and Lob are the two local fairies. It is still the custom to bring all the carts and gates that can be obtained on the night of 30 April to Bolton Cross, where they are piled up in a heap for a bonfire. This is locally stated to be the work of Lob and Michil; who now, however, fortunately confine their labours to erecting the pile, without setting fire to it.

Skelhorne, a limestone hill in which are the remains of lead works, is in Rimington, a township near Bolton, then belonging to William Pudsay. The lead was said by Johnson to contain silver at the rate of 25 lb. a ton.

Rainsbee Scaur, down which Pudsay is said to have leaped, is a rock overhanging the Ribble, about 90 feet high, and a few hundred yards from Bolton Hall.

These notes are from *Pudsay's Leap*, by H. A. Littledale, privately printed in 1856, and lent me by his granddaughter, Mildred Bosanquet, Wrotham, Sevenoaks, Kent (a descendant of William Pudsay).

Aithera Hoile, or Arthur's Hole, is a cavern in the woods at Bolton. See "West Molland House".

THE PUPPY UNDER THE TABLE

Ruth L. Tongue.

There was a foolish lad from Long Sutton who was led away by the excitement, and joined in the Monmouth Rising. He found the excitement of Sedgemoor Battle not at all to his taste and he ran for home terrified and bereft of the few remaining wits he had. Regardless of the fatal danger to any who befriended him, he rushed into the kitchen of a Pitney farmer he had known all his life. The family and servants were just sitting down to supper when the fugitive burst in, and they could hear the shouts of his pursuers in the orchard. The farmer gave one look at him and thrust him under the great oak table among the forest of family legs, and by the time the first soldier reached the door he was kicking the clamorous farm dogs under the table too, then he sat down heavily himself and the family fell to in a silence punctuated by loud champings and growls. When the serjeant insisted on searching the farmhouse there was an audible groan from under the table. The farmer drew back his boot and kicked heavily. "Thic pup did ort tew know better by now," he said. "That'll meake un bide quiet." The soldiers searched, the dogs growled ceaselessly, the family sat stolid as their own cattle and ate a hearty meal and the "pup" lay still as a mouse. Meeting with a wall of silence and finding no one, the soldiers rode off, whereupon the farmer hauled out the trembling fugitive and fetched him a further heavy clout for his folly in endangering all their lives. Then he fed him royally, hid him in the hay-mow till nightfall and sent him safely home to Long Sutton, where he lived to a good age.

Local tradition, Pitney. See "Local Legends". *Langport Herald*, 1894.
TYPE ML.8000. MOTIFS: K.515 [*Escape by hiding*]; P.322 [*Guest given refuge*].
¶ This is another of the "Duking Days" traditions. See "Swayne's Leaps", "The Parish Chest".

THE RECTOR OF RINGMORE

J. R. W. Coxhead, *The Devil in Devon*, pp. 48–9.

At the outbreak of the Civil War the Rector of the parish of Ringmore was the Rev. William Lane. He was an ardent supporter of King Charles, and when the Royalist garrison in Salcombe Castle was beleaguered by a force of Parliamentarians he wished to find a way to hinder the enemy from receiving reinforcements.

The besiegers were getting their supplies by convoys which travelled along the road that crossed the Avon by the bridge just below Loddiswell. Now, in addition to being Rector of Ringmore, Mr Lane also held the incumbency of the neighbouring parish of Aveton Giffard, from which a commanding view of the bridge in question could be obtained.

The high-spirited Rector soon evolved a daring plan which he was convinced, when put into action, would cause the Roundheads considerable embarrassment. By some means or other, he managed to acquire some small brass cannons, and then, having trained a number of his boldest parishioners in the art of war, he placed the weapons in a strong position, cunningly protected by earthworks, from which the bridge could be kept continually under observation.

Every time an enemy convoy was seen crossing the bridge the guns fired on it with such good effect that the besieger's supply system was considerably dislocated. Urgently needed supplies of food and ammunition were so seriously delayed, and so many casualties occurred among the troops guarding the convoys, that the officer in charge of the besieging force sent a request to the commander of the Parliamentary garrison in Plymouth for aid.

As soon as he was able to spare the men from the defence of the town, the commander of the Plymouth garrison sent a strong force by sea to Bigbury Bay to capture the warlike Rector—dead or alive.

The Roundheads are said to have landed at Ayrmer Cove, from whence they proceeded without delay to Ringmore, in search of their quarry.

The intrepid Mr Lane, however, had received timely warning by a swift messenger of the approach of the soldiers, so he took refuge in the secret room within the tower of Ringmore Church.

The Roundheads completely ransacked the parsonage in their eager haste to discover the man they had been sent to capture, and then they searched the village and surrounding countryside with great thoroughness, but all their efforts met with no success.

The Rector's faithful parishioners smuggled food to him in his hiding-place for three months, and, according to tradition, his most painful experience during that anxious time was to hear the minister appointed by the Parliamentary Army preaching in his church on Sundays. Mr Lane had the greatest difficulty to restrain himself from leaving his place of concealment and rushing into the church to refute what he considered to be the man's heresies, and to denounce him for his disloyalty.

From *A Book of the West*, S. Baring-Gould, 1899.
TYPE ML.8000. MOTIF: K.515 [*Escape by hiding*].

THE RESCUE OF KINMONT WILLIE

E. Bogg, *Lakeland and Ribblesdale*, p. 7.

William Armstrong, of Kinmont, or in the more endearing name of the Borders, Kinmont Willie, was a man of great personal strength and stature, and had four sons—Jock, Francie, Geordie, and Sandie—each of them as brave as his father. Their exploits and feuds were dreaded over the whole district, and he was the most lawless and terrible moss-trooper thief on the Borders. His capture, according to the rules and usage of truce, was illegal. He had been attending a Warden's meeting, held on the little Kershope river, and was returning home in the company of a few other Scotchmen; but on the Englishmen becoming aware of his presence at the meeting, they had determined on capturing him, and accordingly a troop followed, and after a long, stern chase up Liddles-dale, arrested and bound him, and brought him, heavily ironed, into Carlisle Castle. This, as we have said, was in direct violation of Border Law.

Scott of Buccleugh, with whom Armstrong was a great favourite, at once wrote to Lord Scrope, the Governor of Carlisle and Warden of the English Border, demanding his instant release, but he refused to release him. So bold Buccleugh swore to bring Kinmont Willie out of Carlisle, quick or dead, with his own hand. Choosing a dark and stormy night (the 13th April), he assembled two hundred of his bravest men at the tower of Norton, a fortalice on the "debateable land" on the water of Sark, about ten miles from Carlisle. Amongst these, the leader whom he most relied on, was Awd Wat Scott of Harden; but along with him were Wat Scott of Branxholm, Wat Scott of Goldielands, Jock Elliott of the Copeshaw, Sandie Armstrong, son to Hobbie, the Laird of Mangerton, Kinmont's four sons, Rob of the Langholm, and Will Beck of the Red-cloak—every one a Scott, except Jock Elliott.

They were well mounted and armed, and carried with them scaling-ladders, besides iron crowbars, sledge-hammers, hand-picks, and axes, etc. Favoured by the extreme darkness, they passed the river Esk, and through the Graham's country, forded the Eden, and came to the brook Caday, close by Carlisle, where Buccleugh made his men dismount, and silently led eighty of them, with the ladders and iron tools, to the foot of the wall.

Everything favoured them; the heavens were as black as pitch, and the rain descended in torrents. The ladders proving too short, they under-mined a postern in the wall of the base, and soon made a breach large enough for a soldier to squeeze through. In this way several of them passed into the outer court, and disarmed and bound the watch, wrenched open the postern from the inside, and thus admitting their companions, were masters of the place. Twenty-four troopers now rushed to the Castle jail (Buccleugh meantime keeping the postern), forced the door of the chamber where Kinmont was confined, carried him off heavily ironed, and sounding their trumpet, the signal agreed on, were answered by loud shouts and the trumpet of Buccleugh, whose troopers now filled the outer court. All was terror and confusion, both in town and castle. The alarm-bell rang out on the stormy night, and was answered by the clang of the Cathedral and Townhouse bells; the beacon blazed from the top of the great tower, and red tongues of flame flitted ominously on the blackness of the night, and the shadowy forms, hoarse shouts and flashing armour rather increased the horror and their numbers. Willie was carried down the scaling-ladders on the shoulders of Red Rowan, "the starkest man in Teviotdale".

Lord Scrope, believing, as he afterwards wrote to Burghley, that five hundred Scots were in possession of the castle, kept himself within his chamber. Kinmont Willie himself, as he was carried on his friends' shoulders beneath the Warden's window, roared out a lusty "Goodnight" to his Lordship. Buccleugh remounted his troopers, forded once more the Esk and the Eden, and, bearing his rescued favourite in the middle of his little band, regained the Scottish Border before sunrise. Kinmont, in swimming his horse through the Eden, which was then flooded, was much cumbered by the irons round his ankles, and is said to have drily observed that, "often as he had breasted it, he had never had such heavy spurs before". His Master, Buccleugh, eager to rid him of these shackles, halted at the first smith's house they came to within the Scottish Border; but the door was locked, the family in bed, and the knight of the hammer so sound a sleeper, that he was only awakened by the Lord Warden thrusting his long spear through the window, and nearly spitting both Vulcan and his lady.

. . . No one admired bold, brave, and doughty deeds more than Elizabeth, and when Buccleugh was brought before her she demanded of him, with lion-like glance, how he had dared to assault and storm her castle at Carlisle? In no way daunted, the renowned Border chieftain replied, "Madam, what is there that a brave man may not dare?"

This answer so impressed her that, turning to her courtiers, she exclaimed: "This is a man, indeed! With ten thousand such men, our brother of Scotland might shake the firmest throne in Europe."

MOTIFS: R.100 [Rescues]; R.51.2 [Prisoners confined in chains]; R.41.1 [Captivity in Castle]; R.121 [Means of rescue from prison].

¶ The story of this is told racily and very much the same in detail in Child, 186, "Kinmont Willie". "Jock o' the Side", Child, 187 is an even better ballad with substantially the same plot, except that the rescuers are only three. Child suggests that it is founded on the Kinmont Willie episode. A similar tale of rescue (Child, 188) is "Archie o' Cawfield".

THE ROBBER UNMASKED

Augustus Hare, *In My Solitary Life*, p. 186.

...A lady in Wales...looked up suddenly one day, after reading the obituary in *The Times*, and exclaimed, "Now, at last, my lips are unsealed." Then she told this:

One day she had been alone at her country-house in Wales, with her son and a friend of his. She had received all the money for her rents that day—a very large sum—and put it away in a strong box. Being asked, she said she did not mind the least having it in her room, and should sleep with the key under her pillow.

When she had been in bed some time, she was aware that her door opened, and that a man in a cloak came into her room with a candle. He passed the candle before her face, but she lay with closed eyes, perfectly motionless. Then he felt for the key; he felt for a long time, but somehow he failed to find it. At last he went away.

As soon as the door closed, she sprang out of bed, intending to go to her son's room to warn him that a robber was in the house. But his room was a long way off, and she thought it would be better to go instead to the friend, whose room was nearer.

As she opened the door suddenly, she saw a figure muffled up in a long cloak put down the candle. It was the same figure who had come into her room. She looked at him fixedly. "Tomorrow, at 9 a.m.," she said, "the dogcart will come to the door which was to have taken my strong-box to the bank: you will go in that dog-cart, and you will never enter my door again. If you never attempt to do this, I will never say a word on what has happened as long as you live." And she never did, even to her son.

MOTIFS: K.1860 [*Deception by feigned sleep*]; K.420 [*Thief is detected*]; M.295 [*Bargain to keep secret*].
¶ A somewhat similar tale was told of a woman in Galloway who had been forced to keep secret the identity of a coven of witches, and as each one was reported dead she said, "That's one", until the whole coven had died, and she told the story.

A ROYAL ESCAPE

J. R. W. Coxhead, *The Devil in Devon*, pp. 55–6.

The historical facts connected with Charles II's escape after his defeat at the Battle of Worcester, on the 3rd September 1651, and his subsequent wanderings through England, are well-known. There are, however, many unproven stories, and local legends, concerning his adventures before he finally escaped from the country by sea to the Continent. One of these legends is attached to an estate called Coaxdon, in the parish of Chardstock, four miles north of Axminster, which in the year 1651 was owned by an Irish family named Cogan.

According to the legend, Charles had gone to Lyme Regis in the hope of securing a ship to take him to France, but finding himself recognized he was forced to beat a hasty retreat hotly pursued by his enemies. Arriving at Coaxdon, he entered the house, and finding Mrs Cogan sitting alone in the parlour, he implored her to hide him.

In those days it was the fashion for ladies to wear dresses which were greatly extended by the use of large hoops, and as there was no time to be lost she quickly concealed him under her voluminous skirt.

Mrs Cogan was a staunch Royalist, but her husband, who was out working on the estate, was a supporter of the Parliamentary cause. Seeing the rapid approach of the soldiers, he returned to the house, and asking them to follow him took them into the parlour where Mrs Cogan was quietly sitting doing some embroidery. She expressed great surprise at such a sudden intrusion upon her privacy, but remained seated quietly in her chair. The leader of the military detachment informed the Cogans that Prince Charles had been traced to the house, and as he was very probably concealed somewhere in the building they were authorised to make a strict search for him.

Mrs Cogan readily agreed to their intention, but remained in her chair and continued with her sewing. Meanwhile, her husband, accompanied by the soldiers, went into every room, and having examined the whole of the house in vain, they all went outside to make a search of the grounds.

When all appeared to be safe, and the soldiers had departed, Mrs Cogan gave Charles some food, and a change of clothes, and he proceeded on his way to Trent. It is said that when he reached France he rewarded Mrs Cogan for her loyalty by sending her a gold chain and locket engraved with the royal arms. This treasured possession was long preserved in the family as an heirloom, until the last owner exchanged it for silver plate with a Jew at Exeter. Repenting his action, he made an attempt soon afterwards to recover it, but the purchaser informed him that he had melted it down for the gold.

How much truth there is in the tradition it is hard to say, but one thing which is quite certain is that the episode is not mentioned in the historical account of the events leading up to the Prince's escape to the Continent.

From James Davidson, *Axminster during the Civil War in the Seventeenth Century*, 1881.

MOTIFS: K.515 [*Escape by hiding*]; P.322 [*Guest given refuge*].

¶ Tales of a lover hiding beneath a lady's hoop are fairly common, though no instance is cited in the motif index. It is unlikely to be true in this case, however, for the farthingale went out with James I and the hoop came in with Queen Anne. Petticoats were heavy and voluminous in the Commonwealth times, but not very convenient for hiding under.

For other royal escapes see "Grey Goose Feathers" and "Methwold Severals".

ST DAVID'S FLOOD

Ruth L. Tongue, *The Folktales of England*, p. 80.

St David's Flood is a name for the spring tide which in the old days brought Christian saints to Somerset. They came up river on St David's Flood. Later on there was a fishing hamlet down by the shore, and one day all the men were out fishing and a little herd boy came running back to the village in terror to say that six Danish galleys were sailing along and would come up the river on St David's Flood. Well, the women and the children scampered away to the nearby village of Uphill, which could give them some safety, and they could warn the farming folk there. But one old granny was down by the riverside gathering gladdon* for thatching her cottage, and as the long ships sailed by she crouched down among the rushes and watched the Danes landing and scattering to plunder. They had tied up their boats and left them without even a guard. St David's Flood had brought them up, the very flood that carried the saints up in olden days, but it was turning now, it was not waiting for the pirates to finish their work.

When they had gone the old woman crept out from her hiding-place and watched the tide. It runs out very quickly there, and she saw that it was on the turn. So she undid the mooring of each of the galleys, and then she stood and watched them jostling against each other, going down river and out into the Severn Sea. In the meantime the men of Uphill had done their work well. They had ambushed the loaded pirates and driven them back towards their boats. But no boats were there, and not a hurd-yed† survived that bloody day. And that, they say, is why the village is called Bleadon.

Recorded from Ruth L. Tongue, 9 September 1963. Heard many times in Somerset from 1906 to 1960. This version is from a farmer's daughter who used to hear the story from her grandfather.
TYPE ML.8000. MOTIFS: N.825.3 [*Old woman helper*]; F.1084 [*Furious battle*]; A.1617 [*Origin of place-name*].
¶ This is one of many traditions of the Danish invasions. A Hampshire legend rather similar to this is preserved in a poem by Charlotte Yonge, "The Cat of Cat Copse" (*Monthly Packet*, Christmas, 1879, p. 17). A Somerset tradition is used by Wordsworth in "The Danish Boy", composed in 1799.
See "The Red-Heads" (B), V, "King Alfred and the Cakes".

* *gladdon* = iris leaves.
† *hurd-yed* = red-head, and it is supposed to show either Danish or Pixy blood in Somerset.

A SECRET MARRIAGE AT ELIE

Wilkie, *Bygone Fife*, p. 219.

In the town of Elie...there stood for about two hundred years after its enlargement by the Gillespies of Nether Riras in 1682 a building known as "the Muckle Yett". It is gone now, and only a few carved stones built into adjoining walls survive to remind the passer-by of vanished glories. Here it was that the last of the Stewart dynasty to rule was wont to take up his abode. During the three years he acted as Governor of Scotland, he found in Fife, as his ancestors had done, relaxation from the cares of office....

The best remembered incident of James's visits to Elie is perhaps that of the secret marriage and flight across the water of the daughter of Thomas Turnbull of Bogmill, whose "town-house" or "lodging" was at the lower end of the street.

The coxswain of the royal barge may often have passed the old dwelling with the turnpike stair, and caught a glimpse of a fair face at a window. How it came about is forgotten, but the gallant sailor fell in love with the Laird of Bogmill's daughter, and she with him. Bogmill does not seem to have approved; the suitor was beneath the station his daughter should have adorned. In the words of the song, sung in other days by those who could recollect the circumstances of the wooing:

> Up the lang turnpike,
>   And at the brass ca';
> The leddy liked the sailor weel
>   And wi' him she ran awa'.

The minister of Kilconquhar, or "Curate" as he was called by the people in those days...was none other than the Reverend William Hay, D.D., afterwards translated to Perth and for eighteen months Bishop of Moray....Dr Hay appears to have had no scruples about solemnizing a secret marriage:

> "O woe be to Kinneuchar priest,
>   And ill death may he dee;
> He's wed my lass to an English loon,
>   And that has ruined me."

A more serious difficulty was the flight. The Governor of Scotland could not be openly implicated in facilitating the runaway match. Yet the barge in the harbour of the Elie presented the only way if the bridegroom were not to desert his new-made bride. An ingenious solution of the problem suggested itself. A barrel was prepared, with a head of open spars, to convey one of the swans from Kilconquhar Loch to Duddingston, Dunsappie, or some other of the sheets of water in the King's Park at Holyrood. In that barrel the lady was smuggled across in her husband's charge.

So the Duke was able to answer with assurance when he received the indignant father at the palace that no woman crossed with him "that ever he did see".

All ended happily:

> "Stand up, stand up noo, gude Bogmill,
>   From off your bended knee;
> I'll mak your son a captain,
>   And he shall sail wi' me!"

MOTIFS: T.97 [*Father opposed to daughter's marriage*]; R.225 [*Elopement*].
¶   The unusual feature of this elopement is the smuggling away of the bride in a swan's cage, which must have been an ample one to allow a human being to crouch in it. It is pleasant to see James II in this genial character as a patron of lovers. He was always fond of children; perhaps this indulgence extended to young lovers.

A SERMON UPON MALT

Memorials of the Rev. John Dod, M.A., pp. 20–3.

John Dod, a famous Puritan preacher, once met four drunken cavaliers who stuck him up in a tree, and commanded him to preach a sermon. They gave him the text: it was "Malt".

He immediately spoke as follows:

"Beloved, I am a little man, come at a short warning—to deliver a brief discourse—upon a small subject, to a thin congregation, and from an unworthy pulpit.

"Beloved, my text is MALT, which cannot be divided into words, it being but one; nor into syllables, it being but one; therefore, of necessity, I must reduce it into letters, which I find to be these; M.A.L.T.

M, my beloved, is Moral, A is Allegorical, L is Literal, and T is Theological. The moral is set forth to teach you drunkards good manners, therefore—M—is My Masters, A—all of you, L—Listen, T—to my Text.

"The allegorical is when one thing is spoken and another is intended; the thing expressed is MALT; the thing signified is the Oil of MALT, which you Bacchanals make, M—your meat, A—your Apparel, L—your Liberty, and T—your Text. The literal is according to the letter. M—Much, A—Ale, L—Little, T—Thrift. The Theological is according to the effects it produces, which I find to consist of two kinds. The First respects this life, the Second, that which is to come. The effects it produces in this world are in some, M—Murder, in others, A—Adultery, in all L—Licentious Lives, in many T—Treason. The effects consequent in the World to come, are, M—Misery, A—Anguish, L—Lamentation, T—Torment. Thus, sirs, having briefly opened and explained my *short* text, give me leave to make a little use and improvement of the foregoing, and first, by way of exhortation. M—My Masters, A—All of you, L—Leave off, T—Tippling. Secondly, by way of commination,—Or M—My Masters, A—All of you, L—Look for, T—Torment."

At that he got down from his tree, and went home in triumph.

From *Tracts* (*Real and Curious Reprints, MS, etc.*) *Relating to Northamptonshire.*
2nd series.
The Author gives three other versions from B.17. 1755.
¶   It is unusual in the many jests about Sermons for the Parson to triumph, although the Card-playing Parson (see MOTIF: 1839B) extricated himself successfully. This anecdote illustrates the way in which the sermon of that period was built up. John Dod was born in 1549, and died in 1645.
See "Parson Spry's Sermon", "The Parson and the Cards" (A, III).

SIR JOHN DE COURCEY

Ruth L. Tongue, *Somerset Folklore*, p. 192.

Sir John de Courcey was a gigantic warrior to whom King John gave the village of Stoke. In those days, for safety from the robber-baron of Nether Stowey, it was built on the top of Farringdon Hill.

Sir John, however, raised himself a stronghold which was named Courcey Castle and the villagers made their homes close to it. No one could harm them with a lord whose "breakfast mug"* held over a quart of cider at a time.

Fulke de Bréauté was the lord of Nether Stowey Castle, and he had no wish for a neighbour. So he set out one day to ambush the Lord of Stoke Courcey, as he rode back downhill from making a truce with the outlaws of Danesboro'.

Now, Sir Fulke had not yet seen Sir John and he had laughed at all the tales that his men brought in....

So the Lord of Stoke Courcey was King John's champion, was he? The King must be hard put to it to make such a choice....

And what was this tale of his meeting the French King's champion in combat? Now, was that likely? Everyone knew he was a giant of a man. Nobody lived who dare challenge him!

And now these fools of his insisted that when he caught sight of Sir John de Courcey the terrible French champion turned and ran away. Here, through the distant trees, Sir Fulke caught his very first glimpse of Sir John. And did the very same thing!

* Sir John's (Courcey's) "breakfast mug" was an eighteenth-century ale-taster's quart mug. He was believed to empty it at one swallow.

Stogursy: The Quantocks. Oral Tradition.

MOTIFS: F.610 [*Remarkably strong man*]; P.14.15 [*King's champion enforces respect*].

¶ According to Collinson's *Somersetshire*, I, p 251, the Lord of Stogursy in King John's reign was Waring Fitz-Gerald, King John's chamberlain, who had married Alice, the heiress of William de Courcy. There is no mention of a Fulke de Bréauté at Nether Stowey either, but a Falk de Brent, who married Alice de Courcy's daughter, Margaret, was an ill-conditioned person who fortified the Manor of Stogursy and made himself obnoxious to the neighbourhood by his depredations.

Perhaps this is enough fact for a tradition to build upon. See "Sir John de Hauteville" (B, VII).

SIR TARQUIN

Legends and Traditions of Lancashire, Harland and Wilkinson, p. 277.

It is said that Sir Tarquine, a stoute enemie of King Arthur, kept this castle (of Manchester), and neere to the fooarde in Medlock, about Mabhouse, hung a bason on a tree, on which bason whosoever did strike, Sir Tarquine, or some of his companye, would come and fight with him; and that Sir Lancelot de Lake, a Knight of King Arthure's Round Table, did beate upon the bason—fought with Tarquine—killed him—possessed himselfe of the Castle—and loosed the prisoners. Whosoever thinketh it worth his pains to reade more of it may reade the history of King Arthur. It is certain that about A.D. 520 there was such a Prince or King, and it is not incredible that hee or his Knightes might contend about this castle when he was in this countie; and (as Minius sayeth), hee put the Saxons to flight in a memorable battle near Wigan, about twelve miles off.

Quoted from Hollingworth: *Chronicles of Manchester*.

¶ The tale of Sir Tarquin in Malory is the same as that given here, but it is not localized.

SIR THOMAS CHALONER

H. Bett, *English Legends*, p. 129.

A very curious tradition about the introduction of a foreign trade to England is concerned with alum. The manor of Longhull, in Yorkshire, belonged for generations to the Chaloner family. It was granted to Sir Thomas Chaloner in the reign of Queen Mary. His son, also Sir Thomas is reputed to be the man who first began alum works in England. The ruins of many of these are still to be seen in the neighbourhood of Whitby and Guisborough. Before Chaloner's enterprise the trade in alum had been for more than a century a papal monopoly. In May 1462 Giovanni de Castro discovered alum at Tolfa. He had lived at Constantinople and had made a fortune by dyeing Italian stuffs, using Turkish alum in the process.

On the fall of Constantinople he fled to Italy, and the Pope made him Treasurer of the Patrimony. He noticed a plant on the wooded hills of Tolfa that he had seen growing in Asia Minor in the districts where alum was found, and when the ground at Tolfa was explored he discovered an enormous supply of the finest alum there. Several thousand men were shortly employed in the alum works, and henceforth they produced an annual revenue of 100,000 gold florins for the Pope. . . .

Now when Sir Thomas Chaloner was travelling in Italy it is said that he was struck by the resemblance of the soil about the alum works of the Pope near Rome to the soil of Guisborough, and also by the fact that in both places the leaves of the trees were of a specially pale green. On his return to England he began works here, but in order to learn the secrets of the industry he had to bribe some of the Pope's workmen to enter his service, and he smuggled them out of Italy hidden in barrels on board his ship.

For this it is said that Sir Thomas Chaloner was solemnly cursed by the Pope. The curse is a really magnificent effort in the way of commination. The offender is cursed in the name of God the Father, the Son, and the Holy Spirit, in the name of the Virgin Mary, in the name of angels and archangels, of cherubim and seraphim, of patriarchs, prophets, apostles, evangelists and saints. He is cursed in the house, in the church, in the field, in the highway, in the path, in the wood, in the water; in living, in dying; in eating, in drinking, in hunger, in thirst, in fasting, in sleep, in waking, in walking, in standing, in sitting, in lying, in working, in resting, in the hair of his head, in his brains, in his temples, in his ears, in his eyebrows, in his eyes, in his cheeks, in his jaws, in his teeth, in his lips, in his throat, in his breast, in his heart, in his fingers, in his hips, in his knees, in his legs, in his feet, and in his toe-nails.

This terrific curse of the Pope's has won a place in our literature, for it is textually the very curse of Ernulphus in *Tristram Shandy*, which Dr Slop read, "while my Uncle Toby whistled *Lillibullero* as loud as he could all the time".

MOTIFS: N.440 [*Valuable secrets learned*]; M.414.11 [*Man who betrays secrets cursed*]; M.411.14.1 (ca) [*Pope curses family for stealing secret process from Pope's alum works*] (Baughman).

¶ The Jackdaw of Rheims was cursed by much the same formula, but it seems to have been less operative on Sir Thomas Chaloner.

THE SONS OF THE CONQUEROR

E. S. Hartland, *English Fairy and Folk Tales*, p. 57.

I

One day, it being observed that William was absorbed in deep thought, his courtiers ventured to inquire the cause of such profound abstraction. "I am speculating," said the monarch, "on what may be the fate of my sons after my death." "Your majesty," replied the wise men of the court, "the fate of your sons will depend upon their conduct, and their conduct will depend upon their characters; permit us to make a few inquiries, and we shall soon be able to tell you that which you wish to know." The king signifying his approbation, the wise men consulted together, and agreed to put questions separately to the three princes, who were then young. The first who entered the room was Robert, afterwards known by the surname of Courthose. "Fair sir," said one of the wise men, "answer me a question. If God had made you a bird, what bird would you wish to have been?" Robert answered: "A hawk, because it resembles most a courteous and gallant knight." William Rufus next entered, and his answer to the same question was: "I would be an eagle, because it is a strong and powerful bird, and feared by all other birds, and therefore it is king over them all." Lastly came the younger brother, Henry, who had received a learned education, and was on that account known by the surname of Beauclerc. His choice was a starling, "Because it is a debonnaire and simple bird, and gains its living without injury to anyone, and never seeks to rob or grieve its neighbour." The wise men returned immediately to the king. Robert, they said, would be bold and valiant, and would gain renown and honour, but he would finally be overcome by violence, and die in prison. William would be powerful and strong as the eagle, but feared and hated for his cruelty and violence, until he ended a wicked life by a bad death. But Henry would be wise, prudent, and peaceful, unless when actually compelled to engage in war, and would die in peace after gaining wide possessions. So when King William lay on his death-bed he remembered the saying of his wise men, and bequeathed Normandy to Robert, England to William, and his own treasures, without land, to his younger son Henry, who eventually became king of both countries and reigned long and prosperously.

Chambers, *Book of Days*, p. 328.

¶ This story, which most probably is of Eastern origin, is frequently told under various circumstances by medieval writers. A Latin manuscript of the thirteenth century relates it in the following form:

II

A wealthy English baron, whose broad lands extended over a large extent of England and Wales, had three sons: when lying on his death-bed he called them to him, and said: "If you were compelled to become birds, tell me what bird each of you would choose to resemble?" The eldest said: "I would be a hawk, because it is a noble bird, and lives by rapine." The second said: "I would be a starling, because it is a social bird, and flies in convoys." The youngest said: "I would be a swan, because it has a long neck, so that if I had anything in my heart to say, I should have plenty of time for reflection before it came to my mouth." When the father had heard them, he said to the first: "Thou, my son, as I perceive, desirest to live by rapine; I will therefore bequeath thee my possessions in England, because it is a land of peace and justice, and thou canst not rob in it with impunity." To the second he said: "Because thou lovest society, I will bequeath thee my lands in Wales, which is a land of discord and war, in order that thy courtesy may soften down the malice of the natives." And then, turning to the youngest, he said: "To thee I bequeath no land at all, because thou art wise, and wilt gain enough by thy wisdom." And as he foretold, the youngest son profited by his wisdom, and became Lord Chief Justice of England, which in those times was the next dignity to that of king.

TYPE 920B. MOTIFS: J.412.1 [*Prince of democratic tastes chosen*]; H.508.1(*a*) [*William the Conqueror asks sons what bird each would choose if he could be a bird, etc.*) (Baughman).
¶ In both the son most commended is not the one to be chiefly endowed, though he came to the highest honours in the end.

Tale II is to be found in a little book, *Short Stories*, published by Chambers in 1878, but the book is not of much use, since it gives no sources. This tale was probably retold from Hone. Professor Archer Taylor is making an exhaustive study of this type.

SQUIRE BIDLAKE AND THE CLOCK

J. R. W. Coxhead, *The Devil in Devon*, pp. 34–5.

Among the foothills on the north-western fringe of Dartmoor, in the parish of Bridestowe, there is an estate called Bidlake, which was owned by a family of the same name for over five hundred years from 1268 to 1792.

At the outbreak of the Civil War, the property was in the possession of Henry Bidlake—a staunch Royalist. He joined the King's western forces early in the conflict, and in 1643 was made a captain of horse under Colonel Sir Thomas Hele. He was one of the members of the gallant garrison of Pendennis Castle, in Cornwall, when John Arundell surrendered the stronghold to the Roundheads on 17th August 1646. The defenders were allowed the honours of war, and marched out of the fortress with drums beating, colours flying, and trumpets sounding.

An interesting tradition relates how he escaped being caught, about the year 1647, when a detachment of Parliamentary soldiers was sent to Bridestowe with orders to surround his home and take him prisoner.

Being warned of the approach of the soldiers by a faithful servant, Bidlake dressed himself up in some ragged old clothes, left the house by a back way, and walked boldly through the ranks of his enemies as they were in the process of drawing a cordon round his home. As he passed by, one of the troopers asked him if he had seen Squire Bidlake. "Aye, tu be sure I 'ave," he replied. "Squire were a-standin' on his own doorstep a few minutes agone."

In order to allay suspicion, he walked at a normal pace until he was well out of sight of the soldiers, and then he proceeded as fast as he could go to the house of one of his tenants named Veale, in Burley Wood.

Somehow the soldiers discovered that they had been cleverly tricked, and were soon hot on his trail. After a while they came galloping up to the house in the wood, and there was a thunderous knocking on the door, accompanied by shouts for admission.

Alarmed for the safety of the Squire, Mrs Veale made him conceal himself in the clock-case. The troopers hunted high and low, but were unable to find their quarry. Just before they left one of the soldiers happened to look at the dial of the clock, and, seeing the hand was pointing to the hour, said to Mrs Veale, "What doan't 'ee strike?" "Aye, aye, maister," she replied, "there be a hand there as can strike, I can tell 'ee."

Bidlake suffered from a chronic cough, and just at that very critical moment it began, but he had the presence of mind to lower his head, let the weight down behind his back, and thus allow the chiming mechanism to work. As the clock struck the hour, the loud tones of the chime drowned the sound of his cough, and he was saved from capture.

After Bidlake's narrow escape it is said that the Veales hid him in a secret place in Burley Wood, and supplied him with blankets and food for several weeks, until it was safe for him to return to his own house. In gratitude for their loyalty, he arranged that they should hold their farm in perpetuity, on a tenure of half-a-crown per annum, so long as there remained a male heir in the family. The last member of the family is supposed to have died between the years 1829 and 1866, during the time the estate was owned by the Rev. John Stafford Wollocombe.

From S. Baring-Gould, *Devonshire Characters and Strange Events.*
TYPE ML.8000. MOTIFS: K.515 [*Escape by hiding*]; P.322 [*Guest given refuge*]; Q.46 [*Reward for protecting fugitive*]; M.207 [*Land grant*].
¶ See "A Royal Escape", "The Puppy under the Table".

SWAYNE'S LEAPS

Ruth L. Tongue, *Folktales of England*, p. 86.

This here Tom Swayne he weren't much of a chap to have around a farm, but he could jump wonderful and he was surprising fond of his dear wife and little ones.

Now there was a lad, out over, could run so fast as his father's hoss, and there was to be a match between the pair, see—who was champion. Then "the war" come—down over there on the moors, and Tom Swayne and this young chap they was both took. Well, they cruel devils did promise the young chap he was to be spared if he can match with a bay colt and win, which he did. Then they devils hang him high with other honest men! Oh, 'twas a time of tears and sadness, 'twas.

Now, Tom Swayne, he's in a turrible fright in case he do swing then and there, but they marches him along this here road to Street. Well, his dear wife and the children run out to beg and pray for his life and his heart do nearly break in two.

Then he say to they sojers, "Looky zee, have 'ee ever heard tell of a man as could jump from where we do stand now right to the edge of this wood in dree leaps?" They wouldn't have it, but he say, "Let's have a try and you can bet on it. I'd a-wish my little children to remember my powers."

Now, a Moorlynch man would ha' been looking out for a bit of a trick, but they sojers didn't know he. They loosed his bonds and he do leap. One: fifteen feet. Then he do leap. Two: eighteen feet. Then he do leap. Dree: twenty-one feet—right over edge of wood and down in under the fern—and they'd a-lost their prisoner. When all them days was gone by, Tom Swayne he come home to his own dear souls all safe and sound.

Recorded from Ruth L. Tongue, 29 September 1963.
Heard by her from a labouring man in the Polden Hills, Somerset, 1947.
TYPE ML.8000. MOTIFS: F.1088 [*Extraordinary escape*]; F.551.28 [*Captors give captive respite in order to witness alleged marvel*]; F.1071 [*Prodigious jump*].
¶ See "The Puppy under the Table", "The Legend of the Sword", "Marshall's Elm".

A TRUE STORY ABOUT A BARBAROUS NAVVY [summary]

Thompson *Notebook* III, from Gus Grey.

Navvies working on cutting through wood. Two of them, with white bulldog, met young lady who went that way to work each day. Owner of dog tied her to tree, and set dog on her to test it. Other man protested, but not strong enough to insist. Dog tore girl to pieces. Owner said he was satisfied with dog.

They went to a pub. Man entered and offered to buy dog. £2 agreed on; man said he must go and get money. Ordered beer for two men, secretly ordered landlord to lock door, as there were murderers in the house. Warned police, who came and arrested them.

At trial, the man proved to be a gamekeeper who had seen the whole thing from behind a tree. Had had gun, but only one cartridge, so did nothing. Murderer hanged; other man transported.

(Gus said he would have shot dog, and tried butt-end of gun on the men.)

MOTIFS: S.100 [*Revolting murders or mutilations*]; Q.211 [*Murder punished*].

UTHER PENDRAGON

Roger of Wendover, *Chronicle*, I, pp. 27-8.

Gillomannius and Pascentius fought a well-contested battle with Uther, the king's brother, in Wales. At length Uther prevailed, and Gillomannius and Pascentius were slain. After this there appeared a star of wonderful size and brightness, with a single ray, on which was a ball of fire extended like a dragon, out of whose mouth proceeded two rays, one of which seemed to extend its length beyond the regions of Gaul, and the other, verging towards the Irish Sea, terminated in seven smaller rays. Struck with terror at this sight, Uther anxiously inquired of his wise men what this star portended. They made answer, "The star, and the fiery dragon under the star, are thyself; the ray which stretches towards the region of Gaul portends that thou wilt have a very powerful son, who will possess the extensive territories which the star covered; the other ray signifies thy daughter, whose sons and grandsons shall successively possess the kingdom of Britain. Hasten, therefore, most noble prince; thy brother, Aurelius Ambrosius, the renowned king of Britain, is dead; and with him has perished the military glory of the Britons." Immediately thereupon came a messenger with the tidings of the king's death, and that he had been buried in royal state, by the bishops and abbats of the kingdom, beneath the Giant's Dance, according to his own directions.

MOTIF: D.1812.5.1.2.1 [*Vision as evil omen*].

¶ In these visions of the early Arthurian legends dragons were symbolic of both the Britons and the Saxons.

See "The Youth without a Father" (B, III).

WALLACE AT LONGFORGAN

From *Our Meigle Book*, p. 51.

...In 1292, young William Wallace, who was completing his education in Dundee, stabbed the son of the Constable of Dundee, who had insulted him: daggers were quickly out in those old days! Seeing what he had done, Wallace fled, pursued by the English soldiers. He ran till he came to Longforgan, and, seeing a little cottage, sat down wearily on the grain knocker which stood at the door. This cottage was the home of one of the Smiths, a decent man who, with his wife, worked a small farm. They owned also a hand-loom, and while the husband was attending to the work of the farm, his good wife was busy at her spinning-wheel. This is how she was employed as Wallace sought a moment's rest at her door. Thinking she heard, above the burr of her wheel, steps passing her door, she got up to see who it might be. What was her surprise to see a young man, breathless and weary, sitting on the stone by the door. Longforgan must be some six miles from Dundee! Six long miles when the race is for life or death!

We suppose Wallace must have seen a kindly glint in Mrs Smith's eye (we know what charm of personality he possessed), for he told her hurriedly why he was there and in such a condition. Mrs Smith quickly invited him in, and, taking off the large loose overall which she had worn while spinning, made him put it on, and set him down to spin. Almost immediately the soldiers arrived, and searched the cottage, but so disguised was Wallace, so covered with fluff from the spinning, that they failed to recognize him, and soon left the cottage to continue their search elsewhere.

When the goodman came in for his dinner he was told of the adventure. Wallace was given food and rest, and at dark they started him on his way in safety.

MOTIFS: K.1836 [*Disguise of man in woman's dress*]; K.514 [*Disguise as girl to avoid execution*].

¶ This early act of violence by Wallace is generally accepted as a true tradition, but the accounts of his youth are scanty and not well-authenticated.

THE WARDEN OF THE MARCHES [shortened]

The Book of Scottish Story, pp. 88–95.

In the reign of King James V the duty of guarding the Marches against English raiders was entrusted to Sir John Charteris of Amisfield, near Dumfries, a brave but arrogant man, whose public duties were apt to be sacrificed to his private interests.

A young farmer of Annandale, George Maxwell, was particularly active against the English, who, in reprisal, raided and plundered his house, and drove off all his livestock. In hot pursuit Maxwell overtook the raiders, but in the battle which ensued, he was killed, and his widow, Marion, was left with the charge of their nine-year-old son, Wallace. Generous neighbours replaced her in a small farm, but in successive raids she lost so much that by the time her son reached the age of twenty, she was reduced to the occupation of a small cottage, and possessed only one cow. But the lad was brave and industrious, and a kindly farmer gave her cow pasturage, so they lived in reasonable comfort and contentment.

Wallace Maxwell had his father's courage and patriotism, and he had won the love of a girl, Mary Morrison, poor as himself, but endowed with beauty and goodness, so that all who knew them thought them a pair well worthy of one another. She was an orphan, and they were fellow-servants to the farmer in whose cottage the widow Maxwell lived. Both had wisdom and prudence to know that it would be long before their circumstances permitted them to marry.

It happened that the leader of the English in a certain raid, the son of a rich Borderer, had been taken prisoner, and a heavy ransom paid for his release, the money having been pocketed by Sir John Charteris, who considered it a perquisite of his office. In the following raid, Wallace Maxwell was captured in his turn, and the man who had so recently paid a high price for his own son's ransom kept Wallace a close prisoner till an equal price should be paid for Wallace's release. Since there was not the least hope that either his widowed mother nor any of their friends could ever raise such a sum, the poor woman appealed to Sir John, begging him to send some of his forces after the raiders, and rescue her son. But Sir John had a grudge against young Maxwell, and contemptuously rejected her request, saying that the matter was altogether too trifling to command his attention; and the desolate mother then went and told all her tale to Mary Morrison, whose distress was no less than her own. Mary, indeed, went so far as to renew the suit to Sir John, and herself, having begged leave from her employer, went to plead with the hard-hearted Warden, who received her in very different fashion. He explained that it would be a hard task to rescue one who had rendered himself an object of vengeance to the English Borderers, and who must by now be under close surveillance. But he offered to pay the ransom, high as it was, in return for what he termed her gratitude. Mary, filled with joy, promised that all in their power should be done to show this, and prayed that Heaven should be his reward. He, however, replied that she herself had it in her power to show a more immediate thankfulness, and made it all too clear what reward he had in mind. But when she, with due modesty and courtesy, rejected every advance, he told her roughly that Wallace

Maxwell might perish in a dungeon, or at the hands of his enemies, for he should never be rescued by him. Mary returned home indignant and sorrowful, and next she and the widow resolved to appeal to their kind friend, the farmer, for leave for them both, in order that they might lay their complaint before the King himself. The farmer was in full agreement; for the Warden's insolence and neglect of his duties had become the subject of general complaint, and he thought that such an appeal might be for the good of the whole countryside. King James was always easy of access to any of his subjects, and he received the woman with great kindness, promising that on his approaching visit to Annandale, their case should be attended to; and that when he sent a certain nobleman to them, they should come at once to the hearing of their case.

It was a favourite custom with the King to go about among his subjects in disguise and, when asked his name on these occasions, to give it as "The Gudeman of Ballengeich". In this character he visited Annandale, and, seeing a girl washing linen in a stream, whom he recognized as Mary Morrison, he sat down on a nearby stone, groaning as if in dire pain. Mary at once came up to offer help, and helped him to walk, leaning on her arm, to the farm. He declared that a drink of milk and a rest would soon cure his distemper, and while lying there, he contrived to learn of the general sympathy for Mary and the widow Maxwell, and the equal dislike and distrust of Sir John.

In due course the King marched back towards Dumfries, and, after passing a night in the small village of Duncow, he left his retinue there, and made his way in beggar's guise to Amisfield, where he requested the porter to procure him an immediate audience with Sir John. The reply was that Sir John was at dinner and could by no means be disturbed for two or perhaps three hours. The King gave the man a groat, and bade him tell Sir John that his business was urgent, and on receiving the same reply, produced two more groats, bidding his messenger say that in crossing the Border he had seen the English massing for an attack; and that it was Sir John's duty to fire the beacons immediately, and alarm the countryside. Sir John only replied, "If he chooses to wait two hours, I will then see whether he is a knave or a fool; but if he send such another impertinent message to me, both you and he shall have cause to regret it."

The kindly porter then offered food and ale to help the stranger pass the time until the Warden should be ready to receive him; but the King now gave him three groats, bidding him return and say that the Gudeman of Ballengeich insisted upon seeing him immediately. As the man went off on this errand, King James winded his bugle horn loudly, and, casting aside his beggar's garb, stood in his royal insignia, while his men-at-arms came galloping up in all haste. The terrified Warden stood trembling, pleading his ignorance of the King's presence, but James sternly replied that the meanest of his subjects had access to him at all times. But to give Sir John his fair chance of clearing himself of the charges brought against him, the King appointed him to attend for the hearing of his case at Hoddam Castle. He added that, if Wallace Maxwell were not produced within a week, the Warden himself should be hanged from a tree before his own window.

Meantime, the King's retinue was to be entertained at the Warden's expense, in the Warden's own castle. The King now sent the young nobleman, as he had arranged to the widow at Stirling, to bring her and Mary Morrison to him at once. When they arrived, he gave the widow a cow, worth double the price of the one stolen from her, with blankets and other presents; but even in the height of her gratitude she could not forbear asking for her son; but he sent her away in the joyful hope of seeing him again very soon.

The Warden's distress was daily increasing, but in the nick of time Wallace Maxwell was brought before him, when, allowing him no rest at all, he sent him on in hot haste to Hoddam Castle. The King now confronted Sir John with all three of his victims, and compelled him to acknowledge his guilt before them all. The Warden could do nothing but confess to it all; and the King decreed that he should establish Wallace in a fifty-acre farm, rent-free, for his lifetime and his wife's, fully stocked and furnished within three months, on pain of immediate death by hanging. Sir John submitted, and the King sent the three away with his blessing.

MOTIFS: R.4 [*Surprise capture*]; K.1353 (variant) [*Woman deceived into sacrificing honour: ruler promises to release her husband*]; N.836 [*King as helper*]; K.1812 [*King in disguise*].
¶ See "The Court Cave", "The Goodman of Ballengiech".

WEST MOLLAND HOUSE

J. R. W. Coxhead, *Legends of Devon*, p. 24.

About a mile off the River Yeo, and on the fringe of the southern slopes of Exmoor, is the village of Molland. A mile to the west of the village, on a spur of the hills rising to a height of over 700 feet above sea-level, stands the ancient house of West Molland Barton.

Above the entrance doorway on the north side of the building there is a crest, carved in stone, representing a hawk, with wings that appear to be clipped.

This crest is the subject of an amusing legend connected with a member of a branch of the Courtenay family.

According to the legend, the Manor of Molland belonged at one time to the powerful family of Courtenay, and one day, many years ago, a member of the family living at West Molland House happened to kill a man.

He was tried at Exeter for the crime, and, because of his very influential position in the county, he was placed on the raised platform in the court-room by the side of the judge who was to try the case.

After hearing all the witnesses, and carefully sifting the evidence, the judge condemned him as guilty, whereupon Courtenay, who was an arrogant and hot-tempered man, leapt up from his chair and knocked the judge head over heels down into the court.

Complaint was made to the King about Courtenay's disgraceful behaviour, and a letter was despatched to London by a trusty messenger.

The truculent Lord of the Manor of Molland, hearing of this and thinking that things were likely to go hard against him unless he could get to London before the messenger, decided to go and see the King and ask for a pardon.

Mounting his mettlesome steed, he galloped off to London, as hard as his horse would carry him, and managed to reach the city before the messenger who was carrying the news of his bad behaviour.

When he asked to see the King, he was told that the King and Queen were being rowed in the royal barge on the Thames.

Thinking it would be fatal for any time to be lost, because the messenger might arrive at any moment, Courtenay galloped swiftly to the river, and, seeing the royal barge in midstream, he rode his horse into the water and made his way towards the boat without delay.

The Queen happened to look across the water, and when she saw a man swimming his horse towards the royal barge, she turned to the King and said: "Look! There is a horseman swimming out to us. Who do you think he is?"

The King had a good look and replied: "I think it must be old Courtenay. I wonder what mischief the old ruffian has been up to now?"

The Queen evidently had a soft spot in her heart for Courtenay, because she turned to the King and said: "You won't be too hard on him, will you?"

So the King replied: "All right, my dear. I won't have his head chopped off, but I'll jolly well clip his wings."

When Courtenay came up to the boat, he bowed respectfully to the King—or as best as the water would allow him to do—and then told the whole story of his misdoings.

The King, with a severe look on his face, said to him: "You are a troublesome old ruffian. I shall have to clip your wings a trifle. You shall be deprived of several of your fine manors as a punishment."

Courtenay was very glad to get off so lightly, and, in memory of the

King's words, he had the emblem of a hawk with clipped wings carved in stone and placed above the entrance to his home at Molland.

The Manor of Molland Bottreaux was originally the property of the Bottreaux family. Later it was held by the Hungerfords, whose heiress married Sir Phillip Courtenay, a younger son of Sir Phillip Courtenay of Powderham.

...As it happens, no hawk in any shape or form was ever used by the Courtenays as a crest, but a falcon with outspread wings was the crest of the Throckmortons. Therefore the story would appear to have arisen during the latter part of the eighteenth century, and the hawk with clipped wings above the doorway of West Molland Barton is really the falcon crest of the Throckmorton family with wings shortened by the weathering storms of the passing years.

Nevertheless, there is a strong possibility that there is some truth in the story which forms a background to the legend, because a fine of manors was often imposed by the King, during medieval times, for a crime committed by a person of exalted position.

MOTIFS: J.1193.2.1 (variant) [*Defendant strikes judge*]; N.837 [*Queen as helper*].
¶ This is very like "Pudsay's Leap" without the supernatural element. See also "Adam Bel, Clym of the Clough and William of Cloudesley" (A, IV).

WHITTINGTON AND HIS CAT

Jacobs, *English Fairy-Tales*, p. 167.

In the reign of the famous King Edward III there was a little boy called Dick Whittington, whose father and mother died when he was very young. As poor Dick was not old enough to work, he was very badly off; he got but little for his dinner, and sometimes nothing at all for his breakfast; for the people who lived in the village were very poor indeed, and could not spare him much more than the parings of potatoes, and now and then a hard crust of bread.

Now Dick had heard a great many strange things about the great city called London; for the country people at that time thought that folks in London were all fine gentlemen and ladies; and that there was singing and music there all day long; and that the streets were all paved with gold.

One day a large waggon and eight horses, all with bells at their heads, drove through the village, while Dick was standing by the sign-post. He thought that this waggon must be going to the fine town of London; so he took courage, and asked the waggoner to let him walk with him by the side of the waggon. As soon as the waggoner heard that poor Dick had no father or mother, and saw by his ragged clothes that he could not be worse off than he was, he told him that he might go if he would, so off they set together.

So Dick got safe to London, and was in such a hurry to see the fine streets paved all over with gold, that he did not even stay to thank the kind waggoner; but ran off as fast as his legs would carry him, through many of the streets, thinking every moment to come to those that were paved with gold; for Dick had seen a guinea three times in his own little village, and remembered what a deal of money it brought in change; so he thought he had nothing to do but to take up some little bits of pavement, and should then have as much money as he could wish for.

Poor Dick ran till he was tired, and had quite forgot his friend the waggoner, but at last, finding it grow dark, and that every way he turned he saw nothing but dirt instead of gold, he sat down in a dark corner and cried himself to sleep.

Little Dick was all night in the streets; and next morning, being very hungry, he got up and walked about, and asked everybody he met to give him a halfpenny to keep him from starving; but nobody stayed to answer him, and only two or three gave him a halfpenny; so that the poor boy was soon quite faint and weak for the want of victuals.

In this distress he asked charity of several people, and one of them said crossly: "Go to work for an idle rogue." "That I will," said Dick. "I will go to work for you if you will let me." But the man only cursed at him and went on.

At last a good-natured looking gentleman saw how hungry he looked. "Why don't you go to work, my lad?" said he to Dick. "That I would, but I don't know how to get any," answered Dick. "If you are willing, come along with me," said the gentleman, and took him to a hayfield, where Dick worked briskly, and lived merrily till the hay was made.

After this he found himself as badly off as before; and being almost starved again, he laid himself down at the door of Mr Fitzwarren, a rich merchant. Here he was soon seen by a cook-maid, who was an ill-tempered creature, and happened just then to be very busy dressing dinner for her master and mistress; so she called out to poor Dick: "What business have you there, you lazy rogue? There is nothing else but beggars. If you do not take yourself away, we will see how you will like a sousing of some dish-water; I have some here hot enough to make you jump."

Just at that time Mr Fitzwarren himself came home to dinner; and when he saw a dirty, ragged boy lying at the door, he said to him: "Why do you lie there, my boy? You seem old enough to work. I am afraid you are inclined to be lazy."

"No, indeed, sir," said Dick to him, "that is not the case, for I would work with all my heart, but I do not know anybody, and I believe I am very sick for the want of food."

"Poor fellow, get up. Let me see what ails you."

Dick now tried to rise, but was obliged to lie down again, being too weak to stand, for he had not eaten any food for three days, and was no longer able to run about and beg a halfpenny of people in the street. So the kind merchant ordered him to be taken into the house, and have a good dinner given him, and be kept to do what work he was able to do for the cook.

Little Dick would have lived very happy in this good family if it had not been for the ill-natured cook. She used to say: "You are under me, so look sharp; clean the spit and the dripping-pan, make the fires, wind up the jack, and do all the scullery work nimbly, or..." and she would shake the ladle at him. Besides, she was so fond of basting that, when she had no meat to baste, she would baste poor Dick's head and shoulders with a broom, or anything else that happened to fall in her way. At last her ill-usage of him was told to Alice, Mr Fitzwarren's daughter, who told the cook she should be turned away if she did not treat him kinder.

The behaviour of the cook was now a little better, but besides this, Dick had another hardship to get over. His bed stood in a garret, where there were so many holes in the floor, and the walls, that every night he was tormented with rats and mice. A gentleman having given Dick a penny for cleaning his shoes, he thought he would buy a cat with it. The next day he saw a girl with a cat, and asked her, "Will you let me have that cat for a penny?" The girl said, "Yes, that I will, master, though she is an excellent mouser."

Dick hid his cat in the garret, and always took care to carry a part of his dinner to her; and in a short time he had no more trouble with the rats and mice, but slept quite sound every night.

Soon after this his master had a ship ready to sail; and as it was the custom that all the servants should have some chance for good fortune as well as himself, he called them all into the parlour, and asked them what they would send out.

They all had something that they were willing to venture except poor Dick, who had neither money nor goods, and therefore could send nothing. For this reason he did not come into the parlour with the rest; but Miss Alice guessed what was the matter, and ordered him to be called in. She then said, "I will lay down some money for him from my own purse," but her father told her: "This will not do, for it must be something of his own."

When poor Dick heard this, he said: "I have nothing but a cat, which I bought for a penny some time since of a little girl."

"Fetch your cat then, my lad," said Mr Fitzwarren, "and let her go."

Dick went upstairs and brought down poor puss, with tears in his eyes, and gave her to the captain; "For," he said, "I shall now be kept awake all night by the rats and mice." All the company laughed at Dick's odd venture; and Miss Alice, who felt pity for him, gave him some money to buy another cat.

This, and many other marks of kindness shown him by Miss Alice, made the ill-tempered cook jealous of poor Dick, and she began to use him more cruelly than ever, and always made game of him for sending his cat to sea. She asked him: "Do you think your cat will sell for as much money as would buy a stick to beat you?"

At last poor Dick could not bear this usage any longer, and he thought he would run away from his place; so he packed up his few things, and started very early in the morning, on All Hallows Day, the first of November. He walked as far as Holloway; and there sat down on a stone, which to this day is called "Whittington's Stone", and began to think to himself which road he should take.

While he was thinking what he should do, the Bells of Bow Church, which at that time were only six, began to ring, and their sound seemed to say to him:

"Turn again, Whittington,
Thrice Lord Mayor of London."

"Lord Mayor of London!" said he to himself. "Why, to be sure, I would put up with almost anything now, to be Lord Mayor of London, and ride in a fine coach when I grow to be a man! Well, I will go back, and think nothing of the cuffing and scolding of the old cook, if I am to be Lord Mayor of London at last."

Dick went back, and was lucky enough to get into the house, and set about his work, before the old cook came downstairs.

We must now follow Miss Puss to the coast of Africa. The ship with the cat on board, was a long time at sea; and was driven at last by the winds on a part of the coast of Barbary, where the only people were the Moors, unknown to the English. The people came in great numbers to see the sailors, because they were of different colour to themselves, and treated them civilly; and when they became better acquainted, were very eager to buy the fine things that the ship was loaded with.

When the captain saw this, he sent patterns of the best things he had to the king of the country; who was so much pleased with them that he sent for the captain to the palace. Here they were placed, as it is the custom of the country, on rich carpets flowered with gold and silver. The King and Queen were seated at the upper end of the room; and a number of dishes were brought in for dinner. They had not sat long when a vast number of rats and mice rushed in, and devoured all the meat in an instant. The captain wondered at this, and asked if these vermin were not unpleasant.

"Oh, yes," said they, "very offensive; and the king would give half his treasure to be freed of them, for they not only destroy his dinner, as you see, but they assault him in his chamber, and even in bed, so that he is obliged to be watched while he is sleeping, for fear of them."

The captain jumped for joy; he remembered poor Whittington and his cat, and told the king he had a creature on board the ship that would despatch all these vermin immediately. The king jumped so high at the joy which the news gave him, that his turban dropped off his head. "Bring this creature to me," he said. "vermin are dreadful in a court, and if she will perform what you say, I will load your ship with gold and jewels in exchange for her."

The captain, who knew his business, took this opportunity to set forth the merits of Miss Puss. He told his majesty: "It is not very convenient to part with her, as, when she is gone, the rats and mice may destroy the goods in the ship—but to oblige your majesty, I will fetch her."

"Run, run!" said the queen; "I am impatient to see the dear creature."

Away went the captain to the ship, while another dinner was got ready. He put Puss under his arm, and arrived at the palace just in time to see the table full of rats. When the cat saw this, she did not wait for bidding, but jumped out of the captain's arms, and in a few minutes laid almost all the rats and mice dead at her feet. The rest of them in their fright scampered away to their holes.

The king was quite charmed to get rid so easily of such plagues, and the queen desired that the creature who had done them so great a kindness might be brought to her, that she might look at her. Upon which the captain called, "Pussy, pussy, pussy!" and she came to him. He then presented her to the queen, who started back, and was afraid to touch the creature who had made such a havoc among the rats and mice. However, when the captain stroked the cat, and called: "Pussy, pussy!" the queen also touched her, and cried, "Putty, putty!" for she had not learned English. He then put her down on the queen's lap, where she purred, and played with her majesty's hand, and then purred herself to sleep.

The king, having seen the exploits of Mrs Puss, and being informed that her kittens would stock the whole country, and keep it free from rats, bargained with the captain for the whole ship's cargo, and then gave him ten times as much for the cat as all the rest amounted to.

The captain then took leave of the royal party, and set sail with a fair wind for England, and after a happy voyage arrived safe in London.

One morning, early, Mr Fitzwarren had just come to his counting-house, and seated himself at the desk, to count over the cash, and settle the business for the day, when somebody came tap, tap at the door. "Who's there?" said Mr Fitzwarren. "A friend," answered the other. "I come to bring you good news of your ship *Unicorn*." The merchant, bustling up in such a hurry that he forgot his gout, opened the door, and who should he see waiting but the captain and factor, with a cabinet of jewels and a bill of lading; when he looked at this the merchant lifted up his eyes and thanked Heaven for sending him such a prosperous voyage.

They then told the story of the cat, and showed the rich present that the king and queen had sent to poor Dick for her. As soon as the merchant heard this he called out to his servants:

"Go send him in, and tell him of his fame;
Pray call him Mr Whittington by name."

Mr Fitzwarren now showed himself to be a good man; for when some of his servants said so great a treasure was too much for him, he answered: "God forbid I should deprive him of the value of a single penny, it is his own, and he shall have it to a farthing."

He sent for Dick, who at that time was scouring pots for the cook, and was quite dirty. He would have excused himself from coming into the counting-house, saying, "The room is swept, and my shoes are dirty and full of hob-nails." But the merchant ordered him to come in.

Mr Fitzwarren ordered a chair to be set for him, and so he began to think they were making game of him, at the same time said to them: "Do not play tricks with a poor simple boy, but let me go down again, if you please, to my work."

"Indeed, Mr Whittington," said the merchant, "we are all quite in earnest with you, and I most heartily rejoice in the news that these gentlemen have brought you; for the captain has sold your cat to the king of Barbary, and brought you in return for her more riches than I possess in the whole world; and I wish you may long enjoy them."

Mr Fitzwarren then told the men to open the great treasure they had brought with them; and said: "Mr Whittington has nothing to do but put it in some place of safety."

Poor Dick hardly knew how to behave himself for joy. He begged his master to take what part of it he pleased, since he owed it all to his kindness. "No, no," answered Mr Fitzwarren. "This is all your own, and I have no doubt but you will use it well."

Dick next asked his mistress, and then Miss Alice, to accept a part of his good fortune, but they would not, and at the same time told him they felt great joy at his good success. But this poor fellow was too kind-hearted to keep it all to himself; so he made a present to the captain, the mate, and the rest of Mr Fitzwarren's servants; and even to the ill-natured old cook.

After this, Mr Fitzwarren advised him to send for a tailor and get himself dressed like a gentleman; and told him he was welcome to live in his house till he could provide himself with a better.

When Whittington's face was washed, his hair curled, his hat cocked, and he was dressed in a nice suit of clothes, he was as handsome and genteel as any young man who visited at Mr Fitzwarren's house; so that Miss Alice, who had once been so kind to him, and thought of him with pity, now looked upon him as fit to be her sweetheart; and the more so, no doubt, because Whittington was now always thinking what he could do to oblige her, and making her the prettiest presents that could be.

Mr Fitzwarren soon saw their love for each other, and proposed to join them in marriage; and to this they both readily agreed. A day for the wedding was soon fixed, and they were attended to church by the Lord Mayor, the court of aldermen, the sheriffs, and a great number of the richest merchants in London, whom they afterwards treated with a very rich feast.

History tells us that Mr Whittington and his lady lived in great splendour, and were very happy. They had several children. He was Sheriff of London, thrice Lord Mayor, and received the honour of knighthood by Henry V.

He entertained the king and his queen at dinner after his conquest of France so grandly, that the king said: "Never had prince such a subject;" when Sir Richard heard this, he said: "Never had subject such a prince."

The figure of Sir Richard Whittington with his cat in his arms, carved in stone, was to be seen till the year 1780 over the archway of the old prison at Newgate, which he built for criminals.

TYPE 1651. MOTIF: F. 708.1 [*Country without cats*]; N.411.1 [*Whittington's cat: a cat in a mouse-infested land without cats sold for a fortune*]; L.160 [*Success of the unpromising hero*]; L.161.1 [*Marriage of poor boy and rich girl*].
¶ Type 1651 is widespread, but finds its best-known example in the tale of Dick Whittington, though it is a matter of conjecture how it became attached to this story. Richard Whittington was probably the son of Sir William Whittington of Pauntley near Newent, and Joan Mansell, daughter of the Sheriff of Gloucestershire. In 1379 he was already a substantial citizen of London and he married the daughter of Sir Ovo Fitzwaryn of Dorset, but died without issue in 1423, leaving very considerable legacies to various charities. Descendants of a collateral branch of the family are still in existence. It is interesting to see the development of a fairy-story plot out of this prosperous history. The tale had its present form by the seventeenth century.

WINDLESHAW ABBEY [summary]

J. Roby, *Lancashire Traditions*, II, p. 115.

After his defeat before York, in the autumn of 1644, Prince Rupert came in disguise with one companion, named Chisenhall, to a country inn near the old ruined Abbey of Windleshaw. They were bound for Knowsley and the coast, but they delayed their departure, for the prince had fallen in love with Marian, the beautiful daughter of the landlord, Nathan

Sumner, and she was, though a Puritan by upbringing, charmed by the attention of this courteous stranger, whom she only knew as "Captain Egerton".

One evening the Prince was passing through the cemetery of the Abbey chapel, when he noticed the sexton, a strange-looking, hunchbacked creature, digging a grave. He asked him who was to be buried there, and was answered, "The first fool that asks."

The startled prince questioned the man further; but was the more perturbed when he found that the sexton apparently knew his secret, for he told him that his uncle "waited for him in Oxford; but he might wait till his porridge cooled". Suspecting that the man was privy to some plot, the Prince attempted to hold him prisoner; but the sexton eluded him, and escaped with a speed astonishing in view of his seeming infirmity.

Failing to overtake him, the Prince returned to the inn, and on relating his encounter he was told that the sinister sexton had the strange power that every grave he dug was so soon filled, that he was known as "the live man's sexton". Marian begged the two men not to go to Knowsley, for the sexton's words seemed to her to indicate that he knew of some plot against their lives. They set off, however, helped by a thick mist which concealed them from their pursuers. The region was a stronghold of Roundheads, and their identity, though not certainly known, was suspected. Hearing the sound of horse-hoofs behind them, they turned aside into a copse, and the enemy passed them by. But they lost their way in the mist, and found themselves back almost at Windleshaw, and just as they made this discovery, they were accosted by the strange sexton, who so startled the Prince's horse, that he stumbled, and threw his rider. The sexton disappeared as suddenly as he had come, and Chisenhall, dismounting, found his master lying unconscious, and bleeding heavily from the nose. He galloped to the inn for assistance, but on returning found no trace of the Prince. Marian, who had ridden back with him, now told him that since their departure, men had been inquiring for them at the inn, accusing her father of sheltering Cavaliers, and sons of Belial, and she warned him that he must by no means be seen in that place. She took him home and concealed him; though his anxiety for his friend made confinement almost unendurable to him. Meanwhile, Marian went to consult a zealous minister, Gilgal Snape, a trusted friend, who had all along felt great concern for the soul of the poor sexton, and now told her his story. He was an orphan, Stephen, or "Steenie", Ellison by name, and, growing up much in company with bell-ringers and grave-diggers had somehow picked up their trade; but his uncanny foresight over the digging of graves roused suspicion that he was in league with the powers of darkness. The good minister by love, and great striving, succeeded in driving out the evil spirit once, and Ellison became gentle and docile.

But from time to time, it seemed, his dark mood returned, and there was fear that he was again falling under the old evil influence.

Marian perceived that the minister, though he knew that the two strangers had been followed after leaving the inn, had no further knowledge of what had befallen them. She therefore concluded that the sexton must have concealed "Egerton", and she next went in search of him. She came upon him, secretly digging a grave at dead of night, singing strange chants as he threw up the spadefuls of earth. He professed to her that he had foreseen the stranger's approaching doom the previous night, and therefore was preparing his grave. He had locked him into a tower of the old Abbey, and held him prisoner, to await his death. He had forgotten, he said, in reply to her urgent question, to provide any food for his captive, but made no objection when Marian went home to bring supplies from the inn; for it was no part of his plan to murder his victim, but only to wait for his fate to be fulfilled. Marian returned with the food, and persuaded him to lead her up the winding stair to the prisoner's room. As they went, the hunchback confessed to her, for he was now again in one of his gentler moods, that the fiend had indeed won him back, and had given him a golden coin, which, as long as he kept it, would preserve his life. If it once passed into other hands, however, he would himself be the next occupant of the last grave he had dug.

The Prince, who had almost fallen into despair, was amazed to see Marian enter his cell with food and drink. She promised to help him to escape, and even begged a loan from the sexton, whose avarice was well-known, and who always carried a hoard of small coin about his person. He grudgingly counted out a few coins, and then, with one of his sudden changes of temper, dropped into her hands all the contents of his pockets, saying it was no longer worth his pains to count them. Hardly had she passed them on to the Prince when a wild shriek startled them, followed by an agonized cry, "Lost! Lost!" The sexton had handed his talisman, the gold coin, to her, not perceiving it among the others. The grave he had dug for "Egerton" was now doomed to be his own. Marian tried in vain to calm him, saying that the Lord could still save him if he would turn to Him, but at last she left him, and went in search of Gilgal, who came and bade them leave him alone with the unhappy wretch. While the two were wrestling in prayer with the evil demon, the Prince and Marian returned to the inn. He now earnestly begged her to become his wife, but, though still ignorant of his real name, she told him that their stations were plainly too far apart, and that her own pride would never suffer her to marry one so far above her. Though it was plain that she returned his love, nothing would change her resolve. They were now joined by Gilgal, who told them that the long struggle was at an end. The sexton had freed his spirit from his tormentor, but in escaping he had surrendered it to

God, begging the minister to stay with him to the end, and had died a quiet and peaceful death. While they rejoiced for him, the minister added that he had also a message for Prince Rupert (calling him by his right name), for the spirit with which he had been wrestling had told him that if the Prince should marry, his son should inherit the kingdom. If not, his sister's son should beget a line of kings who should come to reign over the land. It was for Marian to choose—yet in saying this, Gilgal knew that the revelation he had made was from the devil; for if she wedded the Prince, she would betray the principles of those among whom she had lived, and who had brought her up. Without hesitation, she threw her arms round the old man's neck, and declared her loyalty to her faith. Yet she must procure the safety of the Prince and his companion; and this the minister declared she had earned by her constancy. He promised them his own safe-conduct, in return for their undertaking not to return to that place.

Thus it was that Prince Rupert rode south, to join the King at Oxford, and to help him retrieve his defeat at Newbury.

TYPE ML.8000. MOTIFS: R 200 [*Escapes and pursuits*]; D.1810.2 [*Magic knowledge from devil*].

¶ There are endless local traditions of Prince Rupert's escapes and adventures, many of them may be true, though most of them are unsubstantiated. The interesting part of this one is that it is interwoven with a supernatural belief about the dangers to the digger of an open grave.

See "The Open Grave" (B, XII).

IX LOCAL LEGENDS

LOCAL LEGENDS

Local Legends are of two main types, historical and supernatural.

(I)

Some of the local legends hover on the brink of being Historical Traditions. These might be headed *Local Traditions about Famous People*. An example is "How Littleport began", in which King Canute is the *deus ex machina*, but it is so obviously concerned with local interests that it should come among Local Legends.

Local Repercussions of History is another doubtful section, which rather depends on the stature of the actors. "The Mayor's Last Banquet" may be given as an example of these.

Local Worthies is a third division. These vary from people who are known to history, such as Sir William Pudsay, to legendary characters like Sir Bevis of Hampton and Sir Guy of Warwick, who have hardly a right to be included at all. There are, besides, worthies who are strictly local, famous in their own small place and unknown elsewhere.

There are also tales of individual tragedies that are more local than historical, such as "A Legend of Weem Castle".

The historical legends that are undoubtedly local are those concerning the origin of place-names—generally wildly erroneous, like "Osmotherly", those about the founding of families, and freakish land-tenures, and also those dealing with the origin of local rights and customs, like the Lady Godiva story. Legends of the founding of churches and abbeys and the building of castles sometimes introduce a supernatural element, but not always.

(II)

The local legends founded on supernatural beliefs are more variable than the matter-of-fact historical traditions, though actual happenings often form the preliminary to a haunting.

Among the most fascinating of these tales are variants of TYPE 766, "The Sleepers under the Hill". Often in Britain these are King Arthur and his Knights, but sometimes they are mysterious characters like the sleeper in "The Hunter and His Hounds", or anonymous, like those in "The Wizard of Alderley Edge". There are many tales of magical or curative wells, some connected with saints, some with fairies. There are tales of lakes and rivers, their origin and the spirits that haunt them. There are innumerable ghost stories, most of them, however, not in this section. There are places specially connected with witches and the devil. Among the most numerous are tales of standing stones, stone circles and barrows.

Traditions of buried treasure nearly always have some connection with the supernatural, if only in the tale of the revealing dream, best known as "The Pedlar of Swaffham". We have also tales of the treasure guardian, and of the supernatural disappearance when a tabu is broken. The same applies to church bells, which play a very special part in English folk-tradition. There are sinister but rather vague stories of bells that kill their man, or have a particular grudge against men of ill character.

It seems possible that Dorothy Sayers had such a tradition in mind when she wrote *The Nine Tailors*.

Tales are to be found, too, of shadows cast by tragedy, places where the grass will never grow. "The Brothers' Steps" is an example of these.

Certain places have the reputation of being particularly haunted— by ghosts, by witches and the devil. Because each of these has a section of its own, they are not so richly illustrated in this section.

There are also rumours of such supernatural creatures as the Dun Cow and the Monster Fish of Bomere Pool. We have besides, prodigies, prophecies and curses, so that it will be seen that supernatural beliefs hold an important place in local traditions.

A third, not very important, section might be called "Trivia", and contains such tales as "Ting, Tong, Pluff", but most of these have taken their place among the jocular tales as being frankly invented local libels.

It is clear that every place in England has its own traditions, and a good number of them, too. It is hoped that those assembled here are representative specimens.

THE ABBOT OF WHALLEY [summary]

J. Roby, *Lancashire Traditions*, I, p. 138.

John Paslew was the last Abbot of Whalley, and had ruled it for twenty years before the Dissolution took place. At the time of the Pilgrimage of Grace, he and his monks, though taking no open part in the rebellion, had repossessed themselves of their former dwelling.

About this time, when the rebel army was encamped at Doncaster, with the open support of the Archbishop of York and Lord D'Arcy, their hopes were high of forcing the king to restore the ancient religion, and having arranged a system of beacons, by which their forces could again be mustered, the troops were dispersed, while negotiations with the king were in progress.

One night Abbot Paslew was visited by two strangers, the leader of whom handed him an unsealed letter. This man was richly dressed, and carried a hooded falcon, but he declined to give his name. He was in fact a monk from Kirkstall, travelling in disguise, for it was unsafe for monks to be seen abroad at that time. His errand was to summon Paslew to declare openly for the rebel cause, but still the Abbot hung back, and the strangers had to go on their way uncertain where he stood. Leaving the Abbey, they climbed a steep hill, the Pendle, passing through thick forest, until they came to a rough hut in a clearing, where two of the Abbot's servants watching the beacon site challenged them. The guide who had brought them up from the Abbey vouched for them, and the second of the strangers, Ralph Newcome, who passed for the servant of the other, engaged the guards in conversation, while the other secretly lighted the beacon fire, which flared up, and was quickly acknowledged by the lighting of others on the surrounding heights. The stranger turned swiftly and plunged back through the darkness to return to the Abbey, where he confronted the Abbot with the fact that he would be known as the first mover in the rebellion, since his beacon had been the first to be lighted. There was now no hope for him from the king, and perforce he agreed to go with them to York, and throw in his lot with the rebels.

In the meantime Ralph Newcome, moving more slowly than his companion, had fallen into the hands of the two guards in the hut, and they now appeared, holding him prisoner, and without further inquiry, threw him into the dungeon, where he lay for a night and a day, stubbornly refusing to disclose his master's name, though the Abbot threatened him with torture. Only when he brought the torturers and their instruments into the cell did Ralph produce a parchment which gave him safe-conduct in all circumstances, as one charged with a secret message touching the success of the pilgrimage. It was signed by the Archbishop of York, and the reluctant Abbot dared not hesitate longer.

He accompanied Ralph to Doncaster, where they arrived on the evening of the day before that fixed by the rebels for their first general uprising. The Archbishop received him in audience, with the rebel leaders, Aske and Norton, seated on either side of him, and compelled Paslew to join in the toast wishing confusion to the heretic king.

That night there was a mighty storm, and the river around the town rose to a flood. This so terrified the troops that they would not stir from the town, and in the panic and turmoil Paslew succeeded in slipping away on foot. After ten days he regained his Abbey, footsore and exhausted. But the collapse of the rebellion brought his doom, in spite of this escape. By the king's orders, abbots and monks were dragged from the Abbey, convicted at Lancaster of high treason, and Paslew was hanged at the Abbey gate.

¶ The tragedies of the Pilgrimage of Grace held something the same place in the Northern traditions as Monmouth's Rebellion holds in Somerset, although they appear to be less present to popular memory. This story, though a good deal embellished, seems to be in the main true to history. It seems likely that John Paslew was a reluctant recruit to the insurgents. Thomas Holden, the last surviving monk of Whalley Abbey, died as a Protestant minister thirty-seven years after its dissolution.

THE BAREFOOT PILGRIMAGE:
DUNSTER COMMON

Ruth L. Tongue, *Somerset Folklore*, p. 201.

There was once a Lord of Dunster who was hard on his people and hated all churchmen. He had a lady who was as gentle as he was rough, and who was much beloved by the people. It happened one time that the Lord had the notion of enclosing Dunster Common for his own use. The poor of Dunster went to the monks about it and they went to the Lady. She was ill of fever at the time, but she got up and went to ask the Lord to change his mind. He was obdurate, but at last he said as a kind of joke that she could have as much of the Common for the poor as she could walk round barefoot on a winter's night. Ill as she was, the Lady set out that evening. The poor people, who loved her, begged her to stop and go home, but she limped on. At length they went to fetch the Lord, and he came to stop his Lady, but it was not yet dawn and the circle was not finished, so she went on until she fell fainting. The Lord carried her home in his arms, and the men of Dunster kept their Common.

MOTIF: H.1584.2 [*Land measured according to amount encompassed during certain hours*].
¶ This is the same theme as the Lady Godiva story.
See also "Lame Haverah" and "Crawls".

BARLINCH BELL

Ruth L. Tongue, *Somerset Folklore*, p. 18.

At Barlinch Priory they say there was a bell tower with several bells by which the Exmoor and Brendon folk ordered their remote lives and in which they took great pride. Then came the end of the Priory, and the bells were separated, and left their home of centuries. The Tenor Bell went to Dulverton, near its old home, and it still rings the sweetest note in the town, but Exeter Cathedral bought the Great Bell. It was loaded with immense difficulty behind a team of oxen and began its long journey into exile, and as the cart moved off it sent out one long, heart-breaking note so sweet and sad that Exmoor folk recall it with sorrow to this day. At last it arrived in Exeter, and with great excitement was placed in Exeter Cathedral. Crowds collected to hear the deep, sweet note so famous in West Somerset, but the Great Bell remained dumb. Silent it hung there, until one day an exasperated ringer gave it so lusty a strike that it spoke once more. So heavy and direful a note rolled from it that all the Devonshire cream in Exeter turned sour at the sound.

TYPE ML.7070. MOTIF: V.115 [*Church bells*].

¶ There are many bell-legends in England, many of them connected with sunken bells. There is a short but useful section on bells and bell-ringers in *Somerset Folk-lore*, pp. 17–20.

See "The Bells of Brinkburn", "The Bells of Forrabury Church".

BARNOLDSWICK AND KIRKSTALL ABBEYS

[summary]

Parkinson, *Yorkshire Legends and Traditions*, 1st series, p. 59.

Barnoldswick Abbey in Craven was an offshoot of Fountains—twelve monks from which were sent out in A.D. 1147 with ten lay brethren, under the Prior, Alexander.

The foundation of Barnoldswick had been laid by Henry de Lacy, Lord of Pontefract and of other great estates, both in Lancashire and Yorkshire. This Lord fell dangerously ill, and vowed, should he recover, to erect an abbey for monks of the Cistercian order, in honour of the Blessed Virgin Mary.

But at Barnoldswick both the climate and the neighbours proved unfavourable, and the monks began to look for more congenial surroundings. On one of his journeys, the Abbot came upon a small community of hermits, whose leader, Seleth, told him that they had come there in response to a dream in which he had heard a voice saying, "Arise, Seleth, go into the province of York, to a valley called Airedale, and a place called Kirkstall. There shalt thou provide a dwelling for me and my son." To his question, the voice replied, "I am Mary, and my son is Jesus of Nazareth."

Seleth had obeyed the vision, and for some time had lived at Kirkstall alone; afterwards a few monks of like spirit had joined him.

The Abbot of Barnoldswick hastened home and described to his patron, de Lacy, the advantages of removing to Kirkstall. Barnoldswick was abandoned, and Alexander became the first Abbot of Kirkstall, Seleth being incorporated into his brotherhood.

TYPE ML.7060 (variant). MOTIF: V.111.3 [*Place where a church must be built miraculously indicated*].

¶ This is a more prosaic version of the re-siting of a church or abbey than the common one in which the building materials are miraculously moved.

See "Winwick Church", "North Otterington Church", "The New Church at the Marske".

THE BATTLE OF VELLAN-DRUCHAR*

Hunt, *Popular Romances*, p. 305.

The Sea Kings, in their predatory wanderings, landed in Genvor Cove, and, as they had frequently done on previous occasions, they proceeded to pillage the little hamlet of Escols. On one occasion they landed in unusually large numbers, being resolved, as it appeared, to spoil many of the large and wealthy towns of Western Cornwall, which they were led to believe were unprotected. It fortunately happened that the heavy surf on the beach retarded their landing, so that the inhabitants had notice of their threatened invasion.

That night the beacon-fire was lit on the chapel hill; another was soon blazing on Castle-an-Dinas, and on Trecrobben. Carn Brea promptly replied, and continued the signal-light, which also blazed lustrously that night on St Agnes Beacon. Presently the fires were seen on Belovely Beacon, and rapidly they appeared on the Great Stone, on St Bellarmine's Tor, and Cadbarrow, and then the fires blazed out on Roughtor and Brownwilly, thus rapidly conveying the intelligence of war to Prince Arthur and his brave knights, who were happily assembled in full force at Tintagel to do honour to several native Princes who were at that time on a visit to the King of Cornwall. Arthur, and nine other kings, by forced marches, reached the neighbourhood of the Land's End at the end of two days. The Danes crossed the land down through the bottoms to the sea on the northern side of the promontory, spreading destruction in their paths. Arthur met them on their return, and gave them battle near Vellan-Druchar. So terrible was the slaughter that the mill was worked with blood that day. Not a single Dane of the vast army that had landed escaped. A few had been left in charge of the ships, and as soon as they learned the fate of their brothers, they hastened to escape, hoping to return to their own northern land. A holy woman, whose name has not been preserved to us, "brought home a west wind", by emptying the Holy Well against the hill, and sweeping the church from the door to the altar. Thus they were prevented from escaping, and were all thrown by the force of a storm and the currents either on the rocky shore, or on the sands, where they were left high and dry.

* *Vellan* = mill. *Druchar* = wheel.

It happened on the occasion of an extraordinary spring tide, which was yet increased by the wind, so that the ships lay high up on the rocks, or on the sands; and for years the birds built their nests in the masts and rigging.

Thus perished the last army of Danes who dared to land upon our western shores.

King Arthur and the nine kings pledged each other in the holy water from St Sennen's Well, they returned thanks for their victory in St Sennen's Chapel, and dined that day on the Table-men.

Merlin, the prophet, was among the host, and, the feast being ended, he was seized with the prophetic afflatus, and in the hearing of all the host proclaimed:

> " The northmen wild once more shall land,
> And leave their bones on Escol's sand.
> The soil of Vellan-Druchar's plain
> Again shall take a sanguine stain;
> And o'er the mill-wheel roll a flood
> Of Danish mix'd with Cornish blood.
> When thus the vanquish'd find no tomb,
> Expect the day of dreadful doom."

¶ Hunt marks his surprise that so few legends of King Arthur are to be found in Cornwall. In this one King Arthur is put considerably later than usual, and is fighting the Danes instead of the Saxons. The Danes are vividly remembered in the West of England, and particularly in Somerset. Scattered traditions of Arthur do remain in Cornwall, though not so many as Hunt expected. The Cornish chough is supposed to be a reincarnation of Arthur, and an old man of Pendean, quoted by Hunt, said: "The land swarmed with giants till Arthur, the good king, vanquished them all with his good sword."

Merlin's prophecies are given at length in Geoffrey of Monmouth, and became a feature of political propaganda. See Rupert Taylor, *Political Prophecy in England*.

See "The Youth without a Father" (B, III) and "A Prophecy of Merlin" (B, VIII).

THE BEASTS' THORN

Ruth L. Tongue, *Somerset Folklore*, pp. 29–30.

A pilgrim who went from Ilminster to Glastonbury was asked by the villagers to bring back some holy relic to bless the village. They were all much disappointed when he brought back a single thorn which might have been plucked from any hedge. He told them that it was part of the Crown of Thorns, but no one believed him. He planted it, however, and prayed beside it morning and evening. The strange thing about the thorn was that it began to shoot and grow at an uncanny rate, and people began to draw away from the pilgrim and look at him with suspicion. The thorn still grew, and by Christmas it was quite a little tree. The pilgrim promised that it would bloom on Christmas Day, but Christmas Day passed and nothing happened. But on Old Christmas Eve at night the whole village was wakened by a great clatter in the street. People threw on their clothes and ran to the windows, and there below them went all the sheep and cattle of the place, which had been securely shut in folds and bartons hours before. The richest farmer's master bullock was at the head of them. People tumbled out into the streets and followed their cattle. They went straight to the little thorn tree, which stood blossoming white in the moonshine. The pilgrim was kneeling there already. Just as the crowd came up the first stroke of midnight chime sounded. At that the great master bullock lowed aloud and knelt down on the frosty ground and every beast knelt with him. The stiff knees of the villagers were loosened and they knelt too, among the beasts. And that is how Ilminster knows that it has a holy thorn.

A homelier version of this was told to L. Key in Taunton in 1948. The old man who told it has since died. His experience could be dated about 1888–90:

"When I was a bwoy we did make up our minds to take a look-see on Chrissmus Eve to find if the tree did bloom and cows come to kneel to 'en. So we went along lane to Nailesbourne like, and 'twas dark, couldn't see nothing at all. Proper black, and we had no light, zee, and all to a zudden there was breathings all round us, zeemlike, whichever way we'd turn. Thic lane were vull of cattle, and we just turn and run for it. No, we never zee no thorn blossom nor I wouldn't go now if I was asked. Vull of cows thic lane was."

MOTIFS: F.971.5.2.1 [*Tree blossoms at midnight on Twelfth Night*]; B.251.1.2.3 [*Cows kneel in stable at midnight on Eve of Old Christmas*].
¶ See "The Apple-Tree Man", (A, II).

THE BELLS OF BRINKBURN

Denham Tracts, II, p. 132.

Centuries ago one of the priors of Brinkburn presented the bells of that building to the Priory of Durham. They had been the pride of the secluded sanctuary on the Coquet, for their tones were possessed of great power combined with sweetness, and many tempting offers had Durham made to secure them, but hitherto to no purpose. But she prevailed at length, and the bells so coveted were removed from the tower and dispatched on horseback on their way to Durham under the care of some monks. They journeyed till they reached the River Font, which, owing to a quantity of rain having fallen, was much swelled.

However, they prepared to ford it; but when the horses reached the middle of the stream the bells by some means fell, or, according to the popular belief, were removed from the backs of the horses by miraculous interposition, and sank to the bottom. Owing either to the dangerous state of the stream or from the bells being unwilling to be removed, the exertions of the monks to recover them proved unavailing; so they returned to Brinkburn and reported the disaster. But the Brinkburn prior, determined not to be baffled, sent forthwith a messenger to Durham to request the presence of his brother prior, and both ecclesiastics proceeded with a full attendance to liberate the imprisoned bells; and lo! the superior abilities of high church functionaries over humble monks was manifest to everyone; for they had no sooner ridden into the stream than the bells were lifted with ease; and being conveyed to Durham, were lodged there in safety. To this day it is a saying in Coquetdale that "Brinkburn bells are heard in Durham"; and Wallis, in his *History of Northumberland,* assures us that the bells of Brinkburn were removed to the Cathedral on the banks of the Wear. Still, there are doubters. Walter White in 1859 says "the deep pool where the bells were lost is still to be seen in the river" [Coquet]; and Mr Wilson is positive that some years ago "a fragment of the bell was found buried at the root of a tree on the hill on the opposite side of the river".

Of the bells, William Howitt, in his *Visit to Remarkable Places,* etc., p. 526, note, says: "The Bell Tower looks down upon the Bell Pool, a very deep part of the Coquet, lying concealed beneath the thick foliage of the native trees that jut out from the interstices of the lofty, craggy heights, impending over either side. Tradition says that into this pool the bells were thrown in a time of danger in order to place them beyond the reach of the invading Scots. It is still a favourite amusement among the young swimmers of the neighbourhood to dive for the bells of Brinkburn, and then it is generally believed that when the bells are found other treasures will be recovered with them".

TYPE ML.7070. MOTIFS: V.115.1 [*Church bells sunk in river*]; V.115.1.2 [*Raising sunken church bell*].

¶ See "The Bells of Forrabury Church", "Whitby Abbey Bells".

THE BELLS OF FORRABURY CHURCH

Hunt, *Popular Romances,* p. 438.

The inhabitants of the parish of Forrabury—which does not cover a square mile, but which now includes the chief part of the town of Boscastle and its harbour—resolved to have a peal of bells which should rival those of the neighbouring Church of Tintagel, which are said to have rung merrily at the marriage, and tolled solemnly at the death of Arthur.

The bells were cast; the bells were blessed; and the bells were shipped for Forrabury. Few voyages were more favourable; and the ship glided, with a fair wind, along the northern shores of Cornwall, waiting for the tide to carry her safely into the harbour of Bottreaux.

The vesper bells rang out at Tintagel; and the pilot, when he heard the blessed sound, devoutly crossed himself, and bending his knee, thanked God for the safe and quick voyage which they had made.

The captain laughed at the superstition of the pilot, as he called it, and swore that they had only to thank themselves for the speedy voyage, and that, with his arm at the helm, and his judgment to guide them, they should have a happy landing. The pilot checked this profane speech; but the wicked captain—and he swore more impiously than ever that all was due to himself and his men—laughed to scorn the pilot's prayer. "May God forgive you!" was the pilot's reply.

Those who are familiar with the northern shores of Cornwall will know that sometimes a huge wave, generated by some mysterious power in the wide Atlantic, will roll on, overpowering everything by its weight and force.

While yet the captain's oaths were heard, and while the inhabitants on the shore were looking out from the cliffs, expecting, within the hour, to see the vessel, charged with their bells, safe in their harbour, one of these vast swellings of the ocean was seen. Onward came the grand billow, in all the terror of its might. The ship rose not upon the waters as it came onward. She was overwhelmed, and sank in an instant. close to the land.

As the vessel sank, the bells were heard tolling with a muffled sound, as if ringing the death-knell of the ship and sailors, of whom the good pilot alone escaped with his life.

When storms are coming, and only then, the bells of Forrabury, with their dull, muffled sound, are heard from beneath the heaving sea, a warning to the wicked; and the tower has remained to this day silent.

TYPE ML.7070. MOTIFS: Q.221.4(*b*) [*Ship captain rebukes sailor who prays to God on the sea. He tells the sailor he must thank the ship and canvas on the sea. Ship sinks*] (Baughman); V.115.1.3.2 [*Church bells cannot be raised because person blasphemes*]; F.993 [*Sunken bell sounds*].

¶ See "Whitby Bells".

BESSIE BELL AND MARY GRAY

Scott, *Minstrelsy of the Scottish Border*, I, p. 26.

These two beautiful women were kinsfolk, and so strictly united in friendship that even personal jealousy could not interrupt their union. They were visited by a handsome and agreeable young man, who was acceptable to them both, but so captivated with their charms that, while confident of a preference on the part of both, he was unable to make a choice between them. While this singular situation of the three persons of the tale continued, the breaking out of the plague forced the two ladies to take refuge in the beautiful valley of Lynedoch, where they built themselves a bower, in order to avoid human intercourse and the danger of infection. The lover was not included in their renunciation of society. He visited their retirement, brought with him the fatal disease, and, unable to return to Perth, which was his usual residence, was nursed by the fair friends with all the tenderness of affection. They followed him to the grave, lovely in their lives and undivided in their death. Their burial-place, in the vicinity of the bower which they built, is still visible in the romantic vicinity of Lord Lyndoch's mansion, and prolongs the memory of female friendship which even rivalry could not dissolve. Two stanzas of the original ballad alone survive:

> Bessie Bell and Mary Gray,
>   They were twa bonnie lasses;
> They bigged a bower on yon burn brae,
>   And theekit it ower wi' rashes.
>
> They wadna rest in Methven Kirk,
>   Amang their gentle kin;
> But they wad lie in Lednoch braes
>   To beek against the sun.

There is to a Scottish ear so much tenderness and simplicity in these verses, as must induce us to regret that the rest should have been superseded by a pedantic modern song, turning upon the most unpoetic part of the legend, the hesitation, namely, of the lover, which of the ladies to prefer. One of the most touching expressions in the song is the following exclamation:

> "Oh, Jove! She's like thy Pallas."

TYPE ML.7080. MOTIF: T.92.1 [*The triangle plot and its solution*].

THE BEVERLEY BABE IN THE WOOD:
THE DISTRESSED CHILD IN THE WOOD
or THE CRUEL UNKLE

Gutch, *County Folk-Lore*, VI, p. 168.

Being a true and dismal Relation of one Esq. *Solmes* of *Beverly* in Yorkshire; who dying left an only Infant Daughter of the Age of two Years to the care of his own Brother; who with many Oaths, Vows and Protestations promised to be Loving to her; but the Father was no sooner Dead, but out of a wicked Covetousness of the Child's Estate of three hundred Pounds a Year carry'd it into a Wood, and there put it into a Hollow Tree to Starve it to Death: Where a Gentleman and his Man being a Hunting two Days after, found it half Famish'd, having gnawed its own Flesh and Fingers end in a dreadful manner.

With an Account how the Cruel Unkle to hide his Villany had caused the Childs Effigies to be buried in Wax, and made a great Funeral, as if it had been really Dead; With the manner of the whole discovery by a Dream, and taking the Wax Child out of the Grave; with the Unkles Apprehension, Examination, Confession before Justice *Stubbs* and his Commitment to Gaol, in order to be try'd the next Assizes, for that Barbarous Action. To which is added his Tryal, Examination, and Sentence before Judge *Powis* at *York* Assizes the 4th of March 1706.

London, Printed by J. Read, behind the *Green-dragon Tavern* in *Fleet Street*.

MOTIFS: S.71 [*Cruel uncle*]; S.143.1 [*Child abandoned in hollow tree*].
¶ See "The Babes in the Wood" (A, IV).

THE BISHOP'S BREAD AND CHEESE

J. R. W. Coxhead, *The Devil in Devon*, p. 31.

On the north-easterly slope of Amicombe Hill, overlooking the fine ravine of the West Okement River, in the north-western part of Dartmoor, are two places named respectively Slipper Stones and Branscombe's Loaf. Both these spots play a part in an amusing legend connected with Walter Bronescombe, who was Bishop of Exeter from 1258 to 1280.

One day, so the story goes, while the Bishop was on a visit to some parishes in the neighbourhood of Dartmoor, he decided to ride over the hills from Widecombe-in-the-Moor to the little village of Sourton.

The prelate and his retinue laboured through bogs, crossed rapidly flowing streams, and traversed wild, rock-strewn hillsides until they eventually reached the eastern side of Amicombe Hill. There they came to a place, opposite Black Tor, where their progress was barred by an area of extremely difficult ground, so the attendants dispersed in order to look for some way of passing the obstruction.

The bishop, overcome with fatigue and hunger, turned to his chaplain, who had remained at his side, and said, "Our Master in the wilderness was offered by Satan bread made of stones. If he were now to make the same offer to me, I doubt if I should have the Christian fortitude to refuse."

"Ah!" sighed the chaplain. "And how about a nice hunk of cheese as well?"

"Bread with some prime farm-house cheese I could not hold out against," replied the bishop.

The words were hardly out of his mouth when a moorman with a pack on his back emerged from a peat dyke, and trudged slowly towards them.

"Master!" called the chaplain. "Have you by any chance a snack of food with you?"

"Aye, for sure," replied the moorman as he hobbled up, for he was apparently lame. "I have in my wallet some bread and cheese, but naught else."

"Please give it to us, my son, and I will repay you well," said the famished prelate.

"Nay," replied the man. "I be no son of thine. And the only payment that I require is that you should alight from your fine steed, doff your hat, and salute me with the title of 'master'."

"That I will gladly do," said the bishop, and he immediately dismounted. Then the moorman, who was strangely dark and fierce of aspect, produced a crusty loaf and a large hunk of cheese.

The bishop was just about to remove his hat and address the man in a tone of entreaty and by the title of "master" when the chaplain noticed that the swarthy stranger possessed one cloven hoof very similar to that of a goat. He instantly cried out to God for protection, and drew the bishop's attention to the foot in question.

Alarmed and horrified at the sight, the worthy prelate quickly made the sign of the Cross, and the dark stranger, his eyes flashing fire, glared for a moment with suppressed rage, and then, without a sound, he suddenly vanished, leaving behind the bread and cheese transformed into stone.

In order to make atonement for having so very nearly yielded to temptation the bishop commenced to rebuild Exeter Cathedral about the year 1275, spending great sums of money upon the project until his death in 1280.

The Slipper Stones are supposed to be so named because it was there that the good prelate lost one of his shoes shortly before his meeting with the Evil One.

Walter Bronescombe was a member of a very distinguished family who produced three sheriffs of the county, and owned, until the fourteenth century, an estate called Edge, in the parish of Branscombe in East Devon. He was one of the greatest of Exeter's medieval bishops, and lies buried beneath a magnificent, canopied tomb situated in the interval between the Lady Chapel and the little chapel in the south-east corner of the beautiful Cathedral he helped to rebuild.

From *A Book of Dartmoor*, S. Baring-Gould.
MOTIFS: G.303.9.4.4 [*Devil tempts cleric*]; G.303.3.1.10 [*Devil as a peasant*]; G.303.4.5.4.1 [*Devil is betrayed by his goat-hoofs*]; A.977.4 [*Devil turns object to stone*].
¶ See B, III for many stories similar to this.

BLADUD OF BATH

Ruth L. Tongue, *Somerset Folklore*, p. 199.

Prince Bladud was the eldest son of King Lud of Britain. He was greatly beloved and so wise that all men looked to him to reign gloriously when his turn came. Wishing to gain greater knowledge, he travelled to Greece and spent many years there.

The day came when he turned from Athens to Britain and was welcomed joyfully—when alas! a fearful tragedy occurred. He found he was a *leper*!

With all haste, he journeyed away from men and their kindness—only living on such food as was left by the wayside for such as he. At last he came to Swainswick, where a farmer allowed him to herd his hogs and live afield with them.

Bladud was thankful to feel that there was still something a poor outcast could do, and under his care the swine began to thrive. But when the winter came some of them became restless and sick, their skins cracked and chapped and Bladud could find no herbs to ease them. Suddenly the herd began to move purposefully down the hillside to the marsh where faint steam arose, and by the time Bladud had caught up with them they were wallowing happily in slime and warm mud.

Yes, it was warm—for Bladud waded into it to drive out the herd.

The next day they came back again; the coats of the sick pigs shone with health, and Bladud, looking upon his own feet and hands, found them healed. Filled with joy, he too bathed in the hot springs and was cured of his leprosy.

He returned, a healthy man, to his father's court amid great jubilations, and when he became King of Britain he built a city by the springs that cured him. It was a sign of his gratitude and his thought for the sick among his people. (Oral tradition, 1912).

Hogs Norton. Norton Malreward.

When Prince Bladud became King of Britain he sent for a Somerset farmer. This was the old man who in charity had given him charge over his swine when all men shunned him because he was a leper. Now that Bladud had built the city of Bath to cure the sick, meat and fruit were wanted from the countryside daily. In gratitude, King Bladud made the old farmer lord of a village, which the country people promptly called Hogs Norton.

Later on, when the Normans came everyone was still agreed that a whole village wasn't a bad reward—and since that time it has been called Norton Malreward. (Oral tradition, Bath and Clifton.)

Norton Malreward should be Malregard from the Norman lord who had an "evil eye".

MOTIFS: L.112.7.1 [*Leper hero*]; D.150C.1.1 [*Magic healing fountain*]; B.414 [*Helpful hogs*]; A.1617 [*Origins of place-names*].

THE BOAR OF ESKDALESIDE

Parkinson, *Yorkshire Legends and Traditions*, 1st series, p. 27.

On the 16th day of October, in the fifth year of Henry the Second, the lords of Ugglebarnby and Sneaton, accompanied by a principal free-holder, with their hounds, staves, and followers, went to chase the wild boar, in the woods of Eskdaleside, which appertained to the Abbot of Whitby. They found a large boar, which on being sore wounded and dead run, took in at the hermitage of Eskdale, where a hermit, a monk of Whitby, was at his devotions, and there the exhausted animal lay down. The hermit closed the door of the cell, and continued his meditations, the hounds standing at bay without. The hunters, being thrown behind their game in the thick of the forest, followed the cry of the hounds, and at length came to the hermitage. On the monk being roused from his orisons by the noise of the hunters, he opened the door, and came forth. The boar had died within the hermitage, and because the hounds were put from their game, the hunters violently and cruelly ran at the hermit with their boar-staves, and of the wounds which they inflicted he subsequently died. The gentlemen took sanctuary in a privileged place at Scarborough, out of which the abbot had them removed, so that they were in danger of being punished with death. The hermit being a holy man, and at the last extremity, required the abbot to send for those who had wounded him; and, upon their drawing near, he said, "I am sure to die of these wounds." The abbot answered, "They shall die for thee." The devout hermit replied, "Not so, for I freely forgive them my death, if they be content to be enjoined to a penance for the safeguard of their souls." The gentlemen bade him enjoin what he would, so he saved their lives. The hermit then enjoined that they and theirs should for ever after hold their lands of the abbot of Whitby and his successors, on this condition, that upon Ascension Eve they, or some for them, should come to the wood of the Strayhead, which is in Eskdaleside, the same day at sun-rising, and there the officer of the abbot should blow his horn, that they might know where to find him, who should deliver to them *ten stakes, ten strout-stowers,* and ten *yedders,* to be cut with a knife of a penny price, which were to be taken on their backs to Whitby, before nine of the clock on that day; and at the hour of nine o'clock, as long as it should be low water (if it be full sea the service to cease) each of them to set their stakes at the brim of the water, a yard from one another, and so make a hedge with the stakes, stowers, and yedders, that it stand three tides without being removed by the force of the water. And the officer of Eskdaleside shall blow his horn, "Out on you! Out on you! Out on you!" Should the service be refused, so long as it is not full sea at the hour fixed, all their lands should be forfeited. Then the hermit said, "My soul longeth for the Lord, and I do freely forgive these gentlemen my death as Christ forgave the thief upon the Cross." And in the presence of the abbot and the rest, he said, "*In manus tuas, Domine, commendo spiritum meum: a vinculis enim mortis redemisti me, Domine veritatis. Amen.*" And then he yielded up the ghost on the 18th December.

The Gentlemen's Magazine Library, 1885, ed. G. L. Gomme, p. 117.

MOTIF: Q.520.1 [*Murderers do penance*].

¶ This is the explanation of a custom which was still observed in Whitby in 1888.

BOLTON PRIORY AND THE
BOY OF EGREMOND [summary]

Parkinson, *Yorkshire Legends and Traditions,* 1st series, p. 41.

In the year 1251 the Lady of Craven was Adeliza, widow of William FitzDuncan, who was a nephew of King David of Scotland. Her only surviving child, a son, was out with a companion on a hunting expedition, and came to the spot on the River Wharfe known as the Strid. Through this cleft, so narrow that it seems possible to cross it in one stride, the water rushes with terrible force, and the young man, known as the "Boy of Egremond", attempted to step over it with a hound in leash. Suddenly the hound hung back and dragged his master into the water, where he, like many others, was swept to his death. A terrified forester bore the news to his mother, who, learning that she, the heiress of the de Romilles, whose ancestor had been a friend of William the Conqueror, was now childless, devoted the rest of her life to works of piety. Amongst these, she removed her ancestor's foundations of Embsay to the nearest possible spot to the fatal Strid, increasing its endowments, until by degrees it became the great Priory of Bolton.

One tradition says that the lady Adeliza's spirit continued to haunt the spot in the form of a white doe, which every week came over from Rylstone, but in Wordsworth's poem another story of the White Doe is recorded.

¶ Most of the church-building legends follow the lines of ML.7060 (The disputed site for a church).

This story is a straightforward account of a memorial building, too simple to have earned a motif. See "Wroxall Abbey".

BOMERE POOL

C. Hole, *English Folk-Lore*, p. 104.

When Uriconium was a flourishing town, there was another city at Bomere, the inhabitants of which reverted to paganism. A Roman soldier tried to reconvert them, but none would listen to him except his betrothed, the Governor's daughter. On Easter Eve a flood overwhelmed the city, and only the soldier was saved. He sought desperately for his betrothed, but without success, and eventually his boat overturned and he, too was drowned. Whenever Easter Eve falls on the same date as it did that year, tradition says that the soldier's ghost is seen rowing over the lake, and the church bells are heard ringing in the drowned city. Another version of the legend puts the flood in Saxon times. The people of the lakeside village of those days turned back to Thor and Woden and mocked the Christian priest. After a season of heavy rains, he noticed the barrier which held back the mere was giving way. He urged the local men to strengthen it, but they were carousing at the heathen Yule-tide festival and would not listen. As he was saying Midnight Mass on Christmas Eve, the water burst into the church, putting out the altar lights and destroying the entire village as it rushed down the hill. Those who sail on Bomere on the anniversary of the flood are said to hear the Sanctus bell ringing under the water.

MOTIFS: A.920.1.8 [*Lake bursts forth to drown impious people*]; F.993 [*Sunken bell sounds*].

¶ Most of the lake-origin tales are versions of the Philemon and Baucis story, in which the hospitable house is the only one saved. In this story the good suffers with the wicked. See "Simmerwater".

BONE-MEAL IN THE FLOUR

W. H. Barrett, *More Tales from the Fens*, p. 9.

You all know that the old churchyard at Southery is so high that it makes the church look as if it was built in a hole. Well, that's because so many folk have been buried one on top of the other, that the church doorstep is six feet lower than the topmost body, and it's been like that for years and years. Now, my grandfather, who was a miller like me, told me that when he was a boy there used to be a mill standing close by the churchyard wall, and it stood there in the days when only those who'd got a few gold coins put by were allowed to be buried in the churchyard. Poor folk, and there were a lot of them, were thrown into a pit near the mill, and when one pit was full another was dug, so, in time, the poor's piece was raised as high as where the mill stood. The mill, at the time I'm telling you about, belonged to the Bishop of Ely, and the miller had to pay a rent of twelve sacks of flour a year to the Bishop, who ate so much bread that he was as round as he was high; and so was the Southery parson, who got three sacks of free flour a year.

One day, the parson, who was a very great crony of the Bishop because they'd been to the same school together, came and told the miller that there was a war on with Spain and as soon as it was dark, he was to go up to the top of the mill, and look to see if there was a light shining from Ely Tower; if there was then he was to hurry down and run to tell the parson. Well, the miller kept a look-out for several nights and then, one night, he did see a light shining out of Ely way. He ran over to the parson's house, and found him and his wife, with their money-bags, getting ready to do a moonlight flit because they'd already seen the light from their bedroom window. The parson was back next day, because the light had only been someone's thatch afire, and he brought a message from the Bishop that the miller's last quarter of rent was overdue. Now the miller only had two sacks of corn in his mill, so he wondered how in the world he was going to be able to send three to Ely. It just so happened, though, that the parson had had a barge load of chalk sent over from Brandon, which he was going to burn into lime to mend the flint walls of the church.

That night, when everything was quiet, the miller wheeled a couple of barrow loads of this chalk into the mill, set his sails into the wind and started grinding. Next day the Bishop's rent was ready and there was a sack of flour for Parson, too, as a bit off the rent that was owing to him. The only thing that happened was that a lot of stewed rhubarb was needed in the Bishop's palace and the parsonage after the bread made from this wheat and chalk flour had all been eaten. And once the chalk had found its way into the mill it went on doing so, and folks who could pay for it were able to have some white bread.

A good many years after this there was another war, this time with France, and my grandfather, who worked the mill then, had to climb up to the top of it every night to see if there was a light in Ely Tower. One day, as he was standing by the mill door a stranger rode up on horseback; Grandfather recognized him as a chap who'd been riding all over the Fens buying up hay, which he sold to the Government in London for twice the price he gave for it. He asked Grandfather why the mill wasn't working.

"There's nothing to grind," said Grandfather, "farmers won't sell their corn."

"They would if you hit a high enough price," said the chap. "But what's under that big mound over there?"

"Bones," said Grandfather. "It's the Poor's Piece; the poor have to be buried there as there's no room for them in the churchyard."

"Who does the mill belong to?" asked the man. "I want to buy it, bones and all."

When he heard that it belonged to the Bishop, he hurried off to Ely to see him, but the Bishop wouldn't sell.

Now, out in Sedge Fen, there was a knacker's yard and for over a hundred years dead horses and cattle had been boiled down for cart grease. This sold well in the towns, and so did the hides and the skins, but the bones weren't worth carting away, so they'd been thrown into a huge heap till there was tons and tons of them lying there. Well, believe it or not, that chap bought the knacker out, built a mill with a twin set of stones, and put in a bone-crushing machine worked from the shaft pulley of the mill.

The barns on all the farms round about, Grandfather used to say, were full of corn, but, though wheat was selling at three pounds a sack, the farmers were holding on, hoping to get ten shillings more. That chap paid the price they asked and soon his mill was working away day and night, if there was wind enough. Once a week he had a load of lime delivered and he used this to bleach the bones white, and after these had gone through the crusher a bushel of them was put through the hopper with every bushel of corn. He sold all his flour to the Government to feed the soldiers and sailors, and he got twice as much for the flour as the corn had cost, so the bones and lime were all profit.

The farmers round about here were so pleased at getting such a good price for their corn that they asked the parson to hold a special service in the church; farmers came from miles away, and made so much noise singing that it was a week before the jackdaws could get back into the belfry.

When the war was over that bone-miller was a very rich man, but he didn't last long, because the lime settled on his chest. He was taken a long way away to be buried, as he'd said before he died that he didn't want to be put on top of a lot of other folk in Southery churchyard, but Grandfather and the other Southery people used to say it was because he didn't want to have his bones laid too close to the flour mill in case there was another war.

MOTIFS: K.149 [*Sale of worthless objects*]; K.486 [*Cheating miller*].
¶ Millers have always had a reputation for hard-dealing and dishonesty, as in the folk-song, "The Miller's Four Sons". This tale carries the tradition from the sixteenth to the nineteenth century. It is in the Fenmen's macabre style.

BOW BRIDGE

J. R. W. Coxhead, *Legends of Devon*, p. 119.

At the western border of Axminster the main road to Honiton passes out of the town and crosses the River Axe near the railway station at Bow Bridge. The name of this bridge was originally Stoford Bridge, and there is an extraordinary legend attached to it, which gives a grim reason for the change of name.

Long ago, there lived at the village of Kilmington a certain quack doctor named Bow. He had discovered a miraculous antidote for the poisonous bite of the viper, which never failed.

In olden times adders were far more numerous in the countryside than they are today, because such large areas of land were wild and uncultivated, and thus afforded the secluded and undisturbed existence so much loved by this beautiful, although poisonous, snake.

Many people used to be bitten by adders (more often than they are today), so that a cure for the poison injected by their fangs would have been very eagerly sought by the countryfolk of long ago.

In order to proclaim his skill as a doctor and to increase the sales of his various medicines, Bow adopted a method which both terrified his audience and also impressed them with his powers as a healer.

At fairs and markets he used to stand on a platform, allowing himself to be bitten repeatedly by irate adders, and having been bitten enough for his fate to be apparently sealed, he would produce his wonderful antidote.

The crowd, naturally thinking that he would die in agony in front of their eyes, were amazed to see that after the application of the remedy the wonderful man came to no harm.

Bow's fame spread far and wide until, on one fateful day, disaster overtook him. On that day there was a fair at Axminster, and the famous quack doctor was going through his thrilling ordeal. He had been severely bitten by several vipers on the neck and arms but, unbeknown to him, a pickpocket had removed the jar of antidote from his pocket.

Not being able to find his precious remedy, the poor man at once realized that he was doomed to die an awful death unless he could reach his home at Kilmington, a mile and a half away, where he had a further supply of the antidote.

Uttering piercing shrieks, he leapt from the platform, burst through the astonished crowd of spectators, and ran as fast as he could in the direction of his home.

The poison, however, was rapidly doing its deadly work; when he reached the bridge over the Axe which was formerly called Stoford Bridge, he fell to the ground in a delirious state and was very soon dead.

Ever after this terrible tragedy the bridge had been called "Bow Bridge".

MOTIFS: D.1515.4 [*Antidote for snakebite*]; D.861 [*Magic object stolen*]; D.860.0.1 [*Death to follow loss of magic object*].

¶ This unfortunate man seems to have been not so much a quack as an empiric, for his remedy worked, and he was really bitten by the snakes.

THE BRAVE MAID-SERVANT

E. G. Bales, *Folk-Lore*, I, March 1939, p. 74.

The master and mistress of a house went out and left the servant-girl behind to look after the house. She heard a knock on the door; the girl opened it and found a woman there who asked to come in. It was pouring with rain. The girl said she could not let her in as her master and mistress were out. However, she did eventually let her in. The stranger went and sat in a chair near the fire, and soon the girl noticed that this stranger was a man. She thought she would find out. To do so she offered "her" an apple, but, instead of giving it to her, she copped it to her. The stranger brought his legs together quickly. The girl's suspicions were now confirmed, as she knew that if the stranger had been a woman she would unconsciously have opened her legs, as if to catch the apple in her lap. After some time the stranger fell asleep with his mouth open.

The girl was cooking a joint for her master and mistress when they came home. Seeing the stranger had fallen asleep, she poured boiling fat down his throat and killed him. When the master learnt what had happened, he rewarded the girl by keeping her without her being obliged to work.

¶ This story was told to Mr R. Crawford by Mr F. Buck, who said that it was true and that it took place near King's Lynn; he did not know when.

TYPE 956B (variant). MOTIFS: K.1836 [*Disguise of man in women's dress*]; H.1578 [*Test of sex*]; K.955.1 [*Murder by scalding*].

¶ See "The Cook at Combwell", "The Servant-Maid at High Spital", "The Housekeeper and the Robber" (A, IV).

THE BROTHERS' STEPS

Gentleman's Magazine Library, "English Traditional Lore", p. 121. (1804, Part II, 1194).

I send you for insertion a copy of an old letter in my possession, respecting "The Brothers' Steps". If any correspondent can give any farther account of them, it will be esteemed as a favour.

Wm. Herbert.

To Mr John Warner, near Holborn Bridge, London.

July 17 1778

My Dear Friend,

According to your request I shall give you all the particulars I have been able to collect concerning the Brothers' Steps. They are situate in the field about half a mile from Montague House, in a north direction; and the prevailing tradition concerning them is, that two brothers quarrelled about a worthless woman, and as it was the fashion of those days, as it is now, they decided it by a duel. The print of their feet is near three inches in depth, and remains totally barren; so much so that nothing will grow to disfigure them. Their number I did not reckon, but suppose they may be about ninety. A bank on which the first fell, who was mortally wounded and died on the spot, retains the form of his agonising posture by the curse of barrenness, while the grass grows round it. A friend of mine showed me these steps in the year 1760, when he could trace them back by old people to the year 1686; but it was generally supposed to have happened in the early part of the reign of Charles II. There are people now living who well remember their being ploughed up, and barley sown, to deface them; but all was labour in vain; for the prints returned in a short time to their original form. There is one thing I nearly forgot to mention; that a place on the bank is still to be seen, where, tradition says, the wretched woman sat to see the combat. I am sorry to say I can throw no more light on the subject; but am convinced in my own opinion that the Almighty has ordered it as a standing monument of His just displeasure of the horrid sin of duelling.

Thos Smith.

Since the above was written, they have been enclosed from public view, or nearly built over.

Wm. Herbert.

MOTIF: F.974 [*Grass refuses to grow on certain spot: extraordinary event has happened there*].

THE BUILDING OF ST CHADS, ROCHDALE

Harland and Wilkinson, *Legends and Traditions of Lancashire*, p. 52.

Towards the close of the reign of William the Conqueror, Gamel, the Saxon thane, Lord of Recedham, or Rochdale, being left in the quiet possession of his lands and privileges, was "minded for the fear of God and the salvation of his immortal soul, to build a chapel unto St Chadde", nigh to the banks of the Rache or Roach. According to Mr Roby in his *Traditions*, a place was set apart on the north bank of the river, in a low and sheltered spot now called "The Newgate". Piles of timber and huge stones were gathered in profusion; the foundations were laid; stakes having been driven, and several courses of rubble stone laid ready to receive the grouting or cement. In one night the whole mass was conveyed, without the loss of a single stone, to the summit of a steep hill on the opposite bank, and apparently without any visible signs of the mode of removal.

The Saxon thane was greatly incensed at what he supposed to be a trick of some of his own vassals, and threatened punishment; to obviate which, a number of the villeins and *bordarii*, with great difficulty and labour, conveyed the building materials back to the site for the church; but again were they all removed in the night to the top of the hill. Gamel having learned the truth, sought counsel from Holy Church, and it was thereon resolved that the chapel should be built on the hill-top, as the unknown persons would not permit it to be erected on the site originally selected. This explains the chapel or church of St Chadde, still standing on a hill so high that one hundred and twenty-four steps were cut to accomplish the ascent, and enable the good people to go to prayers. Such are the outlines of the tradition as dramatically told by Roby in his popular work under the title of "The Goblin Builders". We find no vestige of the tradition in Baines's *Lancashire* or Dr Whitaker's *Whalley*. There is a belief and a saying in Rochdale, which Roby connects with

173

his tradition, but which seems to have no natural relation to it, that "in Rochdale strangers prosper and natives fail".

TYPE ML.7060 MOTIFS: V.111.3 [*Site where a church must be built miraculously indicated*]; F.531.6.6.1 [*Giants by night move building built by men in day*].
¶ See "North Otteringham Church".

BULL-DOG BRIDGE

Burnt Fen. Collected by Miss Porter from W. H. Barrett.

This is a tale of the old days, when the Friars used to go along the Friars' Way, begging and bullying among the scattered houses. It happened in late autumn, when the sheep and lambs were killed and smoked, that the Lady of the Manor of Littleport sent one of her maids to gather mint for the curing. The maid filled her basket, and made her way back to the track, but she grew drowsy on the way home, and fell asleep.

She woke to find a Friar stripping back her clothes, and preparing to have his way with her. She shrieked in despair, "Holy Mother, have mercy on me!" At once a great dog leapt out from the long grasses, and made for the Friar. He stuck his knife into it, but it tore him to pieces, then it came up to the girl, licked her hand, and died. When the girl struggled home and told her story, they threw what was left of the Monk into the Red Mere, which has stinked ever since, but the dog they buried near White Horse Drain, and many have claimed to see it as they crossed Bull-Dog Bridge.

MOTIFS: V.465.1.1 [*Incontinent monk*]; B.421 [*Helpful dog*]; B.339 [*Death of helpful animal*]; E.521.2 [*Ghost of dog*].
¶ Friars, priests and monks nearly always seem to be evil characters in these Fenland traditions; they are much more kindly thought of in the West Country.
See "The Nun's Ring", "How Littleport Began".

BULSTRODE

H. Bett, *English Legends*, p. 102.

When William the Conqueror came over, he allocated the manor of the Shobbington family in Buckinghamshire to one of his retainers, who came with a retinue of armed men to take possession. The Saxon owner entrenched himself behind an earthwork, which still exists in the park, and resisted stoutly. Then, as he had no horses, he mounted his liegemen upon bulls, and sallied out upon the Normans. The King heard of the affray, and sent for the valiant thane, with a promise of safe-conduct. The Saxon went to the Conqueror, accompanied by his seven sons, all mounted upon bulls. The result was that he kept his manor, and assumed a bull's head as his crest, along with the name of Bulstrode.

MOTIF: B.557 [*Unusual animal as riding-horse*].

CALLALY CASTLE

Denham Tracts, I, pp. 323–4.

> "Callaly castle stands on a height,
> Up in the day and down in the night,
> Set it up on the Shepherd's Shaw,
> There it will stand, and never fa'."

Like many other ancient structures Callaly Castle was not built without the manifestation of supernatural agency. It was originally designed to erect it on a hill, not far from that on which the present castle stands, but the interposition of an invisible agent compelled the builders to adopt a new site. At the first commencement of the building, the work done during the day was in unaccountable manner levelled with the ground during the night. To discover the reason of this mysterious interruption a watch was set, which remained till midnight without witnessing any symptoms of injury or hostility to the work; suddenly, however, a strange commotion was perceived to have commenced among the closely compacted materials. Each individual stone gradually rose upon its end and fell noiselessly to the ground. No agency was discernible; but the process of demolition gradually proceeded till the whole masonry was once more reduced to a ruinous heap, and then a loud voice giving utterance to the above prophetic rhyme was heard issuing from the midst of the ruins. The site was forthwith abandoned, and, the work being recommenced on the spot pointed out, Callaly Castle in due season became proud in the grandeur of her stern battlements and defended with the valiant arm of a warlike race bade, during a lengthened period, defiance to both foe and time.

CALLALY CASTLE [2nd version]

From Mr George Tate, F.G.S., "Whittingham Vale", *Alnwick Mercury*, 1862.

A lord of Callaly, in the days of yore, commenced erecting a castle on the hill; his lady preferred a low, sheltered situation in the vale. She remonstrated; but her lord was wilful, and the building continued to progress. What she could not achieve by persuasion, she sought to obtain by stratagem, and availed herself of the superstitious opinions and feelings of the age. One of her servants, who was devoted to her interests, entered into her scheme; he was dressed up like a boar, and nightly he ascended the hill and pulled down all that had been built during the day. It was soon whispered that the spiritual powers were opposed to the erection of a castle on the hill; the lord himself became alarmed, and he sent some of his retainers to watch the building during the night and discover the cause of the destruction. Under the influence of the superstitions of the times, those retainers magnified appearances, and when the boar issued from the wood and commenced overthrowing the work of the day, they beheld a monstrous animal of enormous power. Their terror was complete when the boar, standing among the over-turned stones, cried out in a loud voice:

> "Callaly Castle built on the height,
> Up in the day and down in the night,
> Builded down in the Shepherd's Shaw,
> It shall stand for aye, and never fa'."

They immediately fled and informed the lord of the supernatural visitation, and, regarding the rhyme as an expression of the will of heaven, he abandoned the work, and, in accordance with the wish of his lady, built his castle low down in the vale, where the modern mission now stands.

J. H.

TYPE ML.7060. MOTIF: F.531.6.6.1 [*Giants by night move building built by men by day*]; SECOND VERSION MOTIF: K.0 [*Contest won by deception*].

¶ Here are two examples of the often-repeated resited castle; or, rather, the same story with two explanations.

See "The Castle of Melgund", "Garmstone Castle".

CANOBIE DICK AND
THOMAS OF ERCILDOUN

Gibbings, *Folk-Lore and Legends, Scotland*, p. 1.

Now it chanced many years since that there lived on the Borders a jolly rattling horse-cowper, who was remarkable for a reckless and fearless temper, which made him much admired, and a little dreaded amongst his neighbours. One moonlight night as he rode over Bowden Moor on the west side of the Eildon Hills, the scene of Thomas the Rhymer's prophecies, and often mentioned in his history, having a brace of horses along with him, which he had not been able to dispose of, he met a man of venerable appearance, and singularly antique dress, who, to his great surprise, asked the price of his horses and began to chaffer with him on the subject. To Canobie Dick, for so we shall call our Border dealer, a chap was a chap, and he would have sold a horse to the Devil himself, without minding his cloven hoof, and would have probably cheated Old Nick into the bargain. The stranger paid the price they agreed on, and all that puzzled Dick in the transaction was that the gold which he received was in unicorns, bonnet-pieces and other ancient coins, which would have been invaluable to collectors, but were rather troublesome in modern currency.

It was gold, however, and therefore Dick contrived to get better value for the coin than he perhaps gave to his customer. By the command of so good a merchant, he brought horses to the same spot more than once, the purchaser only stipulating that he should always come by night and alone. I do not know whether it was from mere curiosity, or whether some hope of gain mixed with it, but after Dick had sold several horses in this way, he began to complain that dry bargains were unlucky, and to hint, that since his chap must live in the neighbourhood, he ought, in the courtesy of dealing, to treat him to half a mutchkin.

"You may see my dwelling if you will," said the stranger; "but if you lose courage at what you see there, you will rue it all your life."

Dickon, however, laughed the warning to scorn, and, having alighted to secure his horse, he followed the stranger up a narrow footpath, which led them up the hills to the singular eminence stuck between the most southern and the central peaks, and called, from its resemblance to such an animal in its form, the Lucken Hare. At the foot of this eminence, which is almost as famous for witch-meetings as the neighbouring windmill of Kippilaw, Dick was somewhat startled to observe that his conductor entered the hillside by a passage or cavern of which he himself, though well acquainted with the spot, had never seen or heard.

"You may still return," said his guide, looking ominously back upon him; but Dick scorned to show the white feather and on they went. They entered a very long range of stables; in every stall stood a coal-black horse; by every horse lay a knight in coal-black armour, with a drawn sword in his hand; but all were as silent, hoof and limb, as if they had been cut out of marble. A great number of torches lent a gloomy lustre to the hall, which, like those of the Caliph Vathek, was of large dimensions. At the upper end, however, they at length arrived, where a sword and horn lay on an antique table.

"He that shall sound that horn, and draw that sword," said the stranger, who now intimated that he was the famous Thomas of Ercildoun, "shall, if his heart fail him not, be king over all broad Britain. So speaks the tongue that cannot lie.

"But all depends on courage, and much on your taking the sword or horn first."

Dick was much disposed to take the sword, but his bold spirit was quailed by the supernatural terrors of the hall, and he thought to unsheath the sword first might be construed into defiance, and give offence to the powers of the mountain.

He took the bugle with a trembling hand, and blew a feeble note, but loud enough to produce a terrible answer. Thunder rolled in stunning peals through the immense hall; horses and men started to life; the steeds snorted, stamped, ground their bits and tossed their heads; the warriors sprang to their feet, clashed their armour, and brandished their swords. Dick's terror was extreme at seeing the whole army, which had been so lately silent as the grave, in uproar, and about to rush on him. He dropped the horn, and made a feeble attempt to seize the enchanted sword; but at the same moment a voice pronounced aloud the mysterious words:

"Woe to the coward, that ever he was born,
Who did not draw the sword before he blew the horn!"

At the same time a whirlwind of irresistible fury howled through the long hall, bore the unfortunate horse-jockey clear out of the mouth of the cavern, and precipitated him over a steep bank of loose stones, where the shepherds found him the next morning, with just breath sufficient to tell his fearful tale, after concluding which he expired.

TYPE 766. MOTIFS: F.721.2 [*Habitable Hill*]; E.502 [*The Sleeping Army*]; D.1960.2.2 [*Man gains entrance into cavern, etc.*] (Baughman).

¶ In this version of the Sleeping Army there is no King; but the tabu about touching the sword and horn in the wrong order still holds. Here Thomas of Ercildoun takes the place of Merlin.

See "The Wizard of Alderley Edge", "Potter Thompson", "King Arthur at Sewingshields".

THE CASTLE OF MELGUND

Chambers, *Popular Rhymes of Scotland*, p. 337.

Melgund [is] in Forfarshire, the ancient and now ruined seat of a branch of the family of Maule. The situation of this building is remarkably low, and perhaps it is to this circumstance, setting the wits of the vulgar to account for it, that we are to ascribe the existence of the legend. It is said that the site originally chosen was a spot upon a neighbouring hill, but that, as the work was proceeding there, the labours of the builders were regularly undone every night, till at length, on a watch being set, a voice was heard to exclaim:

"Big it in a bog,
   Where 'twill neither shake nor shog."

The order was obeyed; and behold the castle standing in the morass accordingly! It is, of course, easy to conceive reasons in human prudence for adopting this situation, as being the more defensible.

TYPE ML.7060 MOTIF: D.2192 [*Work of day magically overthrown at night*].
¶ See "Callaly Castle".

THE CHURCH OF FORDOUN

Chambers, *Popular Rhymes of Scotland*, p. 337.

...the church of Fordoun [is] in Kincardineshire. The recently existing structure was of great antiquity, though not perhaps what the monks represented it—namely, the chapel of Palladius, the early Christian missionary. The country-people say that the site originally chosen for the building was the top of the Knock Hill, about a mile north-east from the village. After, as in the former case, the walls had been for some time regularly undone every night by unseen spirits, a voice was heard to cry:

"Gang farther down,
   To Fordoun's town."

It is added that the new site was chosen by the throwing at random of a mason's hammer.

TYPE ML.7060 MOTIFS: D.2192 [*Work of day magically over thrown at night*]; V.111.3 [*Place where church must be built miraculously indicated*].
¶ See "The Church of Old Deer".

THE CHURCH OF OLD DEER

Chambers, *Popular Rhymes of Scotland*, p. 335.

When the workmen were engaged in erecting the ancient church of Old Deer in Aberdeenshire, upon a small hill called Bissau, they were surprised to find that the work was impeded by supernatural obstacles. At length the Spirit of the River was heard to say:

"It is not here, it is not here,
   That ye shall build the church of Deer,
   But on Taptillery,
   Where many a corpse shall lie."

The site of the edifice was accordingly transferred to Taptillery, an eminence at some distance from the place where the building had been commenced.

From *Notes to the "Lay of the Last Minstrel"*.

TYPE ML.7060

¶ See "The Church of Fordoun".

CHURCH TREASURE

Ruth L. Tongue, *Somerset Folklore*, p. 203.

In the dark days when Glastonbury Abbey was dissolved one of her priests hid a quantity of church treasure at Ivythorn, uttering a terrible curse on any sacrilegious man who should find and raise it. The priest died or was executed, and centuries later a farmer of Ivythorn dug up the treasure. Laughing at all the old wives' tales, he proceeded to spend it wildly. He got neither pleasure nor peace from it for the curse rested upon him until he lost farm, family and his own wits and died raving. (Local traditions.)

TYPE ML.8010. MOTIFS: N.511 [*Treasure in ground*]; N.591 [*Curse on treasure*].

¶ Many of the abbeys and monasteries from which the monks were driven were supposed to be under a curse. Levens Hall in Lancashire is an example.

CLITHEROE CASTLE [summary]

J. Roby, *Lancashire Traditions*, I, p. 507.

The castle of Clitheroe, originally held by the family of Lacy, who came to England with the Conqueror, passed on the death of Robert de Lacy, the last of the direct line, to his half-sister Awbrey, the wife of Richard Fitz-Eustace, Lord of Halton and Constable of Chester.

This Richard had two grandsons, Richard, who became a leper, and Roger, believed to have been lost while returning from the Holy Land, besides three younger children, not concerned in this story.

In the year 1193, when King Richard Coeur de Lion was a prisoner in the hands of the Duke of Austria, another lord of Clitheroe lay dead, and the chief mourner was Robert de Whalley, the Dean of the Abbey, and descendant of a distant branch of the Lacys. This powerful priest had secretly cherished the hope of himself inheriting the great Lacy estates, which extended over many miles of Lancashire and Yorkshire. He believed that the leper son would be passed over, and that Roger being presumed dead, there would be none to dispute the possession. But even while he was celebrating the funeral rites of the dead lord, a loud knocking at the castle gate announced the arrival of a deputation from house of Fitz-Eustace, headed by its seneschal, Adam de Dutton, who claimed the castle and estates in the name of the lady who was now the head of the family.

The cunning Dean now entered into secret conference with a hermit who lived nearby—a reputed worker of miracles, known as Sir Ulphilas, whose influence with the late Lord had been greater than the Dean himself knew. He begged the holy man's help in recovering the inheritance for the survivors of the de Lacys, only to find that the hermit himself had sent to inform the Fitz-Eustaces of what had occurred, and that, by his gift of prophecy he now foretold that the Dean himself should never enter into that inheritance, though one of his blood should do so, Roger Fitz-Eustace, whom all had believed dead in the Holy Land. He told the Dean also that the true will of the former master of the castle was in his keeping.

The crafty Dean now resolved by any means to possess himself of this document. His first attempt was to send two confederates dressed as monks to the hermit's cell, who claimed to have been sent by the old Lady Fitz-Eustace, to inquire of the Abbot at Kirkstall whether de Lacy's will was in his keeping. The pretext did not deceive Sir Ulphilas, who plainly told them that he himself had charge of the will, and bade them return to the Dean, their master.

In the meantime Adam de Dutton was exercising so tyrannical a rule over the castle and its inmates, that at last the old seneschal, Oliver de Wortshorn, went to the hermit for counsel and comfort, and persuaded him to accompany him back to the castle, where they found Adam inflicting summary punishments on a variety of wretched people without regard to their deserts. The hermit peremptorily bade him stop, and dismissed his victims before the astonished Adam could prevent him. But, recovering his senses, he called loudly for the hermit's arrest. But such was the terror of the hermit's presence that he was suffered to return unmolested to his cell. It was observed that Adam's duties were thereafter carried out in a more seemly fashion, and many believed that some secret sign had been given to him by the holy man, which had brought about this strange alteration.

Adam was addicted to hunting, and on his excursions to the forest he was often accompanied by Geoffrey, the Dean's only son. One day when they were absent on one of these expeditions, the Dean again visited the hermit, to beg him outright for the document he guarded so tenaciously, and to ask him of a rumour that Roger Fitz-Eustace (or de Lacy, for the old name was still in use by many members of the family) was indeed alive and on his way back to England. The hermit was adamant, and at last the enraged priest drew a sword and attacked him.

The steel glanced aside, and the hermit withdrew with a glance of contempt. Next day he appeared in the hall of the castle, and bade the seneschal, Adam, prepare for the arrival of his lord, Roger, who would be with them by the following day. Not daring to disbelieve or disobey, Adam went about his tasks, and by the next evening the hermit's forecast was vindicated, for Roger de Lacy rode up to the castle, accompanied by his daughter Maud, with whom the Dean's son, Geoffrey, instantly fell in love.

The next day Roger gave audience in the castle hall, and the Dean was the first to prefer his complaint. He denounced the hermit, Sir Ulphilas, as a traitor and a sorcerer, who had wilfully concealed the true will of Lord Robert his master. On this the hermit himself appeared unannounced, and the Dean, without ceremony, seized the parchment from his bosom, and on being read aloud, it proved to bequeath the whole estate to Robert de Whalley and his heirs. In triumph, the Dean immediately ordered the hermit to be thrown into prison, but before this could be done, the hermit strode up to him, and, thrusting his hand into the Dean's robe, drew forth yet another parchment, the true will, a copy of which the hermit had already dispatched to Halton, and so summoned the Fitz-Eustace family to the castle. Yet, having promised protection to the Dean, this strange hermit insisted that he should not be immediately put to death, as the imperious Roger demanded. This led to the disclosure of the whole truth. The hermit was in fact, the leper, Richard de Lacy, who by prayer and bathing in the holy well near his cell had been miraculously healed, and had by secret passages been enabled to visit the former lord of the castle, to act as his confessor and counsellor. He now formally renounced his inheritance in favour of his brother, stipulating only that the Dean's life should be spared, since, for all his avarice, he had in earlier days done him some service and charity. He counselled that Maud and Geoffrey should be wedded, and so his former promise that the Dean's blood should enter into the estate he coveted would be fulfilled; and so it shortly afterwards was enacted.

MOTIFS: L.112.7.1 [*Leper hero*]; K.2280 [*Treacherous churchmen*]; X.905.3 [*Claim of property based on a lie*].

CONTRABAND AT CARNBEE

Wilkie, *Bygone Fife*, p. 279.

Many are the tales in Carnbee of the old smuggling days when contraband, after being concealed in the vaults of Newark, the cellars of Largo, the caves of Pittenweem and Pitcaiplie, was conveyed inland with the connivance of the farmers. On one occasion, a considerable quantity of tea, then a very valuable commodity, had evaded duty. It had been successfully deposited at a certain steading to await distribution. The season was spring and the sowers were busy in the fields, sowing as their predecessors did in Palestine thousands of years before. The sacks of seed stood ready to their hands.

Then hot-foot came rumour. Some loose-tongued hind or sailor, incautious in his cups, had given away the secret. The gaugers were on their way. No time was to be lost. The sacks were promptly emptied, the tea filled in instead, and on the top the grain laid thick. The Revenue men arrived, confident that at last they would be able to make an example. They found the farmer and his "hands" peacefully engaged in their ancestral occupation, ignorant of the illicit proceedings of the adventurous Free Traders. Search was in vain. Even a handful taken from the sacks showed only seed. Evidently the Custom House had been hoaxed again. The officers could but withdraw with what grace they might.

MOTIFS: K.400 [*Thief escapes detection*]; K.419.6 [*Husks replaced in granary so theft of grain is unnoticed*].

¶ There are a good many smuggling traditions all over the country. Few of them can be described as stories, but it seems worth while to include a representative anecdote which illustrates the co-operation of the whole countryside with the smugglers.

THE COOK AT COMBWELL

Norton Collection, III, p. 19.

In the days of the Civil War, when the country was frequently infested with travelling bands of marauders, one of these villainous gangs made an attempt on Combwell whilst the family were in church, there then being no one but the cook left in the house. According to tradition one of the robbers, disguised as a beggar-woman, appealed to the cook for admission, and the cook, being a kind-hearted woman, allowed him to enter the kitchen. He begged a piece of bread to satisfy his hunger, and was granted permission to cook it in the boiling fat in the frypan. Whilst her unwelcome visitor was stooping over the pan, the cook noticed that he was wearing boots and spurs and, with a sudden gleam of inspiration, the sinister situation burst upon her, with all its horrible possibilities. Seizing the kitchen poker, which was the most formidable weapon near at hand, she struck him a tremendous blow upon the head, which laid him lifeless at her feet, and, rushing upstairs to the bell turret, she vigorously tugged at the bell-rope, thereby giving the alarm. The hoarse-throated clang of the bell was clearly heard in the peaceful precincts of the sacred edifice at the top of the hill, and its portent in those troublous times was only too patent that danger threatened. The male members of the family, accompanied by a band of stalwart neighbours and dependents, made all haste to the house, and so opportune was their arrival that they succeeded in dispersing the scoundrels, who in the meantime had laid siege to the house and, through the open bell turret, had, from the rising ground a short distance away, employed their time in taking pot-shots at the gallant domestic, whose presence of mind and courageous action had been the means of summoning help, which arrived in the nick of time to prevent the robbers from carrying out their nefarious designs. It was afterwards discovered that the robbers, in order to trick their pursuers in the event of their scheme failing, had had their horses' shoes removed and put on the opposite way, in order to make it appear that they were proceeding in another direction. It is stated that the head of the family, in recognition of the cook's courage, caused the bust to be executed and placed over the doorway.

"Over the entrance to the house is carved a woman's bust", Igglesden, *A Saunter through Kent*, XII, p. 42.
TYPE 958D*. MOTIF: K.1817.1 [*Disguise as beggar*]; K.1836 [*Disguise of man in woman's dress*]; K.534.1 [*Escape by reversing horse's shoes*].
¶ See "The Brave Maidservant", "The Long Pack", "The Robber and the Housekeeper" (A, IV).

COWTHALLY CASTLE

Chambers, *Popular Rhymes of Scotland*, p. 336.

Near Carnwath stands Cowthally, Cowdaily, or Quodaily Castle, an early residence of the noble family of Somerville.

The first Somerville, as tradition reports, came from France, and dispossessed the former proprietor of Cowthally, some of whose vassals he subjected to his authority, though, it appears, without succeeding in attaching them very faithfully to his interests. Somerville demolished the outer walls of the castle, and a good part of the castle itself, before he could make himself master of it; and he afterwards saw fit to rebuild it in a different place. But against this design he found circumstances in strong opposition.

As the country people say, "what of the wall he got built during the day, was regularly *dung down* at night". Suspecting the fidelity of his watchmen, he undertook to wake the castle in person. It would appear that this had no effect in saving the building; for who should come to demolish it but the Evil One himself, with four or five of his principal servants, who, without heeding Somerville's expostulations, or even his active resistance, fell to and undid the work of the day, chanting all the while, in unearthly articulation, the following rhyme:

> "'Tween the Rae Hill and Loriburnshaw,
> There ye'll find Cowdaily wa',
> And the foundations laid on ern."

It is added that, in compliance with this hint, Somerville was obliged to rebuild the castle of Cowdaily on its original foundations, which were of iron.

TYPE ML.7060. MOTIF: G.303.14.1 [*The Devil destroys by night what is built by day*].
¶ An explanation rather like that in the second version of Callaly Castle is half implied here.
See "Callaly Castle", "The Castle of Belburn", "Mauldslie Castle".

CRAWLS

Burne and Jackson, *Shropshire Folk-Lore*, p. 91.

Many hundred years ago there was a young lady, her father's only daughter and heiress, whom a gallant knight wooed and sought for his bride. And she loved him well, and gave him her promise. But when her father came to hear of it, he would by no means give his consent, for the knight was a younger son and landless. The young lady, though, was firm, and held to her word. One day she came and told her father that she and her true love would be married the next morning at Bromfield Church. The father was angry, as he might well be. He upbraided her for a headstrong lass, who must e'en take her own way, but of all his broad lands he vowed she would have none but what she could crawl round by morning light. She said not a word, but went quietly away. An old servant brought her a pair of leathern breeches to guard her poor knees ("else they would ha' wore out"), and thus strangely equipped she crawled round the fields all through that dark cold winter's night, and came in covered with mud to her father at his breakfast, saying that she had taken him at his word, and crawled round so much fair meadow land as reached nearly to Downton. The old man was so much delighted at his girl's brave spirit that he forgave her obstinacy, and took her back into favour. He made her heiress of all his estates, which continued to belong to her descendants for many generations, and the land she crept round during that long dreary night still bears the name of "Crawls".

MOTIF: H.1584.2 [*Land measured according to the amount encompassed during certain hours*].
¶ See "The Barefoot Pilgrimage", "Lame Haverah".

CROOKED CROOKHAM

Denham Tracts, I, p. 10.

There is a Presbyterian meeting-house at Crookham, of which a legend is told of its building. After the ground was marked out, and the foundations were begun to be laid, somebody moved the marks that had been stuck in the ground (and everybody thought they were spirits who did it) and put them in another place, making the place nearly twice as big as it was intended to have been. At the first sacrament, a being declared that the place would always be cursed with fightings and contentions, and then vanished.

Matthew Paxton, II, p. 173.

TYPE ML.7060.

¶ See "The New Church at Marske", "The Building of St Chad's", etc.

THE DANGEROUS SWINE or 'CAULD IRON'

Wilkie, *Bygone Fife*, p. 240.

St Monans was...composed of two populations. Down on the shore the inhabitants were seafaring and such as supplied the wants of seafaring men. There they had lived and intermarried through countless generations. Up on the top of the cliff, where of old the windmill stood, resided a different class, a landward people who found in agriculture and its needs their chief occupation. The territory of the nether town had gradually been diminishing, for here the sea, which farther west at Leven is rapidly receding, has been encroaching. Once a stretch of links extended in front of the dwellings, and there the fishers were wont to spread their nets to dry.

While the folk of the nether town abhorred swine, the rearing of them came naturally to those who dwelt above, a fact which in itself precluded friendly intercourse between the two sections of the burgh. Occasionally a pig broke loose, and, following Scriptural example, rushed down the steep brae. Instantly a panic arose in the invaded territory, for, did the eye but rest on the evil beast, a tide must ebb and flow ere it was safe for the unwilling witness to put to sea. Every door was shut, every face averted, till the squeaks of the monster gradually growing fainter carried assurance of its capture and removal to the unhallowed region of the upper town.

It is told how these incursions became so numerous that the avocation of the fishermen was seriously impeded. Exasperation grew, and finally reached such a pitch that it was resolved to teach the owners of the invading animals a lesson. The sailors seized their boat-hooks and marched in a body up the cleft that gives access to the landward. They were a fierce and formidable horde, and, armed as they were, might have wrought serious mischief. How they intended to proceed was probably not apparent even to themselves.

Happily, bloodshed and destruction of property were averted by an inspiration of genius. The host had not been marshalled without some rumour of its purpose reaching the cliff-top, and when the army was seen debouching from the defile, the gate of every cruive was opened. In a moment the warlike assailants had disappeared, racing in panic-stricken rout for the shelter of their own abodes, while the air resounded with the squeaks, squeals and grunts of the pigs and the hoarse triumphant laughter of the victorious defenders.

The triumph was short-lived. The Laird of Newark, finding it impossible to convince the fisher-folk of the innocent nature of swine, was forced to decree the extermination or exile of the dreaded creatures. It is said that for over a century no pig was to be found within the territories of St Monans. And when the skein of true love was ravelled, was not the appropriate metaphor that "the swine had run through it"?

There remains a taboo on the name among the fishing communities. Even the utterance of the word was sufficient to ensure a boat abandoning its projected voyage for that tide. To speak of a minister while at sea was equally unlucky, as doubtless it has been since the time of Jonah. Consequently, there was never heard among the natives of the nether town of St Monans a story well known beyond its bounds.

It is still held throughout Christendom that to touch wood or iron is to avert retribution for incautious speech. To touch "cauld iron" was considered among the Fife fishing communities particularly effectual.

At some time after the Church of St Monans became the parish church of Abercrombie, it happened, through the death or translation of the minister, that a successor was inducted. Who he was is of little consequence, though he might not be difficult to identify by a process of exclusion. Certainly neither the Reverend John Cook, born in Elie, nor the Reverend Robert Swan, son of the minister of Scoonie, was likely, however unwittingly, so to outrage the feelings of his hearers, nor were those who had worn the gown in St Andrews, where there was a fishing quarter that shared the beliefs of St Monans.

On the first Sunday of the new ministry there was, as always except in the days of the hated "curates", a thronged kirk. The three galleries were filled to overflowing. By an unhappy chance, the preacher chose the parable of the Prodigal Son. It was doubtless the sermon he fancied his best, but he never gave it again. The reading of St Luke, chapter XV, at the 11th verse, was announced. An uneasy wave of feeling seemed to surge over choir and galleries. The occupant of the pulpit thought no evil; but when he pronounced the last word of verse 15 he was startled beyond measure. For at once, like a response in the abandoned liturgies of unenlightened days, there burst forth a hoarse murmur which sounded in his ears like "Touch cauld iron!"

Vague thoughts of the red rags of Popery still, by some chance, fluttering in backward quarters and intruding into the cleansed temples of Presbyterianism flashed across his mind. He must make allowances. He recovered himself and repeated the last words, when again the same response burst forth with a fervour that exceeded the ejaculations of "Revival Meetings".

He paused once more, for a moment at a loss. Then he proceeded with verse 16. He never reached its conclusion. Ere he could pronounce the fatal word, the congregation leapt from its seat and scrambled in a seething and struggling mass for the door. Men despairing of exit by ordinary means from the galleries dropped over their front, descending on the crowd below, to the increase of their panic. It is said that few of the folk of the nether town ventured again within the venerable walls for many a day to come.

(Quoted from *Dean Ramsay's Reminiscences*.)

MOTIF: B.147.1.2 [*Beasts of ill omen*].

¶ Curiously enough, the pig is not explicitly mentioned in the Motif Index as a beast of ill-omen, nor is the hare or rabbit. Yet all three were considered very unlucky among fishermen, so much so that they could not be mentioned by name. Donald Mackenzie, in *Scottish Folk-Lore and Folk-Life*, devotes two chapters to the consideration of the pork tabu and pig cult. In Chapter I, pp. 47–9, he gives an amusing account of the arrival of the first pig in Dumfriesshire and the horrors it inspired. The tabu was widespread, though not universal, throughout Scotland. Even in Somerset the mention of swine is avoided among the fishermen, though pork is eaten.

See "The Fishermen of Worle", "The Pilots of Pill".

THE DEVIL AND JOSEPH GOULD

J. R. W. Coxhead, *The Devil in Devon*, pp. 26–8.

On the easterly slope of Mockham Down, in the parish of Charles, amongst the high hills of western Exmoor, lies the ancient Domesday estate of Mockham.

Early in the nineteenth century the property was being farmed by a man named Joseph Gould, who was greatly respected in the surrounding district. He was a staunch Baptist, and he died at his home on 21st August 1817. In view of the fact that in those days there was no burial-ground for members of his denomination in the parish, special permission was obtained from the ecclesiastical authorities for his body to be interred in Charles churchyard.

Religious prejudices were extremely strong, and sometimes violent, in remote country places at the beginning of the nineteenth century, and, because of the peculiar fact that the farmer had never been baptized, the burial service had to be conducted by a Baptist minister at Mockham, while the actual interment was carried out in the churchyard at Charles in solemn silence.

Many of the parishioners were highly indignant that a Dissenter should have been buried in their churchyard, and when they heard that the man had never even been baptized they were greatly shocked.

Shortly after the funeral, a tombstone bearing the following inscription was erected over the grave by friends of the deceased:

"In memory of Mr Joseph Gould, a respectable farmer of this parish who died August 21st 1817, aged 72 years. He was a man of piety, given to hospitality, a lover of the poor, but above all a promoter of vital Christianity and a humble follower of the Lord Jesus on Whose obedience he confidently hoped for salvation and through Whose grace he triumphed over death. He was for many years a worthy member of the Baptist Denomination."

The last phrase of the inscription caused a sense of outrage to spread amongst the rather narrow-minded and bigoted inhabitants of the secluded little village, and the presence of the offending stone filled many of them with a feeling of foreboding.

Abe Moggridge, the Sexton, and many of the more superstitious villagers were quite convinced that the Devil would shortly snatch both tombstone and body from the churchyard and carry them off to the Nether Regions.

Early one dark December morning, as Abe was walking up the road to Broad Park Common, on his way to work, he caught his foot against a stone as he passed the west wicket gate of the churchyard and almost fell, exclaiming as he recovered himself, "I bet a ha'penny that's old Gould's stone."

Going to the nearest cottage for a lantern, Moggridge returned with several witnesses to find the hated gravestone lying broken in the road, with the two halves about a foot apart, just as it must have fallen from the air as the Devil was in the act of carrying it away.

When he heard of what had happened, one of the dead man's closest friends, named John Winzer, went to Charles with a horse and cart and picked up the two pieces of the tombstone, and brought them back to Mockham.

Meanwhile, an old farm-worker named Anthony Dallyn, who treasured the memory of a good and kind master, seeing the broken gravestone in the yard at Mockham, and not being of a superstitious nature, decided that its desecration was due to human animosity and not to the Devil.

"If they won't 'ave the poor old Maister's stone in the churchyard," said he, "be damned if they shall 'ave 'is body neither."

So, with the help of another man, he went to the churchyard, after dark on Christmas Eve, with a horse and cart and the necessary tools, intended to dig up the body from the grave.

In order to make the abduction of the body more secret, they had made a packing-case large enough to contain the coffin. This case they placed on top of a wall by the footpath at the south side of the churchyard. Then they commenced to dig a hole large enough for the removal of the coffin, which was some six feet below the surface of the ground.

When the arduous task was nearly finished, and the two men were completely hidden from view in the deep hole they had excavated, the Church Choir, returning from a carol-singing expedition, stopped outside in the road to sing a carol. As soon as they had finished singing the party of choristers started to walk up the footpath leading to Charles Town Barton. Suddenly one of them noticed the huge coffin-shaped case on the wall. Plucking up courage, he went up and touched it, whereupon it commenced to rock to and fro in the moonlight as though it were alive.

Then one of the boys saw the open grave, and in no time at all the youngsters were filled with panic, running in all directions, and screaming at the tops of their voices:

"The Devil's in the churchyard, a-digging up old Joseph Gould!"

Doors and windows were opened all down the village, and anxious voices were heard asking to know what all the trouble was about, but no one was able to summon up the courage to investigate the mystery for at least half an hour. Meanwhile, Anthony Dallyn and his faithful companion got the coffin into the packing-case with all possible speed. Carrying it to the north-west gate of the churchyard, they put it on the cart, and were soon on their way back to Mockham, without being seen by anyone.

When the frightened villagers finally mustered up the courage to go to the churchyard, they saw a yawning pit in the place of the farmer's neat grave—a sure sign that the Devil had taken Joseph Gould, coffin and all.

While Abe Moggridge and the rest of the inhabitants of the village were discussing the subject of the vanished coffin, events moved quickly elsewhere.

Carefully, and with reverence, Anthony Dallyn and his friend bore the coffin along by Wilcombe and Shutscombe farms, down Brayford Hill, and into the Baptist chapel. They carefully buried the coffin in the same way in which it had been buried in the churchyard, and placed the broken tombstone against the wall. Then, when their task had been successfully completed, they returned to Mockham, and told John Winzer what they had done.

For many years the tombstone remained in the chapel by the grave, but eventually it was removed to a burial-ground acquired by the chapel authorities at a later date. The broken stone, patched together, may still be seen, and the inscription upon it can be easily read.

From *The Moorside Parish of Charles*, by Rev. W. W. Joyce. Preserved at Exeter. MOTIF: J.1781 [*Objects thought to be the Devil*].
¶ This tale skirts round a good many motifs. It illustrates the intolerance of country places even in the last century.

THE DOG THAT DISAPPEARED

Ruth L. Tongue.

"Old Dapper" was a wise dog who belonged to a good old man. They had guarded and folded their sheep securely for years, and every night Old Dapper had sat with wrinkled brow and watched the shepherd draw a criss-cross at the door of the fold to fend off evil hill-spirits from the Abbey flock. With a cock to scare off ghosts and a dog to drive off witches and a criss-cross at his door, man and beasts could live safe even in Burrington. The old man had a fine chanticleer, and wise Old Dapper, and the flock had their criss-cross. This did not please the evil spirits of the Mendips. They gibbered and peered out of their swallet holes and at last went to the Witch of Wookey for help. The best she could do was to trip the old man up and hurt his leg. The Abbey took him in to nurse him and sent another shepherd. But he wasn't a good man, and the sights he saw so frightened him that he ran back to Wells, leaving Old Dapper and the cock to mind the sheep. They did very well. The cock watched while Old Dapper slept and he kept guard while the bird napped, and nothing evil came near. So one of the demons called Aveline turned himself into a rabbit and hopped out of his cave right by flock and dog. "He'll never resist chasing me," chuckled Aveline. "*And once he's inside the hill——*" "Yur's one of they spurrits hopping 'bout a gurt deal tew near they sheep," says Old Dapper. "I'd best go chase him off!" The cock was nodding sleepily when he heard a fiendish chuckle and looking up saw Old Dapper disappear into Aveline's Hole. He gave a mighty crow of warning which made Aveline scream in a very different fashion, but Old Dapper didn't return. Sadly the cock guarded the flock, when to his joy the old man limped up, and together they went the rounds. The sheep were all quite peaceful and safe—for in the very entrance of Aveline's Hole was a clumsy criss-cross scratched by a big dog's paw. Old Dapper had not forgotten how to save them.... Three weeks after a quarryman at Cheddar heard a faint whimper and, leaning into a hole in the cliff face, pulled out a starving dog without a hair on him. Old Dapper had come through safely. No evil spirits ever tried to face the three again in Burrington Combe.

Aveline's Hole, Burrington, Somerset.
From a school friend, who was told it by her Mendip great-grandmamma of 90.
See also Knight, *Heart of Mendip*, p.246
MOTIFS: F.402.6.4.1 [*Spirits live in caves*]; F.460.4.4 [*Malevolent mountain men*]; B.121.1 [*Dog with magic wisdom*]; F.405.5.1 [*Dogs protect house from spirits*]; A.2493.16 [*Friendship between cock and dog*]; G.303.17.1.1 [*Devil flees when cock crows*].

¶ Local tradition about long caves, so narrow that a dog put in at one end emerges with all its fur rubbed off, are to be found in various parts of the country. It is this tradition that Knight mentions, not the old dog's valiant combat with the spirits.

DOMNEVA

H. Bett, *English Myths and Traditions*, p. 64.

Minster owed its name to the nunnery and church founded here in Saxon days by Domneva, who was a princess of Kent, and the wife of Merwood, the son of Penda, the King of Mercia. In her childhood she was left with her sister Ermengitha, and her brothers Ethelbert and Ethelbright, under the guardianship of her uncle Erwinbert, who had usurped his brother's throne. His son and successor, Egbert, counselled by Thunor, one of his liegemen, determined upon the murder of both the princes, to make sure of the succession. The murder was done by Thunor in the King's palace at Eastry, and was discovered by a miraculous light from Heaven which indicated the very spot where the bodies were buried beneath the King's throne! On the direction of Theodore, the Archbishop of Canterbury, and Adrian, the Abbot of St Augustine's, Egbert promised to give Domneva whatever she should ask for in compensation for the crime.

Domneva and her husband (who had three children) had both by this time taken the monastic vows. She asked the King to grant her as much land as her tame deer could run over at one course, so that she might found a nunnery in memory of her murdered brothers. The King agreed, and in the presence of many of his nobles and people the deer was turned loose at Westgate, on the sea-coast, in the parish of Birchington, and ran right across Thanet, though Thunor rode across the hind's course to stop it. "This impiety", says the chronicler of St

Augustine's Abbey, "so offended Heaven, that the earth opened and swallowed him up, *et in infernum cum Dathan et Abiram absorbetur*," leaving the name of Thunor's Leap to the place where he fell.

Meanwhile, the deer did not stop until it came to the estuary of the Stour, now called Sheriff's Hope, near Monkton, having crossed the isle, and encircled a tract of land amounting to more than ten thousand acres. This was immediately granted by the King to Domneva, and afterwards confirmed by his charters, which contained a fearful curse against all who infringed her right. Soon afterwards the nunnery was founded on the spot where the present church now stands. It was completed about the year 680, and consecrated by Archbishop Theodore in honour of the Virgin Mary. Domneva became the first Abbess, and when she died she was buried in the grounds of the nunnery.

MOTIFS: S.70 [*Cruel relative*]; F.1061.4 [*Flame indicates place where innocent person was murdered*]; Q.520.1 [*Murderer does penance*]; H.1584.2 [*Land measured according to amount encompassed during certain hours*]; Q.220 [*Impiety punished*]; Q.552.2.3.1.2 [*Earth swallows man as punishment for sacrilege*].

¶ For another story of the foundation of a religious house as a penance, see "The Bishop's Bread and Cheese".

DREEL CASTLE

Wilkie, *Bygone Fife*, p. 289.

At some time or other the Lord of Anstruther built the castle beside the Dreel Burn, not far from St Ethernan's Kirk.... Inside the gates... according to tradition, was slain Sir Niel Cunningham of Barns, who had plotted the death of Sir William Anstruther, and might have accomplished his aim but for an intervention of Fate—whether supernatural or not does not clearly appear. Sir William had been asked by Barns to visit him at his fortalice, which, like that of Dreel, exists now only in visions of the past. As he was riding east there appeared before him a venerable man, who warned him that if he went farther on his errand he should return no more. Unlike the "fey" monarchs of Scotland, he obeyed the injunction to go back, and, on reaching Dreel, wrote Cunningham in his turn, inviting him. Barns appeared, unsuspecting, in answer to the call. His welcome was a stroke from a battle-axe wielded by Anstruther's own arm.

From that incident, it is said, came the heraldic bearings of the family and their motto, "*Periissem ni periissem*".

The tale proceeds that Sir William found shelter on the Bass till the storm blew over.

MOTIFS: N.825.2 [*Old man helper*]; Q.211.8 [*Punishment for desire to murder*].

THE DRUMMING WELL AT HARPHAM

[summary]

Parkinson, *Yorkshire Legends and Traditions*, 1st series, p. 207.

In the thirteenth century, when all young men were skilled in archery, it was the custom to hold occasional field-days in every village, where gentry and peasants contended together. The family living in the old manor house at Harpham was named St Quintin, and in the same village was a widow, reputed to have uncanny powers, named Molly Hewson. Her only son, Tom, had been trained by the squire as a drummer, and taken as an inmate into the manor house, for he was a promising, soldier-like young man.

On a certain field-day, when the sports were at their height, and a large company of spectators were there, the squire was more than usually irritated by the clumsiness of one of the peasant performers. He sprang forward to rebuke the man, and as he did so, accidentally stumbled into Tom the drummer, who staggered backwards, and fell head first into the well. Before he could be rescued, the boy was drowned.

His mother quickly appeared upon the scene, and in her frantic grief she cried, "Squire St Quintin, you were the friend of my boy...You intended not his death, but from your hand his death has come. Know then, that through all future ages, whenever a St Quintin, Lord of Harpham, is about to pass from life, my poor boy shall beat his drum at the bottom of this fatal well." Her word was fulfilled; from that time, as long as the house of St Quintin survived, the master's death was preceded by the sound of drumming from the well, and heard by all who listened for it.

MOTIFS: E.402.1.3 [*Invisible ghost plays musical instrument*]; D.1827.1.3 [*Noise warns of approaching death*].
¶ See "The Drummer of Airlie" (B, VI).

THE DRUMMING WELLS

C. Hole, *English Folk-Lore*, p. 99.

Many waters have prophetic powers. Near Brampton in Northamptonshire, Marvel-sike Spring predicted death or trouble by running in great gluts of water. It never ran at any other time, and was regarded as an infallible prophet of evil. In the same county the famous Drumming Well at Oundle gave out the sound like the rolling of drums before an important happening. Baxter, in *The World of Spirits*, relates how he heard it as a schoolboy before the Scots came to England in the Civil Wars. He says it continued for several days, and was audible from a distance. Later, when Charles II died, he went to Smithfield to meet the Oundle carrier, who told him their well had drummed before the King's death, and many had come to hear it. There was another drumming well at Harpham, Yorkshire, but this only predicted a death in the St Quintin family. The legend was that, during an archery contest in the reign of Edward II or III, a drummer named Tom Hewson was pushed by the Squire, in a fit of irritation, into the well. His mother, a woman suspected of witchcraft, swore that whenever any of the family were to die her drowned lad would roll his drum from the depths of the well. Tradition says that this drumming was heard before every death as long as the St Quintins owned the property.

MOTIF: V.134.1 [*Oracles and auguries from sacred well*].

THE DUN COW OF KIRKHAM AND THE
OLD RIB [summary]

Harland and Wilkinson, *Lancashire Legends*, p. 16.

"The Old Rib" is now the name of an old farm at Whittingham, in the parish of Kirkham, five miles north of Preston. The name comes from an enormous rib, said to have been that of an extraordinary cow, which is placed over the door of the farmhouse. The house is remarkable for its four turrets and the heavily studded oak door. There are remains of a moat round the house, and the date above the door is 1615.

Long before that time, it is said, a huge dun cow used to roam over the moors near this house, and drink at the well known as "Nick's Water Pot".

Her supply of milk was so great that from many places within reach people came with their pails, and she filled them all; until at last a witch from Pendle, whose motive none ever explained, instead of a pail, brought a sieve, and sat down all day long milking the dun cow. At night the sieve was still empty, and at last the stream of milk ran dry. After that the dun cow appeared no more on those moors. How her rib (still about a yard in length, in spite of decay, exposure, and depredations of souvenir-hunters) was found and placed above the farm door is not made clear.

From *Curious Corners round Preston*, Anon.

MOTIFS: D.1652.3.1 [*Cow with inexhaustible milk*]; C.918.1 [*Marvellous cow offended: disappears*].

¶ According to another version given by Harland and Wilkinson in *The Traditions of Lancashire*, pp. 16–19, the cow dropped dead after being milked all day. There are many Irish traditions of supernatural cows. Lady Wilde devotes a chapter to them in the second volume of *Ancient Legends of Ireland*.

DUNCOMBE

Gutch, *County Folk-Lore*, II, p. 413.

It is said that many years ago the lord of the manor [of Duncombe], an ancestor of the present Lord Feversham, riding one day home to Duncombe, saw a girl in a sun-bonnet swinging to and fro on the gate of the park. He reined up his horse, and as she swung he heard her sing these words to herself:

"It may so happen, it may so fall
  That Ah may be laady o' Duncombe Hall."

Then she turned and showed the wondering squire the prettiest face he had ever seen. He fell headlong in love with the beautiful face. The girl was about fourteen, and he persuaded her parents to send her to school at his expense for several years; when she returned to her home well-educated and more lovely still, he married her—and made her mistress of Duncombe.

Macquoid, *About Yorkshire*, pp. 294, 295.
TYPE 870A. MOTIFS: T.55 [*Girl as wooer*]; T.15 [*Love at first sight*]; L.162 [*Lowly heroine marries prince*].

THE EBBING AND FLOWING WELL
AT GIGGLESWICK [summary]

Parkinson, *Yorkshire Legends and Traditions*, 1st series, p. 205.

About a mile from Settle, at the foot of the high limestone cliff named Giggleswick Scar, is a well whose water periodically ebbs and flows, at longer or shorter intervals, sometimes as often as several times in an hour, sometimes only once in several hours.

The legend says that this spring was once a nymph, whom a satyr pursued, having fallen in love with her for her flowing silver hair. She fled before him, but was slowly losing ground, so she prayed to the gods of the place for protection, and they, in pity, changed her into this spring, whose ebb and flow is believed to be due to her sobbing, irregular breath as she fled from her pursuer.

MOTIFS: A.941.0.1 [*Origin of a particular spring*]; A.427.1 [*Goddess of springs and wells. In Greek myths nymphs regarded as deities of springs*]; F.425 [*Fountain spirit*].
¶ This legend is so much imbued with the spirit of Greek myths that it is clear that it has passed through educated hands. It is the kind of legend to be found in Drayton's *Polyolbion*. If there is a folk-foundation to it, the satyr was probably a hobgoblin, and the nymph a mortal girl; but it seems more likely that it arose as a fancy of a local schoolmaster or scholar.

A FALSTONE STORY

F. Grice, *Folk-Tales of the North Country*, p. 44.

The farmstead of Woodhouses near Falstone was once the home of a good-living shepherd named Matthew Robson, whose wife was famed for many miles around for her industry. Never was there so industrious a wife. She milked and churned, cooked and baked, cleaned and washed, knitted and sewed, and seemed to do the work of a dozen housewives. She even found time to card enough wool to keep two maidens all day at the spinning-wheel. She was always the last to go to bed, but no one ever rose earlier than she. She seemed to thrive upon work.

Matthew had every reason for being proud of his wife. She was never behind with her work. His meals were always prepared for him; the house was always swept and smelling pleasantly of new things fresh from the oven; his good shirts were fragrant with the smell of the wild thyme flowers that she laid in the drawers; and when he came home from the hill, wet-shod, there was always a pair of warm, dry stockings for him. Yet Matthew was not entirely happy; for his wife was so hungry for work that often she would not stop when the Sabbath Day came round, but kept on carding her wool well into Sunday morning. "Wife," he said to her more than once, "you should not work on the Sabbath morning. One of these days you will be punished for it." But his wife took little heed of his remonstrances. "The Lord also looks upon idleness as a sin, Matthew, and I cannot be idle. Off with you now, and let me get on with my carding."

Nothing unlucky did befall the hardworking Mistress Robson; but Matthew was so sure some punishment would overtake her one day that he determined to lay a plot to make her mend her ways. One Saturday he saw his opportunity. Mistress Robson was away with her basket of eggs and butter to the village of Falstone, when there came to Woodhouses a travelling piper called Miles. It was Miles' habit to travel all the year round from farm to farm, helping each shepherd in turn. Sometimes he helped to cut the peats, sometimes he came at lambing time, sometimes he helped to drive the ewes away at speaning time, and sometimes he did nothing but entertain the family with his pipes. Miles was always welcome, but never more welcome than at clipping time. On those days some ten or twenty shepherds would gather at one farm and spend all the day clipping the hundreds of sheep that were brought down from the fells; and then after the shearing there would be a great feast, and after the feast the tables were cleared and the room prepared for dancing. Every shepherd was pleased to see Miles on those days, for not only could he clip a sheep like the best of them, but he was also the sweetest piper in the countryside. When he played, the clumsiest shepherd danced like a lamb, and the surliest smiled and beat time with him. O it was a joy for all to hear him playing on his sweet Northumbrian pipes and singing to his music:

> "A shepherd sat him under a thorn,
>   He pulled out his pipe and began for to play;
> It was on a midsummer day in the morn,
>   For honour of that holiday.
> A ditty he did chant along
>   That goes to the tune of Cater Bordee;
> And this was the burden of his song,
>   If thou wilt pipe, lad, I'll dance to thee."

This day, however, Matthew did not intend to give Miles the pleasant job of entertaining him and his household. "Miles," he said, "you could not have come at a better moment. Can you help me to teach my wife a lesson that she needs to learn?" "You have always been my patron, Master Robson," replied Miles, "and I will help you if I can."

"Well then," said Matthew, "tonight my wife will be at her work again, and she will not stop, Sabbath or no Sabbath, till she has finished her carding. Before she returns, hide in the cellar beneath the kitchen, and when you hear the grandfather clock in the kitchen strike twelve, strike up the weirdest music that ever piper played, and play till she throws down her wool and runs for fear."

"That I will," said Miles. "I shall play the song of the Brown Men of the Moors when they are in full cry, I shall play the songs of the Bad Fairies, and I shall play the screeching of the witches of Wallsend."

"Good, and when you hear me stamp on the floor, stop as if someone had slit your pipes with a knife. Then, in the morning when the first cock crows, meet me behind the peat-stack."

"I will," said Miles, and went down to his cellar.

No sooner had Mistress Robson returned than she took out her fleeces and began carding the wool ready for the maidens to spin.

"Wife," said Matthew, "I see you are going to be at your work again. I can see no harm in your working on Saturday evenings, but I hope you are not going to desecrate the Lord's Day again."

"Whisht, Matthew," replied his wife. "Go and mend the broken hay-rake, and leave me to my work."

"Some day you may change your tune," said Matthew, and went out to look for hazel wood to make new teeth for the broken hay-rake. He mended the rake, had his supper, and sat a while before the fire, but Mistress Robson was still at her work. When he went to bed, she was still busy.

Eleven o'clock came, and half-past eleven, and a quarter to twelve, and still she worked. At last the old grandfather clock wheezed like an old man going to cough, and struck midnight; and no sooner had the last stroke died away than there arose from underground sounds that made Mistress Robson shake with fear. First it was like the song of the Brown Men of the Moors when humans trespass on their land; then it was like the song of the Bad Fairies when they are enraged; then it was like the screeching of the witches when they go round their cauldron. Mistress Robson flung down her fleece and ran upstairs as fast as she could, crying, "Matthew, Matthew, come quick and lay the Devil! Lay the Devil!"

"What on earth is the matter?" said Matthew.

"O Matthew, lay the Devil, and never again will I work on the Sabbath Day."

"Ah, I knew some such thing would befall. Come with me, and I will speak with him." And Matthew took the Bible in his hands and led his trembling wife downstairs. Then he stamped his foot on the floor, and immediately the eerie music stopped. Then he called out in a loud voice:

> "If my wife this promise give,
> Ne'er to work while she do live
> On another Sabbath Day,
> Devil, wilt thou go away?"

And from underground came the answer in a hollow voice:

> "If your wife will keep her trust,
> Leave this house and go I must;
> If her promise be not true,
> I'll come again and claim my due."

"Come then, wife," said Matthew, "you must swear your oath."

"O that I will," said the wife, and, putting her hand on the Bible, she swore that she would keep the Sabbath Day from that time on. And when she had finished she heard the eerie music fading and fading, as if it was sinking into the middle of the earth.

"Now to bed," said Matthew, "and be thankful you came off so lightly."

For the first time Matthew was the early one to rise the next morning. When the first cock crew, he rose to meet Miles behind the peat-stack, and gave him one of his handsomest fleeces for helping to cure his wife.

MOTIFS: c.631 [*Tabu: breaking the Sabbath*]; K.1838 [*Disguise as Devil*]; G.303.6.2.14 [*The Devil appears to Sabbath-breakers*].

¶ This tale of a spoof Devil embodies a real belief in the Sabbath tabu, but entails no serious consequence, so that it might well be placed among the jocular tales. As a rule, this masking brought down a punishment on the maskers.

See "The Croydon Devil claims His Own" (B, III), "Black Bucca and White Bucca" (B, II).

THE FARMER AND THE FOOTPADS

Ruth L. Tongue, *Somerset Folklore*, p. 197.

The farmer from Bullers Farm went to Taunton Market one wintry day. He returned late with his market-money in his breeches pocket, not in his saddle-bags, as was customary.

At the foot of Buncombe Hill he came up with a well-dressed foot-passenger who asked him for a lift behind on the horse. The night was getting dark and the way among the trees even darker, but the farmer dare not refuse. There might be more of the gang ahead. There was only one thing to do. He pretended to be still cider-hazy. He told the man to mount behind and hold on to his belt, warning him that the horse might not "stand" for him. Then he slyly spurred his old horse into a most uneven and spirited gait, and the fellow clinging behind got the benefit of all the buck-jumps and had rather a rough passage. He did gasp out a warning to the farmer, who was singing drunkenly as the old horse jinked and propped along, "Don't 'ee whistle on no account." Hearing this, the farmer knew a gang lay in wait ahead, so, stealthily drawing a pocket-knife, he sliced through his belt and spurred the horse frantically to the top of the hill. His unwelcome passenger landed so heavily he could not get his breath to whistle until the flying pair had passed the Traveller's Rest. At the signal four mounted men rode out of the wood and galloped after their terrified prey, who fled down Broomfield Road and along by Ruborough Camp. Just ahead of the pursuit the farmer finally rode the old horse into the middle of a gorsey field and ran to the ditch to hide. The pursuers came up with the horse and emptied the saddle-bags, but, finding nothing, rode off cursing. The farmer crept home along the hedges and so saved the market-money. I am told that, according to the Session Papers in Taunton Museum, this gang was tried and sentenced in 1830.

Oral collection, 1955. Told to William Chidley by Mr Sanders, carter, aged 70, who was told the story when a boy by the farmer himself.
TYPE 968. MOTIF: K.437 [*Robber overcome*].
¶ A similar story is told in the folk-song, "The Silly Old Man".
See "The Boy Who outwitted the Robber" (A, IV), "A Robber's Cunning against Another Robber" (A, IV).

THE FIDDLER AND THE MAIDS

Ruth L. Tongue, *Somerset Folklore*, p. 16.

There are three stone circles in Stanton Drew. The smallest is called "The Fiddler and the Maids", but all three are marked as "The Wedding" in Stachey's map of 1736. The story is that a wedding party gathered in the Church Field below Dundry Hill on a Saturday evening. The local harper played for them until nearly midnight, and then reminded them that it would soon be Sunday. They were very merry, however, and one of them cried out that they would go on dancing even if they had to get the Devil himself to play. The harper put up his harp and turned to go, but heard piping behind him, and, looking back, saw that a tall piper had joined the company. He piped faster and faster, so that they danced on, whether they wanted to or not. Their cries and shrieks and curses were heard during the night, but in the morning nothing was to be seen of them but the three rings of stones.

This tale still survives in oral tradition. E. Boger, *Myths, Scenes and Worthies of Somerset*. MOTIFS: A.970 [*Origin of rocks and stones*]; D.231 [*Transformation: man to stone*]; G.303.6.2.14 [*Devil appears to Sabbath-breakers*]; G.303.9.8.2 [*Devil plays fiddle at wedding*]; Q.386.2 [*Girl who dances on Sunday is turned to stone*]. (Baughman).
¶ See "The Giants' Dance", "The Rollright Stones".

FIDDLER'S WELL [summary]

Douglas, *Scottish Fairy and Folk Tales*, p. 97.

Two young men of Cromarty, who were fast friends, both fell ill about the same time of consumption. In one of them the disease progressed so fast that within two months he was dead. The other, though weak and wasted, had just strength to follow his friend's body to its burial. But later, in the evening, he felt so distressed that he could not sleep in peace. His dreams were haunted by fearful images of graves and coffins. Towards morning, however, he fell at last into a calm and happy sleep. He dreamed that he was walking on the sea-shore, on a clear day in summer, and that someone approached from behind, and whispered in the voice of his dead friend, "Go on, Willie, I shall meet you at *Stormy*." This was a rock nearby, named for the violence of the east winds that often beat against it. The young man turned and, seeing no one, he went on towards the rock, hoping to meet his friend there. Suddenly he remembered that his friend was dead, and at the thought he burst into tears. Just then a great field-bee came humming from the west, and circled and buzzed round his ear, "Dig, Willie, and drink. Dig, Willie, and drink." Willie obeyed the voice, and as soon as the first sod came up out of the bank, a spring of clear water gushed forth, and the bee, circling more and more widely round him, and humming triumphantly, at last flew away. As he watched its flight, his dream slowly faded and he awoke in his own room. But he went to the rock, dug the well and, after drinking its water, recovered from his sickness. This young man's name was Fiddler, a common name of sailors in those parts, and from this fact the well is still called Fiddler's Well. Its water, drunk early in the morning, together with the pure air and the exercise involved, is still said to work cures.

From Hugh Miller, *Scenes and Legends of the North of Scotland.*
MOTIFS: D.1500.1.1 [*Magic healing well*]; E.734.2 [*Soul in form of bee*].
¶ See "Bladud of Bath", "Nether Stowey Blind Well".

FIGHTING CHARLIE ARMSTRONG
AND MEG MERRILEES

E. Bogg, *Lakeland and Ribblesdale*, p. 44.

Mump's Ha'...was formerly an alehouse...It was here...that Fighting Charlie, an Armstrong of Liddlesdale, stayed to refresh himself when returning from Stagshawbank Fair. Meg was unusually kind and gracious, and played the hostess well; watching her opportunity, however, she adroitly withdrew the charges from his pistols, and rewadded them with tow; but all her blandishments and smiles could not prevail on Charlie to stay for the night, for he had been warned of the evil reputation the inn-keeper and his wife bore. So he mounted and rode off at a sharp trot in the darkness; but suddenly remembering that under Meg's bland face there had lurked a sinister smile, he felt for his pistols, and, to his anger and astonishment, found the charges had been withdrawn, and the space filled with tow. Fully convinced that he was to be waylaid, he carefully reloaded the pistols, and spurred his steed over the wild waste, scanning the moor in every direction. Suddenly two mounted fellows, disguised and armed to the teeth, confronted him, and a glance over his shoulder proved that two other men had taken up the rear. The men in the front called on him to stand and deliver, but Charlie, spurring his horse, went boldly on, and covered the robbers with his pistols.

"D—n your pistols," shouted one of the robbers, "Aw care not a curse for it."

"Aye, lad," said the deep voice of Fighting Charlie, "but the too's oot noo." This was enough for the highwaymen; they had often heard of Charlie's prowess, but had never expected to meet a man so cool and daring. They turned and fled over the moor, and Armstrong reached home without further molestation. But he always swore that the robber who charged him was none other than the landlord of Mump's Ha'.

MOTIFS: K.2241 [*Treacherous innkeeper*]; K.437 [*Robber overcome*].
¶ See "The Treacherous Innkeeper" (B, III).

THE FIRST CROP

Norton Collection, III, p. 100.

It has been reported that Sir —— bought a field and stipulated with the vendor that payment was to be made when the first crop was taken off. The calculating purchaser had the field sown with acorns, and the first crop would be oak timber.

Cumberland, Dickinson, p. 32.

TYPE 1185. MOTIF: K.221 [*Payment to be made at harvest of first crop*].
¶ In the Scandinavian and German versions of this type the bargain is not with a human seller, but with the Devil. See Kristensen, *Danske Sagn*, III, 1895, p. 382; German, S. Kanfach und Müller, *Nieder Sachsische Sagen und Märchen*, 4, p. 170.

THE FISHERMAN OF WORLE

Ruth L. Tongue, *Somerset Folklore*, p. 149.

At Worle, when the fishermen go down to sea, they each put a white stone on the cairn or "fairy mound" on the hillside and say:

> Ina pic winna
> Send me a good dinner.

And more times than not they come with a load of fish. Now in the old days, there was a clever Dick of a fellow who said he didn't believe in luck. He wasn't going to put a stone on the fairy mound, not he. And his catch would be as good as theirs. They'd all see! They did! First go off, *he went to sea on a Friday*, yes he did. And he'd hardly gone a quarter mile when blest if his old woman didn't come *running after him* in her white apron *calling his name*. You'd think that would have been enough to bring the fool up short. But he wouldn't go home, not he! On he goes and his addlehead of a wife *watches him out of sight*, and *he doesn't put any stone on the cairn*, and he doesn't even say the rhyme, so it just serves him right when he comes *face to face with*

Parson, and what's more, *Parson says "Good day" to him*. But he still wouldn't go home. Down by the Harbour what should run across the road but a *black pig* and you should have heard the fool swear but still he went on down to the boats, and as he sailed out he heard a voice from the cliffs shouting, *"Good dog, after that rabbit now."* But even then he wouldn't turn back.

Out he went and down Channel, and whether he was wrecked or picked up by a Bristol slaver and sold in the West Indies nobody knows. He never came back to Worle, and nobody cared!

Note: This is compiled from a Weston-super-Mare fisherman, the cairn story only. The rest of the tale came from such people as a maid-servant with sailor brothers, the driver of a tourist waggonette, a retired sea captain, a weaver of lobster-pots and a carter of kelp for farm manure. The versions were often fragmentary. This is the best, but many of the superstitions are still alive from Clevedon to the Exmoor sea-board. Phrases in italics are bad luck omens.

MOTIFS: V.11.3 [*Sacrifice to stone*]; N.128 [*Unlucky days*]; C.435.1 [*Taboo: uttering spouse's name*]; C.493.1 [*Wishing sailor good luck*]; C.433.2 [*Dangerous animals not to be named*]; C.494 [*Tabu: cursing*].

¶ This is not a complete story, but a collection of fishermen's superstitions.

FITZHUGH OF COTHERSTONE [shortened]

From E. Bogg, *Lakeland and Ribblesdale*, p. 78.

The ruins of Cotherstone Castle stand on a green hill, above the confluence of the Balder and the Tees. It was the home of the Fitzhughs, between whom and the Kerrs of Roxburghshire there was a long and deadly feud. This feud began on the battlefields of France, in the early part of the fifteenth century, when many Scotch knights fought on the side of the French. One of the Kerrs captured a Fitzhugh in battle, and thus the feud arose.

Later, during a Border raid, the Fitzhughs surprised the house of the Kerrs, and the lady of the house was slain, in the absence of the Lord and his son. The only other child, a daughter, was carried away by the enemy, and for many years no news of her reached her parents. She, however, grew up beautiful and accomplished in the house of the enemy, in ignorance of her true parentage. The heir of the Fitzhughs fell deeply in love with her, she returned his love, and a marriage was about to take place between them when it chanced that Mabel at last learnt the truth about her birth. She seemed inconsolable, but the Fitzhugh, who had been like a father to her, persuaded her that the marriage plan should go forward, and that as soon as it was accomplished they should journey to Scotland, and be reconciled to her father. But a few nights before the marriage-day the Kerrs again descended on the Fitzhugh castle, and in the ensuing battle, the young heir was mortally wounded. Mabel, in her agony, threw herself on the body of her lover, and herself also received a mortal wound. But in the first light of morning, the dying man asked for the leader of the enemy, and when he came, told him all the story, and of their intended reconciliation. It was a sorrowful victory for the Kerrs.

MOTIFS: R.10.3 [*Child abducted*]; T.80 [*Tragic love*]; T.81.3 [*Girl falls dead on lover's body*].

FOUNTAINS ABBEY

Parkinson, *Yorkshire Legends and Traditions*, 1st series, p. 29.

In the year A.D. 1132, Richard, the Prior of St Mary's Abbey at York, with twelve brethren of the house, left the brotherhood to adopt a stricter way of life than the Benedictine under its rather easy-going Abbot. Archbishop Thurston took them under his protection, and eventually gave them land to found a monastery in the valley of the Skell, near How Hill.

There, in the depths of winter, their only shelter at first was a ring of seven yew trees, two or three of which still stand. Soon they built a hut round the trunk of a great elm, their food being bark and leaves, and their drink water from the neighbouring springs.

They adopted the Cistercian rule, and were presently joined by two or three men of some property, so that things improved with them a little. But while they were still enduring great privation, a traveller one day knocked at their gate and asked for food. There were only two and a half loaves in the house, and the porter tried to refuse the man, but he persisted in asking in the name of the blessed Saviour, so the porter at last went to the Abbot, who told him to give the man one loaf; that would leave one and a half for the carpenters and other workers. As for the monks, he said, God would provide for them as He saw best.

Scarcely had this been done when there came to the gate of the convent a cart loaded with bread, sent to their relief by Eustace Fitzhugh, the Lord of Knaresborough Castle.

And so began better times for the monks of Fountains Abbey.

MOTIFS: V.410 [*Charity rewarded*]; Q.111.2 [*Riches as reward for hospitality*].

GARMSTONE CASTLE

E. M. Leather, *Folk-Lore of the Shire. The Memorials of Old Herefordshire*, p. 56.

The builders began on the site of the old castle, but the fairies carried away the stones every night, and at last the castle was built in a new place, lower down.

    The same story is told of the Devil's Churchyard at Ibsden on the Chilterns, where St Bertin started to build, but the Devil carried away the stones every night until he was forced to build in the valley below.

TYPE ML.7060, MOTIF: D.2192 [*Work of day magically overthrown at night*].
¶ See "Callaly Castle", "The Castle of Melgund".

THE GIANT'S DANCE

Roger of Wendover, *Chronicle*, I, pp. 22-24

[Aurelius Ambrosius] proceeded to the monastery of Ambrus, near Kaercaradauc, now called Salisbury, where lay the nobles who had falled victims to Hengist's treachery. He was moved to tears at the sight, and, considering within himself how he could make the spot memorable, he gave orders that the prophet Merlin should be diligently sought, that with the aid of his counsel he might effect his purpose. When Merlin was brought before the king, he declared to him the death of the nobles, the treachery of the Saxons, and his own desire to do honour to the spot. After remaining a little while in mental abstraction, Merlin at length replied, "If thou wishest, my lord king, to grace this burial spot with a lasting monument, send for the Giant's Dance, which is on Mount Killaraus in Ireland, where there is such a structure of stones as no one of this age has ever yet set his eyes on. The stones are of vast size, and so admirably set, that if they were to stand fixed here in precisely the same manner, they would stand for ever and constitute a wonderful monument." At this the king laughed, and asked Merlin whether the stones of Ireland were better than those of Britain, that they must needs be fetched from such a distance. Whereupon Merlin replied, "Thy laughter, O king, is ill-timed; for there is a mystery in these stones, which are endued with healing qualities. Giants in times past brought them thither from the remotest parts of Africa, that they might bathe beneath them when afflicted with any malady. They washed the stones with various confections of herbs, which they then cast into the bath, and the sick were thereupon cured; nor is there a single stone of them without its virtue." On hearing this, the Britons determined to send for the stones; and for this purpose they chose Uther, the king's brother, to go with fifteen thousand warriors, and if any resistance were offered, to bring off the stones by force. Moreover, Merlin was appointed to go with them, that everything might be done by his counsel and direction. Having prepared ships, they put to sea, and had a prosperous voyage to Ireland. On learning the object they had in coming, Gillomannius, king of Ireland, called his people to arms, declaring that, while he lived, he would not suffer the smallest stone of the Dance to be taken away from them. Straightway both parties engaged, but the victory remained with the Britons. Whereupon they went to Mount Killaraus, and laboured in vain to remove the structure of stones; at which Merlin laughed, and then applying expedients of his own, he took down the stones with incredible ease, and, placing them on shipboard, brought them with joy to Britain. On hearing which, Aurelius came to Mount Ambrius, attended with his bishops, and abbats, and other nobles, and there wore his crown on the day of Pentecost.... He commanded Merlin to set up the stones around the burial place of the nobles; which he did accordingly, in a marvellous manner, exactly as they were placed on Mount Killaraus.

MOTIFS: D.1814.1 [*Advice from magician*]; F.309 [*Extraordinary stones*]; A.977 [*Origin of groups of stones*]; D.2136.1 [*Rocks moved by magic*].
¶ The name "The Giant's Dance" seems to suggest that the origin of Stonehenge was once ascribed to giants turned to stone, but there is nothing of this in Merlin's account.

GIFFARD'S JUMP [summary]

J. R. W. Coxhead, *Legends of Devon*, p. 20.

On 28 October 1537, Thomas Giffard of Halsbury was married to Margaret, daughter of Anthony Monk, Esq, of Potheridge, in the parish church of Parkham.

This event, with its sequel, was recorded in 1791 by Sir A. Hardinge Giffard, in a long poem, from which the following account is derived:

After their marriage, the bridegroom took his bride to view the sea from the neighbouring cliffs. She ventured too close to the edge, and he seized her arm to pull her back, but as he did so, his foot slipped, and, though she was saved, he himself plunged over the precipice. Margaret fainted with horror, and was borne by her attendants back to Halsbury. She revived, and was told of her husband's dreadful fall; but her horror was turned to joy, for suddenly his voice was heard outside her room. He entered, and told them that a stunted oak-tree, growing out of the cliff, had saved his life. He had been caught in its branches, and, grasping a projecting piece of rock, had gradually made his way to a less dangerous part of the cliff, from which he was able to climb back to safety.

The cliff, at the point known as "Giffard's Jump", is about 130 feet high.

MOTIF: A.968.2 (variant) [*Cliff from Lovers' Leap*].

¶ There are many cliffs named from lovers' leaps in Britain, but none that are supposed to be actually formed by them. An example is "The Maiden's Leap" in Huntingtower, Perthshire, a narrow gap between two high towers, supposed to be leapt by a maiden to gain access to her lover. Giffard's jump was rather a fall than a leap.

GILSLAND WELL

Denham Tracts, I, p. 164.

> In Cumberland there is a spring,
>   And strange it is to tell,
> That many a fortune it will make,
>   If never a drop they sell.

The prophetic rhymes are popularly understood to allude to Gilsland Spa, respecting which there is a very curious tradition, viz. that on the medicinal virtues being first discovered, the person who owned the land, not resting satisfied, as would appear, with his profits which the influx of strangers to the place had caused, built a house over the spring with the intention of selling the waters. But his avarice was punished in a very singular manner, for no sooner had he completed the house than the spring dried up, and continued so until the house was pulled down; when lo! another miracle, it flowed again as before.

Whether true or false, this story of antiquity enforces a most beautiful moral and religious precept.

MOTIFS: D.1500.1.1 [*Magic healing well*]; Q.272 [*Avarice punished*].

¶ See "Skimmington Well", "Nether Stowey Blind Well".

GLAMIS CASTLE: A LEGEND

R. Macdonald Robertson, *More Highland Folk-Tales*, p. 53.

The Hill of Denoon in Strathmore was at one time believed to be the abode of fairies, and the frequent scene of their midnight revelries. It was part of the code of the "Sith" that no building for human habitation should be allowed to be erected upon the enchanted ground; and, being unable by their own efforts to guard against sacrilegious encroachment on their territory, these Strathmore fairies were believed to have made a compact with a company of evil spirits, whose motive was the doing of mischief to mankind and bringing trouble to anyone unfortunate enough to incur their displeasure.

Three demons, it is said, solemnly bound themselves to prevent the erection of any building whatever on the Hill of Denoon. One evening, in the moonlight certain indications of the commencement of building operations were revealed to the midnight revellers on the hill. We must presume a council of war to have followed between the fairies and their allies, for the well-laid foundations of Glamis Castle were demolished in a single night and sent hurtling over the steep rock into the valley below.

On their return to work the following morning, the builders were sorely puzzled, but proceeded to prepare new foundations of a more durable character. These were allowed to rise to a degree higher than the former ones; then a mighty earth-tremor shook the hill, and the stones were ground to powder.

Additional and more highly skilled workmen were engaged, and for a time all went well, the walls of the castle rising to view in solidity and grandeur. The evil spirits bided their time, and then ruthlessly swept away, as if by a whirlwind, every vestige of the walls. The master-builder then ceased to attribute these successive disasters to either an act of God or to the forces of Nature; and decided rightly that evil influences were at work. He was a man of courage and determination and, after operations had been commenced for the fourth time, resolved to keep watch every night until the expected onslaught came, and defy all the hosts of Hell to prevent the rebuilding of the castle. But when the appointed night came:

> His courage failed when on the blast
> A demon swift came howling past,
> Loud screeching wild and fearfully,
> This ominous, dark, prophetic cry...
> "Build not on this enchanted ground;
> 'Tis sacred all these hills around;
> Go, build the castle in a bog,
> Where it will neither shake nor shog."

For a fourth time the partially completed edifice was demolished and there were no further attempts to build a castle on the fairies' hill, which, however, bears to this day scattered remains of the foundations of a large castellated building. There are several other traditional accounts of how members of the human race, unaware that the hillock on which they were about to build was already an "occupied" building, were obliged to desist because of the opposition of the fairies. A former Grant of Ballindalloch, in Strathspey, who attempted to build a castle on a "Sithean" (fairy mound) found every morning that the previous day's work had been undone and the stones removed from the site.

One night he kept watch for the vandals, and heard a voice telling him to "Build on the cowhaugh" (meadow) instead of on the hill. This he accordingly did, and was subjected to no further interruptions.

TYPE ML.7060. MOTIFS: C.93.7 [*Tabu: erecting fort on holy ground*]; D.2192 [*Work of day magically overthrown at night*].

¶ There are various other legends of Glamis, of the Devil's visit, for instance, and a never-ending card-party, with many modern legends about the blocked-up room, but the "monster" is said to have died, and the legends are perishing of inanition.

See "Callaly Castle", "The Castle of Melgund", "Mauldslie Castle".

GODSHILL

Abraham Elder, *Tales and Legends of the Isle of Wight*, p. 222.

Certain pious men once contributed a sum of money to build a church, and a spot was chosen at the foot of a hill now known as Godshill. They sent a message to the owner of the land, and told him to accept with humility and gratitude the great honour being conferred to him.

But this man was a poor franklin, not given to godliness, and a hater of all priests and monks, except for one jolly friar, who visited him from time to time, and would shrive him without too much attention to details. He did not dare, however, to refuse outright to have the church built on his land; but he pointed out that there was a splendid position available at the top of the hill. They informed him that it had already been carefully considered, and rejected as being too exposed.

The franklin next suggested that he himself was a great sinner, unworthy to have a hallowed building erected on his ground; whereas his neighbours on either side were pious men, and fit for so great a distinction. They replied that, by the laying of the foundation stone of the church alone, he would receive absolution from his sins, and that no taint of sin would remain on the land once it had been consecrated.

At last the franklin owned that by losing the best piece of his small farm he and his family would be reduced to poverty, but the monks turned a deaf ear to his fears. The bishop's architect next arrived to mark out the site, and some stones from the quarry at Binstead were piled up ready for the work to be begun next day. When they arrived the next morning, however, not a stone was to be seen on the bare surface of the field. The franklin appeared as much amazed as the rest, and as they stood there in wonder, the owner of the land at the top of the hill appeared among them declaring indignantly that, without a word to him, the foundations of a church had been marked out on his land, and building stones heaped up in readiness for the work.

The bishop was due to come the same afternoon to lay the foundation stone, so, without further discussion, everyone set to work to remove the stones, and mark out foundations again on the original spot. He arrived in due time, riding on a mule, and with a company of monks walking in procession behind him, chanting solemnly. But on reaching the site of the new church, as the bishop was about to alight, his mule, refusing to stop, carried him at a breakneck speed halfway up the hill, and was only checked by the utmost efforts of two strong men hanging on to its reins. After this, however, the ceremony was completed: the bishop laid the stone over a small silver coin, a psalm was sung; and the franklin was duly acquitted of all his sins. As they rode home, the monks debated the strange events, and the behaviour of the bishop's mule; and the bishop determined, for the truth's sake, to set two men to watch by the new church that night, and he sent one of his attendants back to direct that this should be done, with his blessing.

In the morning these two men were found lying helpless on the ground, as if in a drunken stupor; the stones had again moved to the top of the hill, and all traces of foundation marks had disappeared under the smooth turf.

The watchers reported that, about midnight, they had been startled by a low, rumbling noise, and the stones begun to move. They skipped or rolled away one by one, to the foot of the hill, and then began to scramble up it. The little stones moved quickly; the rest more slowly. One great stone got stuck fast in a hole; they eased it out, and it followed the rest with no further trouble; the architect's pegs followed the stones, a spade followed the pegs, and eventually the foundations had marked themselves out at the top of the hill, just as on the previous night. One of the two watchmen showed a large wound on his shin, which he said had been made by one of the rolling stones, and which certainly had not been there the previous day.

The bishop and his council now decided that in face of this evidence he could do nothing but reconsecrate the church on the new site. Accordingly, two days later, this was done, the bishop relating at length the miracle which had led to the event; the church was duly completed, and the ground on which it stood had ever since been known as Godshill.

TYPE ML.7060. MOTIFS: V.111.3 [*Site where a church must be built miraculously indicated*]; D.2192 [*Work of day magically overthrown at night*].
¶ A similar explanation to that given in the second version of "Callaly Castle" is indicated here.

GOLD HILL

W. H. Barrett, *Tales from the Fens*, p. 133.

Hundreds of years ago King John, who had heard of the fine goings-on at Wisbech Fair, thought he might have a bit of fun there himself, so he came to the Castle and put up there for the night. Then he joined the crowd at the fair and made as much noise as anyone else. After the frolics were over, the king was just sober enough to find his own way back to the Castle, taking a Wisbech wench with him to keep him warm from the cold fen wind. But when he woke up in the morning, he found that all his money and jewels were missing and that the girl had gone, and his servant too.

John flew into a terrible temper and ordered the Castle to be searched from top to bottom, but all that was found were six Wisbech wenches down in the soldiers' quarters, and they swore they knew nothing of any jewels or treasures; they'd only come to the Castle to do the weekly wash. So the king fretted and fumed, and ordered the sentry who'd been on duty at the gate to be hung from the Castle wall; then he clattered out of the Castle, leaving orders that the search was to go on. No one remembered to change that order, and that's why people are still looking for the treasure today.

Next morning a man came into the Castle yard with his cart, to take the dung away from the stables, and he was just bending down to lift up a load when a dagger was pushed between his ribs and he fell down dead. Then the king's servant and the girl who'd shared John's bed that night lifted up the corpse and dumped it in the cart. The girl nipped in beside it, and the servant pulled down the top. Then he led the horse to the Castle gate, which the sentry unbolted for him, and came out on to the road and into the market-place. There he took the horse out of the shafts and left the cart standing by the hot-eel stall. When the stall-holder came back from the tavern, not liking the smell of the dung in the cart he put himself between the shafts and pulled the cart along to the river bank and toppled it into the river, where it sank.

Now, as the servant and the girl were riding along on the horse, they were seen by two Fenmen, who were lying hidden in the reeds near the trackway just outside Wisbech. By making the sound of bird-calls, the two men passed on the news to others, hidden farther along the track, that two travellers were on their way. These others passed the message on until the servant and the girl had come to a group of huts standing hidden in tall reeds and osiers. A crowd of Fenmen were waiting for them here and they surrounded the pair and made them get off the horse. The servant knew that the men would recognize the livery he was wearing, so he told them that he and his wife were royal servants; they had lost their way and were wandering along the track trying to find their master.

"And what have you got in the two leather bags?" asked the Fenmen.

"Money," said the servant. "Gold and silver money and a lot of jewels and precious stones which I stole last night from the King when he was asleep." And he emptied out the bags to show his haul.

"Well," said the Fenmen, "we certainly don't want to kill a man who seems to be better than ten of us when it comes to thieving. So you'd better come and live here with us. There is plenty of work going in your trade with all the money that's lying about in the manors on the edge of the Fens."

So the man and the girl were taken to a mound where the Fenmen lived and were given a hut and a cooking-pot. They were also taught the law of the Fens, which was that they must never steal from a neighbour and must always help each other in time of need. They soon settled down in their new home, and one of the first things they did was to pack up the royal livery inside two leather bags, and send them by boat down to Lynn. From there the bags were sent on to the king, who, when he saw them, flew into such a rage that he had a fit and died. Then, just nine months after Wisbech Fair, the girl had a lusty boy, who, when he grew up, was called the Prince, and he became the greatest thief the Fens have ever known.

Meantime, of course, the Fenmen made the most of all the gold and silver coins which the servant and the girl had brought. Most of the money went on paying the Abbot of Ely so that the Fenmen he held in prison could be set free, and so much gold was paid out that the monks began to wonder where it all came from. But the Fenmen could never use the jewels, so they divided them among themselves, and each man hid his share under the floor of his hut. Years afterwards a great flood came and swept right over the Welney Fens and washed away all the huts. Later on a Dutchman came to drain the Fens and dig wide ditches, and one of these went right across the fen, where the huts had been. While they were working on the ditch they came across a few bits of jewellery and, later on, a few more bits were turned up by the plough. When folks heard of this, they began to call the mound where those old Fenmen had lived "Gold Hill". So you see, John didn't lose all his treasure in the Wash. Some of it disappeared at a place between Littleport and Wisbech, on the Welney Wash.

MOTIFS: A.1617 [*Origin of place-name*]; K.301.2 [*Family of thieves*]; K.331 [*Goods stolen while owner sleeps*].

¶ The character given King John in this legend is not a good one; but here, as in Somerset, a tradition survives of him as a jovial character, ready to share his subjects' pleasures.

THE GOLD OF CRAUFURDLAND

T. F. Thistleton Dyer, *The Ghost World*, pp. 401–3.

It is popularly believed that for many ages past a pot of gold has lain at the bottom of a pool beneath a fall of the rivulet underneath Craufurdland Bridge, about three miles from Kilmarnock. Many attempts have been made to recover this treasure, but something unforeseen has always happened to prevent a successful issue. "The last effort made, by the Laird of Craufurdland himself", writes Mr Chambers, "was early in the last century, at the head of a party of his domestics, who first dammed up the water, then emptied the pool of its contents, and had heard their instruments clink on the kettle, when a voice was heard saying:
    "'Pow, pow!
     Craufurdland Tower's a' in a low!'

"Whereupon the Laird left the scene, followed by his servants, and ran home to save what he could. Of course, there was no fire in the house, and when they came back to renew their operations, they found the water falling over the lin in full force. Being now convinced that a power above that of mortals was opposed to their researches, the Laird and his people gave up the attempt. Such is the traditional story, whether", adds Mr Chambers, "founded on any actual occurrence, or a mere fiction of the peasants' brains; but it was curious that a later and well-authenticated effort to recover the treasure was interrupted by a natural occurrence in some respects similar".

Chambers, *Popular Rhymes of Scotland*, pp. 241–2.
TYPE ML.8010 (Legends about hidden treasure). MOTIFS: N.513.4 [*Treasure hidden in river*]; N.564 [*Magic illusion prevents men from raising treasure*].
¶ See "The Gold of Largo Law", "The Treasure of Castle Rach" (B, III).

THE GOLD OF LARGO LAW [abbreviated]

Wilkie, *Bygone Fife*, p. 166.

Largo is peculiarly endowed with [such] legends...Best known is the tradition of a treasure or a gold-mine reputed to be either under or near the Law. The locality is tantalizingly vague, but that one or the other exists is proven by the fact that the sheep grazing on the hill pastures are occasionally seen to have their wool tinged yellow. The cottars know that they have been lying above hidden gold.
   ...While the origin of the hill is familiar, it is not so widely known that one of the tasks set by the Wizard of Balwearie to his familiars was

its removal. They had only begun their labours when the happier idea of a never-ending employment of their turbulent energies occurred to Sir Michael...otherwise, surely, the gold under the Law must have been laid bare. Enough soil, as it happened, had been removed to form Norrie's Law.

...The story told around the ingle-neuk ran thus:

Once, lang syne, the shepherd of Balmain came near solving the mystery of the gold. Balmain, as everybody knows, lies at the north-western slope of Largo Law, and the shepherd had brooded for years over the problem. He had watched the resting-places of the sheep for a clue, but it evaded him. His chance came in another way. The ghost of some forgotten denizen of the region haunted the vicinity, and was popularly believed to be possessed of the secret, but to be tongue-tied till a mortal sought of him enlightenment. Many would have fain put the question, but when the opportunity was given fear fell upon them and they fled.

Dazzling visions of future grandeur opened before the shepherd while he sat on green hillock or feal dyke with his collie at his feet, or took his way homeward after a spell at lambing-time. He had seen the dread shape more than once and quailed. But at last he took his courage in his hands, and when again the spectre stood beside him accosted it. In quavering tones he demanded what kept it from its rest. The answer was that the uncommunicated secret troubled its repose. The promise was given that if the mortal were brave enough to come to a certain part of the hill on a night indicated, precisely at eight o'clock (the tradition is exact as to the hour, though the day is not mentioned), he would learn all he ought to know.

There were, however, two conditions:

> "If Auchindowie cock disna craw,
> And the herd of Balmain his horn disna blaw,
> I'll tell ye where the gowd is in Largo Law".

The shepherd was elated. He saw himself the equal of the Laird of Largo, to say nothing of those of Montrose and Lundin. He was a man who left naught to chance. Every cock, young and old, in Auchindowie perished mysteriously; and Tammie Norrie, the cowherd, was enjoined by his colleague to refrain, on peril of his life, from blowing the horn that called the cows together for their return from the pastures.

Whether it was forgetfulness or dourness on Tammie's part that led to the catastrophe can never be known.

The shepherd was at the spot appointed. Eight o'clock was indicated by the place of the westering sun. The visitant from the world beyond stood punctually by his side.

At that moment, ere either could address the other, there floated down from the height above the notes of the cowherd's horn. Mortal and immortal were alike struck dumb by dismay and wrath, if indeed the dead suffer the emotions of the living. Then, regaining the power of utterance, the spectre pronounced doom:

> "Woe to the man that blew that horn,
>   For out of that spot he shall never be borne!"

The shepherd stood alone.

No more did Tammie Norrie call the cattle home to Balmain. The blast he sounded had not re-echoed from Largo Law ere he fell, where he stood, a lifeless corpse. Nor could his body be moved. The strength went out of every arm that attempted the task, and men struggled as in a dream. So they abandoned it, and piled a cairn above the luckless cowherd.

TYPE ML.8010 . MOTIFS: E.415.1.2 [*Return from dead to uncover secretly hidden treasure*]; E.371 [*Return from the dead to reveal hidden treasure*]; E.452 [*Ghost laid at cockcrow*]; N.555 [*Time favourable for unearthing treasure*]; N.550.1 [*Continual failure to find or unearth hidden treasure*]; E.384.3 [*Ghost summoned by horn*]; E.411.0.3.1 [*Dead body cannot be moved from where it lies*].

¶ It is not certain if the ghost was summoned away by Norrie's horn, but from the killing of Norrie it seems likely. There are many features of interest in this story.

See "The Treasure of Castle Rach".

GRAYSTEEL [summary]

A Traditional Story of Caithness (summary). *The Book of Scottish Story*, pp. 136–8.

The small mountain tarn known as the Loch of Raenag, in Caithness, is protected to the north by a hill of Bencheildt, and to the south by the chain of lofty mountains named Scarabine, Morven, and the Pap, which divide Sutherland from Caithness. Near the north edge of this loch is a small island, on which stand the ruins of an old keep, where once lived a noted freebooter, known as Graysteel, whose raids from the Ord to Duncansbay Head kept all the countryside in alarm.

He was an expert swordsman of great physical strength, and no trespasser escaped him alive.

A young man of the family of Rollo, out hunting one day, had the misfortune to encroach unwittingly on Graysteel's land; and he, being informed by some of his men, came out to challenge the intruder. Young Rollo faced him boldly and, after a long struggle, was mortally wounded; Graysteel stripped his body of all that was of value, and then threw it into the loch.

When at last the news of his death reached his family, amid the general

distress the young Laird of Durie, his bosom friend, who had lately
become betrothed to Rollo's sister, a beautiful girl of sixteen, vowed to
avenge him. He set out alone across a trackless moor, without having
disclosed his intention to any of the family of the murdered man, and
had not gone many miles before he was caught in a violent storm, so
fierce as to drive him to seek shelter in a lonely cottage on the edge of
the moor. He was kindly received by a poor and aged widow, who
lived there only on the bounty of her neighbours, yet whose appearance
and manner told of better days in the past. She promised him shelter
for the night, and gave him all the comforts she could. In the corner of
the room where they sat, the young man noticed a most unusual sword,
its blade and hilt chased all over with strange characters. In answer to
his eager questions, the old woman told him that it had once belonged
to a noble Saracen, and had been given to her husband by a Polish Jew,
whose life he had saved, while serving as a volunteer in the Highland
Regiment which had gone to Holland under the command of Lord
Reay.

She added that her husband had strictly warned her never to part
with the sword, but to preserve it as an heirloom in the family. Durie
then told the old woman of his errand, and begged her to let him use
the sword for one single day. She consented, though reluctantly, and on
strict condition that he must return it to her.

The next day, when the storm had blown itself out, the young man
joyfully girded on the wonderful sword, and, setting out in the early
morning, he soon reached the brow of Benchieldt; and halfway down
the slope he was met and challenged by Graysteel himself. They
fought fiercely, and at last Durie dealt the robber a mortal wound.
He returned home, and raised a troop of followers, with whom he
marched back to Raenag, captured the castle, and almost levelled it
with the ground.

Shortly afterwards he married the sister of his friend, and they took
the old woman of the moor, now repossessed of her sword, into their
protection, and cared for her to the end of her life.

MOTIFS: Q.211 [*Murder punished*]; D.1C81 [*Magic sword*]; D.821 [*Magic object
received from old woman*].

GRIM AND HIS MAN BÖNDEL

Mrs E. Rudkin, *Folk-Lore*, December 1935, p. 375.

A long time ago, they say it was afore the Deans [Danes] first cam inta
Lindsey, there was a man they called Little Grim, but a big man he was
and a great sea-capting like all his forefathers, I've heerd. This Grim

used to sail about to furrin parts, and sometimes fought and sometimes traded wi' the furrin folks. It was i' one o' his voyages he heerd tell o' two magic stanes belonging to the King o' the Deans country wod wheniver they were basted wi' hazel rods made the rain fall an' the grass an' cows an' everything else plentiful. At that time there was d'arth an a'most famine i' this country. So Grim bethowt him he'd hev 'em anyhow an' bring 'em home wi' him. So thowt, so done. Grim an' his best man Boundel as big as hissen, went ashore after dark, and shouldering a stone apiece, carried 'em off to his ship. Then a strange thing happened—the ship began sinking as soon as the stanes were aboard an' they had to throw overboard ivery stick o' cargo t'keep afloat—an' so wi' water up to th' gunwale they made their voyage home. It was at Tetna they say Grim landed, and from there he wanted to send the stanes to King Lud, but then nobody but him an' his man Boundel could lift 'em, so they showdered 'em agean, an' set off for the royal toon. The stane seem'd to git heavier an' heavier till they got to Grainsby brig, but the brig broke under Grim, an' he went souse inta the mud, there war little water i' the Old Fleet then. Boundel had gone ower fust an' war risting i' Thoresby, so he went back an' helped Grim out wi' his load. Then Grim went on till he came to Audeby, where he stay'd to rest, but the stanes never went fother, for nayther Grim nor Boundel could iver lift 'em agean. So much the better fir th' men o' the wolds and the marsh, Boundel told the secret of the magic, and the stanes were basted—Boundel's for rain an' Grim's to make the corn grow... till there was plenty in the land. Ivery year for a long while after the folks cam' fra far an' wide to a grand feast aboot the stanes, an' they were whipt till everybody went wicked wi' prosperity. Then the Devil come an' flew away wi' Grim's stane.

MOTIFS: F.610 [*Remarkably strong man*]; D.931 [*Magic stones*]; D.1542.1.1 [*Magic stone produces rain*]; D.1347 [*Magic object produces fertility*]; D.1654.1 [*Stone refuses to be moved*].

¶ See "The Giants' Dance", "Havelock and Grim".

GUINEVERE'S COMB

H. Bett, *English Legends*, p. 4.

There are two high points on a ledge of rock near Sewingshields known as the King's Crag and the Queen's Crag. The legend is that King Arthur was once seated on the first and was talking to his queen, who was combing her hair. Angry at something she said, he seized a huge rock and threw it at her, where she was standing some hundreds of yards away. She caught it on her comb, and so warded off the missile, and it lies where it fell, a large block of many tons weight, with the marks of her comb still upon it.

MOTIFS: A.972.5 [*Indentations on rocks from marks of various persons*]; A.977.1 [*Giant responsible for certain stones*].

¶ This legend is an example of the way in which people important in tradition grow in size. An example is "Macbeth's Grave" at Dunsinnon. "Cabal's Paw-mark" MOTIF: A.972.5.3. (*Indentations on rock from paws of King Arthur's dog*) is another example in Welsh tradition of Arthur's potency.

See "King Arthur at Sewingshields" and "The Silver Horseshoe" for other Arthurian legends.

GUY OF WARWICK

H. Bett, *English Legends*, p. 104.

About a mile north of Warwick, on the road to Coventry, is Guy's Cliff, a mansion beautifully situated on a rocky eminence rising abruptly from the Avon. Here St Dubritius, it is said, built a small chapel and dedicated it to the Virgin, and it was here, according to tradition, that the famous Guy, Earl of Warwick, came to seek a religious solitude after his heroic exploits. . . .

When Winchester was besieged by the Danes, in the reign of Athelstan, it was agreed that the fate of the city should be decided by a single combat between a Saxon and a Danish champion. This took place in a meadow outside the east gate, and a projecting turret on the wall of the city, called "Athelstan's Chair" (it does not now exist), was long pointed out as the place from which the King watched the fight.

Guy was the Saxon champion, and his opponent was a gigantic Dane named Colbrand.

Guy was assisted by a friendly crow, which flew about the head of Colbrand, and helped to confuse the giant. Guy slew Colbrand, and the Danish army raised the siege.

Another legend says that the combat took place in a valley near Chilcombe in Hampshire.

After he came back from the Holy Land, Guy resolved to end his days as a hermit, and he took up his abode in a cave at Guy's Cliff. His wife, whose name was Felice, was ignorant of her lord's return from abroad, and lived in loneliness at Warwick Castle. He daily begged alms from her at the gate of the castle, but she never recognized him. Shortly before he died, he made himself known to his wife by sending her a ring, and she went to the cave in time to close his dying eyes. She only lived for a fortnight afterwards. There is an inscription carved on the rock at Guy's Cliff, which is possibly the real origin of some part of the legend. It may be rendered: "Cast away, O Christ, this burden from Thy servant Guhti".

MOTIFS: H.217.1 [*Decision of victory by single combat between army leaders*]; B.451.4 [*Helpful crow*]; V.462.0.3 [*Husband abandons wife to become ascetic*]; D.2006.1.10 [*Forgotten wife gives food to beggar*]; H.94 [*Identification by ring*].

¶ The part of the story in which Guy of Warwick begs from his wife and finally sends her a ring is near to the Hinde Horne story, which also appears in the "St George for England" tale (A, IV).

THE HANGMAN'S STONE

Norton Collection, VI, p. 19.

A noted poacher and sheep-stealer named David was out one moonlight night on his usual errand, accompanied by his little boy, whom he was trying to bring up in the way he should not go. He had already got one sheep slung over his shoulder, and was on the way home, when he heard a wood-pigeon cooing "Take two, do, David, take two; take two, do David, take two." "All right," said David, only too willing, "mid so well take two whiles I be about it; mid so well be hanged for a sheep as a lamb, they say, and I can't get no wuss hanged for two sheep than for one." So he took two. Further along the road he was a bit tired with the weight of the sheep slung over his shoulders, and sat down to rest on the step of an old stone wayside cross. Here his load slipped back over, and the connecting rope throttled him. His boy could not shift the avenging sheep, nor release his father, and he ran away to get help. By the time that he had roused the people at the nearest cottage, and got them to understand what was amiss, their help was no longer needed, and David was found lying on the "Hangman's Stone" dead.

From F. W. Mathews', *Tales of the Blackdown Borderland*.
TYPE 1322A* (variant). MOTIFS: J.1811 [*Animal cries misunderstood*]; A.2426.2 [*Cries of birds*]; Q.424.5* [*Sheep-thief is strangled as he rests sheep on post behind him, etc.*] (Baughman).
¶ See "The Sheep-stealers of the Blackdown Hills", "Take Two Wi't" (A, III).

THE HAUNTED MANOR HOUSE [summary]

J. Roby, *Lancashire Traditions*, I, p. 482.

Ince Hall is the name of two manor-houses, both near Wigan, and about a mile from one another. The following story is told of them both, but probably belongs to the lesser-known house, once the property of the Gerards of Bryn.

A traveller returning to the home of his childhood found it deserted, the grounds overgrown and neglected, the house cold and cheerless. He nevertheless went through it and, climbing the stairs to the nursery, he saw on one of its walls a paper covered with a drawing made by himself many years before, and firmly pasted to the wall, so that no effort of succeeding owners had succeeded in dislodging it. The traveller determined to take it away as a keepsake, but to do so he was obliged to cut away the paper with his knife; and thus was revealed a door, plastered over long before, with rusty hinges, which groaned as he forced them open. A dark closet lay behind the door, and as there appeared to be nothing inside it, the traveller withdrew and was about to leave the room when, looking out of the window, he saw two men approaching the house. They entered, and he soon heard their footsteps on the stairs. In sudden panic, he took refuge in the closet he had just discovered and, peering through its keyhole, he saw the two men come into the room, and recognized them, with some difficulty, since he had not seen them since childhood, as an uncle of his own, and his serving-man, Gilbert, a man whom, as a child, he had instinctively disliked and shunned. He soon learnt from their talk that they had come there to secure a document—a will made by the listener's father—which they were now resolved to destroy, and so rob the heir of his inheritance. The heir was the traveller himself, whom they had believed dead from his long absence, and whose continued existence had lately become known to them. The uncle even spoke of his intention to burn the whole of the old house, that the will might perish with it; and subsequently to produce a forged will, by which he would inherit the property. Gilbert went to fetch matches, and a light was set to a corner of the will, which the two produced from an old iron box hidden in an adjoining closet. They were uneasy, for all their lack of scruples; the house had a reputation of being haunted, and as they spoke of this, the listener in the closet scratched hard against the door. The men started. A louder scratch followed, and they tried to persuade themselves that it was made by rats. But the listener in a hollow voice called out, "Beware!" and at that the two took to their heels, and fled down the stairs, leaving the parchment still smouldering. It was hardly damaged as yet; and the heir, leaving his hiding-place, soon extinguished it. He bethought him to kindle some of the other papers, leaving their ashes to give any intruder the impression that all had been destroyed.

Then he made his way from the house, and sought advice from a trustworthy lawyer, to whom he handed the will. On this man's advice, he next visited his uncle who, after a brief conversation, produced the false will, telling his nephew that he had already made himself responsible for clearing heavy family debts, and taken possession of the estate as the lawful heir. He had left the house to a tenant who, however, had found it untenable, and left it about three years before. "Is it haunted?" asked the nephew, and the uncle, pretending disbelief in all such things, replied that there had been some superstition to that effect, but he felt sure it had been only a pretext to get out of a bargain of which the tenant had grown tired.

At this moment the lawyer was announced, and said that he had come to inquire about the manor-house for a prospective tenant. The "owner" demurred, saying that he had some thought of demolishing the property altogether. From this point the nephew and the lawyer led the talk to the question of the will, and on its being produced, the lawyer remarked that the witnesses—a long-dead sister of the uncle, and the man Gilbert Hodgson—were hardly such as to inspire confidence in the heir-apparent. The uncle flew into a passion, and stamped on the floor to summon his man, only to learn that the lawyer had taken the precaution to send him out on an errand, and so prevent any collusion between them.

The lawyer finally produced the true will, accusing the uncle of having forged the other, and this so robbed the forger of all power of defence that he consented to destroy the false document on the spot, in return for his nephew's promise not to expose him to public knowledge. It is said that, having obeyed, the wretched man held out his hand to his nephew, as if to beg his forgiveness, and in the act, his head sank on his breast, his arm dropped to his side and he fell dead to the ground.

MOTIFS: K.362.7 [*Theft by forgery*]; H.1581 [*Test to determine heir*]; K.1833 [*Disguise as ghost*]; E.236.4.1 [*Ghost foils counterfeiting of will*]; Q.274 [*Swindler punished*].

HAVELOC AND GRIM [summary]

Gutch and Peacock, *County Folk-Lore*, v, Lincolnshire, p. 320.

It is generally believed that the town of Grimsby owes its name to one Grim, variously described as a merchant or a fisherman, who was at first a scullion in the Danish King's kitchen. He discovered a child in swaddling clothes, floating down the Humber in a little boat. Grim took pity on the child, and brought it up in his own home and named it Haveloc. When the child grew up he excelled at every kind of sport and feat of valour, and was at last discovered to be the King's son. He married the King of England's daughter, Goldeburgh, and in gratitude to Grim he conferred many immunities upon his town when it was founded.

One of the ancient seals of Grimsby shows the gigantic figure of a man with a drawn sword in one hand and a circular shield in the other. Near him is written the word "GRYEM". On his right is a youth with a crown on his head, and near him the word "HABLOC". To the left of Grim is a woman, with a royal diadem above her head, encircled by the word, "GOLDEBURGH".

The legend says that when a hostile fleet threatened the town, Grim threw down three towers of the church in an attempt to stop it. The first fell among the enemy, the second in Wellowgate, where it became Haveloc's Stone, and the third crashed into the churchyard, a fourth stone remained on the tower.

Others say that Haveloc's stone was brought by the Danes from their own country, and that it is made of indestructible material.

Bates, *Gossip about Old Grimsby*, pp. 32, 33. Camden, *Britannica*, pp. 338. *Linc. Arch. Soc.*, V, p. xv. W. White, *History of Lincolnshire*.

MOTIFS: S.331 [*Exposure of child in boat*]; R.131 [*Exposed or abandoned child rescued*]; H.80 [*Identification by tokens*]; F.531.3 2 [*Giant throws a great rock*].

¶ The full story of Haveloc and his lady Goldburgh is told in *The Lay of Haveloc the Dane*, a Middle-English poetical romance edited by W. Skeat in 1902. This part of the tale is to be found in pp. 44–52. In the Grimsby legends, Grim is sometimes described as a merchant, sometimes as a fisherman, but even here he is given giant's strength in his feat of plunging down the great stones. In other legends he is clearly either a giant or a god. It may be remembered that Grim was one of Odin's nicknames. (Brian Branston, *The Lost Gods of England*, p. 29).

See "Grim and His Man Böndel".

HEDGES THE GAMESTER

W. E. A. Axon, *Bygone Sussex*, pp. 218–22.

At Tunbridge, in the year 1715,....Mr J. Hedges made a very brilliant appearance; he had been married about two years to a young lady of great beauty and large fortune; they had one child, a boy, on whom they bestowed all that affection which they could spare from each other. He knew nothing of gaming, nor seemed to have the least passion for play; but he was unacquainted with his own heart! He began by degrees to bet at the table for trifling sums, and his soul took fire at the prospect of immediate gain. He was soon surrounded with sharpers, who with calmness lay in ambush for his fortune, and coolly took advantage of the precipitancy of his passions.

His lady perceived the ruin of her family approaching, but at first, without being able to form any scheme to prevent it. She advised with his brother, who at that time was possessed of a small fellowship at Cambridge. It was easily seen that whatever passion took the lead in her husband's mind seemed to be there fixed unalterably. It was determined therefore to let him pursue Fortune, but previously take measures to prevent the pursuit being fatal.

Accordingly, every night this gentleman was a constant attender at the hazard tables. He understood neither threats of sharpers, nor even the allowed strokes of a connoisseur, yet still he played. The consequence is obvious. He lost his estate, his equipage, his wife's jewels, and every other moveable that could be parted with except a repeating watch. His agony upon this occasion was inexpressible; he was even mean enough to ask a gentleman who sat near to lend him a few pieces in order to turn his fortune; but this prudent gamester, who plainly saw there were no expectations of being repaid, refused to lend a farthing, alleging a former resolution against lending. Hedges was at last furious with the continuance of ill success, and pulling out his watch, asked if any person in the company would set him sixty guineas upon it. The company were silent; he then demanded fifty; still no answer; he sank to forty, thirty, twenty, finding the company still without answering, he cried out, "By God, it shall never go for less!" and dashed it against the floor, at the same time attempting to dash out his brains against the marble chimney-piece. This last act of desperation immediately excited the attention of the whole company; they instantly gathered round, and prevented the effects of his passion; and after he became cool, he was permitted to return home, with sullen discontent, to his wife. Upon his entering her apartment, she received him with her usual tenderness and satisfaction; while he answered her caresses with contempt and severity, his disposition being quite altered with his misfortunes. "But, my dear Jemmy," says his wife, "perhaps you don't know the news I have to tell. My mamma's old uncle is dead, the messenger is now in the house, and you know his estate is settled upon you." This account seemed only to increase his agony, and, looking angrily at her, he cried, "There you lie, my dear; his estate is not settled upon me." "I beg your pardon," said she. "I really thought it was; at least, you have always told me so." "No," returned he, "as sure as you and I are to be miserable here, and our children beggars hereafter, I have sold the reversion of it this day, and have lost every farthing I got for it at the hazard table." "What, all?" replied the lady. "Yes, every farthing," returned he, "and I owe a thousand pounds more than I have got to pay." Thus speaking, he took a few frantic steps across the room. When the lady had a little enjoyed his perplexity, "No, my dear," cried she, "you have lost but a trifle, and you owe nothing; your brother and I have taken care to prevent the effects of your rashness, and are actually the persons who have won your fortune; we employed proper persons for this purpose, who brought their winnings to me. Your money, your equipage, are in my possession, and here I return them to you, from whom they were unjustly taken. I only ask permission to keep my jewels, and to keep you, my greatest jewel, from such dangers for the future." Her prudence had the proper effect. He ever retained a sense of his former follies, and never played for the smallest sums, even for amusement.

Truly a lucky gambler. Few possessed by the demon of chance have been so fortunate.

From Goldsmith's *Life of Beau Nash*.

TYPE 888A (distant variant). MOTIF: J.1545.6 [*Wife by cleverness wins back fortune overbearing husband has foolishly lost*].

THE HERMIT'S CAVE [summary]

Abraham Elder, *Tales and Legends of the Isle of Wight*, p. 11.

Woolverton Wood lies on the shore of Brading Harbour, and runs right down to the water's edge. In the heart of it, fragmentary ruins and carved stones indicate that an important building must have stood there long ago. On a nearby knoll it is believed that there was a church; skeletons and broken gravestones have been found. The legend of the place was found among the papers of an old man who died at Brading some years ago.

It is said that at the beginning of the reign of Edward the Third, an old pedlar, dressed always in a rusty black suit of clothes, used to visit the borough of Woolverton every month. His pack was small, yet it always held something to charm the people who came to buy from him. His prices were reasonable, and he soon sold all his goods. At the day's end, however late it was, he took up his stick and empty pack, and walked away, never seeking a night's lodging, and never, it appeared, arriving at any of the neighbouring villages. He became something of a favourite at Woolverton; sometimes he would tell a fortune, or forecast future events, always with strange accuracy. He would lend gold to any who were in difficulties, and often refused repayment when the time came. But instead of the money, he would sometimes urge the debtors to fire the ricks of a farmer against whom he had a grudge; and as this became known, people's liking for him gradually turned to fear; but they had become accustomed to asking his help in their troubles, and continued to do so.

Once a young man named Edgar met the pedlar, or "hermit of the Culver", as he was often called, and confided to him that Matilda, the girl he loved, was preferring the advances of a wealthy knight, the knight of Yaverland. Again the hermit offered to help Edgar, if he, in return, would set light to the thatch of the knight's manor house.

Before he had decided whether to do this, Edgar met another of the occasional visitors to Woolverton, a pious man named Friar John, who seems to have dissuaded him, for the manor-house was not burned.

After this the pedlar, or hermit, apparently gave up his wicked ways, but he continued his odd benefactions; he told the people that his good intentions were always being frustrated by another old man, a hermit in a grey cowl, whom no one ever saw. At last he said that this man was coming to poison the holy water of their well. This well, of which the village was always proud, had beside it on a small knoll the remains of a stone cross. On it were inscribed some mysterious lines:

> While the oose flows pure and free,
> Burg and tune shall happy bee,
> The net bee heavy in the sea,
> And wheaten seed shall yield plentie.
> When sained blood in the burn shall well,
> It shall light a flame so hot and snell,
> Shall fire the burg from lock to fell,
> Nor sheeling bide its place to tell,
> And Culvert's Nass shall ring its knell.

Culver's Nass is a high cliff overhanging the sea not far from Woolverton, and it was always in its direction that the hermit used to turn after his mysterious visits, though none could ever make out where he really lived, for all feared to follow him far outside the village.

The well was believed to possess certain mysterious powers of healing or changing bad fortune to good; no one knew precisely what they were; but all united in saying that the threat of poisoning its waters must be withstood, and before the appointed time all the village gathered at the spot to await the coming of the hermit in the grey cowl. The hermit of the Culver was there among them, but suddenly it was found that he had disappeared, though, as so often, none had seen him go.

After more than two hours, the old man was seen tottering towards the well. With his left hand he leaned heavily on a long staff, of whose support he seemed in dire need, for his steps were slow and feeble. In the right he carried a withered branch from some tree. He reached the broken cross, and stood before it, with hands clasped, and fingers pointed upwards, murmuring words of prayer—or, as some feared, curses—then turned towards the well, as if unaware of the people gathered round to watch him.

He laid down his staff and withered branch, knelt, and leaned over the well. "He is poisoning the water," they began to murmur then, and one threw a stone, which threw the old man senseless to the ground. A shower of stones followed, many of which struck him, and slowly his blood began to trickle from the wounds, and fall drop by drop into the well. He was dead before they well realized what they had done, and as they gazed in alarm at the old man, Friar John appeared among them. "Is this murder?" he said sternly, and bending down he lifted the grey cowl, and, seeing the face beneath it, buried his own in his hands in grief and horror. When he could speak again, he told them that it was a most holy man whom they had killed; one whom he would have given all he had to meet again. He demanded to be told the whole story, and in return told the villagers that they had slain the only man who knew the secret of their well; that he had even then returned from a pilgrimage to the Holy Land (from where he had brought the withered branch); and that now, by shedding his blood, they had brought the curse of the well upon themselves and their homes.

The holy man's funeral was celebrated with all the solemnity and penitence in the power of the villagers to give. Their wrath was now kindled against the hermit of the Culver, and they were amazed when, shortly afterwards, he appeared again amongst them, as smiling and cheerful as ever. He refused to see their cold looks, and walked through the little town as though all were as usual. As he reached the farther gate, Edgar, who had resolved to find out more of the strange old man, overtook him, and, walking at his side, offered to accompany him to his home. The other, quite unlike his usual affable self, replied curtly and disagreeably, but did not refuse; and they walked on together, climbing the down, until at last they reached the highest point of Culver's Nass, and a precipice running sheer down to the sea lay at their feet. The old man tapped the ground with his stick; the earth began to quiver, and presently a large oblong opening appeared at their feet, with light streaming from it, and a flight of steps, down which Edgar followed the old man, till they reached a large vaulted gallery, richly but grotesquely carved, and brilliantly coloured and lighted, with pictures on the walls, including, at the far end, a full-length portrait of the hermit himself. Many of the portraits were of Edgar's acquaintances, but all had the peculiar feature of a black mark, like a horseshoe, or a small pair of horns, on their foreheads.

A countless troop of small, dwarf-like creatures swarmed about the old man, attending to his wants and Edgar's but he rebuffed them in the same surly manner as he had used to Edgar himself, until some further need made him recall them. It grew so cold that Edgar boldly demanded a fire. "We do not often complain about *cold* here!" exclaimed the hermit, but he called out, "Light a fire!" and a crowd of the ugly little creatures jumped up, and scampered down the hall, crying: "Cooky, Cooky, Cooky. Daddy wants a fire!"

A withered and hideous old hag entered, carrying a small phial in one hand, and dragging a broom in the other. She walked three times round a spot in the centre of the hall, then poured out a few drops from the phial, and at once a fire sprang up. The old woman leapt through its flames once, and hobbled away. Soon the heat from the fire became so intense that Edgar begged for it to be put out. "Put out the fire!" ordered the old man, and at once the old woman was recalled by the grotesque creatures and, squatting beside it, she blew out the fire with a single puff. Edgar demanded music, and strange instruments and players at once appeared to provide it; he asked for the company of some ladies, and a dozen beautiful young women at once appeared. One of these, dressed in green, danced with him, and so charmed him that for once he forgot his loved Matilda. But soon a fight sprang up between two of the dwarfs, and suddenly Edgar was aware of their hideously long nails, and black tails, which uncoiled as they fought from the petticoat-like garments they all wore. So his eyes were opened: he knew now that even his lovely partner had a tail curled up under her green dress, and that the hermit of Culver himself might well have one under his gown. Now, anxious to return home, but in doubt how he might get there, he asked the hermit whether they might not have some supper. An immense bill of fare was brought by a man in a cook's tall white hat, but Edgar asked for only a broiled bone and a mug of light ale. They were brought, and, remembering Friar John's teaching, he repeated the Latin Grace which he had been taught. The lights grew dim, and at the holy name a wild shriek arose from all the company. There was a clap of thunder, the whole building rocked and fell; and Edgar fell senseless to the ground.

When he came to himself, it was daylight, and he was lying in a small cave halfway up the cliff-face. He scrambled along a narrow path, and came to the point where the door had opened in the rock. But the whole cliff-face was altered, for the great projection of Culver's Nass had fallen in the night, and lay in a ruinous heap far below. He could see into what must have been the great hall where he had spent so many hours, but not a trace of the carvings remained. In bewilderment he looked out to sea, and was still more astonished to see a large fleet of ships sailing round the neighbouring headland of Dunnose. He soon knew them for French ships of war, and made the best of his way back to Woolverton to warn the inhabitants. But on seeing him they demanded to know what had happened to him when he followed the hermit, and he lost precious time in trying to recount his night's adventures; so that, when the Frenchmen landed, no preparations had been made to shut them out of the little town. One and all had refused to believe any part of Edgar's story, and when he came to the sight he had had of the French fleet, they all took it to be part of the make-believe. At last he gave up the attempt, went home, and collected all his belongings, and made his way into the forest to hide, leaving the rest to their fate. A hopeless battle followed, in which the knight of Yaverland fell fighting bravely, and an arrow of Edgar's avenged him; but the French attacked from two sides, and the men of Woolverton were hopelessly outnumbered. The whole town was destroyed by fire and the spirit of the grey hermit began to haunt the place of his desecrated grave. Only Edgar and Matilda escaped unhurt; his cottage stood out-side the town, and some of their descendants may still be found living in another cottage nearby.

MOTIFS: G.303.3.1 [*The Devil in human form*]; G.303.9.4 [*The Devil as a tempter*]; G.303.4.6 [*The Devil's tail*]; V.134 [*Sacred well*]; G.303.16.8 [*Devil leaves at mention of God's name*]; D.1563.2.2.1 [*Well polluted by blood*].
¶ It is probable that this tale has been a good deal adorned.

HOGHTON TOWER [summary]

J. Roby, *Lancashire Traditions*, I, p. 312.

On 15 August 1617, King James left Preston for a royal progress, and stayed first at Hoghton Tower, the home of Sir Richard Hoghton, a hilltop castle, four and a half miles west of Blackburn. Sir Richard was already in attendance on the king, but his eldest son, Sir Gilbert, rode out to meet them and escort them to the house, along a long drive lined on either side by javelin-bearers in the Hoghton livery. Among the many gentlemen in the king's retinue were his favourite, the Duke of Buckingham, Sir George Goring, the lieutenant of the Gentleman Pensioners, and Sir John Finett, acting as Master of the Ceremonies. Sir John was descended from an ancient Italian family of Siena, a witty and hospitable gentleman, well versed in the arts of entertainment.

The pathway up the avenue was laid with purple velvet, and the splendour of the king's reception was all in accordance with his dignity and expectation. A hunting expedition filled the afternoon, in the course of which Sir John Finett, absenting himself from the chase, found occasion to deliver a letter with which a friend had charged him to the lady Grace Gerard, a daughter of the Gerards of Ashton Hall, near Lancaster, who was a guest at the castle during the present festivities. So well did these two like one another, that the bell for dinner, ringing out from the tower, surprised Sir John, who should have been attending on the king in preparation for the banquet. Dinner had indeed begun without the Master of Ceremonies, and the king was greatly incensed at his prolonged absence. He threatened to dismiss him from his service, and send him to the Tower, when a masked figure, rep-resenting one of the household gods, entered the hall, and in a hollow voice proclaimed in rhyme:

> "The knight ye speak of, mark me well,
> I've just drawn from the castle well!
> How came he thus, I dare not tell;
> My brother may the mystery dispel."

He stooped down, and immediately rose up again, but now clad in a forester's green cloak and doublet, and continued:

"Sir John to be forgiven would hope,
He had been drowned, but for the rope."

This quickness of wit so pleased the king, that, merely threatening to employ the same rope to hang him, he bade the forester bring Sir John to his presence. Instantly shedding his green attire, Sir John now stood before the company, and assured the king that this was part of a device of his which had been bungled, compelling him to assume all these parts himself. The king thanked him for his diligence, and forgave him for the delay.

The next day passed in more hunting, sight-seeing, and another banquet; but on the day following, which was Sunday, the King received a deputation imploring him to relax the severe restrictions on Sunday games imposed by the Puritans. The king heard them graciously, and proclaimed that that very evening he would have a masque and an allegory with dancing, to be provided by the lords and noble gentlemen there present.

This gave Sir John Finett and Sir George Goring so much to do that the day was almost at an end before they had finished drilling all the actors in their parts as beasts or humans, in the chosen pageant, which was to be "The Bower of Beauty". Grace Gerard had consented to play the Queen of Beauty, and Sir John was to be her knight, wearing a black mask and a silver cloak. His duties, however, at the last moment, prevented his taking his part, and he sent Grace a despairing letter of regret, saying that his friend Weldon would take his place, and he himself would be there in time for the dancing.

Almost at the same moment Grace received another letter, in the same hand, warning her to beware of the "snake in the Bower of Beauty", but time was too short for her to pay heed to this. A bell summoned the actors to their places, and Grace's masked knight came forward to claim her, and led her to a raised platform on wheels, on which she was to sit with her ladies. A curtain concealed them from the onlookers for the first part of the pageant, during which a performance of Morris dancers and capering beasts was leading up to the appearance of the fair ladies behind the arras. At last the curtain was withdrawn. There sat the ladies, all but the Queen. Neither she nor her knight was to be seen. The ladies said he had led her away, promising to return, but none knew where the two had gone.

Sir John, whose heart had been utterly captured by the lovely Grace, was compelled by his duties about the king to make light of the matter, and to provide other distractions, which the king took in good part. His usual attendant, Buckingham, had declared his wish to join the throng of masked revellers on this occasion, and Sir John was constrained to fill his place. Buckingham presently returned, unmasked, and seemingly perturbed, but the king still required Finett's attendance, and his anxiety grew greater as no word came from Grace. At last a horseman approached him; it was his friend Weldon, who, to Finett's eager question, replied that he had been to Myerscough with a message from Sir John to his hostess, and received no thanks for his pains. "I sent no message!" exclaimed Sir John, instantly suspecting foul play; but all they could discover was a page, who said he had been given a written message by someone unknown to him, who bade him deliver it to Weldon from his master. They suspected Buckingham, always envious of Finett's popularity and success, but his influence and wealth were so great that it was well-nigh impossible to bring any charge against him. But so it was. Buckingham, like Finett, had been captured by the loveliness and charm of Grace Gerard, he had contrived to send Weldon on a false errand and to take his place; and had wandered with Grace up the hill in the moonlight, delaying her with unwelcome love-making, till she broke away from his clasp, clinging for strength to a slender tree that grew on the edge of a steep cliff. The tree was uprooted by her weight, and fell with her to the very edge of the precipice. Before Buckingham could seize her she had plunged into the torrent below. He rushed down through the entangling bushes, and leapt into the water, but, finding no trace of her, at last made his way back to the castle, where he changed from his dripping garments and rejoined the king's company.

Meantime, the distracted Finett had sent pages and messengers over the castle to find what news they could of the missing girl. Her maid, when questioned, said she had retired early, and that she had taken her a hot posset from the kitchen. But this was not to be believed—no other news was to be heard, and after his pressing duties were at last over, Sir John could only make the best of what remained of the night. He rose early next morning and, hurrying down the stairs, was astonished to meet Grace herself, who at once told him that it was her purpose to leave the castle immediately. Her short glimpse of the ways of the court had so disillusioned her that even her dawning love for him could not pursuade her to stay. She had escaped death as by a miracle, and had stolen back to the castle by a longer route to avoid being seen. But her resolve was taken. She left him, and they never met again.

MOTIFS: T.92 [*Rivals in love*]; T.92.4 2 [*Letter falsified and elopement with false lover arranged*].

¶ An account of the entertainment at Hoghton is to be found in Nicholl's *Progresses of King James I*, III, pp. 398–402. It does not, of course, correspond with this tradition, except in the mention of the petition, which was issued in the Proclamation of the Book of Sports.

AN HONEST STRANGER

E. Bogg, *Lakeland and Ribblesdale*, p. 46.

A farmer, a native of the district between Bewcastle and Cannobie, a great original in his way, and remarkable for his fondness of a "big price" for everything, attended at Langholm Fair, and notwithstanding his parsimonious habits, actually sold his lambs to a perfect stranger upon his simply promising to pay him punctually at the next market. On his return home, the farmer's servants, who regularly messed at the same table, and seldom honoured him with the name of master, inquired, "Wee'l, Sandy, ha'e ye sel't the lams'?" "Atwell ha'e I, and I gat a saxpence a heed mair than ony ane else in the market." "And a'weel paid siller?" "Na, the siller's nae paid yet, but it's share [sure] eneuch." "Wha's yer merchant, an what's yer sakerity [security]?" "Aye, aye, I ne'er fashed mysel' ta speer, but he's a weel fae'd mon, wi' muckle tap bits [top boots] and a bottle-green coat."

The servants at this laughed outright, and tauntingly told him he would never get a farthing. Sandy, however, thought differently, and, having hurt his leg, so as to prevent him from travelling, he sent a shepherd to Langholm, with instructions to look for a man with a bottle-green coat, whom he was sure, he said, to find standing near a certain sign. The shepherd did as he was bid, and strange to say, discovered a person standing at the identical spot, who, on learning his errand, inquired kindly for his master, and paid the money to the uttermost farthing. Sandy, who piqued himself on his skill in physiognomy, heard the news without emotion, and merely said, "I wad ony whiles lippen [trust] mair to looks than gabs [words] and whan I seed Colly smirking sa blithely and kindly aboot'm I ken't weel eneuch he couldna' be a scoondr'l."

MOTIF: J.1661.1.9 [*Recognizing honest merchant*].

THE HOOTING CAIRN [summary]

Hunt, *Popular Romances of the West of England*, p. 216.

Cairn Kenidzhek, pronounced Kenidjack, is on the north road from St Just to Penzance, and appears much more wild and rugged than the other cairns of the neighbourhood.

Two miners who had been working in one of the old mines near Morvah, were returning home one evening from the public house in Morvah Churchtown. They were quiet men, and perfectly sober, and like all inhabitants of the region they were deeply aware of the solemn influence of the Cairn. As they were walking past it in silence, a low moaning sound seemed to come from it, which at times rose to a hoot. The night was dark, but a gleam seemed to come from the rocks, and by its light the two thought they could distinguish gigantic shapes moving between the stones. Soon they heard a horse galloping behind them and, turning, they recognized a lean horse that often worked in their own mine. On his back rode a cloaked, hooded figure, in black, with his face partly covered.

"Hallo! Hallo!" they shouted, fearing to be run down.

"Hallo, to you," replied a gruff voice.

"Where be'est going then?" asked the braver of the two men.

"Up to the cairn to see the wrestling," replied the rider. "Come along, come along!"

They were strangely compelled to follow, and found themselves keeping up without much difficulty with the galloping horse.

At last they came to a mass of rocks at the foot of the hill, and in the darkness they could not cross it. The rider, however, scaled it unconcernedly. As he climbed, it seemed that horse, rider and the rocks themselves were joining in a "three man's song", and that its chorus was a piercing hoot.

Many strange figures were now gathering, of great size and strength, with long, straggling locks of hair, and skin painted in colours. And when the giant rider joined them with two more huge creatures at his sides, a circle was formed, and the rider threw off his black cloak, and revealed himself as the Devil in person. He put the two miners into a good position for watching what was to happen, and sat down in an odd position on the ground.

A wrestling bout now took place between two great demons, lighted by the fiery gleam from the Devil's eyes. At last one of them threw his adversary to the ground with such force that the earth shook, and the rocks echoed like thunder with the shock. No one went near the defeated giant; they all crowded round him who had won. But the two miners from love of fair-play climbed over the rocks, and approached to see whether any help could be given. The giant was clearly dying, and the elder miner, hoping that even now, though he had sold himself to the Devil, repentance might be possible for him, ventured to whisper words of Christian hope in the ear.

Instantly the rocks shook, the darkness became more intense, and there was a sound of wild rushing in every direction, and suddenly, dying man and all, they were all gone. The two men alone were left, clinging in terror to one another, and, as if in the air they saw the burning eyes of the demon disappearing into the west, and vanishing in a black cloud. Utterly lost, even in that familiar place, they lay close under the shelter of a mass of granite, praying for protection until the daylight came to relieve their terrors.

MOTIFS: F.531.6.8.3.3 [*Giants wrestle with each other*]; G.303.7.1 [*Devil rides horse*]; G.303.16.4 [*Words of religious comfort cause Devil and his crew to vanish*]. ¶ See "The Hermit's Cave", "The Demon Wrestler" (B, III).

THE HORN OF EGREMONT

H. Bett, *English Legends*, p. 23.

Sir Eustace de Lucy, the Lord of Egremont (in Cumberland), and his brother Hubert left home to go on a Crusade in the Holy Land. On his departure Sir Eustace blew the horn which always hung by the gateway of the castle, and which could only be sounded by the rightful Lord of Egremont, saying to his brother, "If I fall in Palestine, return and blow this horn, and take possession, that Egremont may not be without a Lucy for its Lord." When they were in the Holy Land, Hubert bribed three ruffians to seize his brother, and throw him into the Jordan. Believing him to be dead, Hubert returned to England and took possession of the castle, but did not venture to blow the horn.

One day when he was giving a banquet he suddenly heard a blast from the horn at the castle gate, and, knowing that only his brother as the rightful owner could have sounded it, he started from his seat and fled by the postern. The gate was then opened to Sir Eustace, who resumed possession of Egremont. His brother is said to have died in a monastery.

MOTIFS: D.1222 [*Magic horn*]; H.31 [*Recognition of unique ability*]; K.2211 [*Treacherous brother*].

HOW DUNDONALD CASTLE WAS BUILT

Chambers, *Popular Rhymes of Scotland*, p. 237

> Donald Din
> Built his house without a pin.

According to tradition, it was built by a hero named Donald Din, or Din Donald, and constructed entirely of stone, without the use of wood ...Donald...was originally a poor man, but had the faculty of dreaming lucky dreams. Upon one occasion he dreamed, thrice in one night, that if he were to go to London Bridge, he would become a wealthy man. He went accordingly, saw a man looking over the parapet of the bridge, whom he accosted courteously, and, after a little conversation, entrusted with the secret of the occasion of his coming to London Bridge. The stranger told him that he had made a very foolish errand, for he himself had once had a similar vision, which directed him to go to a certain spot in Ayrshire, in Scotland, where he would find a vast treasure, and, for his part, he had never once thought of obeying the injunction. From his description of the spot, the sly Scotsman at once perceived that the treasure in question must be concealed in no other place than his own humble *kail-yard* at home, to which he immediately repaired, in full expectation of finding it. Nor was he disappointed; for, after destroying many good and promising cabbages, and completely cracking credit with his wife, who esteemed him mad, he found a large potful of gold coin, with the proceeds of which he built a stout castle for himself, and became the founder of a flourishing family.

TYPE 1645. MOTIF: N.531.1 [*Dream of treasure on the bridge*].
¶ See "The Pedlar of Swaffham", "The Swaffham Tinker".

HOW LITTLEPORT BEGAN [summary]

W. H. Barrett, *Tales from the Fens*, pp. 150–62

When Canute was king, the monks of Ely had grown corrupt and idle. When the river was brim full of water, from the heavy rains, they once sent for the king, as their landlord, to come and see what he could do to improve matters.

Canute first took a punt, and put out some lines to catch eels for his wife, but a storm overtook him, and the punt ran aground on a hill. There was a small hut nearby, and the king knocked at the door, and was taken in and given shelter. The owner of the hut was a brewer to the monks at Ely Grange, and he told the king a terrible story of their cruelty. They had abducted his young wife when their child was only a baby; and when he went to seek her, they had tied him to a post and flogged him nearly to death, rubbing salt into the wounds; and meanwhile they had set their dogs on his wife, and she had been so badly mauled that, when at last they dragged themselves home, she only lived for a few hours. That had been eighteen years before, and on the child's birthday every year, the brewer had cut a notch to mark the death of a monk lost in the swamps of the fen (or at least that was what the Abbot was always told).

The king soon proved for himself what the monks and nuns of Ely had become; for after the storm he went up to the Grange, and asked for a night's shelter. The monk who answered his knock, when he heard that it was the king, said that the monks were too busy with their revels to let him in; for it was the last night of their stay there.

The next day they were to make way for a new lot to come in, so they had no time to waste; he threatened them with whips and dogs unless they went away immediately.

The brewer, whose name was Legres (claimed as an ancestor by Chafer Legge), took the king home with him for the night. But the fleas made him so restless that he crept out to his punt, and spent the rest of the night there. Early in the morning he was awakened by a noise, and was surprised to see a lovely young woman washing herself in the river. When she had finished, she plastered herself with mud, and walked away. Legres ran out of the cottage with a knife in his hand, and forbade the king, whose absence he had just discovered, to follow the girl. The truth was, as he now confessed, that his child was a daughter, but to save her from the predatory monks he had disguised her as a boy. They breakfasted on frumenty, which the king praised, as, the night before, he had praised Legres' beer; and then he led the man and the girl back to the Grange. There, the new company of monks and nuns had arrived, and were clamouring for admittance.

Seeing the king's shining crown (with which he had just named Crown Lane) they fell on their knees, and began to feel for their rosaries, which they had omitted to bring with them, but Canute gave his sword to Legres, to protect himself and the girl, while he himself walked to the top of Portly Hill, and, flashing his crown as a signal, he soon saw answering flashes from boats which were being rowed from every direction towards him.

These were those of his own men, who, as he had guessed, had been all night searching the Fen for their missing king. There was a battle with the monks, and when it was over, the king entered the Grange, which was in so filthy a state that the nuns were ordered to set up tables in the back-yard, which was the cleanest part, and to bring food and drink from the cellars. There the king feasted, with Legres at his right hand, and the girl at his left, and he called for a toast to the brewer of the beer they were drinking, who had taken in his king, when the monks refused him shelter. By the king's order, Legres now became a freeman. And to punish the wicked monks and nuns, the Grange was pulled down, and a new house built by the Abbot of Ely, for Legres who was to become the King's brewer. This was the beginning of Littleport. (The further details of the story, giving the origin of various sites and place-names, are of less interest and relevance.)

When the new town was nearly completed, under the king's own supervision, a nephew of his fell in love with, and married, the daughter of Legres, now to all appearance a fine young lady, and soon after, the brewer himself married one of her bridesmaids.

The nuns from the old Grange were condemned to make shirts for the men whom the king left behind to guard his new community, and a boatload of pretty girls from Ireland was imported to make them for the rest, and for the king himself. These girls soon became the wives and mothers of Littleport, as the town was named, for the king said it had proved a good port to him in the storm. From that time on, for many hundreds of years, the eldest son in the Legres family was always named Canute.

MOTIFS: L.414 [*King vainly forbids tide to rise (Canute)*]; S.400 [*Cruel persecutions*]; S.185 [*Cruelty to pregnant woman*]; S.186 [*Torturing by beating*]; Q.414.0.3.1 [*Monks' monastery burned for incontinence*]; L.156 [*Unpromising hero kills those who scorn him*]; K.1812.4 [*Hospitality to incognito king rewarded*].
¶ The story of King Canute is usually told as his rebuke to flattering courtiers, but there are traces of a belief that a king can control the tides, and some remnant of that belief is shown in this story. The strong bias against the monks of Ely is shown in this, as in several other Fenland stories.
See "Bull-dog Bridge", "The Nun's Ring".

HUGH HIRD, THE GIANT OF TROUTBECK

E. Bogg, *Lakeland and Ribblesdale*, p. 225.

There is a story anent the building of the present Kentmore Hall. Ten men had long been trying to lift the very heavy chimney beam of the kitchen into position, but failed to do so. During the attempt, Hugh Hird, the Troutbeck giant, came past, and took the beam and placed it into position, six feet from the ground, where it still remains, and is 30 feet long, and 13 inches by 12 inches thick. A pastime of this man was that of tearing up trees bodily by their roots, an herculean task, which ultimately killed him. This took place in the days of bluff King Hal, and Lord Dacre, wanting a quick messenger to carry news of a Scotch freebooting expedition to the king, then at London, sent Hugh Hird on foot thither.

A rough and long journey in those days. When he arrived, the King received him graciously, and, on being asked what he would have for dinner, he said, "The sunny side of a wether." This puzzled the King and his attendants most sadly. At last they found out that a wether was a sheep, but it was a long time before they could tell which was the sunny side. At length the King bethought himself that the sun shone on all sides of a sheep, and he therefore ordered the whole sheep to be cooked, which Hugh Hird devoured for his dinner. When he had done, he stroked down his waistcoat, and told the King he had not had such a good dinner since he left Troutbeck. A few such men, says one, would soon cause a famine in the country.

MOTIFS: F.631.6 [*Strong man carries huge beam*]; F.621 [*Strong man: tree-puller*]; F.632 [*Mighty eater*].

¶ See "Tom Hickathrift" (B, VII), "Grim and His Man Böndel".

THE HUNTER AND HIS HOUNDS

A LEGEND OF BRINKBURN

Denham Tracts, II, p. 121.

Under a grassy swell, which a stranger may know by its being surrounded with a wooden railing, on the outside of Brinkburn Priory, tradition affirms there is a subterraneous passage, of which the entrance remains as yet a secret, leading to an apartment to which access is in like manner denied; and as these visionary dwellings are invariably provided with occupants, it is asserted that a hunter who had in some way offended one of the priors was along with his hounds, by the aid of enchantment, condemned to perpetual slumber in that mysterious abode. Only once was an unenthralled mortal favoured with a sight of the place and of those who are there entombed alive. A shepherd, with his dog attending him, was one day listlessly sauntering on this verdant mound, when he felt the ground stirring beneath him, and springing aside he discovered a flat door, where door had never before been seen by man—yea, that door opening upwards of its own accord on the very spot where he had been standing. Actuated by curiosity he descended a number of steps which appeared beneath him, and on reaching the bottom, found himself in a gloomy passage of great extent. Groping along this warily, he at last encountered a door, which, opening readily, he along with the dog was suddenly admitted into an apartment illumined so brilliantly that the full light of day seemed to shine there. This abrupt transition from darkness to light for some minutes deprived him of the power of observing objects correctly, but gradually recovering, he beheld enough to strike him with astonishment, for on one side at a table, with his head resting on his hand, slept one in the garb of a hunter, while at some distance another figure reclined on the floor with his head lying back, and around him lay many a noble hound, ready as ever to all appearance to renew that fatal chase which consigned them all to the chamber of enchantment. On the table lay a horn and a sword, which, seeing all was quiet, the shepherd stepped forward to examine, and taking up the horn first, applied it to his lips, to sound it; but the hunter, on whom he kept watch, showed symptoms of awaking whenever he made the attempt, which alarming him, he replaced it, and the figure started no longer. Reassured, he lifts the sword, half draws it, and now both men became restless and make some angry movements, and the hounds began to hustle about, while his own dog, as if agitated by the same uneasiness, slunk towards the door. Alive to the increased commotion and hearing a noise behind him very like the creaking of hinges, he suddenly turned round and found to his dismay that the door was moving to. Without waiting a moment, he rushed through the half-closed entrance followed by his dog. He had not fled ten paces when, shaking the vault with the crash, the door shut behind him, and a terrible voice assailed his ears, pouring maledictions on him for his temerity. The fugitives traversed the passage at full speed, and gladly hailed the light streaming in at the aperture above. The shepherd quickly ascended the steps, but before he got out the cover had nearly closed. He succeeded, and that was all, in escaping perhaps a worse fate than those victims of monkish thraldom which he had just left; but his poor dog was not so fortunate, for it had just raised its foreparts to come up when the door fastened on it and nipped it through!

MOTIFS: D.1960.2 [*King asleep in mountain*]; D.1962.1 [*Magic sleep through curse*].
¶ See "Potter Thompson", "King Arthur at Sewingshields", "The Silver Horseshoe".

THE IDIOT

Norton Supplementary Collection, No. 11, p. 21.

There was a small inn standing a short way off [from Acorn Bridge] on the roadside, kept by one named Ricks, whose son, being half-witted, and not to be managed, was despatched off to the workhouse at the neighbouring village of Stratton St Margaret. Being here intractable also, and refusing to eat, the master of the place, thinking to frighten him into submission, shut him in the dead-house all night with the corpses. But the idiot was not to be overcome so easily, and was far from being terrified with the presence of the dead. During the night he lifted one of these from its coffin, stripped off his own clothes and dressed the corpse in them and stood it against the wall, just inside the door; then he put the dead man's shroud on himself, and lay down in the coffin, and remained silent. By and by the workhouse master came, bearing food for the prisoner. Unlocking the door, he approached the corpse, standing up, and held out the food, at the same time saying: "Will you have it now?" As there was no answer forthcoming, he asked again: "Will you have it now?" Then, before he could realise anything, up jumped the idiot, clad in the white shroud and cried, "If he won't have it, I wull." The workhouse chief dropped the food and ran off, but so great was his fright and the shock so severe, that he died from it soon afterwards.

Williams, *White Horse*, pp. 201–2. Acorn Bridge, Wiltshire.

TYPE 1676 (variant). MOTIF: K.1833 [*Disguise as ghost*].

¶ This is like "Big 'fraid, Little 'fraid", in that the man trying to frighten the idiot fails to do so and is himself terrified.

See "White Bucca and Black Bucca" (B, II).

JOHN OF HORSILL [slightly abbreviated]

Choice Notes from "Notes and Queries", p. 134.

I

Tradition states he held the manors of Ribbesford and Highlington, near Bewdley (Worcestershire), about the twelfth century.

Hunting one day near the Severn, he started a fine buck, which took the direction of the river; fearing to lose it, he discharged an arrow, which, piercing it through, continued its flight, and struck a salmon, which had (as is customary with such fish in shallow streams) leaped from the surface of the water, with so much force as to transfix it. This being thought a very extraordinary shot (as indeed it was) a stone carving representing it was fixed over the west door of Ribbesford Church, then in course of erection.

II

The great lord of that part of the country had but one child, a daughter, who was passing fair to see, and who was beloved by a young hunter, who seems to have had nothing but his handsome face and bow to depend upon. She returned his love with all the passionate fervour of, etc., etc., and they often contrived to meet in secret in one of those romantic spots on the Severn's banks, where doubtless, according to established custom, they mingled their tears, and said soft nothings, and abused the maiden's paternity.

But one day in came the maiden and said that she had lost the ring that her father had given her: and as it was a magical ring, that possessed a complete pharmacopoeia of virtues and healing properties, and had been a family relic for many generations, Papa was so concerned about its loss that he caused a proclamation to be issued, that whoever should bring him back the ring might claim the hand of his daughter.

Everyone searched for the ring, and everyone confessed that their search was hopeless; and the handsome young hunter laughed in his sleeve, and went on his way to the great lord's castle, to beg his acceptance of a fine Severn salmon, which he had just shot. Not that the Waltonians of that day killed their salmon in that manner, but according to the young hunter's account, he had been walking on the west bank of the river, when a fine stag had suddenly started upon the eastern bank, and that he had shot an arrow at it; that when his arrow had got about halfway over the river, it pierced the salmon, which had chosen that unlucky moment for his last summerset; and that thereupon the young hunter had waded into the water, and secured his unlooked-for prey. In consideration of its being killed in such a singular manner, he begged his lord's acceptance of it, and also offered his services to the cook, to help to prepare it for the table. Having thus procured his witnesses, the young hunter cut the salmon open, and, with a well-affected tone of wonder, exclaimed, "Here's the young lady's ring inside the salmon!" and so, sure enough, there was; and the young lady on being questioned, said she supposed that she must have lost the ring off her finger while she was bathing in the river, and that the enamoured salmon had then and there taken it to heart...They were married and were very happy, and were soon surrounded by many miniature duplicates of themselves.

TYPES (I) 1890, (II) 930D. MOTIFS: X.1110 [*The wonderful hunt*]; T.68 [*Princess offered as prize*]; N.211.1 [*Lost ring found in fish*].

¶ The thing which distinguishes this story from those like "The Bride Who had never been Kissed" (A, IV) is that the finding of the fish and the lucky shot are both tricks by which the lovers secure consent to their marriage.

KENTSHAM BELL

Hartland, *English Fairy and Folk-Tales*, pp. 204–5.

Great Tom of Kentsham was the greatest bell ever brought to England, but it never reached Kentsham safely, nor hung in any English tower. Where Kentsham is I cannot tell you, but long, long ago the good folk of the place determined to have a larger and finer bell in their steeple than any other parish could boast.

At that time there was a famous bell-foundry abroad where all the greatest bells were cast, and thither too sent many others who wanted greater bells than could be cast in England. And so it came to pass at length that Great Tom of Lincoln, and Great Tom of York and Great Tom of Christchurch and Great Tom of Kentsham were all founded at the same time, and all embarked on board the same vessel, and carried safely to the shore of dear old England. Then they set about landing them, and this was anxious work, but little by little it was done, and Tom of Lincoln, Tom of York, Tom of Christchurch were safely laid on English ground. And then came the turn of Tom of Kentsham, which was the greatest Tom of all.

Little by little they raised him, and prepared to draw him to the shore; but just in the middle of the work, the captain grew so anxious and excited that he swore an oath. That very moment the ropes which held the bell snapped in two, and Great Tom of Kentsham slid over the ship's side into the water, and rolled away to the bottom of the sea.

Then the people went to the cunning man and asked him what they should do. And he said: "Take six yoke of white milch-kine which have never borne the yoke, and take fresh withy bands which have never been used before, and let no man speak a word either good or bad till the bell is at the top of the hill."

So they took six yoke of white milch-kine which had never borne the yoke, and harnessed them with fresh withy bands, which had never been used, and bound these to the bell as it lay in the shallow water, and long it was ere they could move it. But still the kine struggled and pulled and the withy bands held firm, and at last the bell was on dry ground. Slowly, slowly they drew it up the hill, moaning and groaning with unearthly sounds as it went; slowly, slowly, and no one spoke, and they nearly reached the top of the hill. Now the captain had been wild with grief when he saw that he had caused his precious freight to be lost in the waters just as they had reached the shore; and when he beheld it recovered again and so nearly placed in safety, he could not contain his joy, but sang out merrily:

"In spite of all the devils in hell,
We have got to land old Kentsham bell."

Instantly the withy bands broke in the midst and the bell bounded back again down the sloping hillside, rolling over and over, faster and faster, with unearthly clanging, till it sank far away in the very depths of the sea. And no man has ever seen it since, but many have heard it tolling beneath the waves, and if you go there you may hear it too.

TYPE ML.7070. MOTIFS: C.494 [*Tabu: cursing*]; C.401.4 [*Tabu: speaking while raising sunken church bell*]; V.115.1.3.2 [*Church bell cannot be raised because person blasphemes*]; F.993 [*Sunken bell sounds*].
¶   See "The Bells of Brinkburn", "The Bells of Forrabury".

KILGRIM BRIDGE

Gutch, *County Folk-Lore*, II, p. 19.

Regarding the building of this bridge is the following curious legend.

Many bridges having been built on this site by the inhabitants, none had been able to withstand the fury of the floods until his "Satanic Majesty" promised to build a bridge which would defy the fury of the elements, on condition that the first living creature who passed over should fall a sacrifice to his "Sable Majesty". Long did the inhabitants consider, when the bridge was complete, as to who should be the victim.

A shepherd, more wise than his neighbours, owned a dog called "Grim". This man having first swum the river, whistled for the dog to follow, poor "Grim" unwittingly bounded across the bridge and thus fell a victim to his "Sable Majesty". Tradition says, from this circumstance the spot has ever since been known as Kill grimbridge.

Bogg, *Wensleydale and the Lower Vale of York*, p. 96, footnote. *From Eden Vale to the Plains of York*, p. 274.
MOTIFS: G.303.9.1.1 [*Devil as builder of bridges*]; S.241.1 [*Unwitting bargain with Devil evaded by driving dog over bridge first*]; K.219.6 [*Devil gets an animal in place of a human being*].
¶ See "The Curious Cat" (B, III).

KING ARTHUR AT SEWINGSHIELDS

Denham Tracts, II, p. 125.

Sewingshields lies between the Roman Wall and the military road, near the twenty-eighth milestone from Newcastle, and at the western extremity of Warden Parish. Of Sewingshields Castle...the walls have been uprooted and the vaults removed, but the following tradition relating to it will not readily perish:

"Immemorial tradition has asserted that King Arthur, his queen Guinevere, his court of lords and ladies, and his hounds, were enchanted in some cave of the crags, or in a hall below the Castle of Sewingshields, and would continue entranced there till someone should first blow a bugle-horn that lay on a table near the entrance of the hall, and then, with 'the sword of the stone', cut a garter also placed there beside it. But none had ever heard where the entrance to this enchanted hall was till the farmer at Sewingshields, about fifty years since, was sitting knitting on the ruins of the castle and his clew fell and ran downwards through a rush of briars and nettles, as he supposed, into a deep subterranean passage. Full in the faith that the entrance into King Arthur's hall was now discovered, he cleared the briary portal of its weeds and rubbish, and, entering a vaulted passage, followed, in his darkling way, the thread of his clew. The floor was infested with toads and lizards; and the dark wings of bats, disturbed by his unhallowed intrusion, flitted fearfully around him. At length his sinking courage was strengthened by a dim, distant light, which as he advanced grew gradually brighter, till at once he entered a vast and vaulted hall, in the centre of which a fire without fuel, from a broad crevice in the floor, blazed with a high and lambent flame that showed all the carved walls and fretted roof, and the monarch and his queen and court reposing around in a theatre of thrones and costly couches. On the floor, beyond the fire, lay the faithful and deep-toned pack of thirty couple of hounds, and on a table before it the spell-dispelling horn, sword and garter. The shepherd reverently but firmly grasped the sword, and as he drew it leisurely from its rusty scabbard the eyes of the monarch, and his courtiers began to open, and they rose till they sat upright. He cut the garter; and as the sword was being slowly sheathed the spell assumed its ancient power, and they all gradually sank to rest; but not before the monarch had lifted up his eyes and hands and exclaimed:

'O woe betide that evil day,
   On which the witless wight was born,
Who drew the sword—the garter cut,
   But never blew the bugle-horn.'

"Of this favourite tradition the most remarkable variation is respecting the place where the farmer descended. Some say that after the King's denunciation, terror brought on a loss of memory, and he was unable to give any correct account of his adventure or the place where it occurred. But all agree that Mrs Spearman, the wife of another and more recent occupier of the estate, had a dream in which she saw a rich hoard of treasure among the ruins of the castle, and that for many days together she stood over workmen employed in searching for it, but without success."

Hodgson's *History of Northumberland*, Part II, Vol. III, p. 287.

TYPE 766. MOTIFS: D.1960.2 [*King asleep in mountain*]; D.760 [*Disenchantment by miscellaneous means*]; D.1960.2.2* [*Man gains entrance into a cavern where a king, his warriors, dogs and horses lie asleep. The man sees articles (sword, garter, bugle, etc.) on a table before the king. He begins to unsheath the sword, the king stirs, and he sheaths it again. They go back to sleep, etc.*]; (Baughman).

¶ The sleeping hero in a cave under a mountain is a theme common in Europe. Sometimes the hero is Barbarossa, sometimes Charlemagne, sometimes King Marko, or Holger the Dane. The subject has been treated by Krappe, Feilberg, and others, and Hartland devoted a chapter of his *Science of Fairy Tales* to it. Macculloch has treated the Arthurian part of the legend. A paper by A. L. Brown, "Camlaun and the Death of Arthur", *Folk-Lore*, LXXII, pp. 612–21, retells the legend of Sewing-shields.

Sometimes the heroes are anonymous, as in the introduction to Durrant Hotham's *Works of Jacob Behmen* and "The Hunter and His Hounds". A Welsh legend, "The Gold of Craig-y-Ddinas" (Betts, *English Legends*), makes King Arthur the guardian of treasure (MOTIF: N 573).

See "The Hunter and His Hounds", "Potter Thompson", "The Silver Horseshoe", "Guinevere's Comb".

LADY GODIVA

Hartland, *English Fairy and Folk-Tales*, p. 55.

The Countess Godiva, who was a great lover of God's mother, longing
to free the town of Coventry from the oppression of a heavy toll, often
with urgent prayers besought her husband that, from regard to Jesus
Christ and his mother, he would free the town from that service and
from all other heavy burdens; and when the Earl sharply rebuked her
for foolishly asking what was so much to his damage, and always forbade
her evermore to speak to him on the subject; and while she, on the
other hand, with a woman's pertinacity, never ceased to exasperate her
husband on that matter, he at last made her this answer: "Mount your
horse and ride naked, before all the people, through the market of this
town from one end to the other, and on your return you shall have your
request." On which Godiva replied, "But will you give me permission
if I am willing to do it?" "I will," said he. Whereupon the Countess,
beloved of God, loosed her hair and let down her tresses, which covered
the whole of her body like a veil, and then, mounting her horse and
attended by two knights, she rode through the market-place without
being seen, except her fair legs, and having completed the journey, she
returned with gladness to her astonished husband, and obtained of him
what she had asked, for Earl Leofric freed the town of Coventry and its
inhabitants from the aforesaid service, and confirmed what he had done
by a charter.

From Roger of Wendover, *Flowers of History*, Dr Giles's translation, *sub anno* 1057.
MOTIF: M.235 [*Bargain: woman rides naked through streets to obtain freedom for
citizens (Godiva)*].

¶ Hartland, *Folk-Lore Journal*, I, p. 207, treated the subject of Lady Godiva and
the ritual ride through Coventry. The chief modern scholar to make an exhaustive
study of the subject is Dr. Hilda Ellis Davidson. See Lancaster and Davidson, *Godiva
of Coventry*. The "Peeping Tom" tradition is discussed by both. Tennyson gives it a
poetic treatment in "Godiva".

See, "The Barefoot Pilgrimage", "Crawls".

THE LAIRD OF FORDELL'S PRISONER

Wilkie, *Bygone Fife*, p. 54.

The tapestries that of old hung in Pitreavie came in the days of its desolation to Fordell, where in the mansion house they still cover the walls.

A story is told of the use of the vault in more modern times. A
candidate for Parliament who, it was desired by the family, should not

be returned, was invited to the castle. When dinner was over, his host opened a door in the corner of the room, and courteously invited him to take precedence in passing through. He did so, and at once slid down a sloping shaft into the vault, where he was entertained until nomination day was past, and his opponent triumphantly returned.

The letter is preserved in which an eminent statesman congratulates the Laird of Fordell on the result. The congratulations proved premature, for an election court entirely lacking in a sense of humour unseated the victor on petition and fined him £10,000.

MOTIFS: R.4 [*Surprise capture*]; R.41.1 [*Captivity in castle*].

THE LAIRD OF SNÜSQUEY

Shetland Folk-Book, II, p. 14.

The last Laird of Snüsquey was a man named Thomas Twatt. He let part of his land to a tenant, but, disagreeing with him, he wished to turn him off.

This, however, he failed to manage. Old John Scott of Vaila then came to him and said, "If you will give me the title deeds of your property for a little while I will help you to put your tenant away."

Twatt agreed to this but when the turning-off of the tenant was accomplished with Scott's assistance, he, Scott, refused to give the title deeds back.

Twatt prayed to the Almighty that he might be revenged upon Scott.

Through time he died, and the very day after a boat from Sandness had occasion to go to Vaila. As they were approaching the beach they saw Scott coming down to meet them. "What news from Sandness," said he. "Oh, not much," said the men, "but the Laird of Snüsquey is dead." "Oh God," said Scott. "I might have known that. He was very rude here last night. Had he come west as he went east there would not have been a 'steed' stone left standing."

The Sandness men then saw that the heavy iron entrance gate at the house had been torn away from its hinges and flung a considerable distance away.

MOTIFS: K.453 [*Cheating through knowledge of the law*]; E.234 [*Ghost punishes injury received in life*].

THE LAIRD'S JOCK'S STONE

Scott, *Minstrelsy of the Scottish Border*, II, p. 91

[The Laird's Jock was the *nom de plume* of John Armstrong, a noted cattle-thief of Liddesdale, in the second half of the sixteenth century. Sir Richard Maitland thus writes of him:

> They spuilye puir men of their pakis,
> They leif them nocht on bed nor bakis,
> Baith hen and cok,
> With reil and rok,
> The *Lairdis Jock*
> All with him takis.

· · · ·

Tradition reports that the Laird's Jock survived to extreme old age, when he died in the following extraordinary manner: A challenge had been given by an Englishman, named Forster, to any Scottish Borderer, to fight him at a place called Kersehope-foot, exactly upon the Borders. The Laird's Jock's only son accepted the defiance, and was armed by his father with his own two-handed sword. The old champion himself, though bedridden, insisted upon being present at the battle. He was borne to the place appointed, wrapped, it is said, in blankets, and placed upon a very high stone to witness the conflict. In the duel his son fell, treacherously slain, as the Scotch tradition affirms. The old man gave a loud yell of terror and despair when he saw his son slain and his noble weapon won by an Englishman, and died as they bore him home.... The stone on which the Laird's Jock sat to behold the duel was in existence till wantonly destroyed a year or two since. It was always called "The Laird's Jock's Stone".

MOTIFS: P.233 [*Father and son*]; F.1041.1.3 [*Death from sorrow or chagrin*].

LAME HAVERAH [summary]

Parkinson, *Yorkshire Legends and Traditions*, 1st series, p. 223.

Haverah Park is a region five or six miles to the west of Knaresborough, belonging to the Ingilbys of Ripley Castle. It was probably once an enclosed deer park, made for the benefit of hunters, but the legend assigns the name to a beggar in the time of John of Gaunt.

One day this beggar had the good fortune to meet the great lord as he was hunting in the forest, and begged his leave to enclose a small piece of land, to form a tilth for growing his food. John agreed in the following terms:

"I, John o'Gaunt,
Do give and do grant,
To thee Havera,
As much of my ground,
As thou canst hop round,
In a long summer's day."

The beggar chose Barnaby Day, 11 June, as the longest in the year, and, starting at sunrise, he hopped on his crutches without stopping until sunset, and so nearly completed the circuit of the present park that he was able to throw one of his crutches to his starting-point, just as the sun dropped beneath the horizon, and so won for himself the land which has ever since borne his name.

MOTIF: H.1584.2 [*Land measured according to amount encompassed during certain hours*].
¶ See "The Barefoot Pilgrimage", "Crawls".

THE LEGEND OF GLEN GARRY
[slightly shortened]

Hugh Miller, *Scenes and Legends*, pp. 38–9.

On the summit of Knock Ferril, a steep hill which rises a few miles to the west of Dingwall, stand the remains of one of those vitrified forts which so puzzle and interest the antiquary; and which was originally constructed, tradition says, by a gigantic tribe of *Fions* for the protection of their wives and children, when they themselves were out hunting. In one of their excursions, a mean-spirited little fellow, not much more than fifteen feet in height, was so distanced by his more active brethren, that, leaving them to follow out the chase, he returned home and, throwing himself down, much fatigued, on the side of the eminence, fell fast asleep. This hunter, Garry, was no favourite with the women of the tribe; he was spiritless and diminutive, and ill-tempered; and as they could make little other use of him, they converted him into a butt for their teasing; and the sport of many a capricious humour. On seeing that he had fallen asleep, they stole out, and fastened his long hair with pegs to the grass, and then awakened him with their shouts and laughter. He strove in vain to extricate himself; until at length, infuriated by their gibes and his own pain, he wrenched up his head, leaving half his locks behind him, and, hurrying after them, set fire to their stronghold. The flames soon mounted over the roof, but Garry, unmoved by the shrieks and groans of the sufferers, held fast the door, until all was silent. Then he fled westwards into the remote Highlands.

The men of the tribe, who had meanwhile been hunting on that part of the northern part of the Sutor named the hill of Nigg, alarmed by the smoke which they saw ascending from their dwelling, came pressing on to the Firth of Cromarty, and, leaping across on their hunting-spears, they hurried home; only to find a huge pile of embers, fanned by the breeze, amid which the very stones of the building were sputtering and bubbling with the intense heat, like the contents of a boiling cauldron. Wild with rage and astonishment, they concluded that none but Garry could be the author of so barbarous a deed: and they tracked him to a nameless Highland glen, which has ever since been known as Glen Garry, and there they tore him to pieces. And as all the women of the tribe had perished in the flames, there was an end, when this forlorn and widowed generation had passed away, to the whole race of the Fions.

MOTIFS: F.531.2.1.1 [Giant (only) fifteen feet tall]; K.1021.1 [Dupe tied by hair and then attacked]; S.112.0.2 [House buried with all inside]; Q.411.6 [Death as punishment for murder]; A.1617 [Origin of place-name]; F.531.6.12 [Disappearance or death of giants].

THE LEGEND OF THE HOLY WELL [summary]

C. J. Billson, County Folk-Lore, I, Part III, Leicestershire and Rutland, p. 19.

It is said that the Comyns of Comyn Castle were giants long ago. One of them attempted to carry off the only daughter of the lady of Groby Castle, but the girl escaped into the woods, intending to take sanctuary at Grace Dieu.

She lay hidden all night, though a dreadful storm was raging, and her pursuers passed by. In the morning, the hermit of the Holy Well found her lying, apparently dead from the terrors and exposure of the night. He carried her to the Holy Well, sprinkled her with its water from his scallop-shell and prayed that she might recover; which she shortly did, and returned safely to her home. A few months later she was married by the Prior of Ulverscroft to one Edward Grey, a young man of wealth and great promise.

Their first act after their marriage was to visit the good hermit, to ask his blessing, and to promise him, in return for his miracle, certain gifts for his hermitage; three fallow deer each year and the "right of the Challenge drift"; also two hides of land, to be held as long as men continued to visit the Holy Well, and to drink its waters in their hollowed hands.

MOTIFS: T.320 [*Escape from undesired lover*]; D.1713 [*Magic power of hermit*]; V.134 [*Sacred well*]; D.1500.1.1 [*Magic healing fountain*].

THE LEGEND OF LINTON CHURCH

William Henderson, *Notes on the Folk-Lore of the Northern Counties of England and the Borders*, p. 297–8.

There is another legend connected with Linton of exceeding interest. It is sometimes interwoven with that of the Worm, but I am informed that in its more correct form it stands alone.... The church is built on a little knoll of fine, compact sand, without any admixture of stone, or even pebbles, and widely differing from the soil of the neighbouring heights. The sand has nowhere hardened into stone, yet the particles are so coherent, that the sides of newly opened graves appear smooth as a wall, and this to the depth of fifteen feet. This singular phenomenon is thus accounted for on the spot:

Many years ago a young man killed a priest in this place, and was condemned to suffer death for murder and sacrilege. His doom seemed inevitable, but powerful intercession was made for him, especially by his two sisters, who were fondly attached to their brother. At last his life was granted him, on condition that the sisters should sift as much sand as would form a mound on which to build a church. The maidens joyfully undertook the task, and their patience did not fail. They completed it, and the church was built, though it is added that one of the sisters died immediately after her brother's liberation, either from the effects of past fatigue or overpowering joy. Such is the version of the legend, deemed the correct one at Linton. The villagers point to the sandy knoll in confirmation of its truth, and show a hollow place a short distance to the westward, as that from which the sand was taken.

MOTIFS: P.253.8 [*Clever sister saves life of brother*]; H.1129.3 [*Task: carrying soil to cover stony ground*].
¶ See "The Linton Worm" (B, IV).

A LEGEND OF WEEM CASTLE [summary]

School of Scottish Studies, Maurice Fleming, from Bella Higgins, 1954.

There was a laird of Weem, who had lost his first wife, and married a second. His first wife had a daughter and his second wife had a daughter, and the girls were very fond of each other, but the second wife was very jealous of her stepdaughter and wanted her out of the way. Now there was a wild man, a kind of hermit up Weem Hill, and he met the lady and promised to kill her stepdaughter, but the two girls were always together. So the stepmother said she would give a bracelet to her stepdaughter, and he was to kill the one wearing the bracelet.

She gave the girl a beautiful bracelet, and told her to take care of it, and always to wear it. Then she sent the two girls up the hill, to look for a calf that had strayed. As they went, the lady's daughter admired the bracelet so much that her stepsister lent it to her. The wild man leapt out on them, and carried off the lady's daughter with the bracelet on her arm. The other tried to follow, but he drove her off, and she ran home. When the lady knew that her own daughter had been murdered, she went off her head, and they say that she killed herself.

MOTIFS: S.31 [*Cruel stepmother*]; S.322.4.2 [*Evil stepmother orders stepdaughter to be killed*].
A similar motif is K.1613.3 [*Poisoner's own son takes the beverage intended for his step-brother*].
¶ There is no motif in the Motif Index for love between stepsisters and stepbrothers, though this is quite frequent in traditional tales, as, for instance, in " Kate Crackernuts ".
Weem Castle is near Aberfeldy.

THE LINCOLN IMP: I

Gutch and Peacock, *County Folk-Lore*, V, *Lincolnshire*, p. 61.

[At Lincoln Minster] the Angel Choir, though so full of beauty, has one queer little object, typical of the love of the early sculptors for the grotesque. This is the celebrated *Lincoln Imp*. It is a curious little effigy. One leg is bent over the other thigh, the body is dwarfed and hairy, the head is hideous and with large ears, a grinning, ugly little monstrosity.

A legend runs that the Devil wanted to get into the Cathedral, and was out with the wind. He slipped inside, leaving the wind for ever blowing outside, and

> The devil hopped up without a limp,
> And at once took shape as the "Lincoln Imp",
> And there he sits on top of the column,
> And grins at the people who gaze so solemn.

This is taken from Arnold Trost's "The Wind, the Devil, and Lincoln Minster" and other legends lately published. It is certain that the wind is always blowing round some part of the Minster, but that is, of course, only natural.

Wilkinson, *Illustrated Guide to Lincolnshire*, p. 45.

THE LINCOLN IMP: II

Thompson, Notebooks. From Gus Gray, Old Radford, 22 December 1914.

There were four imps. One jumped into a red-hot furnace; one flew up to the moon and played with lightning. The third went into a big church and an angel tried to turn it out. It wouldn't go, so the angel kicked it up into one of the buttresses, and it turned into stone. The fourth one jumped into the sea.

MOTIFS: G.303.8.4 [*The Devil lives in a church*]; G.303.16.19.18 [*Catching the Devil*].

¶ The second version of this legend gives an indication of how the Devil got stuck in the church. This story, as generally told, is something as follows:

The Devil and the wind were going for a stroll one day, looking down over Lincoln, when they came to Killcanon Corner. "Hold on for a minute," said the Devil. "I'll see if I can do any mischief in there. Wait for me outside," and he popped into the Cathedral.

Just as he got in, a full Choral Communion Service started. The Devil was terrified, and crept up to hide among the carving of the Angel Choir. When he got up, one of the angels touched him, and he was turned to stone, and never got out again. As for the wind, it is still hanging round Killcanon Corner, waiting for the Devil to come out.

THE LONE TREE

H. Bett, *English Myths and Traditions*, p. 54.

There is a solitary sycamore by the roadside a mile or two from Dover, known as the Lone Tree, and a singular tradition attaches to it. A soldier of the garrison at Dover is said to have slain a comrade with a staff, and as the two men were alone he struck it into the ground, exclaiming that his crime would never be discovered until that dry staff took root. He served abroad for many years unsuspected; but when once again stationed at Dover he visited the spot, driven by a morbid curiosity, and found that his staff had taken root and was a flourishing tree. Stricken with horror, he avowed his crime, and suffered for it on the gallows. The tree used to be visible from the ramparts at Dover, and it is stated that the story was traditional in the garrison.

¶ There are many stories of staffs that take root and grow, as, for instance, D.1673.1 [*Tree grows from stick Saint has used and cast aside*]. The staff, however, usually blossoms in mercy, not in judgment. Murder is, as a rule, shown by sterility, not by growth.

See "The Brothers' Steps".

LONG LONKIN

Denham Tracts, II, p. 191.

(Nafferton Castle, or Nafferton Old Hall, was built by Philip de Ulecote, but the work was interrupted in 1217 and was never completed.)

A lady, courted by a gentleman named Long Lonkin (whom the Northumbrian ballad makes a Moss Trooper), preferred the lord of Nafferton, whose circumstances made him a more desirable match. One child blessed the marriage. Long Lonkin vowed to be revenged, and, to accomplish his purpose, attached to his interest the child's maid, with whom he concerted his measures. His vengeance was most bitter, for he had determined to stab both the mother and her offspring. It happened that the lord of the place had occasion to proceed to London on business, and Lonkin, apprised of his approaching absence, came in the evening and was admitted by the treacherous maid. In order to induce the lady to descend from an upper chamber, by the advice of the maid, he pricked the child till it cried and then a second time till it screamed. The mother called down the maid to appease the child, but she exclaimed that she could not—she would have to come herself:

> "I can't still him, ladie.
> Till you come down yoursell."

Lonkin pricked the child a third time, and the poor mother appeared on the scene and was killed as well as her child.

The Lord of Nafferton had not proceeded far on his journey when an impression took hold of his mind that all was not right at home. Two of the ballads tell how this alarm was created. The rings on his fingers were bursting in twain, and the silver buttons of his coat would not stay on. Returning with all speed, he called to the servants within to let down the drawbridge, and it being done he was admitted. When Long Lonkin heard the noise of the coach passing over the bridge he sought means to escape; but the bridge was secured, and, as he could not get across the moat he fled to a dean below the castle, in which flows the Whittle Burn, and took refuge in a large tree that overhung a deep pool in the water. When the Lord of the place entered his apartments a horrible scene of carnage was revealed and the guilty maid did not conceal by whose agency it had been effected. The murderer was sought for the whole night, but it was not till morning that he was detected, concealed among the tree branches. The outraged husband called on him to descend, but he refused. He then threatened to shoot him if he did not surrender, but Lonkin recklessly leapt into the black boiling pool beneath and sunk, never to rise. The pool, now called Long Lonkin's Pool, the country people declare, is bottomless. A good swimmer had dived into it from the crags on both sides and had found no bottom, and it was only by great exertions that he escaped the fate of Lonkin. Some suppose that there is a spring at the bottom of it, for in the extremest cold it is never frozen over; but this circumstance others account for from a weill, or continuous eddy, being in the middle of it. Long Lonkin's tree was cut down thirty or forty years previous to 1844.

MOTIFS: T.75.2.1 [*Rejected suitor's revenge*]; K.930 [*Treacherous murder of enemy's children or charges*]; D.1812.5.1 [*Bad omens*].

¶ The best-known version of this tale is the Child Ballad 93, "Lamkin". In all the Child versions Lamkin is a mason who had built the Lord a castle, and could not get his fee. The motif of disappointed love seems more convincing.

THE LONG PACK

John Elliot, *Notebooks*, Yarrowford, Selkirkshire, 1952.

The country miller and his mill is now a thing of the past. In my young days the most of the country mills was going, and seemed to be always busy, there was always plenty meal to be had, and farmers could take their grain to the mill and get it ground in a short time. A mill I was at, called Bengelhirt Mill, below Jedburgh, was kept always busy, and the miller often kept his mill going to late at night.

I used to spend a lot of nights in the mill beside the miller, and I had the chance to see how the meal was made and how the oats were dried on the kiln before the grinding, and I often got the job to take the meal to the farmers' and shepherds' places out on the borders. I used to enjoy these times very much, but now there is little left of the country mills but the ruins. It is strange now, when you pass any of these mills, not to hear the old familiar sound of the mills.

This tale I write about the long pack took place at one of these mills down in Northumberland, not a great distance of Bellingham. It was a led* farm with a mill. A gentleman farmer was tenant, and had another farm some distance off, where he lived. He had at the mill a housekeeper called Alice, a ploughman, a miller and a boy for herding the crows off the fields and doing other jobs. This boy had an old gun for firing at the crows. He called his old blunderbuss Captain Hagin, which he was very proud of. The gentleman had a lot of both gold and silver plate stored at the Big House on the Mill in one of the rooms, and it is strange how this got to be known to other people; but it had been found out by some would-be robber.

* *Led* = lade.

One forenoon when the day was very warm, Alice the housekeeper was busy cooking the dinner for the man and the boy, as they came in for their dinner about twelve o'clock, and this was about eleven o'clock, when a knock came to the door, and she went out to see a big, tall man carrying a pack on his back. He asked her for a night's lodging, as he was overcome carrying his pack in the great heat. She told him she could not give him lodgings, as there was no room in the house for any more than two men, the boy and herself, but he pleaded on her just to let him stay for one night, but she declined and told him it was impossible, as she could not take him in.

Then he asked her to let him leave his pack, as he was so tired carrying it.

Alice looked at his pack, and thought it was the strangest pack she had ever seen, but she thought the pack would not take up much room, and she told him to bring it into the room, and he laid it on the floor, and then went out and shut the door. So after the man was away, she was busy in the kitchen preparing the dinner, she was thinking of this funny pack, she thought she would have a look or a peek at it. She opened the door very gently, and was watching it, when to her horror she saw it moving, and she ran to the door screaming, and told the miller; the miller came in and had a look at the pack, then he told Alice she was just imagining she had seen it move, and told her to let the man's pack alone, as it was all right; and he went back to the mill again. But it was not long or dinner-time and the ploughman came in, and she told him how she had seen it move. He went ben and had a look at it, and him and the miller was telling Alice to let the man's pack alone. When the boy came in, carrying Captain Hagin, he heard them telling Alice the pack was all right. "What pack?" said the boy. "I'll have a look at it." And he gently opened the door and watched it moving. "I saw it moving!" shouted the boy. "I saw it moving!" The miller and the ploughman told the boy to come ben out of that, and let the pack alone, but the boy stood, and getting Captain Hagin to his shoulders, told them, "I'll have a crack at it!" Again the miller and the ploughman warned him to leave the pack alone. But he stood with his gun pointed at the pack. "Yes. I'll shoot it!" Once, twice, and the third time he fired and the groans of a man, and the blood swimming over the floor was terrible.

Alice and the men ran ben to see, and as soon as Alice saw the blood, she gave a scream, and ran outside, in a terrible state. The two men and the boy now examined the pack. There was a big man in the pack, lying shot, and in the pack beside him was pistols, and knives, and a wind-call, a sort of tin trumpet. They saw then that the boy had saved them all by shooting the pack. They knew there would be a raid on the house that night, and they would have to be ready to meet the robbers when they came; so they spent all the afternoon going to nearby places, to get young men to come at night, and help them to fight the robbers. So they got the house all barricaded up, and the young men had guns with them. There was a room upstairs, with a small window facing the road that came down the hill, and three or four of the men went up the stairs to watch the road through the little window. The boy, who had got the wind-call out of the pack, went upstairs also, and they sat there watching the road for the robbers coming, but they were not there a long time, and they all thought they were not coming.

The boy said, "Let me give them a call!" and he put the wind-call out of the little window, and gave a tek-tek with his trumpet, and it was not long or they heard the clatter of horses' feet coming down the road. They saw from the little window a band of robbers coming straight for the mill, and they got their guns out of the window, and fired on them. They turned and fled when they saw they had been found out, and all was quiet after that.

The next day they sent word to their master, who came and conducted the business of getting the man who was shot in the pack buried in Bellingham Churchyard. After some time the farmer removed his gold and silver plates from the mill to safety, and the ploughman married Alice the housekeeper, the boy became the gentleman's gamekeeper, and this ends the tale of the Long Pack.

TYPE 958D* (variant).

¶ The most complete example of this story, of which there is a distant variant in "The Robber and the Housekeeper" (A, IV).

See also "The Hand of Glory" (B, XII).

THE LONTON LASS

Gutch, *County Folk-Lore*, II, p. 207.

About 90 years since, a young woman at Lonton had a lover, who first deceived and then resolved to murder her. Under pretence of arranging for their immediate marriage, he persuaded her to meet him in Park End Wood. On the night appointed he repaired to the place and digged a grave. She slipped out of her parents' house, when all was quiet, and sped on to the place of meeting. The farmer, however, at Park End, was greatly disturbed that night by dreams. He dreamt twice that he saw an open grave and a spade sticking in the soil—in a wood near his house. And so excited was his imagination that he could not think of remaining in bed. He arose, and called up his young men, and ordered them to furnish themselves with bludgeons and accompany him into the wood. They all went, and sure enough there was the open grave and the spade. Their horror and astonishment were inexpressible. They searched the wood, and beat about for some time among the bushes, but could neither see nor hear anybody. After some time had been spent in searching and watching, they returned. And on the old road not far from the farm-house one of them discerned an object approaching. They stood aside. The object came up. A young woman! "Hollo!" said the farmer. "whither are you going so late tonight?" "And what is that to you?" she replied. "Surely I am old enough to know my own business, without having to give an account of it to you."

"Come, come," said the farmer. "I know now, I think, who you are, and guess your errand. Pray let me tell you what has caused us to be astir." She would not believe. They took her to the place, and at sight of the grave and spade she fainted. The whole party then returned to Park End, and the poor hapless girl, after telling her story of the matter, was only too glad to remain all night under the protection of him, who, through his remarkable and providential dream, had been the means of saving her life.

The Lord Fitzhugh and His Neighbour, Lord Baliol.
TYPE 955C (Baughman). MOTIF: D.1810.8.2 [*information received through dream*].
¶ The interesting part of this version of a tale which is common in England is the farmer's warning dream, by which the girl is saved.

See "The Oxford Student", "The Lass 'at seed her Awn Grave Dug", "Mr Fox's Courtship" (A, IV).

MAB'S CROSS or LADY MABEL BRADSHAW

H. Bett, *English Legends*, p. 19.

There is an ancient stone cross in Standish Gate, near Wigan in Lancashire, known as Mab's Cross. The tradition is that it commemorates an incident...in the life of Lady Mabel Bradshaw. She was the heiress of Hugh Norreys of Haigh and Blackrod and married Sir William Bradshaw, who is described as a great traveller and soldier. Apparently he lived in the reign of Edward the Second. Sir William had been away "at the warres" for ten years and was presumed to be dead. His supposed widow then married a Welsh knight. Eventually Sir William returned, dressed in a palmer's habit and sat down among the retainers. Lady Mabel noticed him, and his likeness to her dead husband moved her to tears. For this her new consort chastised her, whereupon Sir William made himself known to his tenants, and prepared for vengeance.

Meantime the Welsh knight fled. Sir William pursued him and, overtaking him near Newton Park, killed him. Then the Lady Mabel was commanded by her confessor to do penance for her bigamy by going once a week barefoot to this cross, which has been known ever since as Mab's Cross.

Cf. similar stories of returning Crusaders on other pages: Sir John Attwood of Wolverley, p. 18; Sir Leonard de Reresby of Thrybergh, p. 19; Sir Ralph de Staveley of Mottram, Cheshire, p. 19.

TYPE 974. MOTIFS: N.681 [*Husband arrives home just as wife is about to marry another*]; H.94 [*Identification by ring*]; Q.526 [*Pilgrimage as penance*].

¶ Roby's version of this story is more flowery and circumstantial than Bett's, and includes recognition by a ring and the imprisonment of the true husband.

The story is on the lines of the "Ballad of Hind Horn" (Child, I, pp. 187 *sqq*). See "Fulke Fitzwarin".

THE MAID'S STRATAGEM or
THE CAPTIVE LOVER [summary]

J. Roby, *Lancashire Traditions*, II, p. 358.

Anthony Hardcastle was the only son of a yeoman, whose early death left this son heir to considerable wealth and lands. He fell in love with Kate Anderton, the daughter of Justice Anderton of Lostock Hall, and wrote her an impassioned letter begging her to return his love.

Kate, however, loved and was loved by the lord of Turton Tower, whose father, like Anthony's, had died young, and the son had lately returned from his travels to enter on his inheritance. But Kate's father had had an implacable feud with the young man's father, and she well knew that he would never entertain the thought of the son as a husband for his daughter. With the help of her maid, Marian, therefore, she devised a way of making Anthony's suit a means to winning her own way. She wrote him a letter bidding him write to her father and ask his leave to woo her. But, however favourable the reply, he was not to come near the castle, her home, for a full month after receiving it, on pain of being refused by her at the end of the time.

Anthony wrote, and received a favourable reply, for his father had been known by repute to Roger Anderton. The days passed, and towards the end of the month Anthony's man, Hodge, came to him and asked for a new suit of clothes, for he had heard that mistress Kate was to be married on the feast of St Crispin, and this was all the talk about the place. Anthony supposed that this was intended as a kindly surprise for him, and that Kate had decided to shorten his month's abstinence. The following evening he and his man set out in their best clothes with dark cloaks to cover them, and Anthony stationed himself under cover of a pear tree in Kate's garden to observe without being seen.

He was disturbed by the sounds of revelry and music coming from the house, but dared not approach it, for his month was not yet at an end. As he waited, two half-drunken men staggered from the house, and, finding him there, arrested him for stealing the pears. To his protests that he was Master Anthony Hardcastle, they only returned that he was lying.

Master Anthony had been there, they said, but had gone home long before. He was to wed Mistress Kate on the following day. With that they threw the luckless Anthony into a filthy den, where he passed a wretched night.

Next day, the Justice, rising early, was surprised to be told by the two men that they had caught the pear-thief at last, and that he was claiming to be Master Anthony Hardcastle. The Justice bade them bring the man to him; Anthony repeated his tale and was told by the Justice that Anthony Hardcastle had been a frequent guest at his house for a month past, that he was a gallant and noble gentleman, who did not in the least resemble the draggled and filthy creature before him. At this moment the maid, Marian, entered and owned that a trick had been played. She was followed by Kate herself, led by a tall and handsome gentleman, who confessed that they had deceived her father, to make him know and accept her real lover, by pretending that he was Anthony Hardcastle. Then, turning to Anthony himself, the gentleman begged his forgiveness also. The Justice was won over, the two were married, and very shortly afterwards, Anthony Hardcastle was married to Mistress Bridget Allport, a lady who had long loved him, and whom he had loved in his boyhood, until ensnared by the charms of the wayward Kate.

MOTIFS: T.70 [*The scorned lover*]; K.1210 [*Humiliated or baffled lover*]; T.92 [*Rivals in love*]; T.131.1.2 [*Father's consent to daughter's marriage necessary*].
¶ Roby is unable to give the date or place of this story.

THE MARDEN HIGHWAYMAN

Sir C. Igglesden, *A Saunter through Kent with Pen and Pencil*, I, p. 47.

I cannot better close my sketch of Marden than by relating a strange tragedy that occurred many years ago along the Hawkhurst road. It was in the halcyon days of the highwayman, and on a certain Christmas Eve towards the close of the last century a notorious desperado named Gilbert, who was the terror of the neighbourhood, owing not so much to his daring exploits as to the cruelty with which he treated his victims, hailed a coach just as it was entering the village of Marden. Its two occupants were an old man and a young girl, and in a bantering tone of voice both were ordered to alight. The lady had just reached the ground when through some unknown cause the horses suddenly bolted and, dashing towards Marden, left the highwayman and his fair captive standing lone in the road. The alarm was raised in the village and the grief-stricken old man returned to the spot with a great number of men. But all they saw by the light of their lanterns was Gilbert lying near the hedge, his hand pressed tightly against his side. Life was ebbing fast away, but he was able to tell his awe-stricken hearers that, recognizing him as the murderer of her brother, the young lady had suddenly drawn a dagger from her belt and stabbed him in the side. Then he fell back dead.

But where was the girl? All night they sought her, and at last, in the early dawn, her huddled form was seen crouched behind a tree some miles away. Her brother's death had been avenged, but she was mad. It is supposed that the highwayman was buried by the wayside, and during the last generation the country folks looked upon the spot with horror, because it was said that every Christmas Eve the ghostly struggle between the highwayman and his captive was repeated in weird silence. I give the story as told me by a descendant of the girl's father, a member of an old Weald of Kent family.

But from inquiries made in Marden I can trace nothing further, so it seems as though this old ghost story is dying out, even in the recollection of the villagers themselves.

MOTIFS: P.253.5 [*Sister avenges brother's death*]; F.1041.8.2 [*Madness from grief*].

MARTIN'S STONE

H. Bett, *English Legends*, p. 97.

North of Strathmartin in Forfar there is a large stone known as Martin's Stone. The legend is that here a dragon was slain by a hero called Martin. The monster had devoured nine maidens, who had been sent out, one after the other, to draw water from a well at Pittempton, a few miles from Dundee. The well is still known as the Nine Maidens' Well. Martin was the lover of one of the damsels. The dragon fled from the place, and Martin and his allies fought it at Baldragon, where there was a swamp. The monster got away again to a place some two miles north-ward, and here Martin fought it single-handed, while his friends cried, "Strike, Martin!" and he struck the dragon so mightily with his club that it was only able to crawl away for another half-mile or so. Here it was slain, and the stone known as Martin's Stone still bears a rude carving of the dragon. The folk rhyme says:

I was temptit at Pittempton,
Draiglit at Baldragon,
Stricken at Strike-Martin,
And killed at Martin's Stone.

MOTIFS: B.11.10.2 [*Dragon eats people*]; B.11.11 [*Fight with dragon*]; A.1617 [*Origin of place-name*].

MARY AND MARGARET

Wilkie, *Bygone Fife*, p. 223.

About the middle of the twelfth century, when David the First was King of Scotland, and Stephen and Queen Maud contended for supremacy in England, Mary and Margaret [Abercrombie] loved in secret the same gallant knight. There is a mention of a Humphrey de Abercrombie in 1150, from whom Mr Wood has it that the "House of Birkenbog" was descended. The tradition, however, goes that it was he who died without a son, and that his daughters succeeded as co-heiresses. They were young when the broad lands and the wealth of the family devolved upon them.

They were beautiful too with the aristocratic beauty of the Norman race, and pious and unsophisticated, for they had been educated by the good nuns of North Berwick, the convent mentioned so often, in connection with territory extending from Aithernie eastward.

Naturally, their charm and their position attracted the young knights and nobles of East Fife and compelled the attention of their elders, who appreciated the prospect of wedding the heirs of their respective houses to maidens as well dowered as they were fair. In character they differed. Mary is said to have been strong and self-reliant, her younger sister gentle and timid.

Among the most gallant of their admirers was Philip de Candelle, the descendant of the William de Candelle who had received the estate of Anstruther when his fellow member of the household was rewarded with that of Abercrombie. He had fought in France and in the Second Crusade.... Love goes by contraries, it is said.

It was the gentle Margaret who won the warrior's heart. To her he sang the passionate songs of Provence and Araby....

Legend, like love, is unconscious of time. It tells how they were married by St Monan himself in the cave near the rocky eminence where his church now stands.

If there be aught of fact in this tale, it was doubtless by the monk who served the altar in the early chapel which preceded that erected two hundred years later by David the Second.

For some reason the projected wedding was kept a secret from all, even from Mary. The bride and bridegroom were beyond the Firth ere she suspected what had taken place.

"Heaven has no rage like love to hatred turned." No poison is so deadly as that of jealousy and thwarted passion. Mary, in the first misery of her seclusion in the castle from which her sister and the man she loved had gone for ever, was tempted by the Devil and vowed revenge. Happily, no opportunity offered for its exercise. Time laid its healing hand upon her heart, and her guardian angel vanquished the powers of evil.

Six long months passed. Then in England hostilities broke out. The Earl of Montague had proclaimed himself King Stephen, and fierce warfare raged between the usurper and Queen Maud, daughter of Henry the First of England and sister of the King of Scots. David at once assembled an army and crossed the Tweed. Among those who followed him was de Candelle. No bravery of Scottish King or noble sufficed to stem disaster in the Battle of the Standard. English guile triumphed, and that mad panic which, as at Pinkie, lost the day when victory was hovering, uncertain, above the combatants. Philip of Anstruther fell, either on the field itself, or in a preliminary skirmish. Margaret was a widow.

When the ill tidings came to Abercrombie, Mary's broodings fled like shadows of the night. Pity and love had conquered and the heart-broken sister was welcomed back with tears.

And now they found consolation in the service of the Church. If the legend runs aright, there was then no sacred building in the parish except that at the mouth of the Inweary Burn. They were impelled by consideration for their tenants and other landward folk to found a chapel. The site in what is now the woodland glade was chosen. There it rose as quickly as they could erect it who, with the devotion of the Middle Ages, laid every stone to the glory of God. As it was free of debt, as well as endowed, the consecration ceremony took place on its completion. The Bishop was at that time, Arnold, who had been Abbot of Kelso till his enthronement in St Andrews in presence of King Malcolm the Fourth in 1159. As we know from Wyntoun, Arnold died in 1163. We should have little difficulty in fixing the date, could the authenticity of the narrative be established. It certainly stands various chronological tests, except, perhaps, that it is difficult to account for the lapse of so many years between the Battle of the Standard in 1138, when the scion of the house of Anstruther fell, and the dedication of the church.

The scattered population of the countryside gathered to witness the sacred rite, watching the procession of clergy and choristers from St

Andrews, the relic of the saint borne in its fertour by four of the noblest laymen, the circling on the outside, the demand for admission, the marking of the consecration crosses, the galaxy of lighted tapers held by the worshippers, and the rest of the prolonged and splendid symbolical ceremonial.

When all was over, Mary and Margaret, sad-eyed and sorrowful, recalling the days that were gone, knelt side by side at the chancel steps, while the aged prelate blessed them. The shadows had been deepening, and, as his voice died away, a jagged lightning flash passed through the narrow windows, blinding for a moment clergy and congregation. Almost simultaneously, as it seemed, the thunder crashed in deafening peal, while the noise of the hail succeeded. When the shock had passed, all still remained in prayer. The echoes of the storm rumbled away over Kellie Law, the sky cleared, the clergy retired, the people passed out. But still the sisters knelt on, their heads buried in their clasped hands, motionless.

Bishop Arnold returned unvested, and, seeing them still kneeling, bent down to raise them from their rigid pose. His efforts were in vain. They had crossed the water of separation, and passed beyond the sorrows and the sufferings of earth.

...Awe-struck, the Bishop and the train, who had re-entered at his bidding, gazed upon the faces, calm with the peace and majesty of death. There seemed to echo from far off the voices of an unseen host chanting the last refrain of the *Dies Irae*—

"*Pie Jesu, Domine
Dona eis requiem*".

MOTIFS: T.92.8 [*Sisters in love with the same man*]; V.110 [*Sacred buildings*]; cf. S.261 [*Foundation sacrifice*].

¶ Implicit in this tradition is the idea that Mary Abercrombie had put herself in the Devil's power in her time of jealous anger, that the storm was his attempt to seize her, but that her forgiveness of her sister had cancelled the bond, though it demanded the sanctified death of the two sisters.

MARY THE MAID OF THE INN

Parkinson, *Yorkshire Legends and Traditions*, 1st series, p. 62.

A story often connected with Kirkstall Abbey relates that at a nearby inn was a maid named Mary. She was betrothed to Richard, a young neighbour, whom others thought idle and unworthy of her; but Mary loved him, and clung to him loyally.

One night two guests at the inn made a wager of a dinner that Mary would venture to the ruins of the Abbey and bring thence a branch of the alder that was growing in the aisle. Mary went fearlessly through the windy night, but just as she was about to pluck the bough she heard a voice and approaching footsteps, and quickly she crouched behind one of the great columns to hide. There she saw in a fitful moonlight two men, carrying a corpse between them. As they came close to the terrified girl, the wind blew off the hat from one of the men's head, and it rolled close to where she crouched. "Leave it, and hide the body first," cried one of them, and as soon as they were past her, she unthinkingly snatched up the hat and fled back to the inn. Only when she got safely inside did she look at it, and immediately knew it to belong to her Richard. He was shortly convicted of the crime, and for many years the gibbet stood on the common nearby to mark the spot of his punishment.

TYPE 955 (variant). MOTIF: K.2232 [*Treacherous lover*].
¶ This tale is loosely allied to two types, "Mr Fox" and "The Oxford Student". There is enough variation, however, to suggest that the tale is possibly true.
See "The Girl who got up a tree", "Mr Fox's Courtship" (A, IV).

MAULDSLIE CASTLE

Chambers, *Popular Rhymes of Scotland*, p. 336.

In Lanarkshire they relate that, in building Mauldslie Castle in a former situation, the work was regularly razed every night, till, a watch being set, a voice was heard to enunciate from the foundations:

> "Big the house where it should be,
> Big it on Maul's Lee."

To which spot the building was accordingly transferred.

TYPE ML.7060. MOTIF: D.2192 [*Work of day magically overthrown at night*].
¶ See "Callaly Castle", "The Castle of Melgund", "Glamis Castle".

THE MAYOR'S LAST BANQUET

J. R. W. Coxhead, *The Devil in Devon*, pp. 16–17.

Henry Lee, Mayor of Great Torrington, was one of the two West Country mayors hanged for complicity in the Western Rebellion in 1549.

The story of the dramatic events leading up to the Mayor's untimely end is preserved in an old local tradition which was first recorded about the year 1568.

The tragic tale opens with Henry Lee receiving a letter from Sir Anthony Kingston, the King's Provost-Marshal. In the letter Sir

Anthony informed the Mayor that he intended to visit Great Torrington, with his retinue, on a certain day, and looked forward to dining with him.

The Mayor was overjoyed at what he thought was the great honour about to be conferred upon his town, so he commenced to make preparations to entertain the Provost-Marshal and his party to a fine banquet.

On the appointed day Sir Anthony Kingston arrived at Great Torrington with his retinue, and was welcomed by Henry Lee and the chief men of the town with considerable ceremony.

As the Mayor was about to conduct his guests to the banquet, Sir Anthony drew him aside, and told him that he would have to perform an execution in the town later in the day, so he would be glad if a gallows could be set up and ready for use, by the time the dinner was over. "Certainly, sir," replied Mr Lee. "I will give the necessary orders at once."

Having issued his grim instructions, the unsuspecting Mayor sat down beside his important guests and the banquet commenced.

Sir Anthony's courtesy and pleasant conversation caused the Mayor to forget the unpleasant activities that were going on in another part of the town, and he was extremely gratified when the knight congratulated him on the excellence of the dinner.

As soon as the banquet was over, the Provost-Marshal requested Henry Lee to take him to the place where the gallows had been erected. When the knight saw the gibbet, he turned to the Mayor and said, "Do you think it will be strong enough for its purpose?"

"Yes," replied the Mayor; "quite strong enough."

"Well," said Sir Anthony, "place yourself beneath it, because it is meant for you."

"Surely, sir, you are making a mistake," cried the horrified Mayor.

"Not so," said the knight sternly. "You took part in a recent rebellion, and the reward for your treason is death."

Then, without any further delay, the noose was placed round the unfortunate man's neck and he was duly hanged.

. . . .

If the dreadful details of the foregoing tradition are true, then Sir Anthony Kingston is revealed as a heartless monster who played with his victim like a cat playing with a mouse.

Historically, all that is known of Henry Lee is that he was Mayor of Torrington in 1549 and that he was one of the eight signatories of the "Articles" presented to Edward VI by the insurgents and that he was hanged for the part he played in the rebellion.

There is no motif appropriate to this legend.

¶ The peculiar cruelty of Kingston's action lay in its entire unexpectedness, and in the lack of preparation for death—a preparation which was, at that time, deemed essential, so that "sudden death" is one of the happenings expressly prayed against. Emotionally, the story is nearest to that of the first gallows in Skye, when the chief beckoned to an old clansman who came up, delighted to be summoned by his chief, and was immediately hanged, to see how the gallows worked. The cat-and-mouse cruelty of the last-minute reprieves of condemned men in the Georgian army is an entirely different kind of cruelty.

THE MERCER'S SON OF MIDHURST [summary]

W. E. A. Axon, *Bygone Sussex*, p. 182.

A Sussex youth went wooing a maid, who vowed she would marry only for money and cared not who her husband might be so long as he was rich. Her lover thereupon induced his father to make over to him "all his house and land", but the married pair treated the father so ill that they were punished by having no child. At last, after thirteen years, the wife strangled herself, and the husband died without making a will, so the old man regained his property and used it with great benevolence for the relief of the poor, constantly declaring that parents who during their lifetime relinquish their possessions to their children can only expect ingratitude in return.

From a seventeenth century broadside, "An Excellent Ballad of the Mercer's Son of Midhurst, and the Cloathier's Daughter of Guildford".

TYPE 980A (variant). MOTIFS: P.236.1 [*Folly of father's giving all his property to children before his death*]; Q.281.1 [*Ungrateful children punished*].

¶ See "The Ungrateful Children" (A, IV).

THE MERCHANT OF CHICHESTER

W. E. A. Axon, *Bygone Sussex*, p. 151.

An English merchant...travelling abroad in the pursuit of trade had the misfortune, though he "was both grave and wise", to kill a man in a quarrel at Emden.

For this he was condemned to die, and came on to the scaffold, where he was to be decapitated, very handsomely dressed, and in a very penitent frame of mind. He orders "a hundred pounds apiece" to be given to the widow and her two children. But at Emden they have a law that a woman who will wed a condemned criminal may thus save his life.

Ten merciful maidens contend for the privilege of rescuing the handsome Englishman from the headsman, but he declines their offer. Then another damsel steps forward, and protests that she acts from love and not from mercy, and, as love begets love, he consents to live.

> "I goe, my love," she said.
>   "I run, I fly for thee.
> And gentle Headsman, spare a while
>   My lover's life for me."
> Unto the Duke shee went,
>   Who did her griefe remove,
> And with a hundred Maidens more,
>   Shee went to fetch her love.
>
> With musicke sounding sweet,
>   The foremost of the traine,
> This gallant Maiden, like a Bride,
>   Did fetch him back againe,
> Yea, hand in hand they went
>   Unto the church that day,
> And they were married presently
>   In sumptuously rich array.
>
> *A sweet thing is love*
>   *It rules both heart and mind*
> *There is no comfort in the world*
>   *To women that are kind*

The belief that a woman might beg a condemned man as a husband is widespread, and may not impossibly have had some foundation in fact in ages when death was the penalty of even comparatively slight misdemeanours.... "Pity is akin to love", and the Englishman and his pretty Dutch wife appear to have "lived happy ever after".

MOTIF: P.512.1 [*Release from execution at woman's request (by marriage to her)*].
¶ There is a note on this tradition by Archer Taylor in the *Journal of American Folk-Lore*, p. 185. A verse of an eighteenth-century jocular song is on something this theme:

> There was a man all in a cart,
>   Was going to be hanged.
> There came a message from the King
>   That caused the cart to stand.
>
> If he would marry with a wife,
>   Oh, then he should be free,
> And he should never decorate,
>   The awful gallows-tree.

He pondered long, for life is dear
To everyone alive,
But bitter is the cup of him,
That foolish takes a wife.
"The bargain's hard, I do admit,
I find it hard to part,
But a wife is not the remedy,
So pray, drive on the cart."

THE MISER OF WINCHELSEA

W. E. A. Axon, *Bygone Sussex*, p. 96.

There was once an avaricious man living in the neighbourhood of Winchelsea who hoarded in a chest money which was of no benefit to either himself or to others. One day, as he went to look at his beloved treasure, he saw sitting on the box a little black demon. If he was startled at the sight, he was still more startled to hear this apparition exclaim: "Begone. This money is not thine: It belongs to Godwin, the smith."

Unable to make use of the treasure himself, he decided that no one else should have it. He therefore hollowed out the trunk of a great tree, put the box in it, closed up the ends, and threw it into the sea. The waters carried the trunk up the door of Godwin, who dwelt in the next town—evidently Rye. Godwin, who was a righteous and innocent man, was preparing to hold a Christmas festival, and the appearance of this log was a source of rejoicing, as it would evidently make a capital Yule log. So the smith carried home the tree-trunk, and put it in his fireplace. On Christmas Eve, the fire was lighted and the heat caused the money within the box to melt and the metal ran out. Godwin's wife saw this and, taking the log from the fire, she hid it. The result was that Godwin the smith became rich, whilst the Winchelsea man was forced to beg his bread from door to door. But the story of the manner in which the miser had lost his wealth became known, and when he begged at the Smith's house the wife of Godwin thought she would give the poor caitiff some help. So one day she baked a loaf, and hid forty shillings in it, and gave it to the beggar. The miser went his way, and soon after met some fishermen on the beach, to whom he sold the loaf unbroken for a penny. The fishermen came to Godwin's house and were about to give the loaf to their horses when the mistress recognized it, and let them have some oats instead. So the miser remained poor to the end of his days.

TYPE 745 A. MOTIF: N.212 [*Money cannot be kept from where it is destined to go. Miser told that his hoard is to go to poor man. He hides it in a trunk and throws it in the sea, but it drifts to the house of the poor man, who tries in vain to restore it to its owner.*]
¶ This is a sparsely but widely spread type. The type-index cites Lithuanian, Irish, Russian and West Indian examples.

MISTRESS ANNE GRIFFITH

S. Baring-Gould, *A Book of Folk-Lore*, p. 193.

Burton Agnes is situated in the East Riding of Yorkshire, and the hall is a noble structure. The estate, which was anciently owned by the De Somervilles, passed in the reign of Edward I to the Griffith family, which died out in three co-heiresses, sisters, in the last years of Queen Elizabeth. As they were very wealthy, they resolved on rebuilding the family mansion in the style of the period, and the youngest sister, Anne, took the keenest interest in planning and furnishing the hall. When this was complete, the ladies took up their abode in it; but one day soon after, Anne was murdered on her way to visit some friends by ruffians, then called wood-rangers, for her purse and rings. She had been stunned by them by a blow over the head with a cudgel, and was carried back to Burton Agnes; but, although she lingered during five days, she never recovered, and finally died. In her last conscious intervals she besought her sisters, when she was dead, to sever her head from her body and preserve it in the house that had been her delight and pride.

The two surviving Misses Griffith thought this an absurd request, and did not comply with it. But the noises in the house, of things falling, of doors slamming, cries and moans, so scared them that they had the family vault opened, the head of sister Anne detached and installed in the hall, whereupon the noises ceased.

MOTIF: E.419.8(*e*) [*Ghost forces fulfilment of promise to keep head on table in new house after person dies before the new house is completed*] (Baughman).
¶ The story of this type of haunting is told in more detail in "The Skull House" (B, VI). See also "The Ghost of Calgarth" (B, VI).

MOLE'S CHAMBER

Ruth L. Tongue, *Somerset Folklore*, p. 203.

I

This version was heard by my father on one of his walks from Kinsford to Watchet to preach on the Sunday. It was told him by a moorman near the Chains 1904.

In the old days there was an inn called the Acland Arms on the drove road from Sandyway to Lynmouth. It stood not far from the much-feared bog. One evening after a day's hunting a young squire named Mole took on a drunken bet that he could ride across it. Before anyone could stop him he spurred his hunter straight for the dreadful quagmire. The horse swerved aside, and the drunken man was slung from the saddle straight into its depths and was sucked under at once.

11

Exmoor. A farmer went to Lynmouth with his pack-horse for a load of lime to put heart in his poor fields. Returning in the mist, he lost the way to Kinsford, and the man and horse were swallowed in the quagmire. When it was drained years later, man and horse were found preserved by the lime. This, probably the true version, was told to my eldest brother by the farmer at Kinsford, near March, 1906.

MOTIF: N.2.2 [*Lives wagered*].

THE MONK OF HALDON

J. R. W. Coxhead, *Legends of Devon*, pp. 61–3.

A long time ago there stood near the town of Dawlish, in South Devon, an ancient chapel dedicated to St Mary, and in the north-east corner of the chancel of the chapel there was a well of exceptional depth known as Lidwell. An extremely gruesome and interesting legend is attached to the ruins of the chapel and the immediate neighbourhood.

It was the custom, in medieval days, for the little building to be in the care of a monk, who would always be in attendance to hear the confessions of the many wayfarers travelling along the road which passes over the great hill of Haldon. At one period, according to the legend, the chapel was in the care of a certain monk, who, at first, carried out his sacred duties with great zeal.

Shortly after his appointment as priest in charge of St Mary's Chapel, an irresistible desire to amass great wealth entered the monk's mind. The desire steadily increased day by day until it became a mania. Eventually he could control himself no longer, his evil thoughts got the upper hand, and he started secretly to lead a double life.

By day he ministered in the chapel with humble sanctity, outwardly appearing to be a man of great holiness, but by night he roamed the wild and lonely heathland on Haldon Hill, watching for any belated wayfarer who happened to be travelling alone.

Lurking in a thicket by the road, the wicked monk would wait until his unsuspecting victim had passed by his hiding-place, and then, darting swiftly from his concealment, he would plunge a poisoned dagger into the back of the unfortunate wayfarer.

Being a man of prodigious strength, the priest would hoist the dead body across his broad shoulders, and make his way back to the chapel without delay. Having carefully searched his victim for money, he would then cast the body down the well.

A secure place had to be found in which to keep his plunder, but it was not long before he thought of a brilliant idea. He removed the old altar in the chapel and made a new one, the top of which opened on hinges to reveal a hollow space, where his booty could remain safely hidden.

To satisfy his insatiable greed for gold and silver, this evil wretch murdered many a weary traveller on the lonely road over Haldon Hill. His ill-gotten hoard, securely concealed in the hollow space within the altar in the little chapel, steadily increased in size and value.

One night, when the moon was riding high in a starry sky, the monk was crouching in a clump of gorse stealthily watching a solitary figure trudging along the moonlit track across the wide heathland. As the man passed him, the monk rushed forward to deal the murderous stroke of death.

He mistimed his blow and the poisoned dagger only inflicted a slight wound on the wayfarer's shoulder.

Drawing his own dagger, the traveller turned quickly on the priest and drove the weapon deeply in to his breast. Before he could strike the monk again, the poison in his own slight wound had done its deadly work, and, sinking to the ground, the poor man cursed the murderer with his dying breath.

Terror and dismay seized the heart of the cruel assassin as he realized his victim had dealt him a mortal wound. Clutching his breast, he staggered towards St Mary's Chapel, determined to have one last look at his golden hoard.

Growing weaker from loss of blood at every step, he at last managed to reach the chapel. With his remaining strength he threw back the top of the altar, thrust both his hands into the gleaming heap of gold and silver coins, and drew his last breath. The Monk of Haldon had murdered his final victim....

On wild stormy nights, the ghost of the villainous priest is still said to haunt the ruins of the chapel, and his strange, moaning cries may be heard as he bewails the loss of his golden treasure.

MOTIFS: K.2058.1 [*Apparently pious man a thief*]; K.2285.2 [*Treacherous anchorite*] S.115 [*Murder by stabbing*]; S.111 [*Murder by poisoning*]; E.411.1 [*Murderer cannot rest in grave*].
¶   See B, VI, for similar stories.

MONKSEATON STONES

M. C. Balfour and N. W. Thomas, *County Folk-Lore*, IV, *Northumberland*, p. 156–7.

Near this village [Monkseaton] stands the pedestal of an ancient cross called the *Monk Stone*....On it is inscribed in modern letters, "O Horor to kill a man For a Piges head'. Mr Grove explains this motto by the following traditionary story, of the truth of which he, however, seems to entertain considerable doubt:

A monk of Tynemouth monastery, strolling abroad, came to the house of a Mr Delaval, an ancestor of the ancient family of that name, who was then absent on a hunting party, but was expected back to dinner. Among the many dishes preparing in the kitchen was a pig, ordered purposely for Mr Delaval's own eating. This alone suiting the liquorish palate of the monk, and though admonished and warned for whom it was intended, he cut off the head, reckoned by epicures the most delicious part of the animal, and, putting it into a bag, made the best of his way towards the monastery. Delaval, at his return, being informed of the transaction, which he looked upon as a personal insult, and being young and fiery, remounted his horse and set out in search of the offender. When overtaking him, about a mile east of Preston, he so belaboured him with his staff, called a hunting-gad, that he was scarcely able to crawl to his cell, the monk dying within a year and a day. Although, as the story goes, the beating was not the cause of his death, his brethren made it a handle to charge Delaval with his murder; who, before he could get absolved, was obliged to make over to the monastery, as an expiation of the deed, the manor of Elsig, in the neighbourhood of Newcastle, with several other valuable estates; and by way of an *amende honorable* to set up an obelisk on the spot where he properly corrected the monk.

MOTIFS: J.514 [*One should not be too greedy*]; Q.520 [*Penances*].

THE MONSTER FISH OF BOMERE POOL

Burne and Jackson, *Shropshire Folk-Lore*, p. 79.

Quite a different type of water-dweller from all we have hitherto met with appears in the legend of the Monster Fish of Bomere Pool. He, of course, lives *in* the mere, not *beneath* it, like the water-witches. He is bigger than any fish that ever swam, he wears a sword by his side and no man can catch him. It was tried once. A great net was brought and he was entangled in it and brought nearly to the side, but he drew his sword and cut the net and escaped. Then the fishermen made a net of iron links and caught him in that. This time he was fairly brought to land, but again he freed himself with his wonderful sword, and slid back into the water and got away. The people were so terrified at the strange sight that they have never tried to take him again, though he has often been seen since, basking in the shallow parts of the pool with the sword still girded around him. One day, however, he will give it up, but not until the right heir of Condover Hall shall come and take it from him.

He will yield it easily then, but no one else can take it. For it is no other than Wild Edric's sword, which was committed to the fish's keeping when he vanished, and will never be restored except to his lawful heir. Wild Edric, they say, was born at Condover Hall, and it ought to belong to his family now, but his children were defrauded of their inheritance, and that is why there is no luck about the Hall to this day. This curse has been on it ever since then. Every time the property changes hands the new landlord will never receive the rents twice—and those who have studied history will tell you that this has always come to pass.

MOTIFS: B.175 [*Magic fish*]; D.1081 [*Magic sword*].

¶ There is some slight resemblance between Wild Edric's sword, committed to Bomere Pool for keeping, and King Arthur's Excalibur, returned to the care of the Lady of the Lake.

A hereditary curse on a property that it could never pass from father to son is common in these islands. Levens Hall is said to be cursed in this way.

THE MONYPENNYS OF PITMILLY

Wilkie, *Bygone Fife*, p. 318.

It is hard to think of Pitmilly apart from the Monypennys, though till the twelfth century their patrimony belonged to the Church.... Probably the canons found it better to sell the estate than manage or let it, for the first Monypenny of Pitmilly would appear to have acquired it from Prior Thomas in 1211. There can have been no sacrilege involved; the direct succession of the Monypennys did not fail for over six centuries and a half. It flowed as placidly on as that of any race in troublous times; nor is there legend or tradition generally known about its doings beyond an explanation of its name....

How old it is we see from a "Genealogy of the Name of Monipennie conformally to an old MS. in the time of James II of Scotland", by William Tulloch, Bishop of Moray, 1472–88. As given there, the story is to the effect that Malcolm Caenmhor, during the days of his exile in England after the murder of King Duncan, lodged with a certain James Dauphin, a Frenchman with a fair daughter whose name, Blanche, has been preserved. This Frenchman was a wealthy London merchant. Malcolm was poor. In his straightened circumstances, he one day ventured to ask his host for the loan of a few pennies and was answered, "Not a few pennies, but monie pennies." In due course the King returned to Scotland and did not forget the friend who had trusted him in his days of need. When he entered his kingdom, Richard and Robert Dauphin, sons of James, rode in his train. Richard is said to have been presented with Pitmilly, Kingkell and Earlshall, and to have married a relative of Macduff, Thane of Fife.

"The name of Monypenny had been given him by the King in memory of his father's reply."

"...A Dolphin occupies the first and fourth quarters of the Mony-penny Arms."

MOTIFS: A.1577 [*Origin of personal name*]; Q.42 [*Generosity rewarded*].

THE MURDER HOLE [summary]

The Book of Scottish Story, pp. 316–20.

About three hundred years ago, on the estate of Lord Cassilis between Ayrshire and Galloway, lay a great moor, unrelieved by any trees or vegetation.

It was rumoured that unwary travellers had been intercepted and murdered there, and that no investigation ever revealed what had happened to them. People living in a nearby hamlet believed that in the dead of night they sometimes heard a sudden cry of anguish; and a shepherd who had lost his way once declared that he had seen three mysterious figures struggling together, until one of them, with a frightful scream, sank suddenly into the earth. So terrifying was this place that at last no one remained there, except one old woman and her two sons, who were too poor to flee, as their neighbours had done. Travellers occasionally begged a night's lodging at their cottage, rather than continue their journey across the moor in the darkness, and even by day no one travelled that way except in companies of at least two or three people.

One stormy November night, a pedlar boy was overtaken by darkness on the moor. Terrified by the solitude, he repeated to himself the promises of Scripture, and so struggled towards the old cottage, which he had visited the year before in a large company of travellers, and where he felt assured of a welcome. Its light guided him from afar, and he knocked at the door, but at first received no answer. He then peered through a window and saw that the occupants were all at their accustomed occupations: the old woman was scrubbing the floor and strewing it with sand; her two sons seemed to be thrusting something large and heavy into a great chest, which they then hastily locked. There was an air of haste about all this which puzzled the watching boy outside.

He tapped lightly on the window, and they all started up, with consternation on their faces, and one of the men suddenly darted out at the door, seized the boy roughly by the shoulder and dragged him inside. He said, trying to laugh, "I am only the poor pedlar who visited you last year." "*Are you alone?*" cried the old woman in a harsh, deep voice. "Alone here—and alone in the whole world," replied the boy sadly. "Then you are welcome," said one of the men with a sneer. Their words filled the boy with alarm, and the confusion and desolation of the formerly neat and orderly cottage seemed to show signs of recent violence.

The curtains had been torn down from the bed to which he was shown, and though he begged for a light to burn until he fell asleep, his terror kept him long awake.

In the middle of the night he was awakened by a single cry of distress. He sat up and listened, but it was not repeated, and he would have lain down to sleep again, but suddenly his eye fell on a stream of blood slowly trickling under the door of his room. In terror he sprang to the door, and through a chink he saw that the victim outside was only a goat. But just then he overheard the voices of the two men, and their words transfixed him with horror. "I wish all the throats we cut were as easy," said one. "Did you ever hear such a noise as the old gentleman made last night?" "Ah, the Murder Hole's the thing for me," said the other. "One plunge and the fellow's dead and buried in a moment." "How do you mean to dispatch the lad in there?" asked the old woman in a harsh whisper, and one of the men silently drew his bloody knife across his throat for answer.

The terrified boy crept to his window and managed to let himself down without a sound. But as he stood wondering which way to turn, a dreadful cry rang out: "The boy has escaped—let loose the bloodhound." He ran for his life, blindly, but all too soon he heard the dreadful baying of the hound and the voices of the men in pursuit. Suddenly he stumbled and fell on a heap of rough stones which cut him in every limb, so that his blood poured over the stones. He staggered to his feet and ran on; the hound was so near that he could almost feel its breath on his back. But suddenly it smelt the blood on the stones, and, thinking the chase at an end, it lay down and refused to go further after the same scent. The boy fled on and on till morning, and when at last he reached a village, his pitiable state and his fearful story roused such wrath that three gibbets were at once set upon the moor, and before night the three villains had been captured and had confessed their guilt. The bones of their victims were later discovered, and with great difficulty brought up from the dreadful hole with its narrow aperture into which they had been thrust.

TYPE 956A. MOTIF: R.200 [*Escapes and pursuits*].

¶ There are many Burker stories after this style.

See "Burker Story" (B, VIII). Here, as in many other stories, a pedlar is the victim.

THE NETHERBURY CHURCHYARD LEGEND

J. S. Udal, *Dorsetshire Folk-Lore*, p. 168.

An old parish clerk and sexton living at the foot of the churchyard, the garden of whose cottage was only divided from it by a low wall, was wont to be much annoyed by a poor half-witted girl of the village repairing to the church porch night after night and disturbing his rest by singing psalms. With the intention of frightening away the intruder, he, one moonlight night, wrapped himself up in a sheet, and walking round the church came upon the girl as usual singing in the porch. Instead of being alarmed, however, at the unexpected apparition as had been fully counted upon, she addressed the supposed spirit as follows: "Here's a soul coming! Whose soul be you? Be you my granfer's or grammer's or——" (naming somebody who had recently been buried there). Then after a pause, and looking round, she continued, "H'm! Souls *be* about tonight! For there's a black 'un too and he's trying to come up to the whit' un; and he's coming on so fast that if the whit' 'un don't take care the black 'un'll catch en." Upon hearing these words, the sexton, who had anticipated the flight and terror of the poor girl on his making his appearance, now felt the effects of that terror recoiling on himself; and, looking upon it as a judgment for his cruel conduct, took to his heels with all possible speed. Upon seeing this, the girl, clapping her hands to encourage him to the upmost, exclaimed, "Run, whit' soul; black soul'll catch 'ee! Run whit' soul; black soul'll catch 'ee!" and repeated this several times with the greatest fervency. The sexton, now becoming perfectly wild with fear on hearing these words, glanced hastily behind him, and, fancying he saw a dark figure close to his heels (which was probably that of his own shadow in the moonlight), tore down the path and over the low wall into his garden, never stopping till he was safe inside his own door. From the effects of this shock, a serious illness followed and, as the legend goeth, he "peeled" from head to foot. It is needless to add that the girl remained unmolested for the future.

TYPE 1676A. MOTIF: K.1682.1 [*Big 'fraid and Little 'fraid*].

¶ See "Black Bucca and White Bucca" (B, II).

See also "Meg of Meldrum" (B, VI) and "The Idiot", which has, like 1676A, a naturalistic basis.

NETHER STOWEY BLIND WELL

Ruth L. Tongue, *Somerset Folklore*, p. 22.

Nether Stowey blind well is a curative fairy well, where rags are left on a tree and pins dropped in the water. In 1935 I collected a story about two brothers which seems influenced by the widespread belief in the sympathy between twin brothers:

. . . .

"There was two brothers and they parted, but they promised to meet again down whoame in seven year. The one he was blinded in the Wars and the other he lost his sight, but for all that they set out. Folks helped them along times, and times they just travelled on in their darkness. And they heard their brother's voice asking for aid, and they both run, and they fell in the spring and it washed their sight back again. Wonderful good for the eyes 'tis."

MOTIFS: D.1785.1* [*Unusual connection between separated twins*] (Baughman); D.926 [*Magic well*].
¶ The mystical sympathy between twins is symbolized in fairy tales by the life-token.

An anecdote illustrating the sympathy between twins was told by H. Fowler of Burford in 1954. Twin brothers both worked at a builder's. One was working up a ladder, when he fell and blinded himself. The other, working at a different job at some distance, suddenly exclaimed: "I'm blind! I can't see!" His blindness, however, was temporary.

THE NEW CHURCH AT MARSKE [summary]

R. Blakeborough, *Wit, Character, Folk-Lore and Customs of the North Riding of Yorkshire*, p. 198.

Many years ago it was proposed to pull down the old church at Marske-by-the-Sea, and use the stone to build a new one. The older people were grieved at this, for their whole lives and the history of their families were bound up with the old church. But they could do nothing, and the work was begun. But on the second morning, to everyone's astonishment, the stone had all been carried back from the new site to the old, and replaced with mortar as firm and hard as that of hundreds of years before.

A second attempt met the same result, so on the third night a watch was set. But though the watchers declared that they had been awake all night, and had seen nothing, the next morning the work was all undone as before, and the old church stood as though it had never been disturbed.

Some of the wiser folk already knew whose work this was, and in time it became known to all that it was the hobmen and their friends. When they had made up their minds to prevent any change, no efforts of architects or builders ever produced the slightest effect.

TYPE ML.7060. MOTIFS: D.2192 [*Work of day magically overthrown at night*]; D.2192.1(*b*) [*Fairies responsible for change of church site*] (Baughman).

¶   The Hobmen of Yorkshire belong to the fairy tribes, and are often associated with oak trees.

See "The Building of St Chad's, Rochdale", "The Church at Fordoun", "The Church of Old Deer", "Crooked Crookham", "Winwick Church".

NO MAN'S LAND

Ruth L. Tongue, *Somerset Folklore*, p. 178.

In Tatworth there is a meadow called No Man's Land, with the best watercress bed in the district. Every year it comes up for sale to the farmers who lay claim to it. Now one old farmer had fallen on poor times, and if he could get the watercress bed it would just about put him on his feet. Everyone wanted him to have it, so when the day came only two farmers turned up to bid against him. The inch of candle was lit and farmer No. 1 made his bid quickly. It was a kindly thought, but to everyone's horror the candle began to splutter. His son gave the old man such a tremendous dig in the ribs that he nearly choked as he got his bid out, if he had coughed it wouldn't have counted and he would have been fined.

The candle recovered and burned brightly on, and everyone looked sadly at the poor old man, now in deep despair. It was no use Farmer No. 2 trying to cough before he spoke, for even the auctioneer would have known what was up (he probably did) but no one had tried to *sneeze*. Farmer No. 2 winked at Farmer No. 1 then his nose began to wrinkle up. Very slowly and surreptitiously out came a red handkerchief. "You can't sneeze in here while the candle is lit," said the auctioneer, looking hopefully at it—it was down to a quarter inch now, and the flame as steady as a rock. Farmer No. 2 rose gingerly and tiptoed to the door with the red handkerchief to his nose.

The candle flickered and recovered, but he was a man of resource. Unseen by the auctioneer he flicked his finger to his sheep dog waiting outside. Barking with joy that the long wait was over it leapt up at him, wagging its tail—and the candle went out. The auctioneer solemnly explained that a poor dumb beast could not be held to blame, and amid great good humour the old man was given the field for the year. Then everyone went cheerfully off for the yearly feast with watercress. The old fellow never guessed.

A local tradition from an informant.

¶ This mention of the old method of auction by candle illustrates "The Devil at Little Dunkeld Manse" (MOTIF: G.303.12.5.4) in B, III.

NO NEED FOR A CLOCK

Norton, Supplementary Collection, No. 53, p. 65.

It is said that once when a farmer was bringing a flock of sheep across the hills from Bolton-by-Bowland a woman on the far moorside came out of her cottage and called, "What time is it?" The farmer shouted back, "Three o'clock," and then added, "Han' yo no clocks up theer?" "Nowe," came the reply, carried down the wind. "Whaw, how dun yo' manage then?" queried the farmer. "Oh" said the woman in a doggerel which is no doubt as mythical in its origin as herself:

> "We eat when we're hungry,
> We sup when we're dry,
> Go to bed when we're weary,
> And get up when we corn't lie."

F. Ormerod, *Lancashire Life and Character*, p. 170.
MOTIF: H.1583 [*Tests of time*].

THE NORTHERN COBBLER

W. E. Axon, *Cheshire Gleanings*, p. 136.

In the Rev. E. Paxton Hood's *World of Moral Anecdote* there is an extract from a *Chester Gazette* of which the date is unfortunately not given. The story is thus told:

Henry Parker at the age of seventeen was, by the death of his Master, left alone in the world, to gain a livelihood as a shoemaker. He shouldered his kit, and went from house to house, making up the farmer's leather, and mending the children's shoes.

At length a good old man, pleased with Henry's industry and steady habits, offered him a small building as a shop. Here Henry applied himself to work with persevering industry and untiring ardour. Early in the morning he was whistling over his work, and his hammer was often heard till the "noon of night". He thus obtained a good reputation, and some of this world's goods. He soon married a virtuous female, whose kind disposition added new joys to his existence and whose busy neatness rendered pleasant and comfortable their little tenement. Time passed smoothly on; they were blessed with a neat little cottage and a piece of land. This they improved, and it soon became the abode of plenty and joy. But Henry began to relax in his conduct, and would occasionally walk down to an alehouse in the neighbourhood. This soon became a habit, and the habit imperceptibly grew upon him until (to the grief of all who knew him) he became a constant lounger about the alehouse and skittle-ground and, going on from bad to worse, he became a habitual drunkard. The inevitable consequences soon followed. He got into debt, and his creditors soon took possession of all he had.

His poor wife used all the arts of persuasion to reclaim him and she could not think of using him harshly. She loved him even in his degradation—for he had always been kind to her. Many an earnest petition did she prefer to Heaven for his reformation, and often did she endeavour to work upon his paternal feelings. Over and over again he promised to reform and at last was as good as his word—for he was induced to stay away from the alehouse for three days together. His anxious wife began to cherish a hope of returning happiness, but a sudden cloud one day for a moment damped her joy.

"Betsey," said he, "give me that bottle." These words pierced her very heart, and seemed to sound the knell of all her cherished hopes; but she could not disobey him.

He went out with his bottle, had it filled in the alehouse and, on returning home, placed it in the window immediately before him. "Now," said he, "I can face an enemy."

With a resolution fixed upon correcting his pernicious habits, he went earnestly to work, always having the bottle before him, but never again touched it. Again he began to thrive, and in a few years he was once more the owner of his former delightful residence. His children grew up, and are now respectable members of society. Old age came upon Henry, and he always kept the bottle in the window where he had first put it; and often, when his head was silvered over with age, he would refer to his bottle and thank God that he had been able to overcome the vice of drunkenness. He never permitted it to be removed from the window while he lived, and there it remained until after he had been consigned to his narrow home.

MOTIF: J.167 [*Wisdom from continual reminder of foolishness in the past*].

¶ The incorrigibility of drunkards is a more usual subject in folk-tales. This same method of combating drink is employed by Mistress Goate in *Sir Gibbie*, a novel by George MacDonald. He used a large amount of traditional material in his books, so that it is possible that this tale was current in Scotland as well as in the North of England.

NORTH OTTERINGTON CHURCH [shortened]

Parkinson, *Yorkshire Legends and Traditions*, 1st series, p. 120.

Near Thornton-le-Moor is a slight eminence where an ancient village is believed to have stood, in the midst of fields known as "the Tofts", with the socket of an old cross nearby.

Here the parish church was to have been erected, but night after night the stones were removed from their foundations and carried by invisible hands for more than a mile across the country to North Otterington. As often as they were brought back and replaced, so often they were again carried away. At last the builders were defeated and the site was transferred, and the Church of St Michael erected at North Otterington.

At Leake, the adjoining parish, a similar tale is told. That church was to have been erected at the top of Borrowby Bank, convenient to the village of Borrowby, but the builders' intentions were again frustrated, and the church had to be built in a much more remote position.

TYPE ML.7060. MOTIF: D.2192.1 [*Supernatural agency moves church foundation or building materials to another site at night*].
¶ See "The New Church at Marske", "The Building of St Chad's, Rochdale", "The Church at Fordoun".

THE NUN'S RING

W. H. Barrett, *Tales from the Fens*, pp. 140–5.

You may not know it, but there was a time when the little hill we call Southery was an island, and in those days anyone wanting to go on it had to row a boat there, unless the water was frozen, and then they went on skates. And there weren't a dozen pubs there like there are now; there was only one then, and it stood where the Bell is now and it was called the Golden Fleece. It was a jolly good name for it, too, because anyone who went into it was fleeced of everything he had. I'm just telling you this in case anyone ever asks you if Southery people have changed since the Fens were drained; you can tell them, then, that if they stay long enough that's a thing they can find out for themselves.

In those days a chap who kept a pub was called Mine Host, and that was because all his customers were lousy, and after they'd left the fleas would nip inside the landlord's shirt, so that when he got into bed with his wife she'd say:

"I bet you've brought a host of fleas with you as usual."

Now, one bitter winter's night, years and years ago, a crowd of fen slodgers* were sitting round the turf fire in the Fleece, and bragging about the number of wild duck they'd brought down in Larman's Fen without losing a single arrow. Suddenly the door opened, and in came One-eyed Porter, carrying a bundle of sheepskins, which he put down in front of the fire and began to unwrap. And, believe it or not, bors, inside that bundle was a handsome young woman, frozen so stiff that they didn't know if she was alive or dead.

Well, someone nipped off to find old Mother Goodge, the white witch, and while they waited for her to come, Porter told how he'd found the bundle on the ice as he was coming from Sedge Fen, where he'd been snaring larks. When Mother Goodge came along, she poured some hot mead down the young woman's throat, and rubbed her chest and hands with hot mutton-fat until she came round. Then, when she felt a bit better, she told them all how she'd come to be out on the ice in that bitter weather.

She said that she and several other young wenches lived in a nunnery at Thetford until, one day, a gang of soldiers came and turned them out and told them it was the King's orders.

The Reverend Mother and herself had managed to escape, and they lay hidden up in the turf-stack, listening to the screams of the other young women as the soldiers had their bit of fun with them before they turned them adrift. Then, when it was dark, the two of them began to walk to Brandon, but they got lost and wandered about till they came to a shepherd's hut. The shepherd took them in, and gave them what little grub he had with two sheep skins to wrap themselves up in, and he hid them up all day. When it was dusk they started off again and walked all through the night until they were on the edge of the Fens. Presently they came across a turf-cutter's hut and, as they were tired and hungry, they knocked at the door and asked if they could have food and shelter.

The turf-cutter gave them a basin of hot barley gruel with bits of fat pork floating about in it, and when they'd eaten it they sat by the fire and went to sleep. When they woke up, the turf-cutter told them that they'd be safe if they took to the ice which covered the Fen, and made for the hill of Southery. No soldiers ever went there, he said, and if they did then none of them would ever come back, because Southery people were a rough crowd who bided by no laws except their own. So they thanked him and said they would do what he suggested; and the man gave them some hide thongs to lash round their sandals so they could walk on the ice without slipping. They'd gone quite a way across the fen when a mist came down and they lost their way. After a time the Reverend Mother lay down, saying she was too tired to go on any further, and she seemed to go to sleep. The young woman had tried to get along

*Slodgers = old name for Fen fowlers and fishermen.

on her own to fetch help, but she'd got so tired too that she just lay down on the ice, and she said she didn't remember anything after that.

Well, next morning Porter took his sledge and, after a good look round the fen, he found the body of the Reverend Mother, or rather what was left of it, because starving polecats and carrion crows had to be driven off before he could lift it up and put it on his sledge.

He saw that there was only one finger left on one hand, and on the finger was a thick silver ring, so he took it off and put it in his pouch, because findings were keepings in those days. Then, when he got back to Southery, several of the men made a turf fire in the churchyard to thaw the ground, so that the body, or what was left of it, could be buried. The village hadn't had a parson for years, because not one would live in a place where all the people were against the church and everything else to do with law and order, but Fletcher, who'd been a friar till he was turned out, said a few prayers over the grave.

After a few days at the Fleece the young woman got tired of having all those hairy Fenmen trying to make a fuss of her, so she asked Porter if, as he'd helped her before, he would do the same again, and try to get her to an uncle of hers, who lived at the Manor of Heacham on the other side of Lynn. Porter said he would, and he pulled her on his sledge till they came to the high land, and there they left the sledge and walked along the trackway of Peddar's Way. They took two days to get to the Manor, but when they got there they had a real warm welcome, and Porter soon felt quite at home, because there were marshes all about where he could enjoy himself with his bow and arrow among the wild-fowl. After a few days of this he set out to go back to the Fens, and before he went the young woman gave him a silver cross to hang round his neck, and her uncle fitted him out in a new suit of clothes made of soft leather. He gave him a pouch, too, with a piece of gold inside it; so Porter put the silver ring, which he'd found on the nun's finger, into the new pouch, and threw his old one away.

On his way home he called into a pub at Castle Acre and asked for food and a night's lodging. He showed the landlord the piece of gold so that he'd know that Porter could pay.

Well, he was given the tuck-in of his life, with plenty of wine to wash everything down, and after he'd finished eating he lay down on some rushes, so that his good supper would lie quiet, and was soon asleep. But it wasn't long before he woke up again, because he could feel someone was touching him and trying to find his pouch, and he saw that it was the girl who'd served him with his supper. So he grabbed her by the ankles and rolled her over on to the floor, where she set up such a scream that the landlord came running in, and knocked Porter senseless with a great big cudgel. When he got his senses back, he found that he

was being carried, bound hand and foot, along the lane to the Priory.
When he got there he was taken to the Prior, who charged him with
raping a young wench on the Priory land, and ordered him to be hung
from the Castle ramparts to stop him from doing it again.

Well, they took him along to the Castle, with a monk to hear his
prayers before he was strung up, and this monk asked Porter if he
wanted to ask for anything before he died.

"Yes," said Porter. "Just feel in my pouch, and put the ring you'll
find there on to my little finger." So the monk fished out the ring, and
when he'd looked at it and seen some writing that was inside the band,
he kissed it and fell down on his knees, saying that no one dare hang a
man who had that ring. So back Porter was taken to the Prior, who not
only kissed the ring, but put his hands on Porter's head and blessed
him. Then he said that rape was rape after all, so he'd have to go to the
Bishop of Thetford to be dealt with.

Porter was put on horseback, with a couple of soldiers to guard him,
and sent to Thetford. When the Bishop saw the ring he said that anyone
who had that didn't need to rape to get the good things of life, because
some of the highest ladies in the land would give anything just to be
touched by a hand that had that ring on a finger. So Porter was put on
horseback again, and with a lot of soldiers bowing and scraping every
time he flashed that ring in the sunlight, he was taken all the way to
London. There an Archbishop called Tom Becket said that if any man
thought that that ring allowed a crime to be committed, then he'd
have to believe that there were buckets of water in Hell, all ready for
damned people to drink out of. But the only man who dare hang Porter,
he said, was the Pope himself, so he was going to send him to Rome.

So Porter started off on his long journey, living on the best that every
land could give him as he passed through. And when he got to Rome
he was met by a brass band, and the chaps with the trumpets nearly
blew their heads off as he went through the streets, holding up his hand
so that everyone could see the ring. Well, after a wash and a shave,
Porter went to see the Pope, who asked him to hand over the ring, so
he could have a good look at it. After he'd had his look, the Pope gave
it to several men, who were all wearing red hats, and after they'd looked
at the ring too, they all kissed it. Then, when the Pope had got the
ring back he put it in his pocket, and said he'd have a talk with Porter
later on, but just now he was to have some wine. So some wine was
brought him in a silver cup and when he'd drunk Porter shoved the
cup inside his shirt.

Then one of the red hats, who were still standing around said to him:
"Years ago, bor, I was a monk at Ely, and we fed on lark pie and eel
stew, and we used to go lark-snaring and babbing for eels."

"Did you ever go to Southery?" asked Porter.

"I was there for three years," said Red Hat, "helping to build the church, and, believe me, that church was needed badly because that village was nothing more than a den of thieves. I had the job of carving the twelve apostles' heads on the roof bosses, but all my tools were pinched, one by one, till I only had a maul and a chisel left. When they went too, I turned the job in. That's why there are only eleven apostles on the church instead of twelve. And if you want to go back to Southery then you'd better hand back that cup I saw you put in your shirt, or you'll never get the chance of counting those heads to prove I'm right."

"Well, what about my ring?" asked Porter.

"I'll tell you about that," said Red Hat. "Hundreds of years ago, St Peter lodged at a house here in Rome, and he was waited on by the landlord's daughter, who was called Agnes. When he was put in prison she used to take him food and drink, and on the night before he was put to death Peter took that ring off his finger, and gave it to her to remember him by. Well, after he died, Agnes and a lot of other women used to spend all their time going round the prisons, bringing a bit of comfort to those who were to die.

"When things got too hot for them, they ran away from Rome and went to live in caves, up in the hills, and they used to nurse the people who were ill, and do a lot of good. When Agnes was dying, she gave the ring to one of her friends and said:

"'You'll be the mother now, and when your time comes hand on the ring to the one who takes over from you.' Well that ring went round about, all over the place, and finished up with the Abbess of Thetford. We heard that it had been lost when the nuns were turned out. Now you've come along wearing it. How did you come by it?"

So Porter told him all about it, and then the Pope sent for him and, after thanking him for bringing the ring back, he gave him a bag of gold and the knife that St Andrew used for fish-gutting. The red hats clubbed together and bought him a jack ass and two female donkeys and a slave called Osler, so he could travel back to the Fens, where the air is noted for breeding. And that's why most of the Southery people are called either Porter or Osler, and they own all the donkeys feeding on the Common.

MOTIF: V.140 [*Sacred relic*].

¶ At the beginning it seems as if this story belonged to the time of the Dissolution of the Monasteries, but as it goes on it becomes obvious that it deals with very early times. In this tale it seems clear that the destruction of the nunnery was due to some such scandal as that by which Earl Godwin, a few generations earlier, is said to have obtained possession of the lands of Berkeley. The possession of the ring seems to have done nothing for the unfortunate Abbess, though it secured immunity for Porter. The tale is coloured by the macabre imagination of the tellers.

See "The Southery Wolfhounds".

THE OLD CHURCH OF ST HELEN'S

Abraham Elder, *Tales and Legends of the Isle of Wight*, p. 8.

The old church of St Helen's was built so close to the shore, that in the course of time the greater part was undermined and washed away by the sea. The steeple, however, had become so valuable a sea mark that it was determined to preserve it, so it was built up with bricks in the inside, and its foundations defended from the sea by additional masonry. It was next directed to be whitewashed, to make it more conspicuous, and some men were sent over from Portsmouth for this purpose.

They erected their ladders against the tower, and one of them went up to commence operations. Upon looking over the top of the building, he was very much astonished to see a little, old fashioned gentleman, in tight leather shorts and black worsted stockings, apparently fast asleep there. The whitewasher burst out into a loud laugh, and his comrades came up to see what was the matter, and they all joined in laughing at the old gentleman, and quizzing him.

"It's a fine day, old gentleman," said one.

The old gentleman, who looked very cross, replied, "Wait and see what the evening will bring, before you call it a fine day. I remember when the first stone of this tower was laid, the masons came over from Portsmouth in a boat, and were drowned going back, and so it will be with the last that touches it."

"Why, this tower has been built at least two hundred years," said a mason; "it's quite impossible that you can remember anything about it."

"It is very difficult to say," said the old man drily, "what is possible, and what is not possible."

Here the conversation ended, and the whitewashers went on with their work—dab, splash—dab, splash.

At length one of them said he would just take a peep to see how the old gentleman got on. He went up and looked, but found nobody there.

"How did he get down?"

"Nay, how did he get up?" said the other. It was altogether very odd.

When they had finished their work, they got into their boat to return to Portsmouth, but at Portsmouth the boat never arrived. They were all drowned.

MOTIFS: E.283 [*Ghost haunts church*]; E.292 [*Ghost causes storm*].

¶ This legend, however effective as a story, cannot be taken seriously as a legend, because no one returned to tell of the ghost, or of the conversation with it.

THE OLD HOUSE OF BALHARY

Our Meigle Book, p. 68.

[Above a door leading into the garden] is the old grey stone, with its curious motto and quaint spelling:

I. shall. overcome. Invy. with. Gods. help. to. God. Be. Al. prais. Honour. and. Glorie.   1660.

Around the stone is a legend of considerable charm. The story is long, but briefly, is something like this:

In a bare old castle (mayhap the old house of Balhary) dwelt a father and son. The son, David, was a hunchback, and in consequence, was disliked and neglected by his father, who favoured a nephew, Ronald. To the castle one day, accompanied by her maid, came Lady Jean, a beautiful girl who had been placed under the guardianship of David's father. David and she became great friends; Ronald arrives on a visit, and Jean and he fall in love. David is again neglected. Came the wars of the Commonwealth, and the father and Ronald are called to the aid of Montrose. On defeat, the father had to flee to France, while Ronald, severely wounded, is brought to Jean to be nursed.

On his recovery they become engaged, and David, in bitter envy and jealously, wanders for hours into the hills. At nightfall he lands at the hut of an aged priest who comforts him. There he spends the night and dreams a dream. In it he sees Jean and Ronald and the people of the place building a castle. No matter how quickly they build up the stones it grows no bigger. David finds someone standing beside him, who says, "It is your envy and jealousy which comes between them and the building of the castle. Overcome that by raising this stone and placing it as a foundation for the castle."

Glancing at his feet, David saw a huge stone. "How can I, a poor hunchback, raise such a stone?" he said. Then he noticed its curious motto, "I shall overcome envy with God's help to God be al prais honour and glorie."

Unexpected strength came to him, and he lifted the stone and put it in its appointed place, and immediately the castle reared forth.

Next morning he went home in a different frame of mind, to find two items of news awaiting him; one, that his father could not again return, and so he made over the castle and lands to David, and the other, that owing to the very active part Ronald had played in the war he had forfeited his estates and money, and so couldn't marry Jean.

With much difficulty David persuaded them to accept the castle and lands, while he joined his father abroad. Many, many years elapsed, and feeling that his days on earth were almost numbered, he returned to his old home. He was welcomed by the two he had left and their family, the youngest of whom, his namesake, David, was a fragile, delicate youth, much as he had been. Between the two a great friendship developed, and the story of the dream was related. "Why not have the motto inscribed on a stone, and when you are gone I shall erect it to your memory?" suggested David the younger. This was done, and that is the legend of the stone, and this is its after-story.... Once a year, so it is said, a figure wearing a long cloak and a beaver hat cocked at one side with a feather appears to pay tribute. If the night be warm and he removes his cloak the outline of the poor hunchback can be seen.

MOTIFS: L.112.3 [*Deformed child as hero*]; H.617 [*Symbolic interpretation of dream*]; W.11 [*Generosity*].

OLD NICK IN THE FENS [condensed]

W. H. Barratt, *Tales from the Fens*, pp. 189–95.

Old Betty Forder lived all by herself. The local women said she was a witch, but the men said she was only a poor, simple soul. One night of full moon, Betty, taking her usual midnight stroll, saw something coming towards her. She thought it was the devil, because she could hear the clanking of iron on the road. She turned tail and ran, but the faster she went, the closer the devil seemed to be behind her. Suddenly she felt a hot breath on her neck, so she dived into a thorn hedge into old Grant's garden, grabbed the chain of the windlass on his well, and dropped a tidy distance to the bottom. There was only a foot or two of water in the well, and she stood in this gazing up at the evil one as he peered down to find out where she had gone. Then Betty remembered a fairy stone, with a hole in it, in her pocket, so she pulled it out, and held it up. The stone seemed to do the trick because presently she heard the iron rattling as the devil went away.

In the morning, Grant's old woman went out early to get some water for his early tea, but the chain seemed to stick. She rattled it against the side of the well, and woke Betty, who had fallen asleep, and was now sure that the Old 'un had come back. She shrieked and Grant, rushing out, saw his wife lying in a dead faint. He carried her indoors, laid her on the bed, pulled out from under the mattress the stocking containing his wife's savings, pocketed it, and set out for work as usual. When she recovered, his wife ran out to tell the parson that she'd heard souls in torment. The parson called his groom and they set out together for the well. When old Betty saw their shadows moving above the top of it, she called out:

"Go away, you wicked old devil."

"Did you hear that?" the parson asked the groom.

"That I did," was the answer; "and whatever's down there knows a lot more than I do about you, and I've not been with you these thirty years without learning a thing or two."

This led to an argument till Betty, recognizing the voice of the groom, called out:

"Is that you, Grimmer? If it is, wind me up."

When she reached the top, she told the Parson what had made her jump down the well, and he went off muttering that she ought to have been shut up years before.

Two nights later, Billy Brown, who lived in Flint Cottage, was wakened by a noise in the garden, and found that someone was smashing up his bee-hives. He woke up his wife, and, peering out, they decided that it must be Old Nick: so they crept back to bed, and by daylight there were swarms of bees buzzing round the smashed hives.

Next, Gallaway, who was a Plymouth Brother, swore he had seen the devil pulling apples from the trees in the next-door garden, while he sat up waiting for his sow to farrow. He had roused his wife, and they spent the rest of the night on their knees.

Next morning the sow's teats showed that she had had fourteen piglets, but there was not a trace of them. Either she or the Evil One had eaten them while he and his wife were praying.

Now there was a great panic, and the blacksmith did a great trade in iron bolts to put on people's doors. But the worst came when the Cambridge-to-Lynn coach, with Joe Murdoch on the box, had just come over the bridge, and was rounding the bend, when suddenly the horses, Joe and the outside passengers saw, standing in the middle of the turnpike what the Archdeacon of Lynn, who was an inside passenger, declared was the Prince of Darkness himself. The two leading horses reared and plunged, then fell, throwing Joe off his box and over their heads. He landed light, so he picked himself up and freed the horses. The Archdeacon was down on his knees in the middle of the road, but Joe made him get up and go with the other passengers to the blacksmith's shop, half a mile back, to bring help. But when the terrified passengers reached the smithy and banged on the door to wake the smith up, he jumped out of bed, thinking that now it was his turn for a visit from the devil. But he had prepared for this, on the advice of a wise woman, two things which the devil most hated—a bucket of soot and a bucket of whitewash. These he now emptied through the open window, upon the heads of those below. The noise which followed convinced him that he had been right; so he jumped on a horse and rode away from it all.

Just after dawn, a man on his way to work saw the coach and horses on the road, and a crowd of piebald beings moving about. Others followed, but they all ran home as fast as they could, to announce that the devil's whole family had come in by coach.

At last Joe did come back with some helpers; but from that day he had the name "Swift" taken off his coach, and "Black and White" written up instead. And whenever he passed that place, he used to tell the outside passengers that this was the "Devil's Stop".

After that things calmed down, but an old soldier named Muten (who was always called "Mutton"), who knew all that was worth knowing about bees, hearing how the devil had visited other bee-hives, made plans to welcome him if he came.

When soldiering in India, he had acquired four silver balls, the size of marbles. He loaded his muzzle-loader with one of these, and put it by his bed, with the other balls close by, and his powder-flask, because he'd found out that black men take a lot of killing.

He was a light sleeper, so when he heard one night a sound like that of a chain being dragged over the stones at his back door, he was out of bed in a flash, and stood at the window with his gun at the ready.

He saw a huge figure walking towards his hives, and called out: "Halt! Who goes there?"

Getting no answer when the figure was near the hives, he fired through the window. Something fell heavily to the ground, but, taking no chances, he reloaded and stood there on guard till daylight. Then he went down to look and found that he had shot a great black bear.

Several weeks later, two boys, out bird-nesting, found two bodies which must have been dead some time. Their ribs were crushed as if by a vice. Then it was remembered that two Germans, with a dancing bear, had paraded the village some time back, and one man said that he had seen them going into the copse as though to spend the night there.

MOTIFS: J.1785 [*Animal thought to be devil*]; B.16.2.5 [*Devastating Bear killed*].

ONE-HORSE FARMERS AT A CHRISTENING

[extracts]

W. H. Barratt, *Tales from the Fens*, p. 120.

There was plenty of work going on in the fens after the floods had gone. All the dykes and drains had to be cleaned out and a great big steam engine was built to pump out the water, so all the drains had to be made deeper. I should say there were forty or more of us settled down to being what the big farmers called "One-horse Farmers", and we weren't all doing what you might call sitting pretty. For the first time the big farmers had to dance to the tune we wanted played. Every job we took on was piece-rate and, by working from seven till two, without stopping, we earned half a crown a day; that wasn't bad money, as the day-men only got two bob. Some of us had a couple of cows too, as well as a horse and a sow. We used to grow corn on five of our acres and mangolds for feed on our sixth and, except at harvest-time, you couldn't say we were overworked. We worked with each other, sharing the few tools we had, and it was a right treat after harvest to see a lot of fair-sized stacks standing on Jack Gotobed's bit of land. We all carted our corn up there because it was the handiest place for the threshing tackle to get to, because we all helped with the threshing....

Some of the young chaps from Cambridge came down one summer and slept in a tent. They used to come and talk to us while we were working and some of them were quite handy, helping us with the harvest; they told us they were on a mission. Two of them, after helping me with some shocking up one day said they'd be glad to come and have a bit of dinner with us. Father was pleased to have someone to talk to, so he asked who they were working for. When they said they were working on a mission, Father, being a bit hard of hearing, thought they said, "Missing," who was the mole-catcher; so he told them they wouldn't get much out of that because the ground was too hard to set traps, and anyway mole skins were twelve a penny at that time of the year. They couldn't make him understand, so I had to tell him the mission they were working for was like that big pork dumpling sitting on the table, all goodness, and the sooner he got on with eating it the sooner he'd find the goodness in it.

These chaps soon got into the Missus's good books by telling her that dinner was the best they'd ever eaten. They worked with me all day, and came back to our place for tea; then they said they'd have to be going, because they had a meeting up at the Creek bridge that evening. They came again, a day or two afterwards, and helped with carting; then they asked if they could have what they called a Cottage Meeting in our house.

I told them they'd have to ask my old woman, but if she said, "yes," then it was all right with me.

Well, those chaps made such a hit with the women and children that it wasn't long before folks were going round with boxes getting money to build a chapel, and in six months a little one was put up at the Creek; it's still there today with a bigger one next to it. At first it was only the women and children who went to it, then one or two men began to go to see what the women were up to and, before winter was over, three parts of the men in the fen spent three parts of a Sunday there. Then they got a regular preacher from Ely, who used to come on

Saturdays and go back on Mondays or Tuesdays; the boxes that had been used to build the chapel were now sent round to get money to pay the preacher.

Then the women started making a terrible fuss because most of the children hadn't been christened. So the preacher said, if someone could give him supper and a bed and some breakfast, then he'd stay every Monday and do some christening. Because there were so many children who'd not been done when they were babies, he said he'd start with those who were ten or twelve years old. My old woman said that meant that my eldest boy, who was called Noah, would be one of the first. I felt a bit sorry for the lad, as he was big for his age, and he as good as told me he'd see me somewhere else before they got him to the chapel. So I had to promise I'd go with him and that if he was christened I'd lend him my old muzzle-loader every Saturday and he could shoot what he liked with it. That did the trick.

There were about a dozen boys, all Noah's age, in the chapel, which was crowded out.

The preacher asked each father or mother to stand behind their boys; then, when someone had given him a basinful of water, he came and stood in front of my boy, who was the first in the line, and asked me what he was to be named.

"Noah," I said; "the same name as he's always had."

Then he shook some of the water on Noah's head, said the words, and moved on to the next boy. When he asked what his name was to be, the father said, "Noah." Well the preacher had christened about six before he tumbled to it what a lot of Noahs there were, as that was the only name he had been given so far. So he moved on to the seventh, and when he found this was a Noah too, he put down the basin and went to ask the chap who looked after the chapel if he thought these people were playing a joke on him. He was told it was all right and he'd better get on, as not one of those fathers would stay later than a quarter of an hour before closing-time; so he'd better take the collection now and then finish the christening.

The preacher thought this a good idea, for he'd told the women that everything put in the collecting box ought to be silver; but when he emptied the box he didn't believe there could be so many threepenny pieces in the fen. Anyway, he picked up the basin again and went on down the line and right to the last one every boy was a Noah.

That night the preacher stayed with Shaver Barber, and after supper he asked him if the fen folk hadn't really been making a fool of him with so many Noahs. Shaver told him not to fret himself, and asked him if he hadn't noticed that all those boys were about the same age, which meant they'd all been born at the time of the flood, and that was why there were all called Noah. Shaver said afterwards that if the preacher didn't say, "Well, I'll be damned," he'd like to know what he did say.

Southery Fens.
There are no types or motifs for this lively anecdote, which is valuable as showing the first arrival of evangelical missions in the Fen Country.

ORD, THE CIRCUS MAN OF EDINBURGH

School of Scottish Studies, John Elliot, *Notebooks*.

It is many years ago since Ord was carrying on his circus work in Edinburgh.

About that time the country was in a bad state of lawlessness; there was often murder and robbery. A robber had taken up his abode in a dense forest close on the public highway, and he was committing roguery about every day at different places around the country about ten miles from Edinburgh. The police tried all they could do to catch him, but he was a very wary man, and bad to catch. They even dressed in lady's clothes to try and entice him, but no, he would not be led into a trap.

About a fortnight after he had done a big robbery, Ord met the Edinburgh Superintendent at High Street, and spoke in the passing. "Oh, by the bye," said Ord, "have you got that man yet?"

"What man do you mean?"

"I mean the robber who has been causing so much trouble lately."

"No; we have not got him yet; he is fairly baffling, as he is a terrible cunning customer, and bad to catch."

"I think I could take him," said Ord.

"I would be awful grateful to you if you could," said the Superintendent.

Ord asked him if he would have a cordon of police round a place at the top of High Street, and be ready to take him from him when he brought him in. So the time, or round about the time, for bringing him in was set. So early next morning Ord set off to catch the robber. He rode on a favourite mare called Fanny. He was dressed like a country gentleman, with lots of jewellery flashing about him. After he reached near the robber's quarters, he went into a quiet road between the big forest, and let his mare go slow, and he pretended to be looking at the birds above, and keeping looking as [if] he was not expecting to see anybody, he rode to the far end of the wood, then turned, and came back.

At a dark bit of the wood, out came the robber, and demanded his money or his life.

293

"Oh," said Ord, "I would rather give you my money than my life."

"Now your jewellery"—pointing the pistol at Ord's head. Ord gave him all his jewellery.

"Now," said the robber, "I want this mare, or your life."

Fanny was one of the best-trained horses in the circus, and that was the very reason he had brought her. Ord handed the reins to the robber, saying, "I would rather give you the mare than my life."

The robber tried to get on, but Fanny would not let him get on. He tried all he could to mount her, but it was no use. Fanny would not let him mount her. Then he cried to Ord to assist him to mount.

"Kneel down, Fanny, and let the gentleman on," said Ord. Down went Fanny, and the robber got on, but all he could do would not make Fanny rise again. The robber kicked and kicked her, but she would not get up. At last he cried again for Ord to make her get up. Ord made a flying jump on behind the robber, with his hands holding the robber's head down. Ord was a crack rider, and did not need a saddle. Now Fanny, she sprang to her feet, and [at] a word from Ord she took the road for Edinburgh as fast as her feet could travel, and Ord holding the robber down, they came in to the trysted place where the police were waiting. They closed in, and he was taken. The Superintendent was awful pleased, the way Ord had outwitted the robber and offered Ord a good sum of money, but Ord refused saying, "It was not for money I took him. It was to let you see I could take [him] with my clever mare Fanny, who I can trust to the last."

MOTIFS: K.437 [*Robber overcome*]; K.427 [*Clever animal betrays thief*].

¶ See "The Boy outwits the Robber" (A, IV).

OSMOTHERLY

Norton Collection, III, p. 14.

Some years ago there lived in a secluded part of Yorkshire a lady, who had an only son named Os, or Oscar. Strolling out one day with her child, they met a party of gipsies, who were anxious to tell her the child's fortune. After being much importuned, she assented to their request. To the mother's astonishment and grief, they prognosticated that the child would be drowned. In order to avert so dreadful a calamity, the infatuated mother purchased some land, and built a house on the summit of a high hill, where she lived with her son for a long time in peace and seclusion. Happening one fine summer's day in the course of a perambulation to have fatigued themselves, they sat down on the grass to rest, and soon fell asleep. While enjoying this repose, a spring rose up from the ground, which caused such an inundation as to overwhelm them and, side by side, they found a watery grave. After this had occurred, the people residing in the neighbourhood, named it "Os-by-his-mother-lay" which has since been corrupted into "Osmotherly".

Yorkshire.

Choice Notes from "Notes and Queries", Folk-Lore, VIII, p. 617. Contributed by R. W. Carter.

TYPES 934, 934A* (O'Suilleabhean). MOTIFS: M.341.2.3 [*Prophecy: death by drowning*]; M.372 [*Confinement to tower to avoid fulfilment of prophecy*]; A.1617 [*Origin of place-name*].

¶ This is a widespread theme, of which examples are cited from all over Europe. In these islands it is most common in Ireland. Many examples of various forms are cited in the Irish Type-Index, among them tales from Hyde, Lover and Kennedy.

OUR LADY'S WELL AT THRESHFIELD

[summary]

Parkinson, *Yorkshire Legends and Traditions,* 1st series, p. 205.

The well of Our Lady of Threshfield had the reputation of being a safe sanctuary from all supernatural beings.

One night a local man, having stayed late at the public house, had seen some strange performances by the Threshfield ghost, Pam, in the course of which he had the misfortune to sneeze. This so angered the spirits that he had to take to his heels to escape their wrath. He came to the well and plunged into it, finding himself almost up to his neck in icy water.

The spirits pursued him, but, not daring to approach the well itself, they lingered near and kept their victim imprisoned until the crowing of the first cocks caused them in turn to flee, vowing dire vengeance should he ever again eavesdrop at their assembly.

MOTIFS: V.134 [*Sacred well*]; E.242 [*Ghosts punish intruders*].
¶ This is the Yorkshire version of the "Tam o' Shanter" story.

OVER

E. G. Bales, *Folk-Lore* Vol. L, p. 75.

One of the horses that used to draw lighters up the river was blind, and had been taught to jump over the stiles whenever the driver shouted, "Over!"

As a result of this, the horse would jump whenever anyone shouted "Over!" to it. Some lightermen were one day waiting at a public house at Downham when a man rode up on a hunter, famous as a jumper.

The lighterman said he had a horse which was a better jumper than this hunter. An argument sprang up between the lighterman and the owner of this hunter, and a wager was made. Both men took their horses into the road, the lighterman laid a piece of straw down, led his horse up to it, and shouted "Over!" The horse jumped as though to clear a style. The hunter was then led up to the straw, and the rider tried to make it jump, but all to no purpose, since the hunter could see no obstacle.

Horse-drawn lighters were used on the River Ouse until about fifteen years ago; I can remember them quite clearly.

Told by Mr R. Crawford.
MOTIF: K.17 [*Jumping contest won by deception*].
¶ See "A Wager Won" (A, III).

OWEN PARFITT

Ruth L. Tongue, *Somerset Folklore*, p. 196.

The memory of this historical mystery still survives in Shepton Mallet. Owen Parfitt was an elderly seafaring man who returned to Shepton Mallet from no one knew where. He was supposed to be wealthy, and rumour went round that he had been a pirate. He and his sister lived together for many years until he became paralysed, and a younger relation came to look after them both. One summer day old Parfitt had been settled outside in his chair, to which he could just shuffle, when a passing neighbour told him that a seafaring man had been inquiring about an old sailor. Old Parfitt turned white, but he said nothing. Next day he was settled as usual, and his cousin went out to her shopping. When she got back his chair and rug and cushion were there, but there was no sign of Parfitt himself. The haymakers were working in the field near and had heard or seen nothing, but he was never found again. The local explanation is that he was not so lame as he pretended and that he had made off with his hoard when he heard of someone who had a right to share it. If so, he had gone off just as he was, without even changing his slippers.

¶ See Andrew Lang, *Historical Mysteries*.
The disappearance is one of the unexplained mysteries, almost as insoluble as that of the *Marie Celeste* or of the adventures of Mr Harrison of Chipping Campden, which has been examined in *The Camden Wonder*.
It is doubtful if a solution of any of them will ever be found.

PARSON SPRY'S SERMON [slightly shortened]

From W. Bottrell, *Traditions and Hearthside Stories of West Cornwall*, 1st series, p. 165.

When Mr Spry was vicar of Botusleming, the great man of his parish was a certain esquire, to whom the parson showed so much less respect than he considered to be his due, that, by way of revenge, the squire took every opportunity to ridicule the vagaries of the parson, and often behaved in church in such a way as was intended to show his contempt. Now, it was said that the squire had acquired a great portion of his lands by unfairly foreclosing a mortgage. Mr Spry soon heard all the particulars, for, notwithstanding all his whims, he was a great favourite with the gossips of his parish.

One Sunday when the squire had been more than usually rude in church, the parson took for his text, "The time of your redemption draweth nigh". He compared the sin-burdened soul of a man to a mortgaged estate, of which the Devil was the mortgagee, and the Old One's wiles to get possession of the sinner's immortal part, with the dishonest tricks which some other mortgagees practise when they hold a small part of a spendthrift's estate, to gain the whole before it is fairly due. The picture he drew of the earthly mortgagee made the squire appear much blacker than the Devil. He continued by saying that the poor dupes are in a far worse case than the sinner in the hands of Old Nick, because no amount of faith or good works can purchase their redemption from the power of one more avaricious than Satan. Before the sermon was half over, all the congregation was pointing or looking towards the squire's pew, where his Satanic Majesty's ensampler looked completely crestfallen.

TYPE 1833 (variant). MOTIF: X.435.5 [*Sermon about a rich man*].
¶ See "A Sermon upon Malt" (B, VIII).

PAYING THE SCOT-ALE

Ruth L. Tongue, *Somerset Folklore*, p. 194.

In the old days the Lord of the Forest and the Ranger could hold a Forest Court to try deer stealers, and people who cut down trees or let their beasts stray beyond the king's boundary: they could fine people for very small offences (and often for nothing at all) and they could hold Scot-Ales to which everyone must come to buy the ale whether they wanted to or no. Altogether in remote places like the Brendons and Exmoor they could do very much as they pleased to raise money for themselves as well as the King. It was very easy to accuse a man of hunting the deer, and then fine him or threaten him with prison until he parted with all his wealth. But one day they caught a tartar—the Ranger accused a train-band Captain, a jovial rascal, leader of sturdy rogues, and the Lord of the Forest as usual sent out a charge for him to appear. But the Captain and his merry men had other notions. They sent in turn all the way to Taunton and got a charge laid against the Ranger. To pay for this, they let it be known in all the churches round that they would hold a Scot-Ale in Skilgate Church, and hold it they did. By the time the Church Ale men arrived, the ale was already sold, and the sermon was half-preached. Everyone was in a merry humour and the Captain had collected £60 to pay his lawyer.

When the case did come up at Taunton it seems to have been dismissed. Taunton was used to lawful ways and it probably decided it was a healthy thing for Exmoor folk to see "the biters bit".

TYPE 1525 (variant).

¶ "Church Ales", from medieval times to the seventeenth century, took the place of the modern church bazaar. The churchwardens brewed ale and dispensed it on a day of festivity, generally the patronal festival date, to the parish, to defray any emergency expenses. The unnamed jovial rogue of this tale merely made himself into a self-appointed churchwarden.

THE PEDLAR OF SWAFFHAM: I

From Abraham de la Pryme, *Diary*, published by the Surtees Society, p. 220.

"Constant tradition says that there lived in former times, in Soffham [Swaffham] *alias* Sopham in Norfolk, a certain pedlar, who dreamed that if he went to London Bridge, and stood there, he should hear very joyful newse, which he at first sleighted, but afterwards, his dream being dubled, and trebled upon him, he resolved to try the issue of it, and accordingly went to London, and stood on the bridge there two or three days, looking about him, but heard nothing that might yield him any comfort. At last it happened that a shopkeeper there, hard by, having noted his fruitless standing, seeing that he neither sold any wares, nor asked any almes, went to him, and most earnestly begged to know what he wanted there, or what his business was; to which the pedlar honestly answered, that he had dreamed that if he came to London and stood there upon the bridge, he should hear good newse; at which the shopkeeper laught heartily, asking him if he was such a fool as to take a journey on such a silly errand, adding, 'I'll tell thee, country fellow, last night I dreamed that I was in Sopham in Norfolk, a place utterly unknown to me, where me thought behind a pedlar's house in a certain orchard, and under a great oak tree, if I digged, I should find a vast treasure! Now, think you,' says he, 'that I am such a fool to take such a long journey upon me upon the instigation of a silly dream? No, no, I'm wiser. Therefore, good fellow, learn witt from me and get you home, and mind your business.' The pedlar observing his words, what he say'd he dream'd and knowing they concenter'd in him, glad of such joyful newse, went speedily home and digged and found a prodigious great treasure, with which he grew exceedingly rich, and Sopham [Church] being for the most part fal'n down, he set on workmen and re-edify'd it most sumptuously at his own charges; and to this day there is his own statue therein, but in stone, with his pack at his back, and his dog at his heels; and his memory is also preserved by the same form or picture, in most of the old glass windows, taverns and alehouses of that town unto this day."

¶ Glyde's *Norfolk Garland*, p. 69, gives the following addition:
"The box containing the treasure had a Latin inscription on the lid, which, of course, John Chapman could not decipher. He craftily put the lid in his window, and very soon he heard some youths turn the Latin sentence into English:

> 'Under me doth lie,
> Another much richer than I'.

"And he went to work, digging much deeper than before and found a much richer treasure than the former".

In *Transactions of the Cambridge Antiquarian Society*, III, p. 318, is another version:

> "Where this stood,
> Is another as good."

THE PEDLAR OF SWAFFHAM: II

Norton Collection, v, p. 173.

The story of the Pedlar of Swafham-Market is in Substance this:

That dreaming one night, if he went to London, he should certainly meet with a man upon London Bridg, which would tell him good news, he was so perplex't in his mind, that till he set upon the journey, he could have no rest. To London therefore he hasts, and walked upon the Bridg for some hours; where being espyed by a shopkeeper and asked what he wanted, he answer'd, you may well ask me that question, for truely (quoth he) I am hither upon a very vain errand, and so told the story of his dream, which occasioned the journey. Whereupon the shopkeeper replyed, Alas good friend, should I have heeded dreames, I might have proved myself as very a fool as thou hast; for 'tis not long since that I dream't that at a place called Swafham-Market in Norfolk dwells one John Chapman, a Pedler, who hath a tree in his backside, under which is buried a pot of Money. Now, therefore, if I should have made a journey thither to dig for such hidden treasure, judg you whether I should not have been counted a fool. To whome the Pedlar cunningly sayd, yes verely, I will therefore return home and follow my business, not heeding such dreames henceforwards. But when he came home (being satisfyed that his dream was fulfilled) he took occasion to dig in that place and accordingly found a large pot full of money, which he prudently concealed setting the pot among the rest of his brasse. After a time it hapned, that one who came to his house, and beholding the pot, observed an inscription upon it, which, being in Latine, he interpreted viz: that under that there was an other twise as good. Of this inscription the Pedlar was before ignorant; or at least minded it not; but when he heard the meaning of it, he say'd Tis very true. In the shop where I bought this pot stood another under it, which was twise as big; but considering that it might tend to his further profit to dig deeper in the same place where he found that, he fell again to work, and discovered such a pot, as was intimated in the inscription, full of old coine. Notwithstanding all which, he so concealed his wealth, as that the neighbours took no notice of it. For not long after the inhabitance of Swafham resolving to reedify their Church, and having consulted with the workmen about the charge, they made a Levy, wherein they taxed the Pedlar according to no other Rate than what they formerly had don. But he knowing his own abilitys, came to the Church, and desired the workmen to show him their modell, and to tell him what they esteemed the charge of the North Ile would amount to; which when they told him, he presently undertooke to pay them for building it, and not onely that but of a very tall and beautifull Tower Steeple.

From William Dugdale to Roger Twysden, 29 January, 1652, in T. Caius, *Vindiciae antiquitatis academiae Oxoniensis*...ed. T. Hearne, Oxford, 1730, I, App., pp. 84–6.

THE PEDLAR OF SWAFFHAM: III

F. J. Norton. Oral.

Told me in 1928 by Mr G. Davey of North Hill, who had it "about 50 years ago" from his grandfather...John Rolle, ancestor of the Lords Clinton, lived at Doble's Cross in St Giles in the Heath in Devonshire, near Launceston in Cornwall. He dreamed time and again that if he went to London Bridge, he would become rich. He went. A man there told *him* of a dream of treasure in a crock at Doble's Cross, under a thorn bush, in a corner of a field called Four Acres. The man returned, dug, and found a crock of gold. On the crock was a Latin inscription, He asked the Parson to tea after his child's christening and got him to translate it. It read "Under me, Lie three!" So he dug and found three more. This founded the Rolls Estate on which Exmouth is built.

A Mr Metherell, about the same time, said he had heard the story about Stannon Farm, near the marsh in St Breward in Cornwall. There were no crocks, only treasure.

A friend in North Hill told me a rather rambling story about a man "in these parts" who dreamed that if he went to London Bridge, he would meet bullocks, have bad luck so and so often, and then good luck. He went. He met a drove of bullocks, one, then two, and three. The man remembered he had dreamed he would have bad luck so and so often. Then came the drover. They talked, and the drover had also had a dream, that if he went to (wherever the other had come from) he would find gold for the digging.

NORTON'S NOTES ON THE PEDLAR
OF SWAFFHAM

The Gentleman's Magazine Library, English Traditional Lore, p. 332.

In the *Antiquary* (1884), Vol. X, pp. 202–5, is given some extra notes on the legend of the Pedlar of Swaffham and the Lambeth Pedlar, mentioned in the text:

"The best account of the Lambeth legend is one given in *Long Ago* for September, 1873 (Vol. I, p. 271) taken from a manuscript in the handwriting of Archdeacon Drune, formerly Rector of Lambeth. A descendant of the venerable Archdeacon, the Rev. Bradford Drune Hawkins, Rector of Riverdale, Witham, forwarded the account to the editor of *Long Ago* and the following is a literal transcript:

"'Among the estates belonging to the parish of Lambeth is a piece of land, antiently called Church Hopys, but since called Pedlar's Acre. For what reasons it was so call'd I cannot learn, finding no historical vouchers to justify what the writer of the *New View of London* says about it in page 381; that a Pedlar gave this acre of land, besides ye following benefactions in money, viz.

To Ye Parish	£6	o	o
To Ye Archbishop	£100	o	o
To Ye Rector..............	£20	o	o
To Ye Clerk & Sexton each...	£10	o	o

for leave (as tradition reports) to bury his dog in ye churchyard. So far is true, that there is a Picture of a Pedlar and his dog in painted glass in ye window over ye Pulpit; wh. suffering by the high wind was renewed at ye Parish expense in 1703 (Vestry Book, fol. 7–19). There appears to have been a like picture there in 1607 (Old Vestry Book, fol. 171–173), tho' this land was not then call'd by ye name of Pedlar's Acre: nor in the lease granted February 20th 1656. The first mention of that name, as far as I can find, was in ye lease August 6th 1690. And might not this story take its rise from another Benefactor? Of whom we have the following account given by Bp. Gibson in his edition of *Camden;* "Henry Smith was once a Silver Smith in London, but he did not follow that trade long; he afterwards went a begging for many years, and was commonly called Dog Smith, because he had a dog wh. always followed him—when he dyed, he left a very great estate in ye hands of Trustees upon a general acct. of Charity, and more particularly for Surrey— After ye Trustees had made a considerable improvement of ye estate, and purchas'd several farms, they settled 50id. per annum or thereabouts upon every market town in Surrey or gave 1000id. in money upon every Parish excepting one or two they settled a yearly revenue. Among ye rest, Lambeth has 10id." (*Camden*, Vol. 1, p. 393) From this acct. I should suspect ye picture of ye *Pedlar and his Dog* to have been put up in memory of Mr Smith, and to have no relation to ye Benefactor who gave Church Hopys; could I acct for its being put up before his death, as it was in 1607, whereas he dyed in 1627, and was bur. at Wandsworth.—And yet such seems to have been ye Temper of ye man, yt he might do this in his own lifetime (as tradition says of ye Pedlar) upon ye burial of his dog in ye churchyard. He was whipped at Mitcham as a common vagrant for which reason this parish was excluded from his Benefactions (*Aubreys History*, Vol. II, p. 142). The Benefactor is unknown; but it appears to have been ye estate of ye Parish befor ye year 1504 for its rent was then brought into the Church Account; and its Title was defended out of the Church Stock agst. the claim of Mr Easton in 1581. It was formerly an osier ground, and then let at small rack rents, but being afterwards severed and inclosed as a meadow, long leases were granted of it, and probably with a view to building; the last whereof dated August 6th 1690, for a term of 61 years at the yearly rent of £4, payable quarterly.'

"This account seems to contain all that is to be found about the Lambeth Pedlar and his acre. In 1851 Mr John Smith asked in the pages of Willis's *Current Notes* (p. 59) whether any information could be obtained which connected the pedlar with the Henry Smith mentioned above, but he obtained no reply in response to his query.

"The earliest account of the Swaffham Pedlar story to be found is that by Sir Roger Twysden quoted in Blomefield's *History of Norfolk* (Vol. VI, pp. 211–213)."

It is rather curious that the following almost identical account is told in the *St James' Chronicle* of 28th November, 1786, which shows that the writer had obtained the legend from the same source as Abraham de la Pryme, and that the traditional form had been faithfully preserved:

"In Glyde's *Norfolk Garland*, p. 69, is an account of this legend, but with an additional fact. The box containing the treasure had a Latin inscription on the lid, which, of course, John Chapman could not decipher. He craftily put the lid in his window."

(Parallels quoted from Johannes Fungerus' *Etymologion Latino-Graecum*, pp. 1110, 1111, told of a man at Dort in Holland. Blomefield, *History of Norfolk;* also from the Persian "Nasnavi", by Jalaluddin, who died *c.* 1260, from W. E. A. Axon in the *Antiquary* (1885), Vol. XI, pp. 167–8, alluding to the *New Help to Discourse* often printed between 1619 and 1696. Found also in Lancashire and Cornwall; and said to have been told by Mr Whately in Oriel Common Room. In this last version, the Latin inscription is translated by the Pedlar's son, whom his wealth had enabled him to send to school.)

TYPE 1645. MOTIF: N.531.1 [*Dream of treasure on the bridge*].
¶ See "How Dundonald Castle was built", "The Swaffham Tinker".

PEG O'NELL'S WELL AT WADDOW [summary]

Parkinson, *Yorkshire Legends and Traditions*, 2nd series, pp. 106–7.

Peg O'Nell was a young servant at the Hall at Waddington, in the parish of Mitton on the River Ribble. Within the grounds of the Hall is the well which bears her name.

One day, when she had had a bitter quarrel with her mistress, she was sent to this well to fetch the day's supply of water. As she went, her mistress wished that, before she could return, she might fall and break her neck. This wish came true, for the ground was slippery with ice, and the girl fell on it, and did break her neck.

From that time her spirit became the evil genius of the place, continually visiting it with shrieks and hideous noises, allowing the inmates of the Hall no rest by day or night. Every accident or misfortune that occurred in the neighbourhood was at once attributed to her agency; and the worst of all was that, every seventh year she required a life to be sacrificed to her. This occasion became known as "Peg's Night", and was solemnly observed by the sacrifice of a living animal, for unless this was done, the life of a human being would certainly be forfeit before morning.

One night a young man, who had stayed late at the inn, declared at last that he must go, for he had to be at Clitheroe before daybreak.

Everyone tried to dissuade him, for it was a wild night, and, moreover, the maidservant reminded him that this was "Peg O'Nell's night, and that no sacrifice had been made to her". But he laughed at their warnings and superstition, and set off, giving his horse free rein, and came to the ford, for at that time there was no bridge over the river. Next morning, the bodies of horse and rider were found drowned, and, though no explanation was ever forthcoming, no one doubted that Peg O'Nell had claimed her usual victim.

MOTIFS: S.264 [*Sacrifice to rivers and seas*]; E.246 [*Ghosts punish failure to sacrifice to them*].

¶ Though Peg O'Nell is said to be a ghost, it seems more likely that she is a transformed water-spirit.

See "The Doomed Rider" (B, V), "The Sea's Victim" (B, XII).

THE PENRYN TRAGEDY [summary]

From Hunt, *Popular Romances of the West of England*, p. 442.

A gentleman living at the farm of Bohelland, near Penryn, was blest with wealth and with a happy and grateful family, except only for his youngest son, who was wild and restless. This son gathered about him a company of like-minded young men, and they went off to sea together, and turned pirates. One day they attacked a Turkish ship in the Streights, but their own gunpowder set fire to their ship. The young leader escaped by skilful swimming and reached the island of Rhodes, with the best of his stolen treasures still about him. A Jew to whom he tried to sell them recognized some of them as the property of the Governor of Algiers, and had the pirate arrested and thrown into a galley to work with the other prisoners. Soon this wretched crew revolted, slew some of the officers, and escaped on to an English ship, bound for London. The young man next apprenticed himself to a surgeon, and went to the East Indies, where he succeeded in saving up a little money. At last he decided to return to Cornwall, and in a small ship from London, westbound, he was cast up on the Cornish coast. He swam safe to shore and made his way to his old home, where he found his parents now much impoverished, living in a humble cottage, in debt and danger.

Before making himself known to them, he went to see his sister, to whom he revealed himself and his wealth, and they agreed that he should go that night to his parents' home, but not tell them who he was until the next day, when she and her husband were to join them, and the family circle would be complete to share in the rejoicings.

The young man accordingly made his way home and begged a night's lodging, which his parents compassionately gave him. But before he bade them good night he showed his mother the gold sewed up inside his belt. This was too great a temptation. She told her husband, and persuaded him to join in a plot to murder the unknown sailor. Unwillingly, he agreed, and they covered the body with the bedclothes intending to make away with it in the morning. But early in the morning the daughter and her husband arrived, and were astonished when the parents denied that any sailor had been there. When they added who the sailor really was, they were horrified at the change in their parents' looks. The truth could not be concealed; the daughter rushed upstairs, and showed a scar on her brother's arm, by which it became certain that his parents had indeed murdered their own son. In horror, the mother and father slew themselves with their son's own knife, and the daughter, overcome with horror, died also, and so this ill-fated family came to an end.

TYPE 939A. MOTIF: N.321 [*Son returning home after long absence unwittingly killed by parents*].

¶ This is a widespread tale. Maria Kosko contributed a paper on this subject, "*Varia à propos du Malentendu*", to *Comparative Literature*, x, 1958, pp. 367–77. She had completed, but not published, an exhaustive work on the subject just before her death.

The Splendid Fairing, by Constance Holme, is a literary treatment of this theme. See "A Lay Ghost-Layer" (B, VI).

PETER BANKS

Shetland Folk-Book, II, p. 15.

About the beginning of the seventeenth century there lived a man in Sandsting whose name was Peter Banks.

The people were very superstitious in those days and believed that the Shetland Hills were inhabited by Trows. Peter took advantage of their superstition as follows:

When any person lost their reason or had long, declining sickness, Peter would assure their relatives that the Trows had carried off the person so afflicted to the hills and left behind instead a supernatural body, but if they supplied him [Banks] with fat mutton, burstin and butter, he knew the places where these Trows frequented, and would bring back the real person out by the hills.

By the belief in Peter's superior powers, some of the sick people got better, and therefore his fame spread, and he was sent for from all over the Islands to take human beings and animals out of the hills and thereby he made a very good living like other quacks. He gave no medicine, but it was just the people's belief in his intercession with the Trows that effected the cures. But this only happened when they supplied him with the food he asked for, as he said he could do no good without the mutton, burstin and butter.

MOTIF: K.1963 [*Sham magician*].

THE PIED PIPER

Jacobs, *More English Fairy Tales*, p. 1.

Newtown or Franchville, as 'twas called of old, is a sleepy little town, as you all may know, upon the Solent shore. Sleepy as it is now, it was once noisy enough, and what made the noise was—rats. The place was so infested with them as to be scarce worth living in. There wasn't a barn or a corn-rick, a storeroom or a cupboard, but they ate their way into it. Not a cheese but they gnawed it hollow, not a sugar-puncheon but they cleared out. Why, the very meal and beer in the barrels was not safe from them. They'd gnaw a hole in the top of the tun and down would go one master rat's tail, and when he brought it up round would crowd all the friends and cousins, and each would have a suck at the tail.

Had they stopped here it might have been borne. But the squeaking and shrieking, the hurrying and scurrying, so that you could neither hear yourself speak, nor get a wink of good honest sleep the live-long night! Not to mention that Mamma must needs sit up, and keep watch and ward over baby's cradle, or there'd have been a big ugly rat running across the poor little fellow's face and doing who knows what mischief.

Why didn't the good people of the town have cats? Well they did, and there was a fair stand-up fight, but in the end the rats were too many and the pussies were regularly driven from the field. Poison, I hear you say? Why, they poisoned so many that it fairly bred a plague. Rat catchers! Why, there wasn't a rat catcher from John o' Groats' House to the Land's End that hadn't tried his luck. But do what they might, cats or poison, terriers or traps, there seemed to be more rats than ever, and every day a fresh rat was cocking his tail or pricking his whiskers.

The Mayor and the Town Council were at their wits' end. As they were sitting one day in the town hall, racking their poor brains, and bewailing their hard fate, who should run in but the town beadle. "Please, your Honour," says he, "here is a very queer fellow come to town. I don't rightly know what to make of him." "Show him in," said the Mayor, and in he stept. A queer fellow, truly.

For there wasn't a colour of the rainbow but you might find it in some corner of his dress, and he was tall and thin, and had keen piercing eyes.

"I'm called the Pied Piper," he began. "And pray what might you be willing to pay me if I rid you of every single rat in Franchville?"

Well, much as they feared the rats, they feared parting with their money more, and fain would they have higgled and haggled. But the piper was not a man to stand nonsense, and the upshot was that fifty pounds were promised him (and it meant a lot of money in those old days) as soon as not a rat was left in Franchville.

Out of the hall stept the Piper, and as he stept he laid his pipe to his lips and a shrill, keen tune sounded through street and house. And as each note pierced the air you might have seen a strange sight. For out of every hole the rats came tumbling. There were none too old and none too young, none too big and none too little to crowd at the Piper's heels and with eager feet and upturned noses to patter after him as he paced the streets. Nor was the piper unmindful of the little toddling ones, for every fifty yards he'd stop and give an extra flourish on his pipe, just to give them time to keep up with the older and stronger of the band.

Up Silver Street he went, and down Gold Street, and at the end of Gold Street is the harbour, and the broad Solent beyond. And as he paced along, slowly and gravely, the townsfolk flocked to door and window and many a blessing they called down upon his head.

As for getting near him, there were too many rats. And now that he was at the water's edge, he stepped into a boat, and not a rat, as he shoved off into deep water, piping shrilly all the while, but followed him, plashing, paddling and wagging their tails with delight. On and on he played and played until the tide went out, and each master rat sank deeper and deeper in the slimy ooze of the harbour, until every mother's son of them was dead and smothered.

The tide rose again, and the Piper stepped on shore, but never a rat followed. You may fancy the townsfolk had been throwing up their caps and hurrahing and stopping up rat-holes, and setting the church bells a-ringing. But when the Piper stepped ashore, and not so much as a single squeak was to be heard, the Mayor and the Council, and the townfolk generally began to hum and to ha, and to shake their heads.

For the town money-chest had been sadly emptied of late, and where was the fifty pounds to come from? Such an easy job too! Just getting into a boat and playing a pipe! Why, the Mayor himself could have done that if only he had thought of it.

So he hummed and ha'ed and at last, "Come, my good man," said he, "you will see what poor folk we are. How can we manage to pay you fifty pounds? Will you not take twenty? When all is said and done, 'twill be good pay for the trouble you've taken."

"Fifty pounds was what I bargained for," said the Piper shortly, "and if I were you, I'd pay it quickly. For I can pipe all kinds of tunes as folk sometimes find to their cost."

"Would you threaten us, you strolling vagabond?" shrieked the

Mayor, and at the same time he winked at the Council "The rats are all dead and drowned," muttered he; and so, "You may do your worst, my good man," and with that he turned short upon his heel.

"Very well," said the Piper, and he smiled a quiet smile. With that he laid his pipe to his lips afresh, but now there came forth no shrill notes, as it were, of scraping and gnawing, and squeaking and scurrying, but the tune was joyous and resonant, full of happy laughter and merry play. And as he paced down the streets, the elders mocked, but from school-room and play-room, from nursery and workshop not a child but ran out with eager glee and shout following gaily at the Piper's call. Dancing, laughing, joining hands and tripping feet, the bright throng moved along up Gold Street, and down Silver Street and beyond Silver Street lay the cool green forest full of old oaks and wide spreading beeches. In and out among the oak trees you might catch glimpses of the Piper's many-coloured coat. You might hear the laughter of the children break and fade and die away, as deeper and deeper into the lone green wood the stranger went and the children followed.

All the while the elders watched and waited. They mocked no longer now. And watch and wait as they might, never did they set their eyes again upon the Piper in his parti-coloured coat. Never were their hearts gladdened by the song and dance of the children issuing forth from amongst the ancient oaks of the forest.

From Abraham Elder, *Tales and Legends of the Isle of Wight.*

TYPE ML.3061*.

¶ Type ML.3060 has the same plot as this, but the charmer deals with snakes instead of rats.

Abraham Elder is an adorner of tales, and it seems likely that this legend owes a great deal to the "Pied Piper of Hamelin", and particularly to Browning's version.

Curiously enough, the Motif Index is very weak on rats. There is no motif for charming rats, either with music or rhymes, none for a plague of rats or for inducing rats to leave a farm by writing them a polite letter. There is not even the tale of the old blind rat led between two others by a straw in its mouth. Rosalind in *As you like it* talks of rats being berhymed. It is probable that some tradition of rat-charming lingered in Francheville, which was amplified by Elder.

THE PILOTS OF PILL

Ruth L. Tongue, *Somerset Folklore*, p. 204.

There was great rivalry between the pilots of Pill and the pilots of Portishead. Severn Channel is one of the most dangerous in the world with its ever-shifting quicksands and its tide, which rises at times to 45 feet at Portishead. Merchantmen bound for the Port of Bristol some miles inland were glad enough to hail a pilot from either village, but their sailors homeward bound after years at sea were becoming wary of being paid off at Pill with its street of taverns, to wake up outward bound again and penniless. "Pill sharks" was the name Portishead used about them, but Pill answered with the one word, "Wreckers", and, as one of the clergy had, in far-off days, been as guilty as his parish, Portishead had no answer for it. Now it chanced that there was a shortage of food one year, meat was unheard of in either village, and when two merchant-men were due the two rival pilots raced down Channel as far as Lundy to get their prize and payment. To the surprise of Portishead, the Pill pilot reached the greater prize first, seemed to hang behind it uncertainly, and then went on to fumble around the smaller vessel before boarding it. The Portishead pilots brought their large West Indiaman safely to Pill, where the horse teams towed it on to Bristol Quays. Having jeered at the clumsy seamanship of the Pill men, they went home well paid, but to face still empty larders. The next day they were assailed by their own furious womenfolk. It seemed that Pill was dining on roast pork—great slabs of it. To be sure it was a bit salt, for it had been towed behind both merchantmen as shark bait, but it was none the worse for that, and if the Pill Sharks had earned the smaller pilot's fee they had secured the bait from both ships.

Pill and Portishead.
From Maurice Adams, lighthouseman, born in Gordano; his father and ancestors were Channel pilots. 1956.
MOTIF: J.242.7 [*Choice of learned crow: a dead cat better than a golden crown*].

THE PINDER OF WAKEFIELD

W. Carew Hazlitt, *National Tales and Legends*, p. 417.

In the days of King Henry the Second, when England was torn by intestine discord, and families were so divided against each other, that father and son, and brother and brother were often times opposed, there lived in the town of Wakefield, one Geoffrey à Green, a rich farmer, that in the wars was adverse to the King, and lost his inheritance; and dying, left one only son of tender age—namely, George à Green.

This young fellow, because his father had forfeited to the king all his goods and lands was brought up hardly, and save that in the parish school he learned to read and write, he was an indifferent scholar, and more studied the advancement of his bodily strength, which soon gained him renown among his equals, and neighbours thereabout. More especially since he began by giving his schoolmaster, that brooked not his high spirit and insolency, a fall, which went nigh to cripple him, so that George left his lessons and broke up school.

For some time he lay idle, nor knew not what calling to choose to his best liking; and whereas a friend counselled him to resort to a famous astrologer that dwelled at Halifax, and for forty pence divined the future of every man, George sought his house. But for that this wise man was then busied with discovering who had done him an ill turn, and could not, George kept his money, holding him no seer that could not attend upon his own needs.

Nevertheless, George, lacking employment, and growing in the love of all in that township, was shortly invited without any suit on his part to take the place of Pound-Keeper, or Pinder, and albeit there were many others who would have fain competed with him, all voices were for George by reason of his crying need of some livelihood, and his excellent qualities.

But he desired that merit should decide the choice sooner than favour; and when he proposed that all such as stood for the pindership should meet on Wakefield Green on a given day after evensong, and join in a match at quarter-staff, the prize to the winner being the office that lay vacant, all agreed; and when the time came, George played the part of champion, and the rest were defendants.

The meeting on the green was to all comers; bakers, butchers, tinkers, everyone; and each challenge was given in its turn to the music of the bagpipes, and a throng of gentlefolks from far and near attended to see the sport. As soon as George had laid one low, another appeared in his place, like Hercules and the hydra; but when he had disposed of some twenty of them, and still appeared as fresh as a daisy and ready for more, the rest perceived the vanity of further trial, and by universal consent the prize was awarded to George.

This victory gained him a great name over all that country, and made many a fair damsel gaze upon him favourably that had been a witness to that evening's doings. But in especial his prowess was marked by the paragon of beauty in the northern parts, Beatrice, the daughter of Justice Grymes; and the Pinder, that had long known her for a great lady, yet far above him in reach, espied her betwixt the bouts in the ring, and figured to himself that her smiles and her glances as she looked towards him, meant no harm.

II

Now when God took to Himself the King of England, that was Henry the Second, and Richard the First, named Cœur de Lion, reigned in his room, this Richard, going to the Holy Land to defend the cross and sepulchre of Jesus Christ from the heathens, left his realm in charge of the Bishop of Ely. Whose covetousness and overbearing, together with the disloyalty of the Prince John, the king's brother, bred sore discontent, in so much that, under the Earl of Kendal a host gathered itself together to defend the rights of the people.

This army consumed much provision and substance, and sent into the shires messengers to require subsidies in money and food; and one Mannering came into the Northern parts, and namely to Wakefield, to solicit the bailiff and justices of that township to grant him under his commission, sealed with three seals, a contribution to the cause.

He stood covered before the bench, as representing the Earl of Kendal; and when they had heard the nature of his suit, and hesitated to deny him or to grant him that he prayed, he waxed mighty insolent, and overawed the magistrates so that they began to lean to yielding to him.

At this juncture, the Pinder stepping forth from the body of the court, where the justices sat, craved liberty to answer the earl's messenger in the behalf of his neighbours and townsmen; and when they had given him liberty, he at first demanded by what title Mannering stood covered in that presence, and when the messenger answered not, he plucked the bonnet from his head, and threw it to a distance.

Quoth Mannering: "How darest thou offer this violence to me, who come armed with such a commission?"

The Pinder begged him to show that to him. Which, the permission of the justices granted, he perused and then, as though he would have kissed it in reverence, tore it, keeping only the three seals wherewith it was sealed. Mannering began to stamp and storm, but George took him by the collar, and shook him, saying, that he would soon cool his choleric blood; whereupon, pointing his dagger at the messenger's breast, he made him swallow the seals one after the other, and then quaff a draught of ale, to wash them well down. "For," cried the Pinder, "it shall never be said that a messenger was sent by such great personages, to the town of Wakefield and that none made him drink."

Mannering perceiving no remedy, and feeling the wax tickle his throat, drank supernaculum. "Now," said George, "commend me to thy master, and the rest, and make known to them that the Pinder of Wakefield, albeit he has torn their commission, has yet sent them back their seals by their servant."

So he, departing in secret ire, went in search of the Earl of Kendal, whom, with others, he found at the house of Justice Grymes, and already incensed by the flout which the same Pinder had offered to a spy sent out to gain secret information how Sandon Castle might be brought into the possession of the rebels.

For George, happening to meet with this spy, that knew him not, showed him how he was accustomed to sell corn to the garrison, and was well known of them, and so agreed with the same for a rich reward, to convey him in a sack into the castle, as he were a bushel of corn; and in the night-time he should leave his concealment, and open the gates to the Earl of Kendal's men. But when the spy had entered the sack, the Pinder made it fast with a strong cord, and cast him over his shoulder, and took him and hoisted him up on the tree before the castle green, where the Musgraves, who kept the castle for the King, might easily see him, with the scroll on his breast setting forth his treason, and who put him there.

Which when Sir William Musgrave and his son perceived from the walls of the castle, greatly raised the Pinder in their conceit.

III

Meanwhile, as George à Green grew more and more famous throughout all the North country, the fair Beatrice, Justice Grymes' daughter, who had been courted in vain by lords and knights, and had had even the Earl of Kendal among the suitors for her hand, was more and more enamoured of him, and his exploits, with which the whole kingdom began to ring, kindled in her breast a violent desire to see him or to write to him; and the Pinder, on his part, waxed melancholy by reason of his passion for that lady and the thought of the great distance between them in birth and fortune. So, when it came to pass that George sent a letter by his boy to Beatrice, and she returned a gracious answer by the same messenger, the Pinder was a joyful man indeed.

Then when certain other letters had passed between these two lovers, and Beatrice was so straitly watched by her father, that she might not meet the Pinder, they devised a plot whereby the Pinder's boy, whose name was Willy, was admitted to the chamber of Beatrice, in the guise of a sempstress' maid, that had laces and the like to sell. Who, changing clothes with the lady, remained in the place, and braved her father's anger, when he should discover the cheat, while the other took flight, and tarried not, till she came to the spot appointed for the meeting with George.

It happened about this time that Maid Marian, that was the Lord Fitzwalter's daughter and sojourned with Robin Hood beneath the broad shade in King Richard's forest of Sherwood, grew pensive and dejected, and so strangely bare herself, that Robin, who was, in very truth, the banished Earl of Huntingdon, deemed it in his secret thought to be for that this fair may was importuned by Prince John, the King's own brother to hearken to his love. But when he asked her, she said Nay, but that it was because the fame of George à Green for valour, and Beatrice his paramour for beauty threatened to outshine theirs; and she had a sore longing that she might accompany him to Wakefield town, and challenge those two to a trial, so that it might be known and allowed of all which was the valianter, he Robin or George à Green, and the fairer, she Marian or George's Beatrice.

To whom Robin yielded compliance, and he, with Little John, Scathlock, and the Friar, set out accordingly, in company with Marian; and their other weapons those outlaws left behind, and carried only their quarter-staves on their necks, as the custom of the country was; and they drew not breath until they came to the cornfields that neighbour upon Wakefield, and crossed them, bearing down the corn. Whom the Pinder, that was abroad thereabout with his Beatrice, shortly noting, sharply accosted, as one who was privileged by his office to warn trespassers in the growing season. But who the strangers were, he yet knew not, for they had not their bows, nor wore their forest livery.

Beatrice entreated him not to be over-bold, since there were four to one: but George, seeing such wrong done, was not to be held back, and taking his staff from his shoulder, barred their way, demanding recompense. The strangers answered that the satisfaction was for him to seek. "Marry, sirs, and so it shall be," quoth the Pinder; "and as you are true men, come not upon me all at a time."

It was a sorry spectacle for those two virgins to view, when the lusty Pinder engaged one by one Robin and his merry men. Scathlock and Little John he soon laid at his feet. The Friar approached, and poised his staff by way of entrance. "O," cried George, "I must refuse nothing to the Church," and placed him where his two comrades were.

Then began the fiercest part of the fray; for the Pinder and Robin set at each other like lions, and Marian made no doubt that George had at last found his match. But the Pinder proved too much even for him: and he had to beg him, after such a bout as had rarely been witnessed in these parts, to hold his hand, and then discovered who he was.

To whom the victorious Pinder courteously addressed himself, saying that, after King Richard, he was the man whom he most honoured; and he craved pardon of Maid Marian, praying Beatrice to do likewise, and these two comely mays embraced and kissed each other, Marian declaring Beatrice to be the glory of the northern parts.

IV

While these events were taking place, King Richard, having left the Holy Land, returned to his own kingdom, and sorely grieved to learn what tumults and rebellions and great abuses had been committed during his absence. But it was a mighty solace to his grace to receive at the hands of the Musgraves the arch-rebel Armstrong, and anon by the hands of Justice Grymes the Earl of Kendal, Lord Bonville, and Sir Nicholas Mannering, who were brought before him, and delivered as prisoners, in the name of George à Green that by stratagem had newly taken the same. And by cause that the Earl of Kendal had been encouraged in his disloyalty by a prophecy that the king would one day vail his bonnet to him in the city of London, Richard uncovered himself before him in mockery thereof, and said unto him, "My Lord, you are welcome to London."

The King's grace, hearing the fame of George à Green so widely and loudly bruited, resolved so soon as his affairs afforded him leisure, to make a progress into the North country with the Earl of Leicester, and with Musgrave, disguised as plain yeomen; and it chanced that they arrived at the good town of Bradford on Trail-staff day, when the sturdy shoemakers are licensed by ancient use to come out, and make all comers vail their quarter staves. Now, when these three seeming yeomen carried their staves on their necks, as not knowing the custom, certain shoemakers rudely beat them to the ground, and to the yeomen demanding why this was done, they replied that they had had the right time out of mind, and that it was to them and their heirs for ever.

Wherefore one of the three that was the king asked them where was their patent. "We have none," quoth they, "nor want it; for staff-end-law suffices us." And the yeomen, because they feared discovery, trailed their staves to avoid a fray. But Robin Hood and Maid Marian and George à Green and Beatrice and the rest, coming up, and the shoe-makers summoning them in like fashion, that was a different matter, for Robin and George and their men set upon the shoemakers, and the whole town was shortly astir; but the shoemakers reckoned without their host, and were fain to cry mercy, saying that they felt it to be no dishonour, or disparagement, to be beaten by such renowned men as Robin and the Pinder.

Then followed the drinking and pledging of healths, and the first was to good King Richard, and George gave it, and Robin, as the next best man in the company, pledged it; and the bowl was then passed round to the shoemakers. Only the three yeomen that trailed their staves were excepted out of it, by reason that they were, quoth George, unworthy to drink to so brave a king. The second health was to Robin and the third was to have been to George, when the three yeomen, casting aside their disguise, stepped forward, and the Earl of Leicester craved leave to let King Richard follow next in order.

Hereupon all fell on their knees; but the King raised them by turns, and first to Robin he said, "Rise, Robert, Earl of Huntingdon. I restore thee thy lands, wrongfully taken from thee by my brother and my lieutenant the bishop of Ely and bestow on thee the hand of thy Matilda, the Lord Fitzwalter's daughter."

Next his grace called for George à Green, and after that he had lustily commended his loyalty and prowess, desired him to kneel, that he might make him knight. But George humbly prayed that he might be suffered to remain, as his father had been before him, a yeoman;

and then the King, assenting, gave him in requital of his worthy services to the crown of England the moiety of his royal right in the good town of Kendal and all his title in chief to the good town of Bradford, to stand, he and his heirs, in the place of the King for ever.

Unto whom anon, as these passages were so happily proceeding, came Justice Grymes, to cast himself at his Prince's feet, and beg worthy punishment for him that had stolen his daughter, and left a boy in her room. But when he understood what the king's pleasure was in respect of George à Green, the justice suffered himself to be persuaded, and to offer no hindrance to the marriage of Beatrice his heiress to the Pinder of Wakefield, whom Richard of the Lionheart had so enriched, that he might forsake his office, and who had generously refused to be higher in dignity than his father Geoffrey à Green, albeit in wealth and in authority he became by royal bounty, one of the greatest lords in his own country.

¶ This rather chaotic and rambling tale has been put into shape by Carew Hazlitt, but even so remains somewhat formless. It is an example of the yeomen's romances, of which Robin Hood is the cream. They were to be found in chapbooks, and were socially, as well as poetically, below the Arthurian romances; perhaps Saxon, rather than Celtic in tone. This story was given dramatic form in the Elizabethan play, *George à Green, the Pinder of Wakefield*. The play does not, however, follow the story very closely. In this tale, George à Green was a law-abiding character on the whole, and would have nothing to do with rebellion, even against such a doubtful character as the Bishop of Ely.

See "Robin Hood" (A, IV), "Haveloc and His Man Böndel", "Adam Bel, Clym of the Clough and William of Cloudesley" (A, IV).

THE POLICEMAN AND THE
GIBBET'S OFFSPRING

W. H. Barrett, *Tales from the Fens*, pp. 33-7.

In the days when pot-holes in the high-road were filled with gravel for the carts and wagons to roll it in, old Becky used to pick up a few coppers by sweeping up the grit and selling it to farmers' wives for putting into the chicken-house to make the hens lay.

Becky was a kind, simple soul and she had no idea she was doing anything wrong, so she had the shock of her life when a young bully of a policeman, who was new in the village, came along one day and caught her with her brush and shovel in her hand, busy filling up her barrow. A few days afterwards she was sent up to the Magistrates for stealing what belonged to the Parish Council. After she'd paid out one half-crown for the fine and another for costs, she found that she'd not only lost her job, but all her savings as well, so she had to go on the parish. She was given four shillings a week and, though she was so old, made to put in three days a week breaking stones on the parish roads. Many the time she'd stop in her work and curse that policeman who was the cause of all her trouble and backache, and whenever he went by she'd straighten up and shout after him: "The curse of the gibbet's offspring on you." But he'd no idea what she meant and no one told him.

Well, before that winter was over, Becky was lying in a pot-hole of her own, put there as cheaply as a pauper could be. The only mourner at her funeral was her old dog, a mongrel who'd hardly ever left her side while she was alive and soon showed it wasn't going to now she was dead. It sat watching the sexton filling in the grave, then, when the last spadeful of earth was patted down on top of the mound, the dog jumped on to the grave, curled itself up and, by its bared fangs, let everyone know it was going to stay there. And stay it did, or at any rate until that young policeman came along and grabbed it by the neck, put it into a sack with a couple of bricks for company, and threw it in the river at Gibbet's Corner; then he sat on a tree-stump and waited till the dog's howls stopped, and no more bubbles came to the top of the water. Then he went off home and wrote down in the book that he'd taken a mad dog from the churchyard, using the churchwarden's tongs, and drowned it.

That night, as the policeman was walking on his beat, he suddenly heard the howls of a dog coming across the fens, then, as he walked on, the noise seemed to be coming from quite close to him. So he stopped and threw the light of his lantern all round him, but he couldn't see any dog; then, remembering what he'd done that afternoon, he felt sure that the ghost of Becky's dog was somewhere near; so he took to his heels and pelted as fast as he could back to his lodgings. Two nights later he set out to meet his inspector at a place four miles away, but he hadn't gone far along the road when the howling started again. Sweating with fright, he turned tail and made for home and it was there that the inspector found him when he came, an hour or so later, in a flaming temper wanting to know why he hadn't turned up where he ought to have done. But when he saw the policeman, with his face all white and his eyes popping out of his head, he stopped swearing at him and told him to stay where he was for the rest of the night and to go and see the doctor in the morning.

Now, it so happened that, the week before, two of the young women in the village had each gone to the doctor and told him that it was thanks to that new police chap that they were soon going to be the mothers of lusty babies. So, when the chap turned up at the surgery next morning, saying he thought he was going mad, the doctor thought he meant he was going mad with worry over working out if he was really going to be the father of two, and gave him a certificate. The policeman took this to the inspector who, after reading it, said it looked as if he'd been doing too much while he was off duty, but that anyway, he was to have fourteen days' sick leave and come back for duty at the end of the fortnight.

After the two weeks were up and the policeman came back, he asked the chap who'd taken over from him, what sort of time he'd had.

"Oh, quite quiet," he said, "except for a blasted dog howling all over the place every night; and the queer thing is I've never been able to set eyes on it, let alone get my hands on it. And we haven't found the publican's daughter yet, though they're still dragging for her—she drowned herself yesterday at Gibbet Corner."

Well, the body was found next day and the doctor came to the inquest and said the young woman had been to him and told him she was going to have a baby and, what's more, who the father was, but he couldn't tell the court that, as that wasn't his job. So the jury decided that she had killed herself while out of her mind through worry.

That night the howls were louder than ever and, to make things worse, every yard dog in the place joined in till no one in the village got a wink of sleep. So, early next morning the parson came round to the policeman's lodgings and told him if he didn't do something to stop that noise everybody would be driven mad if they had another night of it. Hardly had he gone when the other young woman who'd told the doctor that her child would be able to call the policeman "Father", came along and said if he didn't get the banns read as soon as possible then there'd be another splash in the river. There'd be more than that, too, because she'd told her father everything and he'd sworn to throttle that young chap with his own handcuffs if he didn't become his son-in-law before the month was out, and she'd like to remind him that her father was the strongest man in the village. So, what with howling dogs and angry fathers, the policeman gave in and promised to take her to church as soon as possible.

The pair were married one morning and in the afternoon the bride-groom, not having been able to get a honeymoon because he'd only just had time off for sick leave, went to the sale of furniture and stuff which was being held down at the pub. The landlord, who was the father of the girl who'd drowned herself, had had notice to quit because the brewers didn't like their tenants being mixed up in anything like that. Now, everybody liked the landlord and they all knew who was at the bottom of his troubles; so when the policeman turned up at the sale he'd have known, if he'd been a local chap, that the black looks and muttered curses he got meant trouble, and he'd have cleared off before dark. But he stayed on, hanging about outside the pub and hoping that after everybody had drunk a few farewell toasts to the landlord, he'd have a nice little bunch of drunk and disorderlies to put him back into the inspector's good books. Just before closing time the landlord's wife came out and told him that though she knew he was the cause of her girl's drowning herself, yet she and her husband wanted him to know they were ready to let bygones be bygones; so, as it was a cold night, wouldn't he come inside and have a cup of coffee with them. So he went inside, but he'd hardly downed the coffee when he said he was going to be sick. Several chaps in the tap-room helped him outside, and then they stripped him and gave him a good coating of tar, before smothering him in feathers from a couple of pillows.

His wife waited up for him till after midnight, then went to bed, but as her husband still hadn't come home in the morning, she went along to the inspector and told him and a search party was sent out. After an hour or so, when the inspector was walking by a ring of saplings which everyone called the Gibbet's Offspring, he heard a dog howling and when he went into the middle of the clump of trees he found the police-man. He was covered in tar and feathers and was lying on the ground, tied to a hurdle, and swearing away at Billy, the village half-wit, who was standing over him, making noises like the howls of a dying dog, while he poked the policeman with his foot to make him swear louder.

Policemen swarmed all over the fen like flies trying to find out who'd tarred and feathered their mate, but no one split. By the time the last bit of tar had worn off, the baby was born, having come on the very day that the policeman got a letter to say he was out of work. He stayed on in the village for a bit, but he daren't go out in the daylight because of the jeering he got, nor at night because the dog's howls followed him round wherever he went. At last, fed-up with all this and with his wife's nagging him because he wasn't bringing any money in, he put on his running shoes and left the village for ever.

Perhaps you're wondering how old Becky's curse of the Gibbet's Offspring came to work on that policeman. Well, it was this way. Billy the half-wit used to spend day after day in that circle of trees, because he'd heard his mother say that, when the wind was right, those trees talked to each other in a wailing kind of voice, and if anyone heard the sound and repeated it just like they heard it, then they'd be able to lay a curse on anybody. Now, if you showed Billy something that looked like work, he'd be off to the other end of the parish in no time; but let him hear a bird sing or an animal cry, then he'd make the same sound and go on making it time and time again. Well, Billy had been in Gibbet's Offspring, waiting to hear the trees talk, on the day that police chap had drowned Becky's dog, and he'd heard the howls the dog gave as it died. So that night Billy had walked round the village making the same howling noise, and he'd kept it up night after night, till every yard dog on a chain was stiff and sore through being kicked for answering him.

The howling stopped one night and that was because Billy ran home with his shirt tail riddled with shot. While his mother was using a bodkin to dig out the pellets which had sunk into his flesh, she soothed him down by telling him how Becky's grandfather had killed a drunken lighterman in a quarrel and had been hung for it on the same place where the fight had been. The gibbet he hung from was cut from the trunk of a willow tree which was growing close by and the sawn-off branches made the arm to hold the cage. The gibbet post, she said, had gradually rotted away, but its roots still went on living and in time they threw up a circle of trees which people called the Gibbet's Offspring. That's why folks believe that those trees wail and curse the men who put the gibbet up and if a man can only make the sound like they do, then he can put a curse on anyone who does him wrong—just like old Becky did.

MOTIFS: Q.556.11 [*Curse for uncharitableness*]; B.301.1 [*Faithful animal at master's grave*]; J.1782.3 [*Noise thought to be ghost*]; E.631 [*Reincarnation in tree growing from grave*].

¶ The belief in the malevolence of the suckers springing up round a gibbet may be compared with such instances of reincarnation in a tree as occur in the singing game, "Old Roger" in *Sweet William and Fair Margaret*, and in some versions of the Cinderella tales.

POTTER THOMPSON

Gutch, *County Folk-Lore*, II, *North Riding of Yorkshire*, p. 406.

On the south side of the river [Swale, near Richmond] is the remarkable circular hill called the Round Howe, [and] near [that] a large natural cave called Arthur's Oven.

...A person walking round Richmond Castle, was arrested by a "man" who took him into a strange vault beneath the fortress, where a multitude of people were lying on the ground, as if in a deep slumber. In this chamber a horn and a sword were presented to him for the usual purpose of releasing the sleepers of other days from their long listlessness. But when he drew the sword out of its sheath, a stir among them all terrified him to such a degree, that he let the blade fall back to its place and an indignant voice instantly cried:

> "Potter, Potter Thompson,
> If thou hadst either drawn
> The sword or blown that horn
> Thou'd been the luckiest man
> That ever [yet] was born."

The tradition adds that no opportunity of breaking that enchantment will again be afforded before a definite time has elapsed.

Longstaffe, *Richmondshire, Its Ancient Lords and Edifices*, pp. 115, 116.
MOTIF: D.1960.2.2* [*Man gains entrance, etc.*] (Baughman).
¶ See "King Arthur at Sewingshields".

THE PRENTICE PILLAR

Local Tradition, Roslin, Midlothian.

Roslin Chapel, founded as a collegiate church in 1446 by Sir William St Clair, is a magnificent example of fifteenth-century work. It is small, but almost every inch is covered with exquisitely executed carving. The most famous feature in it is the Prentice Pillar, as solid as a Norman pillar, but fluted, and wreathed with carved flowers. There is no other like it in the chapel. The tradition is, that the master carver planned it, but was unable to carry it out, so he travelled overseas to learn the secret. He came back to find his apprentice kneeling at the base of the column, finishing the last flower. In jealous rage, he snatched up a mallet and killed the boy, and, since he had failed to learn the secret of his skill, the pillar remained unmatched and solitary.

MOTIF: W.181.2.1 [*Architect kills pupil who has surpassed him in skill*].

THE PRESS GANG

J. R. W. Coxhead, *The Devil in Devon*, p. 33.

A great many years ago, there lived in the parish of Sheepstor, on the western side of Dartmoor, a landowner called Squire Northmore, whose eldest son was slightly deficient mentally. The Squire considered that the young man was quite unfitted to inherit the family estate, and wanted his second son to become his heir.

Now Squire Northmore was a very unscrupulous man, and he always liked to have his own way, so he soon evolved a plan to get rid of his eldest son.

One day, during haymaking time, he mounted his horse and rode off to Plymouth, where he made secret arrangements with a press-gang to come and kidnap the young man while he was out in the fields helping the haymakers.

The plan worked without a hitch. The press-gang arrived, abducted the young man just as he was in the act of pitching some hay on to a rick, and carried him off to sea.

After a time young Northmore was told by one of his shipmates, who had been a member of the press-gang, that the person responsible for his being kidnapped and taken to sea was his own father. The young man was mad with rage when he heard of his father's treachery, and vowed that if he ever returned to England he would have his revenge.

The frigate on which Northmore was serving was away at sea for a long time, but eventually she returned to Plymouth to undergo a refit. Young Northmore realized that the chance to take revenge for the wrongs he had suffered had come at last, so he made up a party from among his messmates, and went by night to Sheepstor. They ransacked the Squire's house, took all the papers they could lay their hands on, including the title deeds of the estate, and might well have done the Squire severe bodily harm, but for the fact that he hid himself in the roof of the house amongst the rafters.

According to this rather forlorn tradition, young Northmore went back to sea and was never heard of again. His father, stricken by belated remorse, took to drink and used to ride back from the local tavern in such a state of inebriation that he often tumbled off his horse. Frequently he would take his horse into the kitchen, fetch a bottle of gin, and drink to the animal's health, and every time the horse nodded its head the Squire would say, "The same to you Sir; I drinks tu'ee again."

It is said that from the day the Squire's eldest son was abducted the family ceased to prosper; things went from bad to worse, and eventually they left the district.

Rewritten from dialect version in *Transactions of the Devonshire Association*, XXX, pp. 92–3.

MOTIFS: S.11 [*Cruel father*]; S.327 [*Child cast out because of stupidity*]; S.22.2 [*Prince plans to kill wicked father for cruelty*].

¶ There are many tales and traditions of that much-hated institution, the press-gang. See "The Press-gang near Whitby" (B, IX).

THE PRESS GANG NEAR WHITBY

Parkinson, *Legends and Traditions of Yorkshire*, p. 178.

Many years have now passed away since the operations of the press-gang, so dreaded in Yorkshire in the earlier part of the present century, ceased. Still, its doings are not forgotten. There are those yet living who can testify of its cruelties and its abuses, and traditional stories are handed down of the evil purposes to which it was sometimes turned, by the evil-disposed, to avenge a supposed wrong, or get rid of an enemy.

It may be necessary to say that the press-gang was an institution, permitted by authority, by which the army and navy, in the long wars with the French, were supplied with recruits by violence. The gang was permitted to keep up the supply by laying violent hands on whomsoever they could, and then forcing the victims on board vessels, or away from the district, where, in many cases, they were heard of no more.

The districts which suffered most, from these operations, were those contiguous to the sea. The hardy fishermen were already trained seamen, and their abduction was more easily accomplished than that of men from inland places.

The following traditional story of the press-gang's work at one point on our Yorkshire coast, is given by Mrs Macquoid in *About Yorkshire*, who says that it happened within the memory of people now living, and the truth of it was vouched for.

In one of the glens running up from the sea, between Whitby and Robin Hood's Bay, there lived a farmer named Mossburn, and his wife and their two daughters. These two sisters, both pretty and virtuous maidens, were beloved by two brothers engaged in the Greenland fishery. They had "fancied" one another before the last voyage, but the young men had not then ventured to speak, for the farmer was a well-to-do man, and not likely to give his daughters in marriage without being sure of their future. Now both brothers had returned from a successful voyage; they had shown great bravery, and had each been appointed to the command of a vessel by the shipowner in whose ships they had served. On the first evening after their arrival they went off joyfully to the farm in the gully (as these grassed clefts leading to the sea are called). On their way, a short distance from the town, they met a girl named Polly, and stopped to speak a few words to her.

"Ye'll turn wi' me, Bill," she said to the youngest. "'Tis a weary while sin' Ah've seed you."

Bill coloured up. His heart was full of his errand of love. In the old days, when he laughed and joked with Polly, he had never been seriously in earnest, and he had not then seen Hester Mossburn.

"Nay, Polly," he said kindly, for the lad's heart was so brimming over with love that it just poured out of him. "Ah canna gau wi' you. Ah've another fish to fry."

Polly was a tall, strongly-built lass, rough-haired and freckle-skinned, like most Whitby girls. She fixed her pale blue eyes keenly on the young sailor.

"Ista thinking on Hester Mossburn?" she said scornfully. "She's noane for you, Bill."

"Wheest, lass," said the brother, whose name was Peter. "Bill's all right and knows his way. He and Hester agree like bells. They want nowt but hanging and mebbe we'll fix t'matter t'neet."

He gave a sly wink, and Polly wrenched her arm away from the grasp he had laid on it.

"Curse her!" she said passionately. "Curse the pair on 'em!" and she fled away like the wind.

"Curses come home to roost, mah lass," said Peter; but both the lads felt that this meeting had dashed their joy.

When they reached the gully and began to climb upwards to the farm—for they had come along beside the strand—the dogs set up such a notice of arrival, that both Hester and her sister, Dorothy, came to the door to see who the visitors might be. And in the joy of meeting, after such a long absence, restraint was forgotten, words were said, and vows were exchanged—and kisses too—and the two couples walked into the house hand in hand, and made their confession to Dame Mossburn. Soon came in the farmer, and when he heard how matters stood, he gave his consent heartily. Then Bill and Peter both began to press that a speedy day might be named for the double marriage. It was true that they should not go on another voyage till next season, but why should they not be made happy as soon as might be? The father took their side, the girls made faint objection, and before they parted, the tender whispers of their lovers, as they all sat in the firelight round the hearth, prevailed, and a day not far off was fixed for the wedding.

It was growing late, and the farmer, after sundry yawns, told the lovers that they would have a solitary walk to Whitby. Then first Peter and Dorothy stole out to take a fond farewell outside the house. Dorothy lingered long, and her mother, after some bridling and shaking of her head, rose up to fetch her in, when suddenly the door was flung open and Dorothy, pale as ashes, rushed into the kitchen, shrieking with terror.

"T'press-gang," she screamed, "they've gotten Peter fast; nobbut ye're a man, Bill, ye'll save t'lad fra' them."

Her passionate cry, and their own indignation, robbed the farmer and Bill of their judgment. Both rushed out to rescue the sailor, but the farmer was seized and overpowered, while Bill was dragged off to take his place beside his brother in a boat lying in the creek.

In the silence that followed, the two young women crept out to see what had happened, but they only found their father lying speechless with a broken head, and, when he came to his senses, he was utterly ignorant of the fate of their lovers.

Months went by; the country was rife with rumours of glorious victories, but to Hester and Dorothy these only meant a chance of death for their absent lads; for might they not have been in the very thick of one of these great sea-fights? So they grew sadder and paler, and at last both put on mourning clothes for their loved ones.

Polly heard of this, and she mocked openly. One day, at a fish auction on the Straithe, she boasted that if a lad broke faith with her, she knew how to punish him.

"Ye can ask Hester Mossburn," she said.

She was startled by the sudden silence that fell on the noisy group, just now full of laughter and coarse jokes.

Then the oldest fisherman, near whom she stood, gripped her arm.

"Ista false, Polly?" he said. "Ah wud not hav thout sic a steeany heart lived amongst us." And he flung her from him with violence.

The man against whom the push sent her flung her away also, as if she were plague-stricken.

At this Polly gathered herself up with an angry scowl, and as she met the stony glances of the eyes all fixed on her—glances that to her guilty soul seemed to promise a speedy vengeance for her treason—she fled away, and from that day she never showed her face on the Staithes. But the story fled like wildfire over the town and down into the gullies. Polly's landlady turned her out of doors, and not a soul would give shelter or employment to the girl, who had betrayed Whitby sailors to their natural enemies.

At last shame and privation and exposure took away her reason, and "Crazy Polly", as she was called, wandered over the moor, telling wayfarers that she was waiting for her lad.

Hester and Dorothy waited on, rejecting all offers of marriage though four years had gone by, and not one word reached them from their lovers. But at last their constancy was rewarded. One day Bill and Peter stood before them safe and sound, though both had been severely wounded during their service on a man of war; and it is to be presumed that they married and lived happily ever after, as all true lovers should do.

MOTIFS: T.71.2 [*Woman avenges scorned love*]; T.84 [*Lovers treacherously separated*]; T.96 [*Lovers reunited after many adventures*].

¶ The press-gang made a deep impression on folk-tradition and comes into many folk-songs and ballads. Examples are "William Taylor" and "The Banks of Sweet Dundee".

Mrs Gaskell used the motif effectively in *Silvia's Lovers*, which is set in Whitby.

THE PRIEST'S HOUSE AT
BRANDON CREEK [shortened]

W. H. Barrett, *Tales from the Fens*, pp. 163–73.

In the days when the fen in winter was all water and tall reeds, it was a lonely quiet place. But in Ely there were a lot of monks and nuns, and in charge of them was a fat old Abbot. They had a big garden there, called the Vineyards, and a young Frenchman, Brother Francis, was sent over to join the monks, because he had great skill in tending vines, and the Abbot wanted his wine made on the spot.

The young nuns pestered Francis, and he nearly left the community, for the other monks were jealous. But the Abbot persuaded him to stay a while, and promised to send someone to help him in the garden, and lessen his loneliness. This proved to be a pretty young nun, named Angela. She was quiet and shy, and they became very friendly, almost like brother and sister. She told Francis that she had left her father's great estate in Kent because her stepmother and uncle, who had made his home with them, were cruel and treated her like an animal.

Soon Angela grew pale and sad, and each morning her eyes were red with weeping. If ever the Abbot came into the garden, she was terrified, and trembled like a leaf. At last one day Francis found her lying in a dead faint, and had difficulty in bringing her to her senses. He would have brought the Abbess to her, but she clung to his knees saying that if he did, he would never see her again. At last she confessed to him that she was going to have a baby and that the Abbot was its father. He had made her drink a bottle of drugged wine with him at Christmas-time, and she knew no more till she woke and found him in her cell. If the Abbess found out, she would be bricked up alive, which was the usual penalty. At this, Francis determined to save Angela; he found a punt, and they escaped in the darkness of a foggy night, to a little island, where they climbed ashore and slept. In the morning they were awakened by a man, dressed in a sheepskin, who was bending over them. His appearance was terrible; he had no nose, one eye was missing, and his ears had been cropped off close to his head. They told him their story and he said that his name was Theobald, but everyone called him Croppy. He led them through the bog to his small hut, where he fed them, and then told them his story. His father had been a noted flint-knapper near Brandon, but he worked under a cruel task-master, appointed by the vicious Bishop of Thetford. His three sisters were sent away to a nunnery while still very young and his mother had been set upon and killed by a gang of wandering friars.

This gave him an implacable hatred for all monks, and as soon as he was old enough, he was set, with one other man, to work the barges that carried the flints to where a new church was being built. On each trip he carried an old wooden-handled knife, that his mother had used, and every time he made away with a friar, he made another notch in his wooden handle. After a time, he escaped, and took work on a building nearby, where he was well-fed and happy and found himself a wife. But the Bishop's men came up with him, one night, marched him back to Thetford, and shut him up in the old Castle there. Later they thrust a red-hot iron into his eye, cut off his nose and ears for being a runaway, and threw him outside to a pack of dogs. But he still had his knife and managed to cut the throat of each dog, as it came up snarling. After that, he had walked for nearly a week, wounded and blind (for his other eye had swelled up too). At last he stumbled by chance into the hut of a white witch, who tended his wounds, and fed him until he was strong again, and spoke for him to the Fen people, who had no love for monks or nuns in those days.

Having told his story, Croppy went off to this witch and told her about Francis, and the witch took Angela into her own hut to care for her. Francis had to tell his tale to the Fenmen, who allowed him to stay among them and work with Croppy. Francis learned how to catch fish and snare birds, and was as good as the next man with a fish-spear.

Angela's baby was born, but it was dead, and the witch said that was the best that could have happened, for the baby had hooves instead of feet. When Angela was well again, she dressed like the other Fen women, and became so much a favourite, that Croppy warned Francis, and he announced that he and Angela were courting.

When a big lighter, loaded with timber, had stuck fast in the mud at Ely, Croppy and Francis built a fine house of the timber, and of bricks which they baked from the fen clay. They slipped into Ely and helped themselves to some of the Abbot's spare chimney-pots and some of his wine, killed a sheep and a bullock, and, with difficulty, loaded the carcasses, cut into joints, on to their boats, and returning to the new house, all held a great house-warming there. They built another house for Angela and Francis, and made another trip to Ely for Christmas fare. But this time Croppy did not go with them. He went home to Brandon, where he found that his father had died some time before; when he knew this, Croppy went to find his old taskmaster and settle his account with him.

He came upon him dragging a shrieking young girl by the hair, drove his knife into the man's back, and took the girl home to her father. The father offered him the girl for his wife, and she was willing, and on Boxing Day there was held the first double wedding in the Fens. The oldest Fenman made Francis and Angela and Croppy and his bride stand side by side, and swear that they would live together as long as fishes had scales and birds had feathers. Then he tied a bit of eel-skin on a finger of each bride and that was all. After a good many years, Francis' eldest son became a priest, and when his father died, he came back to live in the old house. And the house was called "The Priest's House" ever after until the time came for it to be pulled down.

MOTIFS: S.100 [*Revolting murders and mutilations*]; R.210 [*Escape*]; P.322 [*Guest given refuge*]; S.172 [*Mutilation: nose cut off*]; V.465.1 [*Incontinence of clergy*].

¶ This is another of the Fen tales on the wickedness and incontinence of the clergy. See "How Littleport began", "The Nun's Ring".

THE PRIMROSE PEERLESS

Ruth L. Tongue, *Somerset Folklore*, p. 202.

In a field near the church grows or grew a colony of these lovely flowers —nor were any others to be found on Mendip.

The tale is a sad one.

A Crusader came home to Churchill after years of the heat and blood-shed in the Holy Land. He had gone away rich; he came home poor, but he had brought his beloved wife a carefully cherished present— two bulbs of the Primrose Peerless. She had always loved rare flowers.

Alas, when he reached Churchill the primroses on her grave were blooming for the fourth time. In his despair, he flung the precious bulbs over the churchyard wall and, falling beside his lady's grave, died of a broken heart.

Throughout the centuries, the bulbs have grown and flourished and kept his memory alive.

Another version of the story is to be found at Churchill:

Sir Thomas Latch returned from journeying abroad in the Civil War on the very day that his dear wife died of the plague. As he gazed upon her, his own heart broke and he also died where he stood.

There is a most dramatic painted tomb in the church and the whole tale is set out in local verse, but, as the villagers still say, "It don't explain they bewtivull vlowers."

Churchill.

MOTIFS: T.80 [*Tragic love*]; F.1041.1.1 [*Death from broken heart*].

THE PRIOR OF BURSCOUGH [summary]

J. Roby, *Traditions of Lancashire*, I, p. 64.

Burscough Priory, founded in the reign of Richard I for the Black Canons by Robert Fitzhenry, Lord of Latham, stood about two miles from Ormskirk, on the Preston Road. It had great wealth and influence, and a charter of Edward II granted it a weekly market, and a yearly fair, lasting five days.

In the Patent Rolls (fol. 155, art. 13) is contained a free pardon granted by Edward III to a certain Prior Thomas of Burscough, the cause of which is believed to have been as follows:

The Prior had abducted and violated a beautiful girl, Margaret de la Bech, who was companion to Isobel, daughter of Sir Thomas Lathom of Ormskirk. It was given out that she had gone mad from unrequited love, and drowned herself, in the moat of the castle; and some of her clothing had been found on the bank. But no search ever revealed her drowned body, and the whole circumstances of her disappearance appeared so suspicious that at last a knight named Michael de Poininges resolved to renew the search, and to begin by demanding an interview with the Prior, Thomas de Litherland, himself.

He had almost reached the Priory when his way was blocked, in a narrow woodland path, by a woman of strange and wild appearance, who startled him by speaking his name, though it was many years since he had visited the place, and he had thought that none would recognize him. The woman warned him that the Prior would give him no help, and, seeing that he was determined to go forward (for he thought she could have no true knowledge of his secret purpose), she said slowly, as though in solemn warning of some threatened danger, that they should "meet again at suppertime", and before he could reply, she had vanished among the thick trees of the forest.

De Poininges was admitted to the Priory without question, as were all who sought shelter there, and he found the monks seated at supper, but the Prior was not among them. It was his custom to remain in his own room, save when attendance at chapel compelled him to leave it. De Poininges, however, was led by a monk to his presence, but received only a brusque acknowledgement of his greeting, and a demand to state his business. This he declined to do until they were alone. The Prior briefly bade the attendant monk to leave them, and then repeated his question. De Poininges replied that he held a warrant to search for the body of Margaret de la Bech, for there was much ground to suppose that she was alive and being held captive against her will. The prior heard him out, but angrily denied all knowledge or responsibility in the matter; then he attempted to persuade de Poininges to stay in the Priory that night. But the other declined courteously, and made his way back to Ormskirk, from where he had planned to begin his search. There, as he crossed the churchyard, he met with Thomas the clerk and, knowing him for a popular and active member of the community, he took him with him to the inn, and over their ale persuaded him to go over the tale of the missing lady, asking what grounds there might be for thinking her still alive. The clerk reluctantly replied that she was indeed dead, for he had heard her ghost wailing and shrieking in the woods around the Priory, and especially near a great granary that stood near the Priory mill. Under great pressure, and a generous bribe, he unwillingly led de Poininges to the place, muttering prayers and chants all the while in his terror, and at last confessed that one night, when engaged with a companion in stealing the Prior's corn, he had seen four men, apparently servants of the Prior, carrying a woman, and that they had left the granary, without observing the two thieves, by an underground passage, the entrance to which was concealed under a pile of turf. De Poininges, convinced that the woman had been Margaret de la Bech, began to seek for this passage, but before they could find it they were interrupted by a woman's voice singing in wild snatches, which the knight recognized as that of the woman he had met earlier in the woods. The clerk cried, "It is crazy Isabel," and shrank from approaching her. She seemed unaware of his presence and he was turning away in despair when she suddenly spoke, and setting the clerk to keep watch, she led the knight to a heap of loose earth, and moving it away, led him down a winding and broken stairway by a long passage, wet with slime and lined with stone coffins, to another stair which took them to an arched gateway with an unbarred door, opening into a cell where he saw a woman lying on a wretched pallet of straw. It was indeed Margaret de la Bech, but so wasted and crazed that she showed no sense of his presence, even when he lifted and carried her away from that dreadful place.

As they reached the barn, Isabel, waving a torch wildly towards the entrance, cried to them to ride away without pausing, for the pursuit would soon be upon them. Even as they reached the first shelter of the woods, a random arrow struck down and killed the clerk, and a second with better aim struck de Poininges to the ground with a mortal wound. Crying out to his attendants only the woman's name, and that the Prior was her ravisher, he died at once, and his body was borne away to burial, and Margaret to safe keeping for the rest of her life. No vengeance was ever taken upon the Prior. His great influence, and the fear of a scandal in the Church, were his salvation; yet the evidence of his guilt was so clear that all knew and shunned him for hatred of the deed.

MOTIFS: K.2280 [*Treacherous churchmen*]; R.10.1 [*Maiden abducted*]; R.45.3 [*Captivity in cave*]; R.111 [*Rescue of captive maiden*].
¶ The same opinion of the evil conduct of churchmen is to be found in *Tales of the Fens*. See "Bulldog Bridge" (B, IX).

THE PRIOR OF KIRKHAM'S HORSE

Parkinson. *Yorkshire Legends and Traditions*, 1st series, p. 36.

In the City of York there came to wait upon the Archbishop of Armagh a man of noble parentage, William, Prior of the Brothers Regular at Kirkham, who, seeing that the Archbishop had many in his company, and but few horses to carry them, offered him his own, only adding that he was sorry that it had been bred a draught-horse, and that its paces were somewhat rough. "I would gladly offer you a better," said he, "if I had one, but if you will be contented to take the best I have, it may go with you." "I accept it most willingly," said the prelate, "because you say that it is worth little." Turning then to his attendants, he said, "Saddle me the horse, for it is a seasonable present, and it is likely to serve me long." When saddled he mounted it, and though at first he found its pace rough, after a little time, by a marvellous change, the motion became pleasant, and as gentle an amble as he could desire. And that no word that he had spoken might fall to the ground, the same animal never failed him for more than eight years. And what made the miracle more apparent was that from iron-grey the horse began to grow white, so that not long after you could not find a horse more perfectly white than this had become.

MOTIF: Q.41 [*Politeness rewarded*].

THE PRIOR AND THE NUN

Ruth L. Tongue, *Somerset Folklore*, p. 201–2.

This is the heart-breaking tale of ill-starred lovers that still lingers near Langport and the Levels.

He was the youngest son of an impoverished house and she was the daughter of a wealthy knight, and so their wedding was not to be thought of. She was sent away, and he was told that she had been married to a rich nobleman of her parents' choice. In his despair he entered a monastery —some say it was Glastonbury Abbey—and because he needed to direct his sorrow he worked so well for the Church that he became the Prior of Westover. And here, after years of struggle, Fate again took a hand, for among the nuns in his charge was none other than his lost love. She had refused to marry and had preferred to become a nun for his memory's sake. And now they met face to face, and both found their love was a stronger thing than vows made in unhappiness to the Church. There was an underground passage or cellar-way where they met in stealth and planned their escape. Alas, they were spied upon and reported. On the very night that the Prior was preparing to escape he was removed to a far-off monastery without a word of explanation or time to get a warning to the unfortunate nun. She, waiting in the cellar-way for her lover's arrival, was seized there and bricked up in it. Whether the Prior ever learned what had happened to his true love is not on record.

Muchelney.
Local traditions reported by a Bruton friend 1922–30. A similar tale is told of the Old Abbey House, Barnwell, Cambridge.

MOTIFS: T.80 [*Tragic love*]; Q.455 [*Walling-up as punishment*].

¶ Walling-up in common tradition was the punishment for unchastity in a nun. This punishment is given literary treatment in Scott's *Marmion*. For a comic treatment of the subject see "Brother Jucundus" (A, IV).

RAVEN CASTLE [summary]

J. Roby, *Lancashire Traditions*, I, pp. 429–55.

Some time in the seventeenth century, Sir Harry Fairfax, the lord of Raven Castle, had ridden away to the German wars, and before departing he entrusted the care of all his lands, his wife and their two young children to his trusted secretary and friend, Hildebrand Wentworth. In case of their death, Wentworth was to succeed to the estate.

Soon after her husband's departure, Lady Fairfax became a prey to sorrow, and refused all comfort or company. One day she disappeared from the castle, and search revealed her mantle and headgear lying beside the river. Her body was not found, but all believed that she had put an end to her life.

Four years passed, and no word came from Sir Harry, so that in time he also was presumed to have died. Only the lives of the two children now lay between Wentworth and the succession. He was cruel and avaricious, and he contrived with two rough fellows of the neighbourhood to carry off the children, pretending to have had news of a plot against their lives, and that they were being conveyed to a safer place. The children's old nurse, Alice, who had cared for them entirely since their mother's death, pleaded in vain to be allowed to go with them. They rode away, fearless and full of their adventure, but Wentworth had secretly instructed the worst of the two ruffians to make away with them in a certain wild gulf at the foot of a waterfall.

When the other man discovered this treachery, the children had already won his heart. As they reached the place he attempted to wrest the knife from the other's grasp. A fierce fight followed; at the end of it, the murderer was flung headlong by his opponent into the raging water below them. The other looked round to find the children—they were nowhere to be seen.

Hildebrand Wentworth had not long to enjoy his triumph. A stranger arrived at the castle, and, showing him Fairfax's signet ring, told him that its owner was not dead, but had been held prisoner in a castle in Germany. He had recovered from the wound which had been thought to be mortal, and had now sent this messenger to bring him certain papers by means of which he might be exchanged for another prisoner.

Even now Wentworth's ingenious wickedness sought a way out.

He dismissed the messenger and, under pretence of seeking for the papers in a secret drawer, indicated by the stranger, he forged documents purporting to convict Sir Harry of cowardice and treachery, substituted these for the other papers, and dispatched the foreigner with them to the king, to whom he was bound on the next stage of his mission.

Wentworth had never heard certain news from the two assassins of the children's death, and he now set out to find them. Instead, he found the children themselves, alive and well, tenderly cared for by old Alice, and, stranger still, by their mother. She had fled from the castle to escape from Wentworth's attempts to make her his wife, remaining always in communication with old Alice and hidden in a ruined tower near to her old home.

Alice had informed her of the news that her husband was alive. They had contrived to send him a message, and were hourly expecting his return. Confronted by the truth, Wentworth would have stabbed or put them to some other death, but the sound of horses outside stayed his hand, and Sir Harry Fairfax rode in. His wife had secretly entered the castle and obtained the papers necessary to procure his release. In anguish, Wentworth rushed from the ruined tower, and with one leap, hurled himself into the waters below.

MOTIFS: K.2297 [*Treacherous friend*]; K.512 [*Compassionate executioner*]; T.96 [*Reunion of lovers after many adventures*]; Q.261 [*Treachery punished*].
¶   Like all Roby's stories, this is a good deal decorated.
    See "Clitheroe Castle".

THE RAVENS

J. R. W. Coxhead, *The Devil in Devon*, p. 39.

A great many years ago a young couple lived with their little baby in a small cottage not far from Blackingstone Rock.

One lovely sunny day in July, the woman was sitting in the garden rocking the child to sleep in its cradle while her husband was away at work on a neighbouring farm. Suddenly, she heard the distant sound of bells ringing, and realized that it was fair day at Moretonhampstead. The baby was now sleeping peacefully, so the young mother, unable to resist the temptation aroused by the merry pealing of the bells, and thinking that no harm could befall her little child, slipped quietly away to the fair. She had not been gone long when three great ravens swooped down into the garden, seized the sleeping baby and flew away with it towards Blackingstone Rock.

It was late in the afternoon when the young woman returned to the cottage, and found, to her grief and alarm, that the cradle was empty. She hunted high and low, and was soon joined by her husband on his return from work, but all their efforts met with no success, and with darkness falling the sorrowful couple were forced to abandon the search.

The following morning, helped by kindly neighbours, they scoured the countryside around the cottage in the hope of finding the lost child. At length, as a last resort, someone suggested that they should look on top of the great Blackingstone Rock, and there, in a raven's nest they found the baby, or what was left of it, picked to the bone.

Stricken with shame and remorse, the poor woman cursed the day that she foolishly left her baby unprotected for the sake of going to Moretonhampstead Fair.

From *Transactions of the Devonshire Association*, XC, p. 242.
MOTIFS: A.1579.1 [*Children not to be left alone while asleep*]; R.13.3.1 [*Abduction by ravens*].

THE RAVENS AND THE WRECKER

Baring-Gould, *The Vicar of Morwenstowe*, 1876, p. 117.

There was once a noted old wrecker named Kinsman; he lived in my father's time; and when no wreck was around, he would get his wages by raising stone in a quarry by the sea-shore. Well, he was to work one day over yonder, half-way down the Tower Cliff, when all at once he saw two old Ravens flying round and round very near his head. They dropped down into the quarry two pieces of wreck-candle, just at the old man's feet. (Very often wreckers pick up Neapolitan wax-candles from vessels in the Mediterranean trade that have been lost in the Channel.) So when Kinsman saw the candles, he thought in his mind, "There is surely wreck coming in upon the beach." So he packed his tools together and left them just where he stood, and went his way wrecking. He could find no jetsam, however, though he searched far and wide. Next day he went back to the quarry to his work. And he used to say it was as true as a proverb—there the tools were, all buried out of sight, for the crag had given way, and if he had tarried an hour longer he must have been crushed to death! So you see, sir, what knowledge those ravens must have had; how well they knew the old man, and how dearly fond he was of wreck; how crafty they were to hit upon the only plan that would have shocked him away.

Told to Hawker of Morwenstowe by Tony Cleverdon.
MOTIFS: B.122 [*Bird with magic wisdom*]; B.451.5 [*Helpful raven*].

THE RED COW OF ORIOR

T. G. F. Paterson, *Contributions to Ulster Folk-life.*

The Pass* wus the haunt of a famous red cow in the oul' days. She wus the pride of the place, an' many a narrow escape she had, for it wus well known she wus.

An' she had a special place for drinkin' in a well of her own, an' her hoofmarks wur plain on the rocks where she went down to drink.

An' she wus a great milker—the whole of Orior† got their milk from her, but there wus a fool of a man from Louth who said one day he would test her. An' he milked her intill a riddle. An' after he had milked for days she huffed, an' nobody seen her more—she left in a rage an' niver came back.

MOTIFS: D.1652.3.1 [*Cow with inexhaustible milk*]; C.918.1 [*Marvellous cow, offended, disappears*].
¶ See "The Dun Cow of Kirkham and the Old Rib".

RESURRECTION BOB [shortened]

J. R. W. Coxhead, *Devon Traditions and Fairy-tales*, pp. 83–5.

There is a cave in the limestone cliffs of Berry Head, near Brixham, that is said to have been used for the storing of contraband by a daring band of smugglers led by the celebrated Bob Elliott.

One day when the leader was laid up with a bad attack of gout, the crew of his lugger arrived with a number of kegs of brandy for which they had not been able to find room in the already well-stocked cavern.

After consulting together, the smugglers decided that the kegs should remain hidden for the time being in Bob's cottage.

In the meantime, the suspicions of the authorities had been aroused, and Preventive men called at the cottage.

They were told, however, that poor Old Bob had died during the night, so out of respect for the bereaved family, the Excise men withdrew without making any search of the cottage.

The next day an extremely large coffin arrived at the door of the cottage, and when a bystander made a remark about its unusual size he was told that Bob Elliott was an unusually large man.

During the night, three coastguards met a party of men carrying a coffin along the road leading from Brixham to Totnes. Just as they were

* *The Pass* = the gap of the North.
† *Orior* = the baronies of Upper and Lower Orior.

about to question the men, they saw what appeared to be the ghost of the dead smuggler at the rear of the procession. Overcome with superstitious terror, the coastguards fled in panic.

The next morning, the coastguards reported the incident to their highly experienced commander, whose suspicions were thoroughly aroused by the story of the ghostly escort.

The following night, the officer paid a personal visit to Bob Elliott's cottage, and as he stood listening by a window he heard the wily Bob telling a party of friends about the clever way in which he had completely outwitted the excisemen.

While the company assembled in the cottage were still roaring with laughter, the officer suddenly entered the house, and told them that he had heard the whole story. The resourceful old smuggler's confusion and dismay may well be imagined, but, beyond giving him a sound reprimand, the officer let him off scot free.

Because of this humorous episode, the leader of the Brixham smugglers was known as "Resurrection Bob" for the rest of his life.

The Coasts of Devon and Lundy Island, p. 356.
MOTIF: K.1860 [*Deception by feigned death*].
¶ See "The Smugglers and the Squire".

RICHARD GILPIN OF KENDAL

E. Bogg, *Lakeland and Ribblesdale*, pp. 223-4.

The De Gulespins, or De Gylpins, took their name from a place in Normandy, and are supposed to have emigrated to this part about the time of the Conquest. They were two brothers, Walchelin and Joscelin. According to tradition, near the close of the twelfth century, a ferocious boar, more savage and terrible than the "felon sow of Rokeby", infested this district, its den being in Scout Scar, Underbarrow, at that period situated in the depths of a dark forest which stretched west across Whitbarrow to the shores of Windermere and the mouth of the Kent and the Leven.... Pilgrims or travellers passing to and fro from Kendal (then a small place rising into importance, under the protection of a baron's stronghold), to Our Lady's Chapel, Lady's Holm, Windermere, shuddered with fear, for tales of the boar's malignant aspect and unwonted ferocity were circulated far and wide. Things came to such a state that few dared pass the neighbourhood of Underbarrow after nightfall. A champion at length stepped forth in the person of Richard de Gylpin, who tracked the infernal beast to its lair in the intricate and dense gloom of the forest; a terrific fight ensued, in which, though severely wounded, De Gylpin came off the victor, for the grisly beast was slain, and henceforth pilgrims and wayfarers were free to pass to and fro from Kendal to worship at Furness or Lady's Holm. The knight, after this exploit, took for his arms "In a Field Or, a sanglier, or Boar-sable, armed and tusked Gules", which his posterity have borne ever since.

MOTIF: B.16.2.5 [*Devastating bear killed*].
¶ See "The Wild Boar of Bishop Auckland".

RIEVAULX ABBEY AND KIRKHAM PRIORY
[summary]

Parkinson. *Yorkshire Legends and Traditions*, 1st series, p. 31.

Walter de Espec was lord of Helmsley, Kirkham, and many other fair manors in the early part of the twelfth century. His wife was Lady Adeline, and they had one son, a great horseman and hunter, whose name, like his father's, was Walter.

One morning, Lady Adeline felt a great presentiment of danger, and implored her son not to go hunting that day. But he insisted, and towards evening was seen by a wayfarer riding furiously towards the village of Firby. At a place where a spring gushed from the hillside near a wayside cross, a wild boar suddenly darted across the young man's path, causing his horse to swerve, and throw his rider. His head struck the stone at the foot of the cross, but one foot remained caught in its stirrup. The startled horse dragged him a little way, and when it stopped the young rider was dead.

The despairing father sought counsel from his brother, who was Rector of Garton and, advised by him, devoted the greater part of his estates to the founding of the Priory of Kirkham in A.D. 1122, the Abbey of Rievaulx in 1131 and that of Warden in Bedfordshire in 1136.

In 1138 Walter de Espec played a gallant part in the Battle of the Standard near Northallerton. He took the hand of the Earl of Albemarle, the English Commander, and said, "I swear on this to conquer or die on the field." "So swear we all," said all the barons. They conquered, and de Espec lived for some fifteen years more. But two years before his death he became a monk in the Abbey which he had founded at Rievaulx, where he died and was buried in 1153.

¶ Here we have another tradition of the tragic loss of a son, and the founding of an abbey to his memory.
See "Bolton Priory and the Boy of Egremond", "Wroxall Abbey".

THE RIFLED BARROW

J. R. W. Coxhead, *The Devil in Devon*, pp. 19-20.

The little village of Challacombe is situated amid the high, rolling hills of the westernmost part of Exmoor. On the summits of the surrounding bleak and windswept uplands there are many burial mounds of primitive people of a bygone age. These artificial mounds, often as much as twelve feet in height and three hundred feet in circumference, known as barrows, or tumuli, cover the ashes of warriors who lived on the Moor in the dim and distant past. Attached to one of these ancient graves there is a very strange legend.

It is said that about three hundred and fifty years ago an elderly labouring man, who had saved a little money during a lifetime of hard and honest toil, decided to build for himself a small cottage in which to end his days in peaceful seclusion.

The site chosen by the old man on which to build his cottage was a spot about a mile and a half to the northwest of the village of Challacombe. Close to the site there was a large tumulus, and, thinking that this would provide him with plenty of building material, he commenced to dig into it in order to obtain stones for the walls of his new home. He worked with great enthusiasm, and the building operations proceeded apace, with the result that a large hole soon extended deep into the heart of the barrow.

One day, as he was busy getting stones from the cavity in the tumulus, he suddenly found his progress impeded by what looked like a roughly built wall. Filled with feverish excitement, he began to attack the wall with his pick in an effort to break through to the treasure he felt sure was concealed somewhere behind it. After working for some considerable time, he at length managed to make a hole in the wall sufficiently large to reveal a small chamber containing an earthenware pot. Overjoyed at the sight, he set to work with renewed energy to increase the size of the hole in order to be able to take out the vessel. As soon as his task was completed, he thrust his arm through the opening to seize the coveted prize. Just as he did so, he heard, or seemed to hear, the thudding of hooves, as though horsemen were coming towards the barrow. Stepping back from the hole for fear that the newcomers might take his treasure from him, he looked about for the riders, but to his great astonishment neither horse nor man could he see.

Somewhat disturbed by the strange incident, the old man returned to the cavity, and was just about to put his arm through the aperture in the wall when he again heard the sound of galloping horses approaching the barrow. Once more he started back, and looked all around, but to his amazement no horses were to be seen.

Although the labourer was now extremely frightened, he was loath to lose his treasure, so, gritting his teeth, he plunged into the cavity, seized the earthenware pot, and hurried away with it to his partly finished cottage. Trembling like a leaf, he sat down on a large stone, and, looking inside the vessel, found, to his great disappointment, instead of the expected hoard of golden coins, just a small heap of ashes and a few charred bones.

The terrifying experience with the invisible horses at the tumulus, or the thought that he had desecrated an ancient grave, may have preyed on the old man's mind. Be that as it may, shortly after the episode he became blind and deaf and within three months of finding the earthenware pot he died. It is said, to the day of his death he stoutly maintained that his story of the mysterious occurrence at the tumulus was perfectly true.

The old labourer's cottage probably stood somewhere near Holwell Barrow, which is situated on the moor, a little over one and a half miles to the north-west of Challacombe.

MOTIFS: E.481.3.1 [*Abode of dead in barrows*]; E.235.6 [*Return from dead to punish disturber of grave*]; E.402.2.3 [*Hoofbeats of ghost horse*].

¶ Tales of barrows and standing stones, and of the treasure hidden under them, are common in this country, particularly in the West.

See "The Wimblestones", "Robin Hood's Butts".

ROBIN HOOD'S BUTTS

Ruth L. Tongue, *Somerset Folklore*, p. 13.

Robin Hood's Butts are two sets of round barrows right up on the very top of the Blackdown Hills. Under one of these barrows is a hoard of gold, but it is no use digging for it, everyone knows that. So when a rich man brought a lot of workmen to find the treasure everybody warned them what would happen. The rich man and his labourers just laughed. They worked hard that day; they dug huge trenches and carted away great loads of earth, and propped up the trenches with heavy timber, but every time they looked at the barrows they were still the same size. They left stakes to show how far they had gone, and went home tired out. The next day only half the diggers turned up, and when they climbed to Robin Hood's Butts to carry on with yesterday's work they found that there were no stakes, no trenches, no loads of earth; the gorse was growing on all the barrows. The diggers turned and ran, but the rich man was stubborn. He picked up a spade and began digging a trench again. When at last he stood up to look at his work there was no trench and the very hole his spade had made was not there any more. He burst into tears and no one has looked for the treasure since then.

MOTIF: N.550.1 [*Continual failure to find or unearth hidden treasure*].
¶ See "Church Treasure", "The Treasure of Berry Pomeroy Castle", "The Silver Horseshoe".

ROCHDALE CHURCH

Chambers, *Popular Rhymes of Scotland*, pp. 337–8.

The Church of Rochdale in Yorkshire stands on a height. "The materials laid for the building on the spot fixed upon by Gamel, the Saxon thane, are said to have been removed by supernatural agency. This Gamel, it appears held two ludis—Recedham or Rochdale—under Edward the Confessor. The necessary preparations were made; the banks of the river groaned under the huge beams and massy stones; and all seemed to promise a speedy and successful termination. But there were those—not the less powerful because invisible to eyes of flesh and blood—who did not approve of the site, having resolved that the edifice should raise its head on the neighbouring hill. Accordingly, in one night, all was transferred to its summit. The spectacle was beheld in the morning with universal dismay!

"But the lord was not a man to be easily foiled; at his command, the materials were brought down to their former station. A watch was set; and now all appeared safe. In the morning, however, the ground was once more bare! Another attempt was rewarded by another failure. The spirits had conquered. One who knew more about them than he should have done made his appearance; and after detailing what he chose of the doings of the spirits, presented to the lord a massy ring, bearing an inscription to this purport:

> "'The Norman shall rule on the Saxon's hall,
> And the stranger shall rule o'er England's weal,
> Through castle and hall, by night and by day,
> The stranger shall thrive for ever and aye,
> But in Racheds above the rest,
> The stranger shall thrive the best.'

"In accordance with this ratiocination runs the old and now nearly obsolete remark, that 'strangers prosper, but natives are unfortunate.'"

England in the Nineteenth Century, quoting Roby's *Traditions of Lancashire*.
TYPE ML.7060. MOTIFS: D.2192 [*Work of day magically overthrown at night*]; V.111.3 [*Place where church must be built magically indicated*]; D.1076 [*Magic ring*].
¶ This is much the same as all the other tales about re-siting of a church, except for the prophetically inscribed ring.
See "The Church of Fordoun".

THE ROLLRIGHT STONES

Wright, *Folk-Lore Record*, II, pp. 165-79

There was once a king and his knights who were going to war, and it was prophesied that if ever he came in sight of Long Compton, he would be King of all England, but just as he was labouring up to the big ridge, an old witch met him, and turned him and all his men to stones, even the rebellious knights who were whispering against him. So there they stand to this day, and no one can tell the size of the army, for whoever tries to count the stones, can never count them twice the same. Many or few, they are destined to be there for ever, and ill-luck attends anyone who tries to move them. There was once a farmer who fancied one of the Whispering Knights to build into his big barn. In spite of all the neighbours could say, he yoked up his best oxen to his strongest waggon, and set to work to fetch it. It was mortal heavy, but they somehow got it on to the cart, and began the downhill way home. The oxen laboured under it as if they could hardly move, and when they had got it down to the farm-yard, they all three fell dead, and the waggon crumbled to pieces. But the farmer would have his way; he built the knight into his wall, and from that moment he never had a bit of good fortune. He had to mortgage his land and sell his stock, till in the end he had nothing left but one poor old shaky horse, and a ricketty cart that no one would buy. Then at last it came into his head what anyone could have told him, that all his misfortunes came from that stone. He pulled it out of the wall like a desperate man, and levered it on to the cart. He hitched up the old shaky horse and it stepped out like a four-year old all the way up the hill at a smart pace. The farmer dropped the stone back into its socket, and set off home again with a light heart. And after that his luck turned, and in a few years he was as rich as he had ever been. But he never meddled with old stones again.

MOTIF: D.231(*a*) [*Insurgent leader and his knights are turned into stones by a witch, to keep him from fulfilling old prophecy of dethroning the king and becoming king himself*] (Baughman)

¶ The Whispering Knights are still said to go down to the stream to drink on the night of the full moon.

Informant, Frank Pearman, Burford, 1947.

See "The Evil Wedding" (B, III), "The Wimblestone".

ST AGNES'S WELL

Ruth L. Tongue, *Somerset Folklore*, pp. 23–4.

Most of the saints' wells were curative, but there was a wishing well amongst them, and St Agnes's Well at Cothelstone was resorted to by lovers. This is not surprising, for St Agnes's Eve was traditionally one for love divination, but St David seems occasionally to have played the same part, if we may judge by the following story, told me by two old sisters who had been born at Bagborough and had returned there on a visit when I saw them:

"There were a maid-servant, see, and she were coming on in years and she do serve a farmer's wife as were high in station. Proper tacka-lackey she made of the dear soul and she having no living kin. 'Twas pitiful, and her a-longing for a parcel of children underfoot, even if 'twas only to call her Auntie. But there, 'twadn't to be, and her with a heart so full a-drip with loving kindness as a honey-comb. Oh, she were a proper mannerly maiden, no ways like her mistress, who were just a old ewe dressed up lamb's fashion and spending her days living two-three steps from nothing. But it didn't seem like the maiden couldn't never meet up with a proper man for her. She wadn't no summer morning to look at, poor soul, and her mistress kept her so thin as a yard of pump water. But there, Providence knows best! There were an old fellow over by Aisholt, and he were such a upstanding courageous man he'd a never got round to marrying, let alone finding the bravery to walk arm-in-crook with a maiden. Well, o' course he were lonely like she. And it come to a St Agnes's Eve when maids creepy over to her well at Cothelstone and whisper their heart's desire when 'tis dark, and if St Agnes do fancy the maiden she'll send a husband that year. Now, the poor maid, she were coming to the end of her days of womanhood and beginning to blossom about the head, and she were desperate unhappy about it. Her heart was all a-set on children and she find bravery to slip out after farm's a-locked up. She didn't feel 'twere mannerly to worrit St Agnes over one who was so on in years when there was young maidens as plentiful as blackberries, so what do the dear soul do but go down all in the dimmet to the Wishing Well in Seven Wells Combe. Proper unket well 'tis, and hard tew find. But St Agnes must ha' knowed, for she found'n, though there wadn' but little moon, and old fellow he d'hear summat down in coombe and come to look-see. He were a wise old man and nothing hurted he, but he were shy of folks, seems like. Well, whether 'twere St Agnes I can't say, but in a year the farm was sold up and the maid was a-wed to the old fellow. So quiet as a sheep the man was, wouldn' downarg no one, but he made her a good husband. In a year or two she'd a babe in the cradle and one under her apron, and two clinging to her skirts, and they was all so happy as daisies in the sunshine, so they say. But there, 'they say so is half a liar'."

TYPE 1476. MOTIFS: D.926 [*Magic well*]; D.1761 [*Magic results produced by wishing*].

THE SALE OF A WIFE [summary]

Thompson Notebooks, X.

A cobbler at Blackburn used to ill-treat his wife shockingly, though she was a very decent woman. One day he put a halter round her, and said he was going to sell her. She was ready enough. He put her up to auction and people began to bid in fun, but there was one decent old man who liked the look of her very much. He had no money, but borrowed 2s. from a shopkeeper and, when that was not enough, 2s. 6d.

He got the wife, and she said she was glad to go to him, and said, "You've got me and everything about me, I expect." He said, he didn't care for that, as long as he'd got her. But she put her hand in her bosom, and pulled out a bag with £200 in it. The old man bought a little business with it, and she was set up for life.

The people used to sing at the cobbler:

"Oh Mister Duckworth,
You are a cure.
You sold your wife for beer,
And live at [Cuckold's] Moor."

From Taimi Boswell, Oswaldtwistle, 10 January, 1915.
MOTIFS: T.292 [*Wife sold by husband*]; N.421 [*Lucky bargain*].
¶ It was widely believed in country places that if a man put a halter round his wife, and offered her in the market for half-a-crown, he would be quit of her if he could find a purchaser. An incident exemplifying this belief occurred in Burford (Oxfordshire) in the mid-nineteenth century. A man living in a house near the bridge bought a wife for half-a-crown. Public opinion was against him, and he was serenaded with "rough music". He dashed out with a pitchfork and drove some of the crowd into the river, but the feeling against him was too strong, and he had to send his wife back to her husband in the end. In this tale the purchaser was more fortunate, and the "rough music" was directed against the first husband.
Informant, Mrs Groves, Shipton-under-Wychwood, from her father, G. P. Hambridge.

SALTED DOWN

Theo Brown, *Tales of a Dartmoor Village*, p. 19.

The most famous story connected with this building [The New Horse Inn, Postbridge] was that of the innkeeper who died there one winter when the inn was cut off by snow for many weeks. Eventually the snow melted, and the little daughter struggled into Widecombe to ask the Vicar to arrange for the funeral. "I am so sorry of hear of this, my dear," said the Vicar. "Which day did he die?" "Oh dear," said the little girl, thinking hard. "It must be all of six weeks last Sunday."

"Good heavens!" exclaimed the innocent cleric. "How really appalling. We must get on with the funeral."

"Oh, I don't think there's any need for haste," replied the child calmly. "It happened very lucky like. We'd just killed the pig and we was saltin' 'un down, so Mother, 'er put Father in tu."

Offprint from *Transactions of the Devonshire Association*, XLIII, 1961.

¶ See Mrs Bray, *On the Borders of Tamar and Tavy*, I, pp. 27–33. Baring-Gould, *The Vicar of Morwenstowe*, tells the same story.

See also "The Sons who salted Their Father's Corpse" (A, III.)

SCOONIE BURN

Wilkie, *Bygone Fife*, p. 149.

The rain had been heavy among the hills, and the burn had taken on the appearance of a river. A great waggon piled with sacks of grain approached, and the driver saw nothing for it but to attempt the passage. He accordingly whipped up the reluctant horses. But the wain stuck firmly in the middle of the ford, and, despite its weight, was in danger of being washed down the foaming torrent. The horses were cut loose, and scrambled out a little farther down. The Gudeman of Scoonie had seen the struggle to extricate the heavy vehicle, and he now announced that his four boys would accomplish the task. They were accordingly summoned, and they rushed down from the steading. In a trice they had entered the dun and raging stream and almost as quickly as it takes to tell they had tossed the sacks into safety and pulled the empty waggon well out of the water. Each of the four sons was six feet six inches in stature, and of strength to match his height.

MOTIF: N.832.2 [*Sons as helpers*].

¶ This motif, and indeed the series in which it occurs, is generally applied to a less naturalistic tale, such as TYPE 551 (*The sons seek a magical remedy for their father*).

343

Local legends do, however, often preserve the memory of a family of exceptionally strong brothers, such as the twelve sons of the Duke of Atholl, whose great bed is preserved in Blair Castle, Blair Atholl.

THE SELBYS OF CUMBERLAND
[summarized extract]

A. Cunningham, *Traditional Tales of the English and Scottish Peasantry*, I, p. 59.

In the days when the Stuart kings were in exile, Lady Eleanor Selby was betrothed to her cousin, Walter Selby. They had been out hunting all one long day, and stopped in the evening at Wilton Hall, the home of David Forrester, overlooking Soutrafell. As they sat resting in the evening sunshine, a pedlar arrived with a pack-horse, heavily laden, and a tall, strong man, the owner of the horse, walking behind. He carried a measuring rod of oak, spiked with iron at the lower end, and mounted with brass at the other, which would serve well either to measure or to defend his property. Being greeted as an old acquaintance, and promised lodging for the night, this stranger sat down, and made to open a small casket which he had placed beside him on the grass. The servants at once began to ply him with questions about the state of things in the North, and whether it was true that the Highlanders were soon coming to try to seize for themselves the crown of England. But the stranger, whom they addressed as Simon Packpin, made no immediate reply, but went on taking out his wares from his box, humming to himself, and presently breaking into a strange song, of which the last stanza ran:

> "The cuckoo is a princely bird,
>   And we will wait awhile,
> And welcome him with shout and song
>   In the morn of green April;
> We'll lay our things o'er our good steeds,
>   And gird our claymores on,
> And chase away the hooded crows
>   That croak around the throne."

To those staunch supporters of the forbidden Stuart cause this told much; then the strange pedlar addressed Eleanor Selby, and begged her to accept a cross and rosary made of some dark wood, and decorated with gold, which he took from his pack, telling her that it was no common wood, for a princess had sat under its shade, and seen her kingdom won and lost—and he bade her wear it until she saw a kingdom long lost won back as bravely as ever the Selbys had won their lands of old.

Walter Selby now whispered to Eleanor that the so-called pedlar was in truth a knight who had come to summon them all to march against Preston, and that his pack concealed good swords and knives of steel. He turned to the knight, and asked his name; but the knight gave no reply, and as they talked, Eleanor gazed from the window, and saw, riding down the side of Soutra fell, a body of horsemen where no horse had ever stood. She cried out at the sight, and the others, turning to her, saw it also. Walter Selby exclaimed in delight at the gallant sight, but the others trembled, for they knew that this apparition never appeared but as a presage of disaster. The leaders of the troop all wore earls' coronets, and among them the watchers could pick out many of the Jacobite champions—Maxwells, Gordons, Boyds, Drummonds, Ogilvys, Camerons, Scotts, Foresters, and Selbys.

Eleanor, with grief and horror, made out the form of Walter Selby himself, who sat by the fire, till he sprang up, recognized his counterpart, and was barely prevented by her from addressing it. She fainted, and he caught her in his arms.

They left the house where they had been resting, and about midnight heard a horn sounded a little ahead of them. Walter now begged Eleanor to turn back, but she was resolved to ride on with him, and, unable to resist her pleading, he told her the true meaning of the "pedlar's" songs and words, and how he was confident that nothing but success awaited them at Preston. They were now joined by a newcomer, who proved to be no other than the "pedlar" himself, now free of his disguise, who was in fact Sir Thomas Scott, a valiant knight of great fame. Presently another rider came up with them, an old man on an old horse, who sang as they rode a song in praise of the Selbys. The words and his voice recalled Lady Eleanor's thoughts to her childhood, and suddenly she knew the man for an old soldier of her father's, Harpur Harberson by name. He had heard of the phantom troop on Soutra, and resolved to ride out once more, for the last time, as he believed it must be, in defence of the Selbys.

As they rode, they were joined by many other adherents of the Stuart cause, and met with no serious opposition on their road to Preston. When the battle was joined, Eleanor was led away to shelter with other ladies. Her grief was turned to joy when Walter Selby and Sir Thomas Scott returned safe from the fight. Sir Thomas had saved the young man's life. But conflicting rumours reaching the house soon made it clear that the victory was by no means certain, and presently the two men left the house again, Sir Thomas to lead a charge which was to anticipate the expected attack of the enemy. But it was too late; the enemy, under Captain Willis, broke into the town at two points, and an ignominious surrender of the cavaliers followed, to the grief and shame of the Highland troops. Sir Thomas and Selby, now again joined by Eleanor, were making for the woods, for they were resolved not to give in, when, about dawn, they were waylaid by a body of Colonel Preston's dragoons. In a fierce skirmish, Walter Selby was killed, and his head was cut off and carried away to be displayed on the gate of Carlisle. Eleanor followed, distraught with grief, she entreated the sentries to give her one lock of her lover's hair, but none of them dared do it, until on a wild night of rain and thunder, as she still stood gazing up at the dreadful head, she thought she saw a human form at its side, and a flash of lightning revealed that it was Sir Thomas Scott, who had heard of her vain quest, and to ease her pain had come from a distant place, severed a lock of the hair and brought it to her, with the assurance that his body had been recovered and honourably buried, and the head taken down from the gate, that his enemies might know that so valiant and faithful a warrior was not without true friends.

TYPE ML.8000 MOTIFS: E.723.8 [*Appearance of wraith as calamity omen*]; E.723.7.7 [*Wraith rides horse*]; E.501.20.1 [*Wild hunt as omen of disaster*]; S.139.2.2.1 [*Heads of slain enemies impaled upon stakes*].

THE SEVEN CROSSES

J. R. W. Coxhead, *Legends of Devon*, pp. 27–9.

Isabella de Fortibus, Countess of Devon...was the heiress of the powerful and wealthy family of De Redvers, thereby being Countess of Devon in her own right.

One of her greatest possessions was the Isle of Wight. Her chief residence was Carisbrooke Castle, where she lived in great state.

The most charming of the legends in which the Countess plays a part is connected with a spot situated at the hamlet of Hensleigh, near Tiverton, and known as the "Seven Crosses".

The circumstances giving rise to the legend are supposed to have occurred at some period between the years 1262 and 1293.

The story opens with the Countess staying at her manor of Tiverton on a short visit. One day, as she was taking a walk in the direction of Hensleigh, she met a tailor carrying a large basket.

As the man was passing she heard a whimpering sound coming from the basket, so she called to the man to stop, and asked him to tell her what the basket contained. "Only seven little puppies, that I am going to drown in the Exe," he replied.

"I want a dog," said Isabella. "Open the basket and let me have a look at them."

The tailor made all sorts of excuses in order to avoid having to open the basket, but the Countess insisted on him doing so, and when the lid was raised seven little baby boys were revealed to Isabella's astonished gaze.

"Alas, my lady!" cried the poor tailor. "My wife gave birth to all seven at once, and, as we are so poor, it is quite impossible for us to afford to care for them."

Seeing that they were all fine, healthy babies, the kind-hearted Countess told the tailor to take them back home to his wife, as all would be well, because she, the Countess of Devon, would pay for their upbringing and education.

As soon as the boys were old enough, the Countess sent them to Buckfast Abbey to be trained for the priesthood. They were eventually ordained, and four of them became rectors of the four parts of Tiverton, while the remaining three brothers became their curates.

Because they had all been born together, the seven brothers loved each other dearly and lived in perfect harmony until the end of their days. They all died on the same day, and were buried in the same grave at the spot where their lives were saved by the good Countess of Devon. Seven crosses were placed over the grave, to mark where they lay, but the crosses have long since disappeared.

According to the legend, the only time when the rectors and curates of the four parts of Tiverton have not disagreed was during the time the seven brothers occupied these positions.

Isabella de Fortibus...died at her mansion at Stockwell, near Lambeth, on November 9th, 1293, and her body was buried in the Priory of Braemore.

MOTIF: T.586.1.2 [*Seven children at a birth*].

¶ The beginning of this tale was given me orally by Miss Theo Brown. The father of these seven children had already been father to a large family which he was too poor to support. He had not enough self-control to limit his family, so decided that his only course was to leave his wife and wander about looking for work for a time.

He was away for seven whole years, and at the end of it, he and his wife came together again with great joy and the result was a sevenfold birth. It was after this that he decided to drown the children.

THE SHEEP-STEALERS OF THE
BLACKDOWN HILLS

Ruth L. Tongue, *Somerset Folklore* , p. 49.

There was once a sheep-stealer who had just killed a fat ewe on Blackdown and tied a rope round it to drag it away, when he heard a wood quest begin to talk. "Take two-o-o" it said, "Take two-o-o." "That's good advice," said the thief. "Two will balance better nor one."

So he killed another, and tied the two sheep together and slung them round him, one in front, one behind, and away he went. He got on well enough until he came to the stile at Hangman's Stone, and then, as he was climbing over, the front sheep swung behind him, and the rope slipped up round his neck, and there he hung, a hanged man.

Now, this thief had a brother, who was nearly as bad as he. For a time he kept straight after his brother had been hanged, but by and by he fell off into his old ways. One morning he went up to Blackdown, just where his brother had gone, and he was stealing up to one of the sheep when a wood-quest began to cry again. This time it said, "Rope, r-r-rope! Hang the man!" When the sheep-stealer heard that he ran home as fast as could pelt, and never went sheep-stealing again.

From Sampford Arundel.

TYPE 1322A* (variant). MOTIFS: Q.424.5* [*Sheep-thief is strangled as he rests sheep on post behind him, etc.*] (Baughman); J.1811 [*Animal cries misunderstood*]; A.2426.2 [*Cries of birds*].

¶ See "The Hangman's Stone", "The Wedderstone".

THE SILVER HORSESHOE

Ruth L. Tongue, *Somerset Folklore*, p. 189.

Cadbury Castle be King Arthur's Camelot! Never mind what other folk say! The river near it be the Cam and they two villages is Queen Camel and West Camel. There's King Arthur's Well, so fine a wishing well as you could ask you heart's dear thought at; there's King Arthur's Palace, or the grass-grown mounds of it, and down below there's a drove that goes all the way to Glastonbury and 'tis called King Arthur's Hunting Causeway—so what more do 'ee want?

There's gentlemen say Glastonbury be Avalon, where the great King goed when he got his death-stroke and the barge come for him, and Glastonbury men do boast as he and his bewtifull Queen, poor fulish dear, was burred there.

Then why deny as Cadbury be Camelot? Surely *us* knows best!

Would you believe it, they didn't listen when us told 'en how every seven year on Midsummer Eve the door in the hill do open. And then King Arthur and all the Knights of the Round Table do come riding along the Causeway with lights to their spears, and their horses shod with silver shoes.

No, they wouldn't hear on it—and then one of the gurt fules went a-digging for to find the Round Table—not likely! It just went a-sinking down away out of reach, so it did—but he found a silver horseshoe! That showed 'en.

West Camel and Queen Camel; Cadbury Castle.
Oral tradition, 1906–29; oral collection, Rev. E. Skelton and a gardener, Stoke-under-Ham, 1907.
MOTIFS: D.1960.2 [*King asleep in mountain*]; D.1960.2.1 [*King asleep in mountain will awake when his horse's shoes are worn down*].

SIMMER WATER*

S. O. Addy, *Household Tales*, p. 61.

A long time ago there was a village in the North Riding of Yorkshire called Simmerdale, at one end of which stood a church, and the house of a Quaker woman at the other end. It happened one day that a witch came into the village, and, beginning at the house next to the church, asked for food and drink, but her request was refused. And so she went on from house to house, without getting either food or drink, until at last she came to the Quaker woman's House. There, sitting in the porch, she was regaled with bread, meat, and beer. Having finished her repast, she rose and waved an ash twig over the village, saying:

"Simmerdale, Simmerdale, Simmerdale, sink,
Save the house of the woman who gave me to drink."

When the witch had said these words the water rose in the valley and covered the village, except the old woman's house. Simmer Water is now a peaceful lake, and on fine clear days people in the neighbourhood fancy that they can see down in its placid depths the ruins of the village and the church.

Gutch, *County Folk-Lore*, II, North Riding, etc., p. 37.
T. Whellan, *History and Topography of the City of York and the North Riding of Yorkshire.* vol. II, p. 403, gives the date of this story as "previous to the year of grace 45", and the wayfarer is not a witch, but variously given as an angel, St Paul, Joseph of Arimathea, or Our Saviour in the form of a poor old man.
TYPE 750A.I. MOTIFS: K.1811 [*Gods (saints) in disguise visit mortals*]; Q.1.1 [*Gods (saints) in disguise reward hospitality and punish inhospitality*]; A.920.1.8 [*Lake bursts forth to drown impious people*].
¶ See "Bomere Pool".

SIMON'S BATH

Ruth L. Tongue, *Somerset Folklore*, p. 200.

Old Simon was a wild robber who roamed all over Exmoor, and people in the farms and villages were afraid for their dear lives what he would be after next. So they sent the dodman† to bring them back a saint to go and talk to Simon.

* Semer Water, or Simmer Lake, is near Askrig in the North Riding.
† *Dodman* = Pedlar.

The dodman came back with a Cornish saint who was on the look-out for sinners, and as for being afraid of Simon, he was just aching to meet him. So he went out over the moor alone and there he met the robber, but he was so friendly and unafraid that Simon began to listen, and in the end he wanted to be a Christian. "Then I'll baptize you," said the Saint. "There's a nice deep pool in the Barle over there." "Wouldn't somewhere a bit shallower do?" says Simon. "Tisn' the right time o' year for bathing. There's a 'lazy wind'* and 'twas a 'coat colder' this morning when I woke."

But no, the Saint was adamant. "Deep water for sins as deep as yours," says he, so in Simon went, and it was icy. "Will one bath be enough, zur?" he says, with his teeth chattering like cankervells.† But the Saint was a cunning man, and he looked at the poor fields and wretched, neglected farms around and answered thoughtfully, "One will do for here now; but it will take another two to get your soul clean. We'll both go and try Cornwall—*its warmer!*"

Simonsbath, Exmoor.
Oral tradition, Simonsbath, Sandyway, Withypool; oral collection, Mr March, farmer, Kinsford, 1906.
MOTIF: V.222.16 (variant) [*Robbers who enter saint's garden are caused to spade it up for him*].

SIR BEVIS OF HAMPTON

H. Bett, *English Legends*, p. 106.

Bevis was the son of Guy, the Earl of Southampton, and his wife, who was a princess of Scotland. She was a wicked woman, and with her connivance her husband was slain by her paramour, Sir Murdour, when Bevis was a little child. Then she planned the death of her boy and charged Saber, the child's uncle, to murder him.

Saber, in proof of compliance with her command, sent her the boy's garments stained with pig's blood, but he kept the boy safe, and disguised him as a shepherd. While he fed his sheep on the downs, Bevis was maddened to hear the sounds of wild revelry in which his mother and her lover lived; one day he burst into the hall, and with three blows of a mace laid Murdour senseless before them all. He was seven years old at the time of this exploit.

The guilty mother then sent her child to be sold for a slave in heathen lands. He fell into the hands of a Saracen king named Ermyn, whose daughter Josyan at once fell in love with the young captive. Ermyn proposed to make Bevis his heir and marry him to his daughter, if he

---

* A "lazy wind" is one that can't be bothered to go round a man, so it goes through him.
† *Cankervells* = icicles.

would abjure his religion. Bevis refused, and the King made him a page, promising him advancement in the future. When he had reached the age of fifteen, some Saracen knights quarrelled with him about his religion, whereupon he slew some three score of them with astonishing ease. Ermyn forgave him for this, and a little later Bevis slew a frightful wild boar that had long been the terror of the countryside.

Presently he was dubbed a knight, and given a marvellous sword called Mortglai, and an equally marvellous horse called Arundel. Then the King of Damascus demanded Josyan's hand and threatened to lay waste Ermyn's land if his suit was refused; but Bevis easily routed the hosts of Damascus. Josyan was more deeply in love with Bevis than ever, but Bevis insisted that she must renounce her religion. When the King heard of this he was furious, and he sent Bevis on an embassy to King Bradmond, his late foe, who had sworn to be Ermyn's vassal. He was now commanded, on his allegiance, to slay the bearer of the letter which Bevis carried. When the hero came to Damascus, he found a crowd of Saracens worshipping an idol, which he contemptuously overthrew. Bevis was flung into a dungeon with two dragons to guard him. In a combat which lasted a day and a night, he slew the dragons, but he had to live upon vermin in his dungeon during a weary imprisonment.

At the end of seven years, he escaped and rode off to Josyan, whom he found still in love with him, though married to the King of Mounbraunt. Bevis introduced himself into the king's castle as a palmer, and was welcomed by Josyan for the sake of her former Christian lover, though she did not recognize him at first. Then Bevis and Josyan escaped together, meeting various adventures on the way. They encountered a brace of lions, which Bevis slew at a single blow; and they fell in with a giant named Ascapard, who, after a desperate fight, was glad to save his life by becoming Bevis's page.

Bevis now sailed to Cologne, where the bishop happened to be an uncle of his. Here Josyan and Ascapard were christened. The giant misbehaved during the ceremony, to the grief of the bishop and the amusement of the people.

Bevis then slew a fiery dragon that infested the country; and the bishop equipped him with a hundred knights, with whom he landed in Hampshire, leaving Josyan at Cologne.

He next introduced himself, disguised, into the house of Sir Murdour, and undertook to serve him against Saber, but carried off his best horses and arms to the enemy. Then Bevis had to return to Cologne to rescue Josyan from some perils which beset her. At last he joined his uncle in the Isle of Wight. Murdour was captured, and boiled into hounds' meat in a great caldron. His wicked wife, hearing of his fate, threw herself from the top of a high tower. His army laid down their arms after the death of their leader, and the citizens of Southampton hailed Bevis as their deliverer with joy.

After all this Bevis went abroad once more. Ascapard had proved faithless and had stolen Josyan from him to restore her to her Saracen lord, but after a separation of seven years all this ended happily. While Bevis was abroad, however, he had fallen into disgrace with King Edgar, who confiscated his earldom and estates. So Bevis returned to London to redress his wrongs. He had now two valiant sons, and the three of them slew some sixty thousand foes in a battle fought in the region of Temple Bar and Ludgate Hill; hence the place-name of "Bevis Marks". One of Bevis's sons became the King of England; the other ruled over a kingdom abroad; and Bevis himself returned to another of his foreign domains. Finally, Bevis, Josyan, and the horse Arundel all died within a few minutes of each other.

MOTIFS: S.12 [*Cruel mother*]; K.2213.3 [*Faithless wife plots with paramour against husband's life*]; S.12.1.1 [*Treacherous mother and paramour plot son's death*]; K.512.1 [*Compassionate executioner: bloody coat*]; S.210.1 [*Child sold into slavery*]; T.91.6.4.1 [*Sultan's daughter in love with captured knight*]; G.510.4 [*Hero overcomes devastating animal*]; R.225.2 [*Lovers elope to prevent girl's marriage to undesirable fiancé (to rescue girl from undesired husband)*]; R.151.1 [*Husband rescues stolen wife*]; N.391 [*Lover is detained away beyond stipulated time; returns to find his sweetheart married*]. ¶ More motifs might be found to this extremely long and complicated story, but these are enough to illustrate the type, which has some resemblance to the story of "Amleth, Prince of Denmark".

See "Guy of Warwick", "Hind Horn" (A, IV).

SIR EGLAMORE AND THE LADY EMMA

E. Bogg, *Lakeland and Ribblesdale*, p. 144.

Aira Force is the scene of a sad, yet romantic legend. In the far-off centuries there dwelt, at the tower adjoining the Force, a beautiful lady named Emma, betrothed to a famed knight [Sir Eglamore] who had long been engaged in war in Eastern lands.

His long absence had affected her health, and she was wont in the night-time to wander forth in her sleep by the bank of the torrent, dreaming of her lover. It was in this situation that the knight found her on his returning unexpectedly from the East. He was so struck with her appearance that he watched her for some time plucking the twigs from the trees and casting them into the stream. Uncertain how to proceed, he at length touched her; she suddenly awoke from her slumber, and, starting back affrighted, fell down the deep precipice into the water below. The knight leaped into the torrent to rescue her, and bore the inanimate form to the bank. There was a brief moment of consciousness; she opened her eyes and recognized him, and expired in his arms. The heartbroken man built a cell near the Falls, where he dwelt in solitude, humbling the flesh in prayer and fasting for the repose of her soul.

MOTIFS: T.80 [*Tragic love*]; T.24.1 [*Love-sickness*]; T.93.2 [*Disappointed lover turns hermit*].

SIR GUY THE SEEKER

H. Bett, *English Legends*, p. 6.

A knight whose name was Guy rode towards [Dunstanburgh] Castle [in Northumberland] one stormy night, and was met at the gate by a wizard, who told him of a beautiful damsel imprisoned within, and asked if he were brave enough to rescue her.

He led Sir Guy up a winding stair, and through a brazen door guarded by a serpent, into the great hall. Here were a hundred marble knights, sleeping beside their marble steeds. The lady was in a crystal tomb at the end of the hall, and besought his help with clasped hands and floods of tears. Sir Guy was then offered the choice between a falchion and a horn, and told that the damsel's fate depended upon his making the right choice. He chose the horn, and blew a blast upon it, whereupon the captive lady shrieked, and the knights and horses of stone sprang into life. Sir Guy fell into a swoon, and when he awoke he found himself by the gateway in the midst of the stormy night. All the rest of his life he sought in vain a second chance to rescue the damsel, and hence he was called Sir Guy the Seeker.

TYPE 766. MOTIFS: E.502 [*The sleeping army*]; F.182 [*Mortal held by magic in other world*]; D.1364.10 [*Dagger causes magic sleep*]; D.1222 [*Magic horn*].
¶ See "Potter Thompson", "King Arthur at Sewingshields", "The Wizard of Alderley Edge".

SIR RICHARD BAKER, SURNAMED "BLOODY BAKER"

Choice Notes from "Notes and Queries", p. 138.

The Baker family had formerly large possessions in Cranbrook, but in the reign of Edward VI great misfortunes fell on them; by extravagance and dissipation, they gradually lost all their lands, until an old house in the village (now used as the poor-house) was all that remained to them. The sole representative of the family remaining at the accession of Queen Mary was Sir Richard Baker. He had spent some years abroad, in consequence of a duel; but when, said my informant, Bloody Queen Mary reigned, he thought he might safely return, as he was a Papist. When he came to Cranbrook, he took up his abode in his old house; he only brought one foreign servant with him, and these two lived alone. Very soon strange stories began to be whispered respecting unearthly shrieks having been heard frequently to issue at nightfall from his house. Many people of importance were stopped and robbed in the Glastonbury Woods, and many unfortunate travellers were missed and never heard of more. Richard Baker still continued to live in seclusion, but he gradually re-purchased his alienated property, although he was known to have spent all he possessed before he left England. But wickedness was not always to prosper. He formed an apparent attachment to a young lady in the neighbourhood, remarkable for always wearing a great many jewels. He often pressed her to come and see his old house, telling her he had many curious things he wished to show her. She had always resisted fixing a day for her visit, but, happening to walk within a short distance of his house, she determined to surprise him with a visit; her companion, a lady older than herself, endeavoured to dissuade her from doing so, but she would not be turned from her purpose. They knocked at the door, but no one answered them; they, however, discovered it was not locked, and determined to enter. At the head of the stairs hung a parrot, which, on their passing, cried out:

> "Peepoh, pretty lady, be not too bold,
> Or your red blood will soon run cold."

And cold did run the blood of the adventurous damsel when, on opening one of the room doors, she found it filled with the dead bodies of murdered persons, chiefly women.

Just then they heard a noise, and, on looking out of the window, saw Bloody Baker and his servant bringing in the murdered body of a lady. Nearly dead with fear, they concealed themselves in a recess under the staircase.

As the murderers with their dead burden passed by them, the hand of the unfortunate murdered lady hung in the baluster of the stairs; with an oath Bloody Baker chopped it off, and it fell into the lap of one of the concealed ladies. As soon as the murderers had passed by, the ladies ran away, having the presence of mind to carry with them the dead hand, on one of the fingers of which was a ring. On reaching home they told their story, and in confirmation of it displayed the ring. All the families who had lost relatives mysteriously were then told of what had been found out; and they determined to ask Baker to a large party, apparently in a friendly manner, but to have constables concealed ready to take him into custody. He came, suspecting nothing, and then the lady told him all she had seen, pretending it was a dream. "Fair Lady," said he, "dreams are nothing; they are but fables."

"They may be fables," said she, "but is this a fable?" and she produced the hand and ring. Upon this the constables rushed in and took him; and the tradition further says he was burnt, notwithstanding that Queen Mary tried to save him, on account of the religion he professed.

Various notes from correspondents on the Baker family show that this story is entirely fictitious.

TYPE 955. MOTIFS: K.1916 [*Robber bridegroom*]; H.57.2.1 [*Severed finger as sign of crime. Robber bridegroom thus detected*].
¶ This tale, though very like "Mr Fox", is even closer than "Mr Fox" to Grimm's "Robber Bridegroom", because of the speaking parrot. The exact locality of the house draws it into local legends, though there seems to have been no foundation for the tale.
See "Mr Fox", "The Cellar of Blood" (A, IV).

SIR WILLIAM COFFIN

J. R. W. Coxhead, *The Devil in Devon*, pp. 15–16.

An extremely interesting tradition is attached to the name of Sir William Coffin, who lived during the reign of Henry VIII and was present at the Field of the Cloth of Gold in 1520.

One day, so it is said, he was riding past Bideford Church when he noticed a crowd of people in a state of considerable agitation in the churchyard.

The worthy knight dismounted from his steed and asked a bystander the reason for the commotion. He was informed that the corpse of a poor man awaited burial, but the priest refused to perform the last rites unless the mortuary fees were first paid, and as he was claiming for his fee the dead man's cow it would cause great hardship to the bereaved family.

Sir William immediately ordered the heartless priest to perform the ceremony without further delay, but to his anger the cleric, standing very much upon his dignity, refused to obey his command. Whereupon, the irate knight told the crowd to throw the priest into the grave, and bury him alive.

The bystanders had almost completed their grim task, when the priest begged for mercy, saying that he would carry out the burial ceremony as requested. He was then released from his terrifying predicament, and, having recovered his composure, he conducted the service, but afterwards he sent a report to the Bishop of Exeter, complaining of Sir William's high-handed action.

The ecclesiastical authorities were deeply shocked that such a flagrant insult should be inflicted upon the Church, and in due course the impulsive knight was summoned before Parliament to account for his unlawful behaviour.

Sir William made out such a good case to justify his rough treatment of the priest at Bideford that an Act of Parliament was secured which limited the burial fees chargeable by the clergy to people in poor circumstances.

The details of the above tradition have been taken from the book, *Little Guide to Devon*, by S. Baring-Gould, first published in 1907. The story also appears in *Transactions of the Devonshire Association*, XXXIV, p. 210.

MOTIF: Q.286.2 [*Priest will not bury dead unless paid in advance. Ruler has him buried with corpse*].

¶ The instance cited in the Motif-Index is from an Italian *novella*.
This bears some relationship to type 505 [The Grateful Dead] though it is only the beginning of the tale.

SKIMMINGTON WELL

Ruth L. Tongue, *Somerset Folklore*, pp. 22–3.

The efficacy of some of the wells is still believed in. In June of 1961 I collected two fragments about Skimmington Well, which is spoken of as a fairy well, though there is no mention of tribute in the following story:

"There was a labouring man at Shapwick, and he had rheumatism so badly that he was crippled up. In the end he had to give up working, his limbs were useless. So he went to the old witch. She looked at him, and she said, 'Jack, my man, yew've no need to be this way. Yew go over to Skimmington Well. 'Tis on Rock Hill, over tew hawthorn hedges. Bathe in it at sunrise for dree mornings, and the use will come back to your limbs.' So he went away to Curry Rivel and he bathed dree times, and he was cured of his ailments and worked for years afterwards."

The other fragment seems to contain some memory of revels at the well:

"Skimmington Well is where they go to dance on Midsummer Day and cure all their ills. 'Tis on Rock Hill."

MOTIF: D.1500.1.1 [*Magic healing well*].
¶ See "Nether Stowey Blind Well".

SMUGGLER'S LEAP

J. R. W. Coxhead, *The Devil in Devon*, p. 24.

Above Lee Bay, near Lynmouth, the coast road climbs along the steep slopes of the cliffs to the little moorland hamlet of Martinhoe. At one point, the road passes close to a precipice known as Smuggler's Leap, where the sea has worn a deep chasm in the rocky face of the cliff. It was at this spot that a grim tragedy is said to have occurred many years ago in the old smuggling days.

According to the tradition, a notorious smuggler was riding hard along the road to Martinhoe, closely pursued by a Preventive Officer. The Exciseman's horse was the better of the two, and he was gaining fast. Just as the smuggler came abreast of the precipice the officer drew alongside and endeavoured to lay hold of the fugitive.

In a desperate effort to throw off the Exciseman's grasp, the smuggler turned his horse sharply towards the edge of the cliff. The sudden swerve was too much for the frightened steed, and, with a frenzied snort, the poor animal plunged over the precipice. Clutching wildly at his pursuer in a futile effort to save himself, the smuggler dragged his enemy from the saddle, and the two men, still grappling with one another, were hurled to their doom on the rocks below. It is said that when the bodies were eventually discovered by seaweed gatherers, they were still locked together in a vice-like grip. Ever since this tragic event took place, the spot from which the two men fell to their deaths has been known as Smuggler's Leap.

¶ The above tradition is also given in the book, *The Coasts of Devon and Lundy Island*, by John L. W. Page, published in 1895.

The nearest motif number to this is A.963.2 [*Cliff from Lover's Leap*].

Places down which people have fallen are often described as "leaps", as, for instance, "Giffard's Jump". The name is more correctly used for places like the "Soldier's Leap" at Killiecrankie or "The Tinkler's Loup" on the Ken in Galloway, narrow places, said to have been crossed under stress of fear.

See "Sir Eglamore and Lady Emma", "Giffard's Jump".

THE SMUGGLERS AND THE SQUIRE

Sir C. Igglesden, *A Saunter through Kent with Pen and Pencil*, 1, p. 72.

Chalk-pits abound in the hills [around Lenham] through which great caverns penetrate, and here, in the old smuggling days, much merchandise which had never paid duty was secreted. It was an ideal spot for the smugglers, who, leagued with the villagers, brought their wares from the coast, and disposed of them to the gentry and farmers around.

Even the Justices of the Peace could not resist a deal in cheap spirits and tobacco, while their wives and daughters must needs bedeck themselves in fine lace and silks brought direct from the French shores. Perhaps it was owing to this fact that the squire of the village on one occasion saved the smugglers from arrest by a clever ruse. The latter, so the story goes, had been surprised by revenue officers while carting barrels of merchandise up to the old Roman road kilns, and were in full retreat past Chilston Park, with their pursuers close at hand. It fortunately happened that the squire, struck with an original idea, was having a lake made at the time, the labourers working by moonlight. He was an old sailor, and believed in continuous work by watches. Along the lane came the terrified smugglers, and, certain of the squire's sympathy, explained the danger of their position. Quick in thought, quick in action, the old salt fathomed the situation at a glance. The barrels were thrown into the mud and covered in a trice, the smugglers doffed their coats and, spades in hand, joined the gang of labourers. When the Customs officers appeared all was quiet save for the thud of the spades and the clear, commanding orders of the squire. In respectful tones, the officers asked if the smugglers had passed that way. "No," answered the squire, and truthfully he said it, for they were working away under the very noses of the talkers, grinning among themselves and enjoying the joke, as we can well imagine.

The officers passed on, the barrels were eventually unearthed, the squire was voted a rare good fellow, and many a year afterwards the anniversary of that night was celebrated by the secret delivery of a cask of good old cognac into the cellars of the old squire's house.

MOTIF: K.520 [*Death escaped through disguise or shamming*].
¶   This tale illustrates the friendly feeling towards smugglers, particularly in Sussex and Kent. The notorious Hawkhurst gang, however, made the smugglers less popular. Kipling's "Smugglers' Song" (*Rewards and Fairies*) illustrates the countryman's attitude.

THE SOUTHERY WOLF-HOUND

W. H. Barratt, *Tales from the Fens*, pp. 136–9.

When Southery was an island cut off by what are now the Southery Fens, but what were then all water and reeds, some monks came from Ely and brought stone with them from Barnack to build a church, though they used some bricks as well, which were made on the spot.

Southery folk then were a wild, rough crowd, living in turf-walled, reed-thatched huts and earning their living by catching eels and fish and robbing the boats sailing to Ely and Cambridge. It was a hard life, with the swarms of flies in the summer and the ague in winter.

Well, after a few of the monks who came to build the church had been found with their throats cut, the Abbot of Ely sent a company of armed men to hunt out the murderers, but it was a hopeless job in all those miles of reeds and meres. Soon that lot of armed men had thinned out a good deal, and the men they were hunting had got hold of some first-class butchering tools. They used these so well that the Abbot soon began to realize that keeping up the supply of church-builders was going to be more than he could manage. So he asked the Baron of Northwold if, as Southery was part of his land, he'd take some steps to see that the King's law was kept there. Now, the Baron had already tried, several times, to make that murderous tribe in Southery understand that his laws and orders must be obeyed, but all that had happened was that he had lost a lot of his men. So he told the Abbot that he couldn't send any soldiers, but he'd send a pack of wolf-hounds instead; and they could look after the monks while they were at work and guard them when they were asleep.

The hounds soon arrived, with a couple of servants in charge of them, but they didn't bring any meat with them and so, as the dogs didn't like the fish they were given to eat, they were soon out hunting for their own food. Being the kind of dogs they were, their hunting soon led them to a good supply of meat—the bodies of monks and soldiers which had been left lying about. But soon they'd eaten their way through that lot and were very hungry again, though it wasn't long before they found that a freshly-killed fat monk was just as tasty as one that had been dead for some time. The two servants, frightened at the way the hounds were getting so fat, decided it was time to make themselves scarce, and get back to Northwold. So off they went, but on the way they were stopped and thrown into Larman's Mere by some of the Southery tribe, who believed that it was true that dead men can tell no tales.

The hounds, with no one now to try to stop them, went on hunting for their fresh meat until, when the next lot of boats came with more building stone for the church, the monks who were still left scrambled aboard and went back to Ely. There they told the Abbot that, even if he paid them three times what he had been paying them, they wouldn't go back to finish that job. The Southery people had already gone away from the village and were living right out in the fen, so the hounds, finding all their food supply at an end, began to kill and eat each other, till only the fiercest and most cunning of the pack was left, a young bitch, as big as a full-grown ass.

At last she became so weak from hunger that she crawled into a clump of reeds to die. But one of the Fenmen found her there, got help and, with two or three of his pals, carried her back to his hut and told his wife to feed her up. As the woman had had a baby the week before, she was soon able to get the bitch on her feet again by giving her the same milk as the baby had, and in a few weeks the hound was quite tame. The Fenmen used to take her up to the high ground with them, where she was useful in hunting out and bringing down the Baron's deer, so the Southery people had plenty of venison to eat as a change from their usual fish and gruel. In the meantime, the Abbot made friends again with the Fenmen, and the monks came back to go on with their building but, though the bitch was friendly with the Southery men, she used to snarl and growl whenever she saw one of the monks.

One day the hound couldn't be found, so the Fenman went to the monks and said they must have killed her; but the monks swore they hadn't. She came back after a week or two, with her pads all torn and bleeding, as though she'd walked on stony ground miles out of the Fens. Presently everyone noticed that she was carrying pups, and they were very surprised at this, because they knew there wasn't a dog for miles around. The monks said it must be the Devil's work, and began making the sign of the Cross whenever they saw her.

At last she whelped in a corner of the hut belonging to the Fenman who'd saved her life but she wouldn't let anyone go near her except the man's wife. Then one day she brought the pup out from the dark corner and when they saw it, everyone was amazed, because it didn't look like a dog or a wolf, but something between the two. Some of the monks who could read and write said they knew there weren't any wolves for miles around, so the Devil himself must have fathered it. Well, the pup grew up to be nearly as big as an ox, and was soon wandering about where it liked, friendly with everyone except the monks.

When the old bitch died, the youngster took on the job of getting fresh meat for the Fenmen, and it used to go off on its own and come back with a sheep or a deer in its huge jaws.

Presently the church was finished and there was to be a great feast on the day that the Bishop of Elmham came to open it. The Bishop rode over with a company of soldiers to guard him, and among them was one who had been in Southery when the wolf-pack was there. When he saw the big wolf-hound he remembered what those other animals had done and he made up his mind to kill it. But before he could get within striking distance the dog sprang at his throat, then, getting the taste of blood, began eating the soldier as he lay still kicking on the ground. The other soldiers soon ended his meal with a flight of arrows, and the dog, howling terribly, just like a wolf, crawled off into the fen to die.

Well, all that happened hundreds of years ago, but if you go out at midnight on the 29th May, the day of Southery Feast, you will hear that wolf-hound howl as it pads along, and if you do then you will know that, before the Feast comes round again, you will be dead. And what's more, if you look at the corner-stones of the charnel house on the north side of the church ruins, you'll see that the hard stone blocks have been all gnawed away as if giant rats had been at them. Those marks have been made by the wolf-dog who comes back, one night each year, to try to get at the bones inside. And that's why the strongest Southery man, even if he's filled to the brim with beer, goes a long way round to get home, rather than pass those ruins as the clock is striking midnight on the day of Southery Feast.

MOTIFS: B.16 [*Devastating animals*]; B.16.1.2 [*Devastating hound*]; E.521.2 [*Ghost of dog*]; E.256 [*Ghost eats corpses*]; E.585.4 [*Revenant revisits earth yearly*]. ¶ See "Bull-Dog Bridge".

THE SPECTRAL CAT

THE CHURCH AT WHITTLE-LE-WOODS

James Bowker, *Goblin Tales of Lancashire*, p. 63.

The country between Rivington Pike and Hoghton as far as the sea-coast was formerly very wild and thickly wooded. Here, at Whittle-le-Woods, the inhabitants once decided to erect a Church. The money was collected, and the people themselves dug and laid the foundations. The old priest was full of joy and hope at the results of the first day's work. But arising early the next morning to review the site, he was astounded to find no trace of his church; the grass and flowers were undisturbed and all was as before. A crowd of workers soon gathered, and demanded of the priest what had become of all their work, and the stone which had been piled up for the continuance of the building. Before they could recover from their shock, a messenger arrived in hot haste from Leyland, to say that the foundations of a church had mysteriously appeared there in the night, and that Adam the miller was threatening to prosecute the priest for trespassing on his land. The whole crowd returned with the messenger to Leyland, and between them they cleared the field, and returned their foundations to the original site.

That night the priest set two watchers to guard their day's work. But both of them fell asleep, though they had agreed to watch by turns, and in the morning the foundations of the church had again vanished. All was to be done again, but the efforts of the people were effective, and the second night the priest himself remained with the watchers till nearly midnight. But almost as soon as he had left them, one of them saw a movement, and soon they distinguished a huge cat with fiery eyes, which, without difficulty, picked up a large stone, ran off with it, and immediately returned for another. After watching in astonishment for some time, the younger of the two men seized a large piece of wood, crept up to the cat, and struck it hard on the head. The cat, with a scream, sprang at him, flung him to the ground, and fastened its teeth in his head. The older man fled in terror to find the priest. When they reached the spot, the dead body of the other lay on the ground, but once again there was no trace of church or foundations.

At this, it was agreed that the new church could by no means be built at Whittle-le-Woods, and by common consent it was erected at Leyland, on the miller's field.

TYPE ML.7060. MOTIF: D.2192.1(*cf*) [*Spirit in form of cat causes a change in church site by carrying materials built during day to another site*] (Baughman).

¶ This spirit was more dangerous than any other agencies which moved buildings, for it killed the man who attacked it. It was a diabolic rather than a spectral cat.

See "Winwick Church".

THE SPRING CALLED SLUDACH

[slightly shortened]

Hugh Miller, *Scenes and Legends*, pp. 5–7.

In the upper part of the parish of Cromarty is a curious spring, termed Sludach, which suddenly dries up every year early in summer, and breaks out again at the close of autumn. It gushes from the bank with an undiminished flow until within a few hours before it ceases for the season, and bursts forth on its return in a full stream. Tradition says that some time in the seventeenth century, on a very warm day of summer, two farmers from the adjacent fields were approaching the spring from opposite directions. One of them was tacksman of the farm on which the spring rises, the other tenanted a neighbouring farm. They had lived for some time on no very friendly terms. The tacksman, a coarse, rude man, reached the spring first, and, taking a hasty draught, he gathered up a handful of mud, and flung it into the water. "Now," said he, turning away as he spoke, "you may drink your fill." Scarcely had he uttered the words when the offended stream began to boil like a cauldron and, after bubbling awhile among the grass and rushes, sank into the ground.

Next day at noon, the heap of grey sand which had been incessantly rising and falling within it in a little conical jet for many years had become as dry as dust, and the white-flowered cresses that skirted either side of the runnel that had issued from it lay withering in the sun. Moreover, it was found that a powerful spring had burst out on the opposite side of the firth, which at this place is nearly five miles in breadth, a few hours after the Cromarty one had disappeared. The story spread; the tacksman, rude and coarse as he was, was made unhappy by the forebodings of his neighbours, who seemed to regard him as one resting under a curse, and, going to an elderly person in an adjoining parish much celebrated for his knowledge of the supernatural, he craved his advice.

The seer bade him go to the old hollow of the fountain, as nearly as possible at the same hour as when he had insulted it, clear it out with a clean linen towel, lie down beside it, and await the result. He did so, and waited on the bank above the hollow from noon until near sunset, when the water came rushing up with a noise like the roar of the sea, scattering the sand for several yards around; and then, subsiding to its common level, it flowed on as before between the rows of cresses. The spring on the opposite side of the firth withdrew its waters about the time of the rite of the cleansing, and they have not since appeared; while those of Sludach, from that day to the present, are presented, as if in scorn, during the moister seasons, when no one regards them as valuable, and withheld in the seasons of drought, when they would be prized. We recognise in this singular tradition a sort of soul or naiad of the spring, susceptible of offence, and conscious of the attentions paid to it; and the passage of the waters beneath the sea reminds us of the River Alpheus sinking in Peloponnesus to rise in Sicily.

MOTIFS: C.41 [*Tabu: offending water-spirit*]; D.1641.1 [*Well removes itself*].
¶ See "The Ebbing and Flowing Well at Giggleswick".

STAPLETON OF WIGHILL

E. M. Gutch, *County Folk-Lore*, II, *North Riding of Yorkshire, etc.*, pp. 415–6.

"The feet of the figure [on the monument of Robert Stapleton at Wighill] rest upon a huge Saracen's head, which has given rise to a local tradition that it represents the head of a giant who ate children and the like, and was slain by one of the early Stapletons of Wighill" (Chetwynd-Stapylton, p. 240).

Among many legends connecting this badge with the Stapletons and the lands of Wighill is the following quaintly told by the aged sexton:

Many hundreds of years ago a terrible giant, Turk or Saracen, dwelt on an island near the coast of England, causing fearful havoc far and wide, killing all who came in his path. A manor was offered by the king to the man who would rid the country of this bloodthirsty ogre.

After a long delay, a champion was found in the shape of another David, who went forth alone, armed only with a good sword. The hero crossed to the island, the stronghold of the foe; after leaping ashore, young Stapleton sent the boat adrift. The mighty Saracen, who from his castle had seen the coming of England's champion, came on the scene at this juncture, waxing wrath at the sight of his adversary. Inquiring why the boat was sent out to sea, Stapleton replied that he was determined to rid the country of such a monster or die in the attempt, and if victorious should return in his, the giant's boat. After a long fight, the young hero received a terrible blow, which brought him to the ground; at the moment the giant was in the act of giving the final stoke, with arms uplifted, Stapleton, grasping his sword, with a desperate plunge struck him under the armpit and disabled him. Then commenced the final struggle for victory, which ended in the death of the Saracen, whose head was severed from his body, and was brought along with the giant's sword and boat to Britain as proofs of his victory. For this courageous deed the king did grant him the manor of Wighill, where the Stapletons dwelt for six centuries.

E. Bogg, *A Thousand Miles in Wharfedale*, pp. 63, 64.
MOTIF: H.1561.6 [*Test of valour: fight with giant*].

THE SWAFFHAM TINKER [summary]

T. W. Thompson, Notebooks.

A tinker of Swaffham dreamt three nights running that if he went to London he would hear of something to his advantage. He went, stood all day long and was just going away when a man came up and asked why he was waiting. He said he'd had a dream that he'd learn something to his advantage there, but he was a fool for his pains.

The man said he was a fool too, for he'd dreamt that if he went to London Bridge he'd find a man from Swaffham, who had a treasure buried in his garden. The tinker went home, dug, found the treasure. In the chest was a paper with a writing on it that he couldn't read. He took his knife-grinding barrow, and went to the school, and began grinding away, with the paper stuck on his cart. The schoolboys came out, read the paper, and began to laugh. "I bet you can't read it," said the tinker, "Yes, we can," said the boys. "It says where this comes from, you can find one twice as good." So the tinker went back and dug again, and found a chest twice as big. So he was a rich man, and he built on to the church, and if you go there you'll find a carving of him.

From Reuben Gray, Old Radford, Nottingham, 22 December, 1914.
TYPE 1645. MOTIF: N.531.1 [*Dream of treasure on bridge*].
¶ For full notes see "The Pedlar of Swaffham".
See also "How Dundonald Castle was built", "Upsall Castle".

THE TARBAT FISHERMEN [shortened]

Hugh Miller, *Scenes and Legends*, pp. 179–93.

Early in the reign of Queen Anne a fishing yawl, after vainly labouring
for hours to enter the Bay of Cromarty during a strong gale from the
west, was forced at nightfall to take shelter in the Cova-Green. In it
were only an old fisherman and his son, drenched by the spray and
chilled by the piercing wind, which, with thick snow showers, had
blown all day from the snowy top of Ben-Wevis; and it was with no
ordinary satisfaction that, as they opened the bay on their last tack, they
saw the red gleam of a fire flickering from one of the caves, and a boat
drawn up on the beach.

"It must be some of the Tarbat fishermen," said the old man,
"wind-bound like ourselves; but wiser than us, in having made provision for it. I'll feel willing enough to share their fare with them
for the night."

"But," remarked the younger, "I am much mistaken if that be not
the boat of my cousins, the Macinlas! However, the night is getting
worse, and we have no choice of quarters. Hard up your helm, Father,
or we shall barely clear the Skerries."

He leaped ashore, carrying with him the small hawser attached to
the stem, known technically as the *swing*, which he wound securely
round a jutting crag, and stood for a few seconds until the old man,
who moved but heavily along the thwarts, had come up to him. All
was comparatively calm under the lee of the precipices; but the wind
was roaring fearfully in the woods above, and a thick snow shower had
just begun to descend, circling round and round in the eddy.

The place was occupied by three men—two of them young and
rather ordinary-looking persons; the third a grey-headed old man,
apparently of great muscular strength, though long past his prime,
and of a peculiarly sinister cast of countenance. A keg of spirits, which
was placed before them, served as a table.

There were little drinking-measures on it; and the mask-like, stolid
expressions of the two younger men showed that they had been indulging
freely. The elder was comparatively sober. A fire, composed mostly of
fragments of wreck and driftwood, threw up its broad, cheerful flame
towards the roof; but so spacious was the cavern that, except where
here and there a whiter mass of stalactites, or bolder projection of cliff,

stood out from the darkness, the light seemed lost in it. A dense body of smoke, which stretched its blue, level surface from side to side, rolled onwards like a river. On the entrance of the fishermen, the three boatmen started to their feet, and one of the younger pitched the little cask hurriedly into a dark corner of the cave.

"Ay, ye do well to hide it, Gibbie," exclaimed the savage-looking old man in a bitter, ironical tone as he recognized the intruders. "Here are your good friends, William and Ernest Beth, come to see if they cannot rob and maltreat us a second time. Well, they had better try."

There could not be a more luckless meeting. For years the crew of the little yawl had been hated bitterly by the temporary inmates of the cave; nor was old Eachen of Tarbat one of those whose resentments may be safely slighted. He had passed the first thirty years of his life among the buccaneers of South America: later, he had been engaged among the smugglers who even then infested the eastern coasts of Scotland, and had been deemed one of the most fierce and unscrupulous.

When he returned from America, the country was engaged in one of its long wars with Holland, and William Beth, the elder fisherman, who had served in the English fleet, was lying in a Dutch prison, and was reported to be dead. He had inherited some little property from his father in the neighbouring town—a house and a little field, which in his absence was held by an only sister, who was, of course, regarded as the village heiress, and whose affections Eachen of Tarbat had succeeded in engaging. Their marriage had turned out singularly ill: Eachen was dissipated and of a harsh cruel temper; and his poor wife, after giving birth to two sons, perished in the middle of her days, a care-worn, heart-broken creature. Her brother William returned from Holland, and on her death, claimed and recovered his property from her husband, who had ever afterwards regarded him with the bitterest malice. A second cause of dislike arose when Ernest Beth, William's only son, and one of his cousins, the younger son of Eachen, had both fixed their affections on a lovely young girl, and Ernest, a handsome and high-spirited young man, had proved successful. On returning with his mistress from a fair a few weeks before this evening, he had been waylaid and grossly insulted by his two cousins; and the insult he might have borne for the sake of his relationship to their mother: but there was another whom they had also insulted, and that he could not bear; and as they were mean enough to take odds against him on the occasion, he had beaten the two spiritless fellows that did so.

The old fisherman began: "We have not met for many years, Eachen —not since the death of my poor sister, when we parted such ill-friends; but we are short-lived creatures ourselves; surely our anger should be short-lived too. I have come to crave from you a seat by your fire."

"It was no wish of mine, William Beth," said Eachen, "that we should ever meet: but there is room enough for us all beside the fire."

After a long silence, the old fisherman spoke again: "It has vexed me, Eachen, that our young folk, were it but for my sister's sake, should not be on mair friendly terms; an' we ourselves too—why should we be enemies?" The old man, without deigning a reply, knit his grey, shaggy brows, and looked doggedly into the fire.

"Nay, now," continued the fisherman. "We are getting auld now, Eachen, an' wald better bury our hard thoughts o' ane anither afore we come to be buried oursels."

Eachen fixed his keen, scrutinizing glance on the speaker, there was a tremulous motion of his upper lip as he withdrew it, and a setting of the teeth; but the tone of his reply savoured more of sullen indifference than of passion.

"William Beth," he said, "ye have tricked my boys out of the bit property that suld have come to them by their mither; it's no so long since they barely escaped being murdered by your son. What more want you? But, mayhap, ye think it better that the time suld be passed in making boss professions of goodwill than employed in clearing off an old score."

"Ay," hiccupped out the older of the two sons, "the houses might come my way then; an' if Helen Henry were to lose her ae joe, the tither might hae the better chance."

"Look, ye, Uncle," exclaimed the younger fisherman, "Your threat might be spared. Our little property was my grandfather's and of right descended to his only son. As for the affair at the tryst, I dare either of my cousins to say the quarrel was of my seeking. I have no wish to raise my hand against the sons or the husband of my aunt, but if forced to it, you will find that neither my father nor myself are wholly at your mercy." He rose to his feet as he spoke.

"Whisht, Ernest," said the old fisherman calmly. "sit down: your uncle maun hae ither thoughts. It is now twenty years, Eachen," he continued, "since I was called to my sister's bedside. You cannot forget what passed then. There had been grief and hunger beside that bed. I'll no say you were willingly unkind. Few folk are that but when they have some purpose to serve by it, and you could have none; but you laid no restraint on a harsh temper, and none on a craving habit that forgets everything but itself, and sae my poor sister perished in the middle of her days, a wasted, heart-broken thing. I have nae wish to hurt you; we baith passed our youth in a bad school, an' I owre often feel I havena unlearned my own lessons to wonder that you suldna have unlearned a' yours. But we're getting old men, Eachen. Why suld we die fools? An' fools we maun die if we die enemies."

"You are likely in the right," said the stern old man. "But ye were aye a luckier man than me, William—luckier for this warld, I'm sure— maybe luckier for the next. I had aye to seek, an' that without finding, the good that came in your gate o' itsel'. Now that age is coming upon us, ye get a snug rental frae the little house and croft, and I have naething; an' ye have character an' credit, but wha wald trust me, or wha cares for me? Ye hae been made *an elder* o' the kirk too, I hear, and I am still a reprobate; but we were a' born to be just what we are, an' sae we maun submit. And your son too shares in your luck. He has heart and hand, and my whelps hae neither; and the girl Henry, that scouts that sot there, likes him; but what wonder of that!—William Beth, we needna quarrel, but for peace sake leave me alone—we have naething in common, and friends we canna and winna be."

"We had better," whispered Ernest to his father, "not sleep in the cave tonight."

At length they both quitted the cave, though the night was now stormier than ever, and, heaving off their boat till she rode at the full length of her swing from the shore, they sheltered themselves under the sail. The Macinlas returned next evening to Tarbat; but though the wind moderated during the day, the yawl of William Beth did not enter the Sound of Cromarty. Weeks passed away, during which the clergy-man of the place corresponded regarding the missing fishermen with all the lower ports of the Firth, but they had disappeared, as it seemed, for ever; and Eachen Macinla, in the name of his sons, laid claim to their property, and entered a second time into possession of the house and the little field. For five years William's widow lived alone in her small thatched cottage, which stood near the beach, sheltered by a steeply-rising bank behind, and with a carefully tended garden in front. But the garden and thatch fell gradually into a state of neglect, for the poor woman's strength was failing, and she became more and more ill and helpless. But within the cottage all was still kept clean and cheerful, for the girl, Helen Henry, now found her whole pleasure in life in the care and love of her mother-in-law.

One day in late autumn, when the two were as usual together, Helen said, "Tomorrow, Mother, is Ernest's birthday. Is it not strange that, when our minds make pictures of the dead, it is always as they looked best, and kindliest, and most lifelike? I have been seeing Ernest all day long, as when I saw him on his *last* birthday."

The old woman replied by relating a strange dream she had had in the night. She had seemed to be sitting on a rock, far out in the bay which faced the cottage, with the tide rising around her. Even when the whole rock was covered, she felt no fear, for she knew that her husband and son were both in the water before her, and that she could find rest only with them. At last the water closed over her, and she found herself walking lightly and easily over the sand at the bottom. She came to a cave, and saw bones lying on the sand inside it. But as she stooped to enter, William's voice said, "Lillias, it is not night yet, nor is that your bed; you are to sleep, not with me, but, lang after this, with Ernest. Haste you home, for he is waiting for you." She looked up and saw William, her husband.

"Oh, take me to him," she cried, and all at once found herself on the shore, dizzied and blinded with the light, after the green depths of the sea. She looked up for William, but now it was Ernest who stood by her side, with Helen beside him.

As she was telling her dream, the sky grew darker, and the gulls flew inland, and it was clear that another terrible storm was blowing up. They descried a boat, with only one man in it, just rounding the point of the bay.

"My poor old eyes," said the widow, "are growing dim; but yet I think I should ken that boatman. Is it no Eachen Macinla o' Tarbat?"

"Hard-hearted old man!" exclaimed Helen. "What can be taking him here? But see, he is so worn-out that he can hardly walk over the stones." She would have gone to his help, but just then the old man stumbled his way to the cottage and knocked at the door. The poor widow gave him her seat at the fireside, and such food as she had, and together they listened in terror to the storm.

"Heaven itself hae mercy on them," cried the old man, "My two sons are at the far Firth, and how can an open boat live in a night like this!"

In one of the pauses of the hurricane, a gun was heard out at sea, and then a second. "Wae's me," exclaimed the widow. "Would we no better light up a blaze on the floor, an' draw off the cover frae the window? My Ernest has told me that my light has often showed him his bearings frae the deadly bed o' Dunskaith." They did so, and the gun-shots sounded nearer, and at length came evidently from the interior of the bay.

"She has escaped," said the old man. "It's a feeble hand that canna do good when the heart is willing, but what hae mine been doing a' life lang?"

Towards morning the wind fell, and the moon, in her last quarter, rose, and the old man left the cottage and wandered along the beach, searching for traces of his sons' boat, by which to know its fate. Stooping down, he saw in the midst of a tangle of seaweed the face of his elder son, swollen and lifeless. A few yards farther on, he came on the dead body of the younger son. He staggered back to the cottage, where the two women tended and strove to comfort him, but soon, prostrated with grief and fatigue, he fell gravely sick, and in his delirium, seemed to see William and Ernest Beth standing, one each side of the bed where he lay tossing and in fever.

Meantime, the day dawned bright and calm, and many came to the cottage by the shore. Among them was a tall, handsome man of about twenty-seven, with a slight scar on his left cheek; his dress was distinguished from that of the common seaman by three narrow strips of gold lace on the upper part of one sleeve. At first the widow hardly seemed aware of him, but he laid a gentle hand on her shoulder and said, "I have strange news for you. Your son Ernest is alive, and is now in the harbour of Cromarty. He is lieutenant of the vessel whose guns you must have heard in the night."

He told them how the gale had blown the two men's boat out to sea in the night, and after drifting four days, they had been picked up by an armed vessel, bound for the coast of Spanish America. The poor old man soon sank under the effects of his sufferings and exposure, but Ernest had recovered, and soon rose to be the second man on the vessel. The young officer then anxiously asked, "Is Helen Henry yet unmarried?"

"It is Ernest—it is Ernest himself!" she cried, and in a moment he had seized her in his arms. He told them that he had brought home with him enough gold from his Spanish adventure to keep his old mother in comfort, and that their light had indeed steered them to safety on the evening of the storm.

In the meantime old Eachen Macinla lay muttering unceasingly in his ravings of William and Ernest Beth. "Why trouble me?" he cried. "Why stare with your white dead eyes at me? Was it I who raised the wind and the sea? You were fast asleep, and could not see me cut the swing—I will plead for my life. Please, your Honour, I did not murder these two men—*I only cut the rope that fastened their boat to the land.* Ha! He has ordered them away, and they have both left me unskaithed." At this moment Ernest Beth approached the bed. The wretched man raised himself on his elbow, and shrieked, "Here is Ernest Beth, come for me a second time!" and, sinking back on the pillow, he instantly expired.

MOTIFS: S.141 [*Exposure in a boat*]; Q.581.3 [*Those planning to drown others drowned*] T.96 [*Lovers reunited after many adventures*].

THOMAS OF READING [summary]

From W. J. Thom's *Early English Prose Romances*.

In the days of Henry First, the chief of all the crafts in England was that of the Clothiers. They employed almost half the population of the country, and brought in far more wealth from abroad than any other trade. The younger sons of knights and gentlemen often learnt the craft, and it was everywhere held in high repute.

Of all the clothiers, nine were especially famous. Six of them came from the West Country, and the King named them the Six Worthy Husbands of the West. They were Thomas Cole of Reading, Gray of Gloucester, Sutton of Salisbury, William Fitzallen of Worcester, Thomas Dove of Exeter, Simon of Southampton, nicknamed Supbroth. The other three came from the North; Cuthbert of Kendal, Hodgekins of Halifax, and Martin Byam of Manchester.

At Fair times the six would meet together at Basingstoke, and go on together to London, where they lodged at an inn known as Jarrat the Giant's Hall, from the great size of the innkeeper.

One day, when the King was riding to Wales to put down an insurrection, he met a great train of wagons belonging to Thomas of Reading. They were so many, in fact about two hundred altogether, that he became vexed, and sent for the owner to appear before him the next day. But as he went further, he met another train, and was told it belonged to Sutton. And so throughout the day, till the King, impressed by their wealth, determined not to fail such loyal and profitable subjects, but win their support against all comers; for he was always expecting an attack from his elder brother, Robert of Normandy, who thought he had a better claim than Henry to the English throne.

Gray of Gloucester and William of Worcester one time met Thomas Cole at Reading, where he entertained them generously to breakfast, before riding on with them to London. On the way they discussed reports that the banished Earls of Moraigne and Shrewsbury had joined Robert in Normandy, and that their wives, through the King's severe displeasure, were left to wander the countryside, homeless and friendless. On the road they met Thomas Dove, and the four dined together at Colebrooke. Here the Innkeeper's wife used to entertain her guests by persuading some of her woman friends to come and join them at dinner. The wives would come in spite of their husbands' displeasure, and had persuaded them to trust them thus far; and the custom had become so popular, with all the clothiers, and especially Thomas Dove, that the women had made a song about him:

> Welcome to town, Thomas Dove, Thomas Dove,
>   The merriest man alive,
> Thy company still we love, we love,
>   God grant thee well to thrive,
> And never will [we] depart from thee,
>   For better or worse, my joy,
> For thou shalt still have our goodwill,
>   God's blessing on my sweet boy.

They met at Jarrat's Hall, as was their custom, and dined and made their bargains, and for every bargain made, each clothier would send a token to his wife.

Next day they met the Northern clothiers and four of them began to play at dice. Thomas Cole lost much money, but with Gray's help he won it back, so by a friendly arrangement, he and Gray were to pay for the supper of the other two, for Cole never liked to make profit from his winnings. This dicing and supper were held at Bosome's Inn, named from its slovenly and repulsive keeper, who went about all the year huddled up in layers of thick clothing, and with his head sunk in his bosom. This old man had a young and lovely wife, and Cuthbert of Kendal fell at once in love with her, and she with him. They had secretly agreed that, in order to hide their love from her husband, he should always find fault with her in public, and she should pretend to be distressed at it, and so it came about on this evening. She had prepared a meal with which all the clothiers were well content, and there was music played by the most skilled musician of that time, Reior or Rahere, the founder of St Bartholomew's Hospital. He was already so wealthy that he maintained a company of players of his own, and dressed them all alike. In spite of all this, Cuthbert pretended to find everything amiss, and the other guests were hard put to it to reconcile him and the hostess to one another. Next day they all rode back as far as Colebrooke, where Thomas Cole, as was his custom, entrusted his money to the care of his hostess for the night. This precaution was less wise than at the time it appeared.

During these days at a certain hiring fair, Margaret, the beautiful daughter of the banished earl of Shrewsbury, who had no other means of keeping herself alive, hired herself as a servant to the wife of Gray of Gloucester. Though she had no knowledge of household matters, she was so humble and learned so quickly, that she became a great favourite in the home, and though she never revealed the truth about her birth, many suitors for her hand soon arose, and Gray himself, the master of the house, named her "Margaret of the White Hand", and so she was always called, instead of the humble "Meg".

At this time the King was about to sail into Normandy, to fight against Duke Robert, whom he eventually brought home as his prisoner, and confined him in Cardiff Castle, though he allowed him liberty of hunting and hawking, so that he was always attended by guards. Before he left England, however, the King summoned the nine chief clothiers and asked if they had any requests to make of him.

They made three, and the King granted them all. First they asked for a standard measure of length, to prevent certain flagrant and common injustices, and the King established the length of his own arm as the standard yard. Next they begged that cracked money should be made legal coin, since many traders were refusing to accept it, and the King replied that in future all coins were to be slit, so that all became equally legal tender. The third request came from the men of Halifax.

So common had thefts of their cloth become, that they asked the King for the privilege of hanging any offenders who were caught. Grave as this demand was, for till that time there were no hangings in England, the King granted it, for he wished to prove his faith in the clothiers.

They, in gratitude for these favours, invited the royal Princes to a banquet at Jarrat's Hall, and while this was being prepared, Cuthbert slipped away again to Bosome's Inn. Before its owner he kept up the pretence of enmity with his wife, but the old man became suspicious and at length surprised them together in a locked barn. Cuthbert said that he had come to find a cheese, and the wife said that the door had blown to and locked itself. But old Bosome seized Cuthbert, tied him up, and slung him up in a basket from the smoky rafters of the inn kitchen, swearing that he would never release him unless the King's sons themselves begged for it. So Cuthbert missed the banquet, which was held with great merriment, but when it was over, the other clothiers, knowing where to find him, went in search of Cuthbert; and at last the royal Princes *did* procure his release.

But as a warning, on that date every year afterwards, old Bosome insisted that anyone who chanced to come in search of cheeses, should be treated in the same way as Cuthbert.

The clothiers' wives now took part in the story by insisting that their husbands allow them to visit London in their company; and, once there they were so delighted with all they saw that nothing would content them but that they must each have a new gown, made by a Cheapside tailor (for no other, they swore, could do it half so well) and made of bright-coloured stuff, instead of their plain country browns and greys.

Meanwhile, the King returned victorious from Normandy; and was much delighted by the pageantry of welcome which the clothiers prepared for him, whenever he visited one of their cities. He stayed first at the house of Thomas of Reading, and in gratitude for his lavish entertainment there, he resolved that Reading, and no other place, should be his burial-place. In preparation for this, he promised to endow a great Abbey there. His progress took him to Salisbury, then to Exeter, then Gloucester. Here he was accompanied by Robert his brother, and at Gray's house they saw Margaret of the White Hand spinning. Duke Robert fell deeply in love with her and soon afterwards wrote her letters declaring his love and begging her to return it.

At Worcester the King was welcomed by Fitzallen, who was doing much to retrieve his city from a low state of fortune into which it had sunk. His eldest son now became the King's godson, and in later life was the first Mayor of London, and his son was Mayor after him.

The citizens of Halifax, following the privilege granted to them, at length caught a notable thief of cloth, named Wallis, with some companions. But no man could be found willing to act as hangman, and the bold man leapt down from the scaffold, declaring that the King's privilege conferred the right to hang, but not to imprison them, and so they made their escape. Afterwards a cunning friar devised a form of gin, which would cut off heads without human help, and later thieves were thus put to death.

The least successful of the clothiers at this time was Thomas Dove who, from his love of all kinds of good cheer, had fallen into debt, and was at last arrested by a catchpole, in the name of one of his creditors. Jarrat, the giant innkeeper, became surety for him, and for the time he withdrew to the country, forsaken by friends and servants, and fell into great wretchedness.

Duke Robert, in pursuit of the fair Margaret, at last succeeded in winning her love, knowing nothing of her true birth. They appointed to meet in the forest between Cardiff and Gloucester, and though Margaret waited long, and almost despaired of his coming, he at last succeeded in eluding his guards, and they escaped for a short time, but were later caught, and condemned to death by the King.

But Gray's wife, who had become devoted to Margaret and was greatly distressed at her disappearance, at the last moment procured her reprieve, and took her again into her service; but only after she had, at the King's express command, watched her lover's eyes being put out. He was then to be imprisoned for the rest of his life.

At Colebrooke, Thomas of Reading continued on every visit to entrust his money for safe-keeping to his hostess. She and her husband in reality were cruel, avaricious people, and had a trap-bed, which could be let down through the floor of the bed-chamber so that the sleeper fell into a boiling cauldron under it.

In this way they had made away with many guests and now plotted to kill Thomas. Chance saved him several times, but at last he was there one night, alone and ill, and in his forebodings he wrote a will, leaving all his wealth to his wife, Eleanor, and daughter, Isobel, except for £200 to Thomas Dove, of whose misfortunes he had but lately heard. The host and hostess witnessed the will, and that night they carried out their wicked purpose. But the will had already been despatched by a messenger, and Thomas's horse at last betrayed them, for it had broken out of its stable in the night, and was found wandering about, after the host and hostess had told their usual tale that Thomas had ridden away home early in the day.

The two were caught and put to death, and the King commanded their house to be burnt to the ground. But Thomas's will brought a return of good fortune to Dove, for the other clothiers added to his gift, and Dove was reinstated in his former position. At her death, Cole's wife richly endowed the King's new Abbey at Reading, and it is said that the town of Colebrooke and the River Cole were both named after him.

Fair Margaret soon revealed to the Grays her true history, and obtained their leave to enter a monastery, after giving away all her rich clothing and jewels to the poor. When Duke Robert learnt of this, he begged that at his death he should be buried in Gloucester near her, and where he had seen her first. Gray at his death bequeathed his lands to Margaret's monastery; Fitzallen endowed many houses in Worcester for the poor; Sutton left £100 a year to poor weavers of Salisbury; and Simon of Southampton himself gave a generous gift for the building of a monastery at Winchester.

The Northern clothiers also did good with their wealth—for example, Martin Byam endowed the Free School at Manchester.

From Deloney's *Thomas of Reading now the 4th time corrected and enlarged*, 1612. TYPE 956A. MOTIFS: J.445.2 [*Foolish marriage of old man and young girl*]; K.1550 [*Husband outwits adulteress and paramour*]; K.1816 [*Disguise as menial*]; T.91.6.2 [*Prince in love with lowly girl*]; K.2241 [*Treacherous innkeeper*]; K.735.4 [*Capture in trap-bed*]; R.352 [*Lovers fleeing from slavery are recaptured*]; S.73.3 [*Man blinds brother*].

¶ This is an extraordinary hotch-potch of types and motifs, the chief interest of it being that it is one of those tales exalting the great merchants of England, of which "Whittington and His Cat" is the best-known example.

The story of Robert's blindness seems to have had no foundation, and is not found in any of the chronicles until the thirteenth century. The story of Robert's marriage to Margaret of Shrewsbury is equally unfounded. Anne Neville was supposed to disguise herself as a kitchen-maid after Warwick's death in the same way as Margaret of the White Hand. "Jack of Newbury" is a tale in the same vein. See "Whittington and His Cat".

TING, TONG, PLUFF

Norton, Supplementary Collection, no. 58, p. 70.

Passing through Massingham (really Messingham) in Lincolnshire, a long time ago, a traveller noticed three men sitting on a stile in the churchyard, and saying, "Come to church, Thompson!" "Come to church, Brown!" and so on. Surprised at this, the traveller asked what it meant. He was told that, having no bells, this was how they called folk to church. The traveller, remarking that it was a pity so fine a church should have no bells, asked the men if they could make three for the church, promising to pay for them himself. This they undertook to do. They were a tinker, a carpenter, and a shoemaker respectively.

When the visitor came round that way again, he found the three men ringing three bells, which said, "Ting, Tong, Pluff," being made respectively of tin, wood, and leather.

Gutch and Peacock, pp. 424–5, quoting *Ecclesiastical Curiosities*, edited by W. Andrews, 1899, p. 135.

¶ This seems a commentary on the proverbial phrase, "Nothing like leather", explained in the *Fables* of R. Lestrange (1692), p. 484: "There was a council of mechanics, called to advise about the fortifying of a city…Up starts a currier; Gentlemen, says he, when y'ave said all that can be said, there's nothing in the world like leather."

TOR-BARROW HILL*

Hartland, *County Folk-Lore*, I, *Gloucestershire, Suffolk, Leicestershire and Rutland*, pp. 41–2.

Two men digging a gravel pit at the foot of this hill, having sunk four yards deep, discovered an entrance into the hill, where they found several rooms with their furniture, which being touched, crumbled to dust. In one of them were several images and urns, some with ashes, others full of coins, with Latin inscriptions on them. Entering another, they were surprised at seeing the figure of a man in armour, having a truncheon in its hand, and a light, in a glass like a lamp, burning before it. At their first approach, the image made an effort to strike, so at the second step, but with greater force; but at the third it struck a violent blow, which broke the glass to pieces, and extinguished the light. Having a lanthorn, they had just time to observe that on the left hand (I suppose of the figure) lay two heads embalmed, with long beards, and the skin looking like parchment, when hearing a hollow noise like a groan, they hastily quitted those dark apartments, and immediately the earth fell in, and buried all the curiosities. Camden was informed by credible persons that, at the suppression of monasteries, there was found a lamp burning in the vault of that little chapel wherein Constantius Chlorus was thought to be buried. Lazius, says that antiquarian, tells us that the antients had an art of dissolving gold into a fat liquor, and of preparing it so that it would continue burning in the sepulchres for many ages.

Camden, *Britannia*, v, 2, col. 880, in his account of York city. Rudder, p. 347.
MOTIFS: E.481.3 [*Abode of dead in mountain*]; F.855 [*Extraordinary image*]; D.1652.6 [*Ever-burning lamp*].
¶ See "Potter Thompson".

* Near Cirencester.

TRAPPING THE PLAGUE

Hugh Miller, *Scenes and Legends*, p. 245.

In a central part of the churchyard of Nigg there is a rude, undressed stone, near which the sexton never ventures to open a grave. A wild apocryphal tradition connects the erection of this stone with the times of the quarantine fleet. The plague, as the story goes, was brought to the place by one of the vessels, and was slowly flying along the ground, disengaged from every vehicle of infection, in the shape of a little yellow cloud. The whole country was alarmed, and groups of people were to be seen on every eminence, watching with anxious horror the progress of the little cloud. They were relieved, however, from their fears and the plague by an ingenious man of Nigg, who, having provided himself with an immense bag of linen, fashioned somewhat in the manner of a fowler's net, cautiously approached the yellow cloud, and, with a skill which could have owed nothing to previous practice, succeeded in enclosing the whole of it in the bag. He then secured it by wrapping it up carefully, fold after fold, and fastening it down with pin after pin; and as the linen was gradually changing, as if under the hands of the dyer, from white to yellow, he consigned it to the churchyard, where it has slept ever since.

MOTIFS: F.493.0.4 [*Pestilence in visible form*]; F.493.3.2 [*Pestilence spirit bound by magic*].

¶ There are many legends of the persistence of the plague germs. One such was current in 1926 of a piece of land in the middle of Bristol, in which plague victims had been buried, and in which the infection still persisted. The more picturesque belief was that the plague was a spirit.

See "The Plague in Edinburgh" (B, XII).

THE TRAVELLER'S CORN-SACK

Norton Collection, II, p. 219.

On the road from Caistor to Grimsby, in a field by the highway, there stands, or used to stand, a stone known as the "Traveller's Corn-sack". One winter's day, many years ago, a horseman rode along the road—at that time little more than a track across the open wolds—making his way towards Grimsby. As he pressed forward he saw a man busy at work sowing grain, and drew near to ask him if he would give or sell him some of it for his horse, which, like its master, showed signs of a long journey.

"I am short of corn myself," was the sower's reply. "I can neither give nor sell." But the wayfarer's glance had fallen on a sack which was standing near.

"You have a sack there still full," he urged, "and you have almost done sowing. Give me something for my horse."

"That!" said the sower; "that is a great cobble-stone and no sack of corn!"

Receiving this churlish and untruthful refusal, the rider's wrath was roused, and in his anger he uttered the following words:

> "Saints reward both thee and thine,
> As thou rewardest me and mine,
> A stone, thou sayest, I can see—
> Stone for ever shall it be."

And having spoken thus he passed on his way, leaving the startled husbandman to find that the sack had indeed become stone.

Folk-Lore, XII, p. 164. Peacock, *Folklore of Lincolnshire*. From a Lincolnshire man in Buenos Aires.
MOTIF: A.973 [*Punishment of discourtesy: corn to stone*].
¶ See "The Bishop's Bread and Cheese".

THE TREASURE OF
BERRY POMEROY CASTLE

J. R. W. Coxhead, *The Devil in Devon*, pp. 46–7.

Two miles to the east of the ancient borough of Totnes, in a very beautiful and romantic situation, stand the ruins of Berry Pomeroy Castle. Attached to this historic stronghold, which was built in the early part of the fourteenth century by a member of the great medieval family of Pomeroy, is a most interesting legend about hidden treasure.

Once upon a time there lived in Totnes an honest and worthy young workman named John Nokes, who as a boy must have explored every nook and cranny of the castle from the outermost walls to the innermost recesses. One night he happened to experience a very vivid dream in which he found himself wandering amongst the ruins, and after a while, by some unaccountable urge, he was impelled to examine very closely the chimney of one of those enormous fireplaces which are so often found in old mansions. A short distance up the chimney he noticed something peculiar about a certain piece of masonry, and on removing the mortar there was revealed, to his astonished gaze, an iron crock filled with gold.

When he awoke in the morning, John related the dream to his wife, who treated the whole matter with amused scepticism. On the following night, however, the compelling dream was repeated in every particular. Rising quickly from his bed, he would have gone at once to the place so clearly indicated, but, yielding to his wife's advice, he decided to postpone the visit to some more suitable time.

The third night he experienced the wonderful dream again, and the strong desire to investigate the matter could no longer be resisted, so, without disturbing his wife, who might have tried to dissuade him for his purpose, he dressed himself and quietly left the house.

It was just past midnight. Rain was falling in torrents, and the wind was blowing so hard that Nokes had some difficulty in making his way down Fore Street. When he reached the bridge spanning the river, he met a man on horseback. The rider happened to be a local doctor returning from visiting a patient, who was seriously ill.

Now in those far-off days it was a strange thing for a solitary pedestrian to be seen abroad in such wild weather and at so late an hour, so the horseman drew up, and asked John who he was and where he was going.

"I be Jan Nokes," replied John.

"What calls you away from home at this time of night?" asked the physician.

"Well, Doctor," answered John, recognizing the rider. "I be a-goin' tu Berry Castle."

"Goodness me," exclaimed the doctor in surprise. "Why on earth do you wish to go to Berry Castle in this dreadful weather, and at such a late hour?"

Feeling rather foolish, honest John Nokes told the physician all about his remarkable dream, and how it had been repeated three times. The doctor seemed to be very much impressed with the earnest manner in which John told his story; but when it was over he insisted that the dreams were simply figments of an overheated imagination, and strongly advised the young workman to go back to bed. "Anyhow," he added kindly, "if you really think there is anything in it, you can go to the castle, and make a careful examination by daylight."

Thanking the doctor for his advice, poor John returned home in a somewhat troubled frame of mind, and went quietly to bed. The following morning he arose very early, and hurried to the castle in order to solve the tantalizing mystery.

When he reached the ruined stronghold, he proceeded at once to the chimney in question, and very soon found the place that had been so vividly revealed to him in his dream. As he prepared to climb up to the spot, he found himself stepping on several large lumps of dry mortar. His suspicions were at once aroused, and when he reached the place he had seen in his dream, he discovered that the cavity containing the crock had been broken open quite recently and the golden hoard had disappeared.

To the day of his death John Nokes was firmly convinced that, after leaving him at Totnes Bridge, the crafty doctor went himself to the castle, and seized the treasure. The fact that before the night of the storm the physician had been in rather needy circumstances, whereas soon afterwards he suddenly became very wealthy strengthened his conviction.

From *Transactions of the Devonshire Association*, XI, pp. 346–7.
TYPE ML.8010. MOTIFS: N.517 [*Treasure hidden in building*] N.531 [*Treasure discovered through dream*]; N.563 [*Treasure-seekers find hole from which treasure has recently been removed*].
¶ See "The Pedlar of Swaffham", "Upsall Castle", "The Rifled Barrow".

TREASURE–DIGGING

Ruth L. Tongue, *Somerset Folklore*, p. 14.

Treasure-digging is always attended with some hazard. A field near the old Roman Camp at North Petherton is called the Money Field. A plough turned up several coins here where the old market-place once stood, and they say that somewhere close at hand is a buried treasure-house with an iron door, which holds "wealth untold". If you are desperate enough to dig for it, you must choose a night with a full moon, for it can only be seen then. But they also say that if you hear the thunder of chariot wheels and the crash of galloping hooves fast approaching to run you down—well, "don't blame me".

MOTIFS: F.721.4 [*Underground treasure-chamber*]; N.576 [*Ghosts prevent men from raising treasure*].
¶ See "The Treasure of Castle Rach", "The Rifled Barrow".

UFFAS, SHRUBBS AND SIERBERTS

W. H. Barratt, *More Tales from the Fens*, pp. 54–60.

In the days when the Fens were a sea in winter and a tangle of reeds and rushes in summer, there were three hills which stood out of the flat land a few miles from where the boggy land ended on the edge of the Norfolk high ground. One of these was the Isle of Southery, the second was Shrubb Hill and the third one was Shippea Hill. They were all on outcrops of gravel, and a savage lot of people lived there in clearings, with thickets of thorn and willow and alder all round them.

The folk living at Southery belonged to a tribe called Uffa, and they came from the Danish tribes who had settled there.

The Shrubb Hill people were different; they had been living there ever since the Stone Age. The Shippea Hill folk were tall and big and dark, because they had once lived in Africa, but had deserted from the Roman armies when they came over here, and had stolen and married any woman they could get hold of. In time their black skins, by marrying with white folk, turned to a yellowish colour, which is why Fen people are called "Yellow Bellies". Now, all these three lots of people, who were called the Uffas, the Shrubbs and the Sierberts, were very friendly with each other, and used to help each other whenever there was danger about. The soldiers of the Abbot of Ely had good reason to be afraid of these families when they came in their long boats, which they pushed with long poles through the reeds, to Ely, where they did a lot of damage and then cleared out as quietly as they'd come.

They came to Ely for one thing, and that was to get malt, because those fenmen were thirsty folk. So were the monks, and that's why they brewed once a week in the Abbey brewhouse near the river, but they stored the malt in a barn. Often the monks would come down in the morning and find that the barn had been broken into during the night and that several barrels of malt were missing. This was a great worry to the head brewer, who'd been in trouble before when he was in charge of the brewhouse at Crowland, where he'd been caught adding water to the ale after it was brewed. For this he'd had his ears dubbed and been turned adrift until, after wandering across the Fens, he'd turned up in Ely, where the name of Crowland's special brew was well known. So he was made very welcome by the monks, who called him "Croppy" because of his ears, and made him their head brewer. The raids on the malt store worried him because he had the feeling that the Abbot, when he got to know about them, would say that Croppy had stolen the malt and would cut off his nose.

So, when he saw the Abbot go into the barn one day with the monk who wrote everything down in the Abbey, Croppy left the brewhouse by the back door and ran to hide himself in the tall reeds by the river. It was winter-time and the fen was hard frozen, so he found hiding up a cold job, but he warmed up quickly when he heard the monks shouting out when the Abbot told them there'd be no ale for Christmas because the malt had been stolen.

Croppy set off eastwards, hoping to get across the fen before night came. The sound of dogs baying made him hurry even faster because he knew that the Abbot's soldiers were out looking for him. After running hard for some miles, he stopped to get his breath, and then he found that the air he was breathing in was full of a smell he knew very well; so, heading into the wind, he followed his nose till he came to a wooded island, where he ran slam into a crowd of men in sheepskins who tripped him up, put a knife at his throat and asked him if he was coming or going, and what was his name. Croppy told them and said:

"I'm the brewer of Ely and it was the smell of brewing which made me come here."

The men took him by a roundabout way through the alder and whin bushes till they came to a clearing where several huts were built. There he saw a big pot steaming over a turf fire, because it was the Shrubbs' brewing day. Croppy was given a horn full of some of what was left over from the last brew, and, as he was thirsty, he gulpde it down.

"Call that ale?" he said. "Why, it's no more than good water spoilt. Now, if you can find your way to Ely after dark I'll go with you and fetch the proper tools and make you a proper drop of good ale; but you must keep that pot boiling for two days and nights."

Just before dark, then, Croppy and several of the strongest Shrubbs set off for Ely with a sledge. When they got to the Abbey brewhouse they loaded an earthenware jar of yeast and a wooden cask of honey and some other things on to the sledge and then set off back to the island. Next day Croppy started work, and some of the Shrubbs wondered what in the world he was doing when they saw him throw a lot of willow bark* into the simmering pot. When everything had boiled to his liking, he ladled the liquor out of the pot into the jars they'd brought from Ely and, when it was cool, put in the yeast and honey.

A few days later a white froth bubbled over from the jars and Croppy told the Shrubbs that this was balm and that some must always be kept for the next brew. When the froth had stopped coming, he covered the jars with parchment, and a week later called all the Shrubbs round him and gave them some of the brew to taste. One and all declared it was the best drop of ale they'd ever tasted.

Then Croppy told them that in two weeks' time it would be the thirteenth full moon of the year and it was then that he'd always brewed a special ale for the Abbot's feast; in return for the shelter the Shrubbs had given him, he was going, with their help, to give them the biggest bust-up they'd ever had, but it would mean another trip to Ely. So, a day or two later, every man in the tribe set out for Ely, three men to each sledge, which they lined up outside the brewhouse. Croppy went in first and over to a corner, where he lifted a flat stone slab with a flight of steps under it. These stairs, Croppy said, were the bolt-holes which the monks had used when the Danes came.

---

* Willow bark was a very old Fenland remedy to reduce fever in ague and malaria; our modern aspirin (salicylic acid) is its equivalent.

They all went down in single file and along a passage till they came
to a stone door set in the wall. Croppy opened this and then, with a
finger on his lips to show the Shrubbs they must keep quiet, he went
through the doorway and beckoned the others to follow him, which
they did, and then they found themselves in the kitchen larder. Croppy
loaded each man up with hams, cheeses, sides of bacon, wine-jars and
sacks of flour and kept guard while they went to and from the sledges.
Then he closed the stone door, went along the passage, put back the
stone slab in the brewhouse, and then they all went home across the
fen, dragging the sledges behind them. That Christmas was the best
that the Shrubbs had ever had; the ale was so strong and the food so
good that, by evening, those that weren't making love were either
sleeping or fighting.

By springtime the supply of malt had run out and the Shrubb Hill
tribe were so thirsty that they raided the barn of Thetford Abbey,* a
day's journey each way. What they saw in Thetford, though, filled
them with terror, because hundreds of Norman soldiers were camped
on the heath. It was those soldiers who got blamed by the monks for
stealing the malt, which, though it was safe by then at Shrubb Hill,
couldn't be used because the smoke from the fire would have shown
where the tribe's hide-out was. Every night the sky was red with the
light from camp-fires in the east and the south, and the Shrubb Hill
folk were even more scared when the whole of the Shippea Hill tribe
came over saying they'd been driven out of their homes by Norman
soldiers, who'd swarmed into the Fens from Brandon way. Then, when
outposts, hidden in the reeds, brought back news that soldiers were
trying to cross over to Shrubb Hill, both tribes decided to look for
shelter in Southery, because that island had a belt of thorn and brambles
all round it, as well as two gates which still have names today. The
Southery folk built extra huts to hold the other two tribes, who brought
all their belongings with them. The Shrubbs' malt came in handy and
Croppy soon had a brew going, but the Uffas had a stronger drink called
mead, and when Croppy tried some of this he found it made him so
bold that he got round a young Uffa woman to go back with him to
Shrubb Hill because he didn't like Southery.

Well, Croppy and the woman lived alone till summer was nearly
over and then, one day, they were missing and the look-outs in the
reeds said they'd seen them making their way towards Brandon along
the secret way which only the Fenmen knew gave a firm foothold.

Some months afterwards the woman came back to Southery and told

* The Cluniac Priory at Thetford, Norfolk, was founded in 1104. Little remains of it
except the gateway called Abbey Gate, but the foundations of the monastic church can be
traced.

the tribes what had happened. She said that Croppy, when he got to Brandon, told the Norman soldiers that he knew a way to get into Ely, but they wouldn't believe him. An officer who liked the look of the woman told Croppy to clear off.

"If I do," said Croppy, "you'll never get into Ely."

Now it so happened that the King of the Normans was in Brandon, fed-up because he'd lost so many men when he'd tried to get into Ely from the south; so, when the officer told him that there was a man who used to be a monk in the Abbey, saying he knew a secret way to get into Ely, the King said:

"Bring him in, and the woman too."

So Croppy was brought along and given a flagon of wine and told to start talking unless he and his woman wanted their throats cut. After he'd talked, and been promised a big reward, a great party of officers and soldiers went in single file across the fen two nights later, with the woman leading them because, being an Uffa, she knew all the secret pathways over the boggy land. Croppy was there too, sweating with fright because he had an officer just behind him who was pointing a naked sword at his ribs just in case they were ambushed.

Just before dawn they got to the brewhouse, went through the passage and through the stone door into the larder and then all over the Abbey. Most of the monks were killed as they lay in their beds, but those who were awake rushed for the bolt-hole, where they were set upon by the guard, who'd been left at the brewhouse door, and taken prisoner, the Abbot among them. It was all over by sunrise, and at noon the few Ely men left saw the big gates open and the King ride in. When he saw the handful of Ely men he said:

"You can all go, because a battle's no victory when it's been won by a trick."

Then he ordered Croppy to be sent to him. Croppy had put on a monk's habit which he had found, as he thought that was the best dress to wear for meeting a king and getting the reward he'd been promised. But when the King saw him he shouted to his men:

"Strip off that habit from him and give him back his sheepskin and then hang him from the highest branch of that willow tree."

The soldiers asked Croppy if there was anything he'd like to ask for before he was strung up.

"I could do with a last drink of ale," he said, but the Abbot told the soldiers there wasn't a drop in the place as all the malt had been stolen months ago. So the soldiers, thinking a little was better than nothing, hauled Croppy up so high that the last thing he saw was the brewhouse roof sticking up over the garden wall.

Croppy's woman spent some time with the officer and then made her way back to Southery. Several times the Norman soldiers attacked the place, but they never got into it, because the Southery men were the fiercest fighters in the land, just as they are today. Then, some while after she came back, the woman had a baby boy, but the Fenmen strangled it as soon as it was born because they weren't sure if its father was a traitor or a Norman and, anyway, they said, there were enough slimy snakes in the fen already. The three tribes went on living together and fighting and fishing side by side, and no stranger ever went there of his own accord. Although a lot of marrying was done between them, yet the Uffa men today are still tall and fair and the Shrubbs broad and short, while the Sierberts are huge men with curly black hair. A stranger keeps away from them, and especially from the women—that is, provided he knows what Southery men are like when they see an outsider coming after their womenfolk.

TYPE ML.8000. MOTIF: K.310 [*Means of entering house or treasury*]; Q.261 [*Treachery punished*].

UPSALL CASTLE

Gutch, *County Folk-Lore*, II, p. 408.

Many years ago there resided in the village of Upsall a man who dreamed three nights successively that if he went to London Bridge he would hear of something greatly to his advantage. He went, travelling the whole distance from Upsall to London on foot, arrived there, he took his station on the bridge, where he waited till his patience was nearly exhausted, and the idea that he had acted a very foolish part began to arise in his mind. At length he was accosted by a Quaker, who kindly inquired what he was waiting there so long for. After some hesitation, he told his dreams. The Quaker laughed at his simplicity, and told him that *he* had had that night a very curious dream himself, which was that if went and dug under a certain bush in Upsall Castle in Yorkshire, he would find a pot of gold; but he did not know where Upsall was, and inquired of the countryman if he knew, who, seeing some advantage in secrecy, pleaded ignorance of the locality; and then, thinking his business in London was completed, returned immediately home, dug beneath the bush, and there he found a pot filled with gold, and on the cover an inscription in a language he did not understand. The pot and cover, were, however preserved at the village inn; where one day a bearded stranger like a Jew made his appearance, saw the pot, and read the inscription, the plain English of which was:

Look lower, where this stood
Is another twice as good.

The man of Upsall, hearing this, resumed his spade, returned to the bush, dug deeper and found another pot filled with gold far more valuable than the first: encouraged by this, he dug deeper still, and found another yet more valuable.

This story has been related of other places, but Upsall appears to have as good a claim to this yielding of hidden treasure as the best of them. Here we have the constant tradition of the inhabitants, and the identical bush still remains beneath which the treasure was found; an elder near the north-west corner of the ruins.

Grainge, *The Vale of Mowbray*, pp. 277, 278. Whellan, II, pp. 693, 694.

TYPE 1645. MOTIF: N.531.1 [*Treasure discovered through dream*].

¶ The motif of this inscription on the coffin and the treasure buried below occurs in this example, as well as in "The Swaffham Tinker" and several versions of "The Pedlar of Swaffham".

See also "How Dundonald Castle was built".

VEITCH OF DAWYK

Scott, *Minstrelsy of the Scottish Border*, I, p. 118.

Veitch of Dawyk, a man of great strength and bravery, who flourished in the sixteenth century, is said by tradition to have been on bad terms with a neighbouring proprietor, Tweedie of Drummelzier, dwelling also near the source of the Tweed. By some accident, a flock of Dawyk's sheep had strayed over into Drummelzier's grounds at the time when *Dickie of the Den*, a Liddesdale outlaw, was making his rounds in Tweeddale.

Seeing this flock of sheep, he drove them off without ceremony. Next morning Veitch, perceiving his loss, summoned his servants and retainers, and laid a bloodhound upon the traces of the robber, by whom they were guided for many miles, till, on the banks of Liddal, the dog stayed upon a very large haystack. The pursuers were a good deal surprised by the obstinate pause of the bloodhound, till Dawyk pulled down some of the hay, and discovered a large excavation, containing the robber and his spoil. He instantly flew upon Dickie, and was about to poniard him when the marauder, with the address noticed by Lesley, protested that he would never have touched a *cloot* [hoof] of them had he not taken them for Drummelzier's property. This dexterous appeal to Veitch's passions saved the life of the freebooter.

MOTIF: J.1181.3 [*Condemned man wins pardon by clever remark*].

THE VISION OF JOHN OF KILSTARE

Gutch, *County Folk-Lore*, II, p. 204.

[John of Kilstare, who had been made Abbot of Jervaulx—the Abbey of that name being not yet in existence—set forth from Byland with a few monks and many misgivings to revive an abandoned religious establishment at Fors. They came to a village (unidentified) and] Here the Abbot dreamt he was at Byland, where in the cloister he beheld a woman of beauty surpassing human, and in her left hand a boy, the lustre of whose countenance was as that of the morn in her brightness. The boy plucked a beautiful branch from a tree in the midst of the cloister and vanished. Proceeding on their way they quickly found themselves entangled among bushes and rocks. The Abbot exclaimed, "Since we are impeded, let us repeat our hours and the gospel." Immediately the virgin with her child appeared again; to whom he cried, "Fair and tender woman, what doest thou with thy son in this rugged and desert place?" To whom the woman replied, "I am a frequent inmate of desert places, but now I have come from Rievaulx and Biland, with whose abbots I am familiarly acquainted, and am going to the new monastery [Fors]." Then said the Abbot, "Good Lady, I implore thee to conduct me and my brethren out of this desert place, and lead us to the new monastery, for we are of Biland." She replied, "Ye were late of Biland, but now of Jorevale." Then she said, "Sweet son, be their leader; I am called elsewhere," and disappeared. The boy, holding in his hands the branch plucked from the cloister of Biland, cried aloud, "Follow me." At length they arrived at a barren, un-cultivated place, when the boy planted the bough, which was instantly filled with white birds, and having exclaimed, "Here shall God be adored for a short space," disappeared also. Reflecting on the vision, the Abbot quickly discerned that they were not long to remain at Fors. Passing through a certain village, the barking of the dogs woke the inhabitants, who, perceiving the procession of monks in their white clothing, one said, "These are the Abbot and monks passing from Biland to Jorevale"; and another, looking to the stars, exclaimed, "They have chosen a fortunate time, for within thirty or forty years, they shall attain a state of worldly glory, from which they shall never fall." The Abbot accepted the omen and pursued his way.

Whitaker, *An History of Richmondshire*, I, pp. 410, 411.
MOTIF: V.111.3.2 [*Divine person points out site for church*].
¶ See "Wroxall Abbey".

THE WARDLAWS OF PITREAVIE [abbreviated]

Wilkie, *Bygone Fife*, p. 30.

Almost equidistant between Dunfermline and Inverkeithing stands the Castle of Pitreavie brooding over the departed glory of the Wardlaws, whose family tree bore both a cardinal and a poetess.

The history of the lands of Pitreavie goes back to the days of Robert the Bruce. Then a sister of the king owned them. They became possessions of the Church for a time till the chaplain of St Giles, Edinburgh, who served at the altar they maintained, conveyed them with the consent of the magistrates to a relative.

It was not the "meddling with halie things", however, that brought the curse on the family, for that transaction was before the days of Sir Cuthbert, the first-known Wardlaw of Pitreavie. It was their conduct at the Battle of Inverkeithing.

According to tradition, the tide of conflict on that beautiful July Sunday in 1651 rolled up to the valley before the castle. Under its very walls the Highlanders made their last stand for the king. The Wardlaws sympathized with the Cromwellians, wherefore none seems to know, and showered upon the devoted warriors of the Clan McLean stones and other missiles. With their backs literally against the wall, five hundred brave men, invoking Our Lady's aid, defied their assailants for two long hours. There old Sir Hector, their chief, fought like a lion, guarded by his six stalwart sons, each of whom in turn fell, and, as he fell, shouted with his last breath, "*Has air son Eachin!*" [Death for Hector].

When all was over, the callous occupants of the castle refused shelter to the wounded remnant, wherefore it was predicted that never more should the Wardlaws of Pitreavie prosper, but pass "like snaw aff a dyke". So it befell. The first baronet, Sir Henry, went to his account eighteen months later. On the 2nd of March, 1653, according to Lamont, "he dyed suddenlike, and, as it was said by some, the last word he spake was ane oath". In half a century more the lands had gone for ever from his race.

MOTIFS: Q.291 [*Hard-heartedness punished*]; M.460 [*Curses on families*].
¶ Family curses are particularly common in Scottish tradition.

THE WEDDERSTONE

Denham Tracts, I, p. 328.

The Wedderstone stands in a field near the village of Catton in Allendale. Tradition states that many years ago a notorious sheep-stealer infested this part of the county, who, it appears, was the terror of the whole of the neighbouring farmers; in the first place because he appeared to be a good judge of mutton, from the fact of his generally taking the choice of the flock; and in the second place that, although he paid a visit to every sheepfold for several miles around, and to many where a strict watch was kept, he remained unsuspected; neither was there the slightest suspicion as to who the thief might be. At length, however, the invisible became visible. It appeared that his method of carrying off his booty was to tie the four legs of the animal together, and then, by putting his head through the space between the feet and body, thus carry it away on his shoulders. On his last visit to the neighbour's flock, the animal which he had selected for his week's provision being heavy, he stopped to rest himself, and placed his burden upon the top of a small stone column (without taking it off his shoulders), when the animal suddenly became restive, commenced struggling and slipped off the stone on the opposite side. Its weight being thus suddenly drawn round his neck, the poor wretch was unable to extricate himself, and was found on the following morning quite dead.

M O T I F: Q.424.5* [*Sheep-thief is strangled as he rests sheep on post behind him*] (Baughman).

¶ See "The Hangman's Stone", "The Sheep-stealers of the Blackdown Hills".

WHITBY BELLS

Gutch, *County Folk-Lore*, II, *North Riding of Yorkshire*, pp. 39–40.

A favourite story told in connection with the abbey is one concerning its bells. It runs thus: The magnificent peal excited the cupidity of some sea-roving freebooter, and, landing with a sufficient force, he extracted the bells from the sacred building and conveyed them on board his vessel.

This desecration was, however, not suffered to go unpunished, for ere the vessel had gone many miles she struck and foundered a short distance from a projecting ridge of rock called the "Black Nab". As a fitting conclusion to this, we are told, that he who cares on Hallowe'en to spend some time on the rock, and call his sweetheart's name, will hear it echoed by the breeze, accompanied with the ringing of marriage bells from the sunken chime.

Horne, *Guide to Whitby* p. 13.

VARIANT

The abbey was suppressed in A.D. 1539, and shortly afterwards dismantled. The bells were sold and were to be conveyed by ship to London. They were duly placed on board, and, amid the lamentation of the people, the sails were unfurled and the anchor weighed. But lo!

the vessel refused to bear its sacred burden. A short distance it moved out into the bay, and then—on the beautiful, calm summer evening—it quietly sank beneath the waves; and there under the waters, at a spot within sight of the abbey ruins, the bells still remain, and are still heard occasionally by the superstitious, rung by invisible hands.

Parkinson, *Yorkshire Legends and Traditions*, 1st series, p. 29.
TYPE ML.7070. MOTIFS: V.115.1 [*Church bell sunk in sea*]; F.993 [*Sunken bell sounds*].
¶ See "The Bells of Forrabury", "The Bells of Brinkburn".

THE WHITE DOE OF RYLSTONE [summary]

Parkinson *Yorkshire Legends and Traditions*, 1st series, p. 45.

In 1569 a rising took place in the North against the new Protestant religion, and at its head were Percy, Earl of Northumberland, and Neville, Earl of Westmorland. Many Yorkshire gentlemen from the dales came to join them, amongst them Richard Norton of Rylstone, with eight of his nine sons, bearing a banner embroidered with the five wounds of our Lord.

Whilst they were engaged in the siege of Barnard Castle, the Earl of Sussex came against them with the royal forces from York. The rebel leaders lost heart and dispersed, but the Nortons were captured, conveyed to York, and there put to death.

The eldest son of the family, Francis, had refused to join the rising, and remained at home with Emily, his only sister, for they two had received the reformed faith from their mother, who was now dead. Dreading a disastrous end to the rebellion, Francis had followed behind his father, and watched events from afar. He gained access to their prison at York, claimed the banner, which had become the emblem of the whole rebel force, and escaped with it. But when the others had been executed, Sir George Bowes, with a company of horsemen, was sent in pursuit, and Francis was overtaken and killed. For two days his body lay out on the moor. Then a forester belonging to the family found it, and carried it to Bolton Abbey, hoping to spare the gentle Emily the sight of a mangled body. But she, in restless anxiety, had wandered from home, and came to Bolton, where the burial was even then being made.

In all this time her companion and solace had been a white doe, given to her long before by one of her brothers, but now she left even the doe behind, and, dressed as a pilgrim, she wandered far and wide for many years. When she returned, Rylstone Hall was desolate and her family almost forgotten. As she sat unrecognized under an ancient

390

oak tree, a troop of deer came by in swift flight, and were almost past her when one of them suddenly stopped, came timidly up to her, and laid its head on her lap. At once they became inseparable as before. Emily found a home among the humble folk of the region, and passed her days in visiting spots whose associations with her family made them dear to her. When at last she died, the faithful doe still haunted these places for many years, especially Bolton Priory and the grave of Francis Norton, and ever came to Bolton on sabbath days at the hour of service.

Based on Wordsworth.

TYPE ML.8000. MOTIF: B.301 [*Faithful animal*].

¶ Wordsworth worked on a local tradition in his "White Doe of Rylston", but doubtless reshaped it.

THE WHITE MARE OF WHITESTONECLIFFE

R. Blakeborough, *Wit, Character, Folklore and Customs of the North Riding of Yorkshire*, p. 205.

A white Arab mare (in the days when light-coloured horses were commonly used for racing), belonging to a Yorkshire nobleman, while in training at Hambleton became so unmanageable that at last the strongest lad in the stable boasted that he would either ride her a three-mile gallop along the regular course and "best her" or else ride her to the Devil.

Part of this old gallop (later planted with trees, and so ruined by a Puritanical baronet) lay along the edge of a precipice. At the foot, some three hundred feet below, lies the Lake Formire, a hundred feet above sea-level; and tradition says that the lad was carried over the cliffs, and neither he nor the mare were ever seen again. Hence there is a saying:

> When Formire riggs are covered with hay,
> The white mare of Whitestone-cliffe shall bear it away.

TYPE 813. MOTIF: C.10 [*Tabu: profanely calling up spirit, Devil, etc.*].

THE WILD BOAR OF BISHOP AUCKLAND

F. Grice, *Folk Tales of the North Country*, p. 90.

Once there roamed over the land near Bishop Auckland a wild boar of enormous size, which so troubled the bishop who lived in the castle there that he offered a handsome reward for its capture. Few people were daring enough to attack the beast, but at last a sharp-witted young man named Pollard made up his mind to try for the reward. But before he went out to meet the boar he sat down to consider how best he could master it. "This beast is too fierce and savage for me to overcome with the help of my strength alone," he said to himself. "I must first study its habits, and use my cunning against its force."

So first he spent many days stalking the boar, finding out its favourite tracks, and when it went to feed, and what it liked best to eat; and he discovered that it was fond of roaming in a certain beech-wood, and liked to feed on the beech-mast that fell from the trees. So, when he had made himself familiar with the boar's habits, he put on his sword and climbed into the branches of the finest beech tree in the wood, and shook down as much mast as he could. When the ground lay thick with mast he hid himself in the leafiest part of the tree and waited.

By and by the boar came running through the wood, with its ears pricked and its snout to the ground. But when it came to the heaps of mast it sniffed around and began to feed. Pollard had never seen an animal with so great an appetite. It fed and fed until he thought it would never be satisfied; but at last it lay down and rolled on its side and went to sleep.

This was the moment that Pollard had been waiting for. Slipping quietly down the tree, he attacked it. It was fat and heavy after its great meal, but it turned upon him and drove him back with the fierceness of its charge. For hours and hours they fought. When the sun went down and the last bird stopped its singing, the battle still raged; and long after the stars had climbed up and over the wood, the issue was still in doubt.

It was only when the first rays of the rising sun came shining into the wood that Pollard delivered the last blow, and the boar lay dead. But so exhausted was he with his long struggle that he contented himself with cutting out the boar's tongue. He put it in his wallet and flung himself down to sleep.

He slept very deeply—so deeply that he did not waken when a few hours later a stranger came riding through the wood. Nor did the stranger notice Pollard, for he lay still and quiet amidst a clump of bracken. All he noticed was the dead boar, and when he came upon that he dismounted hastily.

"This is a piece of good luck," he said. "Surely some other animal must have killed the boar. Now, if I take its head to the bishop the reward is mine." So he cut off the head, and rode away with it in a sack.

When Pollard awoke he was filled with dismay, but, remembering that he still had the tongue in his wallet, he made his way as fast as he could to the bishop's castle. He was not a moment too soon, for when he entered the castle the stranger was just presenting the boar's head to the bishop, and the bishop was saying to him, "Yes, you have rid us of a notable pest, and I will reward you as I promised."

"Stop a moment, my lord," cried out Pollard. "It was I and not this stranger who killed the boar."

"But I cannot understand this," said the bishop. "This man has brought me its head. What proof have you to back up your claim?"

"This," said Pollard, and, drawing the tongue from his wallet, he presented it to him. And when he had told his story, and both the stranger and the bishop perceived that the tongue was missing from the boar's head, they agreed that the reward should go to Pollard.

"And this is your reward," said the bishop. "I am now just going to dinner. Return to me when the dinner hour is over, and I will give you as much land as you have been able to ride round while I have been dining."

Then the bishop went to dinner, and he did not hurry, for he was very grateful to the young man for ridding the countryside of the boar. After a leisurely meal, he went into the ante-room, and prepared to wait for the youth's return. But to his surprise, he saw Pollard already there and waiting for him.

"You are soon back," he said.

"Yes, my lord," replied Pollard. "I have not ridden far."

"I am pleased to see that you are not a grasping young man," said the bishop. "How far did you ride?"

"My lord," replied Pollard, "I rode no farther than round your lordship's own castle."

"By St Cuthbert," answered the Bishop, bursting into laughter, "I think you have outwitted me as well as you outwitted the boar and the stranger! If I am to keep my word, this castle is now yours. But come with me." And, leading him to a window, he showed him a wide stretch of land, with pastures and meadows and woodland.

"All this," he said, "I will give you in exchange for my castle. Will you accept it?"

"I will, my lord," said Pollard.

"Then," said the bishop, "it belongs to you and your heirs for ever."

So Pollard got his lands, and ever after they were known to the people of Bishop Auckland as Pollard's Lands.

MOTIFS: B.16.1.4.1 [*Giant devastating boar*]; H.105.1 [*Dragon-tongue proof*]; M.1584.2 [*Land measured according to the amount encompassed during certain hours*]. A similar story is told of Tongueland in Galloway.

See "Richard Gilpin of Kendal".

THE WILD MAN OF CRAIGIEBARNS

Dunkeld. Told by Mary Crerer, a girl of an old Dunkeld family in July 1927.

There was a wild man living among the rocks of Craigiebarns who ravaged the countryside, and put everyone in fear. No one could catch him, for he ran wild and broke all chains. At last the Earl of Atholl promised that the man who should catch him, and bring him in chained, should marry the Earl's daughter and be his heir. There were many that tried, and three that came near to succeeding, but each time the wild man burst his chains and killed his captor. In the end there was one called Murray, and he went to work in a cunning-like way. There was a well that the wild man came to drink at. It may have been the one that was afterwards called Lady Charlotte's Well. It's not a real well: a stream runs through it.

One dark night Murray went to work there, and he turned the stream aside above where it comes down over the rock, and he filled the well with Atholl brose—that is whisky and honey. In the morning the Wild Man came to drink, and he liked the brose fine, and he drank and drank, until he fell fast asleep, and Murray came and put heavy chains upon him, and took him to the Earl.

So Murray married the Earl's daughter, and he got the broad lands of Atholl after the Earl died, and that's how there is a wild man in fetters for the supporter of the Atholl arms, and the motto he took was "Furth, Fortune, and fill the Fetters", and that's the motto they have yet.

MOTIF: K.776 [*Capture by intoxication*].

¶ This is one of a number of legends to explain the adoption of coats of arms. Another example is "Richard Gilpin of Kendal".

See also "Dreel Castle".

WILLIAM OF LINDHOLME

Gutch and Peacock, *County Folk-Lore* v, *Lincolnshire*, p. 322.

In former times the country people believed that this place was the residence of a giant, to whom they have given the name of William of Lindholme. He is supposed, also, to have been a wizard, magician, or enchanter, in league with infernal spirits or demons. His first exploit was performed when a boy. His parents went to Wroot Feast, and left him to keep the sparrows from the corn, at which he was so enraged that he took up an enormous stone, and threw it at the house to which they were gone, but, from throwing it too high, it fell on the other side. After he had done this, William went to Wroot; and when scolded for so doing, said he had fastened up all the sparrows in the barn, where they found on their return in the evening, all dead, except a few which were turned white. One of this breed of white sparrows is fabled to have been seen a few years ago. A farmer on whose land this stone fell which William threw to Wroot, fastened six horses to it, but their united strength was unable to move it, and, as they all died soon after, the inhabitants of Wroot consider it as extremely unlucky to meddle with this or any large stones in the neighbourhood. Two immense boulder stones called the *Thumb Stone* and the *Little Finger Stone* are said to have been brought here by him and an antient unfinished causeway is also said to have been the work of this necromancer. "He undertook", says the legend, "to do it as fast as a man could gallop a horse, on condition that the rider should not look behind him." When the person had proceeded a few yards he heard such a noise and confusion that his fears got the better of his resolution; he looked back and saw stones and gravel flying in all directions and William in the midst of hundreds of little demons, not in blue but in red jackets, macadamizing as fast as possible. The terrified horseman exclaimed, "God speed your work," which, as is usual in all these stories, put a stop to the whole business, and left the good people who had to pass and repass from Lindholme to Hatfield to wade through the bog for two hundred years longer. When the time had arrived for the fulfilment of his contract with Satan, he [William] dug a grave in his cell, and lay down in it; and then, by taking away the prop which supported a large flagstone just over it, buried himself.

W. B. Stonehouse, *History & Topography of The Isle of Axholme*, pp. 393–5.
MOTIFS: A.977.1 [*Giant responsible for certain stones*]; D.2072.0.2.2.1 [*Person charged with keeping birds from the crops confines them in barn by magic while he goes to town*]; G.303.9.1.7 [*Devil builds a road*].
¶ The story of the birds confined to the barn is told of St Adelme and of Jack of Kent.

WILLIE ARMSTRONG OF WESTBURNFLAT

Scott, *Minstrelsy of the Scottish Border*, I, p. 338.

One of the last Border reivers was...of this family [the Armstrongs] and lived within the beginning of the last century. After having made himself dreaded over the whole country, he at last came to the following end: One ——, a man of large property, having lost twelve cows in one night, raised the country of Tiviotdale, and traced the robbers into Liddesdale, as far as the house of this Armstrong, commonly called *Willie of Westburnflat*, from the place of his residence on the banks of the Hermitage water. Fortunately for the pursuers, he was then asleep;

so that he was secured, along with nine of his friends, without much resistance. He was brought to trial at Selkirk; and, although no precise evidence was adduced to convict him of the special fact (the cattle never having been recovered), yet the jury brought him in *guilty* on his general character, or, as it is called in our law, on habit and repute.

When sentence was pronounced, Willie arose; and, seizing the oaken chair in which he was placed, broke it into pieces by main strength, and offered to his companions, who were involved in the same doom, that, if they would stand behind him, he would fight his way out of Selkirk with these weapons. But they held his hands, and besought him to let them *die like Christians*. They were accordingly executed in form of law. This incident is said to have happened at the last Circuit Court held at Selkirk. The people of Liddesdale, who (perhaps not erroneously) still consider the sentence as iniquitous, remarked, that ——, the prosecutor, never throve afterwards, but came to beggary and ruin, with his whole family.

¶   See "West Molland House".

WILLY-HOWE

Gutch, *County Folk-Lore*, VI, *East Riding of Yorkshire*, p. 6.

There is an artificial mount by the side of the road leading from North Burton to wold Newton near Bridlington in Yorkshire, called "Willy-howe", much exceeding in size, the generality of our "hows", of which I have heard the most preposterous stories related. A cavity or division on the summit is pointed out as owing its origin to the following circumstance:

A person having intimation of a large chest of gold being buried therein, dug away the earth until it appeared in sight; he then had a train of horses, extending upwards of a quarter of a mile, attached to it by strong iron traces; by these means he was just on the point of accomplishing his purpose when he exclaimed:

"Hop, Perry, Prow Mark,
  Whether God's will or not, we'll have this ark."

He, however, had no sooner pronounced this awful blasphemy, than all the traces broke, and the chest sunk still deeper in the hill, where it yet remained, all his future efforts to obtain it being in vain.

The inhabitants of the neighbourhood also speak of the place being peopled with fairies, and tell of the many extraordinary feats which this diminutive race has performed. A fairy once told a man, to whom it appears she was particularly attached, if he went to the top of "Willy-

howe" every morning, he would find a guinea; this information, however, was given under the injunction that he should not make the
circumstance known to any other person. For some time he continued
his visit, and always successfully; but at length, like our first parents,
he broke the great commandment, and, by taking with him another
person, not merely suffered the loss of the usual guinea, but met with
a severe punishment from the fairies for his presumption. Many more
are the tales which abound here, and which almost seem to have made
this a consecrated spot.

T. C. Bridlington. Hone, *Table Book*, p. 41.
TYPE ML.8010. MOTIFS: N.512 [*Treasure in underground chamber*]; C.401.3 [*Tabu:
speaking while searching for treasure*]; F.342 [*Fairies give mortals money*]; F.348.7
[*Tabu: telling of fairy gifts*]; N.557 [*Treasure disappears after being uncovered*].

THE WIMBLESTONE

Ruth L. Tongue, *Somerset Folklore*, p. 12.

Zebedee Fry were coming home late from the hay-making above
Shipham. It were full moon, for they'd worked late to finish, and the
crop was late being a hill field, so he had forgot what night 'twas.
He thought he saw something big and dark moving in the field where
the big stone stood, but he was too bone-weary to go chasing any stray
bullock. Then something huge and dark in field came rustling all alongside lane hedge, and Zebedee he up and dive into the brimmles in the
ditch till it passed right along, and then he ran all a-tiptoe to reach
Shipham. When he come to the field gate he duck two-double and he
rush past it. But, for all that, he see this gurt stone, twelve feet and
more, a-dancing to itself in the moonlight over top end of field. And
where it always stood the moon were shining on a heap of gold money.
But Zebedee he didn't stop for all that, not until he were safe at the inn
at Shipham. They called he all sorts of fool for not getting his hand to
the treasure—but nobody seemed anxious to have a try—not after he'd
told them how nimble it danced round field. And nobody knows if
'twill dance again in a hundred years. Not till there's a full moon on
Midsummer Night.

From a school-friend, who heard it from her Mendip great-grandmother, aged
ninety.
MOTIFS: D.1641.2.4 [*Stone moves at midnight*]; D.1641.2.4(e) [*Stone runs round
field when clock strikes midnight*] (Baughman); N.511.6 [*Treasure hidden under stone*].
¶ This is one of many legends of moving stones. The Whispering Knights in the
Rollright Stones are said to go down and drink in the stream at midnight (Frome,
Folk-Lore, 1895, pp. 6–51). A Cornish stone turns round three times at cock-crow
(Hunt, p. 187).

WINWICK CHURCH

Choice Notes from "Notes and Queries" Folk-Lore, p. 2.

The parish church of Winwick, Lancashire, stands near that miracle-working spot where St Oswald, king of the Northumbrians, was killed. The founder had destined a different site for it, but his intention was overruled by a singular personage, whose will he never dreamed of consulting. It must here be noticed that Winwick had then not even received its name; the church, as was not uncommon in those days, being one of the earliest erections in the parish. The foundation of the church, then, was laid where the founder had directed, and the close of the first day's labour showed the workmen had not been idle, by the progress made in the building. But the approach of night brought to pass an event which utterly destroyed the repose of the few inhabitants around the spot. A pig was seen running hastily to the site of the new church, and as he ran he was heard to cry or scream aloud, "Wee-ee-wick, Wee-ee-wick, Wee-ee-wick!" Then, taking up a stone in his mouth, he carried it to the spot sanctified by the death of St Oswald, and, thus employing himself through the whole night, succeeded in removing all the stones which had been laid by the builders. The founder, feeling himself justly reproved for not having chosen that sacred spot for the site of his church, unhesitatingly yielded to the wise counsel of the pig. Thus the pig not only decided the site of the church, but gave a name to the parish.

In support of this tradition, there is the figure of a pig sculptured on the tower of the church, just above the western entrance.

TYPE ML.7060. MOTIF: D.2192, (ce) [*Spirit in form of pig moves foundations at night to the spot church now stands on*] (Baughman).
¶ See "The Church of Fordoun", "The New Church at Marske".

THE WIZARD OF ALDERLEY EDGE

W. E. Axon, *Cheshire Gleanings,* pp. 56–8.

A farmer from Mobberley, mounted on a milk-white horse, was crossing the [Alderley] Edge on his way to Macclesfield to sell the animal. He had reached the spot known as the "Thieves' Hole" and as he slowly rode along thinking of the profitable bargain which he hoped to make, he was startled by the appearance of an old man, tall and strangely clad in a deep, flowing garment. The old man ordered him to stop, told him that he knew the errand upon which the rider was bent, and offered a sum of money for the horse. The farmer, however, refused the offer, not thinking it sufficient. "Go, then, to Macclesfield," said the old man, "but mark my words, you will *not* sell the horse. Should you find my words come true, meet me this evening and I will buy your horse." The farmer laughed at such a prophecy, and went on his way. To his great surprise, and greater disappointment, nobody would buy, though all admired, his beautiful horse. He was, therefore, compelled to return. On approaching the Edge he saw the old man again. Checking his horse's pace, he began to consider how far it might be prudent to deal with a perfect stranger in so lonely a place. However, while he was considering what to do, the old man commanded him, "Follow me!" Silently the old man led him by the Seven Firs, the Golden Stone, by Stormy Point, and Saddle Boll. Just as the farmer was beginning to think he had gone far enough, he fancied that he heard a horse neighing underground. Again he heard it. Stretching forth his arm, the old man touched a rock with a wand, and immediately the farmer saw a ponderous pair of iron gates which, with a sound like thunder, flew upon. The horse reared bolt upright, and the terrified farmer fell on his knees praying that his life might be spared. "Fear nothing," spoke the Wizard, "and behold a sight which no mortal eye has ever looked upon." They went into the cave. In a long succession of caverns the farmer saw a countless number of men and horses, the latter milk-white, and all fast asleep. In the innermost cavern heaps of treasure were piled up on the ground. From these glittering heaps the old man bade the farmer take the price he desired for his horse, and thus addressed him: "You see these men and horses; the number was not complete. Your horse was wanted to make it complete. Remember my words, there will come a day when these men and these horses, awakening from their enchanted slumber, will descend into the plain, decide the fate of a great battle, and save their country. This shall be when George the son of George shall reign. Go home in safety. Leave your horse with me. No harm will befall you, but henceforward no mortal eye will ever look upon the iron gate. Begone!" The farmer lost no time in obeying. He heard the iron gates close with the same fearful sounds with which they were opened, and made the best of his way to Mobberley.

The antiquity of the tradition is not easily ascertainable, the story used to be told by Parson Shrigley, and he placed the meeting of the Mobberley Farmer and the Enchanter at about eighty years before his time. Shrigley was curate of Alderley in 1753. He died in 1776.

TYPE 766. MOTIFS: F.721.2 [*Habitable hill*]; D.1960.2 [*King asleep in mountain*]; E.502 [*The sleeping army*]; F.721.4 [*Underground treasure-chamber*]; F.91.1 [*Slamming door on exit from mountain underworld*].

¶ It is not stated, but one is left to suppose that the wizard was Merlin, and the army which he was equipping with horses belonged to King Arthur.

See "The Silver Horseshoe", "King Arthur at Sewingshields".

WROXALL ABBEY

H. Bett, *English Legends*, p. 18.

The foundation of Wroxall Abbey in Warwickshire was due to the miraculous deliverance of a Crusader from captivity. In the twelfth century, the manor belonged to Hugh de Hatton, a son of the Earl of Warwick. He was long a prisoner in the Holy Land, and when he prayed earnestly for deliverance, St Leonard appeared to him and transported him, with his fetters still upon him, to Wroxall, where he met his wife, who did not recognize him until he had shown her half of a ring, which had been broken between them on his departure from England. He founded the Abbey in gratitude for his deliverance.

MOTIFS: R.121.6 [*Rescue from prison by saint*]; H.94.5 [*Identification through broken ring*].

X ORIGIN MYTHS

ORIGIN MYTHS

The English Origin Legends seem so far removed from their mythological roots as to have become moral exempla, fairy tales, flights of fancy, or half-whimsical explanations of natural features rather than true myths. As such, many have been placed in Part A, under Fables and Exempla, or are even included in the Fairy Tales. Others are among Devil beliefs or Local Legends.

It seemed that it might be a convenience, however, to group them together by their titles, alphabetically arranged as in the rest of the *Dictionary*, giving their relevant type or motif numbers, and reference to the section in which they are to be found.

The main categories into which they fall are, first, an explanation of the position of certain natural features, rocks, hills, pools and streams, and, second, an account of the origin of a few animal and bird characteristics. Basically, these are often an attempt to explain the ritual killing of a creature at a certain time. The explanation is often a false and trivial one, but behind it is probably the feeling that the creature was once sacred. On the Isle of Man, for instance, there is an elaborate legend to account for the Hunting of the Wren, which must once have been a sacred bird. No mythical explanation has been found to account for the hostility shown by Scottish boys to the yellow-hammer, who is said to be given a drop of the Devil's blood on May Day, and whose eggs are scribbled with letters written to the Devil. It seems likely that the yellow-hammer was once sacred to the Sun God. In Scotland the Devil took over most of the activities and characteristics of the earlier gods, some of which were adopted by the saints or worthies in other countries. An English example of this tendency are "The Crowza Stones", and King Arthur seems also to have taken some of the functions of the earlier gods.

An occasional aetiological myth appears briefly in a long fairy tale, as in the origin of some of the larger islands in "Assipattle and the Mester Stoorworm", but these have not been included in this list of origin myths.

THE APRON STRINGS
B, III, Devils.

MOTIFS: A.977 [*Origin of certain stones or groups of stones*]; A.977.3.1 [*Devil drops stones from apron*].

THE CROWZA STONES
B, XI, Saints.

MOTIFS: F.624.0.1 [*Saint as mighty lifter*]; A.977 [*Origin of certain stones or groups of stones*].

THE DEVIL AT LARGO LAW

B, III, Devils.

MOTIFS: A.963 [*Soil dropped to form mountain*]; A.969.9 [*Mountains or hills from actions of devil*].

THE DEVIL AT TOLCARN

B, III, Devils.

MOTIFS: A.977 [*Origin of particular stones or groups of stones*]; A.972.2 [*Indentations on rocks from footprints of Devil*].

THE DEVIL'S DITCH

B, III, Devils.

TYPE ML.5020 (Troll making a causeway). MOTIF: G.303.9.1.7 [*Devil builds a road*].

THE DEVIL'S DYKE

B, III, Devils.

MOTIF: A.963 [*Mountains from sand dropped or thrown*].

THE DEVIL'S LAPFUL

B, III, Devils.

MOTIF: A.977.3.1 [*Devil drops stones from apron*].

THE DEVIL'S SPITTLEFUL

B, III, Devils.

MOTIF: A.969.9(*b*) (Baughman) [*Devil with spadeful of earth to cover town is tricked by cobbler into believing town is a long way off (he tells Devil he has worn out all the shoes in his sack while walking from the town). The Devil drops the spadeful of earth, making a hill still seen to-day*].

THE DEVIL'S WHETSTONE

B, III, Devils.

TYPE 1090. MOTIF: A.977.2(*a*) (Baughman) [*Devil throws down whetstone when beaten in a mowing contest*].

THE EVIL WEDDING

B, III, Devils.

MOTIF: A.974 [*Rocks from transformation of people to stone*].

THE FIRST CORNISH MOLE

A, I, Fables and Exempla.

MOTIF: A.1893(*b*) (Baughman) [*Proud girl blasphemes and remarks about her silky skin. She is transformed into a mole*].

ORIGIN MYTHS

THE GIANT GORM
B, VII, Giants.

MOTIF: A.955.10 [*Islands from transformed person*].

THE GIANT OF GRABBIST
A, II, Fairy Tales.

A, Hawkridge Church

MOTIFS: A.977.1 [*Giants responsible for certain stones*]; F.531.3.2 [*Giant throws a great rock*].

B, The Stones of Battlegore

MOTIF: A.977.2 [*Devil throws stones*].

C, The Whetstones

MOTIF: A.977 [*Origins of particular stones or groups of stones*].

THE GIANT'S HAT AND STAFF
B, XI, Saints.

MOTIF: A.977.4(*a*) (Baughman) [*Saint's hat and staff are turned to stone by Devil*].

THE GREEDY PEASANT WOMAN
A, I, Fables and Exempla.

TYPE 751A. MOTIFS: K.1811 [*Gods in disguise visit mortals*]; D.1652.1.2 [*Cake magically increases*]; Q.1 [*Gods in disguise reward hospitality and punish inhospitality*].

HOW THE DEVIL MADE CHEDDAR GORGE
B, III, Devils.

MOTIF: A.969.9 [*Mountain or hills from actions of the Devil*].

KING ARTHUR AT SEWINGSHIELDS
B, IX, Local Traditions.

MOTIF: A.979 [*Stories about stone origins*].

LAPWING AND RINGDOVE
A, I, Fables and Exempla.

TYPE 240 (variant). MOTIF: A.2247.4 [*Dove and magpie exchange eggs*].

THE MAGPIE'S NEST
A, I, Fables and Exempla.

TYPE 236 (variant). MOTIF: A.2271.1 [*Thrush teaches dove to build nest*].

THE MAN IN THE MOON

A, I, Fables and Exempla.

MOTIF: A.751.1.4 [*Man in the moon banished there for stealing bundle of thorns*].

THE ORIGIN OF THE WREKIN

B, IX, Local.

MOTIF: A.969.9(*b*) (Baughman) [*Devil (Giant) with a spadeful of earth to cover town is tricked by cobbler, etc.*].

THE OWL WAS A BAKER'S DAUGHTER

A, I, Fables and Exempla.

TYPE 751A. MOTIF: A.1958.0.1 (Baughman) [*The owl is a baker's daughter who objected to the size of the dough put into the oven for Jesus when He appeared in her house as a beggar*].

SIMMER WATER

B, IX, Local.

MOTIF: A.920.1 [*Origin of lakes*].

TAMARA, TAVY AND TAW

B, V, Fairies.

MOTIFS: A.930 [*Origin of streams*]; A.934.11 [*River from transformation*].

THUMB MARKS ON THE HADDOCK

B, III, Devils.

MOTIFS: A.2217.3.1 [*Marks on certain fish from St Peter's fingerprints*]; A.2217.3.2 [*Marks on certain fish from Devil's fingerprints*].

WHY THE ENGLISH WILL NOT KILL THE RAVEN

B, XII, Supernatural.

MOTIFS: D.151.5 [*Transformation: man to raven*]; A.522.2.2 [*Raven as culture hero*].

WHY THE ROBIN'S BREAST IS RED

A, I, Fables and Exempla.

MOTIF: A.2221.2.2 [*Blood from Cross on robin's breast*].

THE WOODPIGEON'S NEST

A, I, Fables and Exempla.

TYPE 236 (variant). MOTIF: A.2271.1 [*Thrush teaches dove to build nest*].

XI SAINTS

SAINTS

Most of the saints included here are native to these islands, though a few have been admitted that endeared themselves to Englishmen. England's patron saint, St George, could not be left out, and, indeed, his legend is a local growth that has little to do with what is seriously recorded of him. The chapbook, romantic version of his legend is to be found in Part A, among the Fairy Tales, to which it belongs. In the same chapbook are long, rambling versions of the other six champions of Christendom, all carefully subordinated to St George, of course. They bear no resemblance to the actual lives of the saints. St Aloys is another naturalized saint. English tradition claims him as a Somerset man.

In the main, the saints shown here are either Saxon or Celtic. Small as the gallery is, it shows a remarkable diversity of character, well illustrating the truth of the saying that the Christian profession develops personality instead of flattening it. Some of the saints are hardly edifying characters. We have the peppery St Kevern and the thievish St Just. Some of the Saxons appear to have had sainthood thrust upon them, like King Edmund, who was dragged from his hiding-place under a hedge to be martyred, and who liked the prospect so little that he cursed the couple who betrayed him and any newly wed couple who crossed the bridge after them. Little St Kenelm was another involuntary martyr, as innocent and unwilling as Little Sir Hugh in the Child ballad and in Chaucer's "Prioress's Tale". Others, however, like St Wulfric, were ascetic almost to morbidity. Legend, however, has softened their acerbities in such late, delightful stories as "St Wulfric and the Greedy Boy".

Many of the saints, like St Edmund, were too ready with their curses, and we have miracles of wrath as well as many of healing.

A lot of their time was passed in conflict with demons and devils, and some of them were suspected of being magicians themselves. The same stories were told of St Aldhelm as of Jack o' Kent, Faustus, or William of Lindholm. St Kentigern performed some of the same wonders, and even St Dunstan, whose life rests on a firm historical foundation, has some magical prodigies attached to him, as well as his famous combat with the Devil. St Wulstan is another saint well embedded in history, in spite of the miracle of the staff. The sober, saintly virtues of humility and gentleness belong to him too, and differentiate him from some of the wilder earlier saints.

The Celtic saints here are chiefly from Cornwall, though the undoubted fact that Ulstermen are English-speaking has made it possible to include two delightful fragments of recent oral collection about the lovable St Patrick. Some of the Cornish saints were canonized only in popular tradition, and find no place in Baring-Gould's *Lives of the Saints*, which deals rather with canonical than apocryphal saints.

Some of the most delightful tales of both the Celtic and the Saxon saints are of their relations to animals. Of these only a few can be given; but more can be found in Helen Waddell's *Beasts and Saints*. The sources of each tale are given, but as well as these, and such early books as *The Golden Legend*, Ælfric's *Lives of the Saints* and Bede's *Ecclesiastical History*, there are a number of modern books to consult, among them Hippolyte Delehaye's *Legends of the Saints*, Helen Roeder's *Saints and Their Attributes*, and Christina Hole's *Saints in Folk-Lore*.

COUNTING THE CABBAGES

Ruth L. Tongue, *Forgotten Folk Tales*.

There was a countryman who had green fingers—bright green they was and there was nothing to be done about it, and he did grow the best cabbages in the country. His beans was fine, his apples was grand, but his cabbages were a marvel. Rows and rows of 'em, round as the baby's head, so who'd worry about green fingers? He never minded, but *his wife knew better!* She told everyone so, and she took the yard broom to him, and scrubbed them so sore he couldn't do his planting for a bit, and the cabbages were half-size, but even then they were larger than anyone else's. No doubt there was some would have liked him to lose his luck, but he was a steady, careful chap. His wife was easier to handle.

It was coming on to the fall of the year, and he'd got in his beans, and dug up the taters, and clamped the roots all ready for the hard winter, that his fingers warned him were on its way—*but his wife knew better*! She left the apple-tree loaded till they begun to frost-fall, and was only half-sound, to cut into apple-rings, and then to be sure she was in a great hurry, and blamed him.

So out he goes, a bit put-out like, to count the greenstuff he'd been careful to grow, to see the long winter through.

The herbs was hanging on the fences bunched up and drying, so he starts to count the cabbages.

"I shouldn't do that," says St Peter, leaning over the gate, so friendly as a neighbour. "Leave them be, and cut a criss-cross on each stalk you chop, and you'll do."

"I thought you were a fisherman," says Greenfingers.

"I had a bit of ground by the lake when I wasn't after fish. Grew things a marvel. Dead fish was what that ground liked, and it wasn't too bad, living up-wind as we did."

Then Greenfingers knew he was talking to a real gardener, and stood up to go to the gate, but St Peter had gone on.

"I'd like his opinion on dead eels," he said, so he calls his wife to say she can cut *one* cabbage for supper, and put a criss-cross on the stem, and off he went to ask St Peter.

Well, *his wife knew better.* Of course she did.

She cut the whole lot down, and never made a criss-cross, and then she piled them all in the shed where the cows was kept, and felt quite proud of herself.

St Peter said Eels might do, but cow-muck was handier, and might be better than Galilee goats'. So he went into the cowshed to get a fork-load and saw what was left of the cabbages. There was twenty hungry cows relished them.

Then he goes indoors, looking a bit grim.

"I see how you handled our cabbages for the winter," he said.

"Oh yes. I knew better than that," she said. "I likes my cabbages handy."

"So did the cows," says Greenfingers. "I'll get along with herbs and beans, but I reckon it'll be rotten apples and potatoes and point* for you by next Easter. I've filled the salt-box, and you must make it last till then."

When Easter came he was well and hearty and working in the plot, when his neighbour looked in.

"Who've you got visiting?" he said.

"That skinny old creature? That's my wife," says Greenfingers. "She's just showing she knows better."

From a soldier (farm-labourer). 1940s. St Peter. Bedfordshire.

MOTIFS: V.223.1 [*Saint gives advice*]; T.254 [*The disobedient wife*]; T.251.2 [*Taming the shrew*].
¶ This is outside of the run of ordinary saint stories. St Peter makes an unexpected appearance in it.

* *Potatoes and point:* famine fare—a baked potato dipped in salt and pointed to where the meat should be.

THE CROWZA STONES [summary]

Hunt, *Popular Romances of the West of England*, p. 262.

St Just lived at Penwith, and, finding little to do there, except to offer prayers for the tinners and fishermen, he once went to visit St Keverne in his hermitage near the Lizard headland. The two saints feasted and drank together, and St Just's envy was aroused by the beauty of the chalice from which he was drinking his rich wine. With many professions of undying friendship, he pledged St Keverne to return his visit, and took his way home.

Very soon St Keverne missed his famous cup and, after long search had been made, he could not but believe that his visitor had made away with it; so he decided to pursue him, punish him, and get the chalice back. As he passed over Crowza Down he picked up a few of the "Iron-stone" pebbles which lie on its surface, put them in his pockets, and hastened on his way. Soon afterwards, he caught sight of St Just and, raging inwardly, called to him to stop.

St Just only quickened his pace a little, but made no other sign of having heard. But at last St Keverne was within a stone's-throw, and, taking a stone from his pocket, he flung it at St Just. It fell so near that the saint was alarmed and took to his heels. But as he ran he untied the cup, which he had fastened to his girdle, and dropped it to the ground. St Keverne recovered it and, being wearied he abandoned his long pursuit. But he threw all the remaining stones after the vanishing figure of St Just, one by one, and a curse with each. There the pebbles remained, entirely unlike all the other stones about them, but clearly the same as the stones at Crowza, and so heavy that none but a saint could hope to lift them. By day they have sometimes been removed, but they always return to their places by night.

MOTIFS: A.977 [*Origins of particular stones or groups of stones*]; V.229.20 [*Downfall of saint*]; M.411.8 [*Saint's curse*]; F.624.0.1 [*Saint as mighty lifter*]; D.1602.1 [*Stones, being removed, return to their places*].
¶ The Saints of Cornwall and the Celtic countries were by no means always immaculate characters. To be a hermit and a missionary was qualification enough to be counted a saint.
See "The Giant Bolster" (B, VII).

THE DEATH OF KING LODBROG

H. Bett, *English Legends*, p. 34. St Edmund.

A story about the devotion of animals is connected with the murder of Lodbrog, prince of Denmark, at a place near the mouth of the River Yare —an event to which our old chroniclers attribute the first invasion of England by the Danes. Lodbrog was devoted to the sport of hawking, and one day, when he was near the Danish coast, his favourite bird happened to fall into the sea. The King leaped into a boat that was at hand, and put off to rescue the hawk. A sudden storm arose, and he was driven across the sea to the coast of England, and up the River Yare as far as Reedham in Norfolk. The inhabitants of the country brought the stranger to King Edmund, who then kept his court at Caistor, only a few miles distant.

The King received him with kindness and the respect due to his rank, and directed Bern, the royal falconer, to accompany his guest whenever he chose to go hawking. The skill of the royal visitor in the sport excited Bern's mad jealousy, and one day, when they were together in the woods, he murdered Lodbrog and buried the body. The absence of the royal Dane for three days occasioned much alarm. It was noticed that his favourite greyhound came home for food, and disappeared as soon as his hunger was satisfied.

On the fourth day he was followed by some of the courtiers, and he led them to the grave of his master. There was an inquiry into the affair, and the ferocity of the dog towards Bern led to the discovery of the murderer. He was condemned by the King to be turned adrift, without oars or sails, in the same boat which had brought Lodbrog to England. Strangely enough, the boat drifted safely to the coast of Denmark, where it was recognized as the one in which Lodbrog had left the country. Bern was seized and carried to Hinguar and Hubba, Lodbrog's sons, who questioned him about their father's fate. The villain said that Lodbrog had been cast upon the shore of England, and put to death by Edmund's order. The sons determined upon revenge, and set sail with a large army. They landed at Berwick-upon-Tweed, and marched southwards to Thetford, where the King was. After a bloody battle, they gained possession of the place. According to the chronicles, they killed and beheaded King Edmund, but his head, which had been thrown into a wood, was guarded by a wolf. The animal yielded it up to some of the King's friends, who had gone in search of it. When the head was placed in contact with the body it became reunited with it. The wolf watched the scene, and, after attending the funeral at Hoxne with a decent gravity, returned to his native forest in peace. Many miracles were worked by the body of Edmund, which was removed later to a church at Beodericworth, afterwards called Bury St Edmunds.

MOTIFS: B.301.2 [*Faithful animal at Master's grave avenges his murder*]; Q.466.0.1 [*Embarkation in rudderless boat as punishment*]; K.2247 [*Treacherous lord*]; B.251.2 [*Animal honours saint*]; D.1602.12 [*Self-returning head*]; D.1685 [*Interred body of saint performs signs and miracles*].

¶ See "The Legend of St Edmund", "St Edmund's Curse", "St Edmund's Ghost".

OF THE DEATH OF ROBERT,
BISHOP OF LINCOLN

Matthew Paris, *English History*, III, p. 50.

Thus...departed from the exile of this world, which he had never liked, the holy Robert, the second bishop of Lincoln, who died at his manor of Buckdon, in the night of St Denis's Day.* During his life, he had openly rebuked the pope and the king; had corrected the prelates, and reformed the monks; in him the priests lost a director—clerks an instructor—scholars a supporter—and the people a preacher; he had shown himself a persecutor of the incontinent, a careful examiner of the different scriptures, and a bruiser and despiser of the Romans. He was hospitable and profuse; civil, cheerful, and affable at the table for partaking of bodily nourishment; and at the spiritual table, devout, mournful, and contrite....

During the night in which the said bishop departed to the Lord, Faulkes, bishop of London, heard in the air above a wonderful and most agreeable kind of sound, the melody of which refreshed his ears and his heart, and fixed his attention for a time. Whilst listening to it (he was at the time staying near Buckdon), he said to some persons standing near him, "Do you, too, hear what I do?" Whereupon they asked him, "What hear you, my lord?" The bishop replied: "I hear a supernatural sound, like that of a great convent-bell, ringing a delightful tune in the air above." They, however, acknowledged, although they listened attentively, that they heard nothing of it, whereupon the bishop said to them: "By the faith I owe to St Paul, I believe that our beloved father, brother, and master, the venerable bishop of Lincoln, is passing from this world to take his place in the kingdom of heaven, and this noise I hear is intended as a manifest warning to me thereof, for there is no convent near here in which there is a bell of such a sort, and so loud. Let us inquire into the matter immediately."

They therefore did so, and found, as was proved by the statement of his whole household, that at that very time the bishop had departed from this world. This wonderful circumstance, or rather primitive miracle, was told as a fact, and borne evidence to, to the writer of this book, by Master John Cratchdale, a confidential clerk to the bishop, one held in great veneration, and of high authority amongst his attendants and friends.

On the same night too, some brethren of the order of Minorites, were hurrying towards Buckdon, where Robert, bishop of Lincoln, was staying (for he was a comforter and a father to the Preachers and Minorites),

* A.D. 1253.

and in passing through the royal forest of Vauberge, being ignorant of its windings, lost their road, and whilst wandering about they heard in the air sounds of the ringing of bells, amongst which they clearly distinguished one bell of a most sweet tune, unlike anything they had ever heard before.

This circumstance greatly excited their wonder, for they knew that there was no church of note near. When morning's dawn appeared, after wandering about to no purpose, they met some foresters, of whom, after obtaining directions to regain their right road, they inquired what meant the grand and solemn ringing of bells which they had heard in the direction of Buckdon? to which the foresters replied, that they had not heard and did not then hear anything, though the sound still gently filled the air. The brethren, therefore, in still greater wonder went on, and reached Buckdon betimes, where they were informed that at the very time of the night when they had heard the aforesaid melodious sounds, Robert, bishop of Lincoln, breathed forth his happy spirit.

MOTIF: V.222.6.1 [*Church bells ring without aid of human hands at death of holy person*].

THE DISCOVERY OF TIN

Hunt, *Popular Romances of the West of England*, p. 274.

St Piran, or St Perran, leading his lonely life on the plains which now bear his name, devoted himself to the study of the objects which presented themselves to his notice. The good saint decorated the altar in his church with the choicest flowers, and his cell was adorned with the crystals which he could collect from the neighbouring rocks. In his wanderings on the seashore, St Perran could not but observe the numerous mineral veins running through the slate-rocks forming the beautiful cliffs on this coast. Examples of every kind he collected; and on one occasion, when preparing his humble meal, a heavy black stone was employed to form a part of the fireplace. The fire was more intense than usual, and a stream of beautiful white metal flowed out of the fire. Great was the joy of the saint; he perceived that God, in His goodness, had discovered to him something which would be useful to man. St Perran communicated his discovery to St Chiwidden. They examined the shores together, and Chiwidden, who was learned in the learning of the East, soon devised a process for producing this metal in large quantities. The two saints called the Cornishmen together. They told them of their treasures, and they taught them how to dig the ore from the earth, and how, by the agency of fire, to obtain the metal. Great was the joy in Cornwall, and many days of feasting followed the announcement. Mead and metheglin, with other drinks flowed in abundance; and vile rumour says the saints and their people were rendered equally unstable thereby. "Drunk as a Perraner" has certainly passed into a proverb from that day.

The riot of joy at length came to an end, and steadily, seriously, the tribes of Perran and St Agnes set to work. They soon accumulated a vast quantity of this precious metal; and when they carried it to the southern coasts, the merchants from Gaul eagerly purchased it of them. The noise of the discovery, even in those days, rapidly extended itself; and even the cities of Tyre learned that a metal, precious to them, was to be obtained in a country far to the west. The Phoenician navigators were not long in finding out the Tin Islands; and great was the alarm amidst the Cornish Britons lest the source of their treasure be discovered. Then it was they intrenched the whole of St Agnes' beacon; then it was they built the numerous hill castles which have puzzled the antiquarian; then it was that they constructed the rounds—amongst which the Perran Round remains as a remarkable example—all of them to protect their tin-ground.

So resolved were the whole of the population of the district to preserve the tin workings, that they prevented any foreigner from landing on the mainland, and they established tin markets on the islands on the coast. On these islands were hoisted the standard of Cornwall, a white cross on a black ground, which was the device of St Perran and St Chiwidden, symbolizing the black tin ore and the white metal.

MOTIFS: A.541 [*Culture hero teaches arts and crafts*]; A.515.1.2 [*Sworn brothers as culture heroes*]; A.1432 [*Acquisition of metals*].

¶ St Piran and St Chiwidden play the part of culture heroes rather than saints. Like St Just and St Keverne, they were not very particular about ethical behaviour.

THE DUN COW AND THE
MONKS OF LINDISFARNE

F. Grice, *Folk-Tales of the North Country*, pp. 79–83.

St Cuthbert was a very devout monk who lived many hundreds of years ago on the island of Lindisfarne, which we sometimes call Holy Island. He did great good in his lifetime and when he died his fellow monks buried him on Lindisfarne, hoping that his body would find a resting-place there. And there the body did rest for many years, until the Norsemen invaded the shores of Northumberland. They caused so much havoc, burning down the churches and destroying all before them, that the monks of Lindisfarne had to flee before them. But they did not leave the body of the dead saint behind them.

One of them remembered that, before he died, Cuthbert had said, "I do rather choose and wish that you take up my bones and fly from these places, and take your abode and stay wheresoever God shall provide for you, than that you should submit yourselves."

So they took up his body and laid it in a wooden coffin which one who was specially skilled in carpentry made for them, and fled.

For seven years the monks wandered, sometimes carrying the coffin on their shoulders, sometimes bearing it on a horse-litter. They travelled all over the North Country, and in the seventh year of their travels they even tried to sail across to Ireland, to escape from the plunder of the Norsemen. But a storm drove them back, and they turned inland again and came to Chester-le-Street. It seemed that there at last they had found a place where the invaders would not molest them, and the body of Cuthbert rested there for more than a hundred years. But at the end of that time new invaders landed in the North, and plundered the country, and the monks of St Cuthbert had to take up the coffin and begin their travels again.

They journeyed for a long time, travelling south into the country of Yorkshire, and then turning north again, seeking in vain for a place where the body could rest in peace. At last their wanderings brought them back to Durham, and one day they reached a hill not far from Chester-le-Street, called Wrdelau.

There the wagon upon which the coffin was laid stuck fast, and no effort could get it to move. They yoked more and more horses to the wagon, but without success. No strength could move it, and the monks were forced to conclude that the saint did not wish his body to be carried any farther.

"All that we can do, brothers," said one monk, "is to bide here and spend the time in prayer and fasting, and hope that some guidance will be given to us."

For three days they prayed and fasted, until one of the monks announced that he had been granted a vision, and in the vision he had heard a voice saying, "Take the body of the saint to Dunholm."

"It is plain that God desires that St Cuthbert should rest at this place Dunholm. But I am at a loss what to do, for never in my life have I heard of this place Dunholm."

"Neither have we," replied all the others, and they sat down to ponder what they should do next.

Just at that moment two women passed near. One was driving her cows home to milk, and the other was looking about her anxiously as though she had lost something. Then as they passed, the second called out in a loud voice, "Neighbour, I have lost the red cow with the short horn. Have you seen her?" And the other replied, "Yes. I saw her a few minutes ago. She has strayed to Dunholm."

When the monks heard the word "Dunholm", they jumped up and ran to the milkmaid.

"Dunholm is the very place for which we are searching," they cried. "Can you show us the way?"

"My neighbour is going to that very place," she replied. "Follow her and she will take you there."

Full of new hope, the monks turned to where the coffin lay and tried again to move it. To their joy, the wagon moved as smoothly as if the axles had been newly greased.

Pulling it behind them, they followed the woman, and she led them to a lovely place. It was high and craggy, and covered with trees, and from the height they could see the river twisting round it in a hoop, and almost encircling it. No better resting-place for the saint's body could have been imagined, for it was beautiful and secure. The steep crags and the swift-flowing river seemed to hold off any robbers who might think of molesting the quiet monks. On the spot where they found the red cow with the short horn they fell down on their knees and prayed that they might at last be at the end of their wanderings.

By and by they placed the body of Cuthbert with his cross and his vestments in a shrine, and set to work to build a little church. It was a very humble building, as they had nothing to build with but branches and wands from the trees around them; but the monks did not think lightly of their little church, for they were overjoyed that the body of their saint had at last a secure home.

MOTIFS: D.1654.0.1 [*Magic immovability of saints*]; B.155.3 [*Animal determines burial-place of saint*].

¶ The title given to this tale is "The Dun Cow and the Monks of Lindisfarne", but the cow is described as "a red cow with a short horn". A dun cow could be dark or colourless, but it could never be called red.

THE GIANT'S HAT AND STAFF [abridged]

Hunt, *Popular Romances of the West of England*, p. 264.

Some say it was at Roach, others refer it to St Austell; but all agree in one thing, that the Longstone was once the staff of some holy man, and that its present state is owing to the malignant persecution of the demon of darkness.... The good saint...was returning to his cell across St Austell Downs. The night had been fine, the clearness of the sky and the brightness of the stars conduced to religious thoughts.... The devil was wandering abroad that night, and maliciously he resolved to play a trick upon his enemy. The saint was wrapt in thought. The devil was working his dire spells.

The sky became black, the stars disappeared, and suddenly a terrific rush of wind seized the saint, whirled him round and round, and at last blew his hat high into the air. The hat went ricochetting over the moor; and the saint after it, the devil enjoying the sport. The long stick which the saint carried impeded his progress in the storm and he stuck it into the ground. On went the hat, speedily followed the saint over and round the moor, until, thoroughly wearied out, he at length gave up the chase. He, now exposed to the beat of the tempest, bareheaded, endeavoured to find his way to his cell, and thought to pick up his staff on the way. No staff could be found in the darkness, and the hat was, he thought, gone irrecoverably. At length the saint reached his cell. He quieted his spirit by prayer, and sought the forgetfulness of sleep, safe under the protection of the holy cross from all the tricks of the devil. The evil one, however, was at work on the wild moor, and by his incantations he changed the hat and the staff into two rocks. Morning came, and the saint went abroad, seeking for his lost covering and support. He found them both—one a huge circular boulder, and the other a long stone which remains to this day.

The Saint's or, as it was often called, the Giant's Hat, was removed in 1798 by a regiment of soldiers who were encamped near it. They felt satisfied that this mysterious stone was the cause of the wet season which rendered their camp unpleasant, and consequently they resolved to remove the evil spell by destroying it.

MOTIFS: G.303.9.9 [*Pranks played by the Devil*]; A.977.4 [*Devil turns object to stone, which is still seen*]; A.977.4(a) [*Saint's hat and staff are turned to stone by Devil*] (Baughman).

THE GOLDEN FROGS OF BOVEY TRACEY

J. R. W. Coxhead, *Legends of Devon*, p. 51.

A long, long time ago, there lived in a wee house quite near Bovey Tracey Church a woodcutter and his wife and their one beloved child.

It was a stormy night and the rain came down as only it can in Devonshire. They were very sad, as the child was very ill, and was getting worse, although they had done all in their power to bring about his recovery, including many candles to the blessed saints.

When the storm was at its height, and the night black as pitch, there came a feeble knock on the cottage door. Wondering much who could be abroad on such a night, the woodcutter opened the door to find a tall figure in a long blue cloak, appearing soaked to the skin and in the last stages of exhaustion. He called to his wife, and they helped the poor Lady in—for a lady it proved to be, and a very beautiful one too. They took off her wet cloak, and rubbed her poor chilled hands and feet.

The Lady had the sweetest, gentlest smile, and when she had had a drink of warm milk, she recovered somewhat, and asked them why they were so downcast and sad. They told her of their child's illness, and how they had despaired of its recovery. The Lady asked if she might see him, as she too had a Little Son.

They took her up to where the child lay and, gazing sweetly upon him, she laid her hand upon his head. He stopped tossing restlessly, and as with a puff of wind the fever left him and he was sleeping peacefully. The storm too had hushed.

Overcome with gratitude and astonishment, the good man and his wife turned to pour out their thanks to the Lady—only to find her once again cloaked, and saying she must be on her way. But that they should not think her visit but a figment of a dream, next morning they would find a spring of clear water near their cottage, and in it would be tiny golden frogs.

It was even as she foretold, and to this day, long after the woodcutter and his wife and his child are forgotten, there comes the spring and the yellow frogs. And even now the street up which the Lady sped is called "Mary Street".

From Elizabeth Bate of Bovey Tracy, who had written it down many years before from an old man's tale.

TYPE 750*. MOTIFS: Q.45.1 [*Angels entertained unawares. Hospitality to disguised saint rewarded*]; V.256 [*Miraculous healing by Virgin Mary*].

KING EDMUND AND ST DUNSTAN

Roger of Wendover, *Chronicle*, I, p. 250.

On his elevation to the regal dignity, King Eadmund admitted to his counsels the blessed Dunstan, and had him numbered among his royal courtiers and nobles, knowing him to be of approved life, and of ready speech.... Beholding the undeviating good conversation of the man, many of the king's officers and servants said, "He is a good man"; others said, "Nay, but he deceiveth the people." Wherefore certain persons, envious of his goodness and prudence, began to lessen him in the king's eyes; to whom the king, lending a favourable ear, and not well examining the matter, commanded Dunstan to be deprived immediately of every honour with the dignity of chancellor, and to seek service elsewhere, where he would. On the morrow the king, for his amusement, went out hunting with his attendants; straightway the woods resounded with the hunter's horn and the barking of the dogs; a multitude of deer took to flight, one of which of extraordinary size the King singled out for the chase; and followed with his dogs alone, driving him through difficult paths unto the edge of a precipice, over which the stag and dogs fell headlong and were dashed to pieces. The king following at full speed, and, seeing the precipice, strove to rein in his steed; but not being able to keep back the unruly and stiff-necked animal, he gave up all hope of saving himself, and commended his soul to the pleasure of Almighty God, saying, "I give thee thanks, Lord Jesus Christ, that at this time I do not remember having injured any one but Dunstan only; and this fault I will with ready zeal amend, by a hearty reconciliation, if thou only grant me time." At these words, through the merits of the blessed man, the horse stood still on the very verge of the precipice, and the king, recovering himself, gave God thanks for the restitution of his life. On reaching home he ordered the blessed Dunstan to be fetched, and no sooner was he come than they mounted their horses and rode together on the road leading straight to Glastonbury. On arriving there, having entered the monastery, the king took Dunstan by the right hand, and kissing it, led him to the cathedral seat, in which, with the consent of the monks he set him, with these words, "Be thou a very faithful abbat of this seat and church, and if anything be wanting for the holy religious service, I will supply it of my royal bounty."

MOTIFS: K.2110 [*Slanders*]; V.52 [*Miraculous power of prayer*].

¶ There are many legends of St Edmund. See "The Legend of St Dunstan", "The Death of King Lodbrog", "The Legend of St Edmund".

THE KNIGHT AND HIS WIFE

W. Carew Hazlitt, *National Tales and Legends*, p. 3.

There was in a certain country a knight, who was at one time very rich, and every year he held a great feast in honour of Our Blessed Lady. But he spent so largely that by degrees he became poor. A good woman he had to his wife, who held the Virgin as dear as he did; and sorely the fiend grudged therefore.

The season came round for the yearly jubilee to Our Lady, and the poor knight had not wherewithal to discharge the cost of the same; and he was abashed, that he betook himself to the forest, to dwell there in solitude till the feast-day was passed and gone.

The Devil saw the poor knight's case, and of his wife was secretly enamoured; but naught might his unholy passion prevail through that lady's virtuous living and the love which Our Lady bare unto her.

One day while the knight, her lord, was still in the green forest, came the fiend to his side in human guise, and asked him why he walked there, and why he wore so dejected a mien.

Then the poor knight related to the stranger his story. "I was once," quoth he, "a rich man; but now all is lost. I was wont to celebrate every year the feast of Our Blessed Lady, and at present I lack money—yea, for my very livelihood."

The stranger, answering him, said: "If thou wilt grant me my will, I will give thee greater riches than ever thou haddest before. Go to the place that I shall bid thee, and thou wilt find gold in store. Then come back hither, and speak with me again, and bring thy wife with thee along."

The poor knight wist not that he was a fiend that spake thus unto him, and he promised to do as he bad him. So home he went, and found there forthwith money enough, as the stranger had foretold. Right fain was he hereof, and Our Lady's feast was held with greater spending of gold and silver than had ever been remembered.

The time passed away, and the day arrived when he was to meet the stranger once more, and to bring his wife with him. That gentle lady durst not do other than his bidding, and she made herself ready accordingly, and they mounted their palfreys and rode forth toward the forest. On the way, by the roadside, stood a chapel of Our Blessed Lady, and the knight's wife said to her lord, "Let us enter this chapel, and pray to God to keep us in His fear." But the knight was full of glee and jollity, and recked naught of prayer, and to his lady quoth he: "Thou mayest get down, if thou listest, and pray; but for me I will proceed on my journey. Do not tarry long, however, or I shall wax wrath."

The lady promised not to overstay, and into the chapel she hied, and placed herself nigh an image of Our Blessed Lady, where she reclined, and a drowsiness overtook her, so that she fell asleep.

Now Our Blessed Lady, to requite that good wife of the poor knight for all her love to her, transformed herself into her likeness, and, riding on the palfrey, rejoined the knight, who wist not that it was Our Lady that rode beside him. But when they came where it had been appointed that he should meet the stranger, he stood there; but because he was in truth a fiend, he knew her to be, not the knight's wife, but the Holy Virgin; and he cried to the knight: "Traitor, I bad thee bring thy wife with thee, and in her room thou hast brought Christ's Mother! Hanged shouldst thou be by the neck for thy falsehood!"

These words made the knight wax fearful; and he descended from his horse, and sank on his knees before Our Lady, shedding tears, and imploring forgiveness.

Our Lady said to him: "Knight, thou hast erred. Thou hast delivered thyself to the fiend. Return him his gift. Bestir thyself henceforth in the service of God, and He will reinstate thee in thy goods." She uttered these words and vanished. The knight leapt on his palfrey, and rode to the chapel, where his wife yet slept by the altar.

MOTIF: K.1841.3 [*Virgin Mary substitutes for woman whom husband has pledged to the Devil; Devil flees*].

¶ This beautiful fifteenth-century legend has been used as a subject for a ballet.

A LEGEND OF ST CUTHBERT [summary]

Parkinson. *Yorkshire Legends and Traditions*, 1st series, p. 101.

Cuthbert was one of the brethren who accompanied Eata from Melrose to found a new monastery at Ripon, and he was appointed guest-master to the community.

Early one morning he saw a young man sitting at the gates, and gave him customary welcome—water to wash his hands, and himself bathed his feet, dried them and warmed them. Then he pressed the stranger to stay with them until the third hour, and take food, for it was the depth of winter. But the other replied that he must depart in haste, for he had far to go. Cuthbert, however, adjured him in the name of God to stay; and immediately after the prayers of tierce he laid the table, and went in search of new bread. But when he returned, the stranger was nowhere to be seen, nor could he find any footprints in the fresh snow. In amazement he replaced the table in the inner room, and suddenly was aware of a wonderful fragrance, and saw lying beside him three new-made loaves. He trembled, for he knew that his guest must have been an angel.

From that time Cuthbert so increased in works of grace that he was often allowed to see and converse with angels, and when hungry he was refreshed with food from the Lord.

MOTIFS: Q.45.1 [*Angels entertained unawares*]. V.235 [*Mortal visited by angel*]; V.232.7 [*Gifts from angels*].

THE LEGEND OF ST EDMUND: I

E. S. Hartland, *County Folk-Lore*, I, p. 76. Suffolk.

The circumstances relating to St Edmund, says the historian of Bury, which took place on the retreat of the Danes, and which have formed a favourite theme for the Monkish writers and a favourite subject for their painters and sculptors, are given with miraculous embellishments, and with various degrees of amplification by most of the monastic poets and historians.

To offer the utmost indignity to the martyred King, the pagans cast his severed head and body into the thickest part of the woods at Eglesdene.

When the departure of the Danes removed the terror which their presence had inspired, the East Anglians, prompted by affection for their late sovereign, assembled in considerable numbers to pay his corpse the last duties of attachment. After a sorrowful search, the body was discovered, conveyed to the neighbouring village, Hoxne, and there interred; but the head could not be found. These zealous and dutiful subjects, therefore, divided themselves into small parties, and searched every part of the wood. Terrified by its thickness and obscurity, some of them cried out to their companions, "Where are you?" A voice answered, "Here, here, here!" They hastened to the place whence the sound proceeded, and found the long-sought head in a thicket of thorns, guarded by a wolf, "an unkouth thyng, and strange agwyn nature". The people, almost over-powered with joy, with all possible veneration took the holy head, which its guardian quietly surrendered to them, and carried it to the body. The friendly wolf joined in the procession, and after seeing "the precious treasure" that he had with so much care protected deposited with the body, returned to the woods with doleful mourning. The head was some time after observed to have united with the body; and the mark of separation appeared round the neck like a "purpil thread". His martyrdom is thus described by Langtoft:

> He attired him to bataile with folk that he had,
> But this cursed Danes so grete oste ay lad,
> That Edmund was taken and slayn at the last,
> Full far fro the body lay was the hede kast.
> The body son they fonde, the hede was in doute,
> Up and downe in the felde thei souht it aboute.
> To haf knowing thereof alle thei were in were,
> Till the hede himself said, "Here, here here!"
> Ther thei fonde the hede is now a faire chapelle,
> Oxen hate the toun ther the body felle.
> Ther where he was schotte another chapelle standes,
> And somewhat of that tree thei bond untille his hands,
> The tone is fro the tother moten a grete myle,
> So far bare a woulfe the hede and kept it a grete while,
> Until the hede said "Here," als I befor said,
> Fro the woulfe thee it toke, unto the body it laid,
> Men sais ther he ligges the flesh samen gede,
> But the token of the wonde als a red threde,
> Now lies he in schryne in gold that is rede,
> Seven yere was he Kyng that tyme that he was dede.

... The feast of St Edmund, November the 20th, was ranked amongst the holy days of precept in this kingdom by the national Council of Oxford, in 1222, and was observed at Bury with the most splendid and joyous solemnities. We find that, upon this festival, 150 tapers of 1 lb. weight or more illuminated the abbey church, its altars, and its windows. The "revel on St Edmund's night" was of a character somewhat more noisy, turbulent and unhallowed; a loose being then given to every species of jollity and amusement.

Suffolk Garland, p. 349.

THE LEGEND OF ST EDMUND: II [summary]
ST EDMUND'S CURSE

C. Gurdon. *County Folk-Lore*, I, 2. Suffolk, pp. 74–5.

In the hope of escaping his pursuers, the Danes, King Edmund concealed himself under the arch of a bridge, near that now known as Gold
Bridge, from the bright spurs which he wore; and which, glittering in the
moonlight, betrayed the king to a newly married couple returning home
over the bridge. These two informed the Danes, and the angry king
pronounced a curse upon every couple who should in the future pass
over that bridge on their way to or from their wedding. Even today, this
curse is believed, and the bridge avoided by those on their way to the
church, or from it, after the wedding.

It is thought that the king's bright armour is still to be seen glimmering
through the water of the brook.

THE LEGEND OF ST EDMUND: III [summary]
ST EDMUND'S GHOST

Roger de Hoveden's *Annals*, I, pp. 93–4.

In the year 1014, the tyrant Sweyn laid a heavy tribute on the town where
lay the uncorrupted body of the royal martyr, Edmund, a thing which
no one had dared to do before, since the town had been given to the
church named after him.

Sweyn even threatened to destroy the church itself, unless the tribute
were promptly paid: and he declared that the martyr was in truth no
saint. Later in the day on which he pronounced these threats, he held a
council at Gainsborough, and, as he stood in the midst of a throng of
Danes, he saw coming towards him St Edmund himself, in armour, and
the sight so terrified him, that he cried out, "Fellow-soldiers, to the
rescue, to the rescue! Behold St Edmund has come to slay me!" But none
of the others could see anything strange. The tyrant fell from his seat
pierced by the saint with a spear, as he said; and died three days later,
on February 3rd, in great agony.

I. MOTIFS: B.251.2 [*Animal honours saint*]; V.229.22 [*Severed head of saint speaks
so that searchers can find it*]; D.1602.12 [*Self-returning head*].
II. MOTIFS: M.411.8 [*Saint's curse*]; M.411.17(a) [*Bridge cursed by fugitive king
after newly married couple sees reflections of his spurs in the water*] (Baughman).
¶   According to this legend, King Edmund was not anxious for martyrdom.
III. MOTIF: E.230 [*Return from dead to inflict punishment*].
¶   See "King Edmund and St Dunstan", "The Death of King Lodbrog".

The legend of St Winifred, which belongs to the Welsh legends, is a true example of motif D.1602.12 because, not only was the head joined to the body, but the saint came to life again.

MEN WITH TAILS

H. Bett, *English Myths and Traditions*, p. 86.

There are at least three local legends about the people of different places in England being blessed with tails, and the reason why. One story is that St Egwin, who was bishop of Worcester in the latter part of the seventh century, was much displeased with the blacksmiths of Alcester because they would work on Sundays, and he visited the town on purpose to persuade them to desist. But they drowned his exhortation by hammering on their anvils, whereupon the saint cursed them, and each irreverent blacksmith forthwith grew a tail.

A similar story is told of St Augustine and the men of Dorset. Caxton relates the legend thus in his version of *The Golden Legend*: "After this St Austin entered into Dorsetshire and came into a town whereas were wicked people who refused his doctrine and preaching utterly, and drove him out of the town, casting on him the tails of thornback, or like fishes; wherefore he besought Almighty God to show his judgment on them, and God sent to them a shameful token; for the children that were born after in that place had tails, as it is said, till they had repented them.

"It is said commonly that this fell at Strood in Kent, but blessed be God at this day is no such deformity."*

The third legend is concerned with Strood, and Caxton evidently confused it with his story about those who treated St Augustine so badly. It is said that the townspeople of Strood sided with Henry the Second in his quarrel with Becket, and cut off the tail of Becket's sumpter-mule as he passed through the place, whereupon the angry saint doomed their posterity to be born with tails, "binding them thereby with a perpetual reproach", as Polydore Vergil writes, "for afterward (by the will of God) it so happened that everyone which came of that kindred of men which played that naughty prank were born with tails, even as brute beasts be". The inhabitants of Strood and of the district are still jestingly called "Kentish long-tails".

Coulton, *Life in the Middle Ages*, I, p. 238.
MOTIFS: M.411.8 [*Saint's curse*]; C.94 [*Tabu: rudeness to sacred person or thing*]; Q.227 [*Punishment for opposition to holy person*].
¶ The taunt of having tails was a common accusation against the English in medieval times, and was even occasionally heard in the seventeenth century, in the epithet, "The Tailed English".

* Caxton, *Golden Legend*, III, p. 201.

THE MIRACLE OF THE MEAD

Roger of Wendover, *Chronicle*, I, p. 246.

[In] A.D. 929 King Ethelstan determined to visit the relics of the saints in his kingdom for the sake of devotion, and in the first place he visited the monastery of Glastonbury. Now there was there a noble matron, named Elfleda, a niece of the same king, who on her husband's death had resolved to pass her life in widowhood, and had fixed her abode in the western part of that monastery. This religious woman prepared with much care a dinner for the king, whose pious visit she was forewarned of. The attendants who had gone before, to provide for the king's entertainment, knowing that he had been pleased to grant to his niece the privilege of receiving him for her guest, came the day before to see if all things necessary had been provided; when, after a diligent inspection of everything, they said to her, "There would be abundance of everything, if there were only plenty of mead, which the king loves above all liquors." "The mother of my Lord Jesus Christ forbid," said she, "that there should be any lack of mead at the king's table," and so, entering the church of the mother of God, she prostrated herself in prayer to God and his mother. What then?

The king came, accompanied by a large company of soldiers, and after the celebration of Mass, he was invited in to dinner; but when they began to drink, they greedily drained the vessel to the depth of a hand's breadth at the first onset, and afterwards, by God's supply, and through the merits of the blessed woman, it continued without diminution throughout the day so that to the general astonishment there was enough for all. When this miracle was related to the king by his attendants, he was moved in spirit, and said to them, "We have greatly sinned in needlessly burdening this handmaid of the Lord," and arising, and saluting his niece, he proceeded on his pious journey.

MOTIF: V.262 [*Virgin Mary supplies mead for unprepared hostess of king*].

THE MURDER OF ST INDRACTUS

Ruth L. Tongue, *Somerset Folklore*, p. 186.

St Indractus and his sister Drusa had been on a pilgrimage from Ireland to Rome, and on their homeward journey stopped to visit St Patrick's tomb at Glastonbury. All the pilgrims carried bags filled with millet and other seeds which they hoped to grow in Ireland to help the poor, and they leant on staves tipped with brass.

Some of King Ina's servants, seeing the sun shining on the brass, thought it was gold. They looked at the bulging wallets and believed they were stuffed with money. They followed the pilgrims through the dusk to Shapwick, and when night fell entered the house and massacred them all. Finding their terrible mistake, they threw the bodies into a pit on the Polden Hills, and trusted that everyone would believe the pilgrims had gone back to Ireland.

For three days and nights a pillar of light from Heaven shone over the pit and all was discovered. King Ina had the bodies buried in Glastonbury Abbey, though some say it was at Shepton Mallet.

The murderers who dare not be absent from the burial were there and then so tormented by devils that they tore their flesh in their teeth and died horribly.

There is a tradition that the light still shines if a crime is committed.

Oral collection, Chedzoy, 1945. Labouring man at smithy.
MOTIF: V.222.1.4 [*Lights show where the body of saint is buried*].

PROBUS AND GRACE [summary]

Hunt, *Popular Romances of the West of England*, p. 277.

Two saints are connected with St Probus' Church. St Probus himself, who built it, had not enough money to add a tower, and begged the help of St Grace. She was a wealthy lady, and undertook to build the tower at her own cost. She spared no expense, and the best craftsmen in the land were engaged, and made a tower of outstanding beauty. When all was ready, St Probus opened the Church, with due solemnity; but he made no reference to St Grace's share in the building. While praise and gratitude were being lavished on him, a voice was heard reciting, slowly and distinctly:

"St Probus and Grace,
Not the first, but the last."

And so St Grace too received her share of thanks and recognition.

MOTIF: L.435 [*Self-righteousness punished*].

ROBERT AND ST ALBAN [abridged]

Roger of Wendover, *Chronicle*, II, pp. 37–8.

There was a certain man who lived at his native town, St Albans, and enjoyed a character free from reproach among his countrymen. From his youth up...he lived honestly, as far as the mediocrity of his fortune allowed, and was a devout attendant at the church. While this man lay in bed one night, about the time of cock-crowing, a man of tall and majestic mien entered his apartment, clad in white, and holding in his hand a beautiful wand. The whole house shone at his entrance, and the chamber was as light as at noon-day. Approaching the bed, he asked in a gentle voice, "Robert, are you asleep?" Robert, trembling with fear and wonder, replied, "Who art thou, Lord?" "I am," said he, "the martyr, St Alban, and am come to tell you the Lord's will concerning my master, the clerk, who taught me the faith of Christ, for, though his fame is so great among mankind, the place of his sepulchre is still unknown, though it is the belief of the faithful that it will be revealed in future ages. Rise, therefore, with speed, put on your clothes and follow me, and I will show you the spot where his precious remains are buried." Robert, therefore, rising from his bed, as it seemed, followed him, and they went together through the public streets towards the north, until they came to a plain which had lain for ages uncultivated near the high road.

Its surface was level, furnishing an agreeable pasturage for cattle, and resting-place for weary travellers, at a village called Redburn, about three miles from St Albans. In this plain were two eminences, called the "Hills of the banners", because there used to be assemblies of the faithful people held round them, when, according to an ancient custom, they yearly made a solemn procession to the Church of St Alban, and offered prayers. Here, St Alban turned a little out of the way, and, seizing the man's hand, led him to one of the mounds, which contained the sepulchre of the blessed martyr. "Here," said he, turning to his follower, "lie in the remains of my master," and then, opening the ground a little, in the shape of a cross, with the man's thumb, and turning up a portion of the turf, he opened a small chest, from which a brilliant light came forth, and filled first the whole of the west, and then the whole world with its rays, after which the chest again closed, and the plain was restored to its former appearance.

The man was astonished and asked the saint what he should do. "Notice the spot carefully," said the saint, "and remember what I have shown you. The time shall soon come when the information which I have privately given you shall turn out to the benefit of many. Rise now," continued he. "Let us be going and return to the place whence we came." As they were on their way home, the saint entered his own church, and the man, returning to his house, went to bed again.

In the morning, the man awoke and was disturbed in mind, doubting whether or not he should disclose to others what he had seen in the vision, or, as he rather believed, in reality; for he feared lest he should offend God if he conceal it, and incur the ridicule of mankind if he told it. In this state of doubt, the fear of God prevailed; and, though he did not proclaim it publicly, yet he communicated it to his domestics and private friends. They, however, at once published in open day what had been told them in the darkness, and what they had heard in the ear they proclaimed upon the house-tops. Thus the story was spread throughout the whole province, so that the inhabitants thronged the cloister of St Alban's monastery. At last the happy report reached Simon, the abbat, by whose influence, next to God, it acquired great importance. He immediately gave thanks to God, and having held a council of the brethren, chose some of them to proceed to the spot, to which the man above-mentioned should guide them. Meantime, the whole convent at home prayed devoutly to God; while the brethren, appointed for the purpose, proceeded to the spot where they hoped to find the relics of the martyr. When they reached the spot, they found there a large multitude, who had met together, from divers parts of the country, led by the Holy Spirit, to witness the discovery of the martyr's relics. Whilst they all waited for the event, the man aforesaid led the men to the plain where the bodies of the saints lay. It was the Friday before the feast of St Alban's when this was done. From that day, until the bodies of the saints were removed, there was always a watch kept over that place, the brethren of the abbey assisting the laity in this duty. . . .

On the morning of the day when the bodies of the saints were found, the venerable father, Abbat Simon, approached the holy spot, and . . . commanded the monks who were present to search with greater diligence, and to put on more diggers immediately. . . . When the abbat and brethren had returned to the abbey, and were seated at dinner, one of them read aloud the passion of the saint for whom they were digging, and of his companions. . . . Whilst, therefore, the convent in tears were intent on hearing the cruelty of the judge . . . the patience of the martyrs, and the lengthened details of their death, someone suddenly entered the room and announced that they had just discovered the bodies of Amphibalus and three others. . . . Rising from the table, they all proceeded to the church and offered up praises to attest the joy which filled their hearts. The holy martyr Amphibalus was lying between two of his companions, whilst the third was found lying crossways in a place by itself. They also found near the place, six others of the martyrs, making, with St Amphibalus himself, ten in all. Among other reliques of this champion of Christ were found two large knives, one in his skull, and the other in his breast, confirming the account which was handed down from ancient times in the book of his martyrdom. . . . The abbat and brethren returned to the monastery carrying with them separately the bodies of the saints. The rest of the brotherhood who had remained behind, came out to meet them, bearing with them the body of the blessed martyr, St Alban, which, as his bearers can testify, though generally heavy, was at present so light that it seemed rather to fly along than to rest upon their shoulders. Thus martyr met martyr, the disciple his master, receiving him publicly on his return from whom formerly he had been taught the true faith in a humble cottage.

MOTIFS: V.510 [*Religious vision*]; E.367.2 [*Saint returns from dead to give blessing*]; V.222.1.4 [*Lights show where body of saint is buried*].

'ROOM FOR A LITTLE ONE'

Ruth L. Tongue, *Forgotten Folk-Tales*. St Bridget.

There was an inn near Selwood Forest, and they had a little maidservant called Bridget, and they kept the poor little soul on the go from long afore sun-up till long after sun-down. When everyone else was abed, there she'd still be, at the cleaning and washing dishes. They'd send her into the Forest at all hours to bring in faggots for their fires, and she took her liddle nirrip [donkey] along for the load. Good, hard-working liddle nirrip it were, and they'd come back along again and again, the two of 'en, that weighted with firing you couldn't see the bare feet of the one, and the liddle hoofs of t'other; and when her day's labour were done, and well-nigh midnight tew, Bridget her'd creep into stable straw alongside liddle nirrip's warm back, and sleep safe.

One winter-time, come sundown, they bringed in their last load afore dark, and they found the stables full right up with the horses of a rich party of travellers, and standing in the snow in the yard, weary and hungry and clarty [mud-spattered] were a old ox. Ploughman 'e were well away inside, drinking hisself dizzy at the feast. But little Bridget, she didn't think much of that, and she look around, and there's an old tumble-down shed, with a bit of thatch roof still on it, and she gives a look, and there's hay inside. "This'll do us," say she, and she go and draw water for the two beasts and she brush 'en down with yard broom, and made the mud and snow fly, and then she lead 'en to the little stable. 'Tis a bit of a twistabout for old ox to get hisself inside, then he say, "Thanky, my dears, there's room for a little 'un." So the liddle nirrip, it go in too, and scrooge itself, and call out to Bridget, "There's room for a liddle 'un." So she went in too, and somehow there was, and that hay smelt like a day in June, and a star shone in.

"Summat wonderful be going to happen," say the wise old ox.

"Here?" ask the nirrip.

"Ah, here, and nowhere's else," say the wise old ox.

Well, Bridget, she didn't know what to think, but what did happen was, they call and send her and the nirrip for another load of wood to the Forest, and 'twas getting in to black dark.

"Don't 'ee be feared," say liddle nirrip, "I can kick for 'ee."

"Don't neither of 'ee be afeared," say wise old ox. "Just keep a-looking up at the star, and you'll find your way."

So that's what they done, and the wind didn't seem to blow so bitter cold, and Bridget's feet was snug, as if she was warm shod, and they could see. They got a big load each, and then they see a man and a woman coming along slow, for the woman was very near her time, and Bridget and the man lifts her gentle on the liddle nirrip, and the man he takes the nirrip's wood on his back, and they come on under the star.

"There's no room at the inn," say Bridget and the nirrip, that worried and sad they was. "There's room for more in our stable," call out the wise old ox...and there *was* somehow! Room for them all, and the manger was filled with hay, and girt sweet-smelling heaps for the beasts. When Bridget her dragged herself to her sleep that night, there warn't no sleep for she. There was shepherds standing in wonder at the stable door, and the beasts was kneeling too, and the liddle nirrip were singing:

"I gave him my manger all full of sweet hay,
I knelt with the shepherds on Chrissimas Day,
The star it shone over, and loud did I bray,
Gloria in excelsis, Christ the Lord is born."

MOTIFS: L.113.2 [*Menial heroine*]; B.250 [*Religious animals*]; B.251.1 [*Animals rejoice at birth of Christ*]; B.211.1.5.1 [*Speaking ox*]; B.211.1.3.1 [*Speaking ass*]; B.251.1.2 [*Animals speak to each other at Christmas*]; B.211.0.1 [*Animals speak, praising God on the night of Christ's Nativity*].

ST ADELME [Aldhelm]

Briggs and Tongue, *Folk-Tales of England*, p. 77.

St Adelme, Abbot of Malmesbury; his father was a weaver, who as he rose early to go to worke, walking over the churchyard, when he came to the crosse something frighted him still. He spoke to his wife to goe along with him; she did, and when she came to the crosse she was struck at the botome of her belly, and conceived this Saint.

Miracle. When a boy—one Sundaye as they were at Masse he filled a barn full of little birds.

This Saint gave a bell to the Abbey, which when it was rung, had the power to make thunder and lightning cease.

The Pope, hearing of his Fame sent for him to preach at Rome; he had not above 2 daies warning to goe. Wherefore he conjured for a fleet spirit. Up comes a spirit he askes how fleet.resp: as fleet as a bird in the air.yt was not enough. Another as fleet as an arrow out of a bow not enough either. a 3rd. as swift as thought. This would doe. He commands it to take the shape of a horse, and presently it was so; a black horse on which his great saddle and footecloth was putt.

The first thing he thought on was St Pauls steeple lead: he did kick it with his foot and asked where he was, and the spirit told him etc. When he came to Rome the groom asked what he should give his horse. quoth he a peck of live coales.

This from an old man at Malmesbury.

From John Aubrey's MS. on Wiltshire, *Hypomnemata Antiquaria*, Bodleian MS. Aubrey, p. 251. Aubrey heard the tradition in 1645, from old Ambrose Brown at Malmesbury.

MOTIFS: T.540.1 [*Supernatural birth of saint*]; D.2122.5 [*Journey with magic speed by saint*]; D.2072.0.2.2.1 [*Person charged with keeping birds from crops confines them in barn by magic*].

¶ Some similar tales are told of St Mungo, as also of less saintly characters, such as Jack o' Kent, Faustus, and such worthies as Francis Drake.

ST ALOYS AND THE LAME NAG

Briggs and Tongue, *Folk-Tales of England*, p. 78.

There were a carter 'ad a 'oss. Fine 'oss 'e were, worked wonderful 'till 'e took 'en carting stones, and they broked 'is feet dreadful. 'E 'ad a sand-crack so wide you could 'a' put a finger in it. Well! when 'e took 'en down to blacksmith, he couldn't do nothing for it. 'Ot as fire that foot was, and the butcher 'e began to get 'is axe ready. But the carter, 'e was proper proud 'o' that 'orse, real fond of it, 'e was. So 'e 'ears about St Aloys down to Wincanton, and 'e reckoned as 'ow 'e'd take cart'orse there. Well, it took 'en the best part o' two days to do the two mile, but carter 'e were determined 'oss should 'ave a chance. Well, when they got to Wincanton, St Aloys come out of 'is smithy. "Bring 'oss in 'ere," says 'e, "I'll take care of 'en, and 'ere's a bit o' zider for 'ee, and some bread and cheese." "I'm feared 'e won't stand," says carter, knowing 'ow e'd treated black-smith. "Oh! E'll be all right," says St Aloys.

So carter, 'e sits down to 'ave 'is zider and 'is bread and cheese; welcome as May, it was; and Saint, 'e just put 'is 'and on old 'oss, and then 'e go into smithy. Carter, 'e took a look and then he took another look, and 'e gollops down 'is zider. There's old 'oss, wi' a bit o' 'ay in 'is mouth, what Saint 'ad give 'im, and Saint were busy in the smithy, and 'old oss were standing there wi' three legs!

"'Ere we are, then," says the Saint, coming out, and he brings out fourth leg, and 'e claps it on, and old 'oss stands there, and 'e nuckers quietly wi' 'is bit of 'ay, and 'e worked for years arter that. Ah! that was St Aloys, that was, down to Wincanton.

Proper fine smith!

Recorded from Ruth L. Tongue, 29 September 1963, as she heard it from a carter at Wincanton in Somerset, where the legend is well known.

MOTIF: E.782.4 [*Horse's leg cut off and replaced*].

¶ There is a carving of St Aloys in Wincanton Church, and a fine alabaster in Nottingham Castle Museum representing the miracle. S. Baring-Gould, in his *Lives of the Saints* (XV, p. 9), says: "In art he is represented erroneously as a farrier with a horse's leg in his hand; the story going that he was one day shoeing a horse, the animal proved restive, so he took the leg off, shod it, and put it on again, without evil consequences."

The story is known in France and Germany, and is discussed by F. Saintyves in his *Saints, Successeurs des Dieux* (Paris, 1907, pp. 248–51).

St Aloys was not St Aloysius Gonzaga, but the earlier St Eligius of Noyau.

See "The Old Smith" (A, II).

ST AUGUSTINE AT LONG COMPTON

J. E. Field, *The Myth of the Pent Cuckoo*, pp. 152–3.

Long Compton has...[a] legend pointing to the...conclusion that the Briton still occupied the combe when the Saxon came here. It is not handed down in the traditions of the people, but preserved in the Chronicles of the Yorkshire Abbey of Jervaulx—a compilation, as it supposed, of the time of King Edward III, though commonly attributed to John Brompton, who became Abbot of that house half a century later.

According to this story, St Augustine himself travelled into Oxfordshire, and came to preach "in the town called Compton", where the priest of the town complained to him that the lord of the manor refused to pay tithe of his possessions, and though he had often admonished him, and had even threatened him with excommunication, he still found him obstinate.

When Augustine had called for him and reasoned with him in vain he turned to the altar to begin the Mass, bidding all the excommunicate to depart, whereupon a corpse arose from the churchyard. Augustine asked him who he was, and he replied that he was a patron of the church before the English came and had died excommunicate, for refusing to pay his tithe; and the saint enjoined him to point out the grave of the priest who had repelled him from communion; so he in his turn arose from his grave, and bore out the truth of the story. Then at Augustine's bidding the ghost absolved the other ghost and both returned to their graves in peace, while the obstinate knight became a humble follower of the saint's teaching. At least we may gather from the tale that the memory of the Britons and their church at Long Compton had a place in the minds of the Saxon conquerors.

MOTIFS: E.412.1 [*Excommunicated person cannot rest in grave*]; V.229.1 [*Saint commands return from the dead with supernatural information*].

ST CONGAR'S WALKING-STICK

Ruth L. Tongue, *Somerset Folklore*, p. 185.

One day word was brought to King Ina of Somerset that a strange prince from the East had landed in Weston Bay and come up-country to camp. In fact, the messengers said he was building there. Who was he? And what was he building? The king himself decided to find out, and there on the banks of the River Yeo he found a Byzantine prince and a tiny wattled church sheltered by a magnificent yew tree. It had been the saint's staff until he set it in the ground where he hoped to found his monastery. After such a miracle it is not surprising that St Congar got his town and church from the king. A stump of the "walking-stick" is still there, but St Congar's Church is at Badgeworth.

It is possible, however, that St Congar's was the original church at Congresbury. There is a vague tradition that on May Day, or Midsummer Day, which is the festival, the Congresbury women used to process round the well at Southwells Farm, barking like dogs. The conger eels of the nearby Severn Sea are credited with barking, and there may be a trace here of a fisherman's cult. On the other hand, such a dance may be one of the Cadbury Hill witch rites still remembered. Apparently black magic was practised there on May Eve and Midsummer less than a hundred years ago.

Mrs Clifton, Crowcombe, November 1959; the Rev. W. Griffin, Angersleigh, January 1960.

MOTIFS: F.971.1 [*Dry rod blossoms*]; D.1487.3 [*Magic spell makes tree grow*]; H.1573.2.1 [*Magic manifestations required as proof in test of saintliness*].

ST CUTHBERT'S BIRDS AND BARTHOLOMEW, THE HERMIT OF FARNE

Helen Waddell, *Beasts and Saints*, pp. 93–5.

From ancient time long past, this island has been inhabited by certain birds whose name and race miraculously persists. At the time of year for building nests, they gather here, and such gracious gentleness have they learned from the holiness of the place, or rather from those who made the place holy by their way of living there, that they have no shrinking from the handling or gaze of men. They love quiet, and yet no clamour disturbs them. Their nests are built everywhere. Some brood above their eggs beside the altar. No man presumes to molest them or touch the eggs without leave....And they in turn do harm to no man's store for food. They seek it with their mates upon the waves of the sea. The ducklings, once they are reared, follow behind their mothers, who lead the way, and once they have entered their native waters, come no more back to the nest. The mothers too, their mild and gentle way of life forgotten, receive their ancient state and instinct with the sea. This is the high prerogative of the island, which, had it once come to the knowledge of the scholars of old time, would have had its fair fame blazoned through the earth.

But at one time it befell, whilst a mother was leading her brood, herself going on before, that one of the youngsters fell down a cleft of a creviced rock. The mother stood by in distress, and let no one doubt but that she was then endowed with human reason. For she forthwith turned about, left her youngsters behind, came to Bartholomew, and began tugging at the hem of his cloak with her beak, as if to say plainly: "Get up and follow me, and give me back my son." He rose at once for her, thinking that he must be sitting on her nest. But as she kept on tugging more, he perceived at last that she was asking something from him that she could not come at by voice. And indeed her action was eloquent, if not her discourse. On she went, she first and he after, till, coming to the cliff she pointed to the place with her bill, and gazing at Bartholomew, intimated with what signs she could that he was to peer inside. Coming closer, he saw the duckling with its small wings clinging to the rock, and climbing down he brought it to its mother, who in high delight seemed by her joyous look to give him thanks. Whereupon she took to the water with her sons, and Bartholomew, dumb with astonishment, went back to his oratory.

ST CUTHBERT AND THE RAVENS

Helen Waddell, *Beasts and Saints*, p. 66.

Here might be told a miracle done by the blessed Cuthbert in the fashion of the aforesaid father, Benedict, wherein the obedience and humility of the birds put to shame the obstinacy and arrogance of men. Upon that island for a great while back a pair of ravens had had their dwelling: and one day at their nesting time the man of God spied them tearing with their beaks at the thatch of the hospice of which I have spoken, and carrying off pieces of it in their bill to build their nest. He thrust at them gently with his hand, and bade them give over this damage to the brethren. And when they scoffed at his command, "In the name of Jesus Christ," said he, "be off with you as quick as ye may, and never more presume to abide in the place which ye have spoiled." And scarcely had he spoken, when they flew dismally away.

But towards the end of the third day, one of the two came back, and finding Christ's servant busy digging, comes with his wings lamentably trailing, and his head bowed to his feet, and his voice low and humble, and begs pardon with such signs as he might; which the good father well understanding gives him permission to return.

As for the other, leave once obtained, he straight goes off to fetch his mate, and with no tarrying, back they both come, and carrying along with them a suitable present, no less than a good sized hunk of hog's lard, such as one greases axles with; many a time thereafter the man of God would show it the brethren who came to see him, and would offer it to grease their shoes, and he would urge on them how obedient and humble men should be, when the proudest of birds made haste with prayers and lamentation and presents to atone for the insult he had given to man. And so, for an example of reformed life to men, these did abide for many years thereafter on that same island, nor ever wrought annoyance upon any.

MOTIFS: B.771.2 [*Animal tamed by holiness of saint*]; B.256.5 [*Obedience of feathered creatures to the commands of saint*].

¶ This story is of the time when St Cuthbert was living an ascetic and solitary life on Farne Island.

See "St Werburgh".

ST DECUMAN

Sarah Hewett, *Nummitts and Crummits*, pp. 34–6.

Happy Decuman was born of a good family in the western part of Wales, of parents strict observers of the Christian religion. He, after he had passed his childhood at home, as he advanced in years, was of a very good disposition; and at length crossed the Severn unknown to all his acquaintance, especially to his relations, and to those who seemed to be more nearly concerned for his welfare; trusting in Christ alone for his protection. But not to mention anything more, he paid no freight and had no ship. This good man, relying upon the mercy of God, not doubting that he would protect him, bound shrubs together, which he found growing by the seaside, and making use of such a vehicle committed himself to the ocean. Being by divine providence directed, he was carried to the opposite shore, near Dart's Castle.

There was in that part of the country in which he landed a desert place (presumably Exmoor) beset with shrubs and briars, which were very long and large, and by the hollowness of the *vathes* was wonderfully separated. This place pleased him much: changing his native country for a sort of exile, the luxury of a palace for the dens of a desert. There he began to dwell, and to live upon roots and herbs, leading the life of a hermit, and by such government in the above-mentioned desert, he lived many years.

It is said also that he had a cow, by the milk of which he was more kept alive than nourished, especially upon certain festival days. When the fore* happy Decuman had flourished in virtues of every kind, a certain man, but he a man of Belial, envying the holiness of so great a father, drunk with passion, rushed on, and in brutish manner met him; and as he spoke and prayed, he sent the saint to heaven by cutting off his head.

But this also is not to be passed by in silence, for when he was beheaded with a certain sort of crooked hook, as 'tis reported, his body rose itself up and begun with its dangling arms to carry his head from the place where it was cut off even to a very clear well of water, in which he washed his head with his own hands as he was used to do; which well even to this day, in memory and reverence of the saint, is called the pleasant well of St Decuman, useful and well for the inhabitants to drink. In which place his head together with his body being afterwards sought for by the faithful and found, was delivered to be honourably buried.

* Fore = aforesaid.

MOTIFS: D.2156.2.1 [*Cow supplies sufficient milk for saint and all his disciples*]; D.1602.12 [*Self-returning head*].

¶ See "St Edmund".

ST DUNSTAN

Roger of Wendover, *Chronicle*, I, p. 270.

A.D. 988. The most blessed confessor of the Lord, Archbishop Dunstan, ended his praiseworthy life by a happy death on Saturday, the 19th day of May. His glorious miracles are recorded to have commenced in his mother's womb. For Almighty God, foreshowing by a prodigy his future sanctity, revealed what he would become unto his mother while bearing in her womb her yet unborn son. On the day of the purification of the blessed Virgin Mary, the whole concourse of the city being in church with burning tapers, when the priest had adorned himself with the sacred vestments for the solemn services of the altar, on a sudden whether by chance or by the will of God all the lights were extinguished. In the midst of the general amazement, the taper of Dunstan's mother took light, and, by communicating it to the rest, restored the joy of all.

As he advanced in years a harp which hung on a peg, without any human touch, played the sweet melody of the antiphon, "*Gaudent in Coelis*". By the spirit of God he foresaw all the artifices of the Devil, and when he once came to him in the guise of a beautiful woman tempting him to commit fornication, he seized him by the nose with a red-hot tongs, and held it until he made it appear that he was the Devil by assuming various and terrific forms; and at length being let go, he fouled and corrupted the air, and left his filthy marks on those who stood by.

MOTIF: V.229.2.4 [*Baptism of wonder-child is accompanied by a variety of phenomena*].

ST DUNSTAN AND THE DEVIL

K. M. Briggs, *Pale Hecate's Team*, p. 230.

A reputation of occult powers hovered about St Dunstan from the beginning of his career. When he was only a lay churchman he had to purge himself of an accusation of black magic by the water ordeal, which in those days was the opposite of the later swimming of a witch. When he had been converted by Bishop Alfege and lived a life of great austerity many tales began to be told of his personal conflicts with the Devil. But the most famous seems to have belonged to later times when he was Archbishop of Canterbury and founded the church at Mayfield in Sussex, where there was an archepiscopal palace to which he used often to retreat.

St Dunstan was skilled in all artefacts, and he was specially famous as a smith. He had a smithy of his own in his palace at Mayfield, where he often used to entertain himself with ingenious pieces of metal work. One day the Devil chose to visit him there. He had often been worsted by St Dunstan in his proper form, and knew that it was no good to try straight conclusions with him, so he assumed the appearance of a very beautiful woman, and came gliding into the cell on the pretence that he had some ghostly counsel to seek. It was not long before the lovely creature began to make amorous advances to the saint. Whether he saw something odd in her footwear or noticed that she kept one foot always hidden we are not told, at all events St Dunstan shrewdly suspected that it was not mortal wickedness that inspired her; but he made no sign, but continued working at his forge. At length the lady sidled right up to him and St Dunstan drew a red-hot pair of pincers out of the fire and clipped it on to her beautiful nose. At once there was a stench and shriek, and where the lady had been a hideous devil appeared with flapping wings and lashing tail; but the pincers were still firmly fixed on his nose, and St Dunstan still held the other end of them. Round and round the room he dragged the Devil, until they were both tired, and St Dunstan opened the pincers and let him fly. And with one flap of his wings the Devil fled to Tunbridge Wells, where he cooled his nose in the waters, which have a ruddy, ochreous tinge ever since. But the very pincers that St Dunstan used are still to be seen at Mayfield Palace to witness the tale.

TYPE 330 (variant). MOTIFS: T.332 [*Man tempted by fiend in woman's shape*]; G.303.9.4.4 [*Devil tempts cleric*].

¶ Hilaire Belloc retells the story pleasantly in *The Four Men: A Farrago*, pp. 31–42.

ST DUNSTAN'S DYKE

Ruth L. Tongue.

The miller of Baltonsborough was in trouble. There was not enough water in the Southwood stream to turn his wheel, and folk must have their corn ground. There was plenty of water in the River Brue, only a short distance away; in fact, Barton sometimes had too much of it. He only knew one person who could solve the problem. St Dunstan was a Baltonsborough man, and so it was St Dunstan rolled up his sleeves and started to dig a dyke from Tootle's Bridge. Straight as a die it ran above Catsham, and the mill wheels turned merrily. When Barton complained that it was left high and dry, the saint built a hatch on the Brue. From Saturday night to Monday morning, Barton got all the water it wanted; then it was the turn of Baltonsborough. That is still going on.

Local tradition, Baltonsborough.
MOTIF: A.934.5 [*Rivers originate through saint's prayer during drought*].
¶ In this case, however, St Dunstan is credited with the actual spadework. Drake is supposed to have provided the same amenity, but by the help of the Devil.
    See "Drake and the River" (B, III).

ST EGWIN

H. Bett, *English Legends*, p. 43.

St Egwin, the third bishop of Worcester, was the victim of false accusations, and went to Rome to vindicate himself. He put fetters on his feet, locked them, and threw away the key into a pool of the Avon before setting out. While he was at Rome a salmon caught in the Tiber was being cooked by his attendants, when they found in the fish's maw the identical key, wherewith Egwin promptly unlocked his fetters.

    This miracle was naturally regarded by the Pope as a complete vindication, and the saint was sent home to England in honour. This is the story as it is told in the *Chronicle* of the abbey. William of Malmesbury says that the fish leapt on board the ship on the saint's voyage. After Egwin's return, the shepherd Eoves came to him and told him a vision of the Virgin, who had shown him the spot on which a new sanctuary was to be built in her honour. Egwin accompanied Eoves to the place, and the vision was repeated. So the abbey was founded, and called Eovesham, or Evesham.

TYPE 736A. MOTIFS: V.229.2.11 [*Miracle saves saint from unjust censure*]; N.211.1.0.1 [*Lost articles found in interior of fish through virtue of saint*]; N.211.1.2 [*Key to fetters found in fish*]; V.111.3 [*Place where a church must be built miraculously indicated*].

¶ The lost ring found in a fish, of which this legend is a variant, is a motif common in fairy tales, such as "The Fish and the Ring" (A, II), or novelle, such as "The Bride who had never been kissed" (A, IV). It has even found its way into the jocular tales as a catch story.

ST FILLAN

Scott, *Minstrelsy of the Scottish Border*, IV, p. 155.

St Fillan was, according to Camerarius, an abbot of Pittenweem, in Fife; from which situation he retired, and died a hermit in the wilds of Glenurchy, A.D. 649.

While engaged in transcribing the Scriptures, his left hand was observed to send forth such a splendour as to afford light to that with which he wrote; a miracle which saved many candles to the convent, as St Fillan used to spend whole nights in that exercise.... Lesley, lib. 7, tells us that Robert the Bruce was possessed of Fillan's miraculous and luminous arm, which he enclosed in a silver shrine, and had it carried at the head of his army. Previous to the Battle of Bannockburn, the king's chaplain, a man of little faith, abstracted the relic, and deposited it in some place of security, lest it should fall into the hands of the English. But lo! while Robert was addressing his prayers to the empty casket, it was observed to open and shut suddenly; and, on inspection, the saint was found to have himself deposited his arm in the shrine as an assurance of victory.

MOTIFS: F.552.1.2 [*Fingers of saint give light or fire*]; V.224 [*Miraculous replacement of objects for saint*].

ST FRIDESWIDE AND THE BUILDING
OF HER CHURCH

Roger of Wendover, *Chronicle*, I, pp. 464–5.

Roger, Bishop of Salisbury, gave a place in Oxford, where the body of the virgin St Frideswide reposes, to a canon named Wimund, who formed there a community of canons under regular discipline, and was himself their first prior. The place had been in ancient times dedicated to the use of nuns, out of reverence for that same saint, who despised an earthly for the enjoyment of a heavenly bridegroom; for the son of a certain king, wishing to marry the virgin, and having employed entreaties and blandishments in vain, tried at last to use force, but Frideswide, perceiving his intentions, fled privately into a wood, but did not escape her lover, who was on the alert to find out where she was gone. The virgin, therefore, flying by night, and having God for her guide, arrived in Oxford; and when her ardent lover came there also, she despaired of escape, and being

441

too fatigued to proceed further, she prayed God to protect her and to punish her pursuer. The young man was already entering the city with his followers, when he was suddenly blinded by a heavenly stroke. Perceiving that he was punished for his pertinacity, he sent to Frideswide, and entreated her intercession with the Lord. The virgin prayed to God, and at her prayer the young man recovered his sight as quickly as he had before been struck with blindness. From this cause the kings of England have always been afraid to enter that city, for it is said to be fatal to them, and they are unwilling to test the truth of it at their own peril. The virgin constructed a monastery there and herself presided as abbess over the company of pious virgins there assembled.

MOTIFS: M.131 [*Vow of chastity*]; T.321 [*Escape from undesired lover by miracle*]; Q.571 [*Magic blindness as punishment remitted*].

ST GEORGE

S. Baring-Gould, *Lives of the Saints*, IV, pp. 304-5.

George, a tribune, was born in Cappadocia, and came to Libya to the town called Silene, near which was a pond, infested by a monster, which had many times driven back an armed host that had come to destroy him. He even approached the walls of the city, and with his exhalations poisoned all who were near. To avoid such visits, he was furnished each day with two sheep, to satisfy his voracity. When the sheep at the disposal of the citizens were exhausted, their sons and daughters were cast to the dragon. The lot fell one day on the princess. The king covered his child with royal robes, and sent her forth to meet the dragon. St George was riding by, and, seeing the maiden in tears and the monster rising from the marsh to devour her, advanced, spear in hand, to meet the monster, commending himself to God. He transfixed the dragon, and then bade the princess pass her girdle round it, and fear nothing. When this was done, the monster followed like a docile hound. When they had brought it into the town, the people fled before it; but George recalled them, bidding them put aside all fear.

Then the king and all his people, twenty thousand men, without counting women and children, were baptized, and George smote off the head of the monster. Other versions of the story are to the effect that the princess was shut up in a castle, and that all within were perishing for want of water, which could only be obtained from a fountain at the base of the hill, and this was guarded by the dragon, from which St George delivered them.

TYPE 300. MOTIFS: B.11 [*Dragon*]; G.346 [*Devastating monster lays waste the land*]; B.11.3.1.1 [*Dragon lives in lake*]; B.11.2.11.1 [*Dragon spews venom*]; B.11.10 [*Sacrifice of human being to dragon*]; B.11.11.4 [*Dragon fight in order to rescue princess*]; G.510.4 [*Hero overcomes devastating animal*]; V.351.6 [*Conversion to Christianity out of gratitude*].

¶ The full chapbook version of St George in the *Seven Champions of Christendom* will be found in A, II.

An account of St George, the martyr of Cappadocia, is given on p. 302 of Baring-Gould's *Lives of the Saints*. It is taken from Eusebius, and is an account of the witness of an unnamed martyr, usually taken to be St George.

The substance of the Greek *Acts* is to this effect: George was born of Christian parents in Cappadocia. His father suffered a martyr's death, and the mother, with her child, took refuge in Palestine. He early entered the army, and behaved with great courage and endurance. At the age of twenty he was bereaved of his mother, and by her death came in for a large fortune. He then went to the court of Diocletian, where he hoped to find advancement. On the breaking out of persecution, he distributed his money among the poor, and declared himself before the Emperor to be a Christian. Having been ordered to sacrifice, he refused, and was condemned to death. Here follows a numerous succession of tortures, from which he miraculously recovers, day after day, a succession which accompanies, with wearisome monotony, nearly all the Greek apocryphal acts of martyrdom.

See "St George for Merry England" (A, II).

ST GODRIC AND THE HARE

Helen Waddell, *Beasts and Saints*, pp. 87–9.

He had planted vegetables to feed poor men, and these a little hare used stealthily to devour. He put up with the damage for a long time: but at last the track of its paws betrayed the person of the delinquent: and he came on the thief in his garden and as it turned in headlong flight, he bade it halt. The poor little creature stopped, and waited in trembling and alarm the arrival of its pursuer. The saint caught it, struck it with his rod, and binding a bundle of vegetables on its shoulders sent it off with these words: "See to it that neither thyself nor any of thy acquaintance come to this place again: nor dare to encroach on what was meant for the need of the poor."

And so it befell....

MOTIF: B.250 [*Religious animals*].

ST GODRIC AND ST JOHN
THE BAPTIST'S SALMON

Helen Waddell, *Beasts and Saints*, pp. 84–6.

It was the serene and joyous weather of high summer, and the turning of the year brought nigh the solemn Feast of St John the Baptist. And because the man of God had begged it, and it was the familiar custom, two brothers from the monastery at Durham were sent out to him to celebrate the divine office with all due honour. The office reverently said, and this most solemn Mass ended, the folk who had come for the Feast made their way home; and the brethren came to him to ask his blessing, and leave to return to their monastery.

"Ye may have God's blessing," said he, "but when St Cuthbert's sons have come to visit me, they must not go home without their dinner", and calling his servant-man, "Quick, beloved," said he, "and set up the table, for these brethren are to eat with us today."

The table was set up, and oat-cake laid upon it, such as he had, and bowls of good milk. Yet when he looked at the feast, it seemed to him but poor, and he bade the serving-man bring fish as well.

"Master," said he in amaze, "where should we get fish at a time like this, in all this heat and drought, when we can see the very bottom of the river? We can cross dry-shod where we used to spread the seine and the nets." But he answered, "Go quickly and spread my seine in that same dry pool." The man went out and did as he was told, but with no hope of any sort of catch.

He came back, declaring that the pool had dried up "till the very sands of it were parched"; and his master bade him make haste to fill the cauldron with water, and set it on the hearth to heat, and this was done. After a little while he bade his man go to the bank and bring back his catch. The man went, and looked, and came back empty-handed: he did it again a second time: and then in disgust, refused to go any more.

For a little while the man of God held his peace, and then spoke. "Now go this time," said he, "for this very hour the fish has come into the net, that St John the Baptist promised me; for never could he break a promise by not doing what he said, although our sluggish faith deserved it little. And look you," said he, "but that salmon that is now caught in the seine is a marvellous fine one." So in the end his man went off, and found even as he had been told: and drawing it out of the net he brought the fish alive to where his master sat in the oratory, and laid it at his feet, then, as he was bidden, he cut it into pieces, and put it into the pot now boiling on the hearth, and cooked it well, and brought it to the brethren at the table, and well were they fed and mightily amazed. For they marvelled how a fish could come swimming up a river of which the very sands were dry; and, above all, how the man of God, talking with them and sitting in the oratory, could have seen, by the revelation of the spirit, the very hour when the fish entered the meshes of the net. To which he made reply, "St John the Baptist never deserts his own, but sheds the blessing of his great kindness on those that trust him." And so he sent them home, well fed and uplifted at so amazing a miracle; praising and glorifying God, who alone doeth marvels, for all they had seen and heard.

MOTIF: D.2106.1.1.1 [*Fish caught in a waterless field*].

ST HILDA'S WORMS [summary]

Parkinson. *Yorkshire Legends and Traditions*, 1st series, p. 23.

In the year A.D. 655 Oswy, the Christian king of Northumbria, was about to meet in battle Penda, the heathen ruler of Mercia, and vowed that, if he were victorious, he would dedicate his infant daughter, Ethelfleda, to a monastic life, and give twelve estates to found religious houses. He won the battle, and committed the child to Hilda, whom he also made abbess of his newly founded abbey at Whitby.

As soon as they took possession of this abbey, they were troubled with a plague of serpents. Hilda prayed that they might be driven into the sea, and never return.

She followed up her prayer with a vigorous attack upon them with a whip, which cut off many of their heads. Their bodies thereupon coiled up and became petrified, in which state some of them are still to be found upon the sands, and are known as Hilda's worms.

MOTIF: V.229.24 [*Saint turns snakes to stones*].
¶ See "The Snakes of St Keyna".

ST JOHN OF BEVERLEY [summary]

Parkinson. *Yorkshire Legends and Traditions*, 1st series, p. 72.

St John of Beverley was probably a descendant of a noble Saxon family, born at Harpham on the wolds, about the middle of the seventh century. He was Bishop of Hexham in 688, and was translated to York in 705. In 717 he retired to the monastery which he had founded at Beverley, where he was buried, at first in the porch, but later, after his canonization by Benedict IX, his shrine was erected, and became the chief glory of Beverley Abbey.

The following legends are told of him:

I. WATTON NUNNERY

While he was Bishop of York, St John came on a visit to the nunnery of Watton [Vetadum] in the East Riding. Here the abbess entreated him to bless one of her nuns, who had lately been bled in the arm, and now her arm was swollen and so inflamed that she seemed on the point of death. The saint, after inquiry, said they had done wrong to bleed her when the moon and tides were on the increase. Nevertheless, he gave her his blessing, and said a prayer for her. Shortly after he had left her, the girl sent and earnestly begged him to return. He did so, and found her perfectly recovered from her pain, and soon afterwards the swelling also disappeared, and she was entirely restored to health.

II. PUCH THE EARL OF SOUTH BURTON

Near the monastery at Beverley was the country house of Earl Puch, whose wife had been suffering for forty days from a grievous disease. St John was invited by the earl to consecrate a church, and at the same time he sent some holy water to the sick woman, ordering the brother who took it to her, to give her some to taste, and to wash the place where her pain was worst.... By this water she was instantly cured, and came and waited on the Bishop and his company at table. She also presented to him the cup in which the holy water had been carried.

III. EARL ADDI'S SERVANT OF NORTH BURTON

A similar story is told of Earl Addi, who, when St John had dedicated a church for him, requested him with tears to go in and pray for a servant of his who lay at the point of death. The Bishop said a prayer over the man, who soon afterwards, as they sat at table, sent to ask for a cup of wine. The Bishop blessed the cup, and the man, as soon as he had drunk from it, immediately got up, dressed himself, and joined the company at their dinner.

IV. THE PLEDGED SWORD

After the death of St John of Beverley, many wonders were performed at his shrine, of which a few are given below.

In A.D. 937 when Wulfstan was abbot of Beverley he learned that King Athelstane was on his way north, to chastise Constantine the King of Scotland for giving help to some Danes. With his cellarer, Godruff, Wulfstan devised a way to turn the king's journey to the profit of the abbey. As the king with his chief men around him was approaching Lincoln, he determined to devote the next day to prayer and worship and fasting in the great church there, to ask God's blessing on their enterprise. Just before they entered the city, they met a group of pilgrims singing loudly. They wore blue robes, with leather girdles, from which hung their earthenware bottle, bare heads, and sandalled feet. They approached the king and told him that once they had all been lame, blind or otherwise afflicted, and had sought help in vain at many shrines, until they came to that of St John of Beverlega, where they had all been miraculously restored to health, and so were now returning to their various homes. The king was amazed, and remembered that he had been once well entertained at that monastery. He therefore changed his intention of staying at Lincoln, and decided to visit Beverley instead. He gave a generous gift to the pilgrims, sent his army ahead of him to York, and proceeded with Larwulf, his lieutenant, to Beverley, where the abbot, warned of his approach, entertained him to a great feast. At midnight the king, with the abbot, and all his monks went in procession to the holy house, to pray; and before they left it, the king laid his sword upon the altar, and vowed to give rich gifts to the abbey if he returned victorious from his war. The sword was his pledge of fulfilment.

The king set off next morning to join his army at York; and soon afterwards, Godruff and his fellow pilgrims arrived back at the abbey. Almost at once, however, Godruff set forth again on a journey to the north.

When Athelstan had joined his army, after a hot day's march they found themselves on the eve of a great battle—known as the Battle of Brunnanburg—encamped by a river, and as the king lay half-awake in his tent, brooding over the morrow, a slight sound roused him, and in the moonlight he saw an aged man in a white robe, and with long white hair, standing by his couch. "Who art thou?" he cried; and the figure replied: "I am he whose help thou sought at Beverlega. Thy petition is granted. Lead thine army across the river tomorrow, and all will be well. Forget not thy vow and thy pledge at my tomb."

The figure vanished, and the king, after being assured by his sentinels that no one had entered or left the tent, was persuaded that he had seen a vision; the more so when on the following day he gained a complete victory over the Scots, and drove them back across the Tweed. He returned triumphantly to Beverlega, where he was welcomed by the brotherhood, to whom Godruff had already told of the king's victory.

Godruff seemed to avoid the king, until one day he came upon him by chance, and the king asked his name, saying he thought he had been familiar with all the brothers by that time. Looking more closely, he added: "Thou art marvellously like St John who appeared to me on the eve of the battle." Somewhat confused, Godruff replied that he was a descendant of the same family, and that the likeness had been often remarked before. This contented the king, who thereupon founded a college of canons in the church, with rich endowments, and a place of sanctuary. To both church and town he added many more privileges, and so redeemed the pledge of his sword.

V

The abbey grew in fame and wealth until the time of the Battle of Agincourt, when this same St John was said to have appeared in the ranks of the English army, riding on a white horse, and encouraged the men with his gracious words. At the same time his relics in Beverley were moved in sympathy, and blood was seen to drip from his tomb.

I. MOTIF: V.221 [*Miraculous healing by saints*].

II. MOTIF: D.1500.1.10.2.1 [*Wine blessed by saint or received from saint's hands cures various ills*].

III. MOTIF: D.1685 [*Interred body of saint performs signs and miracles*].
IV. MOTIF: K.1970 [*Sham miracles*];
V. MOTIF: A.185.1 [*God helps mortal in battle*] is the nearest motif to the frequently recurring theme of a saint appearing before a battle to promise victory.

¶   The trickster tale of no. IV is introduced by Parkinson, almost without comment, among the serious beliefs about St John of Beverley.

ST KEA'S BOAT

Hunt, *Popular Romances of the West of England*, p. 270.

St Kea, a young Irish saint, stood on the southern shores of Ireland, and saw the Christian missionaries departing to carry the blessed Word to the heathens of Western England. He watched their barks fade beneath the horizon, and he felt that he was left to a solitude which was not fitted to one in the full energy of young life and burning with zeal.

The saint knelt on a boulder of granite lying on the shore, and he prayed with fervour that Heaven would order it so that he might diffuse his religious fervour amongst the barbarians of Cornwall. He prayed on for some time, not observing the rising of the tide. When he had poured out his full soul, he awoke to the fact, not only that the waves were washing round the stone on which he knelt, but that the stone was actually floating on the water. Impressed with the miracle, St Kea sprang to his feet, and looking towards the setting sun with his cross uplifted, he exclaimed, "To Thee, and only to Thee, my God, do I trust my soul!"

Onward floated the granite, rendered buoyant by supernatural power. Floated hither and thither by the tides, it swam on; blown sometimes in one direction and sometimes in another, by the varying winds, days and nights were spent upon the waters. The faith of St Kea failed not; three times a day he knelt in prayer to God. At all other times he stood gazing on the heavens. At length, the faith of the saint being fairly tried, the moorstone boat floated steadily up the river, and landed at St Kea, which place he soon Christianized; and there stands to this day this monument of St Kea's sincere belief.

MOTIFS: F.841.1.1 [*Stone boat*]; V.331.1 [*Conversion to Christianity through miracle*].

ST KENELM

Hugh Miller, *First Impressions of England and Its People*, p. 169.

When little more than a mile out of Hales Owen, I struck off the high road through a green lane, flanked on both sides by extensive half-grown woods, and overhung by shaggy hedges, that were none the less picturesque from their having been long strangers to the shears, and much enveloped in climbing, berry-bearing plants, honeysuckles, brambles, and the woody nightshade. As the path winds up the acclivity, the scene assumes an air of neglected wildness, not very common in England: the tangled thickets rise in irregular groups in the foreground; and closing in the prospect behind, I could see through the frequent openings the green summits of the Clent Hills, now scarce half a mile away. I was on historic ground—the "various wild", according to Shenstone, "for Kenelm's fate renowned"; and which at a still earlier period had formed one of the battlefields on which the naked Briton contended on unequal terms with the mail-enveloped Roman. Halfway up the ascent, at a turning in the lane, where the thicket opens into a grassy glade, there stands a fine old chapel of dark red sandstone, erected in the times of the Heptarchy, to mark the *locale* of a tragedy characteristic of the time—the murder of the boy-king, St Kenelm, at the instigation of his sister, Kendrida. I spent some time in tracing the half-obliterated carvings on the squat Saxon doorway—by far the most ancient part of the edifice—and in straining hard to find some approximation to the human figure in the rude effigy of a child sculptured on a wall, with a crown on its head, and a book in its hand, intended, say the antiquaries, to represent the murdered prince, but at present not particularly like anything. The story of Kenelm we find indicated, rather than told, in one of Shenstone's elegies:

> Fast by the centre of yon various wild,
>   Where spreading oaks embower a Gothic fane,
> Kendrida's arts a brother's youth beguiled;
>   There nature urged her tenderest pleas in vain.
> Soft o'er his birth, and o'er his infant hours,
>   The ambitious maid could every care employ;
> And with assiduous fondness crop the flowers,
>   To deck the cradle of the princely boy.
>
> But soon the bosom's pleasing calm is flown;
>   Love fires her breast; the sultry passions rise;
> A favoured lover seeks the Mercian throne,
>   And views her Kenelm with a rival's eyes.
> See, garnished for the chase the fraudful maid
>   To these lone hills directs his devious way:
> The youth, all prone, the sister-guide obeyed;
>   Ill-fated youth! Himself the destined prey.

The minuter details of the incident, as given by William of Malmesbury and Matthew of Westminster, though admirably fitted for the purpose of the true ballad-maker, are of a kind which would have hardly suited the somewhat lumbrous dignity of Shenstone's elegiacs. Poor Kenelm, at the time of his death, was but nine years old. His murderer, the favoured lover of his sister, after making all sure by cutting off his head with a long-bladed knife, had buried head, knife, and body under a bush, in a "low pasture" in the forest, and the earth concealed its dead. The deed, however, had scarce been perpetrated, when a white dove came flying into old St Peter's at Rome, a full thousand miles away, bearing a scroll in its bill, and, dropping the scroll on the high altar, straightway disappeared. And on the scroll there was found inscribed in Saxon characters the following couplet:

> In Clent, in Caubage, Kenelm, kinge-born,
> Lyeth under a thorn, his head off-shorne.

So marvellous an intimation—miraculous among its other particulars, in the fact that rhyme of such angelic origin should be so very bad, though this part of the miracle the monks seem to have missed—was of course not to be slighted. The churchmen of Mercia were instructed by the pontiff to make diligent search for the body of the slain prince; and priests, monks, and canons, with the Bishop of Mercia at their head, proceeded forthwith in long procession to the forest. And there, in what Milton in telling the story terms a "mead of kine" they found a cow lowing pitifully beside what seemed to be a newly-laid sod. The earth was removed, the body of the murdered prince discovered, the bells of the neighbouring churches began "to rongen a peal without mannes helpe", and a beautiful spring of water, the resort of many a pilgrim for full seven centuries after, burst out of the excavated hollow.

The chapel was erected immediately beside the well; and such was the odour of sanctity which embalmed the memory of St Kenelm that there was no saint in the calendar on whose day it was more unsafe to do anything useful. There is a furrow still to be seen, scarce half a mile to the north of the chapel, from which a team of oxen, kept impiously at work during the festival of the saint, ran away, and were never after heard of; and the owner lost not only his cattle, but shortly after his eyes to boot. The chapel received gifts in silver, and gifts in gold—"crouns" and "ceptres", and "Chalysses": there grew up around it, mainly through the resort of pilgrims, a hamlet, which in the times of Edward the First contained a numerous population, and to which Henry the Third granted an annual fair. At length the age of the Reformation arrived; Henry the Eighth seized on the gold and silver; Bishop Latimer broke down the well; the pilgrimages ceased; the fair, after lingering on till the year 1784, disappeared also; and St Kenelm's, save that the ancient chapel still survived, became exactly such a scene of wild woodland solitude as it had been ere the boy prince fell under the knife of the assassin. The dream of a thousand years was over, when, some time about the close of the last century, a few workmen, engaged in excavating the foundations of the ruined monastery of Winchcomb, in which, according to the monkish chroniclers, the body of the young prince had been interred, near that of his father, lighted on a little stone coffin, beside a larger, which lay immediately under the great eastern window of the church. They raised the lid. There rested within a little dust, a few fragments of the more solid bones, a half-grown human skull tolerably entire, and beside the whole, and occupying half the length of the little coffin, lay a long-bladed knife, converted into a brittle oxide, which fell in pieces in the attempt to remove it. The portion of the story that owed its existence to the monks had passed into a little sun-gilt vapour; but here was there evidence corroborative of its truthful nucleus surviving still.

TYPE 780 (variant). MOTIFS: S.73.1.1 [*Fratricide in order to gain control of kingship*]; N.271 [*Murder will out*]; B.131.2 [*Bird reveals treachery*]; E.143.0.6 [*Dove as prophetic bird*]; B.155.3 [*Animal determines burial-place of saint*]; A.941.5 [*Spring breaks forth through power of saint*]; V.222.6.1 [*Church bells ring without aid of human hands at death of holy person*].

¶ St Kenelm's martyrdom seems to have been involuntary, as were those of King Edmund and St Hugh of "Saint Hugh and the Jew's Daughter" (Child, p. 155).

ST KENTYGERN'S CROSS

E. Bogg, *Lakeland and Ribblesdale*, p. 145.

The place [Threlkeld] has an ancient history. The name Threlkret, or Threlkeld, is said to have come from a Viking named Thorgell, who, in the tenth century conquered the Cimbric people and settled in this fair valley. Centuries before this time, as early as 553, St Kentygern reared the cross at this place and preached to the inhabitants. This cross, we are told, stood for centuries near the "Priest's Acre". The mother of St Kentygern was a daughter of a King of Cambria, and for her refusal to marry a neighbouring chief, was expelled from home to a life of drudgery in the fields, where she was held in ambush by her former lover, and destroyed of her virtue. Her shame and sorrow being discovered, the punishment of death was pronounced, and her execution was to be carried out in the following manner: bound to a chariot, she was doomed to be hurled from the top of the Traprain Law, the Dun Pelder of bygone days. By some miraculous cause she escaped her doom, so they brought her to the sea-shore and placed her in a coracle, without any oar to guide, and pushed it out to sea. Yet, though the tide ran seawards, she again escaped death, for in the early morning she was cast on the coast of the Firth of Forth. Here Thenew, for that was her name, gave birth to a boy. A hermit, who lived near, had compassion, gave the mother and child shelter, and named the latter Kyentgen, or Kentygern, meaning "Head, or chief of the Lord". For many years the boy remained with his foster-father, gaining in knowledge and piety day by day. At length he journeyed to Cathures, now Glasgow, where for years he was a faithful missionary, until at length one came to the throne, a pagan, who knew not God, and, after undergoing many persecutions during this man's reign, he journeyed southward into Wales, by way of Carleolum [Carlisle], thence for several miles down the vale country; but on learning that most of the people in the mountains were still pagans, he turned west into the lakes, and preached and baptized at Thanet Well—the name of his mother, and so called from his visit. At Threlkeld, he again halted, and set up the cross, and numbers gathered round him to hear this Gospel of Christ. Many there would be who had never heard of the doctrine of redemption, for this was nearly half a century before the Roman missionary landed on the coast of Kent.

MOTIFS: S.141 [*Exposure in a boat*]; S.312.2 [*Violated woman's child exposed*].

¶ Much more is told about St Mungo (or Kentigern), than can be gathered in this brief account. In Sinclair's *Statistical Account of Scotland*, X, 1794, p. 146, in the article on Culross, the saint's ancestry is made somewhat different.

According to this, he was the son of Eugenius, King of the Scots, and of Thametis, a daughter of the King of the Picts. When Thametis found herself with child, she stole away, and embarked in an empty boat. She was carried by the tide to the shores of Fife, and landed at Culross, and there, befriended by the night-watchers of the salt-pans, she was delivered of a child. He was taken to St Serf, who had something between a monastery and a hermitage there. His mother went back to her father's court, and left him in St Serf's charge. St Serf christened him Kentigern, but called him "Mungo" (darling). He was a marvellous child, and various miracles were told of him. An early one was MOTIF: D.2072.0.2.2.1 [*Person charged with keeping birds from crops confines them in barn by magic*], by which he confined the sparrows to a barn, and later in life the fish-and-ring story was also told of him. The arms of Glasgow bear his emblems, and a rhyme describing them begins:

> Here is the tree that never grew,
> Here is the bird that never flew.

See "St Adelme".

ST LEVEN AND JOHANA

Hunt, *Popular Romances of the West of England*, p. 265.

If you walk from Bodellen to St Leven Church, on passing near the stile in Rospletha you will see a three-cornered garden. This belonged to a woman who is only known to us as Johana. Johana's Garden is still the name of the place. One Sunday morning St Leven was passing over the stile to go as usual to his fishing-place below the church to catch his dinner. Johana was in the garden picking pot-herbs at the time, and she lectured the holy man for fishing on a Sunday. They came to high words, and St Leven told Johana that there was no more sin in taking his dinner from the sea than she herself committed in taking hers from the garden. The saint called her "foolish Johana", and said if another of her name was christened in his well she should be a bigger fool than Johana herself. From that day to this no child called Johana has been christened in St Leven. All parents who desire to give that name to their daughters, dreading St Leven's curse, take the children to Sennen.

MOTIFS: C.631 [*Tabu: breaking the Sabbath*]; M.411.8 [*Saint's curse*].
¶ Johana was so far in the right that fishing on Sunday is regarded as specially wrong. See "The Lambton Worm" and "The Man that went Fishing on Sunday" (A, II).

ST MILBURGA'S WELL

H. Bett, *English Legends*, p. 48.

At Stoke Milborough in Shropshire is St Milburga's Well, an unfailing spring. The legend is that the saint was pursued by her enemies, and came hither riding a white horse. Here she fell fainting from her steed, which struck its hoofs upon the rock, and a spring immediately gushed out. Some men who were sowing barley ran to help the saint. She knew that her pursuers were close at hand, and she told the men that when her foes came and asked when the lady on the white horse has passed, they were to answer, "When we were sowing this barley". Then she commanded the corn to spring up, and the men to get their sickles ready. Later in the day her enemies arrived, and the men answered as they had been bidden, but they were then busy reaping the barley. St Milburga's Day is therefore the 23rd February, when this happened, and not the 25th June, the day of her death.

MOTIFS: A.941.5 [*Springs break out through power of saint*]; F.971.7 [*Sowing and reaping in one day*].
¶ This miracle of the marvellous harvest is generally told of the Flight into Egypt. The story of a flight and a miraculous well is also told of the Welsh St Winifred.

ST MILDRED

H. Bett, *English Myths and Traditions*, p. 67.

The nunnery (founded by Domneva) was known as St Mildred's Abbey from St Mildred, one of the daughters of Domneva, who succeeded her as Abbess. St Mildred was famous in the Middle Ages for her sanctity and her miracles. The chronicler says that "She was endowed with Godlyke virtue, that coming out of a traunce, the very stone on which she first stepped, at Ippedsflete, in this Isle, received the impression of her foote, and retained it for ever, having, besides, this propertie, that whethersoever you removed the same, it would within a short time, and without helpe of a man's hands, return to the former place againe". The nunnery was burned by the Danes in 1011, and St Mildred and her nuns all perished. Later the abbey was given to St Augustine's at Canterbury. The monks attempted to carry off the body of St Mildred, which had escaped destruction, but it refused to move at first.

Later, in response to the abbot's prayers, the saint's body became movable, and the monks carried it by night to the ferry, pursued by the inhabitants of the place "with swords and clubs and a great force of arms". The monks got to the ferry-boat first, and the men of Thanet were forced to give up pursuit. The relics of St Mildred wrought many miracles at Canterbury.

MOTIFS: A.972.1 [*Indentations on rocks from imprints of saints*]; D.1602.1 [*Stones, being removed, return to their places*]; V.221.0.1 [*Relics of saint cure disease*].

ST NECTAN'S KIEVE AND THE LONELY SISTERS [summary]

Hunt, *Popular Romances of the West of England*, p. 278.

St Nectan's Chapel stands on a lonely pile of rocks in Tintagel parish, enclosed by forest, and with a clear trout-stream running past it to the sea. Though invisible from the land, it can be plainly seen from the sea, and fishermen always sought the prayers of the saint upon their night's work. He placed a silver bell in his bell tower, and when they heard it sound, the sailors knew that the good saint was about to pray for them, and wished them to unite their petitions with his own.

On his deathbed St Nectan prophesied that a time of sorrow for true believers was at hand; that faith would grow dim in their land, but a spark would be left, and would in time kindle again into a great flame, and the faith arise stronger than before. He promised that his silver bell would never ring for others than the true believers.

He begged his attendants to bring him the bell from its tower, and when he held it in his hands he lay for some time in silent prayer, then, sitting up, he rang the bell sharply and clearly three times, and dropped it into the silent waters of the Kieve.

The waters were troubled on receiving the bell, but when they became clear again no sign of it could be seen.

Two strange ladies soon came to live in the oratory, and took possession of all that had belonged to the holy man. It was believed that they came from a foreign country, and by the saint's own wish, but their seclusion and silence were such that no one ever learned their secret, no one visited them, nor even waited upon them. They lived on what they could find in the woods, gathered snails from the rocks and walls, and fish from the stream.

After many years, one of these strange sisters died: the neighbouring peasants at last entered the chapel unopposed, and carried away the dead body for burial; but still the surviving sister spoke no word. She shed no tears, but her grief was manifest in her face; and for many days afterwards no one saw her again. One day, a child in mere curiosity, climbed to the window of her cell, and looking in, saw the lady sitting so still, with her hands hanging helplessly at her side, that the child was afraid. He told what he had seen, and again the neighbours flocked to the chapel, and found that this sister had followed the other to death. They buried her by the side of the first and no one knows the site of their grave.

St Nectan himself, they knew, lay buried, as did his silver bell, beneath the stream he had loved, placed there in an oaken chest by the devoted sisters, after they had contrived to divert the waters, which they afterwards restored to their customary channel. There he lay for centuries undisturbed, until at last a band of miners determined to seek for the bell, and repeated the feat of diverting the stream. They pierced holes in the rocks, charged them, and proceeded to blast. But the rock resisted their efforts, and after many vain attempts, they heard a voice from beneath the ground proclaiming clearly and solemnly, "The child is not born yet who shall recover this treasure."

The work ceased, the stream returned to its course, and saint and bell lie undisturbed as ever to this day.

MOTIFS: V.115.1 [*Church bell sunk in river*]; V.67.3.1 [*King buried with treasure in the bed of an artificially dried river; later the normal course of the river is restored*]; V.115.1.3 [*Sunken church bell cannot be raised*].

ST NEOT

H. Bett, *English Legends*, p. 53.

I

St Neot in Cornwall and St Neots in Huntingdonshire both owe their name to a very shadowy saint. We know hardly anything about St Neot; the only reference to him appears to be a passing allusion in the life of King Alfred. He is supposed to have lived in the ninth century, and to have been ordained priest at Glastonbury, where he had to stand upon an iron stool to celebrate Mass, because he was so short of stature; according to some accounts he was only fifteen inches in height. He is said to have dwelt at a place ten miles from Bodmin, which was afterwards called Neotestoc, now St Neot. His bones were preserved in the church there until the year 974. Then it happened that a Saxon noble, who was building a priory at Eynesbury in Huntingdonshire, wanted a saint's relics for the new foundation. The guardian of the shrine in Cornwall was bribed, and fled with the relics. He reached Eynesbury safely, and was taken into the Earl's house, as the buildings of the priory were not yet finished. The people of St Neot, when they discovered the theft, flew to arms, and pursued the robber to Eynesbury, where they surrounded the house, and demanded the relics. It is said that the King sent an armed force to drive the Cornishmen away, and to put them to the sword if they resisted. It was proclaimed that the saint had become disgusted with the sins of the people of St Neot, and had miraculously made known his wish to seek a new shrine in the east of England, and so Eynesbury received the name of St Neots. The saint's relics were removed to Crowland about 1003, to save them from Danish plunderers, and later Crowland claimed to possess them still, but in 1078, when the monastery of St Neots was refounded as a cell of Bec in Normandy, St Anselm, the famous Abbot of Bec, certified that the body of the saint was really in the place named after him. One of the stories about St Neot tells that the oxen of the monastery where he was Abbot were stolen, and that he appealed to the wild animals for help, whereupon the stags from the forest came to put themselves under the yoke, and ploughed the abbey fields. Each night they went back to the woods. This miracle was bruited abroad, and when the robbers heard of it they were duly impressed, and returned the stolen oxen. But each of the dutiful stags had a white mark like a yoke round its neck ever afterwards, and was immune to the weapons of the hunter. St Neot had considerable repute in the Middle Ages. Gerveys the smith swears by him in *The Miller's Tale* (3,771):

"By seinte Note, ye woot wel what I mene."

II. ST NEOT'S FOOTSTOOL (summary)

Boger, *Somerset Worthies*, 1888, pp. 110–13.

St Neot was King Alfred's brother, but he was so very small that when he became a monk at Glastonbury Abbey, the only work they could find for him to do was to be doorkeeper to the Sanctuary, and he was so short that he had to have an iron footstool made, so that he could reach the lock. One day some merchants came to the door, seeking sanctuary from a band of robbers. St Neot snatched up the key, and ran to let them in, and found he had forgotten his footstool. The merchants were hammering on the door, the robbers were shouting behind them. There was no time to fetch the footstool, so St Neot prayed, and the lock swung down to his hand. And so it stayed long after St Neot had moved to Cornwall. And the footstool stayed in Glastonbury until the nineteenth century.

Glastonbury.

III. ST NEOT AND THE DOE

Hunt, *Popular Romances of the West of England*, p. 276.

On another day, when the hermit was in his fountain, a lovely doe, flying from the huntsmen, fell down on the edge of the well, imploring, with tearful eyes and anxious pantings, the aid of St Neot. The dogs followed in full chase, ready to pounce on the trembling doe, and eager to tear her in pieces. They saw the saint, and one look from his holy eyes sent them flying back into the wood, more speedily, if possible, than they rushed out of it.

The huntsman too came on, ready to discharge his arrow into the heart of the doe; but, impressed with the sight he saw, he fell on his knees, cast away his quiver, and became from that day a follower of the saint's, giving him his horn to hang, as a memorial, in the church, where it was long to be seen. The huntsman became eventually one of the monks of the neighbouring house of St Petroch.

IV. ST NEOT AND THE FISHES

Hunt, *Popular Romances of the West of England*, p. 276.

On one occasion, when the saint was at his devotions, an angel appeared unto him, and, showing him three fishes in the well, he said, "These are for thee; take one each day for thy daily food, and the number shall never grow less; the choice of one of three fishes shall be thine all the days of thy life." Long time passed by, and daily a fish was taken from the well, and three awaited his coming every morning. At length, the saint, who shared in human suffering, notwithstanding his piety, fell ill; and being confined to his bed, St Neot sent his servant, Barius, to fetch him a fish for his dinner. Barius, being desirous, if possible, of pleasing the sick man's taste, went to the well, and caught two fishes. One of these he broiled, and the other he boiled. Nicely cooked, Barius took them on a dish to his master's bedside, who started up alarmed for the consequences of the act of his servant, in disobedience to the injunctions of the angel. So good a man could not allow wrath to get the mastery of him; so he sat up in his bed and, instead of eating, he prayed with great earnestness over the cooked fish. At last the spirit of holiness exerted its full power. St Neot commanded Barius to return at once and cast the fishes into the well. Barius went and did as his master had told him to do; and lo, the moment the fishes fell into the water, they recovered life, and swam away with the third fish, as if nothing had happened to them.

All these things, and more, are recorded in the windows of St Neot's Church.

V. ST NEOT AND THE FOX

Hunt, *Popular Romances of the West of England*, p. 275.

One day the holy hermit was standing in his bath chanting the Psalms, when he heard the sound of huntsmen approaching. Whether the saint feared ridicule or ill-treatment, we know not; but certainly he left some psalms unsung that day, and hastily gathering up his clothes, he fled to his cell.

In his haste that good man lost his shoe, and a hungry fox, having escaped the hunters, came to the spring to drink. Having quenched the fever of thirst, and being hungry, he spied the saint's shoe, and presently ate it.

The hermit despatched his servant to look for his shoe; and lo, he found a fox cast into a deep sleep, and the thongs of the shoe hanging out of his vile mouth. Of course the shoe was pulled out of his stomach and restored to the saint.

I. This is a succinct account of St Neot as a saint, omitting most of the animal legends and not mentioning the well in which he stood to pray at night. St Cuthbert used the same discipline, and it was told of him that a pair of otters came out of the water to warm his feet and dry his garments by licking them.

See Helen Waddell's *Beasts and Saints*, 1934, pp. 59–61, from the *Vita* by Geoffrey of Durham.

II. MOTIF: F.535 [*Pigmy: remarkably small man*].

¶ Some of the most beautiful of the saints legends are those of their friendship for animals. See Helen Waddell's *Beasts and Saints*. The story of "St Godric and the Hunted Stag" on p. 90 of this book is very like that of St Neot.

IV. MOTIF: D.1652.1.10.1 [*Eaten fishes restored by saint*].

V. MOTIF: B.292.4 [*Stags plough for man*].

¶ See "Robert of Knaresborough".

ST OSWALD'S BONES

H. Bett, *English Myths and Traditions*, p. 130.

There is a curious detail of history behind the saying that used to be current in Lincolnshire, "He must have been born at Bardney!" It was used of anyone who entered a room, or left it, without shutting the door.

King Oswald of Northumbria was slain in battle at Maserfield (possibly Mirfield in Yorkshire) by King Penda of Mercia, who was a heathen. Oswald was therefore regarded as a martyr, and afterwards canonized. His festival is on August 5th, which is supposed to be the day of his death. Oswald's niece, Queen Osthrida, translated his relics to Bardney in 697. "When the waggon in which these bones were carried arrived toward evening at the aforesaid monastery", Bede writes in his *Ecclesiastical*

History of England (III, 11, p. 126): "they that were in it refused to admit them, because, though they knew Oswald to be a holy man, yet, as he was originally of another province, and had reigned over them as a foreign king, they retained their ancient aversion to him even after death.

"Thus it came to pass that the relics were left in the open air all that night, with only a large tent spread over them, but the appearance of a heavenly miracle showed with how much reverence they ought to be received by all the faithful; for during that whole night a pillar of light reaching from the waggon up to heaven was seen by almost all the inhabitants of the province of Lindsey. Hereupon, in the morning the brethren who had refused it the day before began themselves earnestly to pray that those holy relics, so beloved of God, might be deposited among them. Accordingly the bones, being washed, were put into a shrine which they had made for that purpose, and placed in the church with due honour." Then the monks of Bardney resolved that the doors of the monastery should never be closed again, by day or night, and so it was said of anyone who left a door open that he had been "born at Bardney".

MOTIF: V.222.1.4 [*Lights show where body of saint is buried*].

ST PATRICK AND THE BULL: I

T. G. F. Paterson, "Contributions to Ulster Folk-life", *Armagh Miscellanea.*

The bull pushed over during the night all that Patrick had set up be day. An' Patrick wus very annoyed an' cursed the bull an' it went mad. The whole of Armagh wus after it. It raged an' tore for miles roun' but whether it wus killed be Patrick's curses or died of a temper, I don't remember.

When I wus a boy it wus often I'd be on the mountain above wi' oul' Sammy Morrison who wus herd till the Moores of Lisnadill. An' it's often he toul' me brothers an' me, that a bull of the oul' days—mebbe indeed the one that chased Patrick he's self, is buried in under the Grey Stone. The marks of its feet are on stones till this very day.

That wus in the oul' days, an' the oul' people always had it that the "Bull's Track" in Ballymanab wus made be that very animal. They said it went clane mad when Patrick tried to settle on Carrickatuke. An' the dancin' an' roarin' of it put the fear of God in the whole countryside—an' no wonder, for shure ivery night it wud be wreckin' all that Patrick hed built be day on Carrick beyant. Ah sure, only for that bull Armagh wud be on the fine site—that's if the story is true—an' mind ye, there's something in oul' stories or they wudn't be toul'!

The bull went mad, ay, completely crazy, an' he riz at Carrick an' lit at Ballymanab, an' the noise wus awful. It frightened even Patrick, an' he gathered the country from far an' near, an' they slew the baste an' dragged him till Corran. An' they fetched the biggest stone they cud find. An' they dug the deepest hole that iver wus, an' they dumped him in. An' they put the stone on top, they wur so afeared he's rise again. An' when we wur childer we wur so afeared of him rising we niver went near the stone at all.

ST PATRICK AND THE BULL: II

T. G. F. Paterson, "Contributions to Ulster Folk-life", *Armagh Miscellanea.*

The boul' Patrick bate the bull at long last. It give him bother on Carrick, dancin' roun' him, but when the bugger followed him till Armagh, he wus fair angered. Says he till himself, "I must show the baste who's the master here," an' with that he grabbed it be its four pins, an' whirled it into the sky.

When it come down again it bounced leck an injy-rubber ball from one hill till another all roun' the town, an' iverywhere it fell it left its marks. They're plain till be seen in many a place still. There's marks at the Navan itself, an' in a couple of places on the way till Newtown, but the bull wouldn't have been the divil as some people would have it, for feth, the ou' boy's here yet.

Ballyheridan, 1927.
MOTIFS: B.16.1.5.3 [*Devastating bull*]; M.411.8 [*Saint's curse*]; G.510.4 [*Hero overcomes devastating animal*].
¶ These modern Ulster legends are undoubtedly Celtic in origin, but it is equally certain that they are told in English and not in Gaelic. It is probable that "Jamie Freel and the Young Lady" and other Ulster tales have an equal right to be included in this book.
For other Ulster folk-tales see *The Orange Lily*, by Sam Hanna Bell.
See also "Ushen and St Patrick".

ST PATRICK'S PURGATORY [summary]

Roger of Wendover, *Chronicle*, I, p. 511.

When St Patrick was preaching in Ireland, the people refused to believe in the truth of Christ, unless they saw with their eyes the things of which he told them. St Patrick, therefore, after much prayer and fasting, was led by Christ in a vision to a desert place, where He showed him a round dark cave, and told him: "Whoever in true penitence shall enter this cave for a day and a night shall be purified from all his sins, and shall not only behold the torments of the wicked, but, if he persevere in the love of God, shall be a witness also of the joys of the blessed."

St Patrick therefore built an oratory on the spot, and appointed a society of regular canons to guard it, so that no one, unless he came with a licence from the bishop of that place, should be allowed to enter the purgatory.

A certain knight named Owen, who had long served under King Stephen, and now repented of his many violent and lawless acts, having with difficulty obtained the bishop's licence, was admitted by the prior, who alone held the key to the oratory. He first led him into the church, where he remained for fifteen days in prayer. Then the prior celebrated Mass, and gave him the Holy Communion, and, leading him to the door of the cave, sprinkled him with holy water, and said: "You will enter here in the name of Jesus Christ, and will walk through the cave until you come out into an open plain, where you will find a hall; enter it, and God will send you guides who will tell you what to do."

The knight passed bravely through the dark cave, and found the plain beyond. Even there the light was dim, but he found the hall. It was not walled, but supported on pillars, like the cloister of a monastery. As he sat there, fifteen men in white, who looked like monks, entered and greeted him in the name of the Lord. Their leader warned him that a multitude of evil spirits would come to him, and do all in their power to turn him from his purpose, with promises, threats and torments. But if he clung to his faith, and called constantly on the name of the Lord, they would have no power over him.

These good spirits then departed, and at once the hall was filled with hideous apparitions, who rushed upon the knight, and at first tried to deflect him from his purpose by offering to conduct him unharmed to the gate through which he had entered, and so restore him to the world and its pleasures.

When he refused, they subjected him to all manner of tortures; first they dragged him with iron hooks through a blazing furnace; then to a wild plain where lay thousands of naked men and women staked to the ground with nails of hot iron. Next they took him to another plain where their victims lay, this time on their backs, with fiery dragons and serpents crawling over and round them, and gnawing their vitals. In another place of punishment, the sufferers were suspended over brimstone flames by hot iron hooks, passed through their eyes or nostrils, or chains about their feet, and as they hung they were ceaselessly lashed by demons. All these tortures they tried to inflict upon Owen also, but as soon as he spoke the name of the Lord their power over him was at an end, and he passed scatheless through every horror. There were many more forms of torment; an iron wheel to which some sinners were lashed, revolving over a furnace of heat so fast that it was impossible to distinguish one from the others, boiling pitch, baking ovens, frying pans, cauldrons of molten metal, all with their shrieking victims crying out for mercy.

Now a whole crowd was swept away, and the knight with them, into a stinking river of icy water, and when they strove to escape, the demons rushed over the surface, and swept them back. But Owen again called on the name of Christ and immediately found himself on the other bank. Now the demons showed him great flames rising from the mouth of a well, and told him that was the entrance to Hell; but even now, they said, they would take him back to the oratory gate if he would go back through it to the world; if not, he must enter that fiery pit, and be lost, body and soul. He made no answer, and they dragged him into the very midst of the fire, and plunged him so deep into its miseries that he almost forgot God, who had supported him hitherto. At the last moment he recalled it, and at the name of Jesus was driven by the flames straight up to the upper air.

But at once he was beset by a new throng of devils, who told him that the well of fire was not the real approach to Hell; but this they were about to show him. They took him to a river of stinking fire, with a bridge over it, so slippery, narrow and high that it seemed impossible that anyone should cross by it. But setting his foot boldly upon it, in the name of Jesus Christ, the knight found it broader and safer at every step. The demons shook the bridge with their cries of rage, and threw burning iron hooks at him, but they could not touch him, and he passed over in safety.

Thus released from their persecutions, he came to a jewelled gate in a wall of wonderful workmanship, and here a procession of blessed spirits met him, bearing palms, and singing in marvellous harmonies. They led him into a place of light and colour and sweet sounds; the abode of the blessed. They told him that this was the earthly paradise, to which souls returned when purged of the sins they had committed on earth; and that there, by their prayers, they continually lightened the sufferings of those still passing through Purgatory. They in their turn were awaiting their call to the fullness of joy in the heavenly kingdom. They bade him look up to the sky and say what the colour of heaven appeared to him to be. He replied that it was like gold made red-hot in the furnace. Then they said that that was the entrance to Heaven; meanwhile they were sustained with heavenly food sent them by God Himself. As they spoke, a ray of light descended from the sky, covering the whole country, and entering with its rays into each one of them. Owen felt such sweetness and joy pass through his being that he would fain have stayed there for ever; but they told him that it was now his lot to return to the world, and if he there led a good and religious life, the time would come when his spirit, released from the body, would return to the place where he now was. Full of grief, the knight suffered himself to be led back to the gate, where he passed through, and heard it close behind him.

The prior met him, and conducted him with praises and thanksgiving to the church, where he again remained for fifteen days. Afterwards he entered on a pilgrimage to the Holy Land, and on his return was sent by King Stephen into Ireland as interpreter to Gilbert, a monk whom the King had set at the head of his new Abbey at Louth. They built the Abbey together, and by degrees Owen revealed to Gilbert all that he had seen and heard and done in Patrick's Purgatory. It was by the diligence of this monk, Gilbert, that the account was written down, and preserved, confirmed by the testimony of the bishops of that country to the truth of the facts.

MOTIFS: F.2 [*Translation to other world without dying*]; E.755.3 [*Souls in Purgatory*]; A.694 [*Christian Paradise*]; V.511.3 [*Visions of Purgatory*]; V.511.2.2 [*Vision of gate of Hell*].

¶ Motifs about passing through Heaven and Hell are not appropriate to this legend.

The visits—whether supposed to be actual or visionary is not quite clear—were to the intermediate states of Purgatory and Paradise.

St Patrick's Purgatory passed into folk-belief in Ireland, and became a proverbial expression.

ST ROBERT THE HERMIT OF KNARESBOROUGH [summary]

Parkinson. *Yorkshire Legends and Traditions*, 1st series, p. 104.

St Robert, originally a monk of Newminster Abbey, in Northumberland, and born about the year 1160, lived for some time with a companion named Giles in a cave near Knaresborough still known as St Robert's Cave.

St Giles soon gave up the hermit's life, and St Robert obtained from a wealthy lady of the neighbourhood a small chapel and hermitage known as St Hilda's, not far from the cave. Here one day, lying asleep in the grass, he saw in a dream his mother, who had lately died, and who told him that for her sins she was condemned to great torment, and could only be set free by his prayers. For a whole year he offered intercession for her, and at the end of that time she again appeared to him in a dream and with a joyful smile thanked him for her deliverance.

Once, when his hermitage had been attacked by thieves, St Robert, instead of resisting, had abandoned the place for a time, though later he had returned to it. This earned him the enmity of the lord of that region, William de Stuteville, who, on a journey past the hermitage, being told who lived there, angrily accused Robert of being an abettor of thieves, and ordered the place to be demolished, and the hermit banished.

For some time he wandered through the forest, but eventually took up his dwelling in a cave not far from his first one, and now called St Robert's Chapel, only to be again hunted and driven out by his enemy, de Stuteville. This time, however, his (de Stuteville's) persecution was avenged by a vision in the night of three men, "blacker than Ynd", who stood over him with clubs and instruments of torture. They bade him rise and defend himself with one of the clubs, for they were sent to punish him for the wrong he had done to a man of God. So the hermit's dwelling was saved, and de Stuteville came to him there and, humbly begging his forgiveness, gave the land to him and his guest-friends as a gift.

In time St Robert, perhaps mistrusting himself, returned to his original cave, and here his brother Walter, now Mayor of York, built for him the small Chapel of the Holy Cross, the foundations of which are still visible.

Here Robert was joined by a Jew named Ivo, but the two quarrelled and Ivo departed. As he went in haste from the cave, he stumbled over a rotten bough, fell into a ditch and broke his leg. Robert, being mystically aware of his accident, hastened to him and, with smiling rebuke, touched his leg and healed it. St Ivo confessed his fault, and returned with Robert to the cave, from which neither departed again until Robert's death.

Robert had a strange power over wild animals. Once when collecting alms he received from the lord of the forest a cow so wild that no one dared to approach her. Robert put a hand round her neck, and led her home so tamed and gentle that one of the lord's attendants deceitfully tried to get her back.

He pretended to be lame and a beggar, and in this guise he begged the cow from Robert. "God gave, and God shall have, but it shall be with thee as thou hast feigned," he replied, and when the man tried to drive away the cow, he found himself so lame that he could not rise to his feet. "O Robert, thou servant of God," he cried, "forgive my trespass, and the injury I have done." At once he was forgiven, and the use of his limbs restored.

Another time, when the forest stags were gravely harming his crops, he asked the lord of the forest to restrain them and was given leave to shut them all up in his own barn.

With a small stick in his hand he drove them in like lambs, shut the door on them, and went to ask the lord of the forest what he should do with them next. He was told that he might keep three to yoke to his plough, and release the rest. With his three stags, therefore, St Robert ploughed his land, to the admiration of all who saw it.

Satanic visitors came to him in his cell from time to time, but he drove them away, one with holy water, one with the sign of the Cross, and one with his "most hallowed staff".

In 1203 de Stuteville died, and was succeeded in his estates by Sir Brian de Lisle, who received them from King John. Sir Brian proved a good friend to St Robert, and persuaded the king to visit him in his cell.

The king came with a great concourse of nobles, and found the hermit at prayer. He did not rise until de Lisle went to him and roused him, saying, " Our Lord King John is desirous to see thee." "Show me which is King John," answered Robert and, taking in his hand an ear of corn, he asked, "Art thou able, O my king, to create such an ear as this out of nothing?" "No," replied the king. "Then there is no king but the Lord only," said Robert, and the king, pleased with the blunt answer, bade him ask for whatever he needed. Robert replied that he had no earthly needs, but Ivo, mindful of their future, ran after them when they had ridden away, and received as a gift as much land as they could cultivate with one plough, and free liberty to cut firewood and bedding.

St Robert died on 24 September 1218, and was buried by Ivo in the Chapel of the Holy Cross, as he had desired, though the monks of Fountains contended fiercely for his body. A great multitude gathered to do the last honour to one who had been so great a benefactor, praying for them, comforting them in their troubles, and driving away their wolves.

MOTIFS: V.229.2.11 [*Miracle saves saint from unjust censure*]; V.221 [*Miraculous healing by saint*]; B.771.2 [*Animal tamed through holiness of saint*]; Q.591 [*Punishment: lie becomes truth*]; Q.572 [*Magic sickness as punishment remitted*]; B.292.4 [*Stags plough for man*].

Akin to this legend is Q.591.1.1 [*King tests saint by having man feign death: saint perceives trick and causes man to be dead*].

ST UNCUMBER

H. Bett, *English Legends*, p. 51.

[A] saint who had a connection with marital affairs, was St Wigefort, surely one of the most extraordinary saints of the Middle Ages. She was commonly known as Maid Uncumber, and her aid was invoked by wives who wished to be rid of their husbands. It is said that wild oats were usually offered to her. A sixteenth-century writer, describing the resort to various saints for help of different things, says that "if a wife were weary of her husband, she offered otes at Poules, at London, to Saint Uncumber". Another writer of the same period quotes a charm, one stanza of which runs:

> If ye cannot slepe, but slumber,
> Geve Otes unto Saynt Uncumber,
> And Beans in a certain number
> Unto Saynt Blase and Saint Blythe.*

Many altars up and down England were dedicated to this strange saint, including one in Old St Paul's in London, and one, which seems to have

---

* Brand, *Popular Antiquities*, III, p. 149, from Bale's *Interlude*.

been a special centre of veneration, at Chew Stoke in Somerset. There is perhaps no saint with such a variety of names. She is variously described as St Wilgefortus, Uncumber, Kummernis, Komina, Comera, Cumerana, Hulfe, Ontcommene, Ontcommer, Dignefortis, Eutropia, Reginfledis, Livrada, Liberata, and so on. The legend says that she was the daughter of a heathen king of Portugal, and she became a Christian. Commanded by her father to marry a pagan prince, she prayed that her body might be disfigured, so that she might keep her chastity. In answer to her prayer, a beard grew upon her chin, and then her father had her crucified. She is always represented as a bearded woman.

One pretty legend about St Wigefort is that a poor fiddler once played before her image, and it gave him one of its golden shoes. He was condemned to death on the charge of having stolen this from the church. He begged that he might play before the image again before he died, whereupon it kicked off its other shoe towards the fiddler, whose innocence was thus proved.

It has been suggested that Wilgefortis is from *Virgo fortis*. The more probable view is that it is derived from *Hilge Vartz* (*Heilige Fratz*, Holy Face) and that the whole legend has grown out of the fact that copies of the *Volto Santo* of Lucca were multiplied and spread through Europe. This represents Our Lord bearded with long hair hanging down to His shoulders, and clothed in a long tunic. As this was not a familiar type of crucifix, it was probably somewhere taken as the representation of a bearded and crucified woman, and so the legend arose. It does not seem to go farther back than the fifteenth century. The name "Uncumber" and its variants arose from the belief that if the saint were invoked in the hour of death you would die *ohne Kummer*, without anxiety. The feast of St Wilgefort is on the 19th of July. The Roman *Breviary* still commemorates "the holy Virgin and martyr Wilgefortes, who contended for Christian faith and chastity, and obtained a glorious triumph upon the Cross".

MOTIFS: T.321.1 [*Maid pledged to celibacy is given, at her request, a beard*]; D.1622.3 [*Saint's image lets golden shoe fall as sign of favour to suppliant*].

ST WALSTAN

H. Bett, *English Legends*, p. 51.

[A] saint who left traces of himself in running water was St Walstan. He was the especial patron of farm-labourers, and was connected with Costessey in Norfolk.

It is said that he renounced his patrimony, and served as a labourer in the fields. He wrought many miracles. As he was one day mowing in a meadow near Costessey, he was warned by an angel of his approaching death. He then prayed that all "scythe-followers" might gain a blessing for themselves and their cattle by visiting his grave, and the prayer was granted. His body was conveyed in a cart drawn by oxen to Bawburgh, and where the oxen stopped on the way springs of water broke out. The cart passed over deep water in Costessey Wood, as if it had been dry land, and the traces of the wheels used to be pointed out on the surface of the water for centuries after his death. St Walstan is said to have died in 1016. His tomb at Bawburgh was visited by numerous pilgrims, and the church, which was dedicated to St Mary and St Walstan, was rebuilt by their offerings at the beginning of the fourteenth century.

MOTIFS: V.235 [*Mortal visited by angel*]; A.941.5 [*Springs break forth through power of saint*].

ST WERBURGH

H. Bett, *English Legends*, p. 57.

There was a belief which survived until quite recently, and perhaps survives still, that wild geese never settle and graze in the fields around Weedon in Northamptonshire. This is due to a miracle wrought by St Werburgh. She lived in the seventh century, and with the help of King Ethelred founded several monasteries, including one at Weedon, where she spent much of her time. The wild geese were making havoc of the cornfields, and the saint intervened. Her steward, Alnoth, who himself was later reputed a saint, summoned all the geese to assemble within the grange.

St Werburgh ordered them to take flight, and never more to appear at Weedon. They took to the air, but kept hovering round until one of their companions, who had been killed and eaten, was restored to them safe and sound. There is a reference to this banishment in Drayton's *Polyolbion* (XXIII), where he tells us that the River Nen runs by

> Weedon, where 'tis said,
> Saint Werburgh princely born, a most religious maid,
> From those peculiar fields, by prayer the wild geese drove.

MOTIFS: D.2072.0.2.2.1 [*Person charged with keeping birds from crops confines them in a barn*]; V.224.2 [*Animals eaten by saint miraculously replaced*]; B.256.5 [*Obedience of feathered creatures to the commands of saint*].

¶ This tale is very charmingly translated in Helen Waddell's *Beasts and Saints*, pp. 68–70. See "St Cuthbert and the Ravens".

ST WILLIAM OF YORK [summary]

Parkinson. *Yorkshire Legends and Traditions*, 1st series, p. 86.

William Fitzherbert, whose father was Treasurer to King Henry I, was on his mother's side the great-grandson of the Conqueror and nephew to King Stephen. He became Treasurer, and then in A.D. 1140 Archbishop of York. The Cistercians, however, resented his appointment, and for five years he was removed from office. But his saintly behaviour under injury won him the popular favour and sympathy, and in 1154 he was restored to his see. A month later, on Trinity Sunday, while administering the Sacrament, he was suddenly taken ill and died.

In 1283 he was canonized by Pope Nicholas III and, in the presence of King Edward III and his Queen, his bones were translated from the nave to a shrine behind the high altar. Thus York at last gained a saint worthy of comparison with St John of Beverley—an honour it had long desired.

The following tales are among many which are told of his miraculous power:

I. THE BROKEN BRIDGE

When William was restored to his Archbishopric on May 8th, 1154, as he was entering York, the bridge over the Ouse gave way under the weight of the turbulent crowd, and a great number of people and horses were thrown into the swift current below at its deepest part.

The Archbishop turned towards them, making the sign of the Cross, and prayed that they might not be overwhelmed. At once the tossing waters became as a bridge and all passed over in safety, "except that the leg of a certain horse was broken".

II. EYES FOR THE BLIND

A man named Ralph, being accused of having broken the king's peace, was subjected to trial by wager of battle. His adversary was named Besing. Ralph was overcome, and in the duel one of his eyes was put out. As a punishment for his transgression—now proved by being vanquished in wager of battle—he was condemned to be deprived of the other eye. The executioner carried out this sentence, and a lad named Hugh picked up both eyes and carried them away. Ralph, being thus unjustly, as he knew, punished, spent some days in fasting and prayer, and then came to the tomb of the Blessed William, and received back two eyes, smaller, and of a different colour than his former ones, but giving him again sharp and clear sight.

III. THE ORDEAL OF FIRE

Two women were accused of having caused the death of the third. One died in prison and the other was brought to trial. She denied the charge, but was ordered to give proof of her innocence by the ordeal of taking in her hand a piece of red-hot iron.

In this trial, the accused must pick up a piece of red-hot iron, carry it in three strides, a space of nine feet, throw it down, and flee to an altar, where a priest bound up the hand in clean linen, and sealed it with the seal of the church. If after three days the hand was found whole, the man was innocent, if a sore mark was left, he was counted guilty.

This woman, therefore, was found to have a blister the size of half a walnut on her hand, and was given up to the executioners. But she was given leave to visit the shrine of St William before the execution. As soon as she entered the sacred space, the blister vanished, leaving no trace. The Justices therefore decreed her innocent, and handed over to the king's mercy those who had unjustly condemned her to death.

IV. SIGHT RESTORED TO A BLIND GIRL

A young girl of Leeds had been blind for seven years, and was led to the shrine of St William, where she remained for a long time in prayer and fasting. On the night of Pentecost, June 12th, 1177, just as she was beginning to fall asleep, "there appeared to her one most beautiful to look upon, having the white hair of an angel, in comparison with whose raiment snow was black, fragrant with unspeakable perfumes, who, having pity on her misery, touched the pupils of her eyes, and, at the touch of his hand, the darkness of blindness cleared away, and for gloomy night was given her the cheerful day".

V. THE YOUNG STUDENT

A young scholar of Beverley, whose learning and industry had endeared him to all the brotherhood, was ensnared by the Devil and made to fall in love with a young girl of great beauty. When for love of her he could no longer attend to his books or devotions, he took himself to the Blessed John (or William, for this tale is told of them both) and was effectually cured of his love, and restored to his former health.

I. MOTIF: D.2151.2 [*Magic control of rivers*].
II. MOTIF: D.2161.3.1.1 [*Eyes torn out magically replaced*].
III. MOTIF: H.221 [*Ordeal by fire*]; V.221.8 [*Wounds healed by saint leave no scars*].
IV. MOTIF: V.221.12 [*Saint cures blindness*].

SAINTS

ST WULFRIC AND THE GREEDY BOY

Ruth L. Tongue, *Folk-Tales of England*, p. 73.

There was a poor widow with a large family and they all worked hard, even the little ones, and folk were very kind. There was always an egg or two or a sack of teddies, or a cabbage, or a bit of bacon put by to help them out. Then the farmers found work and their food for the biggest lads, and they ought to have managed, but they all went on looking so thin as a yard of pump-water except Dicky—and he grew fat. One day the poor widow crept to St Wulfric's cell. She'd brought him a thin little flat oat-loaf, made from the scrapings of the meal chest. St Wulfric took it, and the three little trots that had come with their mother burst into tears as they saw it go.

The saint looked down at their poor little pinched faces, and whispered gently, "Go down to the spring for me, and see what the birds have left me." So off they toddled—half the size of the pail the baby was—but he would go. And back they staggered with it only half full, their poor little sticks of arms and legs couldn't lift more—but the baby's face was rosy with joy over a big loaf with fresh butter and a crock of cream they'd found there.

"Now, sit down and eat them," said the saint. "My birds must have known you were coming. But I've a use for your mother's oat-cake." Down they sat in the sunshine, and down the good food went—and after that it was easy for the grateful widow to tell her troubles.

"'Tis our Dicky, zur; he do get his vittles all down to Varmer Mellish, where he be bird-boy, and they do give he a-plenty. But never were such a boy to eat, Missus Mellish say, and they be hearty trenchermen down there. But when he do come whoame a-night he do gollop up all in the house if I don't stop him. Then he do sneaky round when all's asleep and there's nought for breakfusses. *And* he do get his dew-bit at farm, no fear! All my others, they do bring a few bits of vittles whoame for me and they little trots, but if Dicky be about 'tis all goed down his throat while they be getting two bites in—and him so fat as a pig!"

"Tell him I want to see him," said the saint. So, after they'd picked the saint a bunch of primroses and he'd blessed them, she took the little trots home. They even ran a bit. Next day, a fat sulky lad came to the cell. "I want you to take any bread you see on my shelf down to your mother," said the saint. "Be very quiet, for it is time I was at my prayers."

Dicky glanced at the shelf and saw his mother's oat-cake. He'd searched for it all night! And she'd given it to an old man who knelt on a cold stone floor—the old fool! Here he looked at the shelf again and there were two large white cottage-loaves beside the oat-cake. Dicky grabbed them in

470

terror and ran for it, scared out of his wits. He was so fat he soon lost his breath, and sat down on the turf—and the loaves smelt delicious. Nobody would know what happened to them. The silly old saint was busy praying and his mother wouldn't expect any food. Down Dicky's red lane went all three loaves, yes, oat-cake and all, and my young raskill strolls off home. He wasn't feeling at all happy inside and there were no end of queer pains so he didn't go indoors, but sat down on the drashel. Out came his mother smiling and handed him a big crust of white bread covered with butter. "There, Dicky," she said. "You shall have a taste for being such a good, kind boy, bringing in they three loaves from the saint. Lovely bread 'tis, like us ate yesteddy, I did wish you others could taste." But Dicky's hair was standing on end. "T-Three?" he gasped. "A girt big oat-cake and two white loaves all a-buttered," she said. "I did find they on table where you did a-put them." With that Dicky took off in terror and never stopped till he got back to the saint's cell. St Wulfric was still kneeling, and there on the shelf above him were a poor thin little oat-cake and two cottage loaves. Dicky stood there and shook with fear. Then St Wulfric stood up, "You must be hungry after your climb," he said "Finish your bread and butter." Dicky dare not refuse, but, oh, how terrible it was. It left him with such a taste in his mouth that he didn't eat for days—until he was as thin as the baby had been. After that he never made fun of saints or took more than his share. He even brought his mother home *three* eggs one evening!

Recorded from Ruth L. Tongue, 29 September 1963, who heard the story as a child at Hazelbury Plunkett in Somerset.
MOTIFS: Q.45.3.1 [*Hospitality to monk rewarded*]; V.411.6 [*Food given away by saint miraculously restored*]; Q.552.3.5 [*Punishment for greed*].
¶ Miss Tongue was told this story by an old retired clergyman of eighty-three. He had heard it from his great-grandmother, who was seventy-three, and she had heard it from her great-grandmother. At a rough estimate, the line of tradition stretches back to 1681.

"Teddies" are potatoes; a "dew-bit" an early-morning snack; "drashel" is a threshold.

ST WULFRIC THE HERMIT

Roger of Wendover, *Chronicle*, I, p. 523.

The same year [1154] a holy hermit, Wulfric of Heselberg, departed this life, thereby completing a happy and triumphant warfare of twenty-nine years against the enemies of mankind, of whose life and virtues we think it not irrelevant to introduce here a short notice to adorn the history. St Wulfric was born of an English family in moderate circumstances at Conton, a village about eight miles from Bristol.

Here was he also educated, and passed some years in holy orders, which he is thought to have received in the careless levity of youth, rather than by the settled purpose of his mind; for he did not yet know the Lord, and was led rather by the flesh than by the spirit. He spent much of his time among hounds and hawks; and one day, whilst he was busily engaged in such occupations, there came to him a man, who by his looks and dress seemed to be needy, and begged a new piece of money of him as alms; for at that time there was a new coinage in England, in the days of Henry I, but still rare on account of its recency. Wulfric replied that he did not know whether he had any of the new coinage or not; upon which the man said, "Look into your purse, and you will find there two pieces and a half." Astonished at this, Wulfric did as he was bidden, and found the money, which he devoutly bestowed in alms. The man, receiving the money, said, "May He, for whose love you have done this, return you a proper retribution. I tell you in His name, that you will shortly remove from this place to another, and from thence to a third, where you will at last find repose; there you will persevere in the service of God, who will at last summon you away to join the communion of saints."

OF THE CONVERSION OF ST WULFRIC AND THE AUSTERITY OF HIS LIFE

After a while, Wulfric attached himself to William, the lord of his native village, and every day ate at his table; where also he prepared himself for austerity of life by abandoning the use of flesh. The man of God was now eager for a life of solitude, and was sent by his lord, the aforesaid knight, to Heselberg, a village about thirty miles to the east of Exeter, inspired, it is believed, to this by the suggestions of the Holy Spirit. Here, buried in a cell near the church, he devoted himself to the service of Christ, whose favour he gained by much labour and affliction, both of the flesh and of the spirit; for he so mortified the flesh by abstinence and watching, that in a short time the skin hardly adhered to the bones, and he presented to the eye of the beholder the appearance not of a carnal but of a spiritual being. He contented himself with a plain dress, under which was a shirt of sackcloth; but when he had worn this for a few days, he began to entertain thoughts of exchanging it for a coat of mail, dedicating an instrument of war to the service of the heavenly warfare. At night he used to plunge naked into a bath of very cold water, and there offer to the Lord the psalmody of King David. In this way he mortified in the coldness of the water the fleshly tendencies which he sometimes felt most strongly. He was humble and pleasant in speech to all men: his discourse always sounded like celestial harmony to those who heard him, though he always spoke to men with his window closed.

A REMARKABLE MIRACLE OF CUTTING THE COAT OF MAIL

Meanwhile, the man of God, Wulfric, whom God alone really knew, broke forth like the early dawn upon the knowledge of mankind by his endeavours to forward their salvation; for when the coat of mail, which he wore, struck against his knees, and prevented his constant genuflexions, he invited to him the knight, who was acquainted with his secrets, and spoke to him concerning the length of his coat of mail.

"It shall be sent to London," replied the knight, "and indented in any way you choose." The man of God replied, "That would cause too long delay; and might be thought a proof of ostentation: take these shears, in God's name, and execute the work with your own hand." Saying these words, he gave the knight a pair of shears, which had been brought from the knight's own house, and seeing him hesitate and think that the hermit was mad, he continued, "Be bold, and do not hesitate. I will go and pray to the Lord about this business; meanwhile, do you set about it confidently."

The two warriors were now busily occupied, the one in prayer, the other in cutting, and the work prospered beneath their hands: for the knight felt as if he was cutting cloth, not iron, so great was the facility with which the shears severed it; but when the man of God left off his prayers, the knight, who had not yet finished his work, could cut no longer. Wulfric stood by him and asked him how he succeeded. "Very well," replied the knight, "so far, but now that you are come, the shears have ceased to cut." "Be not afraid," said the hermit, "cut on, as you have begun, with the same shears."

The knight, resuming confidence, finished his work with the same ease as before, and smoothed off the inequalities without any difficulty. From that time the man of God, without any shears at all, but with his own weak fingers, but with no less faith, distributed rings of the coat of mail to heal the diseases of all who asked it of him in charity; and the knight, seeing its power, was struck with unspeakable surprise, and fell at the feet of the man of God, who in confusion raised him up, and adjured him not to tell it to anyone whilst he himself should be alive; but the fame thereof could not be concealed, since several religious men still boast that they possess rings from that same coat of mail, and the reputation of the man of God has spread to all parts of the kingdom.

HOW A MAN WHO HAD DONE HOMAGE TO THE DEVIL WAS HEALED BY THE MAN OF GOD

In the northern parts of England there was a miserable man, who, not being able to endure poverty, had yielded himself, and done homage to the devil. This miserable wretch, after he had for some time felt the oppression of his new master, perceived his crime and began to repent thereof, looking round for some patron to whom he might commit himself, and be redeemed from spiritual death. At last he determined to pay a visit to St Wulfric, in whose hand salvation was said to lie; and when in his anxiety about it he had revealed his intentions to one of his friends, the devil stood by him in his usual and well-known shape, and charging him with breach of faith, threatened to castigate him cruelly if he ever again thought of such a thing. The man imposed silence upon himself, for he saw plainly that the enemy had not known the secret thoughts of his heart, until he had first developed them by words or signs. He therefor dissembled for some time his intention to repent, and at length set out upon his proposed journey to visit the man of God, Wulfric. When he had completed a great part of the way, he arrived at the ford of a river outside the village of Heselberg, for the Lord had prospered his journey. He now entered the ford, and was certain of St Wuldric's assistance, when the devil appeared, incensed with anger, and laying violent hands upon him, "What didst thou mean to do, traitor?" said he. "Thou art essaying to break our compact, but in vain; for thou shalt now suffer for thy treachery; thou formerly didst renounce the service of God, and art now endeavouring to renounce mine also: thou shalt now be miserably drowned." The devil then seized him, and held him so firmly that he could neither go forwards nor turn himself to either one side or the other. Whilst all this was passing in the river, the man Wulfric was informed of it by God in a vision, and, calling to him his priest named Brithric, said to him, "Go quickly: take the cross and some holy water, and meet a man who is held prisoner by the devil in the ford which is beyond the village; sprinkle him with holy water and bring him to me." Brithric made haste, as he was directed, and found the man on horseback in the river, and unable to move from the place where he was. Brithric immediately sprinkled him with water in the name of the Father, and of the Son, and of the Holy Ghost; the devil was immediately defeated, and the captive, released from his enemy, was led into the presence of the man of God, who in the meantime had been praying anxiously to the Lord in his behalf. Behind them came the devil, who claimed his man and seized him, notwithstanding his cries to the man of God for help. The saint held the man by the right hand, and the devil by the left; but the man of God sprinkled holy water in the face of the enemy, who immediately fled in confusion. The saint then led the man, whom he had saved from the jaws of his enemy, into his cell, and there detained him until he confessed his sins, and cast out from him before the feet of the saint the poison with which the devil had corrupted him. He then was blest with the sight of our Lord, offered to him in the flesh by the man of God; and when he was asked whether he believed with his whole heart, he replied, "I believe, my Lord, that, wretch and sinner as I am, I behold in your hands the body and blood of our Lord Jesus in the flesh." "Thanks be to God," said the saint. "Let us now pray together, that you may be thought worthy to behold Him in his real form." He then administered the Communion, and, having thus confirmed his faith, sent him away in peace.

St Wulfric died on the 20th of February, and was buried in his oratory at Heselberg, where, in honour of God and of the saint, numerous miracles are performed even to the present time.

MOTIFS: V.410.1 [*Charity rewarded above prayer or hearing of masses*]; V.462 [*Asceticism*]; E.754.1 [*Condemned soul recovered*]; V.462.8 [*Ascetic immersion*].
¶ There is no motif allotted to St Wulfric's famous coat of mail. The nearest is V.462.5.1 [*Ascetic wears hair garment*].

ST WULFRIC AND THE MOUSE

Ruth L. Tongue, *Somerset Folklore*, pp. 188–9.

St Wulfric, like all the Somerset saints, was very gentle to small creatures.

A stumpy [wren] made her nest above his fern couch and scolded him terribly for disturbing her eggs by coming so near. He moved his couch into a draughtier spot, where he could not lie down properly.

A squirrel kept his hoard in the saint's wooden cup, so he carved himself another....

But there was one self-willed little mouse who insisted on nibbling pieces off the saint's shortened tunic to make her fleece-lined nest finer, and, worst of all, she went on doing it during his prayers....

At last the good saint looked down and quietly rebuked her and the silly, vain little mouse died of shame.

Oral collection, a maidservant, Bruton, 1905.
¶ There are many tales of the penitence of animals when reproved by a saint, but no motif to fit this penitent mouse.
See "St Cuthbert and the Ravens", "St Werburgh", "St Robert of Knaresborough", etc.

ST WULSTAN'S STAFF

Roger of Wendover, *Chronicle*, I, p. 371.

In the year of Our Lord 1075...Lanfranc, Archbishop of Canterbury... in conjunction with his suffragans, began to correct whatever was amiss, and to set forth for the monks and clergy a more correct mode of life. Before this archbishop St Wulstan was accused as a simple and illiterate man, ignorant of the French language, and unable to assist in the king's councils; for which reasons, with the king's consent and, indeed, by his command, it was determined that Wulstan should be deposed. Wherefore Lanfranc, among other decrees of the council, commanded the man of God, Wulstan, to resign his staff and ring. But that servant of the Lord underwent no change either of look or of feeling, but stood up and holding out his pastoral staff, "Truly, my lord Archbishop," said he, "I know that I am not worthy of this high honour, nor sufficient for the discharge of its labours and duties. You claim from me the pastoral staff which it was not you who gave me; yet, in deference to your judgment, I resign it, though not to you, but rather to St Edward, by whose authority I received it." With these words he rose and, followed by his attendants, approached the marble monument wherein the remains of the glorious king were entombed. "Blessed King Edward," said he, "thou knowest how reluctantly I undertook this burden, and absented myself when I was summoned; I acknowledge that I acted unwisely, but it was thou who didst compel me. For though there was no fault in the election of the monks, in the petition of the people, or in the goodwill and favour of the bishops and prelates, yet thy authority and will preponderated over all these motives; but now we have a new king, a new law, and a new archbishop promulgates new theories: they accuse thee of error in having made me a bishop, and me of presumption in having assented; I therefore resign my pastoral staff, not to those who demand back that which they did not give, but to thee who didst give it me I resign the charge of those whom thou didst entrust to my care." With these words he raised his arm slowly, and struck the staff into the stone by which the saint's body was covered. "Receive, my lord the king," continued he. "And give it to whomsoever thou mayest choose," and so, leaving the altar, he threw off his episcopal robes, and sat down like a simple monk among the monastic brethren who were present. All were lost in astonishment at seeing the pastoral staff sunk in the stone, where, as if it formed part of the marble itself, it stood erect, and turned neither to the right hand nor to the left. Some of those who were present tried to pull it out, but it remained immovable. The story was carried before the Synod, but Lanfranc, refusing to listen to it, sent Gundulf, Bishop of Rochester, to go to the tomb, and bring before the council the staff which Wulstan placed on it. In obedience to this command, Gundulf endeavoured to pull out the staff, but the virtues of Wulstan had fixed it too firmly, and he could not draw it out. Then Lanfranc, in astonishment at so unwonted an occurrence, hastened in company with the king to the tomb. When he came there, he offered up a prayer, and putting his hand to the staff, tried to pull it out, but the attempt was ineffectual. The king exclaimed aloud, the archbishop was distressed; they acknowledged that Edward had not done wrong in promoting Wulstan, and Lanfranc, approaching the bishop, said to him, "Truly, the Lord walketh with the simple-minded, and resteth with the humble; your holy simplicity, my brother, was a subject of derision with us, but, alas for the darkness which blinds us! We call good evil, and evil good. Wherefore, in virtue of our authority, and the judgment by which God has convicted us, we again commit to your hands the office from which we unadvisedly expelled you. . . . Come, therefore, my brother, approach to your pastoral staff, for we have no doubt that the saintly hand of the king, which hath withheld it from us, will resign it easily to you." The holy Bishop Wulstan, hearing these words, following the bent of his simple-mindedness, implicitly did as he was told, and, approaching the tomb said, "Behold! my lord and king, I commit myself to thy judgment, and resign unto thy hands the staff which thou gavest me. Wherefore I pray thee now to give thy decision. Thou hast preserved thy dignity and established my innocence; if then thou still hast the same opinion of me, confirm thy former sentence, give me back my staff, or if thy opinion is altered, show to whom it shall be given." With these words the saint tried to take the staff, but it anticipated his wishes, and yielded to his hand, as if it had been stuck in clay.

The king and archbishop ran up to him, and on their knees begged his forgiveness, commending themselves to the prayers of the saint; but he, who had learned from the Lord to be mild and humble in heart, threw himself in his turn upon his knees before them, and prayed to receive a blessing from so great an archbishop. Then King William, kindling with devotion towards his saintly relative, King Edward, with wonderful zeal adorned his holy tomb, covering it with workmanship of gold and silver.

MOTIFS: V.461.4 [*Submission as clerical virtue*]; V.229.2.11 [*Miracle saves saint from unjust censure*]; D.1654.0.1 [*Magic immovability of saint's possessions*]; cf. D.1654.4.1 [*Sword can be moved only by right person*]; L.144 [*Ignorant surpasses learned man*].

SIR JOHN SCHORNE AND HIS BOOT

Summary from an article by J. L. Nevinson and J. A. Hudson, *Country Life*, 1 March 1962.

Sir John Schorne was Vicar of North Marston in Buckinghamshire from 1290 to 1314. He had a great reputation as a saint, and his church was much resorted to by pilgrims. He was supposed to have produced a miraculous curative spring in a time of drought; but his fame rested on his conflict with the Devil, whom he conjured into his boot and imprisoned there. Stained-glass windows, pictures and carvings show him with the Devil peering out of his boot.

MOTIFS: D.2177.1.1 [*Demons imprisoned by magic*]; D.2177.1 [*Demon enclosed in bottle*].

¶ A bottle was a more usual prison for a devil than a shoe, and ghosts rather than devils were generally confined into bottles. The Devil was confined by the Tailor of Clitheroe in a magic bag, and Yallery Brown (A, II) was confined and buried.

THE SNAKES OF ST KEYNA A.D. 500

Ruth L. Tongue, *Somerset Folklore*, p. 188.

St Keyna was the daughter of Braglan, Prince of Brecknock. She became famous for her holiness and desired to leave the world and become a hermit. To this end she left Wales, and came to the West of England, where she asked permission of a local prince to build her cell in a desert spot. He, either disliking the lady's religion or hoping to make use of it, directed her to a valley near Bath that was shunned on account of the size and venom of its snakes. Undeterred St Keyna went boldly among them and turned them all into stone. Some escaped to Exmoor and the Quantocks, but the laggards on Mendip were overtaken by the saint at Banwell.

Oral tradition. Keynsham.
MOTIF: V.229.24 [*Saint turns snakes to stone*].
¶ See "St Hilda's Worms".

THE TWO BREAMS

Hunt, *Popular Romances of the West of England*, pp. 266–7.

...In St Leven's Church there still remains some of the ornamental work which once adorned it. Much of the carving is irremediably gone; but still the inquirer will find that it once told the story of important events in the life of the good St Leven.

Two fishes on the same hook form the device, which appears at one time to have prevailed in this church. These are to commemorate a remarkable incident in St Leven's life. One lovely evening about sunset St Leven was on his rocks fishing. There was a heavy pull upon his line and, drawing it in, he found two breams on the same hook.

The good saint, anxious to serve both alike, to avoid, indeed, even the appearance of partiality, took both the fishes off the hook, and cast them back into the sea.

Again they came to the hook, and again were they returned to their native element.

The line was no sooner cast a third time than the same two fishes hooked themselves once more. St Leven thought there must be some reason unknown to him for this strange occurrence, so he took both the fishes home with him. When the saint reached Bodellen, he found his sister, St Breage, had come to visit him with two children. Then he thought he saw the hand of Providence at work in guiding the fish to his hook.

Even saints are blind when they attempt to fathom the ways of the Unseen. The fish were, of course, cooked for supper; and, the saint having asked a blessing upon their savoury meal, all sat down to partake of it. The children had walked far, and they were ravenously hungry. They ate their suppers with rapidity, and, not taking time to pick out the bones of the fish, they were both choked. The apparent blessing was thus transformed into a curse, and the bream has from that day forward ever gone by the name, amongst fishermen, of "choke-children".

MOTIF: B.175 [*Magic fish*].

¶ For a prohibition against catching more than one fish from a saint's well, see "St Neot and the Fish". There was apparently something ominous about these two breams.

USHEN AND ST PATRICK

T. G. F. Paterson, *Contributions to Ulster Folk Life, Armagh Miscellanea.*

It wus in the days of Ushen, an' Patrick wus sore tormented for iverything that he'd be buildin' on the Brague wud be down the next mornin'. An' Ushen was jist back from the lan' of niver die, where he might have been livin' still, only that he liked Ireland better. An' that's that.

Shure it wus on the other side of Carrickbroad it all happened. Ushen on he's big white horse wus careerin' up the mountain when a woman with a bag of turf—bad luck to her anyhow, for it wus the greed of her caused it. Why cudn't she be after fillin' what she cud carry an' not be burdenin' herself with the lazy man's load? But shure all the sorrows of Ireland come be the weemin an' if ye ax me, they're the cause of many a heartburn still. An' mebbe some of them are worth it an', more like, some are not. How an' so iver, till be slicin' a long story short, shure Ushen forgot he wus safe on he's horse only so long as he didn't be after droppin' his legs on the groun', an' down he hopped, an' helped her up with the turf on her back. An' och anee, that wus the harm. Ushen soon felt the death upon him, an' down he lay upon the hillside. An' the woman, who wus mebbe the Cally Berry, or someone like her, went away.

An' Patrick wus passin' along an' he heared all about it, an' up he goes. An' says Patrick till Ushen, "It's sorry I am till see ye so wake now. Shure it's yerself can have the wish three times one before ye die now." An' Patrick talked to him of Heaven, but Ushen wasn't in much of a bother. Says he, "Are there houn's an' baygels there?" "The divil one," says Patrick. "Well I'm not going there at all," says Ushen. An' Patrick wus sore put about, for he wus takin' a likin' till him. Says he, "'Tween you an' that brute of a bull on the Brague, I'm like to be breakin' my heart."

An' Ushen had a wish, says he, "Will ye bury me on Slew Gullion? An' will ye bury me high an' dry, an' clap a stone or two above me?" "Deed an' I will," says Patrick. Then says Ushen, "For me last wish I'll have me strength again till I take a look at yer bull. Give me back me strength, an' I'll rid ye of him," says he. An' Patrick says, "Rise, me boul'd boy, an' be after doin' your best."

An' Ushen went an' sarched for the bull, an' when he foun' it he struck it a mortal box in the face that knocked it as stiff as you like. An' it's buried on a mountain somewhere near till the Brague with a stone above it, like a Christian himself. An' when Patrick come till look for him, thinkin' as like as not he wud be totally destroyed, there he wus asleep in the skin of the baste. Usin' it for a blanket he wus. But shure he woke no more. An' they brought him back till oul' Slew Gullion an' buried him there. An' Patrick wus real sorry.

MOTIFS: C.937.1 [*Immortality lost for breaking Tabu*]; D.1761.0.2 [*Limited number of wishes granted*]; U.134 [*Knight doesn't want to go to Heaven if there are no hunting-dogs there*]; B.16.1.5.3 [*Devastating bull*]; H.1161 [*Task: killing ferocious beast*]; V.61.8 [*Burial in grave-mound*].

¶ This is a different account of the killing of the Wild Bull that harassed St Patrick from that given in "St Patrick and the Bull". Even in this broken-down version there is a touch of wistful beauty in the friendship of the Christian saint and the pagan hero.

See "St Patrick and the Bull".

A VISION OF ST WILFRED

Roger of Wendover, *Chronicle*, I, p. 117.

The same year [692] Wilfrid of York was accused to king Alfrid, and was by that king and a number of bishops expelled his bishopric. That he might have an opportunity of defending himself, he came to Rome with his accusers...and letters were written to Alfrid, King of the Northumbrians, that he should cause him to be restored to his bishopric, inasmuch as he had been unjustly condemned. On arriving in the part of Gaul as he was returning to Britain, he was taken with a sudden illness, insomuch that he could not ride on horseback, but was borne in a litter by the hands of his attendants, and in this manner he was brought to Meaux, a town in France, where he lay four days and nights like a dead person. After remaining four days in this distressing condition, without eating or drinking, speaking or hearing, on the dawn of the fifth day he arose as from a deep sleep, and sat up, and then, after a gentle sigh, inquired for Acca, the presbyter, who, coming in immediately that he was called, the former thus addressed him: "I have just had an awful vision, which I wish you to hear and not divulge, until I know what is the will of God respecting me. There stood by me a certain person in white apparel and of noble aspect, who said that he was Michael, the archangel, and added, 'I have been sent to recall thee from death to life; for through the intercessions and tears of thy disciples, and at the entreaty of his mother, God hath granted thee to live; but hold thyself in readiness, for, at the end of four years, I shall return and visit thee; but now thou shalt return to thy country and recover the greater part of thy possessions, of which thou wast stripped, and shalt end thy days in peace'." The bishop recovered accordingly, to the joy of all, and, setting out on his journey, arrived in Britain...Alfrid, king of the Northumbrians, contumaciously refused to receive him. But on the death of Alfrid shortly after, the bishop was, with the concurrence of all, restored to the government of his church; and so, after spending his days in peace, he rested in the Lord four years after, according as it had been foretold him by the angel.

MOTIF: V.513.1 [*Saint instructed through vision*].

THE WELL OF ST CONSTANTINE [abridged]

Hunt, *Popular Romances of the West of England*, p. 287.

In the parish of St Merran, or Meryn, near Padstow, are the remains and the holy well of St Constantine. At one time the people of the region had grown careless and irreligious, and when a hot, dry summer brought them to a serious drought, they turned to their priest for counsel. They had so long neglected their church that it was falling into ruin. They had also allowed the saint's well to become foul, and the arches over it to become broken and decayed. The priest declared that their only hope lay in cleansing the well. They laughed at him, but the drought continued, and again they had no help but to consult the priest. His advice was the same, and in their hunger and thirst, this time they obeyed him. They cleared away the moss and weeds, and were overjoyed when a stream of clear water bubbled up. It was enough for all their wants; they drank, bathed and were refreshed. Then at last the heavens clouded over, rain fell, and in their gratitude to God, the people's hearts returned to their former faith and trust.

MOTIFS: V.134 [*Sacred well*]; Q.552.3.3 [*Drought as punishment for neglect of holy well*].

THE WELL OF ST LUDGVAN

Hunt, *Popular Romances of the West of England*, p. 288.

St Ludgvan, an Irish missionary, had finished his work. On the hill-top, looking over the most beautiful of bays, the church stood with all its blessings. Yet the saint, knowing human nature...prayed over the dry earth which was beneath him as he knelt on the church stile. His prayer was for water, and presently a most beautiful crystal stream welled up from below. The holy man prayed on, and then, to try the virtues of the water, he washed his eyes. They were rendered at once more powerful—so penetrating, indeed, as to enable him to see microscopic objects. The saint prayed again, and then he drank of the water. He discovered that his powers of utterance were greatly improved, his tongue formed words with scarcely any effort of his will. The saint now prayed that all children baptized in the waters of this well might be protected against the hangman and his hempen cord; and an angel from heaven came down into the water and promised the saint that his prayers should be granted. Not long after this, a good farmer and his wife brought their babe to the saint, that it might derive all the blessings belonging to this holy well. The priest stood at the baptismal font, the parents, with their friends around. The saint...signed the sign of the cross over the child, and when he sprinkled water on the face...[it] glowed with a divine intelligence.... But, to the astonishment of all, whenever he used the name Jesus, the child, who had received the power of speech from the water, pronounced distinctly the name of the devil, much to the consternation of all present. The saint knew that an evil spirit had taken possession of the child, and he endeavoured to cast him out; but the devil proved stronger than the saint for some time. St Ludgvan...knew that the spirit was a restless soul, which had been exorcized from Treassow, and he exerted all his energies in prayer. At length the spirit became obedient and left the child. He was now commanded by the saint to take his flight to the Red Sea. He rose, before the terrified spectators, into a gigantic size; he then spat into the well; he laid hold of the pinnacles of the tower, and shook the church until they thought it would fall. The saint was alone unmoved. He prayed on, until, like a flash of lightning, the demon vanished, shaking down a pinnacle in his flight. The demon, by spitting in the water, destroyed the spells of the water upon the eyes and the tongue too; but it fortunately retains its virtue of preventing any child baptized in it from being hanged with a cord of hemp. Upon a cord of silk it is stated to have no power.

This well had nearly lost its reputation once—a Ludgvan woman was hanged, under the circumstances told in the following narrative:

A small farmer, living in one of the most western districts of the county, died some years back of what was supposed at that time to be "English cholera". A few weeks after his decease, his wife married again. This circumstance excited some attention in the neighbourhood. It was remembered that the woman had lived on very bad terms with her late husband ...and that during the farmer's lifetime she had openly manifested rather more than a Platonic preference for the man whom she subsequently married.

Suspicion was generally excited...the proper order was applied for, and the body disinterred.... Enough arsenic to have poisoned three men was found in the stomach. The wife was accused of murdering her husband, convicted on the clearest evidence and hanged. Very shortly after she had suffered capital punishment horrible stories of a ghost were widely circulated. Certain people declared that they had seen a ghastly resemblance of the murderess, robed in her winding-sheet, with the black mark of the rope round her swollen neck, standing on stormy nights upon her husband's grave, and digging there with a spade, in hideous imitation of the action of the men who had disinterred the corpse.... This was fearful enough; nobody dared go near the place after nightfall. But soon another circumstance was talked of...which affected the tranquillity of people's minds in the village where she had lived, and where it was believed she had been born, more seriously than even the ghost-story itself....A woman who had been born close by the magical well, and who had therefore in all probability been baptized in its water...had nevertheless been publicly and unquestionably hanged....Every parishioner determined that the baptismal register of the poisoner should be sought for, and that it should thus be officially ascertained whether she had been christened with the well water or not. After much trouble, the important document was discovered...in a neighbouring parish. She had not been baptized in St Ludgvan's Church, and had therefore not been protected by the marvellous virtue of the local water.... The wonderful character of the parish well was wonderfully vindicated; its celebrity immediately spread wider than ever.

MOTIFS: A.941.5 [*Spring breaks forth through power of saint*]; V.134 [*Sacred well*]; D.926 [*Magic well*].

XII SUPERNATURAL

SUPERNATURAL

The modern researches into the field of extra-sensory perception, pursued in such books as *The Hidden Springs*, by Renée Haynes, cover very much the same ground as do the supernatural legends. The tales in this section are those which cannot be called "ghost stories" and are not precisely about witches, fairies, bogies or devils, yet have, nevertheless, no naturalistic explanation—or at least are not supposed to have such. Many of those to be found in Catherine Crowe's *Night Side of Nature* are supernatural rather than ghost stories. These tales deal with wraiths, second sight, visions of things distant in time or place, judgments and other unexplained, often inexplicable, happenings.

Wraiths are among the commonest of these, and are of various kinds. Sometimes a man will see his own double, and this is often thought to be a sign of imminent death, particularly when the real man and his shadow meet face to face. The danger of this can sometimes be averted by vigorous speech, as in the pleasant story of "The Waff", when the ominous double was fairly scolded away. Most often the wraith appears at the moment of death to friends at a distance. Sometimes the man is seen double, as in "The Doctor's Fetch", when the doctor's wife saw her husband asleep beside her and at the same time standing by the window. Sometimes the wraith is not ominous of death, but merely goes where the person wishes to go, and effects what he is unable in his own body to do. The story of "The Strange Visitant" is an example of this. The appearance of the wraith at death is possibly a form of the same state, as in the story of the dying mother who wished vehemently to see her children once more, fell into a trance, and woke calm and comforted, having visited them and been seen by them.

Another group of stories very similar to these is about people who go back into the past or who visit distant places. Often these are seen as wraiths, as in the story of "The Dream House". Some of these experiences seem well established. The most famous of them is that recorded in *An Adventure*, which is too long and detailed to be treated in a summary and should be studied in the original book. "A Vision at Dunino" is a pleasant version of this type of tale.

The separable soul is not unlike the wraith, but has a slightly different, very primitive philosophy behind it. In these stories, which range over a wide period of time, the soul is conceived of as a tiny creature, often of a different shape from the body—a bee, a lizard, or the like—which issues out of the sleeper's mouth or ear and has adventures suitable to its size, which are remembered by the waking man as dreams. An early and often-quoted example occurs in Saxo Grammaticus, but the belief persisted until the end of the last century, and may yet be found alive somewhere.

There are also explorations into the past which concern heroes rather than places—mighty sleepers in underground caverns, or strange wanderers who come into men's houses and make brief contact with them. There are other stranger contacts still—nature spirits, dangerous creatures from the woodland or mountains, or voices calling out from the sea.

There are some tales here about terrible and appalling judgments which find little echo in our modern theology; some read like pardoners' tales, crude pieces of priestly advertisement. Others are even more outdated, offshoots of Christian beliefs, like the story of the little chapel made of wax by the pious bees which may indeed have been invented for edification and never quite received, even by the most credulous, though other legends of animal piety were firmly believed.

Second sight, prophetic glimpses into the future and visions of Heaven and Hell may be listed as examples of extra-sensory perception, but there are a few other, stranger legends, like "The Anchor" and other queer and freakish tales. The section covers many activities of man's spirit, from the crudest moralities to what seem like upsurgings of the unconscious itself. It is this variety which gives its interest to the whole section.

THE ANCHOR

S. Baring-Gould, *A Book of Folk-Lore*, p. 153.

On a certain feast-day in Great Britain, when the congregation came pouring out of church, they saw to their surprise an anchor let down from above the clouds, attached to a rope. The anchor caught in a tombstone; and though those above shook the cable repeatedly, they could not disengage it. Then the people heard voices above the clouds discussing apparently the propriety of sending someone down to release the flukes of the anchor, and shortly after they saw a sailor swarming down the cable.

Before he could release the anchor he was laid hold of; he gasped and collapsed, as though drowning in the heavy air about the earth. After waiting about an hour, those in the aerial vessel cut the rope, and it fell down. The anchor was hammered out into the hinges and straps of the church door, where, according to Gervase (of Tilbury) they were to be seen in his day. Unfortunately, he does not tell us the name of the place where they are to be seen.

MOTIFS: D.1118 [*Magic airship*]; F.30 [*Inhabitant of upper world visits earth*]; F.51 [*Sky-rope*].

¶ This strange early space-men story from Gervase of Tilbury [*Floruit* 1211] shows some glimmering of scientific knowledge about the relative density of the air near the earth. It is one of those strange, unmotivated and therefore rather convincing tales that are scattered through the early chronicles. An example is the story of Nicholas Pipe, the sea-man (B, V).

THE ANXIOUS ENSIGN

Augustus Hare, *In My Solitary Life*, p. 67.

A regiment was lately passing through Derbyshire on its way to fresh quarters in the North. The Colonel, as they stayed for the night in one of the country towns, was invited to dine at a country-house in the neighbourhood, and to bring anyone he liked with him. Consequently, he took with him a young ensign, for whom he had taken a great fancy. They arrived, and it was a large party, but the lady of the house did not appear till just as they were going in to dinner, and, when she appeared, was so *distraite* and preoccupied that she scarcely attended to anything that was said to her. At dinner the Colonel observed that his young companion scarcely ever took his eyes off the lady of the house, staring at her in a way which seemed both rude and unaccountable. It made him observe the lady herself, [who]...seemed, in a manner quite unaccountable, to be listening to someone or something behind her.

As soon as dinner was over, the young ensign came to the Colonel, and said, "Oh, do take me away: I entreat you to take me away from this place." The Colonel said, "Indeed, your conduct is so very extraordinary and unpleasant that I quite agree with you that the best thing we can do is to go away"; and he made the excuse of his young friend being ill, and ordered their carriage.

When they had driven some distance, the Colonel asked the ensign for an explanation of his conduct. He said that he could not help it: during the whole of dinner he had seen a terrible black shadowy figure standing behind the chair of the lady of the house, and it had seemed to whisper to her, and she to listen to it. He had scarcely told this, when a man on horseback rode rapidly past the carriage, and the Colonel, recognizing one of the servants of the house they had just left, called out to know if anything was the matter. "Oh, don't stop me, sir," he shouted. "I am going for the doctor: my lady has just cut her throat."

MOTIFS: D.1825.1 [*Second sight*]; D.1825.3 [*Magic power to see invisible creatures*].
¶ In this section there are various examples of second sight, a gift much discussed in the seventeenth century, and held to be commoner amongst Highlanders than others. Both Aubrey and Kirk discussed it, and many examples are given in Catherine Crowe's *Night Side of Nature*. The gift is often mentioned in the Icelandic Sagas.
  See "The Whinger".

THE ANXIOUS SUBALTERN

Augustus Hare, *In My Solitary Life*, p. 303.

...Mrs Cholmondley Dering...often visited the old house of the Tren-chards, then let to the Misses Foster. The staircase opened from the hall, and below it was a glass door leading to a passage. One day, coming down the stairs, dressed for dinner, she saw through the glass door an old gentleman with a blue coat and pigtail, apparently attired for a masquerade in the dress of the last century.

Going into the drawing-room, she told the Misses Foster what she had seen. "Oh," they said, "you have seen the ghost of the house. He is perfectly harmless, but he often appears, and was a Mr Trenchard, who was excessively cruel to his wife.

"This Mr Trenchard, however, was very hospitable to his neighbours. One day the Colonel of a regiment quartered close by at Weymouth was drinking there with a young subaltern. At dinner the young man's eyes seemed constantly fixed in a very odd manner on the lady of the house, and immediately after dinner he entreated, with great insistence, that they might leave. The Colonel was annoyed, but, thinking he was ill, made an excuse and complied. In the carriage the young man said to him, 'Is it possible that you did not see the figure, which was exactly the double of Mrs Trenchard, standing behind her chair, and that every movement of Mrs Trenchard was repeated by the figure?' The Colonel was beginning to say 'What nonsense' when a servant whom he knew rode by, just stopping to say, 'I am going for a doctor, though it is no use, for Mrs Trenchard has hanged herself.'

"The appearance was several times seen before the death of a Mrs Trenchard. Philip II of Spain slept at the house on his way to marry Queen Mary, and he saw it. Mrs Trenchard of that time died the next day in her confinement."

Variant of "The Anxious Ensign".
MOTIFS the same, with the addition of E.723.6.1*(f) [*Wraith stands behind person at dinner table*] (Baughman); E.723.8 [*Wraith as calamity omen*].

APPARITION AT OXFORD

The Gentleman's Magazine Library, 1885, p. 190.

Mr John Bonnell was a Commoner of Queen's College; he was remark-able in his person and his gait, and had a particular manner of holding up his gown behind, so that to anyone who had but once seen him he might be known by his back as easily as by his face.

On Sunday, November 18th, 1750, at noon, Mr Ballard, who was then of Magd. College, and myself were talking together at Parker's door, I was then waiting for the sound of the trumpet, and suddenly Mr Ballard cried out, "Lord have mercy upon me, who is that coming out of your college?" I looked, and saw, as I supposed, Mr Bonnell, and replied, "He is a gentleman of our house, and his name is Bonnell; and he comes from Stanton-Harcourt." "My God," said Mr Ballard, "I never saw such a face in all my life." I answered slightly, "His face is much the same as it always is; I think it is a little more inflamed and swelled than it sometimes is; perhaps he has buckled his band too tight; but I should not have observed it if you had not spoken." "Well," said Mr Ballard again, "I shall never forget him as long as I live," and seemed much disconcerted and frightened.

This figure I saw without any emotion or suspicion; it came down the quadrangle, came out at the gate, and walked up the High Street; we followed it with our eyes till it came to Cat Street, where it was lost. The trumpet then sounded, and Mr Ballard and I parted; and I went into the hall, and thought no more of Mr Bonnell.

In the evening the prayers of the chapel were desired for one who was in a very sick and dangerous condition. When I came out of the chapel, I inquired of one of the scholars, James Harrison, in the hearing of several others who were standing before the kitchen fire who it was that was prayed for, and was answered, "Mr Bonnell, sen." "Bonnell, sen.", said I with astonishment. "What's the matter with him? He was very well today, for I saw him go out to dinner." "You are very much mistaken," said the scholar, "for he has not been out of his bed for some days." I then asserted more positively that I had seen him, and that a gentleman was with me who saw him too.

This came presently to the ears of Dr Fothergill, who had been my tutor. After supper he took me aside, and questioned me about it, and said he was very sorry I had mentioned the matter so publicly, for Mr B. was dangerously ill. I replied, I was very sorry too, but I had done it innocently; and the next day Mr B. died.

Inquiry was made of Mr Ballard afterwards, who related the part which he was witness to in the same manner as I have now related it; adding, that I told him the gentleman was one Mr Bonnell, and that he came from Stanton-Harcourt.

"E. R. M."

MOTIF: E.723 [*Wraiths of persons separate from body*].

¶ It is generally believed that to see one's own wraith is a sign one will shortly die. In this case the appearance of the wraith to others had the same significance.

See "The Doctor's Fetch".

THE BEES' CHAPEL

W. Henderson, *Folk-Lore of the Northern Counties*, p. 310.

A certain woman, having some stalls of bees which yielded not unto her her desired profit, but did consume and die of the murrain, made her moan to another woman, more simple than herself, who gave her counsel to get a consecrated Host, and put it among them. Accordingly to whose advice she went to the priest to receive the Host, which, when she had done, she kept it in her mouth, and, being come home again, she took it out and put it into one of her hives, whereupon the murrain ceased and the honey abounded. The woman, therefore, lifting up the hive at the due time to take out the honey, saw therein (most strange to be seen) a chapel built by the bees, with an altar in it, the walls adorned by marvellous skill of architecture, with windows conveniently set in their places, also a door, and a steeple with bells. And, the host being set on an altar, the bees, making a sweet noise, flew about it.

From Charles Butler's *Feminine Monarchie*, 1634.
MOTIFS: B.250 [*Religious animals*]; B.259.4 [*Bees build church of wax to contain consecrated Host*].

THE BIRKBECK GHOST

T. Thistleton Dyer, *The Ghost World*, p. 373.

In 1789, Mrs Birkbeck, wife of William Birkbeck, banker, of Settle, and a member of the Society of Friends, was taken ill and died at Cockermouth, while returning from a journey to Scotland, which she had undertaken alone—her husband and three children, aged seven, five and four respectively, remaining at Settle. The friends at whose house the death occurred made notes of every circumstance attending Mrs Birkbeck's last hours, so that the accuracy of the several statements as to time as well as place was beyond the doubtfulness of man's memory, or of any even unconscious attempt to bring them into agreement with each other.

One morning, between seven and eight o'clock, the relation to whom the care of the children had been entrusted, and who kept a minute journal of all that concerned them, went into their bedroom as usual, and found them all sitting up in bed in great excitement and delight. "Mamma has been here," they cried; and the little one said, "She called, 'Come Esther!'" Nothing could make them doubt the fact, and it was carefully noted down to amuse the mother when she came home. That same morning, as their mother lay on her dying bed at Cockermouth, she said, "I should be ready to go if I could but see my children." She then closed her eyes, to reopen them, as they thought, no more. But after ten minutes of perfect stillness, she looked up brightly, and said, "I am ready now. I have been with my children," and at once passed peacefully away.

When the notes taken at the two places were compared, the day, hour and minutes were the same.

From the *Proceedings of the Psychical Research Society*.
MOTIF: E.723.4.4 [*Wraith of dying woman goes to see her children before her death*].
¶ In the title of the story this is called a ghost, but it is clear from the tale that the appearance the children saw was a fetch, or wraith, not a ghost.

K. M. Briggs's Account of a Similar Experience

"I have been told at first hand of someone who desperately wanted a medicine, but felt too ill to fetch it. She lay down on her bed, half asleep, for a time, but presently got up, and found the medicine, neatly wrapped and sealed on the hall table. When she was better, she went to thank the chemist for sending it, and was told that she herself had fetched it. A gardener, working in the small garden in the front of the house, was ready to swear that no one had come out of it. This was told me on All Hallows' Eve, 1950".

THE BISHOP OF THE BUTTERFLY

H. Bett, *English Legends*, p. 5.

The precise locality of the adventure is not recorded, but apparently it was in the neighbourhood of Winchester. The *Lanercost Chronicle* says that Peter des Roches, Bishop of Winchester, was hunting in a forest, and came to a glade where there was a fair mansion he had never seen before. Some attendants came forth, and invited him to banquet with their king. He was prevailed upon to enter and was set down at the king's right hand. He asked the king who he was, and was told that he was Arthur, once lord of the whole realm of Britain. Then he ventured to ask the king if he were among the saved, and received the reply, "In truth I await God's great mercy." Then the Bishop said, "Who will believe me, my lord, when I tell how I have today seen and spoken with King Arthur?" "Close thine hand!" said the king, and he closed it. "Open it!" said the king, and from the opening hand there flew forth a butterfly. Then said Arthur, "All thy life long thou shalt have this memorial of me, that at every season thou mayest do thus, and thou shalt have it in thy hand."

This became so well known that men often begged a butterfly from the Bishop for his benediction, and many called him the Bishop of the Butterfly.

MOTIFS: E.481.4.1 [*Avalon: Happy otherworld where dead are healed*]; A.571.2 [*Culture hero still alive on mysterious island*]; D.1731 [*Magic power received in dream*].

¶ This visit to King Arthur is unlike most others, for he is living, in a castle in a wood, not in an underground cave, and the entrant is given a magical power as a token of his visit. The King, too, is awake and feasting, not asleep.

See "The Silver Horseshoe" (B, IX).

BOGGART HOLE CLOUGH

C. Hole, *English Folk-Lore*, p. 95.

Fern seed worn in the shoe rendered the owner invisible, provided that it was gathered at midnight on St John's Eve, and was not touched by hand. In Lancashire it had to be gathered over the Bible, but it appears always to have been a perilous undertaking. Sometimes it was used for love-charms. In one Lancashire story three men went at the appointed hour to Boggart Hole Clough to gather it for such a charm. They shook it with a forked hazel rod into a dish. The lover succeeded in gaining his girl's affection, but in three months she followed him to the grave; one of the others went mad, and the third lay unconscious for three days. Actually, ferns have no seeds, only spores, which are deposited on the underside of the fronds and are very difficult to find.

MOTIFS: D.971.3 [*Magic fern seed*]; C.401.5 [*Tabu: speaking while gathering fern seed to make wishes come true at midnight on Christmas Eve, when fern-seed ripens and falls immediately*].

¶ C.401.5 has the unusual feature of fern seed ripening at Christmas-time. It is usually supposed to ripen on St John the Baptist's Eve, Midsummer Night, and, because it is invisible at any other time, it confers the powers of invisibility (see Bovet, *Pandaemonium*).

For the theme of this short anecdote, see "The Fairy Follower". BV. Midsummer Night and Christmas Eve were both festivals of the dead, and the watch in the church porch, to see the dead passing by, which was usually kept at Midsummer, was in some places kept at Christmas. One date marks the beginning of the shortening, and the other the lengthening days. Another date for the vigil was St Mark's Eve.

See "Christmas Eve Vigil", "St Mark's Eve".

THE BRAHAN SEER
KENNETH ORE OF ROSS–SHIRE
[slightly shortened]

Hugh Miller, *Scenes and Legends*, pp. 163–5.

Kenneth Ore of Ross-shire, who lived some time in the seventeenth century, is said, when serving as a field-labourer with a wealthy clansman, somewhere near Brahan Castle, to have made himself so formidable to the clansman's wife, by his shrewd, sarcastic humour, that she resolved on destroying him by poison. She mixed a preparation of noxious herbs with his food one day when he was employed in digging turf in a solitary morass, and brought it to him in a pitcher. She found him lying asleep on one of those conical fairy hillocks which abound in some parts of the Highlands; and, her courage failing her, instead of awakening him, she set down the pitcher by his side, and returned home.

He awoke shortly after, and seeing the food, would have begun his repast, but, feeling something press coldly against his heart, he opened his waistcoat and found a beautiful smooth stone resembling a pearl, but much larger, which had apparently been dropped into his breast while he slept. He gazed at it in admiration, and became conscious that a strange faculty of seeing the future as distinctly as the present, and men's real designs and motives as clearly as their actions, was miraculously imparted to him. Thus he became acquainted with the treachery practised against him by his mistress. But he derived little advantage from the faculty ever after, for he led, it is said, till extreme old age, an unsettled, unhappy kind of life—wandering from place to place, a prophet only of evil, or of little trifling events.

There was a time of evil, he said, coming over the Highlands, when all things would appear fair and promising, and yet be both bad in themselves, and the beginnings of what would prove worse. A road would be opened among the hills from sea to sea, and a bridge built over every stream; but the people would be degenerating as their country was growing better; there would be ministers among them without grace, and maidens without shame; and the clans would have become so heartless that they would flee out of their country before an army of sheep. Moss and muir would be converted into corn-land, and yet hunger press as sorely on the poor as ever. During a terrible persecution, a ford in the river Oickel at the head of Dornoch Firth would render a passage over the dead bodies of men clad in the plaid and bonnet, and on the hill of *Finnbheim*, in Sutherlandshire, a raven would drink her fill of human blood three times a day for three successive days.

The greater part of this prophecy still belongs to the future, but almost all his minor ones are said to have been fulfilled. He predicted, it is affirmed, that there would be dram-shops at the end of every furrow; that a cow would calve on the top of the old tower at Fairburn; that a fox would rear a litter of cubs on the hearth-stone of Castle Downie; that another fox, as white as snow, would be killed on the western coast of Sutherlandshire; that a wild deer would be taken alive at Fortrose Point; that a rivulet in Western Ross would be dried up in winter; and that there would be a deaf Seaforth. But it would be much easier to prove that these events have really taken place than that they have been foretold.

Some of his other prophecies have been nearly as equivocal as the responses of the old oracles—he predicted that the ancient Chanonry of Ross, which is still standing, would fall "full of Mackenzies", and as the floor of the building has been used as a burial place by several powerful families of this name, this prophecy can hardly fail of fulfilment. He predicted, too, that a huge natural arch near the Storhead of Assynt would be thrown down with so terrible a crash that the cattle of Led-more (twenty miles inland) would break from their fastenings at the sound. When the tower did fall, it happened that some of these cattle were grazing on the land of another proprietor only a few hundred yards away. Finally, shortly before his death, the prophet is said to have flung his white stone into a lake near Brahan, predicting that it would be found many years later, when all his prophecies had been fulfilled, by a lame, humpbacked mendicant.

MOTIFS: D.810 [*Magic object a gift*]; D.1300 [*Magic object gives supernatural wisdom*]; M.340 [*Unfavourable prophecies*].

¶ Hugh Miller does not mention the cruel death suffered by the Brahan Seer. He is said to have been boiled in a leaden cauldron because he was otherwise invulnerable. His prophecies were published in eighteenth-century chapbook literature with those of Merlin, Sybilla and others.

THE BRICKIN OF LOUGH BRICKLAN

T. G. F. Paterson, *Contributions to Ulster Folk-life, Armagh Miscellanea.*

I remember my Uncle Patrick McGee having an argument with a woman in Ballymacully. She carried the bells for the best-tongued woman for miles, and there was the usual spring-cleaning. He listened to her for a good while and then he said, "Are you a 'Brickin'? You have all the signs of the breed." That dried her up and I wondered why. Said I to my uncle, "Who were the 'Brickins'?" Said he, "Thank God, there's not a drop's blood of them in us, anyway." It was a long time before I learned how the nickname was come by. This is the story:

The real Brickin was a bad one. He lived at Lough Bricklan in the County of Down. He was a petty Chief and the cause of dozens of wars in Ulster. He managed it all by lies and an evil tongue. He was a dangerous sort, for all his lies had a bit of truth in them. Things reached such a pass that the Chief Druid paid him a visit, and threatened to curse him and all his posterity if he did not mend his ways. That gave him a fright, and the Druid imposed a penance on him as well.

He made him build a banquet hall and give a feast to all the kings and chiefs that he had slandered, and the feast lasted for nine days and nine nights. The place selected was the hill of Dundrum, now crowned by an old castle of later days. All the kings and chiefs were there, and he made amends for all he had done, and promised never to cause wars among the men of Ulster again. But he had an evil heart, so he went among the wives of the chiefs and told them tales, and they were soon frightened, and in no time the men were taking sides too, and the feast ended in a great slaughter. When he saw what he had done, and thought of his promise to the Druid, he made for home, but as he crossed the foot of Dehomed Mountain he was attacked by a herd of wild pigs. He was killed by a wild boar and the pigs ate him. That was the last of Brickin, and that was centuries before Patrick's day.

From McCarten, Ballymacully, July 1943.
MOTIFS: Q.305 [*War-making punished*]; W.188 [*Contentiousness*]; Q.523.5 [*Penance: Planting a garden and offering free hospitality to all*]; Q.314 [*Scandal-mongering punished*]; M.460 [*Curses on families*].

BURGESS THE MINER

Ruth L. Tongue, *Somerset FolkLore*, p. 95.

Burgess the miner was a widower who lived with his little daughter in a cottage in White Water Combe. After a time he fell in love with a worth-less woman, and as they found the child a nuisance he murdered it and threw the body down a mine-shaft. This proved no concealment, for a mysterious light shone above the shaft, so Burgess took up the body, buried it hastily in a bank side and left the moor. Two sheep-stealers saw a rag sticking out of some loose earth and thought a sheep had been hidden there, for this was the usual sign. When they began to scrape back the earth, however, they came on a child's hand. Burgess was pursued and caught. He was hanged at Taunton Gaol in 1858. There is still a ghostly light to be seen at the place of the murder, but it is very unlucky to see it. If it is seen by a child it foretells death before twenty-one.

According to Snell, death comes within a year of seeing the light. This seems to be a common belief about seeing spunkies, for in 1909 a maid in our house who had been frightened by a turnip lantern came in crying out that she had seen a spunky and would be dead within the year.

TYPE 960. MOTIFS: E.231.3 [*Ghost light hovers over hiding-place of body of murdered person*]; N.271 [*Murder will out*]; E.530.1.6 [*Ghost light serves as death omen*].

CAEDMON'S DREAM [summary]

From Bede, *Ecclesiastical History*, Book IV, Ch. 24.

Caedmon was a lay brother in the monastery of the Abbess Hilda at Whitby. He had lived in a secular habit till he was well advanced in years, and so had never learnt the art of versifying. At times at some entertainment, when it was agreed that all should take turns in singing, Caedmon would rise up and leave the room as soon as he saw the instrument approaching him.

Once when he had done this, and had gone to the stable, where his duty was that night to look after the horses, he lay down there to sleep, and a person appeared to him and said, "Caedmon, sing some song to me." He replied: "I cannot sing; that was the reason why I left the entertainment." But the other answered: "You shall sing, however." "What shall I sing?" "Sing the beginning of created things," said the other. Caedmon at once began to sing verses to the praise of God, which he had never heard before: "We are now to praise the Maker of the heavenly kingdom, the power of the Creator and his counsel, the deeds of the Father of Glory. How He, being the eternal God, became the author of all miracles, who first, as almighty preserver of the human race, created heaven for the sons of men as the roof of the house, and next the earth."

This is the sense, but not the words in order as he sang them in his sleep; for verses, though never so well composed, cannot be literally translated out of one language into another, without losing much of their beauty and loftiness. Awaking from sleep, he remembered all that he had sung in his dream, and soon added much more to the same effect in verse worthy of the Deity.

In the morning he came to the steward, his superior, and, having acquainted him with the gift he had received, was conducted to the abbess, by whom he was ordered, in the presence of many learned men, to tell his dream, and repeat the verses, that they might all give their judgment what it was, and whence his verse proceeded. They all concluded that heavenly grace had been conferred on him by our Lord. They expounded to him a passage in holy writ, either historical or doctrinal, ordering him, if he could, to put the same into verse. Having undertaken it, he went away, and returning the next morning gave it to them composed in most excellent verse. Whereupon the abbess, embracing the grace of God in the man, instructed him to quit the secular habit, and take upon him the monastic life; which being accordingly done, she associated him to the rest of the brethren in her monastery, and ordered that he should be taught the whole series of sacred history. Thus Caedmon, keeping in mind all he heard, and as it were chewing the cud, converted the same into the most harmonious verse; and sweetly repeating the same, made his masters in their turn his hearers.

MOTIF: D.1731.1 [*Song learned in dream*].

¶ The Anglo-Saxon words of Caedmon's "Song on Creation" have survived to the present day, and are some of the finest in Anglo-Saxon poetry.

THE CAVE AT RHYDWEN [summary]

Thompson *Notebook*, S.

Ben Wood and his brother Godfrey got drunk on money earned by playing in different villages all day. They lay down to sleep on top of a high hill overlooking the sea, called Rhydwen.

In the morning they noticed a row of small white stones on the grass, and when they went closer to look at them, they saw that the stones were moving. They followed them to the edge of the cliff and found some little steps cut out of the rock. They followed the stones down the steps, and came to the mouth of a cave, with a deep well in front of it, in which there was very little water. Inside the cave were three roads, and they started along one of them, but soon turned back, as it was hard to see. This time the well was nearly full.

Later on a farmer told Ben that one of the three roads was broad and easy, and if anyone followed it he never returned; and another had a great hoard of gold and silver at the end of it. Many people (including several of the Woods) tried to enter the cave, but, though they crossed the pool, or well, something then "came over" them and they could go no further.

Told by Matthew Wood at Bala, 28 August 1922.

MOTIFS: D.1641.2 [*Stones remove themselves*]; F.92.6 [*Entrance to lower world through cave*]; F.93.0.2.1 [*Well entrance to lower world*]; F.171.2 [*Broad and narrow road in other world*]; N.511.3 [*Treasure placed in ground by supernatural beings*].

¶ The beginning of this story suggests that some variant of Type 766 will follow. The continuation, however, is more suggestive of the vision of True Thomas, with its three paths leading to Heaven, Hell and Elfland. Slight though the legend is, it expresses ancient and widely held beliefs.

THE CHILD OF BRISTOL

W. Carew Hazlitt, *National Tales and Legends*, p. 6.

He who made both Heaven and Hell in seven days bless us all that are here assembled together, old and young, great and small, if so they lend good ear to my tale! The best tale that ever was told is worth little enough, unless some listen thereto. So, I pray you, as many as are now present, to desist from your talking, and to hear what I am about to say.

There dwelled in England in old days, in the fair city of Bristol, a very rich lawyer, who had gotten into his hands great possessions, and was a lord of many townships, castles and forests, and of much cattle; and he used his craft in law to beguile the poor man, for he had not the fear of God before his eyes.

This rich man, who was both a merchant and an usurer, had only one son, a comely child, of rare promise, and by him he set all his store. For his sake he heaped up riches, and oppressed his neighbours far and wide; for he looked to make him, whenso he himself should die, even richer than he was, and more powerful and great than any in all that country.

It happened, when this youth was twelve years old, that his father sent him to school to learn clergy; and the child grew wise and witty, and in mislike of all ungodliness. Then his father devised in his thought how it would bestead his heir, so that he might not be deceived by men when he came to full estate, and stood in his father's place, to have some learning in law; and accordingly he called the child to him, and said to him thus: "Son, I have it in mind to cause thee for a twelvemonth's space to learn so much of the law of this land as will hinder thy neighbours and all others, when thou comest to manhood, from doing thee wrong."

But the child answered softly: "Father, many prosper well in this world that are no lawyers, and so I trust that I may do. That craft will I never study that may put my soul in jeopardy, and be to God's displeasure. I am loth to follow any calling which is contrary to my spiritual well-being. Ever hath it been my wish to live by merchandise, in which a man may advance himself by honest means in the sight of Heaven. Here at Bristol liveth one who is a good and true man, as I hear tell: let me be his bound prentice seven years, and learn his business, and dwell under his roof."

So his father, seeing his bent, rode to Bristol, and made covenant with the said merchant to take his son for seven years; and the boy went unto that merchant, and by his courtesy and honesty won his love, and the love of all who came into those parts to buy and to sell their goods.

Now, meanwhile, the child's father pursued his godless ways, lending moneys to use, robbing the parson and the vicar of their tenths, and wringing from the poor man all he might, with intent to leave his estate so that his heir would be lifted by his riches above all others without a peer.

But, as all things will have an end, this usurer, who was waxing in years, fell sick and lay on his bed, and doubting that his life might draw to a close suddenly, he summoned to his side some of the chief men of the country, that were his neighbours and acquaintance, and besought them out of charity to be his executors. Then, because his goods had been so ill-gotten, and the fear of the Lord was not in him, no one among them all assented to be his executor, saying that they would not have to do with his affairs from dread of the wrath of God upon them.

This sick usurer lamented sorely his case, that none would for conscience' sake be executor to him; and seeing that he drew nigher and nigher to his end, he sent for his son where he lay at the good merchant's house, seven miles thence, and when he had come to him, he showed him how it was, and begged him, as he was heir to all his fair lands and goods whatsoever, to take that office upon him.

Quoth he: "Son, I have gathered all this together for thee, than whom I have no other heir, and I see well that in friendship there is no trust. Do thou therefore, this thing for me."

His son turned away from him, uttering not a word; and then the dying man, when he perceived his unwillingness, further said: "I charge thee, as thou wilt have my blessing ere I go, obey my behest."

"Ah! Father," cried the boy, "thou layest on me a heavy charge, and thy command I cannot gainsay. But on my part, lo! I enjoin thee, on the fourteenth day after thy passage, to appear before me, and let me behold thy spirit, and see whether it be saved or damned; and further I pray and require thee, both thou and any that shall bear thee company at that time, to do me no trespass."

"Son," answered the father, "I agree."

"Alas," thought the boy, "that for any gold or land of mine a man's soul should stand in peril to be lost!"

The priest came, and gave that rich usurer, as he lay on his death-bed, the glorious sacrament, and shrove him, and prayed to God to be merciful to him; and when God was so pleased, the sick man passed away.

Then his good son brought his father to burial, and spread largesse among young and old, and gave much store of gold to holy priests, so that there was great mourning and many a dirge for the rich usurer; and the boy, who began to draw towards man's estate, sold his father's houses and lands, and with the money he kept in his service a hundred priests, causing them to say for his father's soul thirty trentals of masses. So this pious youth dispossessed himself of almost all that rich usurer's goods, till gold he had none, and where he was heir to so much riches, there was, as the fortnight drew near to completion, no poorer man than him in the whole land.

Now, when the day arrived when he had appointed to meet his father, he repaired to the chamber wherein his father had died, and remained there in prayer nearly to noon; and towards midday, as he knelt praying, there came a flash of lightning and a peal of thunder and he muttered "*Benedicite!*" and called upon God for succour.

And as he thus knelt and prayed, his father's spirit appeared to him, as he had enjoined, flaming like a glowing coal, and the Devil led it by the neck in a gleaming chain.

The boy said: "I conjure thee, whatever thou art, speak to me."

The spirit answered: "I am thy father, that begat thee. Now thou mayest perceive my sad estate."

"It pierceth my heart, Father," answered the boy again, "to behold thee in such a sorrowful plight."

The spirit replied: "Son, I fare thus, as thou seest me today, because I got my estate by deceit and extortion; unless it be restored, I shall go on in this guise a hundred year henceforward. Ease me therefore of my bond, for till then my soul is in durance."

"Nay, Father, not so, if God will give me grace. Pledge me that this same day fortnight ye will return to me in this place, and I shall labour all I can meanwhile to bring thy soul into a better state."

The spirit gave its assent, and in a clap of thunder vanished; and on the next day following, the boy went to Bristol, to seek his former master, the good merchant. To whom "I have served you, sir," quoth he, "many a day; for the love of God, be my friend. My father has passed; and I need a little sum of gold, until I have found a chapman for the residue of my heritage."

But the good merchant blamed him for parting with his patrimony, and said to him thus: "If so it is that need presseth, I will lend thee a hundred marks, and I will not ask for the same again this seven year."

The youth avowed that he must find someone to buy his lands that still remained to him; and when he told the good merchant that his steward held them to be worth a hundred pounds, the other said unto him, "I will give thee three hundred all truly told"; and when the youth consented, he fetched the gold, and counted it out to him, and the son of the rich usurer was right glad in his heart, and thanked his master, and went his way. So now he caused it to be proclaimed and published in all churches and all markets, that whoso, man or woman, had suffered loss by his father, should come to him, and he would satisfy them to the full. And he did as he made promise, till the money was all spent, and the second fortnight passed away.

Then he prepared to meet the spirit, as he had done before, and knelt down and prayed against the hour when it behoved it to appear; and when the youth beheld him, the burning chain was no longer on his neck, and the red flames in which he had been wrapped was turned to blackness.

"Now, Father," said the youth, "tell me how it goeth with thee."

"All the better for thee, son," quoth the spirit. "Blessed be the day that I begat thee! Yet I live still in much pain and woe, and so must continue till my term is fulfilled."

"Father," answered the youth then, "say to me what goeth most grievously against thee?"

"Tenths and offerings that I refused, son, and never would pay," returned the spirit, "are the cause why I remain, all thy good alms deeds not withstanding, thus wretched and forlorn. Give me back my pledge, for there is no remedy, and I must be gone."

The youth replied thus: "I shall still once more essay what I may do, Father. Promise me again that thou wilt be visible to me in a fortnight from this day in the same place, and I will against then try what to amend thy cheer I can do."

To his old master, the kind merchant at Bristol, he betook himself, and said to him: "Sir, it is so, that I lack yet a little sum of money, to make another bargain." And as he spake, he wept.

The merchant replied: "Thou art a fool; thou hast been among bad company, and hast lost money at cards or dice. Thou hast nought left that thou canst sell. Thou art, I doubt, an unthrift."

But the youth offered to become a bond servant to the merchant himself and all his heirs for ever, if he might have that for which he prayed; and the good merchant softened toward him once more, saying, "How much wouldst thou?"

He said, "Forty marks will supply me."

That burgher loved the youth so well in his heart that into his inner chamber he went, and fetched the money, and he gave it to him, saying: "Thou didst ask me for forty marks, and lo! forty pounds I give thee; and God bless thee to boot!"

The youth departed, light of heart, and to all the churches far and near where his father owed tenths and offerings, he went on pilgrimage, and paid them one and all whatso they demanded, till his money was utterly spent; and as he returned home hungry and penniless, he met an old man by the way, who said to him: "Sir, it is so that your father owed me for a measure of corn. I beg thee pay me therefore."

The youth humbled himself before the man, and said to him, kneeling on one knee, that gold he had none; but he stripped off his own doublet, and laid it on the shoulders of the other, saying, "It is all, Father, that I have"; and he went on his journey in his shirt and breeches, till he came to his own house, where his father's spirit was to visit him.

He knelt and prayed long, and presently he became aware of the gladdest song that ever was heard, and when it was ended, by a light which burned more brightly than a thousand torches, a naked child, led by an angel of God, stood before him.

"Son," said the vision, "blessed be thou, and all that shall be born of thee!"

"Father," he answered, "I rejoice to behold thee in that state in which thou now art, and I trust that thou art saved."

"Son," the vision answered, "I go to Heaven. God Almighty reward thee, and make thee prosper! Now yield me up my pledge that I gave to thee, and I go."

And the youth discharged his father from that hour, and to Heaven he went,

Then the child, thanking God and our Blessed Lady, went anon to Bristol; and he was in his poor array, for his gay clothes had he given for the measure of corn. And when the burgher, his former master, espied him, he asked him what he had done to bring himself to such a pass.

He said: "I have come to yield myself to thy service to my life's end."

But the merchant would not take that answer, and said to him: "Now, tell me, son, by the love that is between us, why thou goest thus, and how thou makest thy thrift so thin."

"Sir," answered the young man then, "all my goods have I sold to get my father into Heaven; for through his covetous and unholy life so many had he set against him that no man would be his executor or attorney." And he set before him the whole story of his father's appearances, and how at length he was admitted to bliss. "And so," he said, "now all my sorrow, sir, is healed and assuaged."

"Son," quoth the kind merchant, "blessings on thy name, that thou couldest so impoverish thyself to save thy own father's soul! All the world shall do thee honour. Thou art a steadfast and true friend, the like of which I have seldom seen. Few sons would thus save their fathers after they were gone. Executors know I many a one, but none such as thou art. Now I say unto thee I make thee a partner with me in Bristol, to buy and to sell for me as I should myself do; and seeing that I have no child to come after me, thou shalt be to me a son, and shalt inherit all my goods when I am dead."

And the merchant wedded him to a rich man's daughter of that country, and in the process of time dying, left to him, as he had said, all his lands, cattle and goods; so that he became greater in wealth than before, and through the blessing of God, the treasure which he had restored to holy Church and the poor was given back to him twofold.

MOTIFS: V.413 [*Son's acts of charity save his father's soul*]; V.432 [*Man beggars self by charity*]; V.410 [*Charity rewarded*].

CHRISTCHURCH PRIORY

H. Bett, *English Legends*, p. 78.

There is a legend about the supernatural removal of foundations with a picturesque addition, attached to Christchurch Priory in the New Forest. A site on St Catherine's Hill, about a mile and a half from the present church, was chosen, and the building was begun, but what was built in the day was pulled down in the night, and the materials removed to the present site. So the church was built where it stands, but a strange workman laboured with the rest who never shared their meals, and never took any wages. Once when a great beam was too short, the stranger lengthened it by laying his hands upon it.

It was our Lord, the carpenter's son, and so the church was named Christchurch. The miraculous beam is said to be one over the arched entrance to the south aisle. Unfortunately for the legend, this is one of the latest parts of the building.

TYPE ML.7065 (variant). MOTIF: D.480.0.1 [*Things miraculously stretched or shortened if needed by a saint*].

¶ The story of the stretched beam comes from one of the more obscure apocryphal gospels.

The usual version of TYPE ML.7065 is, that the fellow-worker is the Devil, a troll, or a wizard, and the condition of building it is that his name must be guessed, after the pattern of "Tom Tit Tot".

THE CHRISTMAS EVE VIGIL

J. Bowker, *Goblin Tales of Lancashire*, p. 198.

A certain clergyman of Walton-le-Dale, though kind and considerate to all his parishioners, from his studious and solitary habits, and a habit of talking to himself, gained the reputation of being in league with the Devil. Gradually his friends fell away, and only one remained. This was an old herb-doctor, "Owd Abrum", learned in all the lore of plants, who used to meet the minister on his nightly walks; and they discovered that their interests bound them together, particularly their studies of the stars.

The minister at last confided to Abraham his wish to try a certain experiment. After performing certain ceremonies, if one waited in the church porch on Christmas Eve, he would see the faces of all those who were to die in the following year.

The two determined to prove this; and on Christmas Eve following, they armed themselves with St John's wort, mountain ash, bay leaves and holly, and set out soon after eleven. Many cottage doors still stood open, for the people believed that if on Christmas Eve the way was clear, and one of the family read aloud from the Gospel of St Luke, the saint himself would pass through the house.

The two men reached the church without being seen, and began their strange Latin prayer. There was an icy wind, followed by a strain of music, and they saw a procession coming up to the porch. With horror, they recognized several of the villagers, and then the form of the minister himself, who, at the sight, fell to the ground unconscious.

With help he was carried back to his house, but the story came out, and he had to leave the parish for a time, so much was he persecuted by those who came to ask, if anyone fell sick, whether he had been in the procession.

After some months, news reached the parish that their minister had died from a fever which he caught in visiting a cottage stricken with the disease.

Old Abraham, in spite of many entreaties, would never again perform the experiment.

MOTIFS: D.1825.6 [*Magic power to see who will die during coming year*]; D.1385.2.1 [*Herbs worn to keep off evil spirits*]; D.1385.2.5 [*Rowan protects against spells and enchantments*]; D.1825.6.2*(b) [*The watcher sees his own spirit when he is to die within the year, and realizes he is to die*] (Baughman).

¶ See "Boggart Hole Clough", "Midsummer Eve", "St Mark's Vigil".

THE CONJUROR'S BOOTS

Ruth L. Tongue, *Somerset Folklore*, p. 81.

George Beacham was a cattle-dealer and conjuror. In spite of the fact that his house stood across the lane from the Quaker Meeting House, he owned a wizard's staff and magic books. When his time came to die he was very unwilling to relinquish his power of plaguing his neighbours.

"Yew bury me to cross-roads," he told his poor wife. "I a'nt going to be under no churchyard soil, I tell 'ee. I wants to be where I can keep an eye on the neighbour's doings, so dig my grave to cross-roads. If 'ee don't I'll trouble 'ee."

Whatever the widow might have done, the neighbours were quite determined to be clear of the conjuror, and on July 27th, 1788, they buried him good and proper in Winscombe Churchyard. A year passed by without disturbance, but on July 27th, 1789, the quiet of the Quaker meeting was broken by screams from across the road. A passing woman had looked in at Widow Beacham's cottage and seen chairs and tables dancing with pots and pans, while the kneading trough rocked unaided.

The Friends went across to unravel the mystery, moving out of the way of a large armchair that was gliding across the room. As they stood there wondering, the dead conjuror's boots clattered slowly downstairs and out into the kitchen to meet them.

Both Hannah More and Mr Jones, the curate of Shipham, visited the cottage; but no naturalistic explanation of the phenomena has been found.

Sidcot, local traditions. The historical details of the story are to be found in Knight, *The Heart of Mendip*, pp. 80–2.

MOTIFS: D.1786 [*Magic power at cross-roads*]; F.473.1 [*Poltergeist throws objects*]; F.473.2.1 [*Chair is rocked by invisible spirit*]; E.431.17 [*Criminals buried at cross-roads to prevent walking*]; E.434.4 [*Ghosts cannot pass cross-roads*].

¶ These motifs show the opposite opinion to George Beacham's who wished to be buried at cross-roads so that he could be active. The same contradiction is shown in the beliefs about laying a spirit under a hedge. Some evil men wish to be buried there so that they can do harm to passers-by. On the other hand, many ghosts are laid under hedges.

The main part of the story, empty, walking boots, has no place in the Motif Index.

That boots are considered symbolic of the man in England is shown by such proverbial expressions as "Stepping into his shoes" and such superstitions as the ill-luck of putting boots on a table, supposed to foreshadow the corpse of the owner being laid out there.

See "General Dalzell's Boots", (B VI), "The Haunted Boots" (B.II).

THE CORPSE LIGHT

S. Baring-Gould, *A Book of Folk-Lore*, p. 24.

Mrs Crowe, in her *Night Side of Nature*, tells [a story] which she heard from a "dignitary of the Church", born in Wales. A female relative of his started early in the morning, attended by her father's servant. When she had reached halfway, where she expected to meet the servant of the friend she was about to visit, she dismissed the man who had accompanied her so far.

The fellow had not long left her before she saw a light approach her, moving about three feet above the soil. She turned her horse out of the bridle-road, along which it advanced, to allow it to pass, but to her dismay, just as it came opposite her, it halted and remained flickering before her for about half an hour, and only vanished as she heard steps of the servant's horse as he trotted up to meet and conduct her to her friend.

On reaching the house of her friend, she related what she had seen. A few days later that very servant who had come to meet her sickened and died, and his body was carried along the road upon which the light had moved; and, more curious still, owing to an accident, the coffin halted for an hour at the very spot where she had been delayed confronting the mysterious light.

That light, we may be sure, was supposed to be the soul of a relative come from the grave to meet and welcome a kinsman. In no other way can it be explained.

MOTIF: E.530.1.6 [*Ghost light serves as death omen*].
¶ Baring-Gould is obviously wrong in his interpretation of this story, as the light came from the same direction as the servant, not from the churchyard.
See "The Double Light" (B, VI) "Burgess the Miner".

THE COTTERTOWN MURDER

T. F. Thistleton Dyer, *The Ghost World*, pp. 433–4.

A murder was committed...at Cottertown, of Auchanasie, near Keith, on January 11th, 1797, in connection with which the following facts have been recorded: "On the day on which the deed was done, two men, strangers to the district, called at a farmhouse about three miles from the house in which lived the old folk that were murdered.

Shortly before the tragic act was committed, a sound was heard passing along the road the two men were seen to take, in the direction of the place at which the murder was perpetrated. So loud and extraordinary was the noise that people left their houses to see what it was that was passing. To the amazement of everyone, nothing was to be seen, though it was moonlight, and moonlight so bright that it aroused attention. All believed that something dreadful was to happen, and some proposed to follow the sound.

About the time this discussion was going on, a blaze of fire arose on the hill of Auchanasie. The foul deed had been accomplished, and the cottage set on fire. By next day all knew of what the mysterious sound had been the forerunner!"

Walter Gregor, *Folk-lore of North-east of Scotland*, pp. 205, 206.
MOTIF: D.1827.1.3 [*Noise warns of approaching death*].

THE CRIER OF CLAIFE

E. Bogg, *Lakeland and Ribblesdale*, p. 218.

[At Windermere Ferry.] "Formerly," says Harriet Martineau, "it was impossible to get over by the ferry after dusk, and if you should arrive at the Nab too late, you may call all night, but the boat will not come." On which hangs a tale, known as "The Crier of Claife", the name of a ghost or spirit who, tradition says, long haunted this district.

About the fifteenth century, one stormy night, a party of travellers were making merry at the ferry-house, then a humble tavern, when a call for the boat was heard from the Nab. A quiet, sober boatman obeyed the call, though the night was wild and fearful. When he ought to be returning, the tavern guests stepped out upon the shore, to see whom he would bring. He returned alone, ghastly and dumb with horror. Next morning he was in a high fever, and in a few days he died, without having been prevailed upon to say what he had seen.

For weeks after there were shouts, yells, and howlings at the Nab on every stormy night, and no boatman would attend to any call after dark.

Things came to such a pass that a monk from Furnes, who dwelt on one of the islands of the lake, was applied to to exorcize the Nab. On Christmas Day he assembled all the inhabitants of Chapel Island, and performed, in their presence, services which would forever confine the ghost to the quarry in the wood behind the ferry, now called "The Crier of Claife". Some say that the priest conducted the people to the quarry, and laid the ghost then and there. (Laid though it be, nobody goes there at night.) It is still told how the foxhounds, in eager chase, would come to a full stop at that place; and how, within the last generation, a schoolmaster from Colthouse, who left home to pass the Crier, was never seen more.

MOTIFS: E.265.3 [*Meeting ghost causes death*]; E.443.2.4 [*Ghost laid by priest*].
¶ This is probably a straightforward story of a murdered man, but the haunted ferry and the persistence of the apparition after having been laid suggests some tradition of a water-spirit.

A slightly different version of the legend is given by Harriet Martineau in *A Complete Guide to the English Lakes*, quoted by Bowker in *Goblin Tales of Lancashire*, p. 212.

THE CURATE OF AXHOLME

Choice Notes from "Notes and Queries" p. 52.

At Axholme, alias Haxey, in ye Isle, one Mr Edward Vicars (curate to Mr Wm Dalby, vicar), together with one Robert Hallywell a taylor, intending on St Mark's Even at night to watch in ye church porch to see who should die in ye year following (to this purpose using divers ceremonies), they addressing themselves to the business, Vicars (being then in his chamber) wished Hallywell to be going before and he would presently follow him. Vicars fell asleep, and Hallywell (attending his coming in ye church porch), forthwith sees certain shapes presenting themselves to his view, resemblances (as he thought) of divers of his neighbours, who he did nominate; and all of them dyed the yeare following; and Vicars himself (being asleep) his phantome was seen of him also, and dyed with ye rest.

This sight made Hallywell so agast that he looks like a ghoast ever since. The lord Sheffield (hearing this relation) sent for Hallywell to receive account of it. The fellow fearing my Lord would cause him to watch the church porch againe he hid himself in the Carrs till he was almost starved. The number of those that died (whose phantomes Hallywell saw) was as I take it about fower score.

Thos. Cod, Rector Ecclie. de Laceby.
Bottesford Moors. Edward Peacock, IV, p. 470.
MOTIFS: D.1825.6.1* [*Watching at the church door at midnight on St Mark's Eve, etc.*] (Baughman); D.1825.6.2*(c) [*The watcher does not see his own spirit if he is to die within the year. He goes to sleep during that part of the procession in which his spirit appears*] (Baughman).
¶ See "St Mark's Vigil", "Midsummer Eve".

THE CURSE OF THE SHOEMAKER

Norton Collection, VI. p. XIV

"We shoemakers are a poor slobbering race, and so have been ever since the curse that Jesus Christ laid on us." "And what was that?"..."Why ...when they were carrying Him to the cross, they passed a shoemaker's bench, and the man looked up and spat at Him; and the Lord turned and said: "A poor slobbering fellow shalt thou be, and all shoemakers after thee, for what thou hast done to me."

Henderson, 2nd edition, p. 62. From a Devonshire shoemaker.
MOTIFS: Q.221.2 [*Punishment for opposition to Christ at Crucifixion*]; Q.556.1 [*Curse for participation in the Crucifixion*].
¶ Baring-Gould connects this legend with Type 777 (The Wandering Jew). The Wandering Jew, Cartaphilus or Ahasuerus, was a shoemaker and refused to allow Christ to rest on his doorstep. The punishment is, however, different. (See *Curious Myths of the Middle Ages*, pp. 14, 19, 3).
¶ See "The Wandering Jew in England".

THE DART OF DEATH

Augustus Hare, *In My Solitary Life*, p. 59.

..."I have got a story quite on my mind, and I must really tell it to you." And he said that when he got to Lymington, he found Lord Warwick* ill in bed, and he [Lord Warwick] said, "I am so glad to see you, for I want to tell you such an odd thing that has happened to me. Last night I was in bed, and the room was quite dark (this old-fashioned room of the inn at Lymington which you now see). Suddenly at the foot of the

* George Guy Greville, 4th Earl of Warwick.

bed there appeared a great light, and in the midst of the light the figure of Death just as it is seen in the Dance of Death and other old pictures— a ghastly skeleton with a scythe and a dart; and Death balanced the dart, and it flew past me, just above my shoulder, close to my head, and it seemed to go into the wall; and then the light went out and the figure vanished.

"I was as wide awake then as I am now, for I pinched myself hard to see, and I lay awake for a long time, but at last I fell asleep. When my servant came to call me in the morning, he had a very scared expression of face, and he said, 'A dreadful thing has happened in the night, and the whole household of the inn is in the greatest confusion and grief, for the landlady's daughter, who slept in the next room, and the head of whose bed is against the wall against which your head now rests, has been found dead in her bed'."

Told by Lady Waterford, who heard it from her cousin Charles, 3rd Earl of Somers, who is the narrator.

MOTIFS: D.1825.1 [*Second sight*]; z.111 [*Death personified*]; D.1825.3.1 [*Magic power of seeing death at head or foot of bed*].

OF A DEAD MAN WHO WAS RESTORED TO LIFE FROM THE PAINS OF PURGATORY

Roger of Wendover, *Chronicle*, 1, p. 120.

A certain head of a family in the country of the Northumbrians, was seized with severe bodily illness, and died in the early part of the night; but in the early dawn he revived, and of a sudden sat up, at which all who were weeping around his body fled in consternation. His wife, however, who loved him best, remained, though greatly terrified. Consoling her, he said, "Be not afraid, for in very deed I am risen from the dead, and permitted to live again among men."

Then rising immediately, he repaired to the oratory of the little town, where he remained in prayer until day, and then, dividing all his substance into three portions, he gave one to his wife, another to his children, and, reserving the third to himself, he distributed it forthwith among the poor; and not long after, he freed himself entirely from worldly cares, and received the tonsure in the monastery of Mailros.

After entering the monastery, he made the following narration to the abbat and brethren of the fearful sights he had seen: "I was led by a person of a shining countenance and in bright apparel, and we walked on in silence, as it seemed to me, towards the rising of the sun in summer, until we came to a valley of immense breadth and depth, and of infinite length; on the left side were scorching flames, while the other was no less intolerable by reason of a chilling storm of hail and snow; each was full of human souls, which seemed to be tossed from one side to the other, as if by a violent storm; for when the wretches could not endure the force of the heat, they leaped into the midst of the cutting cold; and finding no rest there, they leaped back again into the midst of the unquenchable flames—a miserable alternation of suffering without any interval of rest; and there was an innumerable multitude of ill-looking spirits. I began to think within myself that this was the infernal place of whose intolerable torments I had so often heard tell; on which my guide, who was going before me, replied to my inward thought, and said, 'Do not think so.'

"When he had conducted me, much frightened at so horrid a sight, to the other end, on a sudden I saw the whole region before us begin to grow dusk, and filled with darkness, which, as we entered became so dense that besides it I could see nothing but the shape and dress of him who went before me. And as we went on through the gloom, on a sudden there appeared before us frequent globes of murky flames, rising as it were, out of a great pit, and falling back into the same. When I was conducted thus far, my guide suddenly disappeared, leaving me alone in the midst of darkness and of this horrid vision. As those globes of fire continued, without any intermission, now to rise on high and then to sink to the bottom of the abyss, I observed that the wreaths of flame, as they ascended, were full of human spirits, which, like embers flying up with smoke, were now thrown on high, and then dropped down into the depths below with the retiring vapours of the fire.

"An intolerable stench, too, came forth with these vapours, poisoning all those regions of darkness. When I had stood there a long time in much dread, and not knowing what to do, all at once I heard behind me the sound of wretched lamentation, and the laughter of insulting demons, which became plainer as it approached me; when I observed a gang of malignant spirits, with much exultation dragging the howling and lamenting souls of men into the midst of that darkness; after which I could not clearly distinguish the lamentation of the men from the laughter of the devils, but had a confused sound of both in my ears. Meanwhile, certain of those dark spirits, ascending from the fiery abyss, ran and surrounded me, glaring on me with their eyes of flame, and distressing me much with the stinking fire which they breathed from their mouths and nostrils, and endeavouring to seize me with the fiery tongs which they held in their hands, yet they did not dare to touch me, though they terrified me much. Being thus on all sides enclosed with enemies and darkness, and looking about on every side for succour, there appeared behind me, in the direction I had come, as it were, a bright star shining through the darkness, which increased by degrees, and came rapidly towards me;

when it drew near, all those evil spirits that would have carried me away with their tongs, dispersed and fled.

"Now he, whose approach put them to flight, was the same who conducted me before; and then turning to the right, he proceeded to lead me towards the quarter of the sun's rising in winter, and soon brought me out of the darkness into an atmosphere of clear light. While he was thus leading me, I saw before us a vast wall, whose height and length appeared to be boundless. I began to wonder why we approached the wall, since there was no apparent way of climbing it. When we were come to the wall, we were presently, I know not by what means, on the top of it, where was a spacious and delightful plain, full of vernal flowers of such fragrance that the wonderful sweetness of their odour immediately dispelled the stink of the dark furnace, which had penetrated my very soul. The entire region was illuminated with such a light, that it seemed to exceed the full splendour of the day, or the beams of the meridian sun; for there were in this plain innumerable companies of men in white, and of souls seated together rejoicing.

"As he led me through bands of happy inhabitants, I thought that this was the Kingdom of Heaven, but he answered my thoughts, and said, 'Do not think so.' When we had passed these mansions of good and happy spirits, and were going further on, I beheld before us a much more glorious light than the former, and therein heard the sweetest voices of persons singing, and so wonderful a fragrance proceeding from the place, that the other, which I had before thought most delicious, now seemed to me but very indifferent; even as that extraordinary brightness of the flowery plain, compared with this, appeared weak and inconsiderable. As I was hoping that we should enter that delightful place, my guide, on a sudden stood still; and then turning round, led me back by the way we had come.

"He then said to me, 'Dost thou know what all these things are which thou hast seen?' I answered, I did not; on which he said, 'That fearful valley which thou sawest, with its consuming flames and cutting cold, is the place where the souls of those are tried who, delaying confession and amendment of life, at length have recourse to repentance when on the point of death, and so departing from the body, they shall all attain to the kingdom of heaven in the day of judgment; numbers too shall be delivered before the day of judgment, by the prayers, alms, and fasting of the living, and especially by the celebration of masses. The fiery and stinking pit, which thou sawest, is the mouth of hell, into which whosoever falls shall never be delivered. The flowery region, in which thou sawest those beautiful young people, so bright and gay, is that into which the souls of those are received who depart from the body in good works, but who, nevertheless, are not so perfect as to be worthy of an immediate entrance into the kingdom of heaven; yet they shall all, at the day of judgment, be admitted to the vision of God, and the joys of the heavenly kingdom; but those who are entirely perfect, in thought, word and deed, enter into the kingdom of heaven immediately on their departure from the body; in the neighbourhood whereof is the place where thou heardest the sound of sweet singing, with the fragrant odour and bright light. As for thee, thou must return to the body and live again among men; and if thou art careful nicely to examine thine actions, and to maintain thy speech and behaviour in uprightness and simplicity, thou shalt have a place among the happy companies of good spirits which thou sawest; for when I left thee for a time, it was to know how thou wast to be disposed of.'

"When he had said this to me, I greatly abhorred returning to my body, being delighted with the sweetness and beauty of the place I had seen, and with the company of those I saw in it; but in the meanwhile, on a sudden, I know not in what way, I found myself alive among men."

For the rest, there was a stream in the neighbourhood of his cell, and in his great desire to chasten his body, he would frequently get in, and there remain as long as he could endure it, singing psalms and praying, standing up to his middle in the water, and sometimes up to his neck; and, when he came out, he could never take off his clothes until they were dried by the warmth of his body. And in winter time, when the pieces of ice were floating around him, those who saw it would say, "I wonder, brother Drithelm, that you can endure such excessive cold"; to which he would simply answer, "I have seen greater cold." And when they said, "It is wonderful that you endure such rigorous austerity," he would reply, "I have seen greater austerity." Thus he continued, through an irrepressible desire of heavenly bliss, to subdue his aged body with daily fasting, till the day when he was called away; and he forwarded the salvation of many by his works as well as by his example.

MOTIFS: E.721 [*Soul journeys from the body*]; E.721.7 [*Soul leaves body to visit hell and Heaven, Purgatory and Paradise*]; E.177 [*Resuscitated man relates visions of beyond*]; V.462.0.3 [*Husband abandons wife to become ascetic*]; V.462.8 [*Ascetic immersion*].

¶ The careful distinctions made between Purgatory and Hell, Paradise and Heaven, show a strong clerical influence here.

A similar experience of a death-trance and awakening is vividly described in *Lady Fanshawe's Memoirs*, as having happened in her infancy to her mother.

See "A Dream of Heaven".

THE DEATH OF DR HARRIS

The Gentleman's Magazine Library, 1885, p. 191.

Having heard a report of the appearance of an apparition a little before Dr Harris's* death, I went on Monday the 14th of this instant, to see my cousin, Ann G., who had been at Mr Godfrey's, at Norton Court, in Kent, some time before, and was there when the Doctor died at his house, and from her I had the following account:

On Monday evening, the 31st of August last, Mr Godfrey sent out his coachman and gardener to catch some rabbits. After their sport was over, as they were coming home with their nets, and what they had taken, and were now not above a field's length from the house, the dogs, who had been running about, came suddenly to them, creeping between their legs as if it were to hide themselves. The fellows immediately took to their heels as fast as they could, not staying till they came within the gate, where they stopped, and accosted one another in the following fashion:

A: "Are you not prodigiously frightened?"
B: "I was never so frightened in all my life!"
A: "What was it you saw?"
B: "Nay, what was it that frightened you so?"
A: "I saw a coffin carried, just by us, on men's shoulders."
B: "I saw the same, as plain as ever I saw anything in my life."

My cousin G. and Mrs Betty H. were gone to bed together; Dr Harris was in bed, and Mr Godfrey in his chamber, just going to bed. A maid-servant, who had heard the two men speak of this in the kitchen, ran up directly, and told Mr Godfrey. He laughed at it; and, desirous to let others partake with him in his mirth, goes into my cousin's chamber, and calling them, tells them, "his men had seen the devil tonight!"

She made answer that "she desired him not to tell them of it then, nor come into their room to disturb them at so unseasonable an hour, when they were just going to sleep; that such a story would, however, serve well enough to divert Dr Harris"—who, by the way, had often expressed a disbelief in such things.

Mr Godfrey went immediately to the Doctor's chamber, and, waking him out of a sound sleep, told him what had passed. The Doctor laughed very heartily at it, but was vexed Mr G. had waked him. The next day the discourse of it served for the entertainment of the family, the Doctor saying, "It was only a tale of the men's devising, in order to frighten the maids, but that in reality they saw nothing." Others thought that, by the strength of imagination, they might take a black horse or a black cow

* Prebendary of Rochester and author of *A History of Kent.*

for a corpse on men's shoulders. Their fellow-servants, however, declared that "when they came in, they both looked as if they had been frightened out of their wits".

At the eating of the rabbits, the subject was resumed, and the Doctor in particular said that "if the Devil had a hand in catching them, he was sure they were good", and ate very heartily. He complained a little on Tuesday, and on Wednesday more, but was very unwilling to have any advice. However, an apothecary was sent for, and afterwards Sir William Boys, of Canterbury; from which time he grew very bad, the distemper lying so much in his head as caused him to be delirious the greatest part of the time he lived, which was till Monday the 7th instant, eleven in the forenoon.

From a memorandum taken the 17th of September by Mr J. B.
MOTIF: D.1825.7.1 [*Persons see phantom funeral procession some time before actual procession takes place*].
¶ See "Dr Harris's Dream".

THE DEATH FETCH OF WILLIAM RUFUS

Hunt, *Popular Romances of the West of England*, p. 373.

Robert, Earl of Moreton, in Normandy—who always carried the standard of St Michael before him in battle—was made Earl of Cornwall by William the Conqueror. He was remarkable for his valour and for his virtue, for the exercise of his power, and his benevolence to the priests. This was the Earl of Cornwall who gave the Mount in Cornwall to the monks of Mont St Michel in Normandy. He seized upon the priory of St Petroc at Bodmin and converted all the lands to his own use.

This Earl of Cornwall was an especial friend of William Rufus. It happened that Robert, the Earl, was hunting in the extensive woods around Bodmin—of which some remains are still to be found in the Glyn Valley. The chase had been a severe one; a fine old red deer had baffled the huntsmen, and they were dispersed through the intricacies of the forest, the Earl of Cornwall being left alone.

He advanced beyond the shades of the woods on to the moors above them, and he was surprised to see a very large black goat advancing over the plain. As it approached him, which it did rapidly, he saw that it bore on its back "King Rufus", all black and naked, and wounded through in the midst of his breast. Robert adjured the goat in the name of the Holy Trinity, to tell what it was he carried so strangely. He answered, "I am carrying your king to judgment; yea, that tyrant William Rufus, for I am an evil spirit, and the revenger of his malice which he bore to the Church of God. It was I that did cause this slaughter; the protomartyr of England,

St Albyn, commanding me so to do, who complained to God of him, for his grievous oppression in this Isle of Britain, which he first hallowed." Having so spoken, the spectre vanished. Robert, the Earl, related the circumstances to his followers, and they shortly after learned that at that very hour William Rufus had been slain in the New Forest by the arrow of Walter Tirell.

MOTIFS: E.723.6 [*Appearance of his wraith as announcement of person's death*]; E.752.2 [*Soul carried off by demon*]; G.303.3.3.1.6 [*Devil in form of goat*].
¶ There were many traditions about the death of William Rufus. This one is probably clerical in its origin, for there was a strong clerical bias against William Rufus. See "The Red King's Deer".

THE DEATH GLEAM

S. Baring-Gould, *A Book of Folk-Lore*, p. 25.

A servant in the family of Lady Davis...had occasion to start early for market. Being in the kitchen at 3 a.m., taking his breakfast when everyone else was in bed, he was surprised by the sound of feet trampling down the stairs; and opening the door, he saw a light. He was frightened and rushed out of the house, and presently saw a gleam pass out of the door, and proceed towards the churchyard.

As Lady Davis was ill at the time, he made no doubt that her death impended; and when he returned from market his first question was whether she were still alive; and though he was informed she was better, he declared his conviction that she would die, and described what he had seen and heard. The lady, however, recovered; but within a fortnight another member of the family died, and her coffin was conveyed by bearers down the stairs. One curious feature in the story is that the man had described how he had heard the sound of a bump against the clock on the stairs; and actually, as the coffin was being taken down, the bearers ran violently against the clock-case.

MOTIFS: D.1827.1.2 [*Sounds heard before death; the sounds are later repeated in connection with the funeral*]; E.530.1.6 [*Ghost light serves as death omen*].
¶ See "The Corpse Light".

A DEATH WARNING

Ruth L. Tongue, *Somerset Folklore*, p. 94.

Very late one night a workman called Marrish was on his way home down Tower Lane. As he came near to the church, he saw that it was fully litten up. It was too late for any service, and so, fearing that evil-doers were robbing the parish box, he turned aside and hammered on the sexton's door. It took some time to rouse the sexton, and longer for him to dress and get the keys. When they reached the church, all was silent and dark. Nothing had been disturbed. A few nights later Marrish died suddenly at the very hour at which he had seen the strange light.

Oral collection, 1909.
MOTIF: E.530.1.6 [*Ghost light serves as death omen*].
¶ In the same way Roslin Chapel in Midlothian is said to be lit up before the death of any of the St Clares.
See "The Corpse Light".

THE DOCTOR'S FETCH

T. F. Thistleton Dyer, *The Ghost World*, pp. 377–80.

In one of our Irish cities, and in a room where the mild moonbeams were resting on the carpet and on a table near the window, Mrs B., wife of a doctor in good practice and general esteem, looking towards the window from her pillow, was startled by the appearance of her husband standing near the table just mentioned, and seeming to look with attention on the book which was lying open on it.

Now, the living and breathing man was by her side, apparently asleep, and greatly as she was surprised and affected, she had sufficient command of herself to remain without moving, lest she should expose him to the terror which she herself at the moment experienced.

After gazing on the apparition for a few seconds, she bent her eyes upon her husband to ascertain if his looks were turned in the direction of the window, but his eyes were closed. She turned round again, although dreading the sight of what she believed to be her husband's fetch, but it was no longer there. She remained sleepless throughout the remainder of the night, but still bravely refrained from disturbing her partner.

Next morning, Dr B., seeing signs of disquiet on his wife's countenance while at breakfast, made some affectionate inquiries, but she concealed her trouble, and at his ordinary hour he sallied forth to make his calls. Meeting Dr C. in the street, and falling into conversation with him, he asked his opinion on the subject of fetches. "I think," was the answer, "and so I am sure do you, that they are mere illusions produced by a disturbed stomach acting upon the excited brain of a highly imaginative or superstitious person." "Then," said Dr B., "I am highly imaginative or superstitious, for I distinctly saw my own outward man last night standing at the table in the bedroom, and clearly distinguishable in the moonlight. I am afraid my wife saw it too, but I have been afraid to speak to her on the subject."

About the same hour on the ensuing night the poor lady was again aroused, but by a more painful circumstance. She felt her husband moving convulsively, and immediately afterwards he cried to her in low, interrupted accents, "Ellen, my dear, I am suffocating; send for Dr C." She sprang up, huddled on some clothes, and ran to his house.

He came with all speed, but his efforts for his friend were useless. He had burst a large blood-vessel in the lungs, and was soon beyond human aid.

In her lamentations the bereaved wife frequently cried out, "Oh! the fetch, the fetch!" and at a later period told the doctor of the appearance the night before her husband's death.

From Patrick Kennedy, *Legendary Fictions of the Irish Celt.*
MOTIFS: E.723 [*Wraiths of persons separate from body*]; E.723.1 [*Person sees his own wraith*]; E.723.2 [*Seeing one's wraith a sign that person is to die shortly*].
¶ This is a complex story, for the doctor sees his own wraith, his wife sees his wraith, and sees him in bed at the same time.
See "An Apparition at Oxford", "The Anxious Subaltern".

DR HARRIS'S DREAM

The Gentleman's Magazine Library, 1885, p. 193.

My cousin A. G. told me at the same time another remarkable circumstance.

It had, it seems, frequently been the practice with one or other of them to tell their dreams in the morning over the tea table. It happened either on Tuesday or Wednesday, that somebody began that subject, whereupon the Doctor said he thought they were always recounting their dreams, and talking of apparitions, and that he would make a collection of them, and have them published "For my part," added he, "if I ever took notice of a dream, it should be of one I had last night. I dreamed that the Bishop of —— in Ireland sent for me to come over to him, and I returned answer that I could not—for I was dead; when methought I laid my hands along by my sides, and so died."

The Doctor's death, and these circumstances attending it, so affected my cousin G., that she resolved to leave the house, and accordingly came away the next morning.

J. B. (Continuation of "The Death of Dr Harris".)
MOTIF: D.1812.5.1.2 [*Bad dream as evil omen*].
¶ See "The Death of Dr Harris".

A DREAM OF HEAVEN

Addy, *Household Tales*, p. 14. From Eckington, Derbyshire.

A girl called Ann Brown who had been very ill, fell into a trance, and it was believed she was dead. When her body had been laid out for ten hours, her mother went into the room where she lay to kiss her, and thought that she felt her daughter's breath warm upon her cheek. Then she fetched the clergyman, and he took a small piece of looking-glass, and held it over her mouth to see whether it was steamed by her breath. In this way he found that the girl lived. So he called all the family into the room, and told them to stand round the bed. He sat at the head of the bed, and took one of the girl's hands into his own, and after a while she opened her eyes, and gave three groans.

Then the clergyman said to her, "Now tell us where you have been."

So after a while the girl opened her eyes and said: "I have been all the way to Heaven, and the first to meet me was the Devil, who held in his hand a black book, and the letters in it were written in crimson. The Devil asked me to write my name in the book, and follow him. But I said, 'Get thee hence, Satan,' and went further on my way. Next I saw an angel dressed in pure white, who took my hand, and led me on a path as soft as down and as white as snow, until we came to the gate of Heaven. And over the gate was written 'Behold the Lamb'. As we came near to the gate it flew open, and the Lord came out and took me in. Then the Lord led me to a place which was full of girls like myself, and after that he took me into another place which was full of soldiers that had spears and bayonets, and the bayonets had seals on them.

"After this another angel came and took me away from the Lord, and led me into another place, which was full of infants singing. I saw the throne of God, which was all bright and shining, but they would not let me see God himself. After I had seen the throne, the Lord came to me again, and took my hand and said, 'It is God's wish that you go back to the earth for a little while longer.' Then I said to the Lord, 'Let me stay here.' But the Lord answered, 'You have served me faithfully from a child, and it is my desire that you go back to the world.'"

MOTIFS: E.177 [*Resuscitated man relates vision of beyond*]; E.721.7 [*Soul leaves body to visit Heaven*].

¶ It is interesting to compare this version with that related by Roger of Wendover in the account "Of a Dead Man Restored to Life". The theological background is markedly different.

THE DREAM HOUSE

Augustus Hare, *In My Solitary Life*, p. 263.

A few years ago there was a lady living in Ireland—a Mrs Butler—clever, handsome, popular, prosperous, and perfectly happy. One morning she said to her husband, and to anyone who was staying there, "Last night I had the most wonderful night. I seemed to be spending hours in the most delightful place, in the most enchanting house I ever saw—not large, you know, but just the sort of house one might live in oneself, and oh! so perfectly, so deliciously comfortable. Then there was the loveliest conservatory, and the garden was so enchanting! I wonder if anything half so perfect can really exist."

And the next morning she said, "Well, I have been to my house again. I must have been there for hours. I sat in the library; I walked on the terrace; I examined all the bedrooms; and it is simply the most perfect house in the world." So it grew to be quite a joke in the family. People would ask Mrs Butler in the beginning if she had been to her house in the night, and often she had, and always with more intense enjoyment. She would say, "I count the hours till bedtime, that I may get back to my house!" Then gradually the current of outside life flowed in, and gave a turn to their thoughts; the house ceased to be talked about.

Two years ago the Butlers grew weary of their life in Ireland. The district was wild and disturbed. The people were insolent and ungrateful. At last they said, "We are well off. We have no children. There's no reason why we should put up with this, and we'll go and live altogether in England." So they came to London, and sent for all the house agents' lists of places within forty miles of London, and many were the places they went to see. At last they heard of a house in Hampshire. They went to it by rail, and drove from the station. As they came to the lodge, Mrs Butler said, "Do you know, this is the lodge of my house." They drove down an avenue—"But this *is* my house!" she said.

When the housekeeper came, she said, "You will think it very odd, but do you mind my showing you the house? That passage leads to the library, and through that there is a conservatory, and then through a window you enter the drawing-room," etc., and it was all so. At last, in an upstairs passage, they came upon a baize door. Mrs Butler, for the first time, looked puzzled. "But that door is not in my house," she said. "I don't understand about your house, ma'am," said the housekeeper, "but that door has only been there six weeks."

Well, the house was for sale, and the price asked was very small, and they decided at once to buy it. But when it was bought and paid for, the price had been so extraordinarily small, that they could not help a misgiving that there must be something wrong with the place. So they went to the agent of the people who had sold it, and said, "Well, now the purchase is made, and the deeds are signed, *will* you mind telling us why the price asked was so small?"

The agent had started violently when they came in, but recovered himself. Then he said to Mrs Butler, "Yes; it is quite true, the matter is quite settled, so there can be no harm in telling you now. The fact is that the house has had a great reputation for being haunted, but you, madam, need be under no apprehensions, for you are yourself the ghost!" On the nights when Mrs Butler had dreamt she was the ghost, she—her "astral body"—had been seen there.

MOTIF: E.723.4 [*Wraith does what person wishes to do, but is unable to do in the flesh*].

ELIZABETH AND HEPHZIBAH

Augustus Hare, *In My Solitary Life*, pp. 19–20.

At Clifton lived a Mrs Fry with her brother-in-law, and his two daughters, Elizabeth and Hephzibah. These were persons who, like many Bristol people, had large property in the West Indies. The elder daughter, Elizabeth, had been born in the West Indies, and when she fell into bad health, her father took the opportunity of taking her back to benefit by her native air, when he went to look after his West Indian property, leaving his younger daughter, Hephzibah, with Mrs Fry.

They had not been gone long when Hephzibah took a chill, and in a very few days she died. Mr Harrison* attended her. Some days after he called as a friend upon Mrs Fry, when she said, "I want to tell you something which has happened to me: I have seen Elizabeth." "Impossible," said Mr Harrison. "No," she said; "it was so. I was sitting reading the Bible when I fell into a state which was neither sleeping nor waking, and in that state—I was not asleep—I saw Elizabeth standing by me. I spoke to her, and, forgetting what had happened in my surprise, I told her to call her sister. But she said to me that she had seen her sister already, and that she was in a box, and had a great deal of sewing about her chest. She especially used the word 'sewing'; then she vanished away, and the place in the Bible where I had left off was changed; someone had turned it over." Mr Harrison noted all this.

Some time after came a letter from the father to Mrs Fry, written before he had heard of Hephzibah's death. After speaking of other matters, he said: "I must now tell you of a very curious circumstance which has occurred, and which is much on my mind. The other day Elizabeth, who has been much better, and who is now nearly well, surprised us by falling

* The second medical authority in Bristol, who told the story.

into a stupor, and when she came to herself, she would insist upon it that she had been to Clifton, and that she had seen you and Hephzibah, and that Hephzibah was in a long box, with a great deal of sewing upon her chest; and she says so still." The dates were precisely the same.

Hephzibah's death was so sudden that there was a post-mortem examination, though it was not considered necessary to distress Mrs Fry by telling her of it. On this occasion, Mr Harrison was unable to be present. He went afterwards to the student of the hospital who was there, and who remembered all about it, and he said—what Mr Harrison had not previously known—that after the examination the body was sewn up, with a great deal of sewing upon the chest.

MOTIFS: E.723.6.1*(d) [*Wraith appears to person in parlour of house*] (Baughman); E.723.4.6 [*Wraith investigates welfare of absent person*].
¶ See "A Strange Visitant".

EPWORTH PARSONAGE

T. F. Thistleton Dyer, *The Ghost World*, p. 430. (Old Jeffrey).

One of the most eccentric instances of spiritual antics was the noises said to have been heard at Epworth Parsonage in the time of the Rev. Samuel Wesley, these sounds having consisted of "knockings" and "groanings", of "footsteps", and "rustling of silk trailing along", "clattering of the iron casement", and "clattering of the warming-pan", and all sorts of frightful noises, which frightened even a big dog, a large mastiff, who used, at first, when he heard the noises, "to bark, and leap, and snap on one side and the other, and that frequently before anyone in the room heard the noises at all, but after two or three days he used to creep away before the noises began, and by this the family knew it was at hand". Mr Wesley at one time thought it was rats, and sent for a horn to blow them away. But this made matters worse, for after the horn was blown the noise came in the daytime as well. Some of the Wesley family believed it to be supernatural hauntings, and explained the cause of it thus; at morning and evening prayers, "when the Rev. Samuel Wesley commenced prayer for the king, a knocking began all round the room, and a thundering knock attended the *Amen*".

Mr Wesley observed that his wife did not say "*Amen*" to the prayer for the king, but Mrs Wesley added that she could not, for she did not believe that the Prince of Orange was king.

MOTIFS: F.473 [*Poltergeist*]; F.473.1 [*Poltergeist throws objects*]; F.473.2 [*Poltergeist causes objects to behave contrary to their nature*]; F.473.3(e) [*Spirit pushes man violently from behind*] (Baughman); F.473.5(a) [*Knockings and rappings that cannot be traced*] (Baughman).

¶ The Wesleys' "Old Jeffrey" is the most famous of all our poltergeists, even surpassing the Demon Drummer of Tedworth. There has been much speculation about it; Andrew Lang, among other people, wrote fully on the subject. It has been suggested that the manifestations were faked by Hester Wesley, but there seems little doubt that they were genuine. There seems no real difference between a boggart and a poltergeist in behaviour.

THE ESCAPING SOUL: I

Norton Collection, VI. p. XXVI.

I remember some forty years ago, hearing a servant from Lincolnshire relate a story of two travellers who laid down by the roadside to rest, and one fell asleep. The other seeing a bee settle on a neighbouring wall, and go into a little hole, put the end of his staff in the hole, and so imprisoned the bee.

Wishing to pursue his journey, he endeavoured to awaken his companion, but was unable to do so, till, resuming his stick, the bee flew out to the sleeping man, and went into his ear. His companion then awoke him, remarking how soundly he had been sleeping, and asked what he had been dreaming of.

"Oh," said he, "I dreamed that you shut me up in a dark cave, and I could not awake till you let me out." The person who told me this story firmly believed that the man's soul was in the bee.

Choice Notes from "Notes and Queries", p. 269. From *F.S.*, III, p. 206.

THE ESCAPING SOUL: II

Norton Collection, VI. p. XXVII.

Two labouring men . . . after their *al fresco* dinner, sat down beside a pond. One dropped off to sleep, and the other noticed a butterfly flitting over the surface of the water, and at times touching it. Whenever the butterfly touched the water, the sleeping man was observed to start. On waking, he said that he had had a fearful dream—that someone had been trying to drown him, and that he was most thankful to awake.

From an old man and his wife at Worle, Somerset. *Notes and Queries for Somerset and Dorset*, III, Sherborne, 1893, pp. 235–6. The correspondent adds "That the man's soul was in the butterfly, my informants had no doubt. They were also firmly of the opinion that the extreme difficulty sometimes experienced in waking, was to be ascribed to the fact that the soul was absent, and that it was impossible to rouse the sleeper until such time as she had winged her flight homeward to 'her mansion in this fleshly nook', at any rate that the attempt to do so might be fraught with some danger to the sleeper".

TYPE ML.4000 I. MOTIFS: E.734.2 [*Soul in form of bee*]; E.721.1 [*Soul wanders from body in sleep*]; E.721.1.2.4 [*Soul of sleeper prevented from returning to his body when soul as bee enters hole in wall beside which he is sleeping*].

II. MOTIFS: E.734.1 [*Soul in form of a butterfly*]; E.721.1.1 [*Sleeper not to be wakened, since soul is absent*].

¶ There are many legends of the separable wandering soul. One from Saxo Grammaticus is retold by many of the seventeenth-century writers.

See the notes on "The Separable Soul" attached to "The Soul as a Bumble Bee".

THE FAITHFUL DOG

Ruth L. Tongue, *Somerset Folklore*, pp. 52–3.

A wretched old pauper died, and was buried on the North side of the Church, and nobody mourned for him but his half-starved and ill-treated dog. He laid himself down on the grave all that day and all that night and howled, and presently the town began to make out the words of his lament.

> "I'll lie on my master's grave
> For lo-o-o-ve, for lo-o-o-ve.
> Because he was all I did ha-a-a-ve,
> Because I was all he did ha-a-a-ve
> To lo-o-o-ve, to lo-o-o-ve."

As the night went on the howls grew fainter, and in the morning the sexton found the dog dead, and, being a Christian soul, he buried it beside its master and told no-one. So that church has two church Grims to guard it now, and no devils will come within miles of it.

MOTIFS: B.211.1.7 [*Speaking dog*]; B.301.1 [*Faithful animal at master's grave dies of hunger*].

¶ See "The Policeman and the Gibbet's Offspring" (B, IX).

THE FETCH

S. Baring-Gould, *A Book of Folk-Lore*, pp. 170–1.

A Mr Macnish. . . tells the following story: "Mr H. was one day walking along the street, apparently in good health, when he saw, or supposed he saw, his acquaintance, Mr C., walking before him. He called to him aloud but he did not seem to hear him, and continued walking on. Mr H. then quickened his pace for the purpose of overtaking him, but the other increased his also, as if to keep ahead of his pursuer, and proceeded at such a rate that Mr H. found it impossible to make up to him.

"This continued for some time, till, on Mr C. reaching a gate, he opened it and passed in, slamming it violently in Mr. H.'s face. Confounded at such treatment from a friend, the latter instantly opened the gate, and looked down the long lane into which it led, where, to his astonishment, no one was to be seen. Determined to unravel the mystery, he then went to Mr C.'s house, and his surprise was great to hear that he was confined to his bed, and had been so for several days.

"A week or two afterwards these gentlemen met at the house of a mutual friend, when Mr H. related the circumstances, jocularly telling Mr C. that, as he had seen his wraith, he of course could not live long. The person addressed laughed heartily, as did the rest of the party; but in a few days Mr C. was attacked with putrid sore throat, and died; and within a short period of his death Mr H. was also in his grave."

MOTIFS: E.723.8 [*Appearance of wraith as calamity omen*]; E.723.2 [*Seeing one's wraith a sign that person is to die shortly*]; E.723.6.2(d)* [*Wraith appears on road*] (Baughman); E.723.7.4 [*Wraith slams gate*].
¶ This was a particularly lethal wraith, for both the people concerned died.
See "The Death of Dr Harris", "Apparition at Oxford".

THE FISHERMAN'S WIFE AND HER BALL OF WOOL [summary]

R. Blakeborough, *Wit, Character, Folk-Lore and Customs of the North Riding of Yorkshire*, pp. 147–9.

A young fisherman, on a visit to some relations inland, fell in love with a girl whom he afterwards took home as his bride. Being strange to the sea and its ways, the girl used to laugh at all the superstitions and beliefs of the sailor folk; and one night, when her husband was away on a voyage, the wife of another fisherman looked in, and found her spinning, and just on the point of winding some wool into a ball. She implored her to stop and several more of the women of the village, who had come in to see her, begged her, in vain, to lay the work aside.

But she laughed at them all, and hung her wool over the back of a chair, and began to wind, inviting them all to stay and watch her. But they were far too much afraid, and ran from the cottage in horror. She wound on, and three times the ball of wool slipped from her hand. Next day the other women asked her how she had fared, and when she told them, they shook their heads, and said it was an evil omen.

Even when the woman's husband returned safely from his voyage, they still said that, as the ball had slipped out of her hand three times, he might return twice in safety, but the third time would be his last voyage.

The young woman told her husband the story, and his face grew pale.

He had been brought up in the same beliefs, and he swore he would make no third voyage. So, after one more safe return, the two set up a small shop in the village, and began to prosper. But three or four years later, a great storm arose; the lifeboat was launched, and the young husband was one of those who volunteered to man it.

Just as he was dragging the last survivor into the boat, a great wave washed him over the side, and he was drowned. Next morning his body was washed ashore. It was duly buried, and all the neighbours showed great kindness to the unhappy widow. But she, overcome with a terrible sense of guilt, believing that she herself had brought about her husband's death, closed their little shop and fled from the village, and was not seen there again.

MOTIFS: C.832 [*Tabu: spinning*]; C.923 [*Death by drowning for breaking tabu*].

¶ The tabu in this case, however, was not against spinning itself, but against winding the wool spun.

THE FIVE WHITE PEBBLES

Gutch, *County Folk-Lore*, II, *North Riding of Yorkshire*, p. 40.

If legends deceive not, anyone who came and threw five white pebbles into a certain part of the Ouse as the hour of one struck on the first morning of May, would then see everything he desired to see, past, present, and to come, on the surface of the water.

Once a knight returning from the wars desired to see how it fared with his lady-love; he threw in the pebbles, and beheld the home of the maiden, a mansion near Scarborough, and a youth wearing a mask and cloak descending from her window, and the hiding of the ladder by the serving-man. Maddened by jealousy, he mounted and rode with speed; his horse dropped dead in the sight of the house; he saw the same youth ascending the ladder, rushed forward and stabbed him to the heart.

It was his betrothed. She was not faithless; still loved her knight, and had only been to a masquerade. For many a day thereafter did the knight's anguish and remorse appear as the punishment of unlawful curiosity in the minstrel's lay and gestour's romance.

W. White, *A Month in Yorkshire*, p. 318.

MOTIFS: D.1273.1.2.1 [*Five as magic number*]; D.926 [*Magic well*]; D.1323.12.1 [*Clairvoyant spring*]; N.340 [*Hasty killing or condemnation: mistake*].

THE FOUR-LEAVED CLOVER

Scott, *Minstrelsy of the Scottish Border*, IV, p. 77.

I remember to have heard (certainly very long ago, for at that time I believed the legend) that a gypsy exercised his *glamour* over a number of people at Haddington, to whom he exhibited a common dung-hill cock, trailing what appeared to the spectators a massy oaken trunk. An old man passed with a cart of clover; he stopped and picked out a four-leaved blade; the eyes of the spectators were opened, and the oaken trunk appeared to be a bulrush.

MOTIFS: D.965.7 [*Magic four-leaf clover*]; D.1323.14 [*Four-leaf clover gives clairvoyance*].
¶ This story is a popular one among the writers of the seventeenth-century, Burton, Heywood, etc.
See "The Four-leafed Clover" (B, V).

THE GHOST THAT DANCED AT JETHART
[summary]

Douglas, *Scottish Fairy and Folk-Tales*, p. 87.

In the year 1285, Scotland, under Alexander III, was at peace, and the king appointed a great pageant to be held at Jedburgh Abbey in celebration of his marriage to Yolande, daughter of the Count de Dreux. A banquet was held in the great hall of the Abbey, and in the midst of the great ball which followed, a spectre, in the form of a skeleton, suddenly appeared, and joined in the dance.

The music ceased, and the masked dancers fled in horror; but, as suddenly as it had come, the spectre disappeared.

Not long afterwards, the king died as the result of a fall from his horse, and Scotland soon returned to its customary warlike condition; this naturally was held to have been foreshown by the dreadful apparition at the marriage feast.

From *The Border Counties' Magazine*.
MOTIFS: D.1812.5.1.17 [*Spectre as evil omen*]; Z.111 [*Death personified*].
¶ See "The Dart of Death".

THE GOBLIN OF LOCH SLIN [summary]

Hugh Miller, *Scenes and Legends of the North of Scotland*, pp. 299–304.

Near the old Abbey of Fearn, famous for its Abbot, the first Protestant martyr, Patrick Hamilton, there stood, more than ninety years ago, a little turf cottage, where lived a poor widow and her daughter.

This woman's mind had been tragically unhinged, about ten years before, by the shock of seeing her husband's dead body carried to her door from the field where he had suddenly died. She wandered like an automaton about her cottage, performing such small tasks as she could, while her little daughter was growing up. The farm passed into the hands of a relation, a hard man, who grew richer as they grew poorer.

When the daughter was seventeen, in 1742, she left her mother in the care of a neighbour, and hired herself as a reaper to a farmer in the neighbouring parish of Tarbat. Her youth and pretty looks, and quiet manners, made her many friends, and at the end of the harvest, she set out for home, proud of her earnings, and full of hope and happiness. Her path wound along the southern bank of Loch Slin. A tall old castle, much worn and ruined by the weather, was reflected in its waters, and as she passed it, the girl heard a continuous knocking which on a week-day she would have taken for the sound of the knocking of clothes at a washing. But this was the Sabbath, yet, at an angle in the bank, not ten yards from her, she suddenly saw a tall female figure, beautiful and yet terrifying, which seemed to be knocking clothes on a stone with a bludgeon such as is still used in the north country. It worked with a malignant pleasure, and on the grass before it lay thirty or more smocks and shirts, all horribly dabbled with blood.

The girl fled in terror, but when she entered her mother's cottage, she fell senseless to the ground. She recovered, however, and as there was no one at hand to whom she could recount her strange experience, she took her mother by the hand, to escape from the gloom of the cottage, and walked with her into the fields in the sunshine. As they drew near the old Abbey, they heard the sound of a psalm from the congregation inside; but suddenly, with a crash like the shock of an earthquake, a dense cloud of dust rose in the air and as it slowly cleared away, it was seen that the roof of the Abbey had entirely collapsed, and fallen on the people gathered to worship.

This horror restored to the poor widow the command of her faculties, and mother and daughter hastened to the place, to find any who might have survived the disaster. They first met two young women, covered in blood, and then an elderly man, badly injured, but they all begged them not to stop to aid them, but to hurry to the church itself, to rescue any they could find, who were not already slain by the ruins. As they were doing what they could among the many wounded, a young man staggered out, with a dead body on his shoulders. It was the girl's young cousin, to whom she was much attached, and the corpse was that of his father, the present owner of the farm on which their cottage stood. The two women gave him what help they could, for he himself was injured, and at last he was able to return to the cottage with them, leaning on his cousin's arm.

Thirty-six persons perished in the ruins, and many more of the injured never recovered. Then the girl remembered the strange sight she had seen on the loch, and the terrible goblin washerwoman. In due time, the young cousin recovered his strength and became her husband; and the old widow retained the faculties restored to her by this second shock. She had now to undergo the grief of realizing fully for the first time the facts of her husband's death; but the rejoicings at her daughter's marriage served to alleviate the pain; and of the ten years between the two events she retained only a dim and dreamlike recollection.

MOTIFS: M.301.6.1 [*Banshees as portents of misfortune*]; D.1812.5.1.1.6 [*Washers at the ford, etc.*]; T.211.9 [*Excessive grief at husband's death*].

¶ This is a Celtic tale, though it has come down to us from a Lowland source. "The Little Washer at the Ford" is the Highland banshee who washes the clothes of those about to die, as this did.

THE GREEN LADY OF CROMARTY [shortened]

Hugh Miller, *Scenes and Legends of the North of Scotland*, pp. 70–1.

There are a few other traditions of this northern part of the country— some of them so greatly dilapidated by the waste of years, that they exist as mere fragments—which bear the palpable impress of a pagan or semi-pagan origin. . . .

A lady dressed in green, and bearing a goblin child in her arms. . . used to wander in the night-time from cottage to cottage, when all the inhabitants were asleep. She would raise the latch, it is said, take up her place by the fire, fan the embers into a flame, and then wash her child in the blood of the youngest inmate of the cottage, who would be found dead the next morning. There was another wandering green lady, her contemporary, of exquisite beauty and a majestic carriage, who was regarded as the genius of the smallpox, and who, when the disease was to terminate fatally, would be seen in the grey of the morning, or as the evening was passing into the night, sitting by the bedside of her victim. I have heard wild stories, too, of an unearthly, squalid-looking thing, somewhat in the form of a woman, that used to enter farmhouses during the day, when all the inmates, except perhaps a solitary female, were engaged in the fields.

More than a century ago, it is said to have entered, in the time of harvest, the house of a farmer of Navity, who had lost nearly all his cattle by disease a few weeks before. The farmer's wife, the only inmate at the time, was engaged at the fireside in cooking for the reapers; the goblin squatted itself beside her, and shivering, as if with cold, raised its dingy, dirty-looking vestments over its knees. "Why, ye nasty thing," said the woman, "hae ye killed a' our cattle?" "An' why," inquired the goblin, "did the gudeman, when he last roosed them, forget to gie them his blessing?"

Fragmentary Legends of North Cromarty.
MOTIFS: F.363 [*Fairies cause death*]; akin to this belief is F.363.2 [*Redcap murders travellers; catches their blood in his cap*]; Z.112 [*Sickness personified*]; A.478.1 [*Goddess of pestilence*]; F.493.0.2 [*Pestilence in human form*].

THE GUARDIAN

Augustus Hare, *In My Solitary Life*, pp. 163–4.

July 14th. Dinner at Lady Charlemont's. Mr Synge, who declared at once his belief in ghostly apparitions, told a pretty story of a clergyman in Somersetshire, who had ridden to the bank and drawn out all the money for his poor-club, which he was taking back with him, when he became aware of another horseman riding by his side, who did not speak, and who, at a certain point of the road beyond a hollow, disappeared. In that hollow highwaymen, who knew the clergyman was coming with the money, were waiting to attack him; but they refrained, "For there are two of them," they said. It was his guardian angel.

MOTIFS: V.238 [*Guardian angel*]; V.232 [*Angel as helper*]; K.1811.4.2 [*Angel takes form of certain person*].
¶ In some forms of this story the guardian is thought to be the man's own wraith going beside him to protect him: MOTIF: E.723.1.1(a) [*Person's wraith walks with him on lonely road to protect him*] (Baughman). In other versions the guardian is a dog.
See "The Guardian Black Dog" (B, I).

THE GUARDIAN COCK [slightly shortened]

Hugh Miller, *Scenes and Legends of the North of Scotland*, pp. 73–4.

THE METEOR

In a small bay off the west coast of Cromarty, towards the end of the reign of Charles the First, a ship-master had moored his vessel while some of his men had gone ashore for the evening. He watched the lights twinkling from the scattered farms, till they all went out except one solitary lamp in the window of a cottage about two miles west of the town. At last this too disappeared, and all was dark round the bay.

Suddenly there was a hissing noise overhead; the ship-master looked up and saw a falling star slanting across the sky towards the cottage he had been watching, increasing in size and brilliancy until it lighted up the whole wooded ridge and the shore as brightly as daylight. A dog howled piteously from an outhouse, and an owl hooted from the wood. When the meteor had almost reached the roof of the cottage, a cock crowed from inside. At once the meteor stood still, rose to the height of a ship's mast, and then began to descend again.

The cock crowed a second time. The meteor rose as before, but this time much higher, and then sank in the line of the cottage. It had almost touched the roof, when a faint clapping of wings was heard over the water, followed by a still louder crow of defiance; at this, the meteor rose with a bound, flew upwards to be lost among the stars, and did not reappear.

Next night, however, the same scene was repeated—the meteor descended, the owl hooted, the cock crowed. On the following morning the ship-master visited the cottage, and, from sheer curiosity to see what would happen, purchased the cock, sailed away before nightfall, and did not return for about a month.

On his return, as soon as he came in sight of the cottage, he eagerly looked out for it; it had disappeared. On going ashore, he was told that it had been burnt to the ground on the night that he had left the bay. No one had been able to find the cause. The ship-master felt that he himself must be in some sense responsible; he therefore had the cottage rebuilt and furnished, and its story was almost forgotten, until many years later, there was dug up nearby a human skeleton, huddled up as if into a hole, with the skull and the feet close together. Then this strange story, remembered for nearly sixty years by a few of the oldest neighbours, was recalled and recorded.

MOTIFS: B.469.5 [*Helpful cock*]; E.452 [*Ghost laid at cock-crow*]; E.200 [*Malevolent return from dead*]; E.530.1.2 [*Ball of fire haunts murderer*] (possible application).
¶ There are motifs about falling stars, but none of the falling star as a vengeful ghost, which this seems to have been.
See "The Dog that disappeared" (B, IX).

THE HAIRY HANDS: I

J. R. W. Coxhead, *Legends of Devon*, p. 55.

One day in June 1921, Dr E. M. Helby, Medical Officer to the prison at Princetown, was riding on his motor-bicycle along the road which crosses Dartmoor from Two Bridges to Moretonhampstead.

In the sidecar attached to the machine there were two children. They were travelling down the slope towards the bridge which crosses the East

Dart near Postbridge, when, according to an account given by the children afterwards, the doctor suddenly shouted out: "There is something wrong. jump!"

The next moment the bicycle swerved, the engine broke away from its fastenings and the doctor was hurled from his seat into the roadway. He landed on his head with such force that he was killed instantly. Luckily, the two children were unhurt.

On August 26th, 1921, a young army officer left the house of a friend on a motor-bicycle, with the intention of visiting some people at a considerable distance. An hour later he returned to his friend's house, cut and bruised, and his bicycle badly damaged. While he was having his hurts tended, his friend asked him to describe how the accident had happened. A queer look came into the young man's eyes, and he said:

"You will find it difficult to believe, but something drove me off the road. A pair of hairy hands closed over mine—I felt them as plainly as ever I felt anything in my life—large, muscular, hairy hands. I fought against them as hard as I could, but it was no use, they were too strong for me. They forced the machine into the side of the road, and I knew no more until I came to my senses lying on my face on the turf a few feet away from the bicycle."

The spot where the accident occurred was close to the place where Dr Helby was killed earlier in the year.

In 1924, three years after the two accidents took place, a woman who is psychic saw one of the "hairy hands" about a mile west of the place where the accidents occurred. She and her husband were in a caravan near the ruins of the Powder Mills, about half a mile to the north of the road. She awoke with a start one cold moonlit night, with a strong feeling that there was something highly dangerous close at hand. The following account of her terrifying experience is taken from the *Transactions of the Devonshire Association*, Vol. 82, p. 115:

"I knew there was some power very seriously menacing us near, and I must act swiftly. As I looked up to the little window at the end of the caravan, I saw something moving, and as I stared, my heart beating fast, I saw it was the fingers and palm of a very large hand, with many hairs on the joints and the back of it, clawing up and up to the top of the window, which was a little open.

"I knew it wished to do harm to my husband sleeping below. I knew that the owner of the hand hated us, and wished us harm, and I knew it was no ordinary human hand, and that no blow or shot would have any power over it. Almost unconsciously, I made the sign of the Cross and I prayed very much that we might be kept safe from harm.

"At once the hand slowly sank down out of sight, and I knew the danger had gone. I did say a thankful prayer, and fell at once into a peaceful sleep.

"We stayed in that spot several weeks, but I never felt the evil influence again near the caravan. But I did not feel happy in some places, not far off, and would not for anything have walked alone on the moor at night or the Tor above our caravan."

The appearance, however, of the "Hairy Hands" in the neighbour-hood of Postbridge, on Dartmoor, is by no means a happening of comparatively recent occurrence. In the days of horse-drawn vehicles, the lonely road over the moor between Two Bridges and Moretonhampstead was greatly feared by benighted travellers because of the danger of a possible materialization of the dreaded spectral hands.

Details supplied by Miss Theo Brown of Heathfield House, Chudleigh, Folk-lore Recorder to the Devonshire Association.
MOTIFS: E.422.1.11.3 [*Ghost as hand or hands*]; E.272 [*Road ghosts*]; E.265.3 [*Meeting ghost causes death*]; V.86 [*The sign of the Cross*].
¶ It is uncertain whether this manifestation was caused by a devil or a ghost.

THE HAIRY HANDS: II

W. H. Barrett, *More Tales from the Fens*, p. 4.

It was reckoned that the tapping of a hammer on a coffin after dark brought the worst of bad luck because it disturbed the rest of those who'd been buried in the fen years ago. Folk round here tell how Mucky's* father was working, once, late at night because he had a coffin to finish off in a hurry. Suddenly a blast of cold wind blew out his rush-light and his hammer was knocked out of his hand and he found himself pinned by a pair of hairy hands against his bench. After that night he was never able to use his hands again, and for the rest of his life his grub had to be put into his mouth and he had to suck up his beer through a reed.

MOTIFS: C.752.1 [*Tabu: doing thing after sunset*]; E.422.1.11.3 [*Revenant as hands*].

THE HAND OF GLORY

Norton Collection, III, p. 21.

I. THE SERVANT MAID OF HIGH SPITAL

One evening, between the years 1790 and 1800, a traveller dressed in woman's clothing arrived at the Old Spital Inn, the place where the mail coach changed horses in High Spital, on Bowes Moor. The traveller begged to stay all night, but had to go away so early in the morning, that if a mouthful of food were set ready for breakfast, there was no need the

* Mucky Porter, a coffin-maker near Southery Ferry.

family should be disturbed by her departure. The people of the house, however, arranged that a servant-maid should sit up till the stranger was out of the premises, and then went to bed themselves.

The girl lay down for a nap on the long settle by the fire, but before she shut her eyes, she took a good look at the traveller, who was sitting on the opposite side of the hearth, and espied a pair of men's trousers peeping out from under the gown. All inclination for sleep was now gone; however, with great self-command, she feigned it, closed her eyes, and even began to snore.

On this, the traveller got up, pulled out of his pocket a dead man's hand, fitted a candle to it, lighted the candle, and passed hand and candle several times before the servant-girl's face, saying as he did so, "Let those who are asleep be asleep, and let those who are awake be awake." This done, he placed the light on the table, opened the outer door, went down two or three steps which led from the house to the road, and began to whistle for his companions.

The girl (who had hitherto had presence of mind to remain perfectly quiet) now jumped up, rushed behind the ruffian, and pushed him down the steps. Then she shut the door, locked it, and ran upstairs to try to wake the family, but without success; calling, shouting, and shaking were alike in vain. The poor girl was in despair, for she heard the traveller and his comrades outside the house. So she ran down and seized a bowl of blue [i.e. skimmed milk] and threw it over the hand and candle; after which she went upstairs again, and awoke the sleepers without any difficulty. The landlord's son went to the window, and asked the men outside what they wanted. They answered that if the dead man's hand were but given to them, they would go away quietly, and do no harm to anyone.

This he refused, and fired among them, and the shot must have taken effect, for in the morning stains of blood were traced to a considerable distance.

Henderson, *Folk-Lore of the Northern Counties*, p. 241–2 (1879) 1st edn pp. 202–8. Spring, 1861. Told by Bella Parkin, an old woman who was the daughter of the servant-maid. Stainmore, Westmorland.

II

Ibid. p. 242 The Baring-Gould Version.

Two magicians having come to lodge in a public-house with a view to robbing it, asked permission to pass the night by the fire, and obtained it. When the house was quiet, the servant-girl, suspecting mischief, crept downstairs and looked through the keyhole. She saw the men open a sack, and take out a dry, withered hand. They anointed the fingers with some unguent, and lighted them.

Each finger flamed, but the thumb they could not light; that was because one of the household was not asleep. The girl hastened to her master, but found it impossible to arouse him. She tried every other sleeper, but could not break the charmed sleep. At last, stealing down into the kitchen, while the thieves were busy over her master's strong-box, she secured the hand, blew out the flames, and at once the whole household was aroused.

Delrio. See also Thorpe's *Mythology*, III, p. 274.

III

Norton Collection, III. p. 22.

One dark night, after the house had been closed, there came a tap at the door of a lone inn, in the midst of a barren moor. The door was opened, and there stood without, shivering and shaking, a poor beggar, his rags soaked with rain, and his hands white with cold. He asked piteously for a lodging, and it was cheerfully granted him; though there was not a spare bed in the house, he could lie along on the mat before the kitchen-fire, and welcome.

All in the house went to bed except the cook, who from her kitchen could see into the large room through a small pane of glass let into the door. When everyone save the beggar was out of the room, she observed the man draw himself up from the floor, seat himself at the table, extract a brown withered human hand from his pocket, and set it upright in the candle-stick. He then anointed the fingers, and applying a match to them, they began to flame. Filled with horror, the cook rushed up the back-stairs, and endeavoured to arouse her master and the men of the house; but all in vain—they slept a charmed sleep; and finding all her efforts ineffectual, she hastened downstairs again. Looking again through the small window, she observed the fingers of the hand flaming, but the thumb gave no light—this was because one of the inmates of the house was not asleep.

The beggar began collecting all the valuables of the house into a large sack, and, having taken all that was worth taking in the large room, he entered another. The moment he was gone, the cook rushed in, and seizing the candle, attempted to extinguish the flames. She blew them all in vain; she poured some drops from a beer jug over them, and that made the flames burn the brighter; she cast some water upon them, but still without putting out the light; as a last resource, she caught up a jug of milk, and dashing it over the four lambent flames, they were extinguished immediately.

Uttering a loud cry, she rushed to the door of the apartment the beggar had entered, and locked it. The whole house was aroused, and the thief secured and hung.

Baring-Gould,-Henderson. Yorkshire.
TYPE 958E*. I. MOTIFS: D.1162.2.1 [Hand of glory]; K.1836 [Disguise of man in woman's dress]; D.1018 [Magic milk of animal].
III. MOTIF: K.1817 [Disguise as beggar].
¶ Milk has a magic quality against enchantments. In "Tamlane" Burd Janet quenched the burning brand into which Tamlane had been transformed in a bucket of milk.

Aubrey has also a story of the Hand of Glory.

HERNE'S HORN

Ruth L. Tongue. *Forgotten Folk-Tales.*

Three silly young chaps were out for mischief. One of them was a Teddy-boy, come for the day, and the other two were from Windsor. So they went in the Forest, and began breaking down the young trees.

Then the Teddy-boy gave a shout. "Coo, look what I've found. Who's been filming Robin Hood now?" The Windsor chaps didn't answer, and looked a bit queer at him. Then he began to feel a bit off himself, no film could have been shot among those bushes.

"Leave it lay," said one of the Windsor lads, "and run like Hell!"

"Don't touch it!" shouts the other, and took off too.

Well, being a Teddy-boy, he had to show off and blow it. The horn gave such a groan and a blast, he nearly fainted, and as he stood shaking, there was a terrible yell among the trees, and great hounds baying. He took off too, but he couldn't catch up with the Windsor lads, who were going hell for leather to church, and, run as he might, he kept stumbling and shivering, and listening to the feet behind him.

The Windsor lads, safe inside the church door, saw him staggering on, and heard the dogs baying. He was nearly to the door when the pursuer stopped, they heard the twang of an arrow, and the Teddy-boy threw up his arms and screamed, and fell flat on his face in the porch quite dead.

There was no arrow through him, and there were no hounds or hunter.

Heard at Cecil Sharp House in 1964. Berkshire.
MOTIF: E.384.3 [Ghost summoned by blast on horn].

THE HERRING–CURER'S VISION

Douglas, *Scottish Fairy and Folk-Tales*, p. 211.

In the year 1665, Alexander Wood, eldest son to the Laird of Nether Benholm, in Angus, having ended his apprenticeship with a merchant in Edinburgh, told Mr James Walker that (in the year 1662 or 1663) he had been employed by his master to go to the Lewis, to make up herring; and being there, and having a good tack of herring, their salt and casks were all made use of, and then they being idle, he began to fret that his master had delayed so long to supply them; and being one day drinking in a country house, and complaining, he went to the door of the house, and there followed him a countryman who said to him, "If you will give me a small hire, I will tell you what has become of the ship you are looking for"; and without more ado he set his foot upon the gentleman's foot, in which time he saw the ship in a great storm, ready to perish, and the seamen casting out their lading to lighten the ship; but when the countryman's foot was off he saw nothing.

The ship at that time was about 100 miles from them, and about forty-eight hours thereafter she came into the same harbour, and had been in the same condition he saw her in at that time the countryman's foot was on his foot.

MOTIF: D.1821.1 [*Magic sight by treading on another's foot*].

¶ Kirk, *Secret Commonwealth*, p. 82, mentions this manner of passing on a seer's vision: "The usewall Method for a curious Person to get a transient Sight of this otherwise invisible Crew of Subterraneans is to put his left Foot under the Wizard's right Foot, and the Seer's Hand is put on the Inquirer's Head, who is to look over the Wizard's right Shoulder."

THE HOOPER, OR THE HOOTER, OF SENNEN COVE

Hunt, *Popular Romances of the West of England*, p. 367.

This was supposed to be a spirit which took the form of a band of misty vapour, stretching across the bay, so opaque that nothing could be seen through it. It was regarded as a kindly interposition of some ministering spirit, to warn the fishermen against venturing to sea. This appearance was always followed, and often suddenly, by a severe storm. It is seldom, or never, seen now. One profane old fisherman would not be warned by the bank of fog. The weather was fine on the shore, and the waves fell tranquilly on the sands; and this aged sinner, declaring he would not be made a fool of, persuaded some young men to join him. They manned a boat, and the aged leader, having with him a threshing-flail, blasphemously declared that he would drive the spirit away; and he vigorously beat the fog with the "threshel"—so the flail is called.

The boat passed through the fog, and went to sea. A severe storm came on. No one ever saw the boat or the men again; and since that time the Hooper has been rarely seen.

MOTIFS: D.1812.5.1.11 [*Grey cloud as evil omen*]; C.41.3 [*Tabau crossing water when spirits are offended*].

¶ See "The Fisherman of Worle" (B, IX) and "The Fisherman's Wife and the Ball of Wool" for fishermen's beliefs.

HOW SAMPSON WAS PUNISHED
FOR SWEARING [summary]

Thompson Notebook, VI.

Reuben's cousin Sampson went fishing to find a gold chair reputed to be drowned in a certain pool. His line tightened, and he drew up the chair, and a silver cradle hanging on to it as well.

"S'help me God, I've got it!" he cried, and with a splash the chair and cradle fell straight back from his line into the water. It was his punishment for calling on God. However often he tried, he never found the chair again.

Told by Reuben Gray, Old Radford, Nottingham, 21 December 1914.
TYPE ML.8010. MOTIFS: C.401.3 [*Tabu: speaking while searching for treasure*]; C.494 [*Tabu: cursing*].
¶ See "The Treasure of Castle Rach" (B, IX), "The Treasure of Berry Pomeroy Castle" (B, IX), etc.

THE IRON CHEST [summary]

Abraham Elder, *Tales and Legends of the Isle of Wight*, p. 158.

Not far from the Needles there is a place known as "the haunted grove", and nearby there formerly lived an eccentric, avaricious person, an attorney, whose favourite interjection was "You say true—you say true —you are in the right." His toadying complacence won him the patronage of a neighbouring squire, and on this man's death it appeared that the old attorney had been left heir to all his possessions, though he had a nephew ten years old, whom everyone had supposed to be his natural successor.

All the documents relating to the estate were kept in a great, locked iron chest. After the old squire's will had been read, amid the astonished protests of the child's parents, this chest was locked again, and the attorney entered into possession of his property. He continued, however, scarcely less parsimonious in his habits than before, occupying a small room covered in cobwebs, and containing no other furniture than his small bedstead, and the iron chest. Only the old woman who made his bed was ever allowed to enter the room, until he was stricken with his last illness.

At last the time came for him to die. His sister, niece, and nephew's wife, whose husband he had named his heir, were gathered at his bedside, when, to their horror, a noise appeared to come from the iron chest, as if the bolt of one of the locks clicked back, and was being opened. Then came another click, and a third, and the lid of the chest gradually lifted itself up, without any apparent cause, until it stood wide open.

At this moment, the old man, who had not spoken for two days, sat up, and, with his eyes staring wildly at the open chest, cried out, "You say true—you say true—you are in the right—I will be with you by and by."

The lid of the chest fell again of its own accord. Click, went the locks one by one, and those who were present tried in vain to reopen the chest.

The attorney never spoke again.

It is believed that the iron chest still remains in the possession of the family, though they carefully conceal its existence.

Several of the descendants of the rightful owner are still living in the island, and will vouch for the truth of this story.

MOTIFS: D.1174 [*Magic box*]; D.1158 [*Magic key*]; E.752.2 [*Soul carried off by Devil*].

¶ A good deal is left to the imagination in this story. Presumably the evidence of the lawyer's trickery was in the iron-bound chest, and the Devil was also there, and at the appropriate moment he made it unlock itself, came out, and carried off the usurer's soul.

THE JOUG TREE AND OTHER WARNINGS

Wilkie, *Bygone Fife*, p. 140.

The Joug Tree warning is known on more than one Fife estate, but the tree at Wemyss fell long ago, worn out by the centuries.

When the owner of Wemyss Castle is nearing death, the event is foretold by the fall of masonry. Here again, as unimpeachable authority, the Countess of Munster* may be quoted. She tells how a recent laird was looking with his sister from a window over the moonlit sea when all was calm. The terraces of that side had been built not very long before. As they conversed the silence was broken by a crash. Before their eyes part of the masonry of one of these broke and fell.

The laird turned to his sister and exclaimed, "I am a dead man." She endeavoured to dispel his foreboding by ridicule. The truth of the warning had been too often verified, and it was hopeless to do so. A few days later they left Wemyss for London, and within a week or two Mr Wemyss was dead.

* *My Memories*, p. 165.

MOTIFS: E.761 [*Life token*]; E.761.3 [*Life token: tree fades*].

¶ The Joug Tree was the local laird's gallows, for in Scotland the feudal lairds had right of life and death. By a kind of revenge, these trees became ominous to the family, and when a limb fell off a death followed. At Wemyss Castle the Joug Tree had fallen, and a piece of the Castle's masonry served the same purpose.

See "The White Bird of the Oxenhams".

LADY ANDOVER'S DREAM

Augustus Hare, *In My Solitary Life*, p. 98.

Lady Andover, who was the daughter of Lord Leicester, was with her husband* at Holkham, and when one day all the other men were going out shooting, she piteously implored him not to go, saying that she had dreamt vividly that he would be shot if he went out. She was so terribly eager about it, that he acceded to her wishes, and remained with her in her painting-room, for she painted beautifully in oils, and was copying a picture of "The Misers" which was at Holkham.

But the afternoon was excessively beautiful, and Lady Andover's strong impression, which had been so vivid in the morning, then seemed to wear off, till at last she said, "Well, really, perhaps I have been selfish in keeping you from what you like so much because of my own impressions; so now, if you care about going out, don't let me keep you in any longer." And he said, "Well, if *you* don't mind, I should certainly like to go," and he went.

He had not been gone long before Lady Andover's impression returned just as vividly as ever, and she rushed upstairs and put on her bonnet, and pursued him. But, as she crossed the park, she met her husband's own servant riding furiously without his coat. "Don't tell me," she said at once. "I know what has happened," and she went back and locked herself into her room. His servant was handing him a gun through the hedge, and it went off, and he was killed upon the spot.

MOTIF: D.1812.5.1.2 (*Bad dream as evil omen*).

THE LAST OF THE KILLIGREWS

Hunt, *Popular Romances of the West of England*, p. 456.

Lady Jane, the widow of Sir John Killigrew, sate in one of the windows of Arwenick House, looking out upon the troubled waters of Falmouth Harbour. A severe storm had prevailed for some days, and the Cornish coast was strewn with wrecks. The tempest had abated; the waves were

* Charles Nevison, Viscount Andover, son of the 15th Earl of Suffolk, died 11 January 1800.

subsiding, though they still beat heavily against the rocks. A light scud was driving over the sky, and a wild and gloomy aspect suffused all things.

There was a sudden outcry amongst a group of men, retainers of the Killigrew family, which excited the attention of Lady Jane Killigrew. She was not left long in suspense as to the cause. In a few minutes two Dutch ships were seen coming into harbour. They had evidently endured the beat of the storm, for they were both considerably disabled; and with the fragments of sail which they carried they laboured heavily. At length, however, these vessels were brought round within the shelter of Pendennis; their anchors were cast in good anchoring ground; and they were safe, or at least the crew thought so, in comparatively smooth water.

As was the custom in those days, the boat belonging to the Killigrew family, manned by the group of whom we have already spoken, went off as soon as the ships were anchored, and boarded them. They then learnt that they were of the Hanse towns, laden with valuable merchandise for Spain, and that this was in the charge of two Spanish factors. On the return of the boat's crew, this was reported to Lady Killigrew; and she, being a very wicked and most resolute woman, at once proposed that they should return to the ships, and either rob them of their treasures or extract from the merchants a large sum of money in compensation.

The rude men, to whom wrecking and plundering was but too familiar, were delighted with the prospect of a rare prize; and above all, when Lady Killigrew declared that she would herself accompany them, they were wild with joy.

With great shouting, they gathered together as many men as the largest boat in the harbour would carry, and armed themselves with pikes, swords, and daggers. Lady Jane Killigrew, also armed, placed herself in the stern of the boat, after the men had crowded into their places, and with a wild huzzah they left the shore and were soon alongside of the vessel nearest to the shore. A number of the men immediately crowded up the side and on to the deck of the vessel, and at once seized upon the captain and the factor, threatening them with instant death if they dared to make any outcry. Lady Jane Killigrew was now lifted on to the deck of the vessel, and the boat immediately pushed off, and the remainder of the crew boarded the other ship.

The Dutch crew were overpowered by the numbers of Cornish men, who were armed far more perfectly than they. Taken unawares, as they were, at a moment when they thought their troubles were for a season at an end, the Dutchmen were almost powerless. The Spaniards were brave men, and resisted the demands made to deliver up their treasure. This resistance was, however, fatal to them. At a signal, it is said by some, given by their leader, Lady Jane Killigrew—although this was denied afterwards—they were both murdered by the ruffians into whose hands they had fallen, and their bodies cast overboard into the sea.

These wretches ransacked the ships, and appropriated whatsoever they pleased, while Lady Jane took from them "two hogsheads of Spanish pieces of eight, and converted them to her own use".

As one of the Spanish factors was dying, he lifted his hands to Heaven, prayed to the Lord to receive his soul, and, turning to the vile woman to whose villainy he owed his death, he said, "My blood will linger with you until my death is avenged upon your own sons."

This dreadful deed was not allowed to pass without notice, even in those lawless times. The Spaniards were then friendly with England, and upon the representation made by the Spanish minister to the existing government, the sheriff of Cornwall was ordered to seize and bring to trial Lady Jane Killigrew and her crew of murderers. A considerable number were arrested with her; and that lady and several of her men were tried at Launceston.

Since the Spaniards were proved to be, at the time of the murder "foreigners under the Queen's protection", they were all found guilty, and condemned to death. All the men were executed on the walls of Launceston Castle; but, by the interest of Sir John Arundell and Sir Nicholas Hals, Queen Elizabeth was induced to grant a pardon for Lady Jane.

How Lady Jane Killigrew lived, and when she died, are matters on which even tradition, by which the story is preserved, is silent. We know, however, that her immediate descendant, John Killigrew, who married one of the Monks, and his son, William Killigrew, who was made a baronet in 1660 by Charles II, were only known for the dissoluteness of character and the utter regardlessness of every feeling of an exalted character which they displayed. Sir William Killigrew, by his ill conduct and his extravagant habits, wasted all the basely-gotten treasure, and sold the manor and barton of Arwenick to his younger brother, Sir Peter Killigrew. With the son of this Peter the baronetcy became extinct. The last Sir Peter Killigrew, however, improved his fortune by marrying one of the coheirs of Judge Twisden. Sir Peter and his wife, of whom we know nothing, died, leaving one son, George Killigrew, who connected himself with the St Aubyn family by marriage. This man appears to have inherited many of the vices of his family. He was given to low company, and towards the close of his life was remarkable only for his drunken habits.

He was one evening in a tavern in Penryn, surrounded by his usual companions, and with them was one Walter Vincent, a barrister-at-law. The wine flowed freely; songs and loose conversation were the order of the night. At length all were in a state of great excitement through the extravagance of their libations, and something was said by George Killigrew very insultingly to Walter Vincent.

Walter Vincent does not appear to have been naturally a depraved man, but of violent passions. Irritated by Killigrew, he made some remarks on the great-grandmother being sentenced to be hanged. Swords were instantly drawn by the drunken men. They lunged at each other. Vincent's sword passed directly through Killigrew's body and he fell dead in the midst of his revelries, at the very moment when he was defending the character of her who had brought dishonour upon them.

This Walter Vincent was tried for the murder of George Killigrew, but acquitted. We are told by the Cornish historian: "Yet this Mr Vincent, through anguish and horror at this accident (it is said) within two years after, wasted of an extreme atrophy of his flesh, and spirits; that, at length, at the table whereby he was sitting, in the Bishop of Exeter's palace, in the presence of divers gentlemen, he instantly fell back against the wall and died."

George Kiiligrew left one daughter, but of her progress through life we know nothing. Thus the Cornish Killigrews ceased to be a name in the land.

MOTIFS: S.110 [*Murders*]; M.411.3 [*Dying man's curse*]; M.460 [*Curses on families*]. ¶ There are no motifs allotted to wrecking, the subject of a good many traditions in the South-west.
See "The Silken Shawl" (B, VI).

THE LEGEND OF MOCKERKIN TARN
[summary]

W. Dickinson, *Cumbriana*, p. 14. seq.

Sir Mochar, the dwarf knight, lived in a castle in the centre of the village of Mockerkin, now believed to lie sunk in the depths of the Tarn which bears its name.

Sir Mochar was fierce and grim and hideous, but of great courage, and he rode a coal-black charger, Black Rook, and wielded a long-handled axe. He had forty yeomen to follow him. As he grew older and greyer, it was remarked with wonder that Black Rook remained, to all seeming, as young and swift and active as ever, and would carry his master in the chase, so that no boar or stag ever could evade their terrible onslaught. And when the beast lay slain on the ground, none ever discovered by what agency it was lifted to the saddle, to be borne home triumphantly before Sir Mochar on the back of Black Rook.

Not content with the pleasure of the chase, Sir Mochar forced his retainers to ride through his lands, and bring back to his castle three maidens for his pleasure. They could not refuse, for he was their overlord, and they were held like prisoners until Sir Mochar had ridden out on one of his periodic forays across the border into Scotland, to replenish his diminished larder. He was gone with his men for many days, and on their return they prepared a great feast. When all was ready Sir Mochar sent for the three maidens. But on his homeward ride he had done an evil deed. He had caused one of his yeomen to unhorse and drown Sam, one of the bravest and handsomest of all his followers, whom the maidens favoured for his youth and high spirits.

This crime had reached the ears of the three, and in terror they had contrived, during the bustle of preparations, to make their escape from the castle, and flee each in the direction of her own home. When Mochar learnt of this, he flew into a rage, sent his men off in all haste, and himself mounted Black Rook and joined in the pursuit. The first maiden he overtook and slew in Hodyoad Ghyl, before the eyes of her father, who had come to lend what help he might in the search. When the old man attempted a protest, Mochar laid him low also, and rode off in the track of the second damsel. But he came up with her too late; his hounds had found her first, and were tearing her to pieces. The third was found drowned in the water of Loweswater Lake; she had flung herself in on hearing the hounds approaching.

Frustrated and enraged, Mochar rode for home, cursing all the race of those maidens, and swearing he would kill every one of them if his castle sank twenty miles deep to atone for the deed. On the word came a fearful crash of thunder, a flash of lightning, and the whole castle, with its occupants, did indeed sink into the earth, to be neither seen nor heard thenceforward.

But it is said that on Michaelmas night a shadowy form comes up out of the lake, encircles the tarn three times, and withdraws again into the dark water. It is the ghost of Black Rook, with the ghost of his master on his back.

MOTIFS: G.303.3.3.1.3 [*Devil as horse*]; Q.211 [*Murder punished*]; Q.244 [*Punishment for ravisher*]; Q.552.2.1 [*Land sinks and Lake appears as punishment*].
¶ Blackmore's tale in *Lorna Doone* of the origin of the Wizard's Slough is something like this tale, though no doubt a real legend of the Doone country.
See "Simmer Water" (B, IX).

THE LIFT THAT FELL

Augustus Hare, *In My Solitary Life*, pp. 297–8.

A gentleman staying at Glamis, and unable to sleep, looked out of his window into the bright, moonlit night. At the extreme end of the avenue he saw a dark object moving, and as it came nearer he saw it was a carriage, but there was no sound of wheels. Noiselessly, silently, it drove up to the door, and, after a minute, drove away again. As it went off, the driver looked up—with a marked and terrible face, which the onlooker felt he should never forget.

At breakfast the next morning, he said to Lord Strathmore, "You had a very late arrival last night." "No. There was no arrival." "But I saw a closed carriage drive up." Lord Strathmore turned pale, said nothing, and his visitor at once changed the subject. Shortly after, he was at Paris. Thoroughly tired with a fatiguing day, he decided to go down from his third floor to the *table d'hôte* in the lift. It stopped at his floor, and he was about to step in when the man who guided it looked at him. It was the face he had seen at Glamis, and he at once drew back. An instant after, there was a frightful crash, the lift fell, and all its inmates were killed.

MOTIFS: D.1812.5.1.17 [*Spectre as evil omen*]; E.723.8 [*Appearance of wraith as calamity omen*]; J.1050 [*Attention to warnings*]; D.1810.8.3.2 [*Dream warns of danger that will happen in near future. Because of the advance knowledge, the danger is averted*]

¶ This is another ghostly story attached to Glamis Castle. There are somewhat similar stories current in Perthshire of heeded warnings that saved life in the Tay Bridge disaster, still vividly remembered. Catherine Crowe in *The Night Side of Nature* (p. 72) tells a similar story.

See "Room for One More".

LORD LYTTELTON'S DREAM
[slightly shortened]

The Gentleman's Magazine Library, 1885, p. 197. seq.

The death of the celebrated Lord Lyttelton, from the singularity of the circumstances, cannot fail to live in the memory of those who have heard it. He professed to have been warned of his death, and the time thereof, as follows:

About a week before he died, he went to bed pretty well, but *restless*. Soon after his servant had left him, he heard a footstep at the bottom of his bed. He raised himself, in order to see what it could be, when one of the most angelic female figures that imagination could possibly paint presented itself before him and, *with a commanding voice and action*, bade him attend and *prepare himself*, for on such a night and *at the hour of twelve*, he would surely die! He attempted to address the vision, but was unable; and the ghost vanished. His valet found him in the morning more dead than alive; and it was some hours before his Lordship could be recovered sufficiently to send for his friends, to whom he thought it *necessary to communicate* this extraordinary circumstance.

Mr Miles Peter Andrews was one of the number thus sent for, being at that time one of his most intimate associates. Every person to whom Lord Lyttelton told the tale naturally turned it into ridicule, *all* knowing him to be *very nervous* and *superstitious*, and tried to make him believe it was *a dream*, as they certainly considered themselves. Lord Lyttelton filled his house with company, and appeared to think as his friends would wish him. Mr M. P. Andrews had business which called him to Dartford, and therefore soon took his leave, thinking Lord Lyttelton quite composed on this subject, so that his friend's dream dwelt so little on his imagination that he did not even recollect the time when it was predicted that the event would take place.

One night after he left Pitt Place, the residence of Lord Lyttelton, he supposed that he had been in bed half an hour, when, endeavouring to compose himself, suddenly his curtains were pulled open, and Lord Lyttelton appeared before him at his bedside, standing in his *robe de chambre*, and night-cap. Mr Andrews looked at him some time, and thought it so odd a freak of his friend that he began to reproach him for his folly in coming down to Dartford Mills without notice, as he could find no accommodation. "However," said he, "I'll get up, and see what can be done." He turned to the other side of the bed, and rang the bell, when Lord Lyttelton disappeared. Mr Andrew's servant soon entered, when his master inquired, "Where is Lord Lyttelton?" The servant, all astonishment, declared he had seen nothing of his Lordship since they left Pitt Place. "Pshaw! You fool!" replied Mr Andrews. "He was here this moment by my bedside." The servant persisted that it was not possible. Mr Andrews dressed himself, and, with the servants, searched every part of the house and garden; but no Lord was to be found. Still, Mr Andrews could not help believing that Lord Lyttelton had played him this trick for his disbelief in the vision, till, about four o'clock the same day, an express arrived to inform him of Lord Lyttelton's death, and the manner of it, and gave the following particular account of it: That, on the morning before Lord Lyttelton died, he entered the breakfast-room between ten and eleven o'clock; appeared rather thoughtful, and did not answer any inquiries made by his friends respecting his health, etc.

At dinner he seemed much better, and when the cloth was taken away, he exclaimed, "Richard's himself again!" But as night came on, the gloom of the morning returned. However, as this was the predicted night of dissolution, his friends agreed that it would be right to alter the clocks and watches in the house. This was managed by the steward, without Lord Lyttelton suspecting anything of it; his own watch, which lay on his dressing-table, being altered by his valet. During the evening, they got him into some pleasant discussions, in which he distinguished himself with peculiar wit and pleasantry. *At half after eleven*, as he conceived it, from the alteration of the clocks (but it was only eleven) he said he was tired and would retire to bed; bid them a good night, and left them all delighted by his calm appearance. As soon as he had withdrawn, the conversation instantly turned upon his dream. The discourse continued till nearly twelve o'clock, when the door being hastily opened, Lord Lyttelton's valet entered, pale as death, crying out, "My Lord is dying!" His friends flew to his bedside, but he expired before they could all assemble round him!

Lord Lyttelton's valet gave them the following statement: That Lord Lyttelton made his usual preparations for bed; that he kept every now and then looking at his watch; that when he got into bed he ordered his curtains to be closed at the foot. It was now within a minute or two of *twelve* by his watch; he asked to look at mine, and seemed pleased to find it nearly keep time with his own. His Lordship then put them both to his ear, to satisfy himself if they went. When it was more than a quarter after twelve by our watches, he said, "This mysterious lady is not a true prophetess, I find." When it was near the *real* hour of twelve, he said, "Come. I'll wait no longer. Get me my medicine. I'll take it and try to *sleep*." I just stepped into the dressing-room to prepare the physic, and had mixed it, when I thought I heard my Lord breathing very hard. I ran to him, and found him in the agonies of death.

MOTIFS: D.1812.0.1 [*Foreknowledge of hour of death*]; E.723.6 [*Appearance of his wraith as announcement of person's death*].

¶ See "Adam Bell" (B, VI), "Apparition at Oxford", "The Doctor's Fetch".

LOST CORPSE END

Gutch, *County Folk-Lore*, II, *North Riding of Yorkshire*, pp. 409–10.

I was taking a holiday stroll, and, passing by a plantation at Upsall, near Thirsk, called "Beechpath Beckstead", I met a garrulous old man. "What do you call this wood?" I asked. The old fellow shook his head solemnly, and whispered: "That part is 'Lost Corpse End!'" "Why?" A very long pause. "I was seventeen years of age, and I am now eighty-four; so you may count how many years 'tis ago. Well! I was one of the bearers of poor Dame ——, and we were to bury her at Kirby Knowle. Just as we arrived at the spot, we set down the body. It was a hot autumnal day, and the nuts were *so enticing*. It was the best nut year I ever remember. We all went off to gather them; and when we returned the corpse was lost!" "Washed away by the burn?" I remarked. "No, sir, wished it had. We should then have got it back. The coffin was there, never moved, never touched by mortal man. We took up the coffin but it was as light as an empty coffin could be.

"We *ran* with it to Kirby Knowle; and the parson buried the *coffin* but the corpse is—is *there*! It is all along o' our nutting."

Eboracum, *Notes and Queries*, 3rd series, II, p. 343.
MOTIF: C.517 [*Tabu: pulling nuts*].

¶ In country tradition nuts are both magical and dangerous. In Somerset girls pulling nuts on a Sunday are likely to meet the Devil (*Somerset Folk-Lore*, p. 31). In *Grimm the Cobbler of Croydon* (Carew Hazlitt's *Old Plays*) the Devil is called up by picking nuts at Hallowmas. It would be unwise for any purpose to leave a corpse in a wood.

THE LOVER'S FETCH

S. Baring-Gould, *A Book of Folk-Lore*, p. 173.

Barham, in his *Reminiscences*, relates the story of a respectable young woman who was roused in the night by hearing somebody in her room, and that on looking up she saw a young man to whom she was engaged. Extremely offended at such an intrusion, she bade him instantly depart if he wished ever to speak with her again. Whereupon he told her that he was to die that day six weeks, and then disappeared. Having ascertained that the youth could not possibly have been in her room, she was naturally much alarmed, and, her evident depression leading to some inquiries, she communicated what had occurred to the family with whom she lived. They attached little importance to what seemed so improbable, more especially as the young man continued in perfectly good health, and was entirely ignorant of the prediction, which was carefully kept from him.

When the fatal day arrived the girl became cheerful, and as the ladies with whom she lived went on their morning ride, they observed to each other that the prophecy did not seem likely to be fulfilled. On their return, however, they saw her running up the avenue towards the house in great agitation and learned that her lover was then either dead or dying.

MOTIFS: E.723.6.1*(c) [*Wraith appears to person in bed in bedroom*] (Baughman); E.723.8 [*Appearance of wraith as calamity omen*].
¶ See "Lord Lyttelton's Dream".

THE MAN WHO BEWITCHED HIMSELF

Strange and Wonderful News
From
EXETER

Giving an Account of
THE DREADFUL APPARITIONS

That was seen by Mr Jacob Seley of Exeter on
Monday, September 22nd, 1690, who gave the full
Account to the JUDGES, the next day, who were
going the Western Circuit.

*

Printed according to Order, October the 2nd, 1690

*

EXON. September 29th, 1690.

British Museum reference, 719.m.17/36. J. R. W. Coxhead, *Legends of Devon*, pp. 145–7.

Sir,

All the Discourse in our Town is concerning Mr Seley's Journey. On Monday 22nd September 1690, at Three of the Clock in the Afternoon he took Horse for Taunton in Somerset-shire, and he took Hinton Clist Road, and so for Black Down; and at a publick House called Cleston, where the Coach and Wagons usually lodge on that Road, he stop't some Time and called for a Pot of Beer, and a Noggin of Brandy, and then went towards Taunton: on his journey he met with a Country like Farmer, being about 7 or 8 at Night, and the Country like Farmer perswaded Mr Seley to ride back a Mile and a half to lodge, telling him there was very good Quarters, but at his return he supposed it to be about 3 Mile; and then he brought him to a Plat of Ground near the House, and the like Country Farmer and his Horse vanished away; and immediately near a 100 or 2 appeared to him Men Women and Childern, some like Judges, some like Magistrates, some like Clergy-men, and some like Country People, and the Country People had Spears who made at him, and then he made use of Scripture, but they made him no Answer; then he did abjure them, In the Name of the Father, the Son, and the Holy Ghost, for it is written, The Seed of the Woman shall bruise the Serpents Head; and over his Head they hung something like a Fishing Net. And by Mr Seley's Account, the bigness of the Plat, wherein he was confined, was not above 4 yards over.

At last he lighted off his Horse, and his Horse laid his Nose over his shoulder as if he had been a Christian, and as he observed they gave his Horse something like to Treacle; then he let go his Horse, and never saw him afterwards. After this he walked up and down from 9 at Night till 4 the next morning, but at several times being assaulted he thrust at them with his Sword, but could find nothing but Shadow, though at length he perceived a Man was cut and his 4 Fingers hung by the Skin, and that a Woman was cut in the Forehead and then he saw them shake their Heads at one another, and the blood did appear upon his Sword.

After this they brought along 10 Funerals one after another, when the last came by he Questioned why they confined him in that place they made him no Answer. Then they dragged along 2 Persons by the Hair of the Head, that look'd as if they were both then Slain; then they came up in a body thrusting at him again, and he drew his Sword at them, but knows not whether he hit any, and this sort of Skirmish continued all Night, and in the Morning he returned to Coldstock; and the Judges then were at that House going to Wells-Sizes, it being Thursday that they went out of Exon, and Mr Seley gave the Judges an Account of the Transaction; and then returned to his own House at Exon, and gave this Account publickly to his Neighbourhood.

If any one desires to be satisfied further of the Truth of this Relation, they may come to Mr William Brown, a Shoemaker, at his House next Door to the Windsor Castle in Charing Cross.

'Tis remarkable that the House where Mr Seley eat The Roast Beef, which is the same House where the supposed Farmer would have him go back to Lodge, was one of Monmouth's Men, and Hanged on the Sign Post; and the spot of Ground where Mr Seley was confin'd being not far from the House where several of them were Buried that were Killed, and Executed on Monmouth's side, and goes by the name of Black Down.

FINIS.

LONDON. Printed by T.M.

MOTIF: F.258.1 ["*The Fairies hold a Fair*"] is of possible relevance here. It seems to refer to the same gathering as that recorded in Bovet's *Pandaemonium* at something the same date, though it is a much more ghoulish affair.

¶ See "The Pixy Fair" and "Pixy Merchandise" (B, V).

MASTER WHITTINTON'S DREAM

A Hundred Merry Tales, ed. Zall, p. 139.

Soon after one Master Whittinton had builded a college on a night as he slept he dreamed that he sat in his church, and many folks there also. And further he dreamed that he saw Our Lady in the same church with a glass of goodly ointment in her hand—going to one, asking him what he had done for her sake, which said that he had said Our Lady's Psalter every day; wherefore she gave him a little of the oil.

And anon, she went to another, asking him what he had done for her sake, which said that he had said two Psalters every day;—wherefore Our Lady gave him more of the ointment than she gave the other.

This Master Whittinton then thought that when Our Lady should come to him, she would give him all the whole glass because he had builded such a great college—and was very glad in his mind. But when Our Lady came to him, she asked him what he had suffered for her sake—which words made him greatly abashed because he had nothing to say for himself. And so he dreamed that for all the great deed of building of that said college, he had no part of that goodly ointment.

By this, ye may see that to suffer for God's sake is more meritorious than to give great goods.

MOTIFS: V.281 [*Devotee of Virgin Mary given present by her*]; Q.20 [*Piety rewarded*]. ¶ In a number of the motifs allotted to the Virgin Mary the recitation of "Aves" plays a very important part.

The "Master Whittinton" of this legend is probably Richard Whittington, who founded a college and gave largely to the Church.

THE MINEHEAD ROOD LIGHT

Ruth L. Tongue, *Somerset Folklore*, p. 96.

Very early in the last century a terrible storm rose in the Bristol Channel, and the Minehead fishermen who were out at sea were given up for lost. But one by one the craft struggled into the safety of the little harbour. They had been guided, they said, by the light in the rood loft of St Michael's Church, which had guided their forefathers for four hundred years. Only, in spite of the cloud and spray, they had never seen it shine so bright. The crowd who heard them knew that the light had been blown out by the storm. The old man who told this tale said that his grandfather and the other fishermen were convinced that the ghosts of drowned Minehead mariners had come to their aid. A carving on the outside wall over the east window of St Michael's runs:

> We pray to Jesus and Mary
> Send our neighbours safety,

and the sailors had come again in time of need.

MOTIFS: E.379.1 [*Return from the dead to rescue from drowning*]; E.530.1 [*Ghost-like lights*].

A MIRACLE OF THE LORD'S CROSS

Roger of Wendover, *Chronicle*, II, p. 390.

[A band of robbers] at the town of Redbourn...pillaged the church of St Amphibalus, and stripped the monks even to their inner clothing; they took also the relics of the saints from above the great altar, and polluted them with their impious hands. One among them seized on a silver-and-gold ornamented cross, in which was contained a piece of our Lord's Cross, and hid it in his wicked bosom unknown to his companions; but before he had left the oratory, he was possessed by a devil, and fell down, grinding his teeth, and foaming at the mouth, then rising quickly on the instigation of the devil, he endeavoured to strike at his companions with his sword; they, however, pitying his agony, tied his hands, and not knowing the cause of it, took him to the church at Flamstead, in a state of the wildest frenzy.

As these robbers were entering that church, for the purpose of robbing it, they were met by the priest, clad in white robes, in order to check the evil disposition of those impious men; however, being alarmed about their mad companion, whom they had brought with them, they refrained from plunder, and there, in the presence of the superior and many others, the aforesaid cross leapt forth from the man's bosom, and fell on the ground; the superior then took it up with reverence and astonishment, and, holding it up, asked the robbers what it was. At length on consideration, they found out, by means of this visitation of God, that he had clandestinely taken it from the monks whom they had robbed in the adjoining town, and they were all in a state of great perplexity and fear, lest the evil spirit should possess them also, and torture them as it had done their companion.

They therefore in great alarm delivered the cross up to the superior, beseeching him by the virtue of God, and in peril of his order, before he took any food, to go to the place and restore the cross to the monks; the superior therefore made all haste to the oratory of St Amphibalus, and with due reverence delivered the cross, and related all the wonderful events connected with it to the prior and brethren.

MOTIFS: V.144 [*Belief in miraculous powers of sacred relics*]; Q.222 [*Punishment for desecration of holy places*]; Q.220.1 [*Devil plagues impious people*].

MR WILLIAMSON AND THE
ROSICRUCIANS

Scott, *Minstrelsy of the Scottish Border*, IV, pp. 73–4.

As for the rencounter between Mr Williamson, schoolmaster at Cowper (who has wrote a grammar) and the Rosicrucians, I never trusted it, till I heard it from his own son, who is present minister of Kirkaldy. He tells, that a stranger came to Cowper, and called for him; after they had drank a little, and the reckoning came to be paid, he whistled for spirits; one in the shape of a boy, came, and gave him gold in abundance; no servant was seen riding with him to the town, nor entering with him into the inn. He caused his spirits, against the next day, bring him noble Greek wine from the Pope's cellar, and tell the freshest news then at Rome; then trysted Mr Williamson at London, who met the same man, in a coach, near to London Bridge, and who called on him by his name; he marvelled to see any know him there; at last he found it was his Rosicrucian.

He pointed to a tavern, and desired Mr Williamson to do him the favour to dine with him at that house; whither he came at twelve o'clock, and found him, and many others of good fashion there, and a most splendid and magnificent table, furnished with all the varieties of delicate meats, where they are all served by spirits. At dinner, they debated upon the excellence of being attended by spirits; and, after dinner, they proposed to him to assume him into their society, and make him participant of their happy life; but among the other conditions and qualifications requisite, this was one, that they demanded his abstracting his spirit from all materiality, and renouncing his baptismal engagements.

Being amazed at this proposal, he falls a-praying; whereat they all disappear, and leave him alone. Then he began to forethink what would become of him, if he were left to pay that vast reckoning; not having as much on him as would defray it. He calls the boy, and asks, what was become of these gentlemen, and what was to pay? He answered, there was nothing to pay, for they had done it, and were gone about their affairs in the city.

Fountainhall's *Decisions*, I, p. 15.

MOTIFS: D.1711 [*Magician*]; D.2100 [*Magic wealth*]; D.2105 [*Provisions magically furnished*].

¶ Some episodes of the Faustus story are reproduced in this legend. The Rosicrucians are represented as black magicians.

See "Faustus" (B, III).

THE MOTHER'S DREAM or
BENJIE SPEDLANDS [summary]

A. Cunningham, *Traditional Tales of the English and Scottish Peasantry*, I, p. 252. seq.

In Annandale there lived a young woman so fair and so kind of heart that she was the joy of all who knew her. She was married to a man worthy of her, but when their son was still an infant, her husband died, and she was left alone, with the child as her only comfort.

On the day when he was two years old, she dreamed a strange dream. In it she seemed to be sitting at her cottage door, with her son on her knees, and her husband standing at her side. He seemed graver than in life, with a pure, strange light shining around him, but he smiled, and they watched the setting sun together. Presently a small black cloud appeared, which spread rapidly till it covered the whole sky, and came half-way down the Ladye's Lowe. Then it began to roll along the earth itself, and hide the fields, and in it were dim shapes of men, and shrill voices. It stopped a stone's-throw from the cottage, and the woman clasped the child closer to her, and knew at the same time that her husband was no longer there. From the cloud there now came forth a black chariot, with a shadowy driver, who cried, "I am the bearer of woes to men; carry these sorrows abroad; they are in number eight." And, tarrying at her door, the phantom cried: "A woe for the son of the widow Rachel."

In the chariot she saw the coffins of eight children, and on the last of them was her son's name, and the number 6, to denote his years. So bitter were her tears that the charioteer passed his hand over the number, and when she looked again it was changed to 9. "I may give no more," he said, and passed on, first laying the coffin at her door.

She awoke, terrified and in tears, and when she told her dream all the women of the parish were in dread. But a woman who dwelt by the Rowantree-burn came to her and said that she could avert the doom if she took her child's undergarment and dipped it at midnight in the water of the Ladye's Lowe, then hung it to dry in the beams of the new moon. The form of a woman would then rise from the water and try to turn the garment. She must forbid it in the name of the Bible, which she must take with her and hold open on her knees.

But another woman came to her, and bade her take no heed of the first woman's words: it might be, she said, that God needed this child for a saint, and his mother would do ill to prevent it. This woman was a mother of two children; one she loved dearly, but her husband was not its father, and the other she hated, and this had driven her husband in his sorrow to leave her, and sail to a distant land. She had not seen him for three years.

The lawful son's name, "John" had been one of those whose names had appeared in the woman's dream on one of the small coffins. A fierce quarrel arose between these two women, and as they argued together a man who was an elder of the Church came up, and told the widow to trust neither of them; the first, he said was an evil witch and the second a faithless wife. The dream was an invention of the Evil One, to tempt the mother to evil ways; if she would but rear her child in the fear of God, he would live to grow up and be her strength and joy.

Nevertheless, three nights later, the unhappy woman took her son's garment to the water, wetted it, and hung it to dry, and as she sat watching, she saw a vision. The lake was covered with ice, and on it she saw her son, now a fair, tall youth, and seven of his companions, hand in hand, singing as they went. Their seven mothers were with her, and they talked of their sons as they watched. Suddenly there was a wild shrieking, the ice had disappeared, and out of the water rose the shape of her son, now deathly pale, and someone, she knew not who, carried him out, and laid him at her feet. She swooned, and when she came to herself it was day, and stiff with cold, she dragged herself home.

All this came true. When her son was nine years old, and surpassed all the other children in beauty and attainments, a great curling match was held in mid-December; and though the Ladye's Lowe had an ill repute among the older people of the village, it was chosen for the sport. There her son, with seven companions, fell through the cracking ice into the deep water below. As they sank, the widow's son put out his hand to a young man, Benjie Spedlands, one of the best-liked and strongest in all the region, and cried: "O Benjie, save me, save me!" But the terror of the dark water was too great; Benjie hung back, though it was he who had led the eight children out to the deepest part of the lake, in heedless daring. He saw them sink; but ever after was haunted by the remembrance of his cowardice; his sleep was broken every night by dreams of the drowning children; shunned by all, he wandered alone about the countryside, cursed by men and by his conscience.

Just a year from the time of the drowning, he was seen running round the side of the lake, stretching out his arms, and crying in agony to some imagined form in the water. Next morning, when his cries had long ceased, his hat was found floating at the lake's edge, but he himself was never seen again.

TYPE 394A. MOTIFS: D.1812.3.3 [*Future revealed in dream*]; M.341.1.4 [*Prophecy: death at a certain age*]; D.921 [*Magic lake*]; M.370.1 [*Prophecy of death fulfilled*]; W.121 [*Cowardice*].

¶ In a Hallowe'en spell a shirt drying by the fire is supposed to be turned by a visionary lover.

A NARROW ESCAPE

Hunt, *Popular Romances of the West of England*, p. 350.

Amongst the mining population there is a deeply-rooted belief in warn-ings. The following, related by a very respectable man, formerly a miner, well illustrates this:

"My father, when a lad, worked with a companion (James, or 'Jim' as he was called) in Germo. They lived close by Old Wheal Grey in Breage. One evening, the daughter of the person with whom they lodged, came in to her mother, crying, 'Billy and Jim ben out theer for more than a hour, and I ben chasin' them among the Kilyur banks, and they waan't let me catch them. As fast as I do go to one, they do go to another.' 'Hold your tongue, child,' said the mother; ''twas their forenoon core, and they both ben up in bed this hours.' 'I'm sure I ben chasin' them,' said the girl. The mother then went upstairs and awoke the lads, telling them the story. One of them said, ''Tis a warning; something will happen in un old end, and I shan't go to mine this core.' 'Nonsense,' said the other; 'don't let us be so foolish; the child has been playing with some strangers, and it isn't worth while to be spaled for any such foolishness.' 'I tell you,' replied the other, 'I won't go.'

"As it was useless for one man to go alone, they both remained away. In the course of the night, however, a run took place in the end they were working in, and tens of thousands of kibblefuls came away. Had they been at work, it was scarcely possible for them to have escaped."

MOTIFS: E.723.8.1 [*Wraith appears before mine disaster*]; D.1812.4.3.1* [*Miner obeys presentiment; saves himself from death or injury*] (Baughman).
¶ See "The Raven and the Wrecker", "The Lift that Fell".

THE NIGHTMARE HOUSE

Augustus Hare, *In My Solitary Life*, p. 302.

To this house of constant hospitality [Baddesley Clinton] three Birming-ham artists had been invited to spend the day. One of them, Mrs King, told us her most extraordinary dream. She had been, with her husband, painting near Bala Lake and they had arranged to go on to Towyn. The night before they were to move, she dreamt that she went to a house most beautifully kept. In her dream she went up a staircase scrubbed to perfec-tion. She entered a large, fresh-looking room, well furnished and hung with very common Scripture prints.

It had a particularly curious carpet, made of large squares of carpet sewn together and involuntarily suggesting trapdoors underneath. The windows were fastened by a row of very large nails, sticking up, but hammered in along the window-sill. She went to bed in her dream, but, when she was there, a terrible-looking woman with long black hair falling down on either side of her face came in and said rapidly, "You are in a very evil place. You must make your escape, now, at once. Leave all you have, only escape."

And the woman touched her to hurry her and she woke with a scream. This aroused her husband, to whom she told all her dream in detail. The next morning her landlady, who had been very kind to her, observed upon her looking ill. She said, "I am not ill, only somehow—I cannot tell why—I cannot bear to go to Towyn: I feel a strange sort of shrinking from it." "Well," said the landlady, "that is very odd, but I see no sort of reason why you should go to Towyn. Why not go to Aberdovey instead?" So they went to Aberdovey. There they saw that lodgings were to let in a house which looked very nice on the outside, and they went in. *There* was the staircase she had seen, and when they ascended it, *there* was the room—the same Scripture prints, the same unusual carpet, the same tall row of nails along the window-sill. On entering, they had ordered tea. "Oh, who will bring it up?" said Mrs King, with horror, to her husband. And it was brought up by the woman with the black hair, exactly the person she had vividly described to him.

They were afraid to drink the tea. They paid their bill and left hurriedly. Years afterwards they were at Aberdovey again. The house was then a shop. They inquired about the former occupants and heard that the house had had a very mysterious and bad reputation, and that the former owners had all left quite suddenly in the night.

MOTIF: D.1810.8.3.2 [*Dream warns of danger that will happen in near future. Because of the advance knowledge, the danger is averted*].

See "The Lift that Fell", "Room for One More", "The Dream House".

THE OLD WOMAN AND THE SPIDER

Henderson, *Folk-Lore of the Northern Counties*, p. 312.

One or two instances, in which popular belief glorifies the world around us with light borrowed from the days when Our Saviour walked on earth, have been given already. I add another of exceeding beauty which has come before me.

In the little town of Malton, in Yorkshire, a few years ago, my friend the late Dr Dykes, while visiting an old woman during her last illness, observed a spider near her bed, and attempted to destroy it. She at once interfered, and told him with much earnestness that spiders ought not to be killed; for we should remember how, when our Blessed Lord lay in the manger at Bethlehem, the spider came and spun a beautiful web, which protected the innocent Babe from all the dangers which surrounded Him. The old woman was about ninety years of age. I have never met with the legend elsewhere, but it may have originated the Kentish proverb:

He who would wish to thrive
Must let spiders run alive.

The spider is curiously connected with the history of Mahomet. He is said during his flight from Mecca to have been saved by a spider and a pigeon. While he was concealed in a cave his enemies came up in pursuit of him, but, perceiving a spider's web across the cave's mouth and a pigeon in her nest just above, they concluded the place to have been undisturbed and did not enter it. There is a Hebrew tradition to the same effect concerning King David. While flying from Saul in the Desert of Ziph, a web, it is said, was spun over a cave in which he rested, and thus the band in search of him were led to believe that no one could be concealed there. Accordingly in the Chaldaic paraphrase of Psalm lvii, instead of "I will cry unto the Most High God, even unto the God that shall perform the cause which I have in hand", we find "I will cry unto the Most High and Mighty God, which sent the spider that she should spin her web in the mouth of the cave to preserve me".

TYPE 967. MOTIFS: B.523.1 [*Spider-web over hole saves fugitive*]; A.2221.5 [*Animal blessed for helping holy fugitive*].

¶ The legend of King Bruce and the spider had this tale added to it in oral tradition. According to this, Robert the Bruce, hidden in a cave, presumably that at Kirkpatrick near Gretna, and despairing at his many failures, learned perseverance from watching a spider. It adds, however, that King Edward's men, who were searching for him, saw the spider's web at the mouth of the cave, and assumed that no one had entered it that day. For this reason, Scotsmen are very loath to kill a spider.

THE ONE WITH THE WHITE HAND

Ruth L. Tongue, *Somerset Folklore*, p. 31.

The One with the White Hand was a terrifying spirit who haunted the moorland near Taunton. It would rise at twilight out of a scrub of birch and oak and come drifting across the empty moor to lonely travellers so fast that they had no time to escape. She was deadly pale with clothes that rustled like dead leaves and her long, white, skinny hand looked like a blasted branch. Sometimes she pointed a finger at a man's head, and then he ran mad, but more often she laid her hand above his heart and he fell dead, with the impress of a white hand on his chest to show what had killed him.

At length a farmer who lived near determined that he would lay the spirit if he could, so he set out near sundown towards the moor with a slice of bread in one pocket and a good quantity of salt in the other. As the sun set he heard the rustling and saw the spirit sweeping towards him, but he stood firm with his hand in his pocket. The white hand came out towards him, but he thrust his own hand, full of salt, right in the thing's face.

"And yur's another white hand to match 'ee," he said. A wind got up in a moment, and the thing vanished, and never troubled that stretch of moor again.

MOTIFS: F.441.2 [*Tree spirit*]; G.303.15.4.1 [*Particular species of tree the abode of devils*]; E.542.1 [*Ghostly fingers leave mark on person's body*]; F.384.1 [*Salt powerful against fairies*].

¶ It is doubtful if this creature is thought of as the spirit of the tree or as a devil inhabiting the copse. Salt is supposed to be powerful against devils, witches and fairies.

THE OPEN GRAVE

Ruth L. Tongue, *Folktales of England*, pp. 117–18.

There was a sexton who cared for a church, and he wasn't at all suitable. The parson was a rich hunting man, and there was very few services he troubled to hold, not more than two–three in the year. So sexton, he had his own way, and a bad way it was. Folk that were curious would notice him dig a grave, so of course they'd ask whose 'twas, and all he'd answer was, "You'll see soon enough," and not a word more.

And sure enough, that open grave was filled with one of them. There was a godly and respected old farmer who was churchwarden and he had his doubts about sexton. One afternoon he came on him digging a grave, unbeknown to all, so he naturally asks whose 'tis. Sexton looked at 'en squinty-eyed, and says, "You'll know soon enough," and not a word more. And in three days farmer himself were buried in it.

By and by folks come to notice that it were those who doubted the sexton filled his open graves, but what to do about it they couldn't tell. Then old Betty, the gifted woman, she was guided to find a way. She came upon sexton in the dimmet, busy digging a new open grave, and she made a criss-cross avore she spoke a word, and she did not waste questions to put herself in his power—no—she pick up a bit of grave-mould, and creeps up all on her tip-toes, and drops 'en down on sexton a-digging. "Hungry earth must be fed, and open graves lie in wait," says she. "You'll see soon enough."

Sexton, he let out a skritch like the foul fiend himself, and he began to climb out arter old Betty, but her skittered off, spry as a robin her-dick, and he took and slipped on grave-edge, and a-fell on his back-spine into 'en. Then he gave out two more fearsome yells. "Dree on 'em," says old Betty. "Aye, he can bide still now," and there wasn't a sound in the grave-yard, but a whisper of wind in the grasses. Old Betty, she say her prayers and go on whoame, and Sexton he lay there with his back a-broked.

Come morning, folks could a-see his dead corpse in the open grave, and they all zee who 'twas vor soon enough.

My great gran she did say, "An open grave must be fed, or the man who digs it will find himself the one to fill it—in a coffin."

Contributed by Ruth L. Tongue to *Folk-Lore*, LXXII (1962), pp. 106–8, as she heard it in Taunton Deane in 1961, and later in Chipstable in 1963.
MOTIFS: K.1601 [*Deceiver falls into his own trap*]; D.1278.1 [*Magic churchyard mould*]; C.411.1 [*Tabu: asking for reason of an unusual action*].

It is supposed to be unlucky to leave a grave open on a Sunday. See song appended to "Mr Fox's Courtship" (A, V).

THE OVERTON HAUNTING

From *County Folk-Lore*, VI, *East Riding of Yorkshire*, edited by Gutch, p. 44.

LETTER WRITTEN BY ONE, EDM. SPENCER to the famous Noncon-formist Divine, RICHARD BAXTER, relating to divers Superstitious Practices and Observances in use in Holderness in the middle of the 17th century. Printed from the Original in the Library at Sledmore, Yorkshire, the seat of Sir Tatton Sykes, Baronet.

. . . .

Rev. Sir,—At the request of my good friend Mr Saunders, I send you here an account of those things which I saw and heard in *Yorkshire*, whereof he saith he gave you some account when you were at Iroton.

About 17 years agoe I went down Chaplain into Yorkshire to Esqr. *Overton* of Easington, in *Holderness*, upon his having married a Gentle-woman in Leicestershire, of my acquaintance. Soon after my coming to his house, I was informed by some of the inhabitants of the town, that his *house was haunted* against the death of any of the family and was at that time disturbed. We had been there but a few nights, but the servants began to talk in the day time of noises they had heard in the night. I was loath to believe it was anything but the Greyhounds walking up and down the garret, and told them sure it must be so. I heard a rush-like noise severall times myself, and I resolved at last to be satisfyed whether it was the dogs or no.

In order thereto I stayed up with the boy late one night, and having turned out all the dogs I lock the door, and tooke the keys into my chamber. That night the noise in the garret was more than ordinary, such a jumping and lumbering, as if the floor would come down on my head.

The rooms commonly said to be disturbed were the garret, and three chambers, betwixt which and the family, I lodged. I heard frequently in the night as if a person came up the back stairs into those rooms, and walked up and down the next roome to me, and when it went down stairs it was as if a woman descended, and her coats swept the stairs. An old servant told me they have some seldome times seen the spirit, and that it was in the likenes of a maid of the family whom their old mr. not permitting to marry one she was deeply in love with, she pin'd away and dyed, and that this disturbance in the house had been from her death.

Against the death of the Gentleman's mother, a servant who then lived there, told me that they filling the copper with water overnight in order to brewing, in the morning it was blood and could not be used, and their milk was spotted with blood severall nights. The last was also when I lived there: the Gentlewoman calling me one morning to see it I told her surely it must be the cats lapping with bloody tongues. She replied that could not be, since it was further than it was possible for them to reach, and more than it can be supposed a cat's tongue should bleed while lapping; we resolved to see how it would be if closely covered, and the next evening she ordered all the milk to be put into one large vessel, which with our own hands we closely covered, and locked the door, and she tooke the key up with her to bed. In the morning when she was about to go in, she was pleased to call me, and the milk was as bloody as any time before, and the inside of the vessel the spots were bigger and less, and the largest as broad as a silver twopence.

The fame of the house being haunted made it difficult for us to get any servants good for anything; and when we had them, they would stay but awhile. A new maid being hired was set to brew. In the daytime she heard a groaning in the celler under her. There being a hole in the floor, she puts her head to see if there were anybody in the celler, when she heard 3 hideous groans, which extremely affrighted her, as appear'd by her countenance and trembling. The maid having been hired a good way of had not heard of the house being haunted.

This last was about two years after I was in the family, and then Colonel Overton dyed at Seaton in Rutland, that day at noon, that the maid heard the groans in the celler and as far as I could gather at that instant, above 80 miles distant. I lived afterwards there three years, but heard no more disturbance within the house.

A person related to the family, and of the same name, a *vicious man*, dyed about eight years before I knew the town. At the instant of his expiring (as I was credibly informed by many) a *spirit* set up a bellowing under the window, and ran up the street into the Church-yard at the end of it, continuing his hideous noise all along till it came thither, and ever since the death of that person, that if any dyed in that street, the spirit made the noise under there window, and ran up so into the Church-yard, and was some times met in one shape, sometimes in another.

Our washerwoman (they told me one day as we were at dinner) had in the night seen and heard the spirit, and was so affrighted that she kept her bed. I urged it might be onely the strength of her imagination, and that I would not believe there was any such spirit unles I *heard it myself*. That very night, we being three of the family, and a gentleman of the next, sat up till one o'clock, and in severall parts of the house, the gentleman and a young lady his mistress upon the stair case, two maids by the kitchen fire fast asleep, I in my study. A spirit came under my study window, and fetched such a groan, as no creature I ever saw could make so loud a noise. It awakened the maids, affrighted the Gentleman and his mistress, set the dogs on howling and trembling, and I thought it might have been heard four or five miles, and yet none heard it but we five. That night a poor blind fellow of the town dyed. It was like his voice, but louder than it was possible for him to grown.

I suppose you may have heard of *Watching the Church-yard on St Mark's Eve*. It was frequently practised by those poor ignorant souls where I was. I have heard the manner of it from severall of them. They go two of them on St Mark's Eve, and stand in the Church-yard, within sight of the Church porch, and at a certain time of night (they say) the likenes of all those of the parish that shall dye that year, passeth by them into the Church, and in that order they will dye, and when they are all in they hear a murmuring noise in Church for a while, and then they have power to return. This they tell me was practised at *Pattrington*, and they that watched saw 140 pass into the Church, and one saw the likenes of the other. That year the *plague* came into the town, and so many dyed, and both the persons that watched.

One of my hearers of *Kelnsey* (which you will find in the map) told me a servant of his being in the field at work, a mile from the town, he went down to him, and while he was with him the bel rang. Saith the master, Somebody is dead. Saith the man, it is such an one. Saith the master, how do you know Saith the man, I was coming over the Church garth one night late, and when I was hard by the Church door, I had no power to stir; by and by there passed by me the likenes of twelve, and this is such an one. I know he is dead, for it is his turn now. And as the man said, so it proved. They told me that Easington Church-yard had often been watched, and that it was so one year that I lived there, and the watchers confidently reported that an old woman who was wont to hear me would dye that year, but they or the devil were mistaken, for she lived more than another.

Sr, I fear I shall tire you with reading wt. I am weary with writing, I pray if you have occasion to make publick anything which I have written concerning the house I lived in, let not the family be named. I am, Sir, your reall friend and unworthy Br. in the Lord work.

Edm. Spencer.

Leicester, July 26, 1673.   Spencer 12.

MOTIFS: F.473 [*Poltergeist*]; F.473.5 [*Poltergeist makes noises*]; E.761.1.10 [*Life token: milk becomes bloody*]; D.1827.1.3 [*Noise warns of approaching death*]; D.1825.6.1* [*Watching at church door at midnight on St Mark's Eve, etc.*] (Baughman); D.1825.6 [*Magic power to see who will die during coming year*]; D.1825.6.2*(c) [*The watcher does not see his own spirit if he is to die during coming year*] (Baughman).
¶ See "St Mark's Vigil", "Epworth Parsonage".

THE PHANTOM FUNERAL

Heather and Robin Tanner, *Wiltshire Village*, p. 164.

When Dr Bennett lived at Kington, Mrs Blanchard, the midwife, was his right hand. When the village lost its resident doctor she became still more invaluable, and even now that there is a district nurse she is often in demand for childbirth, the care of young babies, nursing, and laying-out if need be. The ageing villager while yet in possession of his faculties helps her in this solemn ceremony by putting aside in readiness a best nightgown, a chin-cloth, and long white stockings. She feels hurt if she is not sent for if there is a death.

On one occasion she thought she had been overlooked. It was when the Mintys lived next door to her. Bert Minty was a very small boy then. One winter evening after he had been "'ooding" in Herne Wood he came in, as he loved to do, to share his spoils with Mrs Blanchard. This time the walk had been more exciting than usual. As darkness was falling, he and his mother had crossed Pennycroft and were about to enter Herne Wood when they saw a funeral approaching through the trees, and stood aside, frightened, to let it pass. The procession went through the gate and across the field, but beyond that there was no sign of it.

Now no one lived in Herne Wood except the gamekeeper and his wife, and as far as Mrs Blanchard knew, neither of them was ill. Besides, whoever heard of a funeral taking place at five o'clock? She thought the story one of Bertie's fictions until it was corroborated by Sarah Minty herself. Mrs Blanchard felt aggrieved; she had been cheated not only of the laying-out, but apparently of the whole illness. But she was so busy with the Coles new baby that did not look as though it intended to live that this strange happening slipped her memory until the following week, when she was roused at cock-crow by the frantic knocking of the gamekeeper himself. He had just wakened to find his wife lying dead beside him.

MOTIF: D.1825.7.1 [*Person sees phantom funeral-procession some time before the actual procession takes place*].

¶ See "The Corpse Light".

THE PHANTOM HEARSE

Augustus Hare, *In My Solitary Life*, pp. 49–50.

When Mr Macpherson of Glen Truim was dying, his wife had gone to rest in a room looking out over the park, and sat near the window. Suddenly she saw lights as of a carriage coming in at the distant lodge-gate, and calling to one of the servants said, "Do go down, someone is coming who does not know of all this grief."

But the servant remained near her at the window, and as the carriage came near the house, they saw it was a hearse drawn by four horses and covered with figures. As it stopped at the porch door, the figures looked up at her, and their eyes glared with light; then they scrambled down, and seemed to disappear into the house. Soon they reappeared and seemed to lift some heavy weight into the hearse, which then drove off at full speed, causing all the stones and gravel to fly up at the windows. Mrs Macpherson and the butler had not rallied from their horror and astonishment when the nurse watching in the next room came in to tell her that the Colonel was dead.

MOTIFS: E.535 [*Ghostlike conveyance*]; E.752.1.3 [*Souls of dead captured on leaving corpse*].

¶ See "The Lift that Fell" for the spectral hearse which plays a common part in English tradition.

See also "The Phantom Funeral".

THE PHANTOM SHIP

Hunt, *Popular Romances of the West of England*, p. 358.

Years long ago, one night, a gig's crew was called off to a "Hobble" to the westward of St Ives Head. No sooner was one boat launched, than several others were put off from the shore, and a stiff chase was maintained, each one being eager to get to the ship, as she had the appearance of a foreign trader. The hull was clearly visible; she was a schooner-rigged vessel, with a light over her bows.

Away they pulled, and the boat which had been first launched still kept ahead by dint of mechanical power and skill. All the men had thrown off their jackets to row with more freedom. At length the helmsman cried out, "Stand ready to board her." The sailor rowing the bow oar slipped it out of the row-lock, and stood on the forethought,* taking his jacket on his arm, ready to spring aboard.

The vessel came so close to the boat that they could see the men, and the bow-oar man made a grasp at her bulwarks. His hand found nothing solid, and he fell, being caught by one of his mates, back into the boat, instead of into the water. Then the ship and lights disappeared. The next morning the *Neptune* of London, Captain Richard Grant, was wrecked at Gwithian, and all perished. The captain's body was picked up after a few days, and that of his son also. They were both buried in Gwithian churchyard.

MOTIFS: E.536 [*Phantom ship*]; D.1812.5.1.10 [*Sight of phantom ship a bad omen*].

THE PIRATE WRECKER AND THE DEATH SHIP

Hunt, *Popular Romances of the West of England*, pp. 359–62.

One lovely evening in the autumn, a strange ship was seen a short distance from Cape Cornwall. The little wind there was blew from the land, but she did not avail herself of it. She was evidently permitted to drift with the tide, which was flowing southward, and curving in round Whitesand Bay towards Land's End.

The vessel, from her peculiar rig, created no small amount of alarm amongst the fishermen, since it told them that she was manned by pirates; and a large body of men and women watched her movements from behind the rocks at Caraglose. At length, when within a couple of pistol-shots off the shore, a boat was lowered and manned.

Then a man, whose limited movements showed him to be heavily ironed, was brought to the side of the ship and evidently forced—for several pistols were held at his head—into the boat, which then rowed rapidly to the shore in Priest's Cove. The waves of the Atlantic Ocean fell so gently on the strand, that there was no difficulty in beaching the boat. The prisoner was made to stand up, and his ponderous chains removed from his arms and ankles. In a frenzy of passion he attacked the sailors, but they were too many and too strong for him, and the fight terminated by his being thrown into the water, and left to scramble up on the dry sands. They pushed the boat off with a wild shout, and this man stood uttering fearful imprecations on his former comrades.

* Thus Hunt, but it is possible that "fore-thwart" was intended.

It subsequently became known that this man was so monstrously wicked that even the pirates would no longer endure him, and hence they had recourse to this means of ridding themselves of him.

It is not necessary to tell how this wretch settled himself at Tregaseal, and lived by a system of wrecking, pursued with unheard-of cruelties and cunning. "It's too frightful to tell," says my correspondent, "what was said about his doings. We scarcely believed half of the vile things we heard, till we saw what took place at his death. But one can't say he died, because he was taken off bodily. We shall never know the scores, perhaps hundreds, of ships that old sinner has brought on the cliffs, by fastening his lantern to the neck of his horse, with its head tied close to the forefoot. The horse, when driven along the cliff, would, by its motion, cause the lantern to be taken for the stern-light of a ship; then the vessel would come right in on the rocks, since those on board would expect to find plenty of sea-room; and, if any of the poor sailors escaped a watery grave, the old wretch would give them a worse death, by knocking them on the head with his hatchet, or cutting off their hands as they tried to grasp the ledges of the rocks."

A life of extreme wickedness was at length closed with circumstances of unusual terror—so terrible that the story is told with feelings of awe even at the present day. The old wretch fought lustily with death, but at length the time of his departure came. It was in the time of the barley-harvest. Two men were in a field on the cliff, a little below the house, mowing. A universal calm prevailed, and there was not a breath of wind to stir the corn. Suddenly a breeze passed by them, and they heard the words, "The time is come, but the man isn't come." These words appeared to float in the breeze from the sea, and consequently it attracted their attention. Looking out to sea, they saw a black, heavy, square-rigged ship, with all her sails set, coming in against wind and tide, and not a hand to be seen on board. The sky became black as night around the ship, and as she came under the cliff—and she came so close that the top of the masts could scarcely be perceived—the darkness resolved itself into a lurid storm-cloud, which extended high into the air. The sun shone brilliantly over the country, except on the house of the pirate at Tregaseal —that was wrapt in the deep shadow of the cloud.

The men, in terror, left their work; they found all the neighbours gathered around the door of the pirate's cottage, none of them daring to enter it. Parson —— had been sent for by the terrified peasants, this divine being celebrated for his power of driving away evil spirits.

The dying wrecker was in a state of agony, crying out, in tones of the most intense terror, "The Devil is tearing at me with nails like the claws of a hawk! Put out the sailors with their bloody hands!" and using, in the paroxysms of pain, the most profane imprecations. The parson, the doctor, and two of the bravest of the fishermen were the only persons in the room. They related that at one moment the room was as dark as the grave, and that at the next it was so light that every hair on the old man's head could be seen standing on end. The parson used all his influence to dispel the evil spirit. His powers were so potent that he reduced the Devil to the size of a fly, but he could not put him out of the room. All this time the room appeared as if filled with the sea, with waves surging violently to and fro, and one could hear the breakers roaring, as if standing on the edge of a cliff in a storm. At last there was a fearful crash of thunder, and a blaze of the intensest lightning. The house appeared on fire, and the ground shook, as if with an earthquake. All rushed in terror from the house, leaving the dying man to his fate.

The storm raged with fearful violence, but appeared to contract its dimensions. The black cloud, which was first seen to come in with the black ship, was moving, with a violent internal motion over the wrecker's house. The cloud rolled together, smaller and smaller, and suddenly, with the blast of a whirlwind, it passed from Tregaseal to the ship, and she was impelled, amidst the flashes of lightning and roarings of thunder, away over the sea.

The dead body of the pirate-wrecker lay a ghastly spectacle, with eyes expanded and the mouth partly open, still retaining the aspect of his last mortal terror. As everyone hated him, they all desired to remove his corpse as rapidly as possible from the sight of man. A rude coffin was rapidly prepared, and the body was carefully cased in its boards. They tell me the coffin was carried to the churchyard, but it was too light to have contained the body, and that it was followed by a black pig, which joined the company forming the procession, nobody knew where, and disappeared, nobody knew when. When they reached the church stile, a storm, similar in its character to that which heralded the wrecker's death, came on. The bearers of the coffin were obliged to leave it without the churchyard stile, and rush into the church for safety. The storm lasted long and raged with violence, and all was as dark as night. A sudden blaze of light, more vivid than before, was seen, and those who had the hardihood to look out saw that the lightning had set fire to the coffin, and that it was being borne away through the air, blazing and whirling wildly in the grasp of such a whirlwind as no man ever witnessed before or since.

TYPE ML.5060 MOTIFS: E.536 [*Phantom ship*]; D.1812.5.1.10 [*Phantom ship an evil omen*]; D.1311.11.1 [*River says, "The time has come but not the man"*].
¶ See "The Sea's Victim", "The Spectre Ship of Porthcurno", "The Phantom Ship".

'PITY POOR BRADFORD' [summary]

Parkinson, *Yorkshire Legends and Traditions*, 1st series, p. 198.

During the Civil War, the Earl of Newcastle had succeeded in confining a part of the Parliamentary army, commanded by Sir Thomas Fairfax, in the city of Bradford. The defenders had lost almost all their ammunition in their recent defeat at Adwalton, and were helpless against the Royalist siege-engines. Fairfax and his troops, however, forced their way out through the besieging army one dark night, taking advantage of the smoke and flames and general confusion. The town was thus left entirely helpless, and the Earl of Newcastle issued orders that on the following day they should put to the sword every man, woman and child still left alive within it.

He was sleeping that night at Bolling Hall, and had a strange dream, or vision. A woman, in gauzy white garments, entered his room, and pulled away the coverlets from his bed. This happened several times and the Earl was completely awake and trembling, when his visitant cried out "with a lamentable voice", "Pity poor Bradford! Pity poor Bradford!" So strong was the impression left by the apparition that the Earl immediately after daybreak countermanded the order he had given, and the city was reprieved.

MOTIF: V.235.0.1 [*Mortal visited by angel in vision*].
¶ The capture of Bradford by Newcastle was in 1643. It is unlikely that Newcastle would have had the city put to the sword, since it had not long been sieged, and the garrison surrendered. The account given by Colonel Burne in *The Great Civil War, a Military History*, p. 63, is that Sir Thomas Fairfax and Major-General Gifford broke out with a party of 50 horse, but the rest of the garrison, 300 strong, surrendered next day.

Lady Fairfax was taken prisoner, but the Earl of Newcastle sent her to Hull in his own coach. It is likely that the citizens of Bradford expected dreadful things from the wild Cavaliers, and could only put down their immunity to supernatural interposition.

THE PLAGUE IN EDINBURGH [summary]

Robert Chambers, LL.D., *The Book of Scottish Story*, pp. 104–9.

The last time that Edinburgh was visited by the plague the effects were so severe that the streets lay empty, and grass grew even along the main streets, and around the Cross. A strange feature of this visitation made it even more dreaded and perplexing than usual, for, when it was at its height, it began to be observed that many of the sufferers were dying several days before the sickness had run its full course. No care from the physicians, nor use of salutary drugs, was of any avail; those most carefully tended succumbed, alike with those deserted and neglected. It almost seemed as though some new disease were imposing itself upon the pestilence, making it even more deadly than before. Amid all the uncertainties attending this new development, one thing could be clearly remarked; the greater part of those who suffered from this new disease died during the night, and all of them were unattended.

At last, a poor woman stopped a physician in the street, and begged to speak with him. He tried to shake her off, but she said it was not as a patient that she had approached him; she had something to tell which might help to clear up the mystery of these premature deaths. On the preceding night, she had left her room to attend to a sick neighbour, two floors below her own garret; with a lamp in her hand, she descended the winding staircase, and as she did so, she heard a low groan from her neighbour's room, such as she already connected with the sufferings of those at the point of death. As she reached the door of the room, something seemed to swish past her in the darkness, with a sound like a full garment brushing against a wall, and, drawing in her lamp, she half saw beyond it a tall human figure, gliding out of sight. It was gone in a moment, and she scarcely knew whether she had seen it, or whether it was not a trick of the moving lamplight. But on entering her neighbour's room, she found her already dead, a full three days before the time due; which convinced both her and the physician to whom she now told the story, that what she had seen was something real and active. The report soon spread through the city, and grew into a superstitious belief that what the woman had seen was the image of Death itself, rendered visible by the peculiar horror of the circumstances, and that it would shortly burst forth in open triumph, and roam at large through the desolate streets.

Two days later a strange, armed ship entered Leith Harbour, a Barbary rover, manned by a foreign crew. The plague in Leith was raging as fiercely as in Edinburgh, and there was no resistance when a detachment of the strange crew landed, and inquired for the Provost. On being admitted, they told him their cargo was all of certain drugs, efficacious against the plague, and that they had with them a few men skilled in their administration; and that they were prepared to stay and work for the relief of the sick, on condition of receiving half the wealth of any whom they restored to life. The Provost, whose only daughter was amongst the stricken, and who, besides, was full of care for his citizens, eagerly welcomed the proposal, and the captain himself of the strange ship undertook to attend his daughter.

The Provost, Sir John Smith, lived in this year, 1645, in the Cap and Feather Close, an alley occupying the site of the present North Bridge. The alley itself provided no egress to the North Loch, but the Provost's house possessed one, and had also a back door opening upon an alley to the east, named Halkerston's Wynd. The house at this time was full of treasures; for many citizens had deposited their most precious possessions there, trusting to the Provost's honesty to return them if they should recover their health, and thinking him worthy to inherit them if they did not. The sick daughter lay in a little room at the back of the house, which, besides its main door opening on the great front staircase, had also another, more private one, leading to the narrow spiral staircase at the back. This door was seldom locked, as was the common practice in those days, for simply to close a door was considered sufficient precaution against the entry of fairies.

The Barbary captain administered a certain dose to his patient, which he knew must very soon take effect, either for good or ill; he therefore resolved to watch in her room all night. About midnight as he sat in a far corner of the room, he was surprised to observe a kind of dark cloud interpose itself quite silently between himself and the bed. At first he thought it imagination, or that he was falling asleep; but soon a very slight noise, and something like movement in the dim features of the apparition, convinced him of its reality; and as it stopped over the bed, the patient sighed, and her hitherto regular breathing seemed to cease altogether. The African sprang to his feet with an involuntary cry, and at once the figure, or cloud, rose from the bed, and seemed to contract into a definite human shape, and in a moment it had glided softly from the room. The African said to himself, "In Aleppo, these angels of death are sometimes found to be human. I shall pursue and try it." He followed the phantom with all speed, snatching up his semicircular sword as he went, and, reaching the bottom of the stairs, saw, in the moonlight, a shadow disappearing at an angle of the house, and at once started in pursuit. In the street all was dark, but he followed the way the shadow had seemed to go, and fancied that a beam of moonlight far ahead was blotted out for a moment by its passing. He ran headlong down the steep wynd, and at the bottom, in full moonlight, he clearly saw the figure of a tall man, wrapped in an enormous cloak, gliding towards a small bridge, which here crosses the drain of the North Loch; and connects the town with the village known as the Mutries Hill. Suddenly the flying figure vanished from his sight, as though it had disappeared into a hole in the ground, and left the pursuer alone. He never saw it, or any trace of it, again.

In bewilderment, he returned to his patient, expecting to find her dead, but, to his delight and astonishment, she was already much recovered; and soon afterwards the plague began to abate throughout the city; and many believed that it was through the courage and fidelity of the watcher that the evil demon had been driven away.

An affection sprang up between him and his patient, the Provost's daughter, and on recovery she was married to the foreigner who had saved her life. They inherited, in due time, the Provost's vast property, and the African abandoned his life of piracy and became a devout Presbyterian, and settled finally in Edinburgh, where he eventually rose to high position and won the regard of all. He built a magnificent house for his residence, near the head of Canongate, in front of which was erected a statue of the Emperor of Barbary, which still stands in its original niche, to testify to the truth of the tale.

MOTIFS: F.493 [*Spirit of the plague*]; F.493.0.2 [*Pestilence in human form*]; F.493.3.1 [*Upon destruction of pestilence spirit, plague ceases*].
¶ See "Trapping the Small-pox" (B, IX).

THE POWER OF NAMES

Edward Clodd, *Tom Tit Tot*, p. 137.

The Rev. Hilderic Friend vouches for the genuineness of the following story, the bearing of which on the continuity of barbaric and quasi-civilized ideas is significant:

"In the village of S——, near Hastings, there lived a couple who had named their first-born girl Helen. The child sickened and died, and when another daughter was born, she was named after her dead sister. But she also died, and on the birth of a third daughter the cherished name was repeated. This third Helen died, 'And no wonder,' the neighbours said. 'It was because the parents had used the first child's name for the others.'

"About the same time, a neighbour had a daughter, who was named Marian because of her likeness to a dead sister. She showed signs of weakness soon after birth, and all said that she would die as the three Helens had died, because the name Marian ought not to have been used. It was therefore tabooed, and the girl was called Maude. She grew to womanhood, and was married; but so completely had her baptismal name of Marian been shunned that she was married under the name of Maude, and by it continues to be known to this day."

Folk-Lore Record, Vol. IV, p. 79.
MOTIF: N.131.4 [*Luck changing after change of name*].

THE PRESSING STONES

Hunt, *Popular Romances of the West of England*, pp. 368–70.

Those who are not familiar with the process of "curing" [salting] pilchards for the Italian markets will require a little explanation to understand the accompanying story.

The pilchards, being caught in vast quantities, often amounting to many thousand hogshead at a time, in an enclosed net called a "seine", are taken out of it—the larger net in a smaller net, called the "tuck net", and from it loaded into boats, and taken to the shore. They are quickly transferred to the fish-sellers, and "put in bulk"—that is, they are well rubbed with salt, and carefully packed up, all interstitial spaces being filled with salt—in a pile several feet in height and depth. They remain in this condition for about six weeks, when they are removed from "the bulk", washed, and put into barrels in very regular order. The barrels being filled with pilchards, pressing stones—round masses of granite, weighing about a hundredweight—with an iron hook fixed into them for the convenience of moving, are placed on the fish. By this they are much compressed, and a considerable quantity of oil is squeezed out of them. This process being completed, the cask is "headed", marked, and is ready for exportation.

Jem Tregose and his old woman, with two sons and a daughter, lived over one of the fish-cellars in St Ives. For many years there had been a great scarcity of fish; their cellar had been empty; Jem and his boys were fishermen, and it had long been hard times with them. It is true they went out "hook-and-line" fishing now and then, and got a little money. They had gone over to Ireland on the herring fishing, but very little luck attended them.

Summer had passed away, and the early autumn was upon them. The seine boats were out day after day, but no "signs of fish". One evening, when the boys came home, Ann Tregose had an unusual smile upon her face, and her daughter Janniper, who had long suffered from the "megrims", was in capital spirits.

"Well, Mother," says one of the sons, "and what ails thee a'?"

"The press-stones a bin rolling."

"Haas they, sure enuff," says the old man.

"Ees, ees!" exclaims Janniper; "they has been making a skimmage!"

"Hark ye!" cries the old woman. "There they go again."

And sure enough there was a heavy rolling of the stones in the cellar below them. It did not require much imagination to imagine these round granite pebbles sliding themselves down on the "couse", or stone flooring, and dividing themselves up into sets, as if for a dance—a regular "cows' courant", or game of romps.

"Fish tomorrow!" exclaimed the old woman. The ejaculations of each one of the party showed their perfect faith in the belief, that the stones rolling down from the heap, in which they had been useless for some time, was a certain indication that pilchards were approaching the coast.

Early on the morrow the old man and his sons were on their "stem"; and shortly after daybreak the cry of "Heva! Heva!" was heard from the hills; the seine was shot, and ere nightfall a large quantity of fish might be seen in the cellar, and everyone joyous.

MOTIF: D.1812.5.2 [*Favourable omens*].

THE RED KING'S DEER

Ruth L. Tongue, *Forgotten Folk Tales.*

I'll tell you a new one—and a true one. It happened to us in 1953[?] when King George VI died. (No one but our family knows the tale.)

When my Granny was little (we lost her three years ago) she had an old great-uncle who had been a New Forest verderer all his life. He was over 90 and remembered the Press Gangs and Riding Officers, and Waterloo, and he always said that when the reigning sovereign was going to die, a huge red deer stag haunted the big tree some people call the King's Tree, and say Will Rufus was killed there, because the arrow was deflected on it.

William Rufus was called the Red King, and so Granny's great-uncle called the ghost deer the Red King's Deer, and said you could tell by the size of its slots how heavy it was, and how fast it was going. If it stood still a little while, then the death wouldn't come for nearly a year, but if it galloped it would be in a few weeks.

Granny's great-uncle said only four or five keepers had ever seen it through hundreds of years, and they all died violent deaths, but they had all spoken of a big red stag—not a fallow buck. He also said the slots were seen by keepers in 1820 when the mad old king died, and then the next two kings in 1830 and 1836. My great-great-uncle was dead before Queen Victoria's death, and Granny daren't go and look—but my father, who was very young, went, and no one knew. He never told us until one day Granny was talking, and then he said:

"I went when Teddy [Edward VII] was ill, and I was still a boy—the slots were there, and again for King George V. There wouldn't be any for the Duke of Windsor—he wasn't crowned, and he's still alive. A huge, heavy red deer stag—got all his rights, I should judge—and there aren't any his size or breed in the forest to my knowledge, ever since the park deer got out after the war."

Well, my mother and my sister and I just laughed, but Granny didn't like it, nor did my father, but he never said much anyway. It was such a joke, we kept on and on, just to tease them—then, one day mother jumped up, and said she'd go and look for herself, and so could we. Granny cried, and I felt ashamed, but my sister called, and we hurried to catch up mother, who was a good walker.

We got there, laughing at the joke, all three of us, but the fresh slots *were* there, almost as big as an Exmoor Royal Stag. I've hunted that country, and that stopped my laugh. Then my sister heard an angry snort nearby.

"What's that?" she said.

"Buck in rut," said mother. "We'd better move."

But it wasn't the right time of year.

Then we all heard it—the furious snort of a challenging big red stag, like the Quantock ones we'd heard on the wireless—even my mother recognized it.

We all ran like young girls. I didn't think I could do it—I was forty then, and mother was sixty-one.

When the three of us got home, and fell into armchairs, Granny nodded and father turned on the wireless. "Perhaps you women won't contradict so much now," and the voice of the announcer said King George VI was seriously ill.

From a Hampshire W.I. member. Hampshire, Denman College, 1962.
MOTIFS: B.147.1 [*Beasts furnish omens*]; E.761 [*Life token*]; E.423.2.6 [*Revenant as deer*]; D.1812.5.1.17 [*Spectre as evil omen*].
¶ See "The Joug Tree", "The White Bird of the Oxenhams", "The Death Fetch of William Rufus".

ROOM FOR ONE MORE

Briggs and Tongue, *Folktales of England*, p. 67.

A young woman on her way up to Town broke her journey by staying with friends at an old manor house. Her bedroom looked out to the carriage sweep at the front door. It was a moonlight night and she found it difficult to sleep. As the clock outside her bedroom door struck twelve, she heard the noise of horses' hoofs on the gravel outside, and the sound of wheels. She got up and went over to the window, to see who could be arriving at that time of night.

The moonshine was very bright, and she saw a hearse drive up to the door. It hadn't a coffin in it; instead, it was crowded with people. The coachman sat up high on the box, and as he came opposite to the window he drew up and turned his head. His face terrified her, and he said in a distinct voice, "There's room for one more." She drew the curtains close, ran back to bed, and covered her head with the bedclothes. In the morning she was not quite sure whether it had been a dream, or whether she had really got out of bed and seen the hearse, but she was glad to go up to Town and leave the old house behind her.

It was a shopping expedition she was going on, and she was shopping in a big store which had a lift in it—an up-to-date thing at that time. She was on the top floor, and she went to the lift to go down. It was rather crowded, but as she came up, the lift-man turned his head and said, "There's room for one more." It was the face of the coachman of the hearse. "No, thank you," said the girl. "I'll walk down." She turned away, the lift doors clanged, then there was a terrible rush, and screaming and shouting, and then a great clatter and thud. The lift had fallen from the top to the bottom of the building, and every soul in it was killed.

Heard by K. M. Briggs about 1912 as a child in Dunkeld, Perthshire, from a visitor who lived in London.
MOTIFS: E.723.8 [*Appearance of wraith as calamity omen*]; E.723.7.1 [*Wraith speaks*]; J.1050 [*Attention to warnings*]; D.1810.8.3.2 [*Dream warns of danger that will happen in near future. Because of the advance knowledge, the danger is averted*].
¶ A folder in the Folklore Archives of Indiana University gives five American texts under the heading "Urban Belief Tales: Room for One More".
  Baughman actually allots MOTIF D.1810.8.3.1.1 [*Dream warns of illness or injury. The dream is fulfilled*] to this legend. The next motif, however, seems more appropriate.
  See "The Lift that Fell", "The Nightmare House".

ST MARK'S VIGIL

S. Baring-Gould, *A Book of Folk-Lore*, pp. 174-5.

In Yorkshire the wraith or double is called a waft. There is one night in the year, in which the wafts of those who are about to die proceed to the church and be seen. This is St Mark's Eve, and anyone who is curious to know about the death of his fellow-parishioners must keep watch in the church porch on that eve for an hour on each side of midnight for three successive years. Mr Henderson says in his *Northern Folklore*:

"On the third year they will see the forms of those doomed to die within the twelvemonth passing, one by one, into the church. If the watcher falls asleep during his vigil he will die himself during the year. I have heard, however, of one case in which the intimation was given by the sight of the watcher's own form and features. It is that of an old woman, at Scarborough, who kept St Mark's Vigil in the porch of St Mary's in that town about eighty years ago. Figure after figure glided into the church, turning round to her as they went in, so that she recognized their familiar faces. At last a figure turned and gazed at her; she knew herself, screamed, and fell senseless to the ground. Her neighbours found her there in the morning, and carried her home, but she did not long survive the shock."

MOTIF: D.1825.6.1* [*Watching at church door or church porch at midnight on St Mark's Eve, etc.*] (Baughman).
¶ St Mark's Day is 25 April. This was a day of processions and prayers for the crops. The dead are always clearly linked with agricultural fertility in popular religion, and this makes it natural that the procession of the dead should take place on St Mark's Eve.
  See "The Christmas Eve Vigil", "The Curate of Axholm".

THE SEA'S VICTIM

S. Baring-Gould, *A Book of Folk-Lore*, pp. 114-5.

On the Cornish coast the sea is heard calling for its victims. A fisherman or a pilot walking one night on the sands at Porth-Towan, when all was still save the monotonous fall of the light waves upon the sand, distinctly heard a voice from the sea exclaiming, "The hour is come, but not the man." This was repeated three times, when a black figure, like that of a man, appeared on the top of the hill. It paused for a moment, then rushed impetuously down the steep incline, over the sands, and was lost in the sea.

TYPE ML.4050.MOTIF:D.1311.11.1 [*River says "The time has come, but not the man"*].
¶ See "The Doomed Rider" (B, V), "Jan Coo" (B, V), "The Pirate Wrecker and the Death Ship".

THE SHEPHERD AND THE CROWS

E. M. Leather, *Folk-Lore of Herefordshire*, p. 168.

Years ago, on the Black Mountain above Longton, there lived a hired shepherd, who managed a little farm for his master. There were on either side of this farm two brothers, farming for their father. I can remember in my time there was terrible jealousy and animosity between the shepherds on the mountain, where the sheep all run together. I could always tell my sheep; if I whistled, they would all come running to me every one, while the strangers took no notice. A good shepherd knows his sheep, and they know him.

Well, it was worse nor ever for this man, because the brothers were together and they hated him. He stuck to his master, and they to their father. At last one day they got him alone on the mountain, and caught him, and said they would murder him. They told him there was no one about, and it would never be known. "If you kill me," he said, "the very crows will cry out and speak it."

Yet they murdered and buried him. The body was found after some time, but there was no evidence to show who the murderers were. Well, not long after that, the crows took to come wheeling round the heads of those two brothers, "crawk, crawk, crawk", there they were, all day long —when they were together, when they were apart. At last they could scarcely bear it, and one said to the other, "Brother, do you remember when we killed the poor shepherd on the mountain top there, he said the very crows would cry out against us." These words were overheard by a man in the next field, and the matter was looked into, so that in the end the brothers were both hanged for murder.

From W. Perry of Walbersham, a native of Langton, aged 80. 1903.
TYPE 960A. MOTIFS: N.271 [*Murder will out*]; N.271.3 [*The Cranes of Ibycus*];
N.271.3.1 [*Ravens pursue Murderer*].

SIR JAMES RAMSAY OF BAMFF

Chambers, *Popular Rhymes of Scotland*, p. 77.

Weel, ye see I dinna mind the beginning o' the story. But the Sir James
Ramsay o' that time was said to be ane o' the conspirators, and his lands
were forfaulted, and himsel' banished the country, and a price set upon
his head if he came back.

He gaed to France or Spain, I'm no sure which, and was very ill off.
Ae day that he was walking in a wood, he met an oldish man wi' a lang
beard, weel dressed and respectable-looking. This man lookit hard at Sir
James, and then said to him that he lookit ill and distressed like; that he
himsel' was a doctor, and if Sir James would tell his complaints, maybe
he might be able to do him good.

Syne Sir James said he was not ill but for want o' food, and that all the
medicine he needed was some way to earn his living as a gentleman. The
auld doctor said till him he would take him as an apprentice if he liked;
that he should live in his house and at his table, and learn his profession.
So Sir James went home with him, and was very kindly tret. After he had
been wi' him a while, his master said till him ae day that he kend how to
make the most wonderful medicine in the world—a medicine that would
make baith their fortunes, and a' that belonged to them; but that it was
a difficult business to get the materials that the medicine was made of—
that they could only be gotten frae the river—,that ran through the county
of ——, in Scotland, and at a particular part of the river, which he described; and that it would need to be some canny person, that kend that
pairt o' the country weel, to gang wi' ony chance o' success. Sir James
said naebody kend that pairt o' the country better than himsel', for it was
on his ain estate o' Bamff, and that he was very willing to run the risk o'
going hame for his master's sake, that had been sae kind to him, and for
the sake o' seeing his ain place again.

Then the doctor gied him strict directions what he was to do, and how
he was to make sure o' getting the beast that he was to make the medicine
o'. He was to gang to a pairt o' the river where there was a deep pool o'
water, and he was to hide himsel' behind some big trees that came down
to the waterside for the three nights that the moon was at the full. He
would see a white serpent come out o' the water, and go up to a big stane,
and creep under it. He maun watch it till it came out again, and catch it
on its way back to the water, and kill it and bring it awa' wi' him.

Weel, Sir James did a' that he was bidden. He put on a disguise, and gaed back to Scotland, and to Bamff, and got there without onybody kenning him. He hid himsel' behind the trees, at the waterside, and watched night after night. He saw the white serpent come out the first twa nights, and creep under the stane; but it aye got back to the water afore he could catch it; but the third night he did catch it, and killed it, and brought it awa' wi' him to Spain to his master. His master was very glad to get it, but he wasna sae kind after to Sir James as he used to be. He told him, now they had got the serpent, the next thing to do was to cook it, and he maun do that too. He was to go down to a vault, and there stew the serpent till it was turned into oil. If onybody saw him at the wark, or if he tasted food till it was done, the charm would be spoiled; and if by ony chance he was to taste the medicine, it would kill him at ance, unless he had the proper remedy. Sae Sir James gaed down to the vault, and prepared the medicine just as he had been ordered; but when he was pouring it out o' the pan, into the box where it was to be keepit, he let some drops fa' on his fingers that brunt them; and in the pain and hurry he forgot his master's orders, and put his fingers into his mouth to suck out the pain. He did not die, but he fand that his een were opened, and that he could see through everything. And when his master came down at the appointed time to speer if the medicine were ready, he fand that he could see into his master's inside, and could tell a' that was going on there. But he keepit his ain secret, and never let on to his master what had happened; and it was very lucky, for he soon found out that his master was a bad man, and would have killed him if he had kenned that he had got the secret o' the medicine.

He had only been kind to him because he kend that Sir James was the best man to catch the serpent. However, Sir James learnt to be a skilful doctor under him; and at last he managed to get awa' frae him, and syne he travelled over the warld as a doctor, doing mony wonders, because he could clearly see what was wrang in folks' insides. But he wearied sair to get back to Scotland, and he thought that naebody would ken him as a doctor. Sae he ventured to gae back; and when he arrived he fand that the king was very ill, and no man could find out what was the matter wi' him. He had tried a' the doctors in Scotland, and a' that came to him frae far and near, but he was nane the better; and at last he published a proclamation that he would gie the princess, his daughter, in marriage to ony man that could cure him. Sae Sir James gaed to the court, and askit leave to try his skill. As soon as he came into the king's presence, and looked at him, he saw there was a ball o' hair in his inside, and that no medicine could touch it. But he said that if the king would trust to him he would cure him; and the king having consented, he put him sae fast asleep, that he cuttit the ball of hair out o' his inside without his ever wakening. When he did waken, he was free from illness, only weak a little frae the loss o' blood; and he was sae pleased wi' his doctor, that Sir James kneeled down and tell't him wha he was. And the king pardoned him, and gied him back a' his lands, and gied him the princess, his daughter, in marriage.

TYPES: 673; ML.3030. MOTIFS: B.176.1 [*Magic serpent*]; B.162.1 [*Supernatural knowledge from eating magic fish*].

¶ See "Michael Scott" (B, III).

SIR JOHN ARUNDELL

Hunt, *Popular Romances of the West of England*, p. 373.

In the first year of the reign of Edward IV, the brave Sir John Arundell dwelt on the north coast of Cornwall, at a place called Efford, on the coast near Stratton. He was a magistrate, and greatly esteemed amongst men for his honourable conduct. He had, however, in his official capacity, given offence to a wild shepherd, who had by some means acquired considerable influence over the minds of the people, under the impression of his possessing some supernatural powers. This man had been imprisoned by Arundell, and on his return home he constantly waylaid the knight, and, always looking threateningly at him, slowly muttered:

"When upon the yellow sand,
Thou shalt die by human hand."

Notwithstanding the bravery of Sir John Arundell, he was not free from the superstitions of the period. He might, indeed, have been impressed with the idea that this man intended to murder him. It is, however, certain that he removed from Efford on the sands to the wood-clad hills of Trerice, and here he lived for many years, without the annoyance of meeting his old enemy. In the tenth year of Edward IV, Richard de Vere, Earl of Oxford, seized St Michael's Mount. Sir John Arundell, then Sheriff of Cornwall, gathered together his own retainers, and a large host of volunteers, and led them to the attack on St Michael's Mount.

The retainers of the Earl of Oxford, on one occasion, left the castle, and made a sudden rush upon Arundell's followers, who were encamped on the sands near Marazion. Arundell then received his death-wound. Although he left Efford "to counteract the will of Fate", the prophecy was fulfilled; and in his dying moments, it is said his old enemy appeared, singing joyously: "When upon the yellow sand,
Thou shalt die by human hand."

MOTIFS: M.341.3.4 [*Prophecy: death on seashore*]; M.370.1 [*Prophecy of death fulfilled*].

SIR JOHN DUCK

F. Grice, *Folk-Tales of the North Country*, pp. 127–30.

In the city of Durham there is a very old street called Silver Street. It is narrow and winding, and the houses on either side lean over it and look down upon its cobblestones. Although most of these houses are new buildings, some are almost as old as the street itself and could tell many exciting stories of the ancient city.

One of them is now used as a café, but behind the shop front is a handsome old staircase, which leads to a room containing a very interesting picture. This picture is now dark with age, and you have to look very closely at it to make anything of it. But if you do look closely, you will see that it is a picture of a young man standing by the side of a river with a big bird hovering near him. That man was Sir John Duck, and the people of Durham have an interesting little story about him.

John Duck was not born in Durham, but came there as a stranger many years ago to seek his fortune. But he was young and had no friends in the city to help him to earn a living. He had been apprenticed to a butcher and was skilful at his trade, but in those days the butchers of Durham were jealous of their profession. Most of those to whom he applied for work turned him away, saying, "Already there are more apprentices in this town than we need, and besides, you do not belong to our guild. You had better be off and look elsewhere." And when at last he did find work, the rest of the butchers held a meeting of the guild, and insisted on his being dismissed.

So John Duck found himself penniless and friendless in a strange city. He was worse than friendless, for all the tradesmen seemed to have set themselves up as his enemies. Sadly he turned away from Durham, and began to walk along the riverside, to try his fortune in another city. But he had not gone far before he saw a fine black raven circling round his head, and it seemed to be carrying something in its mouth. However, he took little notice of the raven, except perhaps to envy it the piece of food it seemed to be carrying off. He hung his head and walked on even more sadly.

But the raven kept circling round him, as if it had a message for him. John stopped and looked up at it, and as he looked up it flew closer to him, and he saw something drop and fall close to his feet. At first he thought it was the piece of cheese or crust, but as in falling on the stones it made a tinkling sound, he ran forward to pick it up, and found that it wasn't crust or cheese at all, but a big golden coin. He looked up for the raven to see if there was any further message, but the bird, as if satisfied that it had performed its mission, had already turned and flown away.

To the penniless boy this coin was like infinite riches, and his first thought was to turn back and order for himself a good meal of meat and wine. But just then there came past a man driving two cows slowly towards Durham.

"Are you going to sell those cows?" asked John.

"To the first man that will take them off my hands," replied the man. "These stubborn beasts have led me such a dance today as I have never been put to. I'm footsore and homesick, and the sooner they and I part company the better."

"Then," said John, who was shrewd enough to see that here was an opportunity for a good bargain, "I'll buy them." And the drover was so pleased to find a ready buyer that, as John had foreseen, he sold them cheaply. Overjoyed at his bargain, John drove them immediately to the market at Durham, and sold them at such a good price that he made a handsome profit. And this money proved to be the beginning of his fortunes. He made more and more deals, each with such success that he grew to be a rich man. He bought land here and there, and became so important that in the end he was chosen to be the Mayor of the city and was knighted Sir John Duck.

So John Duck, the penniless boy who had almost starved to death, grew to greatness and popularity, and in that same Silver Street in which he had sought in vain for employment he built himself a splendid mansion. But he never forgot the raven that had brought him so much good luck, and in gratitude to the Providence that had saved him from poverty, he put aside part of his wealth and built at Lumley a hospital for the sick and aged people to whom Fate had not been so kind.

MOTIFS: N.213 [*Man fated to be rich*]; B.451.5 [*Helpful raven*]; N.222 [*First object(s) picked up brings fortune*].

¶ The account of Sir John Duck given in the *Denham Tracts*, I, p. 44, is shorter, but contains one or two additional details, among them the rhyme on Sir John Duck:

> On Duck the butcher shut the door
> But Heslop's daughter Johnny wed;
> In mortgage rich, in offspring poor,
> Nor son nor daughter crown'd his bed.

In this, as in some other ways, his tale was like that of Dick Whittington.
See "Whittington and his Cat" (A, IV).

SIR OSBERT

Scott, *Minstrelsy of the Scottish Border*, II, p. 319.

Osbert, a bold and powerful baron, visited a noble family in the vicinity of Wandlebury, in the Bishopric of Ely. Among other stories related in the social circle of his friends, who, according to custom, amused each other by repeating ancient tales and traditions, he was informed that if any knight, unattended, entered an adjacent plain by moonlight and challenged an adversary to appear, he would be immediately encountered by a spirit in the form of a knight.

Osbert resolved to make the experiment, and set out, attended by a single squire, whom he ordered to remain without the limits of the plain, which was surrounded by an ancient entrenchment. On repeating the challenge, he was instantly assailed by an adversary, whom he quickly unhorsed, and seized the reins of his steed. During this operation his ghostly opponent sprung up, and darting his spear, like a javelin, at Osbert, wounded him in the thigh. Osbert returned in triumph with the horse, which he committed to the care of his servants. The horse was of a sable colour, as well as his whole accoutrements, and apparently of great beauty and vigour. He remained with his keeper till cock-crowing, when, with eyes flashing fire, he reared, spurned the ground and vanished.

On disarming himself, Osbert perceived that he was wounded, and that one of his steel boots was full of blood.... As long as he lived the scar of his wound opened afresh on the anniversary of the eve on which he encountered the knight.

From Gervase of Tilbury. *Otia Imperialia* Vol. I, p. 797.
MOTIFS: E.461.1 [*Revenant challenged to combat*] or G.303.9.6.1 [*Devil fights with man*]; G.303.9.6.0.1 [*The Devil is armed*]; G.303.3.3.1.3 [*Devil as horse*] or G.303.7.1.1 [*Devil rides on black horse*]; G.303.17.1.1 [*Devil disappears when cock crows*]; G.303.20.8 [*Satan injures man*].

THE SOUL AS A HUMBLE-BEE

S. Baring-Gould, *A Book of Folk-Lore*, p. 36.

Two young men had been spending the early portion of a warm summer day in exactly such a scene as that in which he (i.e. a cousin of Hugh Miller) communicated to me the anecdote.

There was an ancient ruin beside them, separated, however, from the mossy bank on which they sat by a slender runnel, across which lay, immediately over a miniature cascade, a few withered grass stalks. Overcome by the heat of the day, one of the young men fell asleep; his companion watched drowsily beside him, when all at once the watcher was aroused to attention by seeing a little, indistinct form, scarcely larger than a humble-bee, issue from the mouth of the sleeping man and, leaping upon the moss, move downwards to the runnel, which it crossed along the withered grass stalks, and then disappeared amid the interstices of the ruin.

Alarmed by what he saw, the watcher hastily shook his companion by the shoulder, and awoke him; though, with all his haste, the little cloud-like creature, still more rapid in its movements, issued from the interstices into which it had gone, and flying across the runnel, instead of creeping along the grass-stalks and over the sward, as before, it entered the mouth of the sleeper just as he was in the act of awakening. "What is the matter with you?" said the watcher, greatly alarmed, "what ails you?" "Nothing ails me," replied the other; "but you have robbed me of a most delightful dream. I dreamt that I was walking through a fine, rich country, and came at length to the shores of a noble river; and just where the clear water went thundering down a precipice there was a bridge all of silver, which I crossed, and there, entering a noble palace on the opposite side, I saw heaps of gold and jewels; and I was just going to load myself with treasure when you rudely awoke me, and I lost all."

I have little doubt that what Cousin George saw was a humble-bee issuing from the mouth of the sleeper, for this is the form the soul is not infrequently supposed to wear.

From Hugh Miller, *My Schools and Schoolmasters.*
TYPE ML.4000. MOTIFS: E.734.2 [*Soul in form of bee*]; E.721.1 [*Soul wanders from body in sleep*].
¶ See "The Escaping Soul".

THE SEPARABLE SOUL

[F. J. Norton's notes]

Gesta Romanorum, no. 72. Guido and Tyrens, "The White Weasel". A version with fuller particulars in Saxo Grammaticus.

English Folk-Lore. The Soul as a Butterfly. *Somerset Notes and Queries*, from Somerset and Dorset, III, Sherborne, 1893.

The Soul as a Bee: *Choice Notes from "Notes and Queries"*, III.

Rhys, *Celtic Folk-Lore:* The Soul as a Lizard, The witch who sent out her soul as a bee.

THE SPECTRE SHIP OF PORTHCURNO

Hunt, *Popular Romances of the West of England*, pp. 362–4.

Porthcurno Cove is situated a little to the west of the Logan Stone. There, as in nearly all the coves around the coast, once existed a small chapel, or oratory, which appears to have been dedicated to St Leven. There exists now a little square enclosure about the size of a (*bougie*) sheep's house, which is all that remains of this little holy place.

Looking up the valley (Bottom), you may see a few trees, with the chimney-tops and part of the roof of an old-fashioned house. That place is Raftra, where they say St Leven's Church was to have been built; but as fast as the stones were taken there by day, they were removed by night to the place of the present church. (These performances are usually the work of the Devil, but I have no information as to the saint or sinner who did this work.)

Raftra House, at the time it was built, was the largest mansion west of Penzance. It is said to have been erected by the Tresillians, and, ere it was finished, they appear to have been obliged to sell the house and lands for less than it had cost them to build the house. This valley is, in every respect, a melancholy spot, and during a period of storms or at night, it is exactly the place which might well be haunted by demon revellers. In the days of the saint from whom the parish has its name—St Leven—he lived a long way up from the cove, at a place called Bodelan, and his influence made that, which is now so dreary, a garden. By his pure holiness he made the wilderness a garden of flowers, and spread gladness where now is desolation.

Few persons cared to cross that valley after nightfall; and it is not more than thirty years since that I had a narrative from an inhabitant of Penberth, that he himself had seen the spectre-ship sailing over the land. This strange apparition is said to have been observed frequently, coming in from sea about nightfall, when the mists were rising from the marshy ground in the Bottoms.

Onward came the ill-omened craft. It passed steadily through the breakers on the shore, glided up over the sands, and steadily pursued its course over the dry land, as if it had been water. She is described to have been a black, square-rigged, single-masted affair, usually, but not always, followed by a boat. No crew was ever seen. It is supposed they were below, and that the hatches were battened down. On it went to Bodelan, where St Leven formerly dwelt. It would then steer its course to Chygwiden, and there vanish like smoke.

Many of the old people have seen this ship, and no one ever saw it upon whom some bad luck was not sure to fall. This ship is somehow connected with a strange man who returned from sea, and went to live at Chygwiden. It may be five hundred years since—it may be but fifty. He was accompanied by a servant of foreign and forbidding aspect, who continued to be his only attendant; and this servant was never known to speak to anyone save his master. It is said by some they were pirates; others make them more familiar, by calling them privateers; while some insist upon it, they were American buccaneers. Whatever they may have been, there was but little seen of them by any of their neighbours. They kept a boat at Porthcurno cove, and at daylight they would start for sea, never returning until night, especially if the weather was tempestuous. This kind of sea-life was varied by hunting. It mattered not to them whether it was day or night; when the storm was loudest, there was this strange man, accompanied either by his servant or by the devil, and the midnight cry of his dogs would disturb the country.

This mysterious being died, and then the servant sought the aid of a few of the peasantry to bear his coffin to the churchyard. The corpse was laid in the grave, around which the dogs were gathered, with the foreigner in their midst. As soon as the earth was thrown on the coffin, man and dogs disappeared, and, strange to say, the boat disappeared at the same moment from the cove. It has never since been seen, and from that day to this no one has been able to keep a boat in Porthcurno cove.

MOTIFS: E.536 [*Phantom ship*]; D.1812.5.1.10 [*Phantom ship an evil omen*]; cf. E.501.15.8 [*Wild huntsman lives in room on farm*]; E.501.15.6.4 [*Wild huntsman's dogs cannot pass over grave*]; E.501.16 [*Phenomena at disappearance of Wild Hunt*]. ¶ See "The Pirate Wrecker and the Death Ship", "The Devil and his Dandy Dogs", (B, III).

THE STOLEN CORN

Roger of Wendover, *Chronicle*, II, p. 600.

When the year [1234] had progressed as far as July, still pressing heavily on the poor, who daily suffered from want, they rushed into the harvest-fields in crowds, and plucked the ears of corn although not yet ripe, and bruising them up with their trembling hands, endeavoured to sustain the spark of unhappy life, which scarcely palpitated in their bosoms; and this fact can scarcely be reprehensible in poor people since we read in the Acts of the Apostles that Christ's disciples did the same.

The labourers of some of the villages, however, who from their avarice always have suspicions of poverty, were much annoyed, on passing through their fields, at discovering this pious theft, and the inhabitants of a town called Alboldesly, in the county of Cambridge, proceeded on the following Sunday, which was the 16th of July, to their church, and tumultuously demanded of their priest to pronounce sentence of excommunication on all those who had picked the ears of corn in their fields. Whilst all the husbandmen were urging this point, one of the townsmen, a religious and pious man, on seeing that the priest was ready to pronounce the sentence, rose and adjured him in the name of Almighty God and all the saints, to exclude him and all his crops from the sentence; he also added that he was well satisfied with the poor people's having taken what they did from his crops in their state of want, and what remained he commended to the Lord's care. Whilst all the rest were persisting in their foolish purpose, and the priest under compulsion had commenced pronouncing the sentence, there suddenly arose a great storm of thunder, lightning, and whirlwinds, attended by inundations of rain and hail; and the corn in the fields was lifted up by a blast from hell; the cattle and birds, with everything growing in the fields, were destroyed as if trodden down by carts and horses.

Aloft in the air, the angels of Satan were seen flying about, who were believed to be the agents of this tempest. But, as the divine goodness is always constant to just and good men, when, after the storm which had caused such loss to his neighbours, that honest and just man visited his fields, he discovered his farms and lands, although in the midst of other people's property, to be without any trace of injury from it; and from this it appears clear as light, that, as glory is given to God on high by His Angels, so there is peace and goodwill on earth towards men. This storm commenced on the boundaries of Bedford and, passing towards the east through the isle of Ely and Norfolk, reached the sea-coast.

MOTIFS: V.410 [*Charity rewarded*]; D.2141.0.3 [*Storms produced by Devil*]; Q.150 [*Immunity from disaster as reward*].

A STRANGE VISITANT

Augustus Hare, *In My Solitary Life*, p. 36.

I

Mr Herman Merivale* told us—

A captain was crossing to America in his ship, with very few sailors on board. One day one of them came up to him on the deck and said that there was a strange man in his cabin—that he could not see the man's face, but that he was sitting with his back to the door at the table writing. The captain said it was impossible there could be anyone in his cabin, and desired the sailor to go and look again.

When he came up, he said the man was gone, but on the table was the paper on which he had written, with the ink still wet, the words "Steer due south". The captain said that, as he was not pressed for time, he would act on the mysterious warning. He steered due south, and met with a ship which had been long disabled and whose crew were in the last extremity.

The captain of the disabled ship said that one of his men was a very strange character. He had himself picked him up from a deserted ship, and since then he had fallen into a cataleptic trance, in which, when he recovered, he declared that he had been in another ship, begging its captain to come to their assistance. When the man who had been sent to the cabin saw the cataleptic sailor, he recognized him at once as the man he had seen writing.

* Herman Merivale, 1806–74; barrister, Professor of Political Economy at Oxford (1837), Under-Secretary for India.

II

Mr Merivale said that a case of the same kind had happened to himself. He was staying at Harrow, and very late at night was summoned to London. Exactly as the clock struck twelve he passed the headmaster's door in a fly. Both he and the friend who was with him were at that moment attracted by seeing a hackney coach at the door—a most unusual sight at that time of night, and a male figure wrapped in black descend from it and glide into the house, without, apparently, ringing, or any door being opened. He spoke of it to his friend, and they both agreed that it was equally mysterious and inexplicable. The next day the circumstance so dwelt on Mr Merivale's mind that he returned to Harrow, and going to the house, asked if the headmaster, Dr Butler, was at home. "No," said the servant. Then he asked who had come at twelve o'clock the night before. No one had come, no one had been heard of, no carriage had been seen; but Dr Butler's father had died just at that moment in a distant county.

I. MOTIF: E.723.4 [*Wraith does what person wishes to do, but is unable to do in the flesh*]. II. MOTIF: E.723.6 [*Appearance of wraith as announcement of person's death*].
¶See "Elizabeth and Hephzibah", "The Doctor's Fetch".

A TEST OF INNOCENCY

Hunt, *Popular Romances of the West of England*, p. 421.

A farmer in Towednack, having been robbed of some property of no great value, was resolved, nevertheless, to employ a test, which he had heard the "old people" resorted to for the purpose of catching the thief. He invited all his neighbours into his cottage, and when they were assembled, he placed a cock under the "brandice" (an iron vessel formerly much employed by the peasantry in baking, when this process was carried out on the hearth, the fuel being furze and ferns).

Everyone was directed to touch the brandice with his or her third finger, and say, "In the name of the Father, Son, and Holy Ghost, speak." Everyone did as they were directed, and no sound came from beneath the brandice. The last person was a woman, who occasionally laboured for the farmer in his fields. She hung back, hoping to pass unobserved amidst the crowd. But her very anxiety made her a suspected person. She was forced forward, and most unwillingly she touched the brandice, when, before she could utter the words prescribed, the cock crew. The woman fell faint on the floor, and, when she recovered, she confessed herself to be the thief, restored the stolen property, and became, it is said, "a changed character from that day".

MOTIF: H.235 [*Ordeal: cock under pot crows when guilty person touches pot*].

¶ A similar test of guilt is a seventeenth-century charm called "The Eye of Abraham", to be found in a seventeenth-century magical manuscript, "The Key of Solomon", MS. Brit. Mus. Addt. 36674. A good many stories deal with mock magical spells, in which the thief betrays himself out of guilt.

THE TREE'S REVENGE

Ruth L. Tongue, *Somerset Folklore*, p. 27.

"There was a old farmer, see, and he had two sons, and him and the eldest they was as cheese-paring a team as you'd a-meet outside Bristol City. Always getting a bit more on the sly they was, though farm were sizeable enough to keep twenty men to work. 'Twas nothing but contrive and worrit to snip off a bit of hedge here and a plot of grass there from what wasn't theirs nohow. Seemed like they couldn't take their meals in contentment at the plenty they had, and the youngest he got so that he wouldn't agree at all. He was one that would sooner give with a kindly word. Now the farm lay by the forest, and the youngest son he'd always been the one as had gone to market through it, but he took care to start at sunrise and was back by sunset, and asked the great oak by the gate if he 'med go droo'. So when the old man begins to take away wood and cut timber without a word to anyone—though he'd fine coppices over-right the farm—youngest son he took himself away from hoame. Trees didn't say nothing—which was bad. If they do talk a bit you do get a warning, but if they'm dead still there's summat bad a-brewing. And zo 'twas. Be danged if gurt oak didn't drop a limb on cart and timber and farmer and eldest son. Killed they two stark dead outright, but when youngest came to rescue the dead the tree rustled fit to deafen he.

"Told he how 'twas, I s'pose; nor it hadn't hurted the cart-hoss on account it was shod. So youngest he gets farm and gives back all the old man nicked, and puts fences to their rightful places, and prospers. And he drove the cart-hoss to market through forest all his days, and tree never followed'n nor closed in about'n, nor let drop branches. But he had a criss-cross of nails on each boot to make sure."

MOTIFS: F.441.2 [*Tree spirit*]; D.950.2 [*Magic oak tree*]; C.43.2 [*Tabu: cutting certain trees lest tree spirits be offended*].

¶ The oak tree is considered formidable, even though good. See *Somerset Folk-Lore*, p. 26.

See "The One with the White Hand".

THE UNBORN SOUL

R. Blakeborough, *Wit, Character, Folk-Lore and Customs of the North Riding of Yorkshire*, p. 110.

Once a soul was permitted to see the body it was soon to inhabit. As it watched, it heard the mother say, "When my baby is born, if it is a boy, we shall have him christened..." The soul returned to its own place, and described the body and the name that were soon to be its own.

But when the time came that the child was carried to the font, to its dismay the soul heard another name spoken. It was sorely troubled at this, and felt that all it could do was to return to its former dwelling-place, and clear itself from the apparent guilt of having given a false name. For this it must free itself from the body; but once a soul and body have parted, they may not be reunited, so the baby died, and the soul fled away.

MOTIFS: E.706 [*Abode of unborn souls*]; E.721.9 [*Soul of embryo wanders*]; E.700.1 [*Names given the soul*]; E.720 [*Soul leaves the body*].
¶ This kind of belief probably accounts for the notion that it is very unlucky to name a child before it is born.

THE UNTOLD SECRET

County Folk-Lore, II, *North Riding of Yorkshire, etc.*, ed. Gutch, pp. 123–5.

A little way from the walls of York, in the direction of Middlethorpe, there stood, in years gone by, a large old house of baronial dimensions and Elizabethan character.... A secret of considerable importance was said to have belonged to one of the families occupying this house, which had been maintained for several generations, but was never known to more than one member of the family, and only transferred from sire to son or daughter at the moment when the holder of the secret was dying.

As the story runs, one of the family, who for the time was keeper of this concealed incident, was taken suddenly and seriously ill, and before she could reveal her keep to some other member of the family, she passed away, and with her the secret so long sustained. The family must have had some experience of ghosts or some suspicions of prospective troubles, for they took especial pains to save themselves from the truant tenant of the grave, and secure for themselves immunity against any intruder. They had learnt the theory prevalent in those days that if a corpse is taken out of a house by some other than the ordinary way of ingress and egress, it will never find a means of access again, and cannot haunt the inmates or even the inside of the dwelling....

They determined to break a hole through the wall at the back part of their home; and then to take the coffin containing the corpse out of the habitation by that new and singular way. Having completed their arrangements they carried off the corpse to the grave, followed by mourning friends. A few nights after, at the witching hour of the night, moaning sounds broke on the night air, as if coming from somebody in distress and, waking the members of the family, they could, on looking out, see a ghost wandering in apparent bewilderment, seeking some way or road into the house. Round about the spot where the hole had been made the spirit wandered, making noises which betrayed anxiety and despair. The family was thrown into a state of deep concern and, after submitting to the trouble for many months, they left the residence, but not so the ghost.

For years the neighbourhood bore the character of being haunted, and persons living close by or passing that way at midnight were persuaded that the belief was well founded. Night by night those who had sat late at their cups, and drunk well if not wisely, and those on whom business or pleasure had made demands only satisfied at midnight, reported visions of the ghost, whilst companies of young folk sometimes made visits to the spot in the hope of seeing the spectre. Occasionally they were gratified, but more generally disappointed, for the ghost was shy and would not do the bidding of a crowd. Many stories were rife of the freaks of this ghost, and many a fireside was encircled in the long winter nights to recite what had been seen, and to guess what was intended by the unrest of the poor dead woman....She invariably appeared in white, with long, flowing hair; her step was quick, yet steady, her aim was unmistakably an entrance into the house she had formerly occupied, and so far as could be deciphered her features bore an expression of anguish mingled with despair. The house was old and unsuitable to general occupancy, with the consequence that it went so much out of repair that some years ago it was razed to the ground, and with its demolition there was an end to the ghost.

Camidge, *The Ghosts of York*, pp. 7–9.

¶ The important part of this story turns on the danger of dying with a family secret undisclosed.

The most relevant motif is E.451.1.1 [*Corpse cannot be laid until he has confided the secret of magic charms*]. Unfortunately, this poor ghost's family did nothing to relieve her of her secret, but selfishly tried to prevent her returning. The applicable motifs are, therefore, E.431.4 [*Coffin carried through hole in wall to prevent return of dead*] and E.451.8 [*Ghost laid when house it haunts is destroyed or changed*].

A VISION AT DUNINO

Wilkie, *Bygone Fife*, p. 325.

Some years ago, when many of the roads in the east of Fife were still used but by few, a visitor to the district chanced to ride from the south coast to St Andrews by that across the uplands. He had heard of Dunino Church, and knew something of its associations. He therefore resolved to make a detour to visit it. A somewhat rough track leads down to a bridge across the Pitmilly Burn, not yet united to her sister streams. Thence there diverges a broad and well-made path, cut in the hillside, and climbing among the trees to the kirk and the manse. Leaving this for the moment he continued on the level track round the flank of the hill, and saw before him on the farther side of the stream a picturesque hamlet. Some of the cottages were thatched, some tiled; but all were covered with roses and creepers. In front a strip of garden, stretching to the burn, was trimly kept, and full of old-world flowers; behind, it took on more the nature of a kail-yard. At the east end, on slightly higher ground, a smithy closed the prospect, save for the trees that shut out the farther windings of the Den.

No sound broke the stillness of the summer noon but the flow of the burn. At one or two of the doors there stood an old man in knee-breeches and broad bonnet, or a woman in a white mutch and a stuff gown, while in the entrance to the forge the smith leant motionless on his hammer.. . .

Peace brooded like a benediction over the hollow. Half in a dream, he turned and climbed to the church, nor, as time pressed when he had seen it, did he return that way.

No sense of the abnormal had occurred to the intruder. He encountered no living thing till he had passed back to the high road. All was solitude.

A year or little more elapsed ere the wanderer came thither again. It was autumn, and tints of russet and gold were stealing into the colour of the woodlands. This time he was accompanied by a companion to whom he had told the story of his glimpse of "the most old-world hamlet in Fife". Where he had left the highway they diverged from it and, crossing the bridge, prepared to sketch the Arcady to be revealed.

The cottages were gone.

The burn flowed through the Den as when last he saw it, but its farther bank was bare. The smithy, like the cottages and those whose simple lives were passed in them, had returned to the world of dreams, and where it had stood appeared a croft, the house on which itself seemed old. The wanderer could but assure his questioning companion of the truth of his vision, and leave the riddle to be solved by other minds than his.

Both the *Statistical Accounts* state that there has been no village in the parish "within living memory"; but the population in Sir John Sinclair's day was only one-half of what it had been, and there were then thirty-one fewer inhabited houses than at an earlier date.

The author is informed on excellent authority that there were at one time at least three or four cottages and a blacksmith's shop at the place described. It is said these were taken down "some time last century".

¶ Glimpses into the past are not unheard of, though not common. The best-known example is described in *An Adventure*, by Miss Moberly and Miss Jourdain, a book which has aroused a good deal of controversy.

See "The Lord Protector" (B, VIII).

THE VISION OF IAN MHOR

Wilkie, *Bygone Fife*, p. 134.

Ian Mhor foretold the victory at Largs won for Alexander the Third by the intervention of his ancestors from their resting graves in Dunfermline Abbey. He had seen it in a dream. Thus writes the nameless monk who penned *The Book of Pluscarden:*

"In the year 1263...the King of Norway landed at Conyngham with a very great host of warriors.... But it came to pass at that time that a certain knight named John de Wemyss dreamt that he went into the Church of the blessed Queen Margaret at Dunfermline, and saw a queen coming clad in gorgeous apparel of gold, wearing a crown on her head; and with her a most comely king, likewise robed in kingly raiment, arrayed in bright armour, wearing a most costly crown on his helmet; and three other kings, equally clad in royal robes, and most gorgeously armed, accompanied the foregoing queen and king. The lady herself was leading the first king by the right hand, keeping step with him, while the others followed step by step, one after the other. So when the said knight beheld them, he marvelled, and kneeling down with becoming reverence, said, 'O glorious lady, I beseech thee, deign to show me who thou art, and these who accompany thee, and whither thou art bound.'

"She said to him with a cheerful countenance, 'I,' said she, 'am Margaret Queen of Scotland; he whom I lead by the hand is my illustrious husband, King Malcolm; the others who follow are my sons, whilom kings of this realm; and we are hastening with them to a place called Largs, to defend our country against the snares of the enemy; and God granting us grace, we shall gain the victory over that tyrant king who is striving wrongfully to invade our realm and subdue it unto him; for, as thou knowest, I have had this realm intrusted to me and my heirs for ever by God.'

"Then said the knight unto her, 'O my glorious lady, give me a token whereby I may know this and that others may believe me.' 'Go,' said she, 'to the church of my burial, and thou shalt straightway recover thee from thy sickness.'

"So the knight, who had long been laid up and suffering from some incurable feverish sickness, at once awoke out of his sleep, made the necessary preparations, and failed not to accomplish on foot a pilgrimage to Dunfermline, though he could hardly stir in bed the day before. But when he came to Dunfermline and gave the prior and the other religious a set account of the vision, he was brought to the blessed Margaret's bier, touched the relics and prayed; and straightway from that hour he was cured of all his sickness and the fever left him.

"Now this was done that it might not be thought that the aforesaid vision was brought about by a trick of evil spirits; but it was in very truth manifested from Heaven, as the result of the affair most clearly showed, for shortly afterwards the King's envoys came thither and brought word of the splendid victory of the said Battle of Largs. So they rejoiced thereat with great gladness, and gave praises unto God and the blessed queen."

From *The Book of Pluscarden*.
MOTIFS: V.516 [*Vision of future*]; V.229.7 [*Invaders miraculously defeated by saints*]; V.221.0.1 [*Relics of saint cure disease*].

THE WAFF

Gutch, *County Folk-Lore*, II, *North Riding of Yorkshire*, p. 83.

Not very many years have gone by since a man of Guisborough entering a shop in this old fishy town [Whitby] saw his own wraith standing there unoccupied. He called it a "waff". Now it is unlucky in the highest degree to meet one's own double; in fact, it is commonly regarded as a sign of early death. There is but one path of safety; you must address it boldly.

The Guisborough man was well aware of this and went up without hesitation to the waff. "What's thou doing here?" he said roughly. "What's thou doing here? Thou's after no good, I'll go to bail. Get thy ways yom, wi' thee, get thy ways yom." Whereupon the waff slunk off abashed and the evil design with which it came there was brought happily to nought.

Norway, *Highways and Byways in Yorkshire*, p. 139.

MOTIF: E.723.2(*b*) [*Person avoids imminent death by giving his own wraith a severe tongue-lashing, sending it home*] (Baughman).

¶ Scolding is often an effective way of dealing with the Devil and ghosts.

THE WANDERING JEW IN ENGLAND

From *Choice Notes from "Notes and Queries"*, p. 150.

Of the many myths which diverge from every little incident of Our Saviour's career, the legend of Ahasuerus, the Wandering Jew, is certainly the most striking and widely distributed. According to the old ballad in Percy's *Collection:*

> He hath passed through many a foreign place,
> Arabia, Egypt, Africa,
> Greece, Syria, and great Thrace,
> And throughout all Hungaria.

All the nations of the Seven Champions have it in some shape or other, and it is amusing to note the way in which the story adapts itself to the exigencies of time and place. In Germany, where he appeared A.D. 1547, he was a king of Polyglot errant, baffling professors and divines, with the accumulated learning of fifteen centuries. In Paris he heralded the advent of Cagliostro and Mesmer, cured diseases, and astounded the *salons* by his prodigious stories, in which he may be truly said to have ventured the entire animal. He remembered seeing Nero standing on a hill to enjoy the flames of his capital; and was a particular crony of Mahomet's father at Ormus. It was here, too, he anticipated the coming scepticism, by declaring, from personal experience, that all history was a tissue of lies.

In Italy the myth has become interwoven with the national art lore. When he came to Venice, he brought with him a fine cabinet of choice pictures, including his own portrait by Titian, taken some two centuries before. In England John Bull had endowed him with the commercial spirit of his stationary brethren, and, to complete his certificate of naturalization, made him always thirsty! But the Jew of Quarter Sessions Reports, who is always getting into scrapes, is not the Jew of the rural popular legends; in which he is invariably represented as a purely benevolent being, whose crime has been long since expiated by his cruel punishment, and who is therefore entitled to the help of every good Christian.

When on the weary way to Golgotha, Christ fainting, and overcome under the burden of the Cross, asked him, as he was standing at his door, for a cup of water to cool His parched throat, he spurned the supplication and bade Him on faster. "I go," said the Saviour, "but thou shalt thirst and tarry till I come." And ever since then, by day and night, through the long centuries he has been doomed to wander about the earth, ever craving for water, and ever expecting the Day of Judgment which shall end his toils:

> *Mais toujours le soleil se lève,*
> *Toujours, toujours,*
> *Tourne la terre ou moi je cours,*
> *Toujours, toujours, toujours, toujours.*

Sometimes, during the cold winter nights, the lonely cottager will be awoke by a plaintive demand for "Water, good Christian! water, for the love of God!" And if he looks out into the moonlight, he will see a venerable old man in antique raiment, with grey flowing beard and a tall staff, who beseeches his charity with the most earnest gesture. Woe to the churl who refuses him water or shelter.

My old nurse, who was a Warwickshire woman, and, as Sir Walter said of his grandmother, "a most awfu' le'er", knew a man who boldly cried out, "All very fine, Mr Ferguson, but you can't lodge here." And it was decidedly the worst thing he ever did in his life, for his best mare fell dead lame, and the corn went down, I am afraid to say how much per quarter. If, on the contrary, you treat him well, and refrain from indelicate inquiries respecting his age—on which point he is very touchy —his visit is sure to bring you good luck. Perhaps, years afterwards, when you are on your death-bed, he may happen to be passing; and if he *should*, you are safe; for three knocks with his staff will make you hale, and he never forgets any kindnesses. Many stories are current of his wonderful cures; but there is one to be found in Peck's *History of Stamford* which possesses the rare merit of being written by the patient himself.

Upon Whitsunday, in the year of our Lord 1658, "about six of the clock, just after evensong", one Samuel Wallis, of Stamford, who had been long wasted with a lingering consumption, was sitting by the fire, reading in that delectable book called *Abraham's Suit for Sodom*. He heard a knock at the door; and as his nurse was absent, he crawled to open it himself. What he saw there Samuel shall tell in his own style:

"I beheld a proper, tall, grave old man. Thus he said: 'Friend, I pray thee give an old pilgrim a cup of small beere!' And I said, 'Sir, I pray you, come in, and welcome.' And he said, 'I am no Sir, therefore call me not Sir; but come in I must, for I cannot pass by thy doore.'

"After finishing the beer, 'Friend,' he said, 'thou art not well.' I said, 'No, truly, Sir, I have not been well this many yeares.' He said, 'What is thy disease?' I said, 'A deep consumption, Sir; our doctors say, past cure; for, truly, I am a very poor man, and not able to follow doctor's councell.' 'Then,' said he, 'I will tell thee what thou shalt do; and, by the help and power of Almighty God above, thou shalt be well. Tomorrow, when thou risest up, go into thy garden, and get there two leaves of red sage, and one of bloodwarte, and put them into a cup of thy small beere. Drink as often as need require, and when the cup is empty, fill it again, and put in fresh leaves every fourth day, and thou shalt see, through our Lord's great goodness and mercy, before twelve days shall be past, thy disease shall be cured, and thy body altered."

After this simple prescription, Wallis pressed him to eat; but he said, "No, friend, I will not eat; the Lord Jesus is sufficient for me. Very seldom doe I drink any beere neither, but that which comes from the rocke. So, friend, the Lord God be with thee."

So saying, he departed, and was never more heard of; but the patient got well within the given time, and for many a long day there was war hot and fierce among the divines of Stamford, as to whether the stranger was an angel or a devil. His coat was purple, and buttoned down to the waist; "his britches of the same couler, all new to see to"; his stockings were very white, but whether linen or jersey, deponent knoweth not; his beard and head were white, and he had a white stick in his hand. The day was rainy from morning to night, "but he had not one spot of dirt upon his cloathes".

Aubrey gives an almost exactly similar relation, the scene of which he places in the Staffordshire Moorlands. He there appears in a "purple-shag gown", and prescribes balm leaves.

So much for the English version of the Wandering Jew. Nothing tending to illustrate a theme to which the world has been indebted for *Salathiel, St Leon, Le Juif Errant*, and *The Undying One*, can be said to by wholly uninteresting.

V. T. Sternberg, *Notes and Queries*, XII, p. 503.

THE WANDERING JEW

Aubrey, *Miscellanies*, p. 83.

Anno 165*. At —— in the Moorlands in Staffordshire, lived a poor old man, who had been a long time lame. One Sunday, in the afternoon, he being alone, one knocked at his door: he bade him open it, and come in. The Stranger desired a cup of beer; the lame man desired him to take a dish and draw some, for he was not able to do it himself. The Stranger asked the poor man how long he had been ill? the poor man told him. Said the Stranger, "I can cure you. Take two or three balm leaves steeped in your beer for a fortnight or three weeks, and you will be restored to your health; but constantly and zealously serve God." The poor man did so, and became perfectly well. This Stranger was in a purple-shag gown, such as was not seen or known in those parts. And no body in the street after evensong did see anyone in such a coloured habit. Dr Gilbert Sheldon, since Archbishop of Canterbury, was then in the Moorlands, and justified the truth of this to Elias Ashmole, Esq., from whom I had this account, and he hath inserted it in some of his memoirs, which are in the Museum at Oxford.

TYPE 777. MOTIFS: Q.502.1 [*The Wandering Jew*]; Q.221.3 [*Punishment for blasphemy*]; Q.45 [*Hospitality rewarded*].
¶ Aubrey's version is appended to Sternberg's notes for the sake of his pleasant narrative style, though it is summarized by Sternberg.

THE WARNING DREAM

E. G. Bales, *Folk-Lore*, Vol. L, March 1939, p. 74.

There were two maids at a farm, and every night the yardman used to bring up the milk, set it just inside the dairy, shut the door and go home. One night when he brought the milk up he put it in the dairy and shut the door, but he stopped in the house unbeknown to the girls. For three nights these girls had dreamed that they would be murdered in bed. They told the gardener, and he said he would sit up and watch. The yardman hid under the bed in the girls' room. The girls went upstairs to bed, and the gardener stayed downstairs to watch with a double-barrelled gun.

After some time he saw the door open, and without waiting to see who was there he shot and killed the yardman. The gardener locked the door and went to inform the police. On the way he met the yardman's wife and he asked her where she was going. She replied: "You haven't shot my husband, have you?" "There's enough done for tonight," he said, and sent her home.

When the policeman and the gardener returned to the house they found both girls with their throats cut.

Told by Mr R. Crawford.
MOTIFS: D.1810.8.3 [*Warning in dreams*]; D.1810.8.3.1 [*Warning in dream fulfilled*].

THE WEIRD OF THE THREE ARROWS
[summary]

Gibbings, *Folk-Lore and Legends, Scotland*, pp. 40–51.

Sir James Douglas, the companion of Bruce, known as "The Black Douglas" during his war against the English, was resting with his troops and his colleague Randolph, at Linthaughlee, near Jedburgh. At night, having completed his round of the camp, he was standing outside his tent, when an old woman approached him with faltering steps. She was leaning on a staff, and held in her hand three English arrows. She told him that the three arrows were stained with the blood of three of her sons, shot in different battles by the English, and that she had vowed to return them to their owners by the same means as she had received them.

Sir James replied that he never used the bow, and that she must apply to another; but she answered that she could not take the arrows back, and added that she would see him again on St James's E'en. She departed, and Sir James put the arrows into an empty quiver amongst his baggage. After a broken night, for he could not put out of his mind the image of the strange old woman, he was roused at daybreak by a message that Sir Thomas de Richmont had crossed into Scotland, and could easily be attacked in a certain narrow defile.

Sir James marched there in haste, and by ordering his men to twist the slender stems of the young birch trees together, he made an impassable barrier for the enemy, and his archers, from hidden positions, inflicted severe injury upon the English, while Sir James, at the head of his cavalry, rushed upon them and himself killed Sir Thomas de Richmont with his dagger.

Shortly afterwards a Gascon knight, Edmund de Cailon, who was Governor of Berwick, was returning to England loaded with plunder from a successful raid into Teviotdale, and was heard to boast that he had sought in vain for the famous Black Knight. Sir James met him by forced marches, and in single combat slew him also.

Sir Ralph Neville, who was defending Berwick, similarly boasted that he would fight the Douglas if he would show his banner before Berwick. Sir James joyfully accepting the challenge, first ravaged the country, and burnt the villages around the town, and then waited for Neville to come out to the attack. In a desperate battle which followed, he again succeeded in bringing his opponent to single combat, and killed him. Neville's army fled in confusion, and the Scots having at last retired to their tents to sleep, Douglas was surprised by the reappearance of the old woman. She reminded him that it was the Eve of St James, and asked whether he had returned the three arrows to the English. He replied, as before, that he never fought with the bow, and she then asked for the arrows, which he produced and was astonished to find that all three were broken through the middle. The old woman cried out in delight that the weird was broken, since one arrow had come from a soldier of Richmont's army; a second from one of Cailon's; and the third from one of Neville's; and thus her sons were now avenged.

She went out, scattering the broken fragments of the arrows on the floor of the tent as she left.

MOTIFS: D.1092 [*Magic arrow*]; D.1700 [*Magic powers*].
¶ It is difficult to classify this mysterious tale with its mixture of magical powers and straightforward fighting.

THE WHINGER

Douglas, *Scottish Fairy and Folk-Tales*, p. 210.

A noble peer of this nation being one morning in his bed-chamber and attended by several persons, when his servant had put a new coat upon his Lord, a gentleman standing by presently cried out, "For God's sake, my Lord, put off that coat," and being asked the reason, he replied that he saw a whinger, or poignard, stick in the breast of it. The noble peer, esteeming this as a mere fancy, replied; "This coat is honestly come by, and I see no reason why I may not wear it."

The gentlemen still entreated, and earnestly craved that it might be put off; upon which debate, the noble peer's lady being not far off, came in, and being informed of the whole affair, entreated her Lord to comply with the gentleman's desire, which he did; meantime, one of the servants standing by desired the lady to give it him, and he would wear it. She granted his request, who put it on; and ere night he was stabbed by a poignard in that very place which the gentleman had pointed to in the morning.

From the Rev. John Frazer, Δευτεροσκοπιά, *or A Brief Discourse concerning the Second Sight, commonly so called,* 17th Century.
MOTIFS: D.1825.1 [*Second sight*]; D.1825.7 [*Magic sight of incident before it actually happens*].

THE WHITE BIRD OF THE OXENHAMS

J. R. W. Coxhead, *Legends of Devon*, p. 44.

Probably one of the best-known of all the many interesting legends of Devon is the strange tradition attached to the Oxenham family. This tradition is the once widespread belief in the white-breasted bird of the Oxenhams.

According to the earliest version of the legend, which undoubtedly dates from medieval times, a certain Margaret Oxenham was about to be married to the man of her choice. On the morning of the wedding, while the preparations for the happy event were at their height, a large white bird appeared and hovered above Margaret's head, to the great consternation of everyone present.

The appearance of the bird was considered to be an omen of forthcoming death. However, in spite of the bird of ill-omen, the preparations for the wedding were continued, and when all was ready the happy bride proceeded to the church of South Tawton. But when she was standing before the altar during the ceremony, a rejected lover, maddened with grief and jealousy, sprang forward from amongst the wedding-guests and stabbed the bride to death before the horrified onlookers were able to intervene.

Ever since the tragedy the white-breasted bird is supposed to have appeared just before the deaths of many of this family, until fairly recent times. The information available regarding the various appearances of the bird is very considerable, so that only the more outstanding evidence is given in this necessarily brief account.

From *Transactions of the Devonshire Association*, 1882, IV, p. 223; also a tract in the British Museum Library and the Gough Collection in the Bodleian Library, from which extracts are given, but are not included here.

MOTIFS: B.147.2.2 [*Bird of ill-omen*]; z.142 [*Symbolic colour: white*]; D.1293.3 [*White as magic colour*]; z.142.1 [*White rose the symbol of death*].

¶ Family death-tokens are fairly common. The Tongues have a pigeon (informant, Ruth L. Tongue). White creatures are often considered ominous. A white rabbit or a white hare is thought to be unlucky or death-bringing. A pure white cat is equally unlucky, and so is a pure white dog. Spectral dogs are generally either black or white. See B, I.

See "The Joug Tree", "The Red King's Deer".

THE WHITE HORSE OF THE STRID

Parkinson, *Yorkshire Legends and Traditions*, 1st series, p. 229.

It is said that on the morning of May Day preceding any fatal accident in the river Wharfe, the white horse of the Fairy Queen is seen rising out of the foam and spray of the cataract of the Strid.

Three sisters, co-heiresses of Beamsley Hall, once stood watching for this fairy horse, and told one another the wishes they would hope to have granted if they saw the Fairy Queen. Claphams and Mauleverers were the great families of the place; they often intermarried, and are buried in the same vault in the Abbey Church at Bolton. The three sisters of the legend believed that if they could see the fairy horse they would also see each her own future husband, and also that whoever was the first to see the fairy horse would be the sole heiress of Beamsley (in those days spelt "Bethmeslie").

The first wished that the elm-tree and the rocks by which they stood might be changed into a knight and his castle, and that she might be the lady of his heart. The second wished for a marble-domed hall and pages in green to tend her horses and hounds, with many ladies to weave pearls into her silk gowns, and a princely knight to be her lover. The third said she had no wish, for she loved best the white roses gathered for her by their father. But she would wish for them all to ride on the white fairy horse straight back home to where their father lay asleep, that he might bless them all in his dream.

At dead of night the white horse came to bear them away, and that was the last that was ever seen of the three sisters of Beamsley.

MOTIFS: F.234.1.8 [*Fairy in form of horse*]; F.341 [*Fairies give fulfilment of wishes*]; F.252.2 [*Fairy queen*]; F.241.1.0.1 [*Fairy cavalcade*]; F.329 [*Fairy abductions*].
¶ This appears to be a case in which the most modest wish is the most dangerous, as in the story of "Beauty and the Beast".

WHY THE ENGLISH NEVER KILL A RAVEN

H. Bett, *English Legends*, p. 10.

"Have not your lordships read," Don Quixote said, "the annals and histories of England, in which are recorded the renowned exploits of King Arthur, whom we, in our Castilian tongue, commonly call King Artus, of whom there is an ancient tradition common in all that kingdom of Great Britain, that this king did not die, but by arts of enchantment, was transformed into a raven, and that in due course of time he will return to reign, and recover his kingdom and sceptre; for which cause it cannot be proved, from that time to this, that any Englishman has ever killed a raven."

Later in the story, the Don returns to the theme: "And if it be a lie, then there was no Hector, nor Achilles, nor Trojan War, nor the Twelve Peers of France, nor King Arthur of England, who goes about yet in the form of a raven but whose return is expected every hour in his kingdom."

MOTIF: E.613.7 [*Reincarnation as a raven (King Arthur)*].
¶ See also Thistleton-Dyer, *The Ghost World*, pp. 79–80. It is interesting to come across the knowledge of this legendary belief in sixteenth-century Spain as well as in fourteenth-century Cornwall.

WILLIE MILLER AT THE DROPPING-CAVE
[summary]

Hugh Miller, *Scenes and Legends of the North of Scotland,* pp. 333–6.

Willie Miller was a Cromarty mechanic of fertile invention, who rarely told the same story twice, save that of his adventure in the Dropping-Cave. There was a local tradition that a man had once passed through the Cave so far that he heard a pair of tongs rattle over his head in the hearth of a farmhouse of Navity, a parish fully three miles from the opening. Willie determined to test this story by experiment. He sewed sprigs of rowan and wych-elm in the hem of his waist-coat, thrust a Bible into one pocket, and a bottle of gin into the other, took a torch and a staff of buckthorn, cut at the full of the moon, and dressed without the aid of iron or steel. And so he set out on a morning of midsummer. It was evening when he returned, his torch burnt out, and his clothes stained with slime and soaked with water.

He said that after lighting his torch, he plunged fearlessly into the gloom and found the cavern lower and narrower as he went on. The floor was of white stone like marble, and was hollowed into cisterns, full of sparkling pure water. From the roof hung clusters of richly embossed white icicles, down which there constantly trickled drops of water from the roof, and these fell into the cisterns, with a tinkling sound like that of rain. In gazing curiously round him at these sights, Willie missed his footing at the ninth and last of these cisterns and falling forwards, he dashed his bottle of gin into fragments against the side of the cave. Unwilling to lose the whole of the precious contents, he lay down, and lapped up what he could from a little hollow in the stone. He paused, and stopped and drank again and again; and when he rose, a circular rainbow had formed round his torch, a blue mist seemed to be gathering in the hollows of the cave, and the living rock seemed to be heaving like a ship in a heavy swell. But Willie went boldly forward.

And now the cavern widened, and the roof rose to such a height that the light reached only the tips of the snowy icicles which hung over his head. His footsteps echoed through countless openings, where the gleam of his torch was reflected in pools, and shining ribs of rock and, besides the echoes of the cave itself, he could hear strange sounds from the world above—the wind moaning through the wood, the scream of a hawk, the deafening roar of a smith's bellows and the clang of his anvil. Then a wind came rushing through the cave, and shook the marble drapery of its sides, as if it were of gauze or linen. The cave seemed to heave and turn till the floor stood upright, and the adventurer fell heavily against it. As his torch hissed and expired in the water, he saw a host of dark shadowy figures around him in the blue mist which now came pouring in dense clouds from the interior.

He fell, and lay long insensible in the darkness. When his consciousness returned, he saw, but as if in a dream, that the gloom had given way to a reddish twilight, which flickered like a distant fire. "It is sunlight," he thought. "I shall find an opening among the rocks of Eathie, and return home over the hill." But, instead, the passage ended in a vast room, lit by an immense fire of whole pine-trees; through it a vast cataract descended, to disappear through a wide gulf far below. The floor of this apartment seemed to be strewn with human bones, half burned, and bloodstained, and gnawed, as if by cannibals; and before the fire stood a vast dark stone, twenty yards in length, covered with grotesque hieroglyphics. Against its upper end rested a huge mace of iron, crusted with rust and blood; and a golden bugle hung by a golden chain from a column at the bottom. Willie seized the bugle, and blew such a blast that the cave re-echoed. The waters of the cataract disappeared, as if dried up at their source, and the ponderous stone began to heave and crackle, and to tip slowly over the edge. He blew again, then an enormous hand, covered with blood, was slowly stretched out of the dark tomb below, towards the mace. Willie's heart failed him at the sight; he flung down the bugle and rushed for the passage. A yell of grief and indignation burst from the tomb as the immense cover again settled over it; the cataract came dashing from its precipice in greater volume than ever; and a hurricane of wind and spray almost dashed him against the side of the cave.

Almost petrified with horror, he stumbled to the mouth of the passage; and, staggering along it in a kind of feverish dream, he came to himself, lying across the ninth cistern, with the fragments of his bottle at one hand, and his buckthorn staff at the other. He could hear the dash of the advancing waves against the rocks below; and, leaping down the beach, found his journey had taken the whole of the day.

MOTIFS: F.92.6 [*Entrance to lower world through cave*]; D.1960.1.1 [*Mighty sleeper*].

¶ This tale has some connection with D.1960.2, that of the Sleeping King under the mountain. As in "Potter Thompson" or "King Arthur at Sewing-shields", there is a magic weapon and a magic horn, but in this tale the sleeper was a horrible ogre. It is noticeable that all these adventures occurred after the hero had drunken a pool full of gin, and that when he awoke he found himself still lying near the broken bottle. Under the circumstances the reeling floor and the swaying walls are hardly surprising.

See "The Cave of Rhyader", "Potter Thompson" (B, IX).

THE WINDING-SHEET

Douglas, *Scottish Fairy and Folk-Tales*, p. 211.

I was resolved to pay a visit to an English Gentleman, Sir William
Sacheverill, who had a commission from the English Court of Admiralty
to give his best trial to find out gold or money, or any other thing of
note, on one of the ships of the Spanish Armada that was blown up in
the bay of Topper-Mory, in the Sound of Mull. And having condescended upon the number of men that were to go with me, one of the
number was a handsome boy that waited upon my own person; and,
about an hour before I made sail, a woman, that was also one of my
own servants, spoke to one of the seamen, and bade him to dissuade me
to take that boy along with me, or if I did, I should not bring him back
alive. The seaman answered, he had not confidence to tell me such un-
warrantable trifles. I took my voyage, and sailed the length of Topper-
Mory; and having stayed two or three nights with that liberal and
ingenuous gentleman, who himself had collected many observations of
the second sight in the Isle of Man, and compared his notes and mine
together, I then took leave of him. In the meantime my boy grew sick
of a vehement body flux, the winds turned cross, that I could neither sail
nor row—the boy died with me the eleventh night from his decumbiture.

The next morning the wind made fair, and the seaman to whom the
matter was foretold related the whole story when he saw it verified.
I carried the boy's corpse aboard with me, and after my arrival, and his
burial, I called suddenly for the woman, and asked her what warrant
she had to foretell the boy's death. She said that she had no other warrant
but that she saw, two days before I took my voyage, the boy walking
with me in the fields, sewed up in his winding sheets from top to toe,
and that she had never seen this in others but she found that they shortly
thereafter died; and therefore concluded that he would die too, and
that shortly.

From the Rev. John Frazer, Δευτεροσκοπιά, *or A Brief Discourse concerning the
Second Sight, commonly so called*, 17th Century.
MOTIF: D.1825.1 [*Second sight*].

¶ This prophetic vision of those about to die already wrapped in their winding-
sheets seems to have been common among second-sighted Highlanders. Douglas
gives another instance from Sir John Fraser's book, from which this is taken.

WITCHES XIII

WITCHES

The witchcraft beliefs are those which are most present to modern consciousness as a proper subject for folk-lore research. The automatic response of a person uninstructed in folk-studies on hearing that some-one is a folklorist is to ask about witches. There is an almost morbid interest in the subject, which was illustrated by the crowded audience, many of them self-declared witches, which attended a lecture given to the Folk-Lore Society by a leading American authority on witchcraft. That the lecturer was entirely and avowedly sceptical made no difference to the fervour of his audience.

There is no doubt that witchcraft beliefs are still alive in this country, though a great deal of the interest taken in witchcraft depends upon scepticism; it is the pleasure taken in quaint, obsolete, horrific stories, which would be no pleasure at all if they were believed in. Hallowe'en parties, children's games about witches, witch fairy stories would have no pleasure about them if the actual witch beliefs and witch persecutions were really present to the imagination. The humour of the witch's curse in *Ruddigore* depends on the complete scepticism of sophisticated people at the end of the last century, just as *Ruthless Rhymes for Heartless Homes* were born in the peaceful days before the First World War. That complacency is not possible to us now; our horror comics are more ruthless and brutal, and something more sinister has crept into the new fashion for witchcraft.

There are two strands in modern witch beliefs, deriving from two very different strains. The first and most widely publicized is the modern cult of self-styled witches, who claim that they are reviving, or even carrying on, a Bronze-Age fertility religion. As far as one can see—though the evasiveness of the propagandists makes it difficult to be certain—the inspiration of this is almost wholly literary and is founded on the writings of Dr Margaret Murray, herself a complete sceptic. It is an ironic thing that Reginald Scot's *Discoverie of Witchcraft*, written at the end of the sixteenth century to expose the groundlessness of the witchcraft persecutions, became a kind of textbook on witchcraft, and disseminated the beliefs it was meant to disprove. In the same way, Dr Margaret Murray's writings have provided a base and groundwork for the modern literary cult of witchcraft. Little of this will be found in the following witch legends, though there are a few lingering traditions of the Rosicrucians, a learned, mystical society of dabblers in theurgic magic, who were popularly credited with all kinds of witchcraft practices.

The real country belief in witchcraft, with its ill-will, forespelling and sympathetic magic, has left plenty of traces all over the country, and the actual belief itself is still lurking among unsophisticated people, though no longer so explicit as it once was. This is the soil out of which the theological, intellectualized beliefs arose, which nourished them and made the witch persecutions possible. The more complicated and thoughtful features of the belief have faded in England and left only the basic assumptions on which they were founded. In Scotland, where the beliefs were more theological and nearer to those held on the Continent, and where the persecutions were more cruel, we find tales of the witches' Sabbat and more instances than in England of the diabolic compact. Tales of imps, familiars and shape-shifting are to be found everywhere. Everywhere dairy produce is tampered with, livestock are injured and human beings bewitched and visited with sickness or death. Everywhere witches are nasty people to annoy, and they are often retaliated on with unnecessary brutality.

The country consciences were not over-sensitive about magical practices. Some people were content to use prayers, good thoughts, the Bible or the sign of the Cross as their defence; others resorted to magic as black as any the witches used, torturing and burning live animals with the intention of thus destroying the witches in slow fires or making them unable to urinate. Some pride and pleasure was certainly taken in the exploits of white witches and wise women, and a few of the tales about them are entertaining enough, but on the whole these stories make us realize the pressures of close proximity, when neighbours have no power to separate, however antipathetic they may be, and show us how easy it would be for ill-will to acquire supernatural powers in the minds of those who were exposed to it.

AALD SIBBIE

Shetland Folk Book, II, p. 3.

Dere's aald Sibbie o' Bronisdaoi shø wis laek hirsel. Ee day shø said ta da servant lass, "I'm gyaan ta kirn, tak a divit aff o' de second slue o' Ole's byre and pit him anunder de kirn." De Lass güde furt bit shø took a divit aff o' Sibbie's ain byre an' pat in anunder de kirn.

Sibbie started ta kirn, shø kirned an' shø better kirned but shø got nae butter. Dan shø loopit laek de fire and shø says, "Whear took du dis divit frae," an' de lass lauchin' til hirsel' says, "Aff o' your nain byre de second slue." Sibbie made fir her wi de dreepin' kirn-staff an de lass tøk de door ower her head.

Yea, bit shø lost de profit o' de milk an' Ole's folk got it an' no fil shø owesed de milk at shø wis been kirnin' in ower Ole's byre door an' brig stanes did shø get it back agen.

Dey're a wife 'at lives at Maill. Her man is awa sailin'. Dey hae a fine peerie horse. Ee day comes Sibbit ta de door an' says shø, "I'm come ta git a len o' your horse fir a oor or twa ta laed hame twa or three paets wi wir een."

"Na," says de wife, kennin wha shø wis spaekin til. "My man bade me no ta len de horse." De day efter Sibbie comes an' spørs fir de horse agen an' de wife denied her agen. Dan Sibbie shø güde ower de rigs an' sharpened ae stane ipo anidder as shø güde. De wife wis a cliver body an' shø made fir Sibbie an' shø says, "Loard grant 'at what doos prayin' fir me comes ipo dysel," an wi dat shø left her.

Whin Sibbie cam hame hir black coo at wis fastened ipo de banks broo wis faaen an' brokken hir neck. An truly dey wir little maen made fir hir loss.

Noted down by Mrs Jane Saxby from a narration of Christina Smith, Troswickness.
MOTIFS: K.1600 [*Deceiver falls into his own trap*]; G.271.6 [*Exorcism of witch by counter-charm*].
¶ In both of these incidents the tables are turned on the witch by reversing her charm. The second one is much like Lochiel's retort to the witch in J. G. Campbell's *Witchcraft and Second Sight in the Scottish Highlands*, p. 198.

AILER WOOD THE WITCH [summary]

R. Blakeborough, *Wit, Character, Folk-Lore and Customs of the North Riding of Yorkshire*, p. 189.

Throughout Bilesdale, some years ago, Ailer, or Alice, Wood would run about in the form of a cat or a hare, and no hounds could ever catch her.

Once a girl whose sweetheart had deserted her for another was sure that Ailer Wood had bewitched him. She went to the wise man, Henry Wilson, who told how to find out whether it was indeed the witch who had cast a spell on her lover. She was to turn upside-down a small four-legged stool, known as a cricket, and stick nine pins close together into the wood; as she pushed in the last, she must say, "There's nine for him and her and the witch." At another spot she must push in another nine, saying, "There's nine for the witch and her and him," and lastly at another place, another nine, saying "And there is nine more for all three of them, wi' her in t'middle." Thus the false girl who had stolen her lover was always named next to the witch. Then the stool was to be set right way up again, and the witch induced to sit on it. She would be unable to get up again until she had answered truly any questions Annie asked her.

All this was done. Ailer was invited in to have tea, but the stool was

39-2

put for her to sit upon just in front of the fire. But Ailer quietly replied that she could not enjoy her tea sitting on a "Pricky-back 'otch'n" (hedgehog). Somehow she had discovered, and escaped the charm prepared to catch her.

MOTIFS: G.211.2.7.1 [*Witch in form of hare allows herself to be coursed by dogs for play or sport*]; G.257 [*Charms to cause witch to reveal self*]; cf. G.254.2 [*Witch known by inability to rise from chair with salt under cushion*].

THE AITH MAN AND THE FINN

Shetland Folk Book, II, p. 5.

An Aith man was once in Norway and, meeting with a Finn, he related to him his success as a fisherman, whereupon the Finn wagered the Fetlar man that he should not taste or have fresh fish in his skjo before Yule.

The winter turned out to be very stormy, so stormy in fact and the sea so violent that not even a lempit could be obtained. But on Tammasmus E'en [20 December new style] there came a break in the weather and the Aith man went to sea in his small boat. He had no bait except a white rag dyed in "drørie" [blood] drawn from his own foot. He pulled to the nearest seat, where he "ran de boddam and turned de stone" with an olik. As soon as the fish was secured the boat was headed for the shore, but the sea rose and threatened to swamp the small craft. He had fortunately taken with him a small keg of oil and this helped to smooth the angry sea, but as he was crossing the "String o' de Minnie Stakk" a wave more terrible than any preceding one came rolling up behind.

Seizing the oil keg, the Fetlar man threw it and its contents into the face of the big wave and thereby he was enabled to get safely to land.

It happened that some time after this the Aith man was again in Norway and, meeting the Finn, he reminded him of the wager. Pointing to the deep scar in his brow and his broken teeth, the Finn replied, "I'm paid dear eneuch fit dat olik. Doo didna only smore we mid dy oil bit du soved me wi dy oli hjulk [a vessel for holding oil]."

Noted down from the narration of William Laurenson, Aith, Fetlar, by E. S. Reid Tait.

TYPE ML.3055. MOTIF: G.275.14 [*Witch out of body while travelling at night is injured; witch's body is injured at home*].

¶ Actually in this case the Finn had turned himself into a wave.

See "The Ferryman".

ALL HALLOWS NIGHT [summary]

J. Bowker, *Goblin Tales of Lancashire*, p. 189.

A farmer who lived in a lonely spot not far from the foot of Pendle began to suffer from every kind of misfortune. First, three of his cattle died, then two of his children; then the crops were blighted. He felt sure that he had somehow incurred the ill-will of the invisible powers, and told his wife that they would fare no better until November. "Why November?" she asked, and he told her that he had resolved on All Hallows E'en, to "leet the witches"—that is, to carry a candle round their meeting-place on Pendle. If anyone could succeed in this without his candle being blown out, it was thought that he would be safe from the witches' power for a year.

Old Isaac, his devoted serving-man, promised to go with him, and when the time came, they set out, soon after ten o'clock, each carrying a branch of ash, with sprigs of bay tied to it as protection against thunder and lightning, and the unlighted candle in the other hand.

They lighted the candles at Pendle foot, and, carefully shielding them against the rising storm, they walked on till they were close to Pendle tower, where the witches' revelry was at its height.

At the end of the hour they turned towards home, when suddenly a Satanic face appeared at the window of the tower, and both candles instantly went out. "God bless us!" they both cried, and the cry broke the spell. The tower was plunged in darkness, and all was silent. The terrified men hurried away, still clinging on to their branches, but in the darkness they got separated. They lay out till dawn; then Isaac awoke with the sun shining on his face, and the old farm bulldog licking his face.

The farmer's wife had sent out a search-party, and it was not long before the missing farmer was found lying with a broken leg at the foot of a gorge into which he had fallen.

Unaccustomed prosperity for the farm followed this brave deed, and the farmer's wife therefore declared that it must have been after midnight when *He* blew out the candles.

MOTIFS: G.263.4 [*Witch causes sickness*]; G.265.4 [*Witches cause disease or death of animals*]; G.272.2.1 [*Rowan wood protects against witches*]; G.272.2.4 [*Bay leaves used as protection against witches*]; G.271.6 [*Exorcism of witch by counter-charm*]; G.271.2.3 [*Name of Deity breaks witch's spell*].

ANN ALLAN

R. Blakeborough, *Wit, Character, Folk-Lore and Customs of the North Riding of Yorkshire*, p. 174.

About the year 1780, a witch named Ann Allan was almost caught in the act of milking other people's cows. Four of the Ugthorpe cows had ceased to give the proper quantity of milk. The villagers consulted the priest, but his help was unavailing; and then a fifth cow went completely dry. Its owner was so angry that he boldly went to Ann's house and accused her of milking their cows. She denied it, and a fierce argument resulted, in the course of which he seized a milking-stool, and was about to hurl it at her head, when a stream of milk began to pour out of one of its legs. A crowd of neighbours had by now collected, and they shouted: "Thou's gitten it! That's what she milks the cows with." And so it proved. Ann's pigs were being fattened on the milk stolen from her neighbours' cows. As her punishment she was made to walk three times through the village in nothing but her chemise, in view of all the inhabitants.

MOTIFS: D.1605 [*Magic thieving object*]; D.2083.3 [*Milk transferred from another's cow by magic*].

AULD SCAIRIE AND THE BLACK AIRT

School of Scottish Studies. Hamish Henderson.

This was a story my father used to tell me about a shoe-maker in Aberdeenshire, and he workit the black airt, an' the wey they fun' oot, like, was there was an auld woman one day went up to his shop, a small shop it wis, an' there was a press in the shop, an' she cam in—she wanted a pair of boots soled, ye ken, and she gien him the boots, ye see,... an old travellin' woman she was—he flings the boots in the press, ye see—just a small press, no-one could be in the press, or anything like that...and she starts (?) newsing him, ye know, about different things, so they carry on for aboot a quarter of an hour, and she was in a hurry to get on with her work, and she told him to hurry up with the boots. "Oh," he says, "all right," he says. "They'll be ready in time for ye."

But she got impatient, and that, and he says, "Jist wait a minute, and I'll get your boots," put his haun in, and here was her boots hauf-soled, ye ken, and heeled.

She got suspicious of this man, ye see, 'cos naebody could get intae this wee press. So she tellt some of the people aboot it, and everything's like that, and the lassies—the young folk of the toon, like, at least a village it wis, and they heard aboot it, and they cried this man "Scairie".

So one night there was a couple cam up to the dance—a young couple —they were goin' to hae some fun wi' Scairie, may be aboot eleven or twelve o'clock at night, and they were going' to Scairie, cryin' him names, and things like that, and he looks through the windae at them an' he told them, "Be quiet!" but they'd take nae heed, and he turned roon, and told them, he said, "May your boots stick to the ground," he says, "and your feet stick to your boots, and be like that till mornin'." An' they were like that till mornin'. They never moved till next mornin', till he cam oot and let them off.

Another thing was told of him was, he got a housekeeper. He'd got books aboot this black airt, and aathing like that, and this housekeeper, she was kinna inquisitive, and she wad look through this books on this black airt, see. So she got kinna on wi' this job whativer it was—this black airt—and one day Scairie comes in and this woman, she had the whole place—tables were gaun up, and the bowls were goin through the hoose—an' she raised the black airt, but she couldnae lay it. She'd read this books, and raised the black airt, but she couldnae lay it, and as Scairie cam in, the hoose was in an uproar—plates and tables were gaun up, floating through the air, and aathing like this, and he knew she was fiddlin'—he'd warned her before aboot this, no to touch his books and leave alone, an' she got that much of a fricht, she never bothered aboot black airt again.

There were a lot mair o't, but I cannae remember—my father used to tell me aboot it, but within the last thirty years the people remembered aboot him here—the local people definitely remember aboot him— auld Scairie, and he supposed to be giftit or learnt in the black airt.

Told by Robert Stewart, Aberdeen, 1955.
TYPE 325. MOTIFS: D.1935 [*Any work touched automatically done*]; D.2072 [*Magic paralysis*]; D.1266 [*Magic book*]; G.297*(*b*) [*Person raises Devil by opening or reading wizard's book*] (Baughman).
¶ See "The Black Hen".

THE BAG OF FLOUR

Burne and Jackson, *Shropshire Folk-Lore*, p. 159.

There was a woman who lived near Cheadle, who went to the mill one day to get a bag of flour for baking, and as she came back she met an old witch.

"Good day," said the witch. "Good day," said the woman again. "What's that you've got on your head?" said the witch. "It's flour I'm taking home for my baking," said the woman. "It isn't flour; its manure," said the witch. "It's good sound flour!" said the woman. "I've fetched it straight from the mill, and I'm going to bake with it as soon as ever I get home."

"It's nothing at all but a bag of manure," said the witch, and off she went.

Now the woman knew very well that it was flour she had in her bag, but this made her feel so uncomfortable that as soon as the witch was out of sight, she put down the bag off her head, and opened it and looked in. And there, sure enough, it was not flour at all, nothing but manure!

Well, she thought, as she had carried it so far, she might as well carry it all the way, so she took it up again and went home, and set it down by the pig-sty. In the evening her husband came home.

"Whatever have you put that bag of flour down by the pig-sty for?" he said as soon as he came into the house. "Oh," said she, "that's not flour; that's only a bag of manure." "Nonsense!" said he. "What are you talking of? I tell you its flour. Why, its sheeding [spilling] all over the place." So they went to look, and there actually it was flour again, the same as at first, and they took it into the house, and very glad the woman was to get it back. And that was the only thing the witch was ever known to *turn* [transform] back again.

She *turned* a many things, but never a one back again like that.

MOTIF: D.2031 [*Magic illusions*].
¶ See "The Four-leaved Clover" (B, XII).

BERNSHAW TOWER AND LADY SYBIL

Harland and Wilkinson, *Legends and Traditions of Lancashire*, pp. 5–7.

Bernshaw Tower, formerly a small, fortified house, is now in ruins, little else than the foundations being visible above the surface. It stood in one of the many beautiful ravines branching off from the great gorge of Cliviger, about five miles from Burnley, and not far from the noted Eagle's Crag. Its last owner, and heiress, was celebrated for her wealth and beauty; she was intellectual beyond most of her sex, and frequently visited the Eagle's Crag, in order to study Nature and admire the varied aspects of the surrounding country. On these occasions she often felt a strong desire to possess supernatural powers; and in an unguarded moment was induced to sell her soul to the Devil in order that she might be able to join in the nightly revelries of the then famous Lancashire witches. The bond was duly attested with her blood, and her utmost wishes were at all times fulfilled.

Hapton Tower was then occupied by a junior branch of the Towneley family, and "Lord William" had long been a suitor for the hand of "Lady Sybil" of Bernshaw Tower, but his proposals were constantly rejected. In despair he had recourse to a famous Lancashire witch, one Mother Helston, and after using many spells and incantations, she promised him success on the next All-Hallow's Eve. On that day he went out hunting, according to her directions, when, on nearing Eagle's Crag, he started a milk-white doe, and his dogs immediately gave chase. They scoured the country for many miles, and, at last, when the hounds were nearly exhausted, they again approached the Crag. A strange hound then joined them which Lord William knew full well. It was the familiar of Mother Helston, which had been sent to capture Lady Sybil, who had assumed the disguise of the white doe.

On passing the Crag, Lord William's horse had well-nigh thrown its rider down the fearful abyss; but just as the doe was making for the next precipice, the strange hound seized her by the throat and held her fast, until Lord William threw an enchanted silken leash around her neck, and led her in triumph to Hapton Tower. During the night the Tower was shaken as by an earthquake, and in the morning the captured doe appeared as the fair heiress of Bernshaw. Counter-spells were adopted— her powers of witchcraft were suspended—and soon Lord William had the happiness to lead his newly-wedded bride to his ancestral home. Within a year, however, she had renewed her diabolical practices, and, whilst enjoying a frolic in Cliviger Mill, under the form of a beautiful white cat, she had one paw cut off by the manservant, Robin, who had been set to watch by Giles Robertson, the miller. Next morning Lady Sybil was found at home in bed, pale and exhausted; but Robin's presence at the Tower, with a lady's hand, soon dispelled the mystery of her sudden indisposition. The owner of the hand, with its costly signet-ring, was soon detected, and many angry expostulations from her husband followed. By means of some diabolical process, the hand was restored to Lady Sybil's arm; but a red mark round the wrist bore witness to the sharpness of Robin's whittle.

A reconciliation with her offended husband was afterwards effected; but her bodily strength gave way, and her health rapidly declined. On the approach of death, the services of the neighbouring clergy were requested, and by their assistance the Devil's bond was cancelled. Lady Sybil soon died in peace, but Bernshaw Tower was ever after deserted. As Mr Roby truly observes, popular tradition "still alleges that her grave was dug where the dark Eagle Crag shoots out its cold bare peak into the sky; and on the Eve of All Hallows the hound and the milk white doe meet on the crag a spectre huntsman in full chase. The belated peasant crosses himself at the sound as he remembers the fate of the witch of Bernshaw Tower.

TYPE ML.3055. MOTIFS: G.224.4 [*Person sells soul to Devil in exchange for witch powers*]; G.211.2.4 [*Witch in form of deer*]; G.225.6 [*Dog as witch's familiar*]; G.252 [*Witch in form of cat has hand cut off: recognized next morning by missing hand*]; D.2161.3.2 [*Magic restoration of severed hand*]; K.218 [*Devil cheated by religious means*].
¶ This tale contains a collection of authentic motifs, but it is rather hard to believe in the whole as a genuine legend.

THE BEWITCHED HORSES

S. O. Addy, *Household Tales*, p. 45. Nottinghamshire.

One day, as a carter was leading his horses along the high road, an old woman came up to him and said, "Please give me a pipe of tobacco." But the carter said, "Nay, thou must buy thy tobacco, like me." So the old woman left him. But after this the horses had not gone many yards before they stood quite still, and could not move an inch. So the carter laid him down by the roadside, and wondered what he was to do next. As he lay thinking, a stranger came by and said, "What's the matter; why doesn't thou get on?" The carter said, "My horses are bewitched. An hour ago an old woman passed me on the road, and asked me for a pipe of tobacco, and I wouldn't give it her. So she has bewitched them."

The stranger said, "You ought to have given her what she asked for, and you were very foolish to refuse. But do as I tell thee. Go to the old woman's cottage, and either beg, borrow or steal something. And when she comes near thee, scratch her arm with a needle and fetch blood."

So the carter did as the stranger told him, and he called at a house on the road, and borrowed a stocking needle. When he got to the old woman's cottage, he said to her, "I've come to buy a penn'orth of thread, mother." So the old woman fetched her the thread, and as she was giving it to him, he took the stocking needle and scratched her arm from the elbow to the wrist. When he had done this he paid for the thread, and took the stocking-needle back to the woman who had lent it him. Then he ran after his horses, and found that they had started at the very moment when he drew blood from the old woman's arm.

MOTIFS: D.2072.0.2.1.1 [*Horse unable to move wagon, paralysed by witch*]; G.273.6 [*Witch rendered powerless by drawing blood from her*].
¶ It is generally said that the blood should be "above the breath" which is sometimes interpreted as above the nostrils and sometimes above the lungs.
See "The Dung Putt", "The Ghostly Hand" (B, VI).

BLACK ANNIS: I [summary]

C. J. Billson, *County Folk-Lore*, I, 3, pp. 4–9.

Black Annis' Bower, a spot near the Dane Hills, is traditionally connected with a woman named Agnes Scott, who lived there long ago, and is said to have hollowed out a cave for herself with her long claw-like nails. The cave, at least, was plainly visible in the early part of the nineteenth century, though now almost filled up with soil carried in by the rains.

In Swithland Church a flat gravestone, inlaid with brass plates, bears the following inscription:

> *Hoc in conclave jacet Agnes Scott camerata,*
> *Antrix devota Dominae Ferrers Vocitata,*
> *Quiquis eris, qui transieris, quero, funde precata;*
> *Sum quis eris, fueramque quod es; pro me, precor, ora.*

"In the east window of the chancel is her picture in glass drawn to the life, in the same habit (as her picture on the gravestone) with a ring on her finger. This *Agnes Scott*, as I guess, was an anchoress; and the word *Antrix* in this epitaph coined from *antrum*, a cave wherein she lived" (*Leicester Chronicle*, 26 February 1842).

The Dane Hills, or Dunes, are low hills about a mile to the west of Leicester, and here in her cave Black Annis is said to have practised cannibalism, and may therefore be identified with the Celtic mother-goddess *Anu* or *Nannu*, since it is believed that the ancient Britons did eat the flesh of human victims offered on their altars.

Children used to be frightened away from the hills by the tale that Anna lay there in wait for them, and would claw them to death, suck their blood and hang up their skins to dry. A huge pollard oak, the last remnant of the forest which once covered the whole region, was her favourite lurking place, and from it she would spring out on any wild beast or child who passed below.

A relic of the tale lingers in the minds of the Leicester people, in the form of "Cat Anna". Some warehouse girls said that she was a witch who lived in the cellars under the Castle, and that there was an underground passage from the cellars to the Dane Hills, along which she ran.

MOTIF: G.219.3 [*Witch has long nails*].

¶ Roger Bacon was said to dig a grave for himself with his long nails. The harmless recluse, Agnes Scott, seems to have become associated with Black Annis, the supernatural hag of the Dane Hills, said by some to be a form of the goddess Danu. She is much nearer to her traditional character in the next story.

BLACK ANNIS: II

Ruth L. Tongue.

Black Annis lived in the Danehills.

She was ever so tall, and had a blue face and had long white teeth, and she ate people. She only went out when it was dark.

My mum says, when she ground her teeth people could hear her in time to bolt their doors, and keep well away from the one window. That's why we don't have a lot of big windows in Leicestershire cottages; she can't get only an arm inside.

My mum says that's why we have the fire and chimney in a corner. The fire used to be on the earth floor once, and people slept all round it, until Black Annis grabbed babies out the window. There wasn't any glass in that time.

When Black Annis howled, you could hear her five miles away, and then even the poor folk in the huts fastened skins across the windows, and put witch-herbs above it to keep her away safe.

My mum told us there was a wicked stepmother who sent her three little children out near Christmastide to gather wood when it got dark earlier than this is (a dark lunchtime, Christmas Eve, 1941). They were ever so cold and frightened, and little Dicky he cried.

"Don't cry, Dicky lad," says Jim. "Don't be frightened. 'Tis Christmas Eve. You can't be hurted, noways."

"Why?" says Dicky.

"There's no bad 'uns about," says Jen.

"Why?" says Dicky.

"'Tis Our Lord's Birthday, and the bells ring," they said. "If the bad 'uns hear them, they die."

So off they went to the wood, and picked a big load each. It was getting dark, and they had a long way back, and they were so tired, and little Dicky cried, and so did Jen.

"It's getting dark, and she may not have gone under the earth yet. I'm going to run."

But she couldn't, with all her load of firewood.

Then Jim said, "I've got a holed stone, and if you like, I'll look through it and see. But she'll be right underground with the covers over her ears, till after Christmas."

But she wasn't. She'd forgotten the day, and Jim saw her five miles off.

It wasn't quite dark yet, and they tried to make haste. Then Jim looked again. "She's only a mile away," he whispered, but they couldn't go any faster until they heard a yell.

Then they did run till they dropped.

"She won't come now," says Jim. "She'll stop to eat that ragged drunken old woman I saw—I think it was stepmother, come to look for us."

"I hope it were," say Jen and little Dicky. "We're nearly home now."

So they rested just a little bit longer, and then little Dicky says, "Its coming on near dark."

And Jen says, "There's something grinding teeth. Look through the stone, Jim."

So Jim looked, and it was Black Annis, only half a mile behind them.

She hadn't liked the taste of that beery old stepmother, so she only snapped off her head, and come on again.

"Drop your faggot across the path, little Dicky, and run for home," says Jim.

So Black Annis bruised her legs, and ran back to her cave to get ointment to stop the bleeding. My mum says, if a witch bleeds, she loses all her power and dies.

And didn't Jim and Jen run too! But she wasn't scratched bad, and back she come. She was only a quarter of a mile away when Jim looked, so they both dropped their faggots to trip her, and ran for it.

Black Annis fell flat on her face over the firing, but she caught up with them at their cottage door, where their dad stood with an axe. And he threw it right in her face, and her nose bled like a pig, and she yelled, and ran for her cave, crying, "Blood, Blood!" but the Christmas bells started pealing, and she fell down far away and died.

Then the children kissed their dad, and he'd brought a great load of firewood himself, and the stepmother was dead, and it was Christmas Eve, so they made a big fire and had kippers and butter for tea.

"Butter?" said a rationed boy, listening. "Coo, what a feast!"

"It was Christmas Eve," said the tale-teller firmly, "And the old stepmother had been hiding all their rations to sell to the grocer's man, so she could buy beer."

"Did they find Black Annis?" I asked.

"The crows picked her bones...but one of my uncles he found a long tooth...ever so sharp it is...that's how I know it's quite true."

Told by an evacuee Leicester girl, 24 December 1941 "as we ate our lunch of war-time sandwiches in Hillfield Barn hay-mow". Leicestershire.

MOTIFS: G.11.3 [*Cannibal witch*]; G.214.1 [*Witch with long teeth*]; G.261 [*Witch steals children*]; G.262 [*Murderous witch*]; G.272.2 [*Magic herb protects from witch*]; D.1331.1.4 [*Stone gives magic sight*]; D.1825.2 [*Magic power to see distant objects*]; G.303.16.12 [*Ringing of Church bells causes Devil to lose his power*]; G.276 [*Escape from witch*]; G.278 [*Death of witch*].

¶ The Black Annis of this story is really more of a supernatural hag than of a mortal witch. Certainly she is. killed, but even the Devil himself can be killed, according to some tales.

The witch in "Hansel and Gretel" is of something the same kind (Grimm, no. 15, Type 327A).

THE BLACK HEN [slightly shortened]

J. R. W. Coxhead, *The Devil in Devon*, pp. 39–40.

A great many years ago, there was a large fairy ring of particularly lush green grass in one of the meadows of a certain remote parish on the western fringe of Dartmoor, and within this magic circle a jet-black hen and chickens were occasionally to be seen at nightfall.

The vicar of the parish was an extremely keen student of sorcery, and possessed a large collection of books and manuscripts dealing with the perilous subject of black magic.

One day, while the parson was conducting a service in the village church, one of his servants happened to visit his study and, finding a large volume lying open on the table, began to read it aloud. He had read no more than half a page when the sky became dark, and the house was shaken violently by a great wind. The servant, deeply absorbed in the book, read on; and as the storm increased in fury, the door flew open, and a black hen and chicken entered the room.

The creatures were of normal size when they first appeared, but they gradually grew larger and larger, until the hen became as big as a prize bullock. At this point the vicar, who was in the midst of his sermon in the pulpit of the church, suddenly closed his discourse, and abruptly dismissed the astonished congregation, saying that he was needed at home urgently, and hoped he would arrive there in time.

When he entered his study the hen had grown so large that it was already touching the ceiling. He quickly threw down a bag of rice which stood ready in a corner of the room, and while the hen and chickens were busily engaged in picking up the grains, he had time to reverse the spell.

From *Notes and Queries*, 1st series, II, 1850, p. 512.
TYPES 325* and ML.3020. MOTIFS: G.303.3.3.3 [*Devil in form of bird*]; D.1266 [*Magic book*]; G.297*(b) [*Person raises Devil by opening or reading wizard's book*] (Baughman); G.297*(ce) [*Spirit terrifies person who raises it until master returns, lays spirit*] (Baughman); G.303.3.5.1 [*Devil becomes larger and longer*].

THE BLACKSMITH'S NAIL

Ruth L. Tongue, *Somerset Folklore*, pp. 87–8.

"There was a old woman to Porlock Weir, they'd call her a witch. She'd keep twoads in her bedroom and up on the shelves like. 'Twas so long ago I can't call it to mind, must be fifty year, but my sister she could tell 'ee. But thur was a woman whose pigs did always get out, no matter! whenever this old witch d'go by. Try how she could they'd always be out and running. So she went and drove a blacksmith's nail into her heel-print in the ro-ad, 'n the old woman she were a-crippled all on a sudden, 'n they had tew half carry her whoame."

Once I was so lucky as to get a hint from a blacksmith about the making of the nail. It is not often that they will betray their magical secrets. This was at Porlock in the 1940's:

"The nail must be specially made, yew see, by the blacksmith. I've a-knowed it done. 'Twas never touched by hand or 'twas no good."

From Mrs Badcock (in her late 70s), Triscombe, 1955.
MOTIFS: D.2089.3.1 [*Swine magically kept from fattening*]; G.273.7.2 [*Steel driven into witch's track immobilizes her*]; G.273.7.2(a) [*Nail driven into witch's track*] (Baughman).
¶ See "Toads on the Road".

THE BLACKSMITH'S WIFE
OF YARROWFOOT

Douglas, *Scottish Fairy and Folk-Tales*, pp. 177–9.

Some years back, the blacksmith of Yarrowfoot had for apprentices two brothers, both steady lads, and, when bound to him, fine healthy fellows. After a few months, however, the younger of the two began to grow pale and lean, lose his appetite, and show other marks of declining health. His brother, much concerned, often questioned him as to what ailed him, but to no purpose. At last, however, the poor lad burst into an agony of tears, and confessed that he was quite worn-out, and should soon be brought to the grave through the usage of his mistress, who was in truth a witch, though none suspected it. "Every night," he sobbed out, "she comes to my bedside, puts a magic bridle on me, and changes me into a horse. Then, seated on my back, she urges me on for many a mile to the wild moors, where she and I know not what other vile creatures hold their hideous feasts. There she keeps me all night, and at early morning I carry her home. She takes off my bridle, and there I am, but so weary I can ill stand. And thus I pass my nights while you are soundly sleeping."

The elder brother at once declared he would take his chance of a night among the witches, so he put the younger one in his own place next the wall, and lay awake himself till the usual time of the witch-woman's arrival. She came, bridle in hand, and flinging it over the elder brother's head, up sprang a fine hunting horse. The lady leaped on his back, and started for the trysting-place, which on this occasion, as it chances, was the cellar of a neighbouring laird.

While she and the rest of the vile crew were regaling themselves with claret and sack, the hunter, who was left in a spare stall of the stable, rubbed and rubbed his head against the wall till he loosened the bridle, and finally got it off, on which he recovered his human form. Holding the bridle firmly in his hand, he concealed himself at the back of the stall till his mistress came within reach, when in an instant he flung the magic bridle over her head, and behold, a fine grey mare! He mounted her and dashed off, riding through hedge and ditch, till, looking down, he perceived she had lost a shoe from one of her forefeet. He took her to the first smithy that was open, had the shoe replaced, and a new one put on the other forefoot, and then rode her up and down a ploughed field till he was nearly worn out. At last he took her home, and pulled the bridle off just in time for her to creep into bed before her husband awoke, and got up for his day's work.

The honest blacksmith arose, little thinking what had been going on all night; but his wife complained of being very ill, almost dying, and begged him to send for a doctor. He accordingly aroused his apprentices; the elder one went out, and soon returned with one whom he had chanced to meet already abroad. The doctor wished to feel his patient's pulse, but she resolutely hid her hands, and refused to show them. The village Esculapius was perplexed; but the husband, impatient at her obstinacy, pulled off the bedclothes, and found, to his horror, that horseshoes were tightly nailed to both her hands! On further examination, her sides appeared galled with kicks, the same that the apprentice had given her during his ride up and down the ploughed field.

The brothers now came forward, and related all that had passed. On the following day the witch was tried by the magistrates of Selkirk, and condemned to be burned to death on a stone at the Bullsheugh, a sentence which was promptly carried into effect. It is added that the younger apprentice was at last restored to health by eating butter made from the milk of cows fed in kirkyards, a sovereign remedy for consumption brought on through being witch-ridden.

TYPE ML.3055. MOTIFS: D.535 [*Transformation to horse by putting on bridle*]; G.241.2.1 [*Witch transforms man to horse and rides him*]; G.211.1.1 [*Witch in form of horse*]; G.211.1.1.2 [*Witch as horse shod with horseshoes*]; G.275.12 [*Witch in the form of an animal is injured as a result of the injury done to the animal*].

¶ See "The Two Fellows".

BLIND BYARD or BAYARD'S LEAP [summary]

County Folk-Lore, v, *Lincolnshire*, Gutch, pp. 81–7.

A witch who was supposed to live on human flesh lived in a cave in a wood, near where the Newark Road crosses Ermine Street. She kept the whole countryside in terror, till at length a knight came forward as champion, and went to a wise man to know what he was to do against her. He had the choice of a dozen horses who watered at a pond near by. He was to throw a stone into the water, and watch which horse threw up his head. The one to do so was Blind Bayard (often called Byard). The knight mounted Bayard, and rode to the witch's cave with a naked sword in his hand. He stopped at the entrance, and invited the witch to take a ride with him. The witch answered:

> "I must suckle my cubs,
> I must buckle my shoes,
> And then I will give you your supper."

and she soon darted out of her door, armed with cruel claws on feet and hands, and leapt on to Bayard's back. The knight sliced at her with his sword, and cut off one of her breasts. She stuck her talons into his neck and chest, and clutched at the horse with the claws on her feet. In his agony the horse sprang sixty feet, and flung her off, and the knight despatched her as she lay on the ground. Bayard's hoof-dints are marked by a stone, and it is the duty of those living at the place to keep his hoof-marks clear.

There are various versions of this story. In some the champion is the knight, in some a trooper, and in some an ordinary farmer. Addy does not give the rhyme.
MOTIFS: G.11.3 [*Cannibal witch*]; L.210 [*Modest choice is best*]; G.219.3 [*Witch has long nails*]; F.989.1.1 [*Horse's tremendous leap*]; G.275.8 [*Hero kills witch*].
¶ See "Byard's Leap".

THE BRIDGWATER RABBIT

Ruth L. Tongue, *Somerset Folklore*, p. 73.

A cottager's pig was bewitched and at last the man visited the White Witch in the Quantocks. He was told to follow these directions implicitly: He was to lance both ears and each foot of the pig in silence, letting the blood drip upon a piece of dowlas; he was then to pierce the dowlas from opposite directions with two pins, after which he must enter his cottage, lock the door, place the bloody rag on the fire, heap some turf over it, and read a few verses of the Bible while the dowlas burned. The man did all this, and when he went out to the pig-sty he found, as the White Witch had promised, that the pig was quite well again. Shortly after the old Bridgwater witch came, as she had often done, to inquire after the pig's health, but this time the pig remained quite healthy. Now every evening a strange white rabbit was seen running up and down a lane in the town and mysteriously disappearing. No dogs would chase it, and the neighbours were certain that it must be the witch, for they noticed that her bedroom window was open every time the rabbit was seen. So the pig's owner collected a party of friends and they went out one evening to catch the rabbit if they could. They found it sampling the plants in a walled garden, set a strong party at the only entry, a narrow drang [passage] between two cottages, and advanced on the rabbit. The pig's owner grabbed it by its ears and took a hearty kick at it. In a moment the rabbit was gone from his grasp, shot past the men at the entry and disappeared, never to be seen again. But the old woman was laid up for three days afterwards, unable to walk about, so the kick had landed somewhere.

From old Bridgwater friends, 1907–12.
TYPE ML.3055. MOTIFS: D.2089.3.1 [*Swine magically kept from fattening*]; G.271.4.4 [*Breaking spell on animal by bleeding animal*]; G.271.4.1 [*Exorcism by burning object for sympathetic magic*]; G.211.2.7 [*Witch in form of hare (rabbit)*]; G.275.12 [*Witch in form of an animal is injured as a result of injury done to the animal*].

THE BULL-DOG PISTOL AND THE HARE

Ruth L. Tongue, *Somerset Folklore*, p. 72.

"Well then, 'nother time when I were young I were working in gardens down to Bratton, 'n there were a bridge in gardens 'n 'ee went up along by a long haige, 'n I seed a vine hare a-sat down in haige, 'n her didn't never move, 'n I says, 'Yew stay thur, my dear, 'n I'll have 'ee.' Now, I tried with my gun same as Ellicombe, and bits of leaf 'n grass did vly

up round whur her did quat, but her just upped 'n jump deown in ditch
t'other side, not hurted a bit, though tree behind were marked. Well
then, I says, 'I'll have 'ee another day,' an' next time I tooked a pistol,
a heavy gurt thing they did call a bull-dog, took a bullet as big as a
currant, from a Winchester gun, an' I goes down over bridge, 'n I do
trip somehow, 'n blows end of me boo-ut raight off! Mid hev been me
gurt twoe. No, I never seed hare no more, nor I 'oodn't want tew."

There was an old woman who lived near Elworthy Barrows who was
suspected of being a hare. Some labourers determined to course her,
but she evaded the dogs and disappeared behind the cottage. When they
marched up to the door boldly to take possession and burn it down the
old lady herself opened it, and with one accord they all turned round
and ran. "Her were turble short in her breathings, they'd say."

From Walter Badcock, an old coachman, 1955.
MOTIFS: G.211.2.7 [*Witch in form of hare*]; G.265.8.3.1.1 [*Gun bewitched so that
it will not hit target*]; G.265.8.3.1.2 [*Witch throws bullets back at shooter*].
¶ See "The Witch Hare".

BYARD'S LEAP

S. O. Addy, *Household Tales*, p. 25.

At Newmarket, near Market Rasen, in Lincolnshire, there once lived a
witch who was a great trouble to the farmers in the neighbourhood.
They bore it for a long time, until one of them made up his mind to
stand it no longer. So he went to the wise man and asked what he was
to do to get rid of her.

The wise man said, "Turn all your horses out of the farmyard, and
drive them to the pond. And when they are drinking throw a stone into
the water, and take notice of the horse which is the first to lift up its
head. You must mount on his back, and in the night you must call at
the hut where the witch lives, and ask her to get up behind you and
ride. But you must take a dagger with you, and keep it sticking out, so
that when the witch leaps upon the horse she may cut her arm."

So the farmer did as the wise man had told him, and took all his
horses to the pond. Now it happened that the first horse to lift up its
head when the farmer threw a stone into the water was a blind one
called Byard. So the farmer leaped on Byard's back, and the same night
be rode straight to the hut where the witch dwelt, and knocked at
her door.

"Mother," said the farmer, "I have come to take thee for a ride, so
get up behind me."

So the witch, whose finger-nails were very sharp and long, tried to leap up behind the farmer. In doing so she tried to catch hold of Byard with her finger-nails, but she fell back twice, and each time that she fell back Byard leaped seven yards forward. At the third leap the witch clung fast to Byard behind, but she grazed her arm against the dagger which the farmer wore by his side. As soon as her arm began to bleed she lost all her power as a witch, and the country was no more troubled by her.

Byard's footprints are still to be seen in the place where he leaped three times. Whoever farms the land where they are is told to keep them clean and never to plough them up. And so they are carefully preserved to this day.

Nottinghamshire.
The word is pronounced Byard, and not Bayard.
MOTIFS: L.210 [*Modest choice best*]; G.219.3 [*Witch has long nails*]; G.273.6 [*Witch rendered powerless by drawing blood from her*]; F.989.1.1 [*Horse's tremendous leap*]; A.972.4 [*Imprint of horse in rocks*].
¶ See "Blind Byard".

A CAT ON A GATE [summary]

Thompson *Notebooks*, B.

Two gypsies went to put their horses into a field, with or without leave. A cat was sitting on the gate of the field, and refused to move; and it was with the greatest difficulty that they forced the gate open and drove the horses inside.

They started off down the lane to their camping-place, but found that the horses were out and following them. Again they drove them into the field, but the cat still refused to move from the gate. The same thing happened again, and the horses were driven into the field for the third time, and this time one of the gypsies beat the cat hard with a stick. It stayed on the gate, however, and again the horses broke out, and they found that one of them had a broken leg. At that, the men gave up the attempt to force them back into the field.

Next morning, when one of them fetched milk from the farm, he saw an old woman who was black and blue, and felt convinced that she was a witch who had changed herself into the cat on the gate.

Told by Phoenix Boswell at Windy Harbour, Siddington, Cheshire, 5 August 1923.
MOTIFS: G.211.1.7 [*Witch in form of cat*]; G.265.5 [*Witch maims animals*]; G.275.12 [*Witch in form of an animal is injured as a result of injury to the animal*].

THE CHRISTMAS BLOCK

E. M. Leather, *The Folk-Lore of Herefordshire*, p. 164.

Once Jack was going to put a Christmas block [a Yule log] on the fire. It was a very large one, and folk said he would never get it into the house. "Wait a bit," said Jack. He went and fetched four goslings, and fastened them to the log; at his bidding they drew it into the house as easily as if they had been horses.

Told by Miss M—— of Orcop, *aetat* 86, in 1909.
MOTIF: D.1691 [*Magic suspension of weight*].
¶ It is possible, however, that it may have been an example of D.2031.2 [*Thread made to appear as a large log carried by a cock*].

This is a stray anecdote about that mysterious character, Jack o' Kent.
See "The Four-Leafed Clover" (B, XII).

CLUB-FOOTED AGGIE

W. H. Barrett, *More Tales from the Fens*, pp. 146–50.

When I was a boy there used to be a witch living round here. She always wore a long cloak, tied with a bit of rope, which, she always said, her mother had taken off her father's neck after he'd been hanged for stealing some sheep. One of her legs was much shorter than the other, and instead of a foot it had a kind of lump at the end of it.

This is why she was always called Club-footed Aggie; but, for all that, she could move along, on a crutch, faster than most men could walk.

Aggie was a great worry to the cobbler. She'd go along to the shed where he sat working, lift her gammy leg over the half-door, and shout to him:

"Make me a shoe to fit that, you old leather-spoiler."

"Only the Devil could do that," the cobbler would say; then a good old row would start between them. This would end when Aggie swung herself off on her crutch, threatening all sorts of things that would happen to the cobbler till the day came when, she said, the carpenter would make a box to fit him better than the shoes he made fitted his customer's feet.

One day, one of the cobbler's pals told him that the only way to stop Aggie annoying him was to draw her blood. So the next time she stuck her leg up over the door he jabbed at it with his awl, which made her fall over backwards. When she picked herself up she leaned over and told the cobbler that for the next few days he'd be too busy scratching himself to be able to get on with his stitching. Next morning, she came to the shed and threw a small bundle of rags on to his lap. When he picked it up, ready to throw back again, it fell apart, and hundreds of fleas swarmed out of it. So that evening, when his pals came along, as usual, to hear one of his stories—because he was a good story-teller, they found him too busy scratching himself to be able to get on with his patching.

It was a full fortnight, too, before he got rid of those fleas.

Then Aggie came to him again, this time with a small sack of vipers, so he rushed out of the shed and into the pub and refused to go home till Ratty Porter had been along and killed the snakes. Even then Aggie didn't leave him alone. The next night, just as he was finishing off a pair of riding-boots for the squire, a bucket of dirty slops came flying through the door, hitting him full in the face. When he was able to see out of his eyes, he saw Aggie swinging along the road as fast as her crutch would take her.

Half an hour later, when the cobbler took up the boots to the big house, he asked the squire if he could have two silver spoons instead of the money, for the boots.

"What on earth do you want silver spoons for?" asked the squire.

So the cobbler told him all about Aggie and said that, if he had some silver spoons, he could get the blacksmith to melt them down and pour metal into his bullet-moulds; then he'd have some silver bullets to load his gun with.

"But why silver?" asked the squire. "Lead ones are cheaper."

"I know they are," said the cobbler, "but lead bullets would fly off that old woman's hide; only silver ones can topple a witch over."

"And you know what would happen to you then?" said the squire. "You'd be hanged for murder. And what sort of a harvest horkey* should we have then, without you telling us some of your good yarns? No; don't you do anything silly. I'll think things over, and perhaps I'll be able to help you."

So next morning the squire took a stroll round the village. The first person he met was the Rector, so he asked him what he thought about Aggie.

"Well," he said, "I can only say that some of the things she gets up to make me wonder if we are living now, or back a hundred years or so. Why, only this morning I found her in the churchyard, putting some filthy, dirty rags over the last Rector's gravestone. And, do you know, she had the impudence to tell me that she'd been talking to him, and he'd asked her to leave the rags there to wipe the sweat off his face, as it was so hot where he was."

Later on the squire met the baker, and asked him if he thought Aggie was a witch or not.

* *Harvest horkey* = A harvest supper.

"I don't think—I know she is. Some time ago I couldn't get my bread to rise for a whole week—all the loaves came out of the oven sappy and stodgy. I happened to tell Aggie about it, and she came into my bakehouse one night, took a bit of dough and made it into the shape of a frog. Then she threw it into the furnace and watched it burn, and, do you know, every batch that I've drawn since has been perfect."

Next the squire called in at the grocer's.

"I reckon that old Aggie does me a lot of good," he told the squire. "Before she started calling in at my shop I always had thirty shillings to two pounds in bad debts every week. Now I don't suppose I'm owed more than five or six shillings, and I put it all down to her."

At the butcher's the squire was told:

"Every time that old hag comes into the shop, my sausages go sour, the lard won't wet, and my pickled pork goes bad in the brine-tub. If I had my way, I'd hoist her on my pulley-hooks and jab her heart out."

Then the squire met the chimney-sweep, who told him that several times, when he'd been pushing his brush out of the chimney, the rods had been pulled out of his hands and the brush had flown up the chimney-pot and dropped half a mile away.

"There's only one person who could make it do that," he said "and that's Aggie."

Then the squire turned into the builder's yard and asked him if he'd any complaints about Aggie.

"Complaints?" said the builder. "I should just think I have. Why, that old gal's done me out of sixty pounds, and I'll tell you how. One of the farmers here asked me to dig him a sixty-foot well at a place where the water-diviner had said there was a spring. I was nearly down to that when Aggie comes along and demands some of the money I was getting for the job. I told her I'd see her in Hell first; so then she spat on the two chaps I had down the shaft, and said I'd as much hope of finding water there as I had in in the place where I'd said I'd like to see her. Well, I was down nearly sixty feet when the shaft caved in, and, as I'd already paid out more than I'd bargained for in wages, I turned the job in. But what made my blood boil was this: I heard that Aggie went to the farmer and told him that, for a sovereign, she'd tell him where to find all the water he wanted, and it wouldn't cost him a penny more. So he gave her the sovereign, and she took six steps with her crutches and then told him to start digging there. The hole he dug, she said, was to be deep enough for three barrels, with their heads and bottoms knocked out, to stand in, one on top of the other. When he'd finished, she told him, she'd come along and get the water flowing. Well, she came along, leaned over those barrels, said the Lord's Prayer backwards three times, and the water came gushing in till it was level with the top of the barrel. And the farmer's been using it ever since, and the water's not fallen more than two inches. I say, only a witch could do a thing like that."

On his way home, the squire called in at the pub, where he found Micky the roadman enjoying his dinner of bread and cheese and a pint of ale.

"Nice morning, Micky," said the squire. "Now what do you think about Aggie? Is she a witch?"

"Yes. I do," said Micky. "But that doesn't really bother me, because in my eighty years I've picked up a good few tricks to stop any of her goings-on."

"Have you now," said the squire. "Well, you have another drink, and then perhaps you'll let me know some of your tricks."

Micky and the squire spent a good hour talking together. Then the squire went home, told his wife all about his walk, and asked if she'd help him with a little plan he had.

That evening he sent for the cobbler and gave him one of his wife's shoes, the right one, and asked him if he'd take the upper away from the sole, and then stitch it on again.

"That's easy," said the cobbler, and he showed how it could be done by taking his pocket-knife and cutting off the upper.

"That's fine," said the squire. "Now you take the sole, drive a few tacks in it, so that anyone wearing it would soon get a few blisters, and then bring it back to me."

The cobbler did as he was told, and later on that day, people passing the green were very surprised to see the squire giving a good curry-combing to Jerry Brown's donkey.

Next day the squire's wife was out in the village when she met Aggie and told her, that if she liked to come up to the house, then she could have a good shoe to wear instead of the broken-down old one she had on. When she got back Aggie was waiting for her, so she gave her the shoe. But Aggie, though the shoe fitted her perfectly, didn't say, "Thank you," but threw her old one at the yard-dog, then went round to the cobbler. She shoved her foot under his nose and told him to have a good look at that shoe and make one like it for her other leg, then she swung off. But before she'd gone very far she started to limp. Two days later she limped into the grocer's shop, sat down on a chair and said she was going to stay there, because the only foot she had to stand on was burning like Hell. So the grocer fetched the baker, who, seeing she couldn't walk, went off to borrow the cart that the butcher used for fetching hogs on killing days. He laid Aggie flat in this and told her he'd drive her home; but instead of doing that he took her along to the workhouse.

Well, for many years after this everyone at the horkey supper enjoyed this tale of how a witch was cured of her wicked ways. And you want to know what the trick was? Old Mickey's been dead for a long time, now, but he'd have told you that he did to Aggie what he did to himself many a time, in India, when he wanted a few days rest from soldiering.

He'd tell you that if a scratch on the hand or foot is rubbed with the hair of a mule or donkey, then it burns and itches and swells for a few days, then gets better and doesn't leave a mark.

MOTIFS: G.273.6 [*Witch rendered powerless by drawing blood from her*]; D.926.1 [*Well produced by magic*]; D.1385.4 [*Silver bullets protect against witches*].

¶ Club-footed Aggie's retaliation against the cobbler had nothing supernatural about it, but it is arguable that this may be because he had drawn blood from her (MOTIF: G.263.8 [*Witch makes person lousy*]). Witches are supposed to cause magical infestation by vermin, also plagues of snakes, so she was following accepted lines.

The squire's methods were also naturalistic, though they had a magical basis, as, for instance, MOTIF: G.273.7.2(a) [*Nail driven into witch's track*] (Baughman), and also the magical quality of hairs from the cross on a donkey's back.

It is clear that Aggie would have been in danger from "common repute" in the days of the witch trials.

THE COUNTER-CHARM [summary]

R. Blakeborough, *Wit, Character, Folk-Lore and Customs of the North Riding of Yorkshire*, p. 191.

A man living at Broughton had a spell cast on him, and went to consult a wise man, who first wished to know whom he suspected of having worked the spell. There were two possibilities: the witch Nancy Newgill and a man known to have the evil eye. If a counter-charm were worked upon the innocent suspect, it would recoil against the victim of the spell, thus adding to his sufferings; so the wise man advised him to go to both of them and accuse them openly. This he did, and was convinced that, for once, Nancy was innocent, for she looked him straight in the face, and swore a fearful oath, while the man's behaviour was so shifty that he felt safe in telling the wise man to act against him.

Just before midnight they lighted a fire of wicken wood, and while it was burning up they took a ball of clay, beat it flat with the back of an old Bible, and scooped out of it a rough figure in the shape of a man.

Into this rough mould was poured a mixture of pitch, beeswax, hog's lard, bullock's blood, and a little fat from a bullock's heart. This was melted and stirred over the wicken-wood fire, and what remained after filling the clay mould was divided into two parts. One part was thrown into water, then worked into a ball, and thrown away; the other was poured on to the fire. It flared up into a tremendous blaze, and when this had died down, the ashes were buried in the churchyard. The figure was then taken out of the mould and two small holes made in it for eyes. Into one of these eyes a pin was driven, a charm was pronounced, and the spell was complete.

As the man was returning home to Broughton, the pain suddenly left him; and in the same night the evil-eyed man of Nunthorpe was seized with a fearful pain in the eye, and by morning that eye was blind. This story was told by one who knew all three men personally.

MOTIFS: D.2071 [*The evil eye*]; G.271.6 [*Exorcism of witch by counter-charm*]; D.2063.1.1 [*Tormenting by sympathetic magic*]; D.2063.1.1.1.1* [*Tormenting by sticking pins into clay figure*] (Baughman).
¶ See "The Pig and the Butcher".

CRAZY MOLL

W. H. Barrett, *More Tales from the Fens*, pp. 119–122.

When Crazy Moll was full up with gin she used to go about shouting that she'd been born in Witchford, and was going to be buried in Witcham. She wasn't, though. She was buried in Southery, as you'll find out when I've finished my tale. She was a terror, was Moll, mad as a March hare when she was sober, and a proper hell cat when she wasn't.

She always wore a long, black cape, buttoned up to her chin to hide her beard, and an old felt hat which she pulled down to hide a big black mark on her forehead. Folks all said that she'd got this mark from the Devil himself; you see, everyone, except the parson, swore that Moll was a witch. The Rector used to let her come and sit by the stove at the back of the church, even though the verger kept telling him she was dirty. The Rector found this out for himself, at last, and this is how it came about.

It was winter and Moll had been sitting by the stove all day, brewing tea in an old pan. When it was dark the verger started getting the church ready for service, so she cleared off when he told her she was in his way. Then the Rector came in, a bit footsore after trudging round the parish all afternoon, so he sat down on the bench where Molly had spent the day. As he sat there warming himself, he thought what a lonely soul the poor old girl must be, with no one to keep her company; but he soon found out she wasn't so lonely as he'd thought because, in a little while, he began to itch, and he went on doing so all through the service. After supper, as he sat by the fire with his wife, she began to itch too, and next morning, after a night of scratching, they found they were both covered with little red spots. So, after breakfast, the Rector went down to the church, and told the verger that the church door must be kept locked.

Presently Moll came along with a little bottle of gin, which someone had given her to keep out the cold, and which she was looking forward to enjoying by the stove. Finding the door padlocked, she drank off the gin, then set off to find the verger. She met him as he was going to the baker's with a bundle of bedding which the baker had promised the Rector he'd put in his oven when his last batch of loaves had been drawn.

"Get out of my way, you flea-bitten old devil," shouted the verger, which made Moll set up such a screeching and cursing, that all the dogs in the road put their tails between their legs and cut off for home as fast as they could go.

The verger pushed Moll in front of him, with his bundle, as far as the baker's. Then the baker, finding she wouldn't go there on her own, pushed her with his bakehouse mop till she'd backed onto the horse-trough standing outside the bakery. Every time she tried to get out of the water he pushed her in again, shoving her well down. A crowd of people gathered round to see the fun, while the Rector, hearing her screams, came up just as the baker was pulling her out with a muck crome.

The next time anyone saw Moll she was leaning over the gate of the meadow where, it being a Sunday and no round to do, the baker's horse was grazing. She was still there when passers-by were going to bed. Next morning the horse was brought up to the stable, but it wouldn't eat its breakfast and, when it was harnessed to the cart, it wouldn't start. The baker tried all ways to make it go, but in the end he had to give up and go and borrow a horse from the butcher.

Well, he started off all right, then, halfway on his round, he tied the horse up while he walked across a couple of fields to take some bread to a farmhouse. On his way back he saw someone standing near the horse, and, when he got near he saw it was Crazy Moll, who walked off cursing, and with her hand held up in the air.

"Git up," said the baker, but the horse, like the other one, stood still and wouldn't move. After half an hour of trying to shift it, the baker gave up and walked back to the butcher, who came along, took the horse out of the shaft and led it home. Then he drove it back in his own cart, and loaded up the loaves from the baker's cart. But, believe it or not, as soon as that horse felt the loaves behind it, it wouldn't stir a foot.

At last the butcher said: "That animal's tudded.* I know it. Well,

---

* *Tudded* = bewitched. The word probably owes its origin to the frequent use of toads in East Anglian witchcraft.

all you can do is to go and borrow Turfman Martin's dickey and cart and carry on your round with that."

So the baker walked along to Turfman's house and asked if he could have his dickey and cart as there seemed to be something wrong with his horse, and he must get on with his bread round. Turfman was only too glad to lend a hand, and the dickey trotted along quite happy. When the baker got near the Ship, he thought it would be a good idea to call in and have a drink after all he'd been through. He was just getting his face down to his pint when, through the window, he saw Crazy Moll talking to the dickey, who seemed to be listening with both its long ears.

"Now, don't you stop that one from going," said the baker, and rushed outside just as Moll was walking away, still cursing him. But, when he jumped into the cart and called out "Get along, Neddy" the dickey started off at a smart little trot.

The baker kept the dickey for a few days, and paid Turfman for the hire of it. Then, the first time he took his own horse out, after he'd found it would go, he hitched the dickey behind in case he met Moll on his round. But he didn't see the old woman again. That ducking in the horse-trough had been too much for her, so she turned her toes up and was buried in Southery, where she did it, and not in Witcham after all.

It was Turfman who told the baker why she hadn't been able to put a spell on his dickey.

"No old witch can ever do that," he said, "because a dickey's the only animal that's as cunning as the Devil himself."

MOTIFS: A.2221.1 [*Animal characteristics reward for pious act*]; D.2072.0.2.1 [*Horse enchanted so that he stands still*]; A.2221.3 [*Markings on animals as recollection of Christ's life and sufferings*].

¶ The reason generally given for the donkey's immunity is the blessing gained by him for carrying Christ on his entry into Jerusalem, for which he was rewarded by a cross on his back. Curiously enough, the Motif Index gives no prominence to this.

See "The Liddle Dunk Foal" (A, II).

THE CROSSED CORN

Shetland Folk Book, II, p. 12.

There were two families in Yell whose houses were very close together, but as neighbours the people did not get on very well.

When the family which can be called No. 1 was cutting their corn they found here and there through the rig handfuls of corn cut and crossed so that the beard was at both ends and tied in the middle.

The young folks went to ask their mother's advice, and she said it was certainly done by someone who wished to harm them, and told them to keep the corn separate and watch what happened. They placed it in a particular scroo and then forgot all about it.

In the winter a newly calved cow fell ill and then they discovered they had been feeding her with the crossed corn. They immediately stopped giving the cow this corn and took some of it to their neighbour's byre and gave it to his cow. Whereupon it took ill and died, and the first cow recovered. This happened nearly sixty years ago.

MOTIFS: G.265.4.2 [*Witch causes illness of animals*]; D.1783.5 [*Magic turned against the makers*].

CURE FOR A WITCH

The Folktales of England, pp. 110–12.

In Fenland a hundred years ago the fens were smothered with witches.

Everybody believed in them, except the Parson, and he had good cause to think there was something supernatural about them.

It happened like this. One night old Billy Bowers, the local poacher, was returning home with his bag heavy with what he'd found in the woods, and as he walked by the churchyard he saw a flittering light. So he stopped on his way, and peered through the fence, and saw that it was one of the so-called local witches gathering earth off of a new-made grave. Well, Billy don't like to see that, so he went home, got his old muzzle-loading gun, put a charge of gunpowder into it, and then filled it up with broken rock-salt which he used to use to cure rabbit skins. So he went back up the lane, and he saw this old girl's behind bobbing up and down in the lantern light. So he took aim, and he fired. Well, the screech the old girl gave woke everybody in the neighbourhood. They all opened their bedroom windows to hear her screaming. Soon they was congregating round the churchyard gate. One said, "This is a job for the parson." So he went along, called the parson up. The parson wanted to know what was the trouble. "Well," he said, "all the devils in Hell are running round the churchyard, shrieking their insides out."

So the parson got up, and he called this man in, and he said, "Before we go, we'd better have something to put some courage into us." So he produced a bottle of whisky, took a good drink himself and then handed a good drink to the other chap, who, by the way, was the sexton. Then the parson put on his surplice, in case there was something, and he picked up one of these new-fangled oil lamps, grabbed a big stick and went across to the churchyard gate. He wanted the sexton to go with him. The sexton said his was a day-job; he wasn't paid for night work. No one else wanted to go. So the parson said he'd go on his own. As he went down the churchyard, the old girl who'd had a dose of rock salt in her buttocks saw something coming the other way. Her gave a scream, and run down the churchyard. The parson followed her. He caught his foot on a tombstone, the lamp flew out of his hand, and burst into flames. Billy thought it was time he took a hand. So he went into the church, and he rang the bells for all he was worth. That caused all the jackdaws in the church steeple to fly out, and hover just over the heads of the people standing in the road with lanterns. So Billy went along and wanted to know what they was all out there for at that time of night. Someone told him that the Devil was in the churchyard. He'd come out of Hell, and when he came out of Hell there was a flame of fire went up into the sky, and they hadn't seen him [the parson] since, so they supposed the Devil took him.

So Billy says, "Well, ain't none of you going in to see what's happened to him?"

They said, "No."

"Well," he said, "I'll go."

So he went along, and he found the parson laying there with his face all covered with blood, where he'd hit his nose on the tombstone as he fell. Billy said, "I'm surprised! That must have been a hell of a fight you was in. I wonder what the other chaps look like, you being so covered with blood."

But the parson said if he'd only help him home, he'd give him whatever he'd like to ask. So Billy helped him home, and the parson promised him that he'd have a brace of pheasants off of him all the time the game season lasted. But Billy used to sit in the pub and tell his tale.

He said: "People as thinks they knows think there's a lot of ways of curing witches." He said: "There's only one—that is, pepper their hams with rock-salt. That'll cure 'em!"

Recorded from W. H. Barrett, 12 October 1963.
MOTIFS: D.1278.1 [*Magic churchyard mould*]; G.271.3 [*Use of salt in exorcism of witch*]; X.410 [*Jokes on parsons*].
¶ The Fenland country was some of the wildest and bleakest in England, and supernatural beliefs were rife there, particularly the more sinister ones.
See "Club-footed Aggie", "Crazy Moll", "The Green Mist" (B, XII).

DICK, DUKE AND MERRYBOY

K. M. Briggs, *Pale Hecate's Team*, p. 225.

There was an old woman near Poundsford who had three toads, Dick, Duke and Merryboy. Mrs Hill's grandfather was reaping with two other men, and they saw a great toad and killed it. The old woman cursed them and said they should not finish that day's work. The first cut his hand and had to go home, the second cut his boot, and her grandfather cut the toe right off his foot. So they none of them finished their reaping.

From Ruth L. Tongue, notes on Somerset witchcraft. Told by Mrs Hill of Poundsford in 1957. The tale was sixty years old.
MOTIFS: G.225.4 [*Toad as witch's familiar*]; G.269.10 [*Witch punishes person who incurs her ill-will*].

DOLLY MAKIN THE WITCH [summary]

R. Blakeborough, *Wit, Character, Folk-Lore and Customs of the North Riding of Yorkshire*, p. 150.

An old woman told how she had once seen a witch, who had, long before, tried to harm her aunt. The witch, Dolly Makin, was over a hundred years old at that time, but when she and the old aunt had been young, a strange thing had taken place. A young man, Tom Pickles, was wanting to marry the young aunt, but she preferred one, William Purkis. So Tommy went to the witch, and paid her to work a spell on the girl.

As she was at her milking one evening, an old fortune-teller came up to her, took her hand, and told her that William Purkis was in love with another girl, and it would be far better for her to take up with Tommy. But the girl replied that she would wed whom she liked, and it would not be Tommy.

The fortune-teller struck the cow with her stick; the cow kicked, and knocked over the milk-pail; the girl flung her milking stool, which just missed the fortune-teller's head, and the two women fought fiercely for some time.

At last the fortune-teller screamed out that the other must be wearing something that belonged to the unburied dead; otherwise, she said, she would have been overpowered long before.

"But I haven't done with you yet," she said; and then the girl saw that she had been fighting with the witch.

Next morning they heard that an uncle of hers had died the day before, and as the girl's brooch held a lock of his hair it had saved her from the witch.

The old woman added that this witch, Dolly Makin, had once crossed from Ingleborough to Whernside at one stride; and when challenged on this, she said, "Mebbee ah was wrang; sha wad loup it."

At the time when she herself saw Dolly, the old woman said, she was walking with her sweetheart to Fetham Holme, a few months before their marriage, when they saw an old woman sitting on a great stone. She looked so strange that the young man burst out laughing; at which the old woman sprang up, shrieking, "Ya arnt wed yet!" She vanished, and the next moment a black cat darted across their path. Terrified by the omen, the girl went next day, without telling her sweetheart, to consult the Wise Man of Reeth. He told her there were only two chances of escape. One was to tear a piece of cloth from the coat of a man on a gibbet, cut it into nine pieces, and burn them at dead of night, with doors and windows securely fastened. But this she declared to be impossible; so he bade her listen to the last words of a man about to be hanged, write them on nine pieces of paper, stick a pin through each, and burn them at midnight, as before. She learnt from the *Yorkshire Gazette*, that a man was soon to be hanged at York, so she travelled there, and stayed in the house of a cousin in the town till the appointed day, then faithfully carried out the Wise Man's instructions. So it was that the witch, Dolly, had never any power to harm her or her children.

MOTIFS: G.269.4 [*Curse by disappointed witch*]; G.275.9 [*Fighting and wrestling with witch*]; G.272.20*(a) [*Person keeps something taken from unburied dead to protect herself from witches*] (Baughman); G.271.8(b) [*Burning at midnight clothes taken from man on gibbet*] (Baughman); G.271.8(a) [*Burning at midnight nine scraps of paper with last words of man about to be hanged. They are stuck with pins*] (Baughman).

THE DUNG–PUTT

Ruth L. Tongue, *Somerset Folklore*, p. 75.

There was an old witch over to Broomfield used to keep cats and toads, and if she didn't like you she'd send the toads after you. She lived in the cottages at Rose Hill—they've fallen down now, and if anyone did anything she didn't like she'd say, "I'll toad 'ee," and people was all afraid, I s'pose. I knew the carter who worked over to Ivyton Farm, and he had to go to Bridgwater with the cart with a load of corn, and she come to the door and asked him to bring her a couple of sacks of coals back. Well, he forgot, and when he come to pass her cottage she came out for her coals, and she shook her fist at him and said, "I'll set the toads on 'ee." When he got to Ivyton, farmer asked him why he looked so bad and when he told him he said, "I sooner have lost the wheat than you should ha' forgot they coals." And after that, if he had to take a load of dung, s'pose too, she'd come to the door of her cottage and cackle at him. And sure enough the pegs sprung and the dung-putt tipped up. Then she'd cackle, "That'll teach 'ee to forget my coals. I'll toad 'ee!" The carter told me he'd tie the pegs down with binder twine, but 'twas no use. Every time he got to the cottage the twine broke, and the pegs sprung, and the old witch she'd come to the door, and stand there and cackle.

From Wilfred Chidley, artisan, Crowcombe, 21 February 1957. The carter, who is a very old man, is still living, but has moved.

MOTIFS: G.225.0.3 [*Familiars do work of witch*]; G.265.8.3.2 [*Witch bewitches wagon*].

THE EARTHENWARE GOOSE [summary]

James Bowker, *Goblin Tales of Lancashire*, p. 167.

Mag Shelton was a lonely old woman, who lived with her cat and her goose in the village of Singleton, near Fylde, and, because she was ugly, was an object of suspicion to all her neighbours. They thought her in league with the Devil, and attributed to her whatever went amiss on their farms or in their homes.

At one time there was a great scarcity of milk in the neighbourhood, and as usual, Mag was blamed for it. At last a company of the local farmers banded themselves together to watch outside her cottage, and see what they could discover.

Very soon after they had hidden in some bushes, the door opened, and Mag came out, followed by her goose and cat. The men waited in hiding, and before long she came back, walking slowly, and alone. As she stopped to unlatch her door they darted out, seized her roughly, and tore off her cloak, demanding, "What have you done with the milk?"

In vain she protested that she was only taking the air, and that the children persecuted her so much it was only at night that she could venture out. They had already started to drag her to the horse-pond, when the goose appeared, hissing loudly, and placed itself at the old woman's side. The leader of the farmers raised his stick, and hit the goose on the head, whereupon it vanished, leaving in its place a large broken pitcher, with milk warm from the cow streaming from it.

They flung the old woman into the pond, and would soon have brought her to trial as a witch, but on the intervention of the Vicar she was allowed to depart, with her goose and cat for company.

Soon afterwards a large jug in which the watchers had carried their beer to the place of ambush was missed by the landlord of the Blue Pig, and was never returned. The landlord, however, often declared that fragments of it were to be seen in the village, carefully treasured as being bits of the jug which had been transformed.

MOTIFS: D.2083.3 [*Milk transferred from another's cow by magic*]; D.423.1 [*Transformation: goose to object*]; D.2083(2083.3.3(a)).3.3(a) [*Witch transfers milk to her pitcher*] (Baughman).

THE EASINGTON HARE

F. Grice, *Folk-Tales of the North Country*, p. 99.

Once the men of Castle Eden were fond of coursing. They bred and trained their own greyhounds and had rare sport. The carpenter would match his dog against the blacksmith's, and the thatcher would challenge the shepherd, and on the first fine holiday they held their coursing matches in the fields around the village.

One year, however, they began to be troubled by a strange hare that threatened to spoil their sport. No sooner had they let slip their greyhounds than this strange animal came loping through the hedge and over the furrows. It was not sandy like the other hares, but darker and greyer-coloured, almost like a mole, and it ran across the path of the hounds as if to say, "Come after me. I am not so fleet as my brothers, and you'll soon catch me." It never failed to turn the hounds from their proper game; but no sooner had they turned to give chase than it led them a merry dance, and drew them after it into the depths of Castle Eden Dene.

It was in vain for the men to whistle the dogs back. They would not leave the hare; and long after it had eluded them they kept coursing through the dene, barking madly and running backwards and forwards. Sometimes they ran their heads against the boles of the trees, and killed themselves, and sometimes they strayed so far that they were lost. Instead of enjoying a day's sport, the men spent many weary hours tramping through the thick undergrowth in the dene, searching for their missing greyhounds.

They soon grew to recognize the mischievous hare, and to wish that they could catch it, and put an end to its pranks, for it brought them nothing but inconvenience and loss. It always outstripped the swiftest of their greyhounds, and no trap or snare was cunningly enough laid to catch it. Day after day it ruined their coursing matches, until it seemed that soon the men would have to give them up altogether.

At last the men held a meeting to discuss what they could do.

"When we try to shoot it," said one, "every bullet seems to miss it."

"When we set traps," said another, "we find the traps closed, but no hare in them!"

"When we course it," said a third, "we only lose another greyhound. What can we do?"

They were all at a loss, but at last one proposed that they should seek the advice of an old man who lived near Castle Eden, and was skilful in healing sick horses and cows.

"He may help us," said the man, "for he is more learned that we are in the ways of animals."

So they went to visit the old man. He listened very carefully to their story, and then he said, "This hare possesses powers that no other hare possesses, and it will not be caught by ordinary means. Tomorrow you must take with you, not a greyhound, but a bloodhound. If it is a black bloodhound, all the better, and if it has been fed on human milk I think you will be sure of catching your hare."

The men thanked the old horse-doctor and obeyed his instructions. The next day they took with them a coal-black bloodhound, and as soon as the hare appeared they loosed it. Immediately the hare made for the dene, and the bloodhound followed it. But so slow did the bloodhound seem, that one of the men cried out, "It is no good. It is like setting a magpie to keep up with a swallow."

Most of the men were of his mind, and when both hare and hound disappeared into the dene, they tied their horses to the branches, and prepared for another weary search. But just when they had given up hope they saw the hare running up the bank at the other side of the ravine, and soon the hound appeared running after it, with its nose to the ground and its big ears flapping as it ran. For once the hare had been hunted out of its refuge in the woods and forced out into the open country. The men remounted their horses and crossed the dene, just in time to see both hare and hound running in a bee-line for the village of Easington.

They gave chase, and though the many hedges and gates prevented them from catching up, they drew close enough to see that the hare was limping, and the bloodhound was gaining on it. On they went, past straggling hedges of tall thorn-trees and haystacks standing like new-cut loaves on a green cloth, and over pasture and pleated plough-land, until they came to Easington village. Then the hare ran straight across the village green. On the opposite side of the green stood a little stone cottage, with curved brown tiles and a cracked and dirty door. There was a little space cut away from the bottom of the door, like an opening left for hens to wander in and out, and through this space ran the hare. It was almost too late, for just as it bolted through the opening the bloodhound caught up with it, and seized it by one of its hind legs. However, the hare shook its leg free, and disappeared into the cottage.

The huntsmen tried the door, but it was locked. Then they knocked, but no one came to let them in. So at last they burst open the door, and rushed into the room. But they could see no hare. Instead, they saw, sitting before the fire, an old woman. She was hastily bandaging her heel, and trying in vain to stop the blood from flowing, and to hide a wound. None of the men spoke to her. Perceiving that the old woman knew that her witchcraft had been found out at last, they turned and left the room; and never again was their sport spoiled by the mischievous hare.

TYPE ML.3055 MOTIFS: G.211.2.7.1 [*Witch as hare allows self to be coursed for pay or for sport*]; G.275.12(*daa*) [*Witch hare is injured by black hunting-dog*] (Baughman); G.275.12(*d*) [*Witch as hare injured when hare is injured*] (Baughman); G.273.6 [*Witch rendered powerless by drawing her blood*].

THE ELDER-TREE WITCH

Ruth L. Tongue, *Forgotten Folk Tales.*

There were a farm not far from Knighton, and 'tis an unket bit of land round there, but farmer took it and he did well. His few cows give the best milk round-abouts. There wadn't any big trees to the farm, but good hedges down to the shores—and no elder bushes.

No one like elder thereabouts.

There was a tale my own great-granddad used to tell and he's a-heard 'en vrom his own girt-grand-dad about a veller as went to chop down an elder tree and it bled and chased 'en—he might h' taken thought, witches can turn into elders if they wish, but he didn't and he got a terrible chasing till he crossed running water.

Well, whether farmer believed the tale or no, there came a time when his cows was being milked unbeknown to him.

He wadn't a rich man, and he couldn't afford the loss, so he gets up by starlight and goes out to make sure his cows was in safe grazing and there was the shadow of a tree up by the hedge.

So all in a cold sweat, he drove cows to the little home pasture, but the chain was gone off the gate, and he couldn't fasten it with iron, so he put a girt stone agin it.

Come morning he tells his women-folk what had been seen and his wife she say, "Thee girt fool, did'n 'ee draw a criss-cross in the mud droo the gate?"

No, he hadn'n.

And his daughter she up and peep out the window, then she turn so pale as curd cheese, and run around cottering the inside shutters safely crying, "'Tis out in the pasture now, right among the cows."

"Oh Lord, save us!" say the wife. "What tree be it?"

"A elder!" says the girl, shivering and shaking, and the old Granny she lays the big iron shovel among the red-hot embers, and raked in a faggot of ash to make a blaze.

"Elder!" say the farmer, and he were all a-shiver too, but he were a courageous man and his cows was dear to him. "Wife, go fetch this silver button as come off my Zunday coat."

Well, she'd a-sewed'en on again but she took and snipped 'en off and brought 'en to 'en, and by time he'd a-load his gun with it the daughter she'd a-swung the cross bar down across back door and the granny she'd got the iron shovel nice and hot.

Then the wife opened vront-door a crack and he took a look. This there tree were right in among his cows now so he couldn' take a long shot.

"I'll have to get upsides with 'en," he says. "Hold the door open and let I out and in again if I has to run for it."

And his wife she done it and out he went trembling all over. But he was bound to save his cows.

Well, the elder tree were right in among they, and he had to get too close for comfort to take aim, and for the life of him he couldn't hold the gun steady and the silver button missed her.

Well she let out a yell, and so did he, and she leapt arter 'en like a stag, and he leapt too, and she come rushing arter him and went rushing vor thic open door. He were a fat old fellow, but he made the pace, and his wife she slammed door so quick she caught his coat-tails in it, but for all that she drop the iron bar safe into its socket. And there they were all safe inside.

They could hear her branches a-scrattling and a-rattling outside and her a-skreeking like a high wind. Wife and daughter they skreeked too, and farmer he bellered like a bull-calf trying to get his coat-tails free and be out to his cows again.

He had the courage, see, but not the right knowledge, or not enough of it. Then they heard her rushing round the house and rap-tapping at the shutters, but she couldn' get in, no more than they could get out—and what was to happen to the pig and the pony?

Then the old Granny she get up vrom hearth-place with a girt shovel of burning coals and she say to the girl, "Open the back door now wide," and she did, and ran back to her mother, but the old Granny she just stood there, and when the elder tree come straight at her a-leaping and a-skreeking, she just up and throw all they red hot coals at her and come in and shut the back door, then they all see blue flames flicker and hear tree crackling into cinders.

After a bit Granny she take the ashen cattle-gad and go out and there was a girt heap of ashes cold already and they women all made a criss-cross on the ashes with the ashen gad, then they ran and opened shutters and vront door again, and Varmer were able to free his coat-tails and go out to his cows.

Then the neighbours all come, and they all rejoiced, for they said that were the end of Madam Widecombe and her coach and the gold pig who pulled it, but 'twasn't to be—she were still around, the Combwich man said, nor it wadn't the old black witch over to Steart, and then someone up and told 'em Raggy Lyddy over to Doddington had valled in her vire, and was burnded dead—so that were who 'twas.

From Mr Burton, Stolford. Somerset.

MOTIFS: G.212.4 [*Witch in form of tree*]; G.271.11(*ad*) [*Magic herb: elder*] (Baughman); D.2083.3 [*Milk transferred from another's cow by magic*]; G.271.5(*e*) [*Shooting witch in person with silver bullets*] (Baughman); G.275.3 [*Witch burned*].

¶ In some parts of the country elders are thought to give protection against witches and fairies, and it is often said that flies will not trouble one under elders. It used to be quite widely thought, however, that if elders are cut they will bleed.

See "The One with the White Hand" (B, XII).

THE ENCHANTED MIST [summary]

J. R. W. Coxhead, *Devon Traditions and Folk-Lore*, p. 71.

Vixen Tor, on the western border of Dartmoor, overlooks the valley of the River Walkham, about half a mile below Merrivale Bridge, and four and a half from Tavistock. It is the highest rock mass on Dartmoor, rising on its steepest side, the southern, to a height of 93 feet.

An evil witch named Vixana once lived in an underground cavern below this tor. She was incredibly old, wizened, and hideous, and all the neighbourhood dreaded to go near her, for it was her delight to raise a magic mist, in which travellers could be lured into the quaking bog at the foot of the tor.

A moor-man, living in a remote part of Dartmoor, heard of her wicked deeds, and resolved to bring about her destruction. He had two great assets—for a service he had once done them, the pixies had given him a gold ring which made him invisible whenever he slipped it on his finger; and they had also given him the power to see clearly through the thickest mist. He placed his ring in his pocket, and set out to trudge the many weary miles between his home and that of the witch.

Watching from above, as she always did, the witch saw him toiling along the path beside the bog. She waved her wand, and at once the treacherous mist hid him and all his surroundings. But to the moor-man this meant nothing; avoiding the bog, he made his way steadily on to the foot of Vixen Tor. Vixana screamed with rage, and began to weave another spell to destroy him, but he slipped the ring on his finger and vanished immediately. While the bewildered witch was looking in every direction for him, the moor-man quietly climbed the tor on the northern side, and when he reached the top he came up behind the witch, who was peering about to the south, and with a fierce thrust of his arm, he drove her, screaming wildly, to her death 93 feet below.

Her death caused rejoicing over all Dartmoor, and the people of the neighbourhood rewarded the moor-man so generously for his valour that he was able to live in comfort for the rest of his life.

MOTIFS: D.902.1 [*Magic mist*]; G.262 [*Murderous witch*]; D.1361.17 [*Magic ring renders invisible*]; F.642 [*Person of remarkable sight*]; G.275.8 [*Hero kills witch*].

THE ENCHANTER OF PENGERSWICK
[summary]

Hunt, *Popular Romances of the West of England*, pp. 322–6.

The first lord of Pengerswick, who built the castle, was ambitious for his son to marry into a high-born family. He chose a lady much older than his son, who was connected with the Godolphin family, and who was passionately in love with the young man. But he had no love for her, and at last, in revenge, she married his father.

The Witch of Fraddam, who had often helped the Lady of Pengerswick with her love-potions, had a niece, Bitha, whom they had both employed to aid them in their spells, and as a result Bitha herself fell in love with the young man. She now ingratiated herself with his stepmother, and was chosen as her lady's-maid.

But the stepmother herself was still in love with the young heir, and when she saw him and Bitha speaking together one day, she became so wildly jealous that she determined to destroy him. Bitha discovered her intent, and set herself to counteract the older woman's schemes. At last, when everything else had failed, the stepmother persuaded her husband that his son had a violent passion for her, which was making her life impossible, and he hired a gang of foreign sailors to carry his son off and sell him into slavery.

The young man escaped, however, and disappeared from the castle, and for many years he was never heard of. Meantime, the two women plotted to secure the wealth of the old lord, and on his deathbed Bitha told him that he was dying from the effects of a poison given to him by his wife.

After many years the young lord returned to Pengerswick, learned in all the magic arts, which he had studied in his travels, and found that his stepmother, from much handling of poisons, had become covered with scales like a serpent, and had shut herself up in a tower in solitude. At last she perished by throwing herself from it into the sea. Bitha had gone to live on the Downs in St Hilary, and from her evil practices, and dealing with the Devil, her skin had become the colour of that of a toad.

The young lord brought with him from the East a lady of great

647

beauty, and in their castle they pursued their magic arts, admitting no one inside its walls except their servants, who were said to be themselves bound by spells to secrecy. It was said that Pengerswick would shut himself up for days at a time in his room, with strange experiments which sent their odours for miles around the country. At night, especially in stormy weather, he would be heard calling up spirits, his voice sounding above the roaring of the storm, and the spirits answering in voices of thunder. The frightened servants would run from the castle, and huddle together in an open courtyard, despite the storm; but when the spirits proved too strong for the man who had summoned them, his lady would play softly on her harp, and the spirits would flee, and be heard moaning as they passed through the air towards Land's End. Then the servants would return to the house unafraid, for they loved and trusted their mistress. She, however, was never seen outside the castle grounds, but would sit in her tower playing her harp, and once and again singing to its accompaniment strange songs of the East. Then the fishes from the waters, and mermaids from the Lizard, and many still stranger spirits, would gather to listen and sometimes joined softly in her singing.

The lord of the castle, though he often rode abroad on a splendid horse, which was so wild to all others except its master that it was reputed to come from the Devil, made no friends in the neighbourhood, and was generally feared, though men respected him for his many good deeds. Among these was his conquest of the Giants of the Mount, for, before he disappeared from the country, they had all died, from grief, as was supposed, and from want of food.

In a mysteriously short time the Lord and Lady had completely rebuilt their castle; some said that the spirits of earth and air helped them to raise a huge structure in only three days. Today there remains only one tower.

After many years, when all those who lived round them had become accustomed to their presence and generous ways, a bronzed stranger appeared in the streets of Market Jew. He answered no questions and gave no hint of his business but a supposition arose that it was in some way concerned with Pengerswick. On dark nights he would wander out and fishermen said they had seen him sitting at the entrance of the Pengerswick Valley on a solitary rock. The lord seemed to be keeping indoors more than was his custom, and the lady's music was not heard through all these days. One night a fearful storm arose, and suddenly a red glare broke out in the eastern sky, lighting up St Michael's Mount. Pengerswick Castle was on fire; the interior of it was entirely burnt out and the servants fled.

No trace of the lord or the lady, nor of the bronzed stranger, was found, but two of the oldest people always declared that, when the flames were at their height they had seen two men and a woman floating in the fire, that they passed through the falling walls, and disappeared like lightning through the air.

MOTIFS: T.418 [*Lustful stepmother*]; K.2111 [*Potiphar's wife*]; K.2213 [*Treacherous wife*]; S.111 [*Murder by poisoning*]; D.1711 [*Magician*]; D.1719 [*Possession of magic powers*]; N.845 [*Magician as helper*].
¶ This is one of the long, rambling Cornish romances. For Pengerwick's final victory over the Witch of Fraddam, see "The Witch of Fraddam and the Enchanter of Pengerswick".

THE FERRYMAN [summary]

The School of Scottish Studies, Maurice Fleming from Mrs Reid.

There was a ferry, and at one time it was not safe for anyone to cross it but the ferryman himself. Everyone else was drowned. One day a shepherd came who wanted to cross to the other side to see his mother and his two sisters. The ferryman told him it was not safe, but the shepherd begged him to take him, and at last the ferryman gave him a sword, and told him to sit in the prow, and cut the waves as they came at the boat. "For three great waves will come against us," he said, "and unless you cut them they will drown the boat." So the shepherd sat in the prow, and when they were halfway across, a great wave came up, and he leant out and cut it, and it died back into the water, and let the boat pass. Then a second wave came up, and the shepherd cut that, and they got safely through. Then a third wave came up against them, far greater than either of the others, and the shepherd leaned far out, and cut into the wave, and it died back into the water, and the boat got safe to land. Then the shepherd paid the ferryman, and went up to his mother's cottage. But when he went in he found his mother and his two sisters lying on the floor, cut in two. They were the witches who had troubled the ferry.

TYPE ML.3055 MOTIFS: D.283.5 [*The transformation: man to ocean wave*]; G.275.14 [*Witch out of body while travelling at night is injured: witch's body is injured at home*].
¶ This story is usually told in Gaelic, but has been transmitted to English-speaking tinkers.
See "The Aith Man and the Finn".

THE FOUR-EYED CAT

Briggs and Tongue, *The Folktales of England*, p. 57.

There was a gentleman had a beautiful daughter who was bad at heart, and they said she knew more than a Christian should, and they wanted to swim her, but no one dared because of her father. She drew a spell on a poor fisherman, and he followed for love of her wherever she went. He deserted his troth-plight maid, though he was to be married in a week, and he ran away to sea with the gentleman's daughter and unbeknown to all the rest (that is the rest of the fleet) took her out with them to the fishing. She did it to spite her father's pride, but he thought himself well rid of her.

A storm blew up and the whole fishing fleet were lost to a man, for they had on board a woman with them at sea, though none knew of it but her lover. It was she that had whistled up the storm that had drowned her own lover, for she hated everyone. She was turned into a four-eyed cat, and ever after she haunted the fishing fleet.

So that is why even now fishermen won't cast their nets before half-past three (cock-crow)—my uncles won't—and they always throw a bit back into the sea for the cat.

Collected by Ruth L. Tongue in 1955 from N. Marchant (*aetat* 12) daughter of a lightship sailor from Harwich and Dovercourt in Essex. She heard it from her grandparents.
MOTIFS: G.229.5 [*Beautiful witch*]; G.211.1.7 [*Witch in form of cat*]; G.283.1.2.3 [*Witch raises wind to sink ships of people who have injured her*].
¶ It is a general belief of fishermen all round the British Isles that it is unlucky to take a woman to the fishing-grounds, and even to meet one on the way to sea. In some places the tabu extends to even mentioning a woman. See "The Fishermen of Worle" (B, XII).

FRIAR BACON

W. Carew Hazlitt, *National Tales and Legends*, p. 77–96.

I (a)

There once lived in the West Country a rich farmer, who had an only son. The farmer's name was Bacon, and his son was called Roger, and, not because his father looked to make him a holy clerk, but for that he should get learning enough to enable him to use his wealth wisely, this Roger was put with the parson of the town where he was born, to learn his letters and to become a scholar.

But the boy discovered so rare an aptitude and so quick a wit, that his master could, after a short time, teach him no more; and as he judged it to be pity that young Bacon should lose what he had gained, he went to the farmer, and exhorted him to suffer Roger to go to Oxford, that he might shew, by taking upon him that charge, his thankfulness to God in having sent him such a son.

The father said little; but as soon as Roger came home, he asked for his books, and taking them and locking them up, gave him a cart-whip in place thereof, saying to him so: "Boy, I will have you no priest; you shall be no better learned than I; you can tell, as it is, by the almanac, when it is best to sow wheat, when barley, peas, and beans, and when the gelding season comes; and how to buy and sell I shall instruct thee anon, for fairs and markets are to me what his Mass and *Ave Maria* are to Sir John. Take this whip; it will prove more useful to you than crabbed Latin. Now do as I bid, or, by the Mass, you will rue it."

The young fellow thought this hard measure; but he made no reply, and within a short space he gave his father the slip, and entered himself in a cloister some twenty miles off, where he was heartily entertained, and continued his studies.

And, ere many years had passed he made such progress in all kinds of learning that he grew famous, and was invited to go to the University of Oxford, where he perfected himself in all the sciences, and was known for a master of the secrets of art and Nature throughout Christendom.

Now the King of England, hearing of this learned friar, and of the wonderful things which he was able to perform and to answer, sent for him at such time as he and the queen were sojourning in Oxfordshire, and he said to the king's messenger: "I pray you, thank his grace from me, and say that I am at his grace's service; but take heed lest I be at the court two hours before thee."

"Scholars, old men and travellers," answered the messenger, "may lie with authority. Scarce can I credit such a thing."

"To convince you, I could tell you the name of the wench you last lay with; but I will do both within four hours."

The gentleman departed in haste; but whether he took the wrong road or not, the friar was there before him.

The king warmly welcomed him, and told him, from what great marvels he had heard of him, that he had long desired to see him. The friar declared that report had been too flattering, and that among the sons of learning there were many worthier than himself. The king prayed him not to be too modest, and to afford him some taste of his skill; and he said that he should be unworthy of possessing either art or knowledge, did he grudge to make his grace and the queen witnesses of his ability. So he begged them to seat themselves.

Frair Bacon then waved his wand, and forthwith there arose such ravishing music that all were amazed.

"This is to please," quoth he, "the Sense of Hearing. All the other senses shall be gratified, ere I have done."

He waved his wand again, and the music waxed louder; and lo! five dancers entered, the first like a court-laundress, the second like a footman, the third like a usurer, the fourth like a prodigal, the fifth like a fool. And when they had given great content by their antics and positions, they vanished in the order in which they came. This was the indulgence of the second Sense, the Sense of Sight.

He waved his wand the third time, and the music was changed, and before them appeared a table covered with all manner of delicious fruits, many not to that season belonging, and when they had partaken fully thereof, they were suddenly removed from view. And this was the Sense of Taste.

Then the wand once more moved, and the most fragrant perfumes filled the air. And this was the Sense of Smell. And presently for the fifth and last time Friar Bacon exercised his mastery, and men of divers nations, as Russians, Polanders, Indians, Armenians, were seen bearing the richest furs, which they offered to the king and queen to handle, and for softness they surpassed all that had ever been seen of that nature. And this was the Sense of Touch.

When it happened that these wonders were at an end, Friar Bacon demanded of his majesty if there was any other thing in which he might do him service; and the king thanked him, and said no, not for that time, and he took a costly jewel from his neck, and gave it to the friar of his royal bounty. And when the friar was about to take his leave of the court, he cast his eyes round, and espied the messenger hurrying in with all speed, covered with mud, for he had ridden through quagmires and ditches, through mistaking his way.

"Be not wrath," said the friar to him. "I shall now fulfil my word that I pledged to thee." And he lifted the hangings, and there stood a kitchen-maid, with her basting-ladle in her hand.

"I trow," quoth the friar, "you have no great store of money in your purse, and I will bear the charges of your wench's journey home." And at his bidding she disappeared, and all laughed at the gentleman's greasy sweetheart.

I (b)

Now Friar Bacon had one servant to wait upon him, and his name was Miles; and he was none of the wisest. So the friar being yet at Oxford in residence with other scholars, all were wont to fast on the Friday; and none so devout as Miles, for when his master offered him bread to eat, he would refuse it, saying that it was holier and meeter not to eat ought. But the friar knowing his craft, and that he secretly ate meat, served him well for his deceit, and it was in this manner following.

On a certain Good Friday, when the friar was accustomed to partake of bread only, he tendered some to Miles; but Miles, with a grave aspect, turned away from it, and desired leave to fast altogether. Then he left his master, and went where he had a delicate black-pudding that he had made the day before, and began to eat the same. But the friar his master so contrived by his art, that when his man had set the end of the pudding in his mouth, he might in no wise remove it again; and when he pulled and pulled, and it stirred not, he cried out for help. The friar ran to him, and taking the other end of the pudding, drew him to the hall, where all the scholars were, and showed them how Miles would not eat meat on Fridays for conscience' sake; and he tied him by the pudding for a while to one of the window-bars, where he looked like a bear fastened by his nose to a stake.

II

Friar Bacon now began to accomplish many other strange and marvellous works. Whereof one was the deliverance of a gentleman in Oxfordshire, that had been a prodigal, and had brought his estate to ruin. This gentleman scarce knew at the last how to earn bread enough to keep him during the rest of his miserable existence, and so he wandered about here and there. Then came to him one day an old penny-father, and besought him that he would say why he was in this piteous case.

The Oxfordshire gentleman told the stranger everything, and the other said that, if he would fulfil certain conditions, he would furnish him with money enough for all his creditors; and when he said that he would swear to return the money, the old man rejoined that it was not oaths he would have, but bonds.

So the gentleman met him the next morning in a wood, as they had appointed, and he was attended by two serving-men carrying money-bags. Then he dictated to him the conditions on which he would lend him what he needed; and they were, that he should discharge all his debts, and when he was no longer indebted to any man, he should become at a word the slave of the lender.

That gentleman, in the plight in which he found himself at that time, yielded to this treaty, and paid all his mortgages and chief creditors, and became richer than he had ever been before. But he was secretly troubled in his mind when he remembered how he had bound himself to the stranger, and had consented to submit to his will; and after a time the old penny-father appeared, and claimed his bond, saying, "Thou hast paid thy debts, now thou art mine." But he replied, "Nay, sir, I have not yet discharged them all." And the userer therefore waxed wrath, and transformed himself into a horrible shape, and cried, "Thou shalt not deceive me; I will come tomorrow morning, and prove to thee thy falsehood, till when I leave thee to despair." And he vanished, and the gentleman now knew that it was the devil with whom he had made that compact.

This caused him to be so sorrowful and downcast, that he would have thrown himself on his sword, and so ended his life, had not Friar Bacon happily interposed, and comforted him; and when he unfolded to the friar what had passed between the devil and himself, the friar said unto him so: "Sir, appoint to meet the devil tomorrow in the wood, and for the rest be content."

So the Oxfordshire gentleman met the devil in the wood, and the devil in sore anger upbraided him with his falsity, and commanded him to tarry no more, but to follow him.

Then the gentleman asked him whether he would suffer someone to be judge in the case, and to deliver an award; and the devil agreed thereto. Whereupon suddenly Friar Bacon was seen by the gentleman walking near at hand, and he called him, and set out how the matter was. Friar Bacon considered, and asked the gentleman whether he had ever paid anything to the devil for all his great goodness to him, and he answered that he had not. Then he told him, as he valued his life, never to do so, for he was his chief creditor; and thereupon the devil vanished with a loud cry, and the Oxfordshire gentleman thanked Friar Bacon for the great boon which he had conferred upon him in so wisely judging between them.

III

The next exploit which Friar Bacon sought to achieve proved him a loyal subject to his prince and a dear friend to England. For reflecting how often England had been invaded by Saxon and Dane and Norwegian, he laboured with a project for surrounding the whole island with a wall of brass, and to the intent that he might compass this, he first devised a head of brass which should speak. And when he could not for all his art arrive at this, he invited another great scholar, Friar Bungay by name, to aid him therein; and they both together by great study made a head of brass, yet wist not how to give it motion and speech. And at last they called to their succour a spirit, who directed them, but gave them warning that, when the head began to speak, if they heard it not ere it had finished, all their labour would be lost.

So they did as the spirit had enjoined them, and were right weary; and bidding Miles to wake them when the Head spake, they fell asleep.

Now Miles, because his master threatened him if he should not make them aware when the head spake, took his tabor and pipe, and sang ballads to keep him from nodding, as, *Cam'st thou not from Newcastle? Dainty, come thou to me,* and *It was a rich merchant-man.*

Presently the Head spake, saying, TIME IS! But Miles went on playing and singing, for the words seemed to him to import nought. Twice and thrice the Head said, TIME IS! But Miles was loath to wake his master and Friar Bungay for such a trifle; and there surely, enough, came in one of his ditties, *Dainty, come thou to me,* and he began to sing:

Time is for some to eat,
  Time is for some to sleep;
  Time is for some to laugh;
  And time is for some to sleep.

> Time is for some to sing,
> Time is for some to pray,
> Time is for some to creep,
> That have drunk all the day.

At the end of half an hour the Head spake once more, and delivered these two words, TIME WAS! And Miles make sport of them as he had done before. Then another half hour passed, and Head uttered this sentence, TIME IS PASSED! And fell down amid flames of fire and terrible noise, whereat the two friars awoke, and found the room full of smoke.

"Did not the head speak?" asked Bacon.

"Yea, sir," replied his man, "but it spake to no purpose. I'd teach a parrot to talk better in half the time."

"Out on thee, villain!" cried his master. "Thou hast undone us both. Hadst thou roused us, all England would have been walled about with brass, and we had won everlasting renown. What did it say?"

"Very few words," answered Miles, "and I have heard wiser. It said, TIME IS!"

"Hadst thou called us then, we had been made forever."

"Then in half an hour it said, TIME WAS!"

"And thou didst not wake us then!" interposed Bungay.

"Alack, sir," answered Miles. "I was expecting him to begin some long tale, and then I would have awakened you; but anon he cried, TIME IS PASSED! and made such an uproar withal that he woke you himself."

Friar Bacon was greatly incensed at what his servant had done, and would have beaten and maybe slain him; but Friar Bungay pleaded for the fellow, and his master said, "Well, his punishment shall be, that he shall be struck dumb for a month."

So it was that England was not girded round with a brazen wall, as had nearly come to pass.

IV

Friar Bacon, this mishap notwithstanding, ever grew more famous as time passed; and it so fortuned that, when the king of England proceeded to his conquests in France, and could by no means take a certain town, but, on the contrary, sustained much loss before it he wox angry, and offered ten thousand crowns truly counted, to anyone who should conquer this town and gain it for him.

So, when proclamation had been made to such effect, and no one came to essay to do what the king desired, Friar Bacon, leaving his studies, crossed over to France, and sought admittance to the king. To whom he recalled how his grace had formerly shown him great courtesy in Oxfordshire, and he was now ready to do his pleasure.

"Bacon!" said our lord the king. "Alas! it is not art, but arms that I now require."

"Your Grace saith well," returned the Friar; "but be pleased to remember that art doth often times accomplish more than force. And speaking of art and nature, pure and simple, without any magical property, consider how ships are made without oars, and large vessels to cross the wide sea, and only one man to guide them; how chariots may be built to move with incredible force without human help to stir them; and how one may fly in the air and turn an engine; or walk in the bottom of the sea (as Alexander the Great did) and, which is more pertinent at this time, how by means of a mirror you may make one man wear the semblance of a whole army, and what is far off seem near at hand, and what is high, low, or the contrary. So Socrates did detect the dragon that lurked in the mountains, and destroyed all round. Then, as Aristotle instructed Alexander, instruments may be contrived by which venomous influences may be brought in contact with a city, and infect its inhabitants every one, even the poison of a basilisk lifted up upon the wall. These things are worth a kingdom to a wise man."

His grace gave leave to Friar Bacon to do as it liked him, and he should name his reward; and the friar caused an earthwork to be raised higher than the city wall, and desiring his grace to be in readiness the next morning to attack the town, when he should wave a flag from the earthwork, on the morrow, at nine of the clock the friar had, with certain mathematical glasses, set fire to the town hall, and while the people and the soldiers were busy in extinguishing the flames, the flag was waved, and the king took the place with little resistance.

He treated the inhabitants with such clemency, that he won the love of his brother the king of France, who, to divert him, summoned a servant of his, a German named Vandermast, to show conjuring sleights before both their graces; and the king of England, understanding what the entertainment was to be, privily sent for Friar Bacon and Friar Bungay to come to him, that they might witness the same. But he bad them keep their counsel.

When the banquet was over, Vandermast asked the king of England if it was so that he would choose to see the spirit of any man that had formerly lived. The king said, "Yea. Above all I would see Pompey, who could brook no equal." And Vandermast made him appear as he was attired at the Battle of Pharsalia, whereat all were mightily contented.

Then Friar Bacon, all without warning given, raised the ghost of Julius Caesar, who could brook no superior, and had beaten Pompey at Pharsalia; and Vandermast, not knowing that Friar Bacon was present, said that there was someone in the hall who was skilled in magic. To whom Bacon discovered himself, and declared that he had brought

Caesar to overthrow Pompey, as he did erst; and therefore Caesar engaged Pompey, and vanquished him. Which pleased all present passing well, and then both disappeared.

The king of England said to the German ambassador, that he thought his man had got the better of Vandermast; but Vandermast said that he would tell a different tale, ere all was done. "Ah!" said Friar Bacon, "my companion, Friar Bungay, shall deal with thee, sirrah; and if thou canst worst him, I will try what I may do, and not till then."

Then Friar Bungay raised the Hesperian tree, laden with golden apples, which were guarded by a fiery dragon, stretched beneath its branches. Vandermast conjured up the ghost of Hercules, and said, "This is Hercules, who in his life gathered the fruit of the tree, and made the dragon crouch at his feet; and so shall he do again."

But when Hercules offered to take the fruit, Friar Bacon raised his wand, and Hercules desisted. Vandermast threatened him and he picked it not: but he said, "Vandermast, I cannot; I am fearful; for here is great Bacon, that is more powerful than thee." Vandermast cursed Hercules, and again threatened him. But Bacon bad him not fret himself, for, since he could not persuade Hercules to do this bidding, he himself would cause him to do some service; and he commanded Hercules to take up Vandermast, and carry him back straightway to Germany.

"Alas!" cried the ambassador, "I would not have lost Vandermast at any price."

"Fear not, my lord," answered Bacon; "he hath but gone home to see his wife, and shall return to you anon."

v

Shortly after, when Friar Bacon had come again into England, a rich man of that country died, and left his estate to that one among his three sons who loved him best; and none could say who that was, for each one avowed that it was he, by reason that to him his father was most dear. So Friar Bacon was asked by the king to help him in this matter, and that learned and famous man, when the three brethren agreed to abide by his judgment, having caused the body of the father to be taken from the ground, and gotten ready three bows, and three arrows, summoned the sons to attend him, and said unto them so; "Sirs, there appeared to be no other method whereby this controversy might be concluded; therefore I have brought hither the dead body of your father, and whoever strikes him nearest to his heart shall have all his goods and lands."

The two elder brothers shot one after the other, and both hit the body, yet did not go near the heart. But the youngest refused to shoot, saying that he would liever lose his patrimony; and Friar Bacon awarded him the estate, because he showed by his loyal act that he loved his father better than the others: and all men commended the friar's wisdom therein.

Now, albeit Friar Bacon had seldom indeed taken any reward for all his great services to our lord the king, and many other, yet the report spread abroad that in his house he kept rich treasure; and certain thieves brake one night thereinat, and demanded of Miles, who admitted them, and of the friar, what money they had. The friar answered that he was poorly furnished with money; whereto they replied, these three thieves, that they must have whatso there was; and the friar gave them one hundred pounds each in a bag.

They heartily rejoiced at their good fortune; and he said to them that they should have music to boot, which still further contented them; and Miles took his tabor, and began to play thereon. Then the three thieves rose and set to dancing, and danced so lustily with their money-bags in their hands that they grew weary, but could not cease, for the friar had set a spell on them; and Miles went out of the door playing the while, and led the thieves over the fields, and over hedge and ditch, and through quagmire and pond, till they were wet to the skin, and weary to death. Then Miles stayed his hand, and they lay down as they were, and slept; and he took the money from them, and returned home to his master.

Meanwhile Vandermast was plotting how he could compass the death of Friar Bacon, to revenge the dishonour which had been cast upon him in France; and the friar, looking into his books, and finding that a great danger would befall him in the second week of the present month, unless he used some means to prevent it, devised this sleight, namely, while he read to hold a ball of brass in one hand, and beneath it a brass basin, and percase he should fall asleep, the loosing of the ball from his hand would awake him.

Now Vandermast had recently hired a Walloon soldier to come over to England, and to kill Bacon, and if he did so his reward was to be one hundred crowns; and when he arrived at Bacon's house, this Walloon soldier found Bacon dozing, yet the ball of brass still in his hand; but as he lifted the sword to slay him, the ball dropped into the basin, and Bacon awoke.

"Who art thou?" he demanded of the Walloon.

"I am a Walloon, and a soldier, and more than that, a villain; and I am come, hired by Vandermast, to kill thee."

"What is thy religion?"

"To go to an ale-house, to abstain from evil for want of employment, and to do good against my will."

"A good profession for a devil! Dost thou believe in Hell?"

"I believe in no such thing."

Then Friar Bacon raised the spirit of Julian the Apostate, with his body burning and full of wounds, whereat the soldier was almost out of his wits for fear. Friar Bacon asked the spirit wherefore he was thus tormented; and he answered, that he had been happy if he had remained a Christian, but he abjured the true faith, and now endured the doom of all unbelieving wretches.

The Walloon soldier that had come to kill the friar stood trembling all this time, and when the friar dismissed the spirit, he begged that he would instruct him in a better way of life, which the friar engaged to do; and this Walloon became a true Christian and died in the Holy War.

VI

It becomes time to relate how Friar Bacon once had a strange adventure, and helped a young man to his sweetheart, that Friar Bungay would have married to another.

An Oxfordshire gentleman had a daughter named Millisant, who was courted by a youth whose love she returned, and whose wife she desired to be; but her father was averse from that match, and would have wedded her to a rich knight.

This knight, when he perceived how loth the maiden was, went to Friar Bungay, and asked him to get her for him, either by his counsel or art; and Bungay, for that he was something covetous, promised, if he would take the lady for the air in a coach, so to direct the horses, that they should bring them to an old chapel in the wood, where they might be secretly married.

But meantime the gentleman had sought Friar Bacon, and implored him to do what he might to further his suit: and Bacon, knowing him to be virtuous and deserving, brought out a beryl, wherein he could see his best-loved and the knight in the chapel, though it was fifty miles thence, on the eve of being joined together in holy matrimony by Friar Bungay. The gentleman was overwhelmed by grief; but Bacon bad him be of good cheer, and seating himself in a chair, they were presently at the chapel door. Friar Bungay was about to join their hands, when Bacon struck him dumb, and raising a mist in the chapel, no one could see his way, but each mistook the other, and amid their bewilderment, Bacon led Millisant to the poor gentleman, and they were married by him in the chapel porch and furnished with a good store of money for their journey; and while they went their way joyfully together, the friar by his magic detained the father, and the knight, in the chapel, until they could not overtake them. And at a certain distance he prepared for them (albeit unseen) a banquet, succeeded by an antic masque of apes with music, wherein first entered three apes, and then three more, dressed in quaint coats, and then six; and all danced in merry and strange wise together, and then, when they had saluted the bridegroom and the bride, vanished.

VII

News had been brought to Vandermast, where he sojourned in Germany, that at length Friar Bacon was dead; and accordingly he came over once more into England, and met Friar Bungay in Kent, whom-of he learned that Bacon yet lived.

Now he bare no goodwill to Bungay, for that he was a friend to Bacon; and when he rose in the morning to leave his inn, he went to the stable where Bungay's horse was, and took it, leaving a spirit in its room. And when Bungay sought his horse to go on his way, he wist not what Vandermast had done, and mounted it, and in the middle of a stream it let him go, so that he perforce returned to his inn, at the door whereof he met the other, who asked him if he had been in a swimming match, and Bungay answered him again that if he had been so well posted as he was when he went to Germany, this would not have so fallen out.

Vandermast bit his lip, but said nought. And then Bungay, knowing that this German loved a wench in the house, and spared no pains to get her, shaped a spirit in her likeness, which yielded unto his advances, that he was enraptured; and when he had gone to bed, the sheet on which they lay was carried into the air, and fell into a deep pond. When Bungay saw him, he asked him how he liked the girl.

"Marry, I wish thee such another," quoth he.

"Nay, the rules of my order forbid it," he replied.

So it came to pass that these two conjurors grew more and more wroth with each other, until at last the Devil wox impatient of not having received from them the money for teaching them all their knowledge, and slew them, so that they were strangely scorched with fire amid a mighty storm of wind and rain; and the country people, finding their bodies, bestowed on them Christian burial, for that Bungay was a friar and Vandermast a stranger.

VIII

You have heard that Friar Bacon, who thus outlived both Bungay and Vandermast, possessed a wonderful glass, in which it was possible to see what was happening some fifty miles away; and this glass had been a source of great profit and pleasure to many, whom Bacon had obliged with the use thereof; till it happened that two youths, whose fathers— being neighbours—were absent from home, wished to know how they did, and besought Bacon to suffer them to look in his glass.

But those gentlemen, since their departure, had grown to be foes one to the other, and when their sons looked, they saw that their fathers were on the eve of fighting together, and as they fought, one killed the other; and this sight so fired one of the youths, whose father was slain, that he began to quarrel with his friend, and they both became so furious that they stabbed each other. Which when Friar Bacon knew, hearing the noise, he was so grieved, that he broke his mirror, the like whereof the whole world could not show; and then arrived the news of the deaths of Bungay and Vandermast, which further distressed him, so that he kept his chamber three days.

He now began to repent his wicked and vain life, spent in the service of the devil, and to turn his thoughts to Divine studies: and calling together many of his friends, he addressed them in these words:

"My good friends and fellow-students, it is not unknown to you how by my art I have attained great credit with all, and have done many wonders, as everyone knows, both king and commons. I have unlocked the secrets of nature, and have laid them open to the view of man, whereas they had been buried and lost since the days of Hermes the philosopher. I have revealed the mysteries of the stars and of every kind of life that is under the sun. Yet all this my knowledge I value so lightly, that I could wish I were ignorant; for what hath it availed me, save to keep me from the study of God, and the care of my soul, which is the immortal part of man. But I hasten to remove the cause of all my error, gentlemen." And, a fire burning in the hearth, before they could prevent him, Friar Bacon threw all his books therein, and consumed them utterly.

Then he gave away all his goods to the poor, and, building himself a cell in the church wall, withdrew from the world, and after two years space died a true, penitent sinner.

I(a). MOTIFS: D.1738 [*Magic arts studied*]; D.2031 [*Magic illusion*]; D.2120 [*Magic transportation*]. I(b). MOTIFS: D.1711.C.1 [*Magician's apprentice*]; W.151 [*Greed*]; cf. W.151.9 [*Greedy Person gets head stuck in food-jar. This is one of many jocular tales about magicians and their servants*].
II. MOTIFS: N.845 [*Magician as helper*]; K.210 [*Devil cheated of his promised soul*].
III. MOTIFS: D.1311.7.1 [*Oracular artificial head*]; D.1711.0.1 [*Magician's apprentice*].
IV. MOTIFS: D.1814.1 [*Advice from magician*]; D.2091 [*Magic attack against enemy*]; D.1719.1 [*Contest in magic*].
V. TYPE 920C. MOTIFS: H.486.2 [*Test of paternity: shooting at father's corpse*]; J.1171 [*Judgment by testing love*]; L.13 [*Compassionate youngest son*].
VI. MOTIFS: There are various magical motifs in this part, such as D.1331.1.5 [*Jewel gives magical sight*]; D.902.1 [*Magic mist*] and others, some already given.
VII. MOTIFS: Among motifs already used are G.303.20.1 [*Devil kills man with fiery sword*]; G.303.6.3.1 [*Devil is followed by thunderstorm*].
VIII. MOTIFS: V.315.1 [*Power of repentance*].
¶ In some chapbook versions Friar Bacon is said to dig his own grave with his nails. The whole story is told in Robert Greene's *Friar Bacon and Friar Bungay*, 1594.

This strange medley of motifs is an example of the traditions by which a famous man is shaped into a magician. Examples are "Virgilius", "Tales of Sir Francis Drake" (B, III, and B, VIII) St Dunstan (B, XI) St Adelme (B, XI).

FRIAR BACON AND FRIAR BUNGAY

E. M. Gurdon, *County Folk-Lore*, I, part 2 p. 90. Suffolk.

..."A gentleman in Oxfordshire, being greatly enamoured of a young gentlewoman, after long courtship, got her Good Will, with the consent of her Father. But whilst everything was preparing for the Marriage, a rich Knight, who had a mind to the young Lady, prevailed with the covetous Father to break off the Match, and marry her to him. The young Gentleman was much grieved at this, and so was the Lady, for she had now settled her affections entirely on him, and was much averse to the Knight's courtship; whereupon he (the Knight) consulted Friar *Bungy* how to get her promising him a great Summ if he accomplished it. Why, says he, do but get her and her Father to ride with you abroad in a coach, and which way soever they direct or design to go, I will so enchant the Coachman and the Horse, that they shall directly pass to such an old chapel, where I will be ready to marry you. This the Knight resolved to put into practice, and it accordingly proceeded so far that they did come to the Chapel, found the Fryer there, and the Marriage was proposed.

[The young lover applies to Friar Bacon who shows him in a "Magic Glass" what is happening; Bacon strikes Bungay dumb, rescues the lady, and marries her to the Gentleman from Oxfordshire.]

"After this, *Vandermaster*, the German Conjurer, came over to *England* and not daring to venture on *Bacon*, he thought to be revenged on *Bungy*; so he privately challenged him into a Wood, to Conjure, thinking to make his Spirit destroy him. They made their circles, and *Vandermaster* raised a Dragon, which, running round *Bungy's* circle, threw so much fire on him that he almost roasted him. *Bungy* raised a Sea-Monster that with spouting Floods almost drowned *Vandermaster;* and to destroy the Dragon, raised up the Spirit of *S George*, while *Vandermaster* raised up that of *Perseus*, to destroy the sea-monster; and so they vanished.

"Then *Vandermaster* raised up *Hector* and *Bungy Achilles*, who trained their Greeks and Trojans to the Battle, and fought so desperately that the whole Element seemed on fire; Thunder and Lightning, and such prodigious Storms ensued that the People for many miles distant, concluded that the World was at an End. The Spirits growing too strong for these Conjurors and their Charms, broke into their Circles, and tore them in a thousand pieces, scattering their limbs about the Fields, and so ended they their miserable lives."

Bungay, Aug. 19, 1896. G. B. Baker, *The East Anglian*
MOTIFS: D.1719.1 [*Contest in magic*]; G.275.1.1 [*Witch carried off by Devil's crew*].

THE GIPSY'S CURSE

K. M. Briggs, *Folktales of England*, pp. 59–61

A dirty old gipsy woman, encamped on a waste piece of ground, used to terrify the children of the neighbourhood, and on her daily round with a basket filled with bits of dirty lace for sale, she so persecuted one woman that she almost had a nervous breakdown. So her husband asked the police to remove her caravan, but they had no power to do this. However, they warned her to stop pestering the neighbours on pain of being imprisoned. That night she met the man who had been to the police and pronounced a curse on him—that neither he nor any of his descendants should die in their beds. He was a religious man and paid no heed to the curse, but some of the neighbours had overheard it. Some time later that man died at his work-bench, and as the years passed, five of his offspring died, four in hospital, and one on active service. Mr Barrett himself was another son.

Recorded by W. H. Barrett, 11 October 1963.
MOTIF: M.411.12 [*Curse by Witch*].

¶ There is nothing definitely supernatural about this story, but it is an evidence of the strength of the witch belief in the Fens. Mr Barrett writes in the course of a letter: "Everyone in those days that lived around my home held firm belief in the power witches possessed, and a lot of good food us children would have been glad to have was wasted by being put outside the door for a wandering witch to collect for her supper, who never appeared in human form. Any seen were disguised as cats or rats, and it was a well-known fact that the dish the food was placed in needed no washing up the next morning, it was so clean. My father, who was in great demand as a lay preacher in the fen chapels, firmly believed that stewed pigs' brains, served on a plate which had contained the witch's supper (unwashed), gave him such power to preach in his sermons that it caused his listeners to sit enthralled."

THE GOODWIFE OF DELORAINE

Henderson, *Folk-Lore of the Northern Counties*, p. 197.

The farmer's wife of Deloraine...engaged a tailor with his workmen and apprentices for the day, begging them to come in good time in the morning. They did so, and partook of the family breakfast of porridge and milk. During the meal, one of the apprentices observed that the milk-jug was almost empty, on which the mistress slipt out of the back-door with a basin in her hand to get a fresh supply. The lad's curiosity was roused, for he had heard there was no more milk in the house; so he crept after her, hid himself behind the door, and saw her turn a pin in the wall, on which a stream of pure milk flowed into the basin. She twirled the pin, and the milk stopped. Coming back, she presented the tailors with the bowl of milk, and they gladly washed down the rest of their porridge with it.

About noon, while our tailors were busily engaged with the gudeman's wardrobe, one of them complained of thirst, and wished for a bowl of milk like the morning's. "Is that a'?" said the apprentice; "ye'se get that." The mistress was out of the way, so he left his work, found his way to the spot he had marked in the morning, twirled the pin, and quickly filled the basin. But alas! He could not then stay the stream. Twist the pin as he would, the milk still continued to flow. He called the other lads, and implored them to come and help him; but they could only bring such tubs and buckets as they found in the kitchen, and these were soon filled. When the confusion was at its height, the mistress appeared among them, looking as black as thunder; while she called out in a mocking voice, "A' ye loons! Ye hae drawn a' the milk fra every coo between the head o' Yarrow and the foot o't. This day ne'er a coo will gie her maister a drop o' milk, though he war gawing to starve." The tailors slunk away abashed, and from that day forward the wives of Deloraine have fed their tailors on nothing but chappit 'taties and kale.

TYPE ML.3040 MOTIF: D.2083.3.1(*da*) [*Visitor in house watches witch use peg to obtain milk. He does as she has done, cannot stop the flow of milk. The housewife returns after he has filled all the containers in the house. She stops the flow, tells him no cow in the neighbourhood will give milk that night*] (Baughman).

¶ See "Ann Allan", "The Earthenware Goose", "The Black Hen".

THE HARE AND THE HARBOURER

Ruth L. Tongue, *Forgotten Folk Tales.*

There was a harbourer lived in a snug little cottage next to the forest. He had a neat little garden plot and the river ran just beyond it—but people never came to visit. As he was always busy, he didn't mind—so that was all right, then.

The neighbours never went into the wood, not even to fetch firing, but he did, as he went about his journeys after the deer and he came out safe and sound—so that was all right, then.

The neighbours were afraid of the river too, and they taught their children to sing:

"Nicky Nicky Nye,
He pulls you down,
Underneath the water,
To drown, drown, die."

664

Which frightened them so much they kept away from all the ditches and ponds as well, and only got fresh water with rain and dew. But the harbourer never minded the green, wicked watching eyes of Nicky Nicky Nye. There was a wishing well in his garden plot and he got his fresh water from that. Besides that he had his dogs, and one dog no one said much about—so that was all right then.

But one day at the Inn the new Landlord said, "Where's that spannel of yours I hear about, then? The others is lying at your feet. Do you always leave him to guard house?"

"*She* wouldn't come away from it," said the harbourer. "She's a special bitch, with a special job—mind that—special." And he got up and went his way.

Then everyone talked—oh, very brave all together they were!

"He needs a spayed bitch to guard him and his house from evil spirits."

"'Tis too ugly herself she is for a luck dog."

"And too ugly-tempered to strangers," said those who liked stolen venison or to go prying, and had found a welcome on the wrong side.

So they all joined in saying the large white-and-gold spannel was not a real dog at all (except those whose breeches she had tasted for them). But they left the cottage alone.

It suited the harbourer. No one tried stealing from his garden. She was there; and no one came after his deer. She was there too. Sometimes she was seen, sometimes she wasn't; but *he* could always see her, and he didn't worry about her looks.

One moony night, to his surprise, a farmer hailed him across the river.

"I glimpsed your spayed bitch as I came, and I take that for a sign my ill-luck has changed. I'm in a bad way, and need her kind of help if only she'd come. My cows is being milked dry and bleeding, and no one dares say who is ill-wishing them. Would she come?"

"She might, at that," said the harbourer, and he crossed the bridge to the farmer, and they walked back to the farm in the moonlight. The farmer couldn't see, and the harbourer took care not to look, but they both heard the pad of a dog's feet. So they took care not to speak a word all night. At midnight something huge and with glowing eyes came hop-hopping along to the poor, uneasy cows. The farmer nearly cried out, but the harbourer stopped him in time, for they could see it was a monstrous hare.

When it saw them standing silent it stopped—*then it came hopping on at them*, but there was a growl from a dog, then a squeal from the hare, and then a scream in an old woman's voice, and they saw the spayed bitch seize the hare and drag it by the throat to the river and fling it in with a splash.

There was another splash as Nicky Nicky Nye grabbed it down and the witch-hare screamed in old Kezzy's voice, and the farmer turned and ran for home as hard as he could pelt.

He never saw the spayed bitch go away, nor did the harbourer, but there she was, waiting for him at his cottage door, wagging her tail. So that was all right then, wasn't it?

Welsh Marches and Monmouthshire. From Annie Jones, Welsh maid, Whitchurch, Salop, 1916. Also from a Welsh member of W.I., Denman College, 1962.

MOTIFS: F.420.1.4.8 [*Water spirits with green teeth, green eyes*]; F.420.5.2.1.5 [*Water spirit drags children into river*]; E.439.6 [*Ghosts cannot come near spayed bitch*]; G.211.2.7 [*Witch in form of hare*]; D.655.2 [*Witch transforms self to hare so as to suck cows*]; D.2083.2.1 [*Witches make cows give bloody milk*]; G.275.2 [*Witch overcome by helpful dogs of hero*].

¶ A continuation of this tale, from Hampshire, is to be found in A, II.

THE HARES' PARLIAMENT

N. Cooper, *Ulster Folk-Life*, 1959.

Mary and Pat lived in a nice wee house. Mary one day bought a looking-glass. When she was admiring herself in the glass she noticed that her ears were growing long and furry, and that she was getting wee-er and wee-er, and when she looked down at herself, she saw she was a hare. She ran out of the house, and started skipping about. She felt herself drawn in a certain direction and skipped along. In the meantime, Pat came into the house, and began to look for Mary; soon he spied the looking-glass. He too began to look at himself, and the same thing happened to him. Out he ran, and he also felt drawn in a certain direction. Soon he overtook Mary, and they skipped along together. They noticed that there seemed to be a great many hares all going the same way as they were. At last they arrived at a big field at Clonmallon, which was filled with hares all dancing round. So Mary and Pat danced round too. A great big hare called them all to order and began to speak. They could understand the hare's talk quite well, and it was a sort of parliament of hares.

Before long the boss hare said, "I can smell strangers. There are some hares that should not be here at all." Mary and Pat felt sort of uneasy at this, and when all the other hares turned and looked at them they turned and ran away, and all the other hares ran after them. But Mary and Pat had a good start, and got away safely and reached home. Mary went to the looking-glass to see what she looked like as a hare, and when she looked into the glass she saw that she was turning back into a woman and Pat into a man again.

Told by Mrs Mulholland, Warrenfoot.

MOTIFS: D.579 [*Transformation by looking in mirror*]; D.117.2 [*Transformation: man to hare*]; B.230 [*Parliament of animals*]; G.211.2.7 [*Witch in form of hare*]; G.303.3.3.2.3 [*Devil in form of hare*]; G.303.6.2.2 [*Devil appears at meetings of witches*].

¶ There are traditions in Oxfordshire and elsewhere of hares' parliaments, which are the meetings of the natural animals, but, in view of the magic transforming mirror, it seems almost certain that this was a gathering of witches. At Kinloch Rannoch, in Perthshire, it was believed at the end of the last century that the witches used to meet in the form of hares in the churchyard, and would scamper away in all directions if anyone passed by (Informant: Mrs J. McIntosh, c. 1946, who had it from her grandfather).

THE HARPTREE WITCH

Ruth L. Tongue, *Somerset Folklore*, p. 79.

There was a celebrated witch at Harptree during the last century who had the power of healing and could cure the King's Evil. But she had other powers which rendered her formidable. She had second sight. Among her prophecies were the following:

Water will one day cross Harptree Combe and treasure be found there. Bristol water-pipes now cross it, and it is said that the workmen found buried silver.

Before a certain tree comes into leaf the Schoolmaster will be laid low in his grave. He died within the month.

A village mason was warned by her not to go to work, but "bide in bed". He went on, and fell off his ladder and broke his arm.

The Vicar wanted to move the pulpit and was told, "If you shift the pulpit you'll shift yourself." He left the parish shortly afterwards.

The Harptree witch was a nasty person to offend. A shopkeeper who asked for her long account to be settled was haunted by a rat in her bedroom until she died. A labourer disagreed with one of her sons and found that he could not take the straight way home. He had to make a long detour across the fields. These traditions come from Mendip friends about 1925, but they are also recorded in Mrs Kettlewell's *Trinkum-trinkums of Fifty Years*.

MOTIFS: G.220.0.1 ["*Black*" *and* "*White*" *witches. The witch may use magic powers either for good or evil*] (Baughman); D.1812 [*Magic power of prophecy*]; M.301.2 [*Old woman as prophet*].
¶ See "Harriet, the Witch of Keenthorne", "Kenneth Ore of Ross-shire".

HARRIET, THE WITCH OF KEENTHORNE

Ruth L. Tongue, *Somerset Folklore*, pp. 63–5.

Harriet was a well-known witch who lived near Stogursey about a hundred years ago. She was blind, and was considered very dangerous, but she had her good days, and others when she wasn't too malicious. Here are three instances, which I was told by the children and grand-children of the protagonists:

White (an old cottage woman, about 80, 1920s):

"My gran, when she were a young maid, she was wishful to know if my grandad did love she, and she got her courage up, and she went by herself, see. She got so far as the path to Harriet's door, and she durstn't go a step further. She could see Harriet a-quot down by fire, in hearth, ever so still, all in black. Then she turn and look at Gran, and her eyes were white. Gran, she couldn't stir a finger, and Harriet she say, 'I d'know what you d'want, my maid. Go whoame, and see who be by briar bush.' Gran, she turn and run, and never mind the brambles, but when she got to whoame, there stood my grandad by briar bush, and he axed her, and her was that out of breath, her couldn't think to say 'No' the first time."

Grey (an old hedger, 1960):

"My mother used to tell me how one of her sisters was foolish as a maid and got herself into bad trouble. 'Twas terrible thought on those days, not like their shameful ways now, and she was so beside herself she went to Harriet to see could she buy summat to rid herself afore 'twas noticeable. When she got near door, her courage failed her and she stood and shook all over. There were Harriet huddled down by vire-place all in black, with white eyes, and her says, 'I do know what you d'want. Go whoame, thee gurt fule, and tell'n tew marry 'ee.' And my auntie done just that and he did, and my mother had sixteen cousins."

Black (a labouring farm couple both told it 1930–40):

"Our grandad were a proper terror of a man, zo wicked a temper as he had no one daren't zo much as cross he. Led my Gran a sad life. His pigs was ailing and he took a notion 'twas Harriet's doing and she'd overlooked'n. Well then, off he marches with a gurt stick and in at her door. Reckoned he were gwine to tan the hide off she and dust her back-side like he done my Gran. And no salt to his pocket. Harriet she just sat there, quite still like and she turn her white eyes on he, and she say quiet and cold like spring water, 'I d'know what yew want. Now will 'ee walk or ride whoame?' And my Gran came and found'n all a-sat

right down in the midden all tore with thorns and twigs and so white
as whey, and he were a-begging all, 'Where be I tew? O, where be I?
I been a-vlying I have, over treetops and droo hedges. O, my dears,
where be I?'

"And my liddle old Gran she up and say quietly, 'Yew be buried in
your own dungheap, and best place vor 'ee.'"

MOTIFS: G.220.0.1 ["*Black*" *and* "*White*" *witches*]. *White:* G.202 [*Beneficent witch*];
N.828 [*Wise woman as helper*]. *Grey:* See above, for this advice was good enough for
a white witch. *Black:* D.2135.0.1(*b*) [*Witch carried person through air against will as
punishment*] (Baughman).

¶ In pp. 65–6 of *Somerset Folklore* Ruth L. Tongue distinguishes between white,
grey and black witches.

JAKEY BASCOMBE AND THE COB

Ruth L. Tongue, *Forgotten Folktales.*

My mother always drove our cob. She took him to market regularly,
and he'd go well. He was very fast and everybody knew him, but he
was so smart and good to handle she could do anything with him.

And all of a sudden he turned. He would become nappy and back
away or just stand for an hour for no reason. In the end he had the dog-
cart over, and broke the shafts, and mother's arm was put in plaster.
They were going to have the Vet. and have him put down. Father
thought he had poll evil. It was hay-carrying time, and the Vet. was too
busy to come.

Grandma (she lived six miles away) was ailing, and she wanted to
see mother. All the horses were working except the cob, and, of course,
mother couldn't drive him. We had a very old man still doing little jobs
on the farm. Father wouldn't part with him, he'd worked for us sixty-
five years, and he said to Mother, "I'll drive cob vor'ee, missus. There's
old putt I can put 'en in, and 'tis heavy enough to steady 'en up."

Well, mother chanced it. Father never knew till after—he'd have
been furious—and old Ben drove to Grandma's without a bit of trouble.

Grandma was better, so they didn't stay too long. They wanted to
get back while the cob was in the right mood, so mother was cross
when old Ben went a roundabout way all through the lanes. "I knows
what I be about, missus" was all he said, and they came home at a fine
smart trot all the way.

When mother did tell father, he had a word with old Ben. Then he
'phoned the Vet. not to come. Mother didn't want the cob put down, so,
of course, she asked why. And father said, "Did you notice which way
old Ben came back?"

Mother said, "Yes. Almost in a circle."

Father said, "Going westwards?"

"Yes. It must have been."

"Well, then," said father, "Ben tells me the cob has been driven along the lower road lately, that goes past Jakey Bascombe's, and it goes wrong-handed. Ben says he reckons Jakey Bascombe won't overlook the cob any more, and his ill-wish will go back on him."

The cob worked for mother for years afterwards, and never misbehaved, but Jakey was tipped out of his putt and kicked, and laid up for a month seven days after old Ben brought mother home, "with the sun".

From the daughter of a Mendip farmer then living on the Gloucester Downs, a member of Brislington W.I., 1962. Gloucestershire.

MOTIFS: G.265.6.3 [*Witch causes horse to behave unnaturally*]; G.271.6 [*Exorcism of witch by counter-charm*]; Q.580 [*Punishment fitted to crime*]; D.1791.2 [*Withershins circuit for ill-luck*]; D.1791.1 [*Dextrorsum circuit for good luck*].

JANE HERD AND HER CAUL [summary]

R. Blakeborough, *Wit, Character, Folk-Lore and Customs of the North Riding of Yorkshire*, 1898, p. 105.

Jane Herd was born with a caul over her head and face, which her mother carefully preserved, and it proved to possess extraordinary powers. If Jane laid it on the Bible, and wished to see anyone, that person was bound to appear. But she was a good girl, and never used it for any evil purpose.

One day a puff of wind blew the caul out of the window, and, try as she would, she could find no trace of it. After this all began to go amiss with Jane. Her lover refused to marry her, though the wedding day had been fixed; her neck swelled, and her right knee became so painful and swollen that she was lame, and her state went from bad to worse. At last someone remembered that, when she had been searching for her lost caul, the only other person in the street had been the witch, Molly Cass. But Molly was by this time living so far away that it seemed she could have no part in Jane's misfortunes.

However, Jane was persuaded to visit the two wise men of Bedale, Master Sadler and Thomas Spence, who made a sign round the swellings, and bade her go and gather certain ingredients, which they then mixed with others, and boiled them in a cauldron over a wicken fire, while Jane stirred the cauldron with a wicken stick. A great smoke arose from this boiling, which Jane was made to inhale nine times, though it nearly choked her. Then, still holding the wicken stick, and laying her other hand on the Bible, she had to ask aloud, "Has...gotten ma caul?" There was no reply, and Master Sadler declared that the person she had named was free of guilt. Master Spence then said: "By the power of the Holy Writ, and the charm of Hagothet and Arcon, mention the name of some other person thou doubtest." After several attempts, at last Jane spoke the name of Molly Cass, and as she did so, the cauldron boiled over, and the stench drove them all gasping out into the yard. There they surprised the witch scrambling down from a settle on which she had been standing to peer through a small hole in the shutters. She was thrust inside, into the suffocating smoke, until she confessed that she had indeed stolen the caul, and had it with her; also that, the moment they had placed the cauldron on the fire, she had found herself compelled to run all the way from Leeming. She begged their forgiveness, but she was shut up all night in a stable, and next day was ducked nine times in the mill-pond.

Told by Ann Caygill of Bedale, aged 75 years.

MOTIFS: G.257 [*Charms to cause witch to reveal herself*]; G.272.2.1 [*Rowan wood protects against witches*].

¶ The items dealing with a caul in the Motif Index are inappropriate to the English folk-tradition, according to which a caul is fortunate for the owner as long as it is in her possession. In Radford and Hole's *Encyclopaedia of Superstitions*, p. 92, among other interesting matter, we find: "If a child is born with his head covered by a thin membrane commonly known as a caul, or a mask, he will be lucky in life, and will never be drowned, provided the caul is kept"; and later: "It is, of course, considered very unlucky to throw away or destroy a caul deliberately".

JANE WOOD OF BASEDALE [summary]

R. Blakeborough, *Wit, Character, Folk-Lore and Customs of the North Riding of Yorkshire*, p. 194.

Jane Wood, supposed to be a witch, lived at Basedale, about seventy years ago. It was said that she often took the form of a hare, and then had no fear of dogs or guns; she could outrun the dogs, and the guns always missed her. But at last one sportsman consulted a wise man, who told him to take some silver coins from a Communion plate, and melt them in an iron ladle smeared with the blood of a hare. This was done over a wicken-wood fire, in the blacksmith's forge. The melted silver was then poured into a bowl of water, which caused it to divide into small particles.

The next evening, this silver was used to shoot at the mysterious hare. It escaped again, but was evidently badly wounded. In the morning the huntsman, with the others, visited Jane Wood in her cottage, but Jane called out that she was too ill to get up and open the door; for she had been badly stung by bees. But those outside burst open the cottage door and broke in; and found that part of Jane's body was covered with small shot-holes. For further proof, it was said that the venturesome hare was never seen again.

TYPE ML.3055. MOTIFS: G.211.2.7.1 [*Witch, as hare, allows self to be coursed by dogs for pay or for sport*]; G.275.12 [*Witch in form of animal is killed or injured as a result of injury to animal*]; D.1385.4 [*Silver bullet protects against witches*].

¶ This is one of the commonest of the witch legends.

See "The Witch Hare", "The Witch and Hare", "The Laird of Littledean".

KENIDZHEK WITCH

Hunt, *Popular Romances of the West of England*, p. 329.

On the tract called "the Gump", near Kenidzhek, is a beautiful well of clear water, not far from which was a miner's cot, in which dwelt two miners with their sister. They told her never to go to the well after daylight; they would fetch the water for her.

However, on one Saturday night she had forgotten to get in a supply for the morrow, so she went off to the well. Passing by a gap in a broken-down hedge (called a *gurgo*) near the well, she saw an old woman sitting down, wrapped in a red shawl; she asked her what she did there at that time of night, but received no reply; she thought this rather strange, but plunged her pitcher in the well; when she drew it up, though a perfectly sound vessel, it contained no water; she tried again and again, and, though she saw the water rushing in at the mouth of the pitcher, it was sure to be empty when lifted out. She then became rather frightened; spoke again to the old woman but, receiving no answer, hastened away, and came in great alarm to her brothers.

They told her that it was on account of this old woman they did not wish her to go to the well at night. What she saw was the ghost of old Moll, a witch who had been a great terror to the people in her lifetime, and had laid many fearful spells on them. They said they saw her sitting in the gap by the well every night when going to bed.

MOTIFS: E.278 [*Ghosts haunt spring*]; E.545.0.2 [*The dead are silent*]; D.2151.6 [*Magic control of wells*].

THE LAIRD OF LITTLEDEAN

Henderson, *Folk-Lore of the Northern Counties*, p. 201.

The Laird [Harry Gilles] of Littledean was extremely fond of hunting. One day, as his dogs were chasing a hare, they suddenly stopped, and gave up pursuit, which enraged him so much that he swore the animal they had been hunting must be one of the witches of Maxton. No sooner had he uttered the word than hares appeared all round him, so close that they even sprang over his saddle before his eyes, but still none of his hounds would give chase.

In a fit of anger, he jumped off his horse and killed the dogs on the spot, all but one large black hound, who at that moment turned to pursue the largest hare. Remounting his horse, he followed the chase, and saw the black hound turn the hare and drive it directly towards him. The hare made a spring as if to clear the horse's neck, but the laird dexterously caught hold of one of her forepaws, drew out his hunting-knife and cut it off; after which the hares, which had been so numerous, all disappeared. Next morning Laird Harry heard that a woman of Maxton had lost her arm in some unaccountable manner; so he went straight to her house, pulled out the hare's foot (which had changed in his pocket to a woman's hand and arm) and applied it to the stump. It fitted exactly. She confessed her crime, and was drowned for witch-craft the same day in the well by the young men of Maxton.

TYPE ML.3055. MOTIFS: G.211.2.7.1 [*Witch as hare allows herself to be coursed*]; G.303.3.3.1.1 [*Devil in form of dog*]; G.252 [*Witch in form of cat has hand cut off; recognized next morning by missing hand*]; G.278 [*Death of witch*].
¶ See "Jane Wood of Basedale", "The Witch Hare".

THE LAIRD OF PITTARRO

SIR JAMES CARNEGIE

R. Chambers, *Popular Rhymes of Scotland*, p. 386.

The Earl of Southesk—better known in Mearnshire as Sir James Carnegie of Pittarro—was an expert swordsman, and vulgar fame attributed his skill in this and other sciences to the gift of supernatural power. In this tradition of Mearnshire, he is said to have studied the *black art* at Padua, a place once famed for its seminaries of magic. The Devil himself was the instructor, and he annually claimed, as the reward of his tuition, the person of a pupil at dismissing his class. To give them all a fair chance of escape, he ranged them up in a line within the school, when, on a given signal, all rushed to the door—he who was last in getting out being the devoted victim. On one of these occasions, Sir James Carnegie was the last; but, having invoked the Devil to take his shadow instead of himself, *it* being the object last behind, the Devil was caught by the *ruse* and was content to seize the shadow instead of the substance. It was afterwards remarked that Sir James never had a shadow, and that he usually walked in the shade to hide this defect. Sir James is also remembered as a griping oppressor of the poor, which gave rise to the following lines, and occasion to his enemies secretly to injure his property:

> The Laird of Pittarro, his heart was sae narrow,
> He wanna let the kaes* pike his corn-stack;
> But by there came knaves, and pikit up thraves,
> And what said the Laird of Pittarro to that!

Note to Lamont's diary, 1660.

TYPE ML.3000. MOTIFS: F.1038 [*Person without shadow*]; K.525.2 [*Man steps aside so that only his shadow is caught*]; F.1038.1 [*Man attends Devil's school to learn witchcraft; has no shadow afterwards*].

THE LITTLE WEE TYKE

Ruth L. Tongue, *Forgotten Folk Tales.*

There was a little wee tyke, and he was black, so nobody wanted him.

He wasn't so big as the house-cat, so nobody wanted him for a house-dog either.

They said he was no use at all, and they were going to drown him when a poor ragged little lassie begged for him and got him.

She ran home with him. "Mammy! I've brought a little wee tyke," she cried.

"There's no water for the porridge," said her mother. "The well's bewitched. He'll die of thirst like us all."

"Not if I'm about," said the little wee tyke. "Let me alone to deal with this."

Then the farmer came in.

"I can't get out to my sheep," he said. "the gate's bewitched, and the ewes and lambs need watching against hill foxes."

"Not if I'm about," said the little wee tyke. "Leave me alone to deal with them."

Then the son came in.

"The cow's bewitched. There's not a drop of milk to see."

Then his little boy came in.

"The hens are bewitched. There's no eggs, and they'll never cackle or walk about any more."

"Not if I'm about," said the little wee tyke. "Leave me alone to deal with this."

"You!" they all cried out angrily. "Get out!" They started to throw things at him. The little lassie picked him up. "You!" said the little lassie. "Could you? Would you?"

* Kaes = crows.

"I would, and what's more I will!" said the little wee tyke, and out the door he went

"He can't get out any more than we can," said the farmer. But he had.

"You can't pass through," said the gate. "Old Witch Nanny laid it on me to keep back all who belong here."

"I don't belong here *yet*," said the little wee tyke, and he went through to the sheep. After he rounded them up so nicely and quietly into the fold by the wall, he went back to the hen-house, and carried the twelve hens safe inside.

"I don't belong here *yet*, so I'll break the mischief on you. When I've fetched your water, you can lay an egg each for me."

Then he went down to the well, and the family were all watching now. He scratched all round where the spring ran out. "Old Witch Nanny laid it on me not to run freely for any who belong here," said the well.

"I don't belong here *yet*," said the little wee tyke, and he kicked away the witchstone, and the water ran all down by the door, and the mother got a pailful for the porridge.

Then the farmer went out to the fold, and the little boy ran and found the eggs, and the cow was milked.

"You all said we needed a dog," said the little lassie.

"I've not done yet," said the little wee tyke.

But they all came running back and crying.

"The witch is on her way here!" and ran to bolt the door, but the little wee tyke said, "Let me out first. I'll deal with her." And they shut him out, and the little lassie cried.

Old Witch Nanny walked widdershins all round the farm.

"That'll hold them fast," she cackled.

"Oh no it won't. Not a bit," barked the little wee tyke. "Because I've come behind you backwards and scratched your footsteps all out."

Old Witch Nanny turned around in terror, and dropped her broom.

"That's clever, that is," said the little wee tyke, and stood *across* it, and then all she dared do was shriek "Scat!" at him.

"I'm not a house-cat," said the little wee tyke. "I can use my teeth as well as bark."

Then Old Nanny the Witch tried to climb up the thatch roof, but the little wee tyke took a bite of her left leg, and hung on as she climbed. When he let go and rolled down to the ground, she sat on the roof bleeding and yelling, and could never do any mischief any more. Then she fell off the roof and lay in the farmyard.

"I'm dying!" she whimpered.

"Not just yet," said the little wee tyke. "Old Nick has got to fetch you, and we don't want him here—and he don't like the look of me and my teeth. Take yourself away, and die Somewhere Else before he takes you there!"

And away she hobbled and crawled right out of sight. And there was thunder and lightning and a great green flame.

Then the little lassie called the little wee tyke to come in.

"I don't belong," said the little wee tyke.

"We all want you," said the little boy.

"But I'm black," said the little wee tyke.

"So is our house-cat," said the mother, "and she is almost as good and clever as you."

"I'm too small," said the little wee tyke.

"You got good teeth," said the father.

"You won't chase me with the poker, or throw things at me, or tread on me when I'm sleeping?"

"Never," they cried, and the little lassie brought him a bowl of milk.

And when he had lapped it all up he came in.

"This is about my size," he said, and went to sleep in one of the farmer's slippers.

Told by a visiting minister from near Carlisle, 1912.
MOTIFS: B.421 [*Helpful dog*]; B.121.1 [*Dog with magic wisdom*]; D.2080 [*Magic used against property*]; D.2083.1 [*Cows magically made dry*]; D.2151.6 [*Magic control of wells*]; D.2072.4 [*Magic prevention of performance of task*]; D.1791.2 [*Withershins circuit for ill-luck*]; G.273.6 [*Witch rendered powerless by drawing blood from her*].
¶ See "The Hare and the Harbourer".

THE LUCKY HORSE-COLLAR

Ruth L. Tongue, *Somerset Folklore*, p. 77.

There was a farmer whose finest cart-horse was bewitched, and he could neither find the witch nor cure the horse, and then his cows and pigs began to pine; so off went his wife to the conjuror in a town miles away. When she came in all the conjuror would say was, "I know what you have come for. Take this horse-collar *without touching it*, and hang it on the wall of your kitchen. So long as no one ever touches it your man will prosper."

Then he handed her the magic collar on the end of a hazel stick, and not another word did he utter.

So the farmer's wife drove home with the collar still on the stick across her knees, and when she got to the farm she went in and straightway hung it on a peg above the clavel tack [mantlepiece] and she wouldn't speak till all was done. Then she told the farmer all about it, and sure enough the beasts were cured from that very day.

She sent the conjuror a great market basket of eggs and butter and chickens, for he would take no money ever. The farm grew richer and richer, and the family never allowed a soul to lay a finger on the horse-collar over the clavel tack, until one day a great foolish maidservant lifted it down and dusted it. You can guess where their luck went after that.

From Mr Wyatt, Chard, 1909.

MOTIFS: G.265.4.2 [*Witch causes illness of animal*]; G.271.6 [*Exorcism of witch by counter-charm*]; D.1380 [*Magic object protects*]; C.401 [*Tabu: speaking during certain time*]; C.500 [*Tabu: touching*].

MADAM JOAN CARNE

Ruth L. Tongue, *Somerset Folklore*, p. 82.

Madam Joan Carne was an Elizabethan witch whose husbands died of suspected poisoning. Her restless spirit was condemned to stay in "The Witch's Pool" half a mile away, but every year she comes one cock-stride nearer home.

There was a lass in Queen Elizabeth's days who was called Joan, and she had a smile and a way with her. It is not surprising that she won the heart of a farmer and got on in the world quite a bit. What was surprising was that, in spite of her smile, he died soon after and left her comfortable.

It wasn't to be thought her taking ways would keep her a widow long, so next time she took a yeoman and he was richer than her first. Nobody knows how it was he died so soon, though some could give a guess. And now the poor soul had lost two healthy, wealthy husbands in a year or two, and was richer than ever. They say luck goes in threes. So whether it was that smile of hers, or whether riches call to riches, it wasn't long before she became Madam Joan Carne of Sandhill Manor, wife to the wealthiest man in the neighbourhood. Would you believe it, in spite of all her care, that strong, hearty man was taken ill of a sudden and, for all the nursing his family gave him, and the watch his servants kept over him, and the broth his lady coaxed him to drink with a special smile, he too died. To be sure he had kept alive longer than the other two, but his family and friends had seen to that. And now Madam Joan Carne had Sandhill Manor for herself as well, and she was the best-served woman in Withycombe. Who knew if she'd smile at *them!*

When at last she died they made sure of her. They nailed her coffin with iron nails, they hurried her body off to the church for Christian burial and when the service was over they came dancing with joy back to Sandhill Manor. One of them flung open the kitchen door, and there stood Madam Joan Carne frying eggs and bacon quite placidly. Then she turned her head and smiled at them... Well, they sent post-haste to Watchet for a priest who was hiding there—their own parson had failed badly and Watchet had succeeded with another ghost. Now, the priest must have known a lot about Madam Carne, for he sent her wicked spirit into a pond not a mile away and she can only return by one cock-stride each year, despite her smile.

"We used to fish and get blackberries by the Witch's Pond but we were always ready to run for our lives.

"Our people are now saying that she turned into a hare and someone shot her with a silver bullet and lamed her, and that she is now a ghost. Some of our older men say she's about if things go wrong."

MOTIFS: G.229.5 [*Beautiful witch*]; K.2213 [*Treacherous wife*]; G.262 [*Murderous witch*]; S.111 [*Murder by poisoning*]; E.431 [*Precautions at funeral against revenant*]; E.411 [*Dead cannot rest because of sin*]; E.437.2(c) [*Ghost laid in pool or pond*] (Baughman); E.443.2.4 [*Ghost laid by priest (minister)*].

¶ The ghosts that have escaped from their captivity and are gradually returning are part of a fairly widespread tradition. It is often connected with some tedious but not eternal task, but the "cock-stride" ghosts, which approach by the length of a cock's stride every year, appear to be peculiar to Somerset.

Madam Joan Carne died in 1612.

MADAM NOY AND OLD JOAN

Hunt, *Popular Romances of the West of England*, p. 334.

They say that, a long time since, there lived an old witch down by Alsia Mill, called Joan. Everybody feared to offend the old woman, and gave her everything she looked for, except Madam Noy, who lived in Pendrea.

Madam Noy had some beautiful hens of a new sort, with "cops" on their heads.

One morning early, Joan comes up to Pendrea, so as to catch Madam Noy going out into the farmyard with her basket of corn to feed her poultry, and to collect the eggs.

Joan comes up nodding and curtsying every step. "Good morrow to your honour. How well you are looking, Madam Noy! And, oh, what beautiful hens! I've got an old hen that I do want to set; will you sell me a dozen of eggs? Those with the 'cops' I'd like to have best."

Madam turned round half offended, and said, "I have none to sell, neither with the cops, nor yet without the cops, whilst I have so many old clucking hens about, and hardly an egg to be found."

"You surely wouldn't send me home empty as I came, madam dear?"

"You may go home the same way you came, for you aren't wanted here."

"Now," croaked Joan, hoarse with passion, "as true as I tell you so, if you don't sell me some eggs you will wish your cakes dough."

As the old witch said this, she perched herself on the stile, shaking her finger and "nodling" her head.

Madam Noy was a bit of a virago herself, so she took up a stone and flung it at Joan; it hit her in the face, and made her jaws rattle. As soon as she recovered she spinned forth:

"Madam Noy, you ugly old bitch,
  You shall have the gout, the palsy and itch;
  All the eggs your hens lay henceforth shall be addle;
  All your hens have the pip, and die with the straddle;
  And ere I with the mighty fine madam have done,
  Of her favourite 'coppies' she shan't possess one."

From that day forward, madam was always afflicted. The doctor from Penzance could do little for her. The fowls' eggs were always bad; the hens died, and madam lost all her "coppies". This is the way it came about—in the place of cops the brains came out—and all by the spells of old Joan.

MOTIFS: G.269.4 [*Curse by disappointed witch*]; G.263.4.0.1 [*Illness caused by curse of witch*]; G.265.4.0.1 [*Witch punishes owner for injury or slight by killing his animals*]. ¶ Presumably Madam Noy's stone had not drawn blood, for Old Joan's curse lodged, and did not return to her.

This scolding match was a subject for one of the Cornish drolls, of which the rhyme given by Hunt was probably a part.

MADGY FIGGY'S CHAIR [summary]

Hunt, *Popular Romances of the West of England*, p. 330.

The great natural piles of rock near St Levan known as Tol-Pedden-Penwith rise high out of the Atlantic; and among them is a mass of almost cubical granite blocks, known as the *Chair Ladder*. At its top is one remarkably shaped stone, called the Chair, where the famous witch, Madgy Figgy, used to sit and work her spells, calling up storms, and uttering curses upon man and beast. From here, too, she would lead flights of witches on their journeys to Wales or Spain.

She and her gang were notorious wreckers, and would lure ships into Perloe Cove, and plunder the corpses of their victims. One such ship was a Portuguese Indiaman, and Figgy with her husband, after stripping off all their valuables, buried the bodies of the passengers and crew in a green hollow, placing a rough stone at the head of each grave. For years afterwards, they and their friends with their families went about in the finery and jewels gathered from this wreck. The richest of all their spoils came from the body of a lady, whose body bore a mark, which Figgy declared would be an omen of evil to them all if the treasures she wore and others which she had secured about her person were separated. She therefore proposed that they should be kept in a chest in Figgy's own hut, and, though her confederates resented the arrangement, Figgy's will prevailed, and the woman's body was finally buried with the others.

That night a light was seen to rise from her grave, and, passing along the cliffs, it came to rest on Figgy's chair. After some hours, it came down and entered her cottage, alighting on the chest of treasure.

Every night for some months this was repeated, to the alarm of all but Figgy herself, who said it would come right in time. Then one day a stranger arrived at the cottage, a foreigner, who showed by signs that he wished to be led to the graves. Figgy's husband guided him there, and he at once made his way to the rich lady's grave, sat down on it, and broke into tears and lamentation. There he remained until, at the usual time, the light from the grave appeared, to rest as it always did, on the chest.

Sweeping aside the fisherman's litter with which it was covered, the dark stranger now opened the chest, and took away everything which had belonged to the Lady. He left costly gifts for the wreckers, and went away without a word.

But Madgy Figgy used to say triumphantly that "One witch knows another witch, dead or living", and that the stranger would have been the death of them all if they had not kept the treasure for him.

MOTIFS: G.283.1.2.3 [*Witch raises wind to sink ships*]; G.266 [*Witches steal*]; E.530.1.3 [*Ghost-light haunts burial-spot*]; E.371.10* [*Ghost-light leads to hidden treasure*] (Baughman).

¶ The dark, mysterious stranger in this story reminds one of the man who appeared at the end of "The Enchanter of Pengerswick". Neither seems to have been a devil; rather a brother magician. It is strange that this one did not avenge the lady or her murderers, but rewarded them for returning the treasure.

THE MAN WHO WAS CURSED

Ruth L. Tongue, *Somerset Folklore*, p. 70.

"You know the Seven Kings. Well, a man went to have his drink, and he had some fish on his bike, and another man came out of the pub and defiled it. When the fish-man saw what had happened he asked who had done it. No one owned up. So he said, 'The man that did it will not get home very easily tonight.'

"So that man that did it tried to get home. He left the pub and he walked home—he lived at Nailesbourne. In fact, he lived where Mrs Bailey lives now. Instead of being able to get through the gate—there is a stream on the left-hand side of the house—he was walking up and down the stream (till) the early hours of the morning unable to get indoors."

MOTIFS: G.269.10 [*Witch punishes person who incurs (his) ill-will*]; D.2172.1 [*Magic repetition; person must go on doing thing till released*].

¶ In the pamphlet, *Dr Lamb's Darling* (1653, pp. 4–5), Anne Bodenham boasts of a similar feat.

THE MISSING MUTCH

Shetland Folk-Book, II, p. 11.

A Fetlar woman called Gairdner who was credited with being able to say "Mair or hir prayers" used to cure rheumatic ailments by tying a "wristen treed" with black woollen thread on which nine knots were tied and uttering a spell.

When she was a girl, one night, she wanted a go to a dance, but was very sad because she had no suitable mutch to wear.

It happened that she said this in a house where a sailor had just returned from a voyage. He said, "I'll gie de somethin' oot o' my kist," and she said afterwards that he handed her the most beautiful mutch she ever saw, and which she wore at the dance.

Before leaving the dance she put her hand to her head and missing the mutch, was greatly upset at having lost it, but was told that she never had one on.

(A clear case of hypnotism)

MOTIF: D.2031 [*Magic illusion*].

THE MISSING WEB

Douglas, *Scottish Fairy and Folk-Tales*, p. 183.

"Some time since, when calling at the house of one of my oldest parishioners, who had been a hand-loom weaver, he fell to speak of other days; and, amongst other things, he told me of the disappearance, some years back, on a fine summer's evening of a web of linen which had been laid to bleach by the riverside at the foot of the glebe. The fishermen, it seems, were 'burning the water' (spearing, or 'leistering', salmon by torchlight) in the Skerry, and the man who had charge of the web went off to see the salmon 'leistered', and on his return the web was gone. Of course, there was a sensation. The story was soon in everybody's mouth, with abundant suspicions of as many persons as there were yards in the web of linen.

"The web belonged to a very important personage, no less than the 'howdie', or the old village midwife, who was not disposed to sit down quietly under her loss.

"So she called in the aid of a wise man from Leitholm, and next day told her friend the weaver, my informant, that she had found the thief, for the wise man had turned the key. The weaver being anxious to see something of diablerie, the howdie brought the wise man to his house; and the door being locked on all within (four in number), the magician proceeded as follows: He took a small key, and attached it to a string, which he tied into the family Bible at a particular place, leaving the key hanging out. Next he read two chapters from the Bible, one of which was the history of Saul and the witch of Endor. He then directed the howdie and another person to support the key between them, on the tips of their forefingers, and in that attitude the former was told to repeat the names of all the suspected parties.

"Many persons were named, but the key still hung between the fingers, when the wise man cried out, 'Why don't you say Jock Wilson?' This was accordingly done, and immediately the key dropped, i.e. turned off the finger-ends.

"So the news spread far and wide that the thief was discovered, for the key had been turned and Jock Wilson was the man! He proved, however, not to be the man to stand such imputations, and, being without doubt an honest fellow, he declared 'he wudna be made a thief by the deevil'. So he went to consult a lawyer, but after many long discussions the matter died away; and my authority, the weaver, says it was believed the lawyer was bribed; 'for he aye likit a dram.'"

From the narrative of the Rev. R. O. Bromfield of Sprouston.
MOTIF: H.251.3.2 [*Thief detected by Psalter (Bible) and key*].
¶ The method described in this tale is slightly different from that given in the Motif Index, which follows the recipe given by Reginald Scot (*The Discoverie of Witchcraft*, ed. Montague Sumers, p. 277). This is rather more elaborate than the one usually followed by village wise women, and also rather less practical.

MOLLY CASS AND THE NINE OF HEARTS
[summary]

R. Blakeborough, *Wit, Character, Folk-Lore and Customs of the North Riding of Yorkshire*, p. 164.

Molly Cass lived for many years in a cottage close to Leeming Mill, possibly in the mill itself. Abe Braithwaite, of Bedale, used to tell a strange story of her, told by his grandfather.

Abe's grandfather, the miller and two others were playing cards in the mill one night, and eight times in succession George Winterfield had the nine of hearts dealt to him. At the ninth deal one of the players laid a guinea on the table, and wagered it with Winterfield against a shilling, that he would not receive the nine of hearts again.

Just then Au'd Molly put her head round the door, and said: "Put thy brass in thy pocket. Thy brass is not for him, and his is not for thee."

So terrified was the man of incurring her ill-will that he at once put back his guinea into his pocket, and Molly said, as the cards still lay on the table: "Thou's gotten it again, George; take thy hand up and see." And so he had. The old woman went on: "Thou's gotten it hard enough; thou's had it eight times already. The Old 'Un's in thee now, and he'll not leave thee till he's gotten thee altogether. Thou'st thrown away thy chance, so I've pitched it into the Swale. The Swale's waiting to be thy bridal bed. Go now; the longer thou waits, the longer thou'll stay."

George turned white as death, and got up, crying: "I'll wed her. Give me another chance. I've rued all I've done." But Molly replied: "I'm not often in the mind to give one chance, let alone two. Go thy way. Thy bride's waiting for thee in a bed of bulrushes. Oh, what a bridal bed!"

George left the mill, saying he would go at once and wed his old sweetheart. Molly shrieked after him: "Good night, George. All roads lead to the Swale to-night." And whether he lost his way in the darkness, or for some other reason, his dead body and his sweetheart's were found the next day, tangled in reeds and sedge, side by side in the water. He had never seen her alive, for she had drowned herself before he came.

For many years afterwards it was said that anyone who ventured near the spot at midnight would see the body of a girl first, and then that of a man, float by, and disappear when they joined one another among the bulrushes.

MOTIFS: G.269.10.1 [*Witch kills person as punishment*]; D.1812.5.1 [*Bad omens*]; M.341.2.3 [*Prophecy: death by drowning*]; T.81.2.1 [*Scorned lover kills self*]; T.86.2 [*Lovers die at the same time*].

MOTHER DARK

J. R. W. Coxhead, *The Devil in Devon*, pp. 53–5.

In the year 1881, when Mrs Milton was seven years old, she was living at a farm called Higher Lea, in the parish of Dalwood, in East Devon. Her father, Mr Thomas Warren, who was the tenant of the farm, had suffered heavy losses amongst his stock for a long time, and what was more, most of the animals concerned had died under very queer circumstances.

One day, for some unaccountable reason, most of the pigs on the farm suddenly became ill and died. A few days later one of the cows in the herd started staggering about in a peculiar manner, then its legs gave way and it collapsed in the yard. Six men tried to lift the animal in order to take it into the cowshed, but, in spite of all their efforts, they were unable to move it an inch from the place where it lay. The farmer immediately sent for the veterinary surgeon at Colyton, who examined the cow very thoroughly several times, but could find nothing wrong with the animal. Nevertheless, during the night, the poor creature expired. One of the men who worked on the farm told Mr Warren that he considered all the trouble to be the work of a black witch, and strongly advised him to seek the services of a famous white witch who lived at Exeter.

In bygone days black witches were the dreaded enemies of the community, and worked much evil, but white witches, often called "wisemen", endeavoured to heal or help anyone in distress at all times, so the worried farmer mounted his horse and rode over to Seaton Junction, from which place he went by train to Exeter to implore the wiseman's aid.

The white witch readily agreed to go to Higher Lea to see what he could do to help in the matter. On his arrival at the farmhouse he asked for a glass of water.

As soon as it was brought to him he placed it on the table and requested the farmer to gaze into it and tell him if he could see anything. Mr Warren did so, and presently in an excited voice he said, "I see a woman's face amid swirling mist." There was a tense silence, and then, in a hoarse whisper, he spoke again, "The mist is clearing and the face I see is the face of 'Mother Dark'."

Now old Mother Dark was a woman of particularly sinister repute who lived alone in a little cottage in the village.

The wiseman told Mr Warren that unless he could defeat the spells cast by Mother Dark all the stock on the farm would eventually die, and possibly some of his children also.

The now thoroughly frightened farmer, aghast at the evil fortune that had befallen his farm and household, beseeched the white witch to use all his great skill in the art of sorcery to break Mother Dark's power. He requested the man to make the black witch suffer in the same manner as she had caused his cow to suffer, but not to the extent of causing her death, and if he succeeded he would be well rewarded.

Time passed, and more animals died on the farm, but at length the wiseman's potent counter-spells were successful, and Mother Dark, afflicted by a mysterious illness, was carried off to hospital.

At the hospital the doctors could find nothing wrong with the wicked old woman; nevertheless, every time she tried to stand up her legs kept giving way beneath her, and the remarkable thing about the whole business was that from the moment she became ill the misfortunes at Higher Lea ceased, and the farmer prospered and never had any serious trouble on his farm afterwards.

It would be very interesting to know the name of the white witch concerned with the case at Higher Lea. Unfortunately, Mrs Milton was unable to remember his name.

He may, however, have been a man from Exeter named Snow, who was working as a wiseman in 1887, or he might well have been Tuckett, the celebrated white witch of Exeter, whose services were much in demand about the time the unpleasant events at Higher Lea were taking place. As a matter of interest, Tuckett stayed for a lengthy period at the Bell Inn at Parkham, about the year 1890, while practising his magic arts in North Devon.

Told to the author by Mrs Jane Milton of Southleigh, near Colyton. She was born at Luppitt near Honiton on 13 April 1874.
MOTIFS: G.265.4 [*Witch causes disease or death of animals*]; G.220.0.1 ["*Black*" *and* "*White*" *Witches*]; D.1821.3.7.1 [*Magic sight by looking into glass of water*]; D.1719.1 [*Contest in magic*]; Q.580 [*Punishment fitted to crime*]; Q.583 [*Fitting bodily injury as punishment*]; G.271.6 [*Exorcism of witch by counter-charm*].
¶ See "Aald Sibbie", "Anne Allen", "The Blacksmith's Nail".

MOTHER KEMP [condensed]

W. H. Barrett, *More Tales from the Fens*, pp. 111–18.

I

I've heard tell of a witch who spat on the door of the chap who was Mayor of Lynn at the time, because he wouldn't give her any money when she asked for it. Then she shouted out:

"May you and all your family shake themselves into Hell before the moon changes." And, do you know, they all got the ague and, before they died in their beds, they shook so much that they couldn't keep the clothes on them. Well, the Lynn folk weren't going to put up with that, so they went out to Stow Bridge way, where the old witch lived, and took her into Lynn and sent word round that they were going to boil her alive in a big copper. Hundreds of people went to see her bobbing up and down like a pork dumpling; and when the broth cooled down it was ladled into jars and sold for a penny a ladle. Some of it came down here and folk stood the jar outside their doors, to keep the Devil away, and it was said that if fish-hooks were dipped in it, there wasn't any need for any other bait to get a good catch. That was long before my time, of course, but I *can* tell you about one old woman I *did* know.

II

Her name was Mother Kemp, and she lived in Burnt Fen; everyone said she was a witch. She'd been married five times and all her husbands had died very suddenly. Then she'd started courting a sixth, but just before the wedding he walked into the drain, and a week afterwards, when the engine chap was cleaning out the grid, he found the body, so he went to tell Mrs Kemp that her future husband had died a bit sooner than she'd expected. This upset her so much that she started shouting out curses at the top of her voice. Men working in a field a mile away stopped to listen, and when they met the engine chap they told him that, if only half the things came true that she'd said, then there'd soon be another stoker needed at the engine. They wouldn't be putting in for the job though, as they'd heard that old hag shout out that anyone who took the job when he was finished would go the same way.

A few weeks later, as the chap was stoking up, the boiler blew and he was thrown into the air, and when he came down he was as dead as could be. And do you know, they had to go miles to find another stoker because none of the local chaps would take the job on. Even when a new stoker did come he couldn't get lodgings anywhere near his work as nobody would take him in for fear of what that old witch might do. So the drainage people sent him an old gault lighter [barge] with a little cabin at one end.

He moored it on the river close by the engine and lived and slept on the boat till, one morning, when the engine-driver went out on to the bank to find out where his stoker was, he found that during the night the lighter had been burnt out and had sunk. When it was raised the man was found lying in his bunk, badly burned as well as drowned; it seems that the smoke-pipe from the little stove had set fire to the cabin roof.

Next Saturday night the men met at the Dog and Duck and, by closing time, six of them were so full of courage that they went down to where Mother Kemp lived, tied up her door with wire, set fire to the thatch and then ran off. When they were back on the hard road they stood and watched the flames till they died down and then they went home to bed. On the Sunday morning they walked down the drove, but, before they got anywhere near the cottage, they could see the old woman pottering about among the hot ashes. Those chaps were so scared that they tore off home and, when evening came, they washed themselves and went into the little chapel just as the service was starting. They said they wanted someone to pray for them as they needed praying for badly, and to learn how to deal with the Devil and with his devils, who were witches. And do you know, bor, those six joined the chapel and stuck to it too. I don't suppose, myself, that they'd have joined if they'd known that, when they set fire to Mother Kemp's cottage that night, she wasn't in bed, but was miles away across the Fen, so she wasn't, as they'd thought, a witch that the flames hadn't been able to hurt.

It wasn't long, though, before she started her tricks again. She moved to an old shack which had stood empty for years; it was miles from anywhere, at the end of a long drove. I saw her once myself when I was out that way; she was wry-necked and had only one eye, so she looked just like what folk said she was, a proper witch. She used to wander all over the Fen at night and a lot of farmers used to find that one of their cows had been milked dry in the morning. They all knew who'd done the milking because Mother Kemp had a couple of dozen cats which used to wander about all over the place, catching a rabbit, a moorhen or a young chicken, which they'd carry back and put on the old girl's doorstone. All the cats were as fat as butter because they lived on fresh milk.

One night four young farmers had been to a wedding and, being full up with the stuff that makes folks do what they wouldn't dream of doing when they are sober, they left the hard road and went down the drove to where old Mother Kemp lived in her shack. They crept up to the window and saw her sitting in the firelight, smoking a clay pipe. The room seemed to be full of cats; one old tom came to the window and spat as if he knew they were skulking outside. Then the old woman took the pipe out of her mouth, reached up to the mantelshelf and took down a tin whistle and began to play a tune, while all the cats started making a terrible noise. After a bit she opened a cupboard door, and, as she played, two snakes, each one over four feet long, slid out into the room and, after listening for a while to the music, reared up on their tails and swayed backwards and forwards, every now and then darting their heads forwards and touching the old woman's face. When she left off playing, the snakes coiled up on the hearth and went to sleep, while the old girl lit up her pipe again and, between puffs, talked and muttered to herself. After a bit she went over to a box and took out a tin, opened it and threw a handful of powder on the fire, which flared up and filled the room with a bright blue light. The cats arched their backs and spat at the fire and the snakes uncoiled themselves and began hissing, while Mother Kemp, with her hands over her head, bowed down every now and then to the flames. Then, when the fire had died down, she took her cloak off a nail on the wall, put it on, picked up a pail, and went out of the back door with the cats and snakes following her. The four chaps outside watched her cut across the Fen towards old Jowler's farm.

Now, one of those four was Jowler's son, and he said he wasn't going to be done out of his milking job by an old woman with cats and snakes; he knew which field the cows were in and that on one side of it was the main drain, twenty foot wide and ten foot deep, and he said he knew the dykes on the other three sides were too wide for the old girl to jump. So the four of them followed, as near as they dared, and young Jowler ran off to the house and woke up his father, telling him it wouldn't be a bad idea to bring his gun, as there was a good chance he might be able to wipe off a few bad debts from his dairy book. So old Jowler got up and dressed and came down with his gun, and they told him that the old girl was among the cows.

"Well, a little exercise won't hurt her," said old Jowler, and he turned the bull into the field, where it made over towards the cows as fast as its chain would let it go.

It was just getting light by now, and Mother Kemp looked up, and, seeing the bull, she bolted off towards the gate, the cats well in front of her and the bull close behind, every now and then treading on its chain, which hurt its nose. When the cats were in range, old Jowler's gun banged twice. The cats swung round, leaving two behind, dead.

The old woman turned as well, and cut along the bank by the drain, but daren't take to the water. The bull got tired of following her, and went back to the cows, and, when the cows had been called up out of the field for milking, old Jowler went back with his gun, and got twenty-three cats. When he had gone home to his breakfast, Mother Kemp slipped out through the gate. And when the men were cutting hay in that field the next year they killed two of the biggest snakes they'd ever seen in the Fen.

After that the old witch used to go down the drove, and stand and curse Jowler and his farm for hours on end, till everyone got so scared that they fetched a doctor and two magistrates to take her away and shut her up.

But after she was gone everything began to go wrong for old Jowler. His wife died, and then his daughter. His animals fell sick and died too, and then he himself fell from a corn-stack and broke his neck. Young Jowler went to America, and was not heard of again. The farm was sold four times in the next six years, for no one would stay in it. No one would go near the place after dark, either, and at last the house stood empty and began to fall to ruins. Children carried off the timber for kindling, but the old woman's shack was verminous, so at last the owner lighted a pile of straw inside it. When the flames reached the tin in the cupboard, a bright blue light flared up and lit all the sky around. Folks said that Mother Kemp died just at that moment, while her cottage was going up in flames.

The farm never prospered again, and when the last of the sheep had gone down with liver-rot, the owner let the shepherd sell their skins for five shillings a piece, and the neglected land reverted to the Fen, with only a patch of blackthorn and nettles to mark where Mother Kemp's cottage had stood.

Some Irishmen who'd come over for the harvest work once attempted to camp in the ruins of the farmhouse, for they were two and a half miles from the nearest pub, but one night they woke up its landlord, who found them huddled together outside, sweating with terror and exhaustion, for they had run all the way from the farm. He took them into his taproom, and gave them whisky, but the next day they drew all their money from the farmer, saying that not for all the gold in the world would they spend another night in a fen so full of devils. But they wouldn't tell anyone what it was that they had seen.

I. MOTIFS: G.269.4 [*Curse by disappointed witch*]; D.2061.2.4 [*Death by cursing*]; S.112.1 [*Burning to death*].

II. MOTIFS: G.262 [*Murderous Witch*]; M.430 [*Curses on persons*]; M.451 [*Curse: death*]; G.269.14 [*Witch causes person to be burned*]; G.225.3 [*Cat as witch's familiar*]; G.225.7.2 [*Magician's familiar a viper*]; E.200 [*Malevolent return from the dead*].

¶ The cats and snakes seem not to have been familiars, since they could be killed by ordinary weapons, and Mother Kemp seems to have milked the cows herself, not by magic.

See "Club-footed Aggie".

MOTHER SHIPTON [summary]

Parkinson, *Yorkshire Legends and Traditions*, 1st series, p. 151.

Most, if not all, of these stories are derived from a book published in 1684, 130 years after the reputed death of Mother Shipton, and it is uncertain how far they were the invention of the author, Richard Head.

It is said that her mother, Agatha, died in giving her birth, and that strange and horrible noises on the occasion terrified and nearly drove away all those who were present. "She was born at Knaresborough, and baptized by the Abbot of Beverley by the name of Ursula Southell. Her stature was larger than common, her body crooked, her face frightful, but her understanding extraordinary."

She was put out to nurse with a poor woman outside the town, but strange manifestations made the nurse's life well-nigh impossible. Once, when the child was about six months old, the woman left the house for a short time, and on returning found the door open and an uproar in progress. She called some neighbours to her help, but as soon as the foremost of them entered the house large yokes, in the form of a cross, were put round their necks, to detain them, and when, after a hard struggle, they cast these off, a staff was laid across their shoulders, from which an old woman clung by heels or toes.

The men of the company made their escape somehow, but the women forced their way in, and were at once compelled to take hold of the four ends of a cross, and dance round, each of them goaded by an imp like a monkey, until they were utterly exhausted. At last the priest with a band of followers, succeeded in crossing the threshold, and searching the house—the child was nowhere to be seen; but was at length discovered hanging with its cradle, both unsupported, halfway up the chimney.

As the child grew, the work of the foster-mother was invariably interfered with in mysterious ways. Chairs and tables would march upstairs, the meat would be spirited away from the table, and the child Ursula would grin and say, "Be contented. There is nothing here that will hurt you."

At school she was a prodigy: she needed no teaching of alphabet or reading; at first sight she read whatever book was shown to her. At twenty-four she was married to Toby Shipton; but little is known of their life together.

Long before her death in 1561, she foretold its day and hour. As the time drew near, she took a solemn farewell of her friends, and when it arrived she lay quietly down on her bed to await her end.

The earliest collection of her prophecies was printed about 1641; they included one to the effect that Cardinal Wolsey should never come to York with the King; in fact, he arrived within eight miles of it, but was summoned to return to the King, and died on his way to London. She is also said to have foretold the Great Fire of London and the plague, and other events of history; but it is uncertain which of the prophecies attributed to her were really hers, and which were fabricated later to fit the events.

MOTIFS: G.303.12.5 [*Devil marries girl*]; G.303.11.5 [*The Devil's daughter*]; T.550.2 [*Abnormally born child has unusual powers*]; T.551.13.2 [*Child born with long beard*]; T.585.5 [*Child born with all his teeth*]; T.585.2 [*Child speaks at birth*]; M.300 [*Prophecies*]; D.1812 [*Magic power of prophecy*].

¶ *Mother Shipton.* Mother Shipton is a kind of homely Merlin. Like him, she was the offspring of a woman and a devil, born toothed and of precocious intelligence. A play printed in 1660, *Mother Shipton*, deals with her mother's history, rather than hers. Mother Shipton is a patroness of washerwomen, and in the Eastern Counties "Mother Shipton's Day" is celebrated by laundresses with a holiday and tea-parties. More can be learned of her in *Mother Shipton Investigated*, W. H. Harrison, 1881.

NAN HARDWICKE [summary]

R. Blakeborough, *Wit, Character, Folk-Lore and Customs of the North Riding of Yorkshire*, p. 176.

These are two stories of Nan Hardwicke, who was once famous, and is still remembered in the Cleveland dales.

One afternoon she called at a house some miles away from her home, and asked for a "shive of bread and a pot of beer". The woman of the house was expecting a baby, and her husband was just about to ride off in search of her sister, who lived about five miles away. Nan, having been given what she asked, put her head in at the door of the room where the woman was lying, and said: "I wish you well; you'll have a lad before morning, and you'll call him Tommy, won't you?"

Neither the wife nor her husband was willing to do this; they had agreed to name the child John; and they decided to take no notice of what Nan had said. About six o'clock the husband drove off in search of his sister-in-law; but all of a sudden, about thirty yards from a small bridge which he had to cross, his horse stopped dead, and when he tried to get out to lead her over, he found that he was quite unable to move. He called out angrily, "Nan, what's thee after? This is thy work." He heard a laugh, and a voice shouted, "Thou'll call the bairn Tommy, won't thou?" "Not for thee nor for all the Nan devils in the country," he answered boldly. "Then you'll bide where thou is till the babe's born, and the mother dies," croaked she. In face of this threat, the farmer promised, and was allowed to go on his way.

Nan occasionally visited a relation who lived at Lowna Bridge. It was twenty miles from her home, and some said she turned herself into a hare to perform the journey. On one of these visits, which proved to be the last, she found that the daughter of the house had just been married; the wedding procession was returning from the church, and Nan was invited to join in their festivity. But every bed in the house was occupied for that night; so a kindly bridesmaid invited Nan to her home for the night, and said she could share her bed, and she would bring her back in the morning. The bride incautiously said: "Relation though she is, I would not sleep with the old thing for anything." Nan, overhearing her, said: "Nay, but thou wouldst sleep with him." Then, shaking her stick, she added:

> "I've let thee be wedded,
> But I'll stop thee being bedded."

So she left the house and was soon forgotten.

Late that evening, when the bride had already retired, the bridegroom's sister told him that there was a plot to keep him up with the revellers all night (a common practice in those days), but that the brides-maids had planned to help him escape to the bride's room by means of a ladder. They had arranged a game of Blind Man's Buff, during which a girl would call out, "Kiss the girl you love best." At this signal all the candles would be blown out, and the bridegroom would be able to slip out and find the ladder. The last bit of the climb, as the ladder was not quite high enough, was to be made by pulling himself up to the bride's window by means of a towel. Just as he reached this towel, one of the guests, half-drunk, pulled the ladder from beneath him, having discovered what was going on. The bridegroom crashed to the ground with a broken leg. So the witch's prophecy was fulfilled.

MOTIFS: D.2072.0.2.1 [*Horse enchanted so that he stands still*]; D.2072 [*Magic paralysis*]; G.269.12.1 [*Witch breaks bridegroom's leg when slighted by bride*].

NANCY CAMEL

Ruth L. Tongue, *Somerset Folklore*, p. 83.

Nancy Camel lived in a cave and sold her soul to the Devil. He came to collect her one stormy night and left hoof-prints in stone on her cavern walls.

Old Nancy Camel lived in a cave in the woods. She was a stocking-knitter, and worked ceaselessly by day and at night by rushlight to gain a few more pence to add to her hoard. Then she began to work on a Sunday and people whispered together and looked sideways at her for a godless old miser.

It is not surprising then that one night the Devil visited her with a sack of gold to increase her hoarding.

And now she was really rich, but she still went on knitting to scrape in a few more pennies; folk dare not refuse to buy her stockings, for they knew she was a witch.

When the seven years were nearly up she went in terror to the priest and confessed. He promised her pardon if she would throw away the Devil's gold, but she found she couldn't bring herself to part with the last coin, and hid it. Then she went back to the priest and told a lie about it—and after that the pardon was no protection at all.

A fearful storm broke out that very night, and above the howling of the wind folk heard the rattle of wheels and the crack of a giant whip. Then a terrible scream rang out from the cave.

In the morning the priest and a few villagers went to find old Nancy. She was gone, but the deep marks of wheels and hooves on the rock of her cave are still there to show who carried her off.

MOTIFS: W.153 [*Miserliness*]; C.631.2 [*Tabu: spinning on holy days*]; M.211 [*Man sells soul to devil*]; D.2141.0.4 [*Storm at death of wizard*]; G.299.2 [*Witch is heard struggling with the Devil*]; G.275.1 [*Witch carried off by Devil*]; A.972.2.2 [*The Devil's footprint*].

NANCY NEWGILL, THE WITCH OF BROUGHTON

R. Blakeborough, *Wit, Character, Folk-Lore and Customs of the North Riding of Yorkshire*, p. 190.

Nancy Newgill used to set hedgehogs to milk the cows of those she had a spite against, and at times, it was believed, she turned into one herself, for there was one hedgehog in those parts that could run as fast as a hare, and no one could catch nor kill it.

Once she cast a spell upon Martha Brittain, and when she could get no relief from it, she went to the wise man, Henry Wilson, who told her first to go to Stokesley and buy a new fire-shovel. On this she was to chalk Nancy's name; then to make a cake, and after closing her doors and windows, bake the cake over the fire on the new shovel. This she did at four in the afternoon. At that time Nancy Newgill was weeding in a field with others a mile away from Martha's cottage, and suddenly she clapped her hand to her stomach, crying, "I must go home!" She left the field, and was ill for many days, but Martha Brittain began to recover immediately, and was soon as well as ever.

MOTIFS: G.211.2.9 [*Witch as hedgehog*]; D.655.2 [*Witch transforms herself to animal to suck cows*]; G.263.4 [*Witch causes sickness*]; G.271.6 [*Exorcism of witch by counter-charms worked by witch doctor*] (Baughman).

NANNY APPLEBY AND THE EVIL SPIRIT
[summary]

R. Blakeborough, *Wit, Character, Folk-Lore and Customs of the North Riding of Yorkshire*, p. 159.

A widow living in the village of Aldfield had an only son, who fell desperately ill. It was supposed that a witch, Nanny Appleby, had laid a spell on him, and his mother, in her despair, determined to visit her and beg her to remove it. She set out early one morning, and before she had covered the half of the long journey across Dalla Moor, she met the old woman herself, and told her trouble.

Nanny swore that she was innocent, but that she knew what had afflicted the lad, and offered to go home with the widow and cure him. The villagers were astonished to see the two women returning together, but when Nanny had been alone with the boy for some time she came out and told his mother that a devil was gnawing his vitals, and that she would try to drive it out. A terrible fight followed, and at last the evil spirit came out, yelling fearfully, and the boy quickly recovered. Nanny then had to dispose of the devil, or it would have been free to enter some other body, so she bade it enter a certain Tom Moss, perhaps because she had a spite against him. About a month later, Tom was found drowned in Grantley Lake.

MOTIFS: G.284 [*Witch as helper*]; G.303.16.14 [*The devil exorcized*]; D.2176 [*Exorcizing by magic*]; E.728.1 [*Evil spirit cast out of person*]; G.303.18 [*Devil enters body of another*].

NANNY PEARSON AT GOATHLAND

R. Blakeborough, *Wit, Character Folk-Lore and Customs of the North Riding of Yorkshire*, p. 186.

The Squire of Goathland had one very beautiful daughter. She had an old rich suitor, but her love was given to a certain young farmer.

The old lover sought the help of Nanny Pearson, for he feared the young pair might elope. Nanny therefore inflicted a dire disease on the girl: she could not leave her bed, and her legs began to die.

Her father told her it was because she had offended one of the female saints by her obstinacy, but she remained firm in her resolve not to marry the rich old man. Then the young lover, in his despair, visited the wise man of Scarborough, who set him in front of a looking-glass, and told him to say if he saw there the likeness of anyone he knew.

Soon the young man swore he had seen the likeness of Nanny Pearson. Then the wise man told him that she was the cause of all the trouble, and said he must procure a drop of her blood, mix it with a few drops of holy water and a cup of milk drawn from a red cow. This, rubbed on the calves and soles of the feet of his lady, would restore her to health. The task was full of difficulty, but an old woman in the village, Janet Haswell, told him how to overcome the worst of them all.

Every night, she said, a hare sat in a certain corner of a field, which neither men nor dogs could catch; and this hare was none other than Nanny Pearson. If he melted down some silver for shot, he would be able to shoot her, and perhaps gather some blades of grass stained with her blood. The young man carefully carried out these instructions, and was successful. Nanny was for some weeks confined to bed; and in the meantime he procured a ladder, climbed up into his sweetheart's room, and applied the remedy to her legs. She was instantly well, and he carried her away, and kept her in a safe place until he could marry her.

MOTIFS: G.263.4.3 [*Witch cripples or lames victim through illness*]; G.271.6 [*Exorcism of witch by counter-charm*]; G.273.6 [*Witch rendered powerless by drawing blood from her*]; G.211.2.7 [*Witch in form of hare*]; D.1385.4 [*Silver bullet protects against witches*].

NANNY PEARSON AND THE GOOSE
[summary]

R. Blakeborough, *Wit, Character, Folk-Lore and Customs of the North Riding of Yorkshire*, p 186.

Nanny Pearson had once been a Roman Catholic, so it was said. Anyhow, she became a witch, and used to go every day with an empty jug to Mrs Webster's farm, carrying away a full jug of milk with her.

At one time Mrs Webster had a goose sitting on a clutch of eggs by her fireside, and in the evening, when Nanny appeared with her jug, the goose flew up from her nest in great agitation, breaking two of her eggs. This happened each time Nanny appeared, and at last someone who happened to be going to Scarborough, called on the wise man there, and asked his advice. He told them to put a few drops of holy water in Nanny's milk, and her power would be broken. This was done the next day, and just as Nanny put out her hand to take the jug, the goose boldly flew up into her face, and knocked the jug out of her hand. It broke, and its contents were splashed over her face and gown; she fled with a shriek and never troubled that goose again.

MOTIF: G.271.2.2 [*Witch exorcized by holy water*].

OLD BETTY SPRY

S. Baring-Gould, *The Vicar of Morwenstow*, p. 158.

Farmer Brown was opposing a lecturer who maintained that witches and witchcraft were mere superstition:

"There was, t'other day, my cow Primrose, the Guernsey, and as gude a cow for milk as ever was. Well, on that day, when my missus put the milk on the fire to scald 'un, it wouldn't hot. She put on a plenty of wood, and turves, and brimmle bushes, but 'twouldn't hot, noways. And sez she to me as I came in, 'I'll tell ye what tez, Richard. Primrose has been overlooked by old Betty Spry. Now you go off as fast as you can to the White Witch up to Exeter.' Well, I did so, and when I came to the White Witch as lives nigh All Hallows on the Walls, I was shown into a room, and there was a farmer stamping about in just such a predicament as me. Sez I, 'Are you come to see the White Witch?' 'Ah!

that I be,' sez he. 'My old cow has fallen ill, and won't give no milk.' 'Why,' sez I, 'my cow's milk won't hot, and the missus has put a lot of fire underneath.' 'Do you suspect anybody?' sez he. 'I do,' sez I. 'There's old Betty Spry has an evil eye, and her's the one as has done it.' Just then the door opens and the maiden looks in, and sez, 'Mr Brown, the White Witch will speak with you.' And then I am shown into the next room. Well, directly I come in, he sez to me, 'I know what you've come for, before you speak. Your cow's milk won't scald. I'll tell y'why. She's been overlooked by an old woman named Betty Spry?' He said so to me, as sure as eggs is eggs, and I never told him not one word. 'Then,' sez he to me, 'you go home and get sticks out of four different parishes, and set them under the milk and her'll boil.'

"Well I paid 'un a crown, and then I came here, and I fetched sticks from Lew Trenchard, and from Stowford, and from German's Week, and from Broadwood Widger, and no sooner were they lighted under the pan than the milk boiled. . . .

"I'll give you another pinch of facts," said Farmer Brown. "Before I was married, I was going along by Culmit one day, when I met old Betty Spry, and she sez to me, 'Cross my hand with silver, my pretty boy, and I'll tell you who your true love will be!' So I thinks I'd like to know that, and I give her a sixpence. Then sez she, 'Mark the first maiden that you meet, as you go along the lane that leads to Eastway House. She's the one, that will make you a wife.' Well, I was going along that way, and the first maiden I met was Patience Kite. I thought she was comely and fresh-looking, so after going a few steps on, I turns my head over my shoulder, and looks back at her; and what in the world should she be doing at exactly the same minute, but looking back at me. Then I went after her, and said, 'Patience, will you be Mrs Brown?' and she said, 'I don't mind. I'm noways partickler.' And now she is my wife. Look at her yonder, as red as a turkey-cock; there she sits, and so you may know my story is true. But how did Betty Spry know this before ever I had spoken the word? That beats me."

MOTIFS: D.1814.1 [*Advice from magician*]; D.2083 [*Evil magic in the dairy*]; D.1812 [*Magic power of prophecy*].

¶ The Wise Woman of Hogsdon in Heywood's play of that name, uses the same method of overhearing her clients' conversations before she admits them to consultation.

OLD MADGE FIGGEY AND THE PIG

[summary]

Hunt, *Popular Romances of the West of England*, p. 332.

Madge Figgey, one of the most renowned of the St Levan witches, once moved to Burian Church-town. There, her neighbour, Tom Trenoweth, had a fine sow, which Madge coveted. It was worth a pound at least, but Madge's offer was five shillings. Tom said he had no mind to sell her to anyone; he was going to fatten her for himself, ready for the winter. Madge replied, "You will wish you had sold her."

Now the sow ceased to thrive, but, though the witch more than once repeated her offer, Tom sturdily refused to sell. But in time the creature, though eating more than ever, became so wasted that he decided to take her to Penzance market, and sell her for whatever he could get. At first she seemed almost too weak to walk, yet, as soon as they reached the high-road, the pig set off at a run, so fast that Tom could scarcely keep hold of her, and she never stopped till she came to Leah Lanes. Then she dropped to a walk, but nothing would make her go where Tom wanted, so he was forced to go her way. They came to Tregenebris Downs, and there the road divided, one part of it going to Penzance.

Tom again attempted to turn the pig in that direction; but she jerked her rope out of his hand, and set off again at a gallop, with Tom in pursuit.

She ran straight to Tregenebris Bridge, which is a sort of long drain, narrowing in the middle; and in the narrow part the sow stuck fast. Tom threw stones, and tried every means to get her out; they were there till nearly sunset, and Tom was just preparing to go home in despair of getting the animal out when Madge came along with her stick, and a market basket on her arm.

Seeing their plight, she asked Tom, "What will you sell her for now?"

"If you can get her out, take her!" Tom replied, "But have you any food in your basket?" He had eaten nothing since five in the morning.

Madge gave him a twopenny loaf, and called, "Cheat, cheat, cheat!" The sow came out of the ditch immediately, and followed her home like a dog.

MOTIFS: G.269.4 [*Curse by disappointed witch*]; D.2089.3.1 [*Swine magically kept from fattening*]; G.265.7.3*(b) [*Witch causes pig to drag its owner all over countryside, etc.*] (Baughman).

THE OUGHTREDS, THEIR HOB, AND PEGGY FLAUNDERS [summary]

R. Blakeborough, *Wit, Character, Folk-Lore and Customs of the North Riding of Yorkshire*, p. 196.

Even as late as the year 1820, the Oughtreds, whose farm was close to Hob Hill, at Upleatham, were greatly helped by a hobman from the near-by hill.

He turned their hay; drove their cattle to pasture and home again; winnowed their grain; topped and tailed their turnips; and much besides. But suddenly all this came to an end. It was thought that a man had left his coat hanging on the winnowing-machine, and forgotten it at the day's end; the Hob mistook this for an offering for himself and, in the manner of all Hobs, when offered clothing, he took offence.

However this might be, at the same time the family were so unfortunate as to incur the ill-will of the witch, Peggy Flaunders, though no one knew how. One evening there was a loud knocking at the back door. The maid went to open it, and saw a fearful thing, like a blazing pig, standing there. Forgetting to close the door, she rushed to her master and mistress, shrieking that the devil was standing on the back doorstep.

They rushed to the door, but it had stood open long enough to allow the evil thing to enter the house, and as they had feared, there was nothing there. But after that evening the house was haunted by disasters: their crockery was smashed, machinery broken, and their cattle died. In despair, they decided to move from the place; and, on their last evening there, a neighbour called in to ask the farmer if it was true that they were going away. A queer little head popped out from the top of the press, and a little voice squeaked, "Aye, we're gahin ti flt ti morn." But the farmer said, "Whya, if thoo's gahin wiv uz, it's teea neea ewse gahin; wa mud ez weel stop."

At last the farmer went to consult the wise man. He told them to pierce a live cock with pins and roast it at dead of night, with every door, window, or other crevice blocked up. By these means, Peggy's power, and the imp, were overcome.

TYPE ML.7020. MOTIFS: G.225.8 [*Minor devil as witch's familiar*]; G.225.0.3 [*Familiars do work for witch*]; G.303.3.3.1.5 [*Devil in form of swine*]; F.482.3.1.1 (variant) [*Farmer is so bothered by brownie that he decides to move, etc.*]; G.271.4.1 [*Exorcism by burning object for sympathetic magic*]; G.271.4.1(*db*) [*Burning live hen*] (Baughman).

¶ This is one of many cruel and grisly counter-spells used by witch-doctors and amateur magicians, which partly justified the witch-hunters in thinking the white witches as bad as the black.

PEGGY FLAUNDERS [summary]

R. Blakeborough, *Wit, Character, Folk-Lore and Customs of the North Riding of Yorkshire*, p. 168.

Peggy Flaunders, who died in 1835 at the age of eighty-five, used to wear a tall hat and a red cloak, and tales are still told of her tricks and miracles.

She cast a spell on Tom Pearson, and all his cattle died. He left his farm, and it was taken over by his cousin. This cousin had once befriended Peggy, and as he crossed the threshold for the first time she passed by, and called out: "Thou hast my good wishes." She turned round three times, threw her red cloak on the ground, jumped over it, mumbled some words, and walked away. From that time everything prospered with that farm and its owner.

Two neighbours, Hannah Rothwell and Mary Parker, went to consult the wise man of Upleatham, Jonathan Westcott; for three weeks Hannah's butter had refused to come, and Mary's cow had given but little milk.

Jonathan bade Mrs Rothwell scald out her churn three times: first with boiling water and salt; next with boiling water into which she had thrown some wicken berries; and last with a large quantity of boiling water alone. Then she must drive a small wicken-wood peg into each end of the churn, and pretend to look if the butter was coming, repeating as she did so:

> "This time it's thine,
> Next time it's mine,
> And mine for ever more."

This must be repeated nine times, with nine turns of the handle between each repetition, and then all would be well.

For the milk charm Jonathan consulted his almanac, and declared that, first, the cow must be given a drench, and not fully milked for nine days. On the tenth day, as she sat down to milk, Mary must whisper in the cow's ear: "I'm milking thee for Peggy Flaunders." This must be done every day, and if the cow still failed to yield the proper amount of milk, she would know that it was through no fault of Peggy Flaunders, and must either find some other cure or get rid of the cow.

Peggy had a son who one day went coursing with some sportsmen in the old close field at the top of Marske. The dogs put up a hare, which they recognized as one they had often tried in vain to catch before.

Peggy had told her son in secret that no hare could escape their own black bitch, and had warned him never to slip it at any hare without her consent. But in his excitement he forgot her words, and after an arduous chase the bitch caught the hare, just as it was trying to enter Peg's worral hole (a drain-pipe let in at the back of the fire for ventilation).

Later, when Peggy was examined, teeth-marks were found on her body in a part corresponding to the haunch of the hare where the bitch had bitten her.

MOTIFS: G.265.4.1 [*Witch causes death of animals*]; G.284 [*Witch as helper*]; D.2084.2 [*Butter magically kept from coming*]; D.2083.3 [*Milk transferred from another's cow by magic*]; G.271.6 [*Exorcism of witch by counter-charm*]; G.272.16.1 [*Salt put into churn before churning to protect cream from witch*]; G.271.11*(aa) [*Magic Herb: rowan; also known as wicken, etc.*] (Baughman); G.211.2.7.1 [*Witch as hare allows self to be coursed*]; G.303.3.3.1.1 [*Devil in form of dog*]; G.275.12(d, aa) [*Witch hare is injured by black hunting-dog*] (Baughman); G.275.12 [*Witch in form of animal is injured as a result of injury to the animal*].

THE PIG AND THE BUTCHER

Ruth L. Tongue, *Somerset Folklore*, pp. 78–9.

A widow living near Chard was certain that her pig had been bewitched by someone passing late on Midsummer Eve, for it had never thriven since that date. She set out rather timidly to ask the local conjuror's help, and hardly gone a quarter of a mile when she met him face to face. "I know what you do want," he said, "and I'll tell 'ee what to do 'bout it, and not a penny for it. Take the pig to the butcher."

Well, it was a great loss, but the widow thought she might save a little bacon, so off she went to the butcher. When the butcher saw her coming he turned pale, but when he saw the pig his eyes rolled in his head.

The widow had a good guess now who it was who had bewitched her pig, so she stood firm, whatever the butcher could say, and fairly forced him to take the knife to the pig. At the first cut such a sheet of flame came out of the beast's mouth, that everyone in the town came running. But all they ever found of the pig or the butcher were two cinders, so the widow was well rid of both of them.

Chard, 1909.
MOTIFS: G.265.4.2 [*Witch causes illness of animals*]; G.271.6 [*Exorcism of witch by counter-charm worked by white witch*] (Baughman); G.275.3.1 [*Witch burned by burning bewitched animal*]; D.1783.1 [*Magic results of reversing a spell*].
¶ This last motif is not an exact parallel, but the principle is clear: that the witch can be injured in the form of her victim, which has possibly been already consumed by the witch, and is only represented by a fading image, as is often the case with a fairy "stock".
See "The Trow-shot Coo" (B, V), "The Counter-charm".

PROFIT FROM THE FISH STORY

Shetland Folk-Book, II, p. 9.

James Omand lived at Vigon. His son was skipper of a fishing boat—
a very handsome man who dressed very well. They bought a new boat
and in the month of February built for themselves a new "lodge" with
a fireplace in it.

In May when they went to draw down their boat they found that the
"back-stane" and the "hert-stane" had both been removed from the
"lodge".

They guessed that someone wanted to harm them, and were not
surprised to find that they failed to get any fish on that or on subsequent
occasions.

When Johnsmas (the day on which the haaf-men held a foy. June
24th, new style) came they had hardly got any fish, and on Saturday
the crew went to look for bait while the skipper prepared the Johnsmas
supper. When the men returned they had only been able to get one sand
eel for bait. They were very disappointed, but Omand had prepared a
splendid supper at the "lodge".

On Sunday James Omand sent a message to one of the crew called
Lowrie requesting him to come to see him, which Lowrie hastened to do.

James said to him: "Lowrie am sent fir dee fir dir naøse spaekin' ta
me son, he only maks a deeresshon o' me. Der some-een taen de profit
o'wir fysh an' der nae hearm getting 'wir ain back agen. Do whit I
tell de an' de luck 'ill come back. Go du aerly i' di moarnin' afore dir
ony idder boddy ipo de beach an' mak dy watter troo de nile o' de boat
an pray at de sin may be apo de ill-willer."

Lowrie did as he was told, although he knew they had only one eel
for bait and that there was no use going to sea with that. By and by
all the other boats' crews arrived and went to sea, unless one small
boat which, for some reason, could not go that day. The skipper of this
boat offered Omand his bait, as his boat did not require it. Omand took
it thankfully and returned with 35 hundredweight of fish and the person
who had willed the harm was discovered, as from that day he caught
nothing.

MOTIFS: D.1449.4 [*Charm prevents fish being caught*]; G.271.6 [*Exorcism of witch
by counter-charm*].

THE SEER [summary]

J. Roby, *Lancashire Traditions*, I, p. 247.

Edward Kelly of Manchester was for long associated as seer with the famous Dr Dee, but they had many quarrels, and at last Kelly pursued his arts alone, and seldom visited his former master. They both had lodgings in the college, and on one of his rare visits to Dee, Kelly met there a handsome youth, whose parents had entrusted his education to the famous teacher. Many maidens fell in love with this newcomer, and among them the petulant, high-spirited daughter of Cornelius Ethelstoun, a merchant of high reputation in the city and abroad. She was too proud to own her love, and had rejected many suitors, to her father's great concern. He was driven by his anxiety to consult Kelly, who foretold that, if the girl were not married on St Bartlemy's Night, which was her birthday, her temper would never amend, and she would never find a husband. Returning with this warning, Cornelius confided in his faithful clerk, Timothy Dodge, a hunchback, who had served him for many years. Dodge procured a charm from Kelly, and when "Kate" (her real name is unknown) came down on the morning of her birthday, he gave her a knot of ribbon, bidding her throw it over her left shoulder, when it would write the first letter of her true love's name. Contemptuously, the girl obeyed, and snatched up the ribbon so quickly afterwards, that Timothy barely had time to make out the letter R, which was indeed the initial of Rodolf, the young man Kelly had met at Dr Dee's lodging.

At Mass that morning, Rodolf met Kate's eye, and her blush gave him hope, for he secretly loved her already. Returning to the college, he learnt from his page that Cornelius Ethelstoun was engaged with Kelly on some business, but that Kelly had desired to see him on his return. He entered Kelly's room, and found the two men in deep consultation, but the merchant left immediately, and Kelly then turned to the young man, and told him that a spirit had warned him that

> "The stranger that hither comes over the broad sea
> Shall wed on the night of St Bartlemy."

He bade Rodolf return at noon, when he would show him some further mysteries. He did so, and himself heard the same words chanted in a low tone, while in the dark chamber a dim form seemed to take shape, in the likeness of Kate, and gaze at him with a gentle, loving look such as he had never seen in her face before. This vision faded, and another showed him her father's hall, with Kate seated, and a lover kneeling at her feet.

The distracted youth now confessed his love to Kelly, who reassured him that the suitor he had seen was not of Kate's choosing. He disclosed also that it was of utmost importance that she should be married that very night; then bade him return once more at sunset, and in the meantime to keep away from Kate's home, or all would be undone.

He returned to the dark chamber, and, warned in a whisper by the magician, kept utter silence. Peering through a crevice, he saw Kate in another room, and saw the seer approach her and demand to know whether she had a lover. As she remained silent, he held before her a richly set miniature, which Rodolf recognized as his own likeness, though he had no knowledge that it had passed into Kelly's possession. At the sight, and the seer's solemn words, Kate's pride broke, and with tears she confessed her love, but she still feared that Rodolf had no heart for her. At this Rodolf flung open the door through which he had been peering, and found that it was indeed herself, and no vision. They were married that same night, and the doom was averted.

MOTIFS: N.845 [*Magician as helper*]; D.1825.1.2 [*Magic view of future lover*]; T.53 [*Match-makers*]; T.66 [*Help in wooing*].

¶ This is one of the more reputable actions recorded of Kelly, whose reputation was generally as bad as his character.

SET THE DOGS ON HER

Ruth L. Tongue, *Somerset Folklore*, p. 80.

An Exmoor farmer had such ill luck with his stock that he went to visit a conjuror thirty miles away. He was told that the old hag who had overlooked him would visit him and that he must be ready to do just what the conjuror told him. The farmer paid the conjuror and returned home to have his revenge. Now, there was a queer old soul in a little cottage up the lane, and when she was seen passing by, the farmer forgot all his instructions and yelled, "Set the dogs on her!" Even as he shouted and the dogs rushed out, his chair, a stout oak chair, rose in the air with him in it until it touched the ceiling. The dogs rushed in again howling and the chair descended; but the farmer had suffered a "fairy stroke", and never moved or spoke again for the rest of his life.

Either the conjuror's charms rebounded on the farmer because he had accepted money or the farmer in his rage had placed himself in danger by omitting any precautions. My informant, however, distrusted the conjuror. Her theory was that the old woman was a white witch, and the conjuror, being a black one, sought to destroy her through the farmer, but his magic rebounded. She was anxious to know if I could tell her what the conjuror's end was. She gave me his name, but as a branch of the family is still alive I cannot put it down.

MOTIFS: C.401 [*Tabu: speaking during certain time*]; D.1783.1 [*Magic results of reversing a spell*]; D.2072 [*Magic paralysis*].

THE SILVER SIXPENCE

H. Henderson, School of Scottish Studies.

There was an old farmer who had a fine herd of cattle, but they gave no milk. At last he asked a wise woman, and she said someone must be milking the cows, and he had better watch in the byre at night. So the old man lay in the byre, but always at midnight a drowsiness would come over him, and he would fall asleep. So at last he made up his mind that he must stay awake, and at midnight the byre door creaked open a little crack, and a brown hare came into the byre, and went from stall to stall. So the next night the old farmer watched again, and he took his gun, and loaded it with a silver sixpence and waited till midnight. In came the hare, and lolloped from stall to stall, and when she got to the door, the farmer took aim and fired, he only hit her front paw, but she gave a great scream, and a flood of milk came out of her, and she scampered away. The next morning the farmer went to see an old woman that lived near. The door was shut, and her granddaughter came to it. "You'll no can see Grannie," she said. "She's ill. She's hurt her hand." "That'll no prevent her seeing me," said the farmer. "An old neighbour like me." He went in, and found the old wife sitting by the fire, with her hand all bundled up.

"Let's look at your hand, Maggie woman," said the old farmer. "Maybe I can cure it." He unwrapped the bandages, and sure enough there was a wound in it, and in the middle of the wound there was a bent silver sixpence. The farmer's cows gave good milk after that.

From Jeannie Robertson.
TYPE ML.3055. MOTIFS: D.655.2 [*Witch transforms self to hare so as to suck cows*]; D.1385.4 [*Silver bullet protects against witches*]; G.275.12 [*Witch in the form of an animal is injured as a result of injury to the animal*].
¶ See "The Witch Hare", "Jane Wood of Basedale".

SPINNING JENNY

W. H. Barrett, *More Tales from the Fens*, p. 129.

Jenny was always called Spinning Jenny because she used to twist about on her toes whenever she talked to anyone. She lived out in the fen in a broken-down, thatched hovel all alone, except for the jackdaws in the chimney and the pigeons under the eaves.

She shared her bed with about a dozen cats, but she never let any of them touch a bird. Living like that, of course, everyone said she must be a witch, and the squire's lady knew she was, and I'll tell you why. She was driving in her carriage one day through the village, when she passed Jenny, who, as usual, had a jackdaw perched on her shoulder. Suddenly the bird caught sight of the cherries bobbing up and down on the lady's bonnet, so it flew at them and pulled them off. The coachman, turning round on his box when he heard his mistress scream, gave Jenny a couple of lashes with his whip and then drove off to the Hall, with the squire's lady half-dead with fright.

When she felt a bit better she told her husband how Jenny's jackdaw had flown at her, so he sent for his gamekeeper and told him to see that all the daws round Jenny's shack were killed.

"I can't do that," said the keeper. "Why, I'd rather lose my trigger finger than shoot one of those birds. You see, I have to be out a lot at night, all on my own, and I don't like to think what might happen to me if Jenny found out what I'd done. After all, I don't want my old woman to be a widow yet."

"I never thought I'd keep a dog and have to bark myself," said the squire, "but if you won't, then I will." And in no time at all he was potting away at the daws on Jenny's roof.

When Jenny heard the shots she came out of the cottage, with all the cats rushing about her feet, scared stiff by the shots. So, after he'd finished off the daws, the squire began on the cats, while Jenny screamed curses at him and told him that his dog, which was mauling her biggest tabby, would get his share of the curses too.

That night the squire was kept awake by his dog howling its head off. This went on for a week until, fed-up with getting no rest, he told the keeper to shoot the dog and put it out of its misery. So the gamekeeper took the dog down into the wood, chained it to a tree and then took up his gun. He was raising it to take aim, though, when he found he had no strength in his arm, so he put the gun down again. His arm seemed all right then, but when he tried to fire a second time the same thing happened. While he was doing this, the squire was going round the estate and came across Jenny. She dropped him a curtsy and said:

"Make the most of being on your feet while you're able to be."

That put him a real bad temper, which got even worse when he met the keeper who told him:

"If you want the dog shot you'll have to do it yourself. I can't."

"All right. I *will* do it, and with your gun," said the squire, and hurried through the wood. But he hadn't gone far along the path when he caught his foot in a rabbit snare and fell flat on his face. There was a loud bang and, when the keeper rushed up, he found his master cursing and groaning with his foot shattered. On the way to get help he passed Jenny, who shouted after him:

"Well, does squire swear on his back as well as he does on his feet?"

When he got to the stable-yard, the keeper told the coachman to hurry up and harness a horse to a cart and then they'd both go back to fetch the master, who was badly hurt.

While the coachman was doing this, the keeper picked up a cast shoe and put it in his pocket, thinking he'd feel a lot safer with a bit of iron about him as a safeguard. Then he and the coachman set off for the wood. They found, when they got there, that the dog had broken its chain and was standing over its master, licking his hands; and while the squire was carried along the path the dog followed behind. Jenny was waiting for them at the gateway leading from the wood to the road, and as they passed by she threw something on to the squire's face. He managed to get his hand up to take it off and then he saw that it was the skin of the tabby cat that the dog had mauled. The dog didn't see Jenny till it was through the gateway, and when it did it let out a howl of terror, and flew off down the road. No one ever saw it in day-light again, but young couples walking in the wood after dusk often heard the rattling of its chain.

Well, the squire got better, but he wasn't able to walk without a stick. He used to sit all day in his chair, and, for hour after hour, he'd hear the scraping of a dog-chain on the gravel drive, but he never saw the dog. Then the shepherd lost his collie bitch, and folk said they'd seen it making for Hangman's Wood. A few weeks later the sound of puppies yelping came from the wood, but no one could gather up courage to go and look for them.

The squire's troubles weren't over, though, by a long way. There was hardly a morning when he wasn't told of his sheep or calves being found killed and half-eaten, until he couldn't stand it any longer and sold all his livestock. Then, one day, as he looked out of his window, he saw Jenny outside. She pointed first at the house and then at the outbuildings and then at him and shouted:

"It won't be long before there won't be a brick on top of another here; everything you have will go. The house will tumble down and where it stood will be a great pond and you'll be the slimiest eel at the bottom of it."

Then she went off to the stables, where the coachman, when he saw her coming, went out to meet her, waving his biggest whip. But Jenny just stood still and pointed, and the whip flew out of his hand, and he saw it slither across the yard, and coil up like a snake at her feet.

"I can see you swinging at the end of a halter," she shouted, "but that won't be till your pal, the keeper, has borrowed a length of cord."

On her way home she passed the keeper, who was coming to ask the coachman to lend him a length of whipcord for a snare. He hid under a bush when he saw Jenny, but she called out to him:

"A halter and a gun are funny things to play with."

When she had gone the keeper came out from under the bush and went on to the stable yard, borrowed the cord and set off toward the wood. But about an hour later the coachman heard a loud bang in the hayloft, and when he went to see what was amiss, he found the keeper had tied the whipcord to the trigger of his gun, put the barrel in his mouth and blown the top of his head off. This so upset the coachman that he tied a halter to a beam, climbed on to the corn bin, put the running noose round his neck and jumped.

Two days afterwards one of the servants found the squire's two sticks, which he just managed to hobble round the house with, lying by the lake, and no sign of the squire.

The house and gardens and the woods were searched and even the lake was dragged, but it had too much mud at the bottom, and the squire was never found. Jenny, too, disappeared a day or two later. Not long after she'd gone an old man, living out in the fen, heard a woman screaming one night, and a dog baying. In the morning, not far from his house, he found some blood-stained bits of rag lying beside the body of a great dog which had been strangled with its chain.

You want to know if Jenny's curse came true? Well, it did. Everything that the squire had owned went to waste, and now there's only nettles and weeds and bits of brick, and a pond which is still called "Squire's Lake".

MOTIFS: M.411.12 [*Curse by witch*]; D.2061.2.4 [*Death by cursing*]; Q.556 [*Curse as punishment*].

¶ See "Club-footed Aggie".

THE STRANGE SHIP AT PAPA STOUR

Shetland Folk-Book, II, p. 15.

A foreign ship came once into Housa Voe, Papa Stour. Not one of the crew could speak English except the cabin-boy. One day he overheard the sailors plotting to burn the houses and plunder the isle.

As his sympathies were entirely with the Papa folk, some of whom had been very kind to him, when he came ashore he revealed the plot to the Papa men, beseeching them not to betray him, as he would assuredly be killed by the crew.

As they had little or no means of defence, the Papa men, in their dilemma, went to an old "witchie" wife and asked her advice. "Der a mukkle ox ipo Fugla Skerry," said she. "If ye gie me de 'Stickin' piece dan Stak-a-baa sall mount de heigher an de ship sall niver hurt you. Only ye maun first secure your coarn, houses and boats an' dan lat me ken whan your düne."

When the Papa man had done this, a small cloud appeared in the north-west which developed into a terrific gale, during which the ship was overwhelmed and the whole crew, with the exception of the cabin-boy, perished.

MOTIFS: G.284 [*Witch as helper*]; G.283.1.2.3 [*Witch raises wind to sink ships of people who have injured her*].

SUNNY CLARA'S CURSE

W. H. Barrett, *More Tales from the Fens*, p. 137.

I'd never have had this story to tell you if Sunny Clara (she was always called Sunny because she was so miserable-looking) hadn't gone into Darky Theobald's wheelwright's shop one day. He was making a wheel for a gig and was trueing up the felloe with hand and eye—a tricky job—when he heard Sunny muttering behind him. So he turned round and shouted at her: "Get out of here, you misbegotten mawther," because Darky loved using long words. When it was his turn to preach in chapel, he'd have everyone gawping at him, wondering what in the world he was talking about.

Sunny took no notice of him, so he gave her a push and sent her sprawling on the floor among the shavings. So, muttering away more than ever, she scrambled up and then walked over to the wheel, spat on her finger and drew a circle round the hub while she called out:

> "Hubs, spokes and rim
> Will never be trim;
> Ash, oak and elm
> I condemn.
> Whoever rides above that wheel
> Will all his days my curses feel,"

and then walked away.

When Darky had finished the wheel he trundled it across to the smithy to be tyred. The smith and he spent all the afternoon getting the tyre to fit, because every time they cooled it down they found there were places where it didn't fit. At last, the smith was so hot and tired that he went down to the inn to cool down while Darky, who was a teetotaller, quenched his thirst in the river. Then they both had another go at the wheel, but still the tyre wouldn't fit.

By this time it was getting late, so the smith threw down his hammer, and told Darky to take the wheel away and make the best do of it he could.

"We can't go on with it any more tonight, anyway," he said, "because no tyre will stay on if it's fixed after sunset; leastways, that's what my old grandfather used to tell me."

Darky took the wheel back to his shop and filled in the spaces, where the tyre didn't fit, with putty, then painted it over so it didn't show. He made such a good job of it that when the farmer, who'd ordered the gig, brought his horse to drive it home, he said it was a first-rate piece of work. He put the cob in the shafts and drove off, and the cob trotted along as if it was proud of the shining, new gig behind it. But it didn't see Widow Mann's pig lying asleep in the middle of the road; it was a sudden jolt which made the farmer think they'd run over something, but he didn't bother to stop.

Now, the farmer owned Widow Mann's house, so when he called, a few days later, to take her rent, she told him that, as he'd killed the pig which was to pay the rent, he wouldn't get any. This put him in a furious temper, because he hated losing money, so he whipped up his horse and drove off up the road at a furious pace. Sunny Clara happened to be sitting by the roadside, so she scrambled up out of the way. This brought the horse to a sudden stop, which sent the farmer over the dashboard and into the road, where he lay groaning with a broken shoulder and a cracked rib or two. Sunny called out to some men who were working in a field nearby, to fetch a hurdle and take the farmer home; then she went over to the gig and scratched two marks on the new, shiny paint.

When the men came with the hurdle and put the farmer on it, he was so heavy that it broke and let him down on the road again. So the men took a gate off its hinges and put him on that, and when they'd carried him away Sunny picked up the broken hurdle for fire-wood. As she passed the wheelwright's shop, she poked her head in and called out:

"Darky, the wheel's started turning."

When the farmer was on his feet again, he went into the stable yard one day, and found Sunny staring at the sides of the gig where she'd put the scratches.

"Get you out of here," shouted the farmer, "and stop using my gig as a looking-glass. Though, with a face like yours, I don't know what you expect to see."

"I've seen all I want to see, thank you," said Sunny, "and that's a picture of you in your coffin, you old skinflint."

When he'd threshed his harvest, the farmer drove to market with some corn samples in little bags. Trade was a bit slow, though, and he tramped from one corn merchant to another, but still by the end of the day, he'd only sold one sample. He drove home in a rage, and after swearing at the groom, who was waiting in the yard for him, climbed out of the gig. As he did so, he staggered and fell down. The groom carried him indoors, and the doctor was sent for, but all he could do was to tell the wife she was now a widow.

The doctor saw that the dead farmer was still clutching one of his sample bags, and when he took it out of his hand it burst, and all the sample scattered on the floor. The wife stared at it and then said:

"That's funny; whyever did he take tares to sell?" and, do you know, when she looked in the other bags there wasn't one had corn in, only tares.

After the funeral the farmer's widow had to get out of the farm and sell up everything. At the sale was a gipsy and when he saw the gig he took a real fancy to it.

He was just wondering if he'd make a bid for it when he saw Sunny go up to it and make a scratch on it. When she'd gone he went over to look, and then he saw the other scratches.

He was scratching his head over this when along came Darky, who opened his shut knife and began jabbing at a wheel just under the tyre. The gipsy couldn't make head or tail of all this, so he decided to fetch some of his tribe to see if they could. As they came along, Sunny walked over to the trap, stroked the spokes of one of the wheels, then pulled out a rag from her pocket and rubbed the paint off the putty that Darky had put in.

"Let's get out of here," said the gipsy's grandmother, "before that old witch starts doing the same to us as she's doing to that cart."

When the gig was put up for sale, the smith bought it for four pounds ten. When he'd got it back to the smithy he thought he'd have another look at the wheel which had been so bothersome. But he'd hardly got hold of it than the tyre came off and knocked him backwards, and as he fell the heavy iron hoop fell too. It wasn't till next morning that someone found him, lying on his back with the edge of the tyre pressing on his throat.

After he'd been buried, it wasn't long before Sunny was scratching away again at the gig, which now belonged to the innkeeper. When he went outside to see what she was up to, he found four straight lines, with another straight down across them, cut in the wood. He didn't like this at all, especially when he remembered what had happened to the two other people who'd had that gig; so he thought the best thing to do was to chop it up for firewood. He was just doing this when Sunny came up and asked him to sell her one of the side panels.

"Pick out what you like," he said.

So she picked up the bit with her tally marks on it and thanked him, because she wasn't used to folks being so nice to her.

A week afterwards it was Darky's turn to preach in the chapel. After he'd finished speaking he went to sit down, but he'd no sooner done that than he was up again, looking at the seat and shouting at the top of his voice:

"Blast that old devil. May she burn in Hell, and this too," and he held up Sunny's side panel from the gig, with rows of tacks stuck in it. Everyone stopped singing and began to laugh, and the more they laughed the more Darky swore and cursed, so that when the chapel people got home they all began talking about it and wondering where Darky had learned to swear like that. Two evenings later the deacons sent for him to ask him about those words. Darky said it was Sunny who had cast a spell over him; it hadn't really been him speaking, but those devils she'd put inside him. As he said this, they heard someone laughing outside the vestry door, and when they opened it there stood Sunny.

Darky dived forward to get at her, but two of the biggest deacons got hold of him and hurled him out on to the road, where he lay, still cursing and swearing. And I can tell you this: never again would the chapel people let him preach.

MOTIFS: M.411.12 [*Witch's curse*]; G.263 [*Witch injures, enchants, or transforms*].

A TAUNTON WHITE WITCH

Ruth L. Tongue, *Somerset Folklore*, p. 77.

"In a farm where granddad worked [Nailesbourne Farm, Mr Biffin] they made cheese and butter. They had a lot of girls then, as they do, and every time they tried to make the butter it wouldn't come. Well, anyway, they sent to Taunton to Billy Brewer, who lived in St James Street, and he came out and went to the farm, and they explained what had happened, the butter wouldn't come. And he had all the girls there that were working there, looked around and walked in, and said to the farmer (and said about a particular girl), 'You get rid of her. She's evil!' After this girl was gone everything was all right. No more trouble with the butter-making."

From Mrs Lowman, carter's wife (70), Kingston St. Mary, 1935.
MOTIF: G.220.0.1 [*"Black" and "White" witches*]; D.2084.2 [*Butter magically kept from coming*]; N.845 [*Magician as helper*]; D.1814.1 [*Advice from magician*].
¶ See "Peggy Flaunders".

THE TELL-TALE SWORD

Augustus Hare, *In My Solitary Life*, p. 263.

A young girl...was with a number of other girls, foolish and frivolous, who went to consult an old woman who had the reputation of being a witch, and who was supposed to have the power of making them see their future husbands.

She said they must say their prayers backwards, perform certain incantations with water, lock their doors when they went to bed, and then they would see whom they were to marry, but they would find their doors locked in the morning.

The girl followed all the witch's directions. Then she locked her door, went to bed, and waited. Gradually, by the firelight, a young man seemed to come in—to come straight through the locked door—a young man in uniform; she saw him distinctly. He went to the end of the room and returned. As he passed the bed, his sword caught in the curtain, and fell upon the floor. Then he seemed to pass out. The girl fainted.

In the morning at first she thought it was a dream, but there, though her door was still locked, lay the actual sword upon the floor! Greatly aghast, she told no one, but put it away, and kept it hidden. It was a terrible possession to her.

The following year, at a country-house, she met the very young man she had seen. They fell violently in love, and were married. For one year they were intensely—perfectly—happy. Then her husband's regiment had to change its quarters. As she was packing up, with horror which was an instinct, she came upon the sword put away among her things. Just then, before she could hide it, her husband came in. He saw the sword, turned deadly pale, and in a stern voice said, "How did you come by that?" She confessed the whole truth.

He was rigid. He said, "I can never forgive it. I can never see you again," and nothing she could say or do could move him. "Do you know where I passed that terrible night?" he said. "I passed it in *Hell!*" He has given up three-quarters of his income to her, but she has never seen him since.

MOTIFS: D.1812.2 [*Power of prophecy induced*]; D.1812.3 [*Means of learning future*]. ¶ These spells to force the appearance of the future bridegroom are believed to be very painful to the man forced to appear.

See "The Spectre Bridegroom" (B, VI).

TOADS ON THE ROAD

Ruth L. Tongue, *Somerset Folklore*, pp. 75–6. Lucott, 1945.

A farmer's wife I knew had words with a black witch who lived at Countisbury, just over the Devon border. She was a redoubtable soul, and determined to outface the old woman, witch or no. She mounted the pony and rode across Lucott Moor, and to Windwhistle Corner to County Gate. A little way beyond this the pony refused, and when she looked for a reason she found the road was swarming with toads. The further she tried to go the more there were. She turned the pony for home, and, when she reached Yenworthy, dismounted to get over her scare. A local tradesman's van drew up beside her, coming from Countisbury. Toads in the road? What toads? He'd seen her in the distance turn her pony back towards Porlock, and he'd caught her up in under five minutes, but there were no toads.

Apparently repeating this tale to me awakened her resentment again, for a little later I rode past her in a lane, hammering a blacksmith's nail into a footprint in the dust, and went by discreetly on the other side of the hedge. I never mentioned the matter, and all I was told about it, some time later, was that the old witch was dead.

MOTIFS: G.225.4 [*Toad(s) as witch's familiar(s)*]; G.271.4.6(*b*) [*Breaking spell by sticking nail into tracks of witch*] (Baughman).
¶ See "The Blacksmith's Nail".

TOMMY LINDUM

E. H. Rudkin, *Folk-Lore*, December 1955, p. 398.

At Lindholme lived a hermit, William of Lindholme, described in the Bishop's Visitations as "gent"; he built himself a chapel of stone, with an altar at one end and a hearth at the other. When the time came for him to die he dug a grave before the hearth, lowered himself into it, and let down a large freestone slab, so practising self-burial. In 1727 this chapel was falling down; the grave was opened by the Rev. Samuel Wesley of Epworth, and Mr Stovin, and was found to contain a few human bones of a tall man, an oval piece of beaten copper and a peck of hemp-seed. Whether this hermit was the original of the popular local hero affectionately spoken of as Tommy Lindum, or whether the island had been previously inhabited by this magician is difficult to say, for the two are so mixed up in the local mind.

At an early age Tommy discovered his unusual powers. Stories about him have been published, but I should like to call a few to mind. It was in July and Wroot Feast was in full swing, some two miles distant. His Father was going to the Feast, and he left Tommy at home to tent the sparrows on the corn. This did not suit Tommy at all, who also wanted to go to the feast; in a rage he took up a large boulder stone and threw it at Wroot. He found another huge stone and threw it at their house, but it went right over the house, and was afterwards known as the Thumb Stone;—the stone that went towards Wroot was the "Little Finger Stone". Next he put all the sparrows in the barn, shut the doors and put harrows up at the windows, and off he went to the Feast. In time he came face to face with his father, who was very angry with him for neglecting the tenting. Tommy said that the sparrows were safe, as they were all in the barn. Next morning his father opened the barn doors: most of the sparrows inside were dead, and those that survived were white—and up to thirty years ago there were always one or two white sparrows to be found in that vicinity.

It was very wet going from Wroot to Lindholme, and Tommy undertook to make a road if a rider on a horse would gallop from one place to another without looking behind him. This seemed an easy task, and a rider came forward; he started off well, but the noise behind him was so awful that he looked behind him—and he saw the air thick with stones flying in all directions and little black imps macadamising as hard as they could. "God speed your work!" said the terrified rider, and immediately the work stopped, and the road remains unfinished to this day.

Tommy's mother became a widow and worked for a local farmer, who said that she could fetch some straw for her pig. She asked Tommy to go and get this; he said that he would if she would get him a wagon rope. The rope was found, and Tommy set off to the farmyard, where he proceeded to throw the rope round a whole straw-stack. The other men in the yard jeered at him, but not for long, for Tommy tied his rope and walked off with the stack upon his back.

Tommy once did some work for a farmer, who went into the field to see how he was getting on with the ploughing; the farmer's only criticism was, "You can go deeper." Next day he went to see if his order had been carried out, and "Believe it or no, boath Tommy *and* his 'osses was so deep that moles was runnin' in 'is smock pockets!"

MOTIFS: D.2072.0.2.2.1 [*Person charged with keeping birds from crops confines them in barn*]; G.303.9.1.7 [*Devil builds road*]; F.624.5 [*Strong man lifts ton of rye*]. ¶ See "William of Lindholm" (B, III).

THE TWO FELLOWS

Maurice Fleming, School of Scottish Studies.

There were two fellows who worked in a manse glebe. The one of them was stout and fat, but he was always weary. One night the thin one happened to be awake late, and he heard someone coming into the bothy where they slept. It was a woman, and she put a bridle over the fat one's head, and he started up, a fine plump horse, and she rode away on him. Just at cockcrow she brought him back, took the bridle off him, and left him exhausted. His fellow said nothing, but next night he changed places with him, and lay awake, waiting. When the woman came in, he pretended to be asleep, but when she came up to the side of the bed, he started up, snatched the bridle out of her hand, and put it on her own head. And there beside him stood a beautiful white mare. The lad got on her back, and if the horse had been ridden fast and far the night before, the mare was ridden faster and farther that night. On the way back he passed a smithy, and saw the smith working early. "I've just bought this fine white mare," he said, "but I'm not sure of the shoes; will you just shoe it all round for me?" So the mare was new-shod all round, and the lad rode her back to the Manse, and hitched her up at the gate, while he had his breakfast.

The Minister was looking everywhere for his lady. It seemed she had risen early, gone out, and was not back yet. "Come with me," said the lad. "Maybe I can show you where she is." He led the way down to the gate, and snatched the bridle off the white mare, and there was the Minister's lady, with horse-shoes nailed to her hands and feet.

TYPE ML.3C55. MOTIFS: D.535 [*Transformation to horse by putting on bridle*]; G.241.2.1 [*Witch transforms man to horse and rides him*]; G.211.1.1 [*Witch in form of horse*]; G.211.1.1.2 [*Witch as horse shod with horse-shoes*]; G.275.12 [*Witch in form of an animal is injured as result of the injuries done to the animal*].

¶ It is interesting to see that this tale has survived in oral tradition, and is virtually the same in plot as that given by Douglas from William Henderson.

See "The Blacksmith's Wife of Yarrowfoot", "The Witch's Bridle".

THE TWO MAGICIANS

Child, *The English and Scottish Popular Ballads*, I, p. 402.

1. The lady stands in her bower door,
   As straight as willow wand;
   The blacksmith stood a little forbye,
   Wi hammer in his hand.

2. "Weel may ye dress ye, lady fair,
    Into your robes o' red;
Before the morn at this same time,
    I'll gain your maidenhead."

3. "Awa, awa, ye coal-black smith,
    Woud ye do me the wrang
To think to gain my maidenhead,
    That I hae kept sae lang!"

4. Then she has hadden up her hand,
    And she sware by the mold,
"I wudna be a blacksmith's wife,
    For the full o' a chest o' gold.

5. "I'd rather I were dead and gone,
    And my body laid in grave,
Ere a rusty stock o' coal-black smith
    My maidenhead shoud have."

6. But he has hadden up his hand,
    And he sware by the Mass,
"I'll cause ye be my light leman
    For the hauf o' that and less

    O bide, lady, bide,"
        And aye he bade her bide;
    The rusty smith your leman shall be,
        For a' your muckle pride.

7. Then she became a turtle dow,
    To fly up in the air,
And he became another dow,
    And they flew pair and pair.

    O bide, lady, bide,
        And aye he bade her bide;
    The rusty smith your leman shall be,
        For a' your muckle pride.

8. She turnd hersell into an eel,
    To swim into yon burn,
And he became a speckled trout,
    To gie the eel a turn.
    O bide, lady, bide, etc.

9. Then she became a duck, a duck,
   To puddle in a peel,
   And he became a rose-kaimd drake,
   To gie the duck a dreel.
      O bide, lady, bide, etc.

10. She turnd hersell into a hare,
    To rin upon yon hill,
    And he became a gude greyhound,
    And boldly he did fill.
       O bide, lady, bide, etc.

11. Then she became a gay grey mare,
    And stood in yonder slack,
    And he became a gilt saddle,
    And sat upon her back

    Was she wae, he held her sae,
    And still he bade her bide;
    The rusty smith her leman was,
    For a' her muckle pride.

12. Then she became a het girdle,
    And he became a cake,
    And a' the ways she turnd hersell,
    The blacksmith was her make.
       Was she wae, etc.

13. She turnd hersell into a ship,
    To sail out ower the flood;
    He ca'ed a nail intill her tail,
    And syne the ship she stood.
       Was she wae, etc.

14. Then she became a silken plaid,
    And stretcht upon a bed,
    And he became a green covering,
    And gaind her maidenhead.
       Was she wae, etc.

MOTIF: D.615.3 [*Transformation combat between lover and maid*].
¶ See "The King of the Black Art" (A, II).

THE UNBIDDEN GUEST

J. Bowker, *Goblin Tales of Lancashire*, p. 37.

"Owd Jeremy" lived in a wretched hovel in a lane leading from the town of Clitheroe. He had the reputation of being a wizard, and claimed to be on familiar terms with the Evil One, and to be able to foretell men's destinies by his help. This cottage was furnished with all the apparatus of a wizard, and would strike awe into those who came to consult Jeremy; but in fact he was a charlatan, and had no faith in the powers he so often invoked.

For all his strange and solitary existence, Jeremy loved the world outside his home, and one day, when an inquirer had just left the cottage, he stood gazing out of the window towards Pendle, and thinking of its ancient beauty, so much more powerful and enduring than the life of a man, and as he turned back to the darkness of the cottage, he saw a stranger sitting in the clients' seat, who said to him, "Devildom first, and poetizing afterwards."

"What do you want?" said Jeremy.

"Security," said the stranger. "For five and twenty years you have been duping fools in my name, and amassing wealth for yourself, and now I want my share."

Jeremy pointed to his poverty-stricken abode, for, in spite of his reputed lore, he remained very poor, but already he suspected who his dreadful visitor was, and, rising in his agitation, he saw from the window that darkness had suddenly fallen, and a terrible clap of thunder broke over the cottage at the same moment. In panic Jeremy murmured, "What security do you seek?"

The stranger produced a written bond, and demanded Jeremy's signature, but the sturdy old man refused to sign. Then the Devil threatened that by the next day he should have a rival who would take the bread out of his mouth, and expose all his pretences and sham wisdom. But if he signed the bond, he was to have twenty-two years of life and success such as he had never dreamed of.

But still Jeremy, after deep thought stoutly refused to sign. The visitor departed, the storm abated, and the sun shone again.

But for five days no one came to Jeremy's house, and when at last he crept out to buy food, the people he passed, instead of shrinking from him in terror, called out jeering remarks, and children went on with their games, as though they had never feared him in their lives.

Next day a shower of stones broke old Jeremy's window, but no one else came to the house, and at last he cried aloud in his misery, "I wish I had another chance!"

Immediately there was a loud burst of thunder, and there sat his visitor as before, with the parchment on the table in front of him.

"Are you ready to sign?" he demanded.

"I cannot write."

The devil seized him by one finger, which he used as a pen, and made a neat X writing beside it, "Jeremiah Parsons, his mark."

He disappeared as mysteriously as he had come, and almost at once a man knocked at the door, wishing to have his future declared to him. He told Jeremy that he had first tried the new wizard's house in Clitheroe, but found it completely deserted. All fell out as the Devil had foretold. For twenty-two years Jeremy's fame continued to soar, till after one wild night, his cottage was discovered in ruins, and no trace of him remained.

MOTIFS: G.303.6.3.1 [*Devil is followed by a thunderstorm*]; G.303.9.4 [*The Devil as a tempter*]; M.211 [*Man sells soul to Devil*]; G.275.1 [*Witch carried off by Devil*]. ¶ This tale illustrates a declension often stressed by the seventeenth-century writers on witchcraft, the steps by which a man, from using the Devil as a tool, descends to signing the diabolic contract.

See "Nancy Camel".

THE WEAVER'S WIFE AND THE WITCH

S. O. Addy, *Household Tales*, p. 43.

Once upon a time a weaver and his wife lived at Sutton-on-Trent in Nottinghamshire. One day the weaver went to Newark to sell his linen, leaving his children in the house, and his wife, who lay ill in bed. Now, at that time there lived at Sutton a witch who had some spite against the weaver's wife. A short time after the weaver had gone one of the children heard a noise, as of something pattering up and down stairs. The child opened the door of the bottom stairs, and there she saw a great ugly cat, which she could not catch, try as she would. As she was trying to catch it, the cat ran upstairs, sprang upon the bed, where the poor woman lay, and clawed her. But the woman roused herself, and knocked the cat down. Now, when the weaver came back from Newark, the children told him about the cat. So he watched all night in an old lumber-room, for the cat came in and went out through a broken pane in the window.

One night the cat came in as the weaver was sitting by the fire, so he picked up a fork, and struck her on the cheek. He then threw her out of doors, believing she was dead. But in the morning, when he went to look for the cat's body, he could not find it. But ever after that the witch had her face tied up, and she had no more power to do harm to the weaver or to his family.

Nottinghamshire.

TYPE ML.3055. MOTIFS: G.211.1.7 [*Witch in form of cat*]; G.275.12 [*Witch in form of an animal is injured or killed as a result of injury to the animal*].

¶ See "The Witch Hare".

THE WHITE WITCH OF EXETER

J. R. W. Coxhead, *Legends of Devon*, p. 149.

At one time a very famous white witch lived in Exeter. People who considered they had been "overlooked" by someone, or were victims of the "evil eye", came from long distances to consult her, in the hope that she might be able to help them in their trouble.

In South Devon there lived a certain man and his wife, who were having a long run of bad luck. They strongly suspected that a relative of the wife had cast an evil spell over them. The wife made the journey to Exeter and consulted the white witch, who at once confirmed the woman's suspicions and named the person who was the cause of all the misfortune.

The white witch told her client that the spell could very easily be broken if she and her husband were to do exactly as she said.

The remedy she prescribed was a queer one. The good people were to go to a butcher's shop and buy a large bullock's heart. Just before midnight they were to bolt and shutter all the doors and windows in the house with the greatest care, and then put the bullock's heart into the fire. The vindictive woman who had bewitched them would then come to the house in great haste, and use every effort to break in. If she succeeded in making an entry, the evil spell would continue to operate, so it was of the utmost importance that she should be kept out.

The couple quickly carried out the white witch's instructions, and awaited the result with bated breath. As the bullock's heart started to burn, a great clamour broke out, the windows were rattled and the doors were heavily beaten upon. The relative who practised the black art was raging round the building, trying to gain an entry.

The terrified man and his wife, hoping only that their doors and windows would hold, watched the burning heart. Gradually all was consumed, and with the fading of the final wisp of smoke a great stillness fell on the house. The spell was at an end, and the evil woman outside had departed with her power broken.

This is one of the few stories encountered by the author in which a bullock's heart has been burnt in order to break an evil spell, but he has heard of several cases where the heart has been hung in a shed or out-building and completely stuck all over with pins.

MOTIFS: G.220.0.1 [*"Black" and "White" witches*]; G.271.6 [*Exorcism of witch by counter-charm worked by "white witch"*] (Baughman); G.271.4.1(*aa*) [*Burning heart of cow or bullock to break spell of witch*] (Baughman).

¶ In this case the spell was broken, but the witch herself was not injured, as was supposed to happen in some cases.

See "The Pig and the Butcher", "Marshall's Elm". (B. VIII).

THE WHITE WIZARD OF PRESTON WYNNE

E. M. Leather, *Folk-Lore of the Shire: the Memorials of Old Herefordshire*, pp. 148–66.

A curious story is told of a visit he once paid to the "Buck" Inn at Woonton, where he had a meal. When he asked what he should pay, the landlady said, "Fourpence for eat, fourpence for drink—eightpence on the whole." The old farmer considered this too much—perhaps it was in those days; so he placed the money in the centre of the table on a piece of paper, and drew a line round it with a piece of chalk. When the landlady tried to take it, she began to run round and round the table, unable to stop, saying, "Fourpence for eat, fourpence for drink—eightpence on the whole." The servant came in and tried to reach the money, but the spell came upon her also, and she ran round after her mistress, repeating the same words. The ostler next made an attempt, with the like result. Another servant went out to the yard, where the wizard was just leading out his horse, and told him what was going on. He said, "You take the money with a pair of tongs—that'll stop 'em." And so it did.

MOTIFS: D.1272 [*Magic circle*]; G.269.21 [*Witch torments person by making him act in a ridiculous manner*]; G.272.1 [*Steel powerful against witches*].

THE WIGGIN STICK

S. O. Addy, *Household Tales*, p. 24.

One night a man came to a toll-bar with a wiggin stick in his hand, and wanted to go through. But the old woman who kept the gate would not open it, so he struck the gate with the wiggin stick. Thereupon it immediately flew open, and let him go through, as well as some others who were waiting behind.

When the old woman saw this she rushed out of the house, and, pointing her hand at the man with the wiggin stick said, "Away wi' thee, thou old devil, wi' thy witch wiggin!"

From Calver, Derbyshire.

MOTIF: G.272.2.1 [*Rowan wood protects against witches*].

¶ Rowan is a protective wood, used against, not by witches. It seems likely that the old woman was the witch, and had closed her gate by a magical spell.

THE WISE WOMAN OF LITTONDALE
[summary]

Parkinson, *Yorkshire Legends and Traditions*, 1st series, p. 135.

An old woman named Bertha lived, some time during the eighteenth century, in a wretched hovel not far from Arncliff. She had the reputation of a wise woman, and a curious traveller once knocked at her door, wishing to see the inside of her cottage.

She greeted him ungraciously, but he confessed his curiosity, and added that he would like her to perform some magical incantations in his presence. His tone suggested that he had no real faith in her powers, but she bade him sit down by her fire, and told him that within half an hour he should see a thing which she had shown to no other mortal.

All the furniture of the cottage was three stools, an old deal table, a few pans, three pictures—of Nostradamus, Merlin, and Michael Scott—a cauldron, and a sack.

As the stranger sat watching, old Bertha began her incantations, first warning him not to interrupt her. She then drew a circle with chalk on the floor, and in the middle of it she placed a brazier of burning embers. On this she placed the cauldron, half full of water. She stationed her guest at the far side of the circle, and then from her sack she threw into the cauldron a skeleton head, various bones, and carcasses of several small animals. All the time she was muttering charms in an unknown tongue, the only recognizable word being "Konig". When the water boiled, the witch handed the stranger a glass, and bade him look through it at the cauldron. He did so, and saw a figure wreathed in the steam. It was that of one of his own friends, looking pale and ill. He trembled, and the figure disappeared.

"Now," said the old woman, "do you still doubt my power?" The stranger bade her a hurried "Goodnight," and would have left the cottage, but she stopped him and said:

"I will show you something still more wonderful. Go to Arncliffe Bridge to-morrow at midnight, and look at the water on the left side of it."

The stranger had no wish to go to such a wild place alone at night, but she said that no companion must go with him, or the charm would be broken. She would say no more, but the other, feeling that she intended him no harm, after passing an anxious day, in which he found attention to his business impossible, obeyed her bidding, and at midnight stood watching the water from the left side of the bridge.

Very soon after midnight had struck from the neighbouring church, he heard a low moaning sound, and observed a violent troubling of the water with no visible cause. After a few minutes, the disturbance ceased, and all was again calm and quiet. He turned homewards, oppressed with a strange fear, and on turning a corner of the lane that led to his father's house, he saw in the path a huge dog, resembling a Newfoundland, looking at him with wistful eyes. It followed him home, and at the door he turned to take it in and give it shelter for the night, but the dog had vanished. He supposed that it must have found its master, and thought no more of it.

The next morning he returned to old Bertha's cottage, and told her what he had seen at the bridge. "Was there nothing more?" she asked, and he replied, "Nothing," but she pressed him, and then he remembered, and told her about the dog.

"That dog you saw was Bargest!" she replied, and he remembered the legend and said that his appearance was reputed to herald a death.

"You are right," she said. "And a death will follow last night's appearance," and when he asked "Whose?" she would only say, "Not yours."

He left her, and less than three hours later received news that the friend whose image he had seen in the steam of the cauldron had that morning committed suicide by throwing himself from Arncliffe Bridge at the very spot where the water had been troubled in the night.

MOTIFS: D.1171.2 [*Magic cauldron*]; D.1323 [*Magic object gives clairvoyance*]; E.423(a) [*Spirit animal*] (Baughman). In Parkinson a note follows giving a list of the bogie dogs, among which the Bargest is mentioned. D.1812.5.1.2.1 [*Vision as evil omen*].

¶ See "The Seer".

THE WITCH OF ASHREIGNEY

J. R. W. Coxhead, *Legends of Devon*, p. 151.

"In the parish of Ashreigney, North Devon, nearly a hundred years ago, there lived a man and his wife, named Bowden, who were considered to be witches by their neighbours, and for that reason avoided.

"At that time it was the custom, now probably unnecessary, on account of reaping machinery, to have upon each farm a great reaping-day, to finish off the cutting of the wheat. It was known by general report when each farmer would have his reaping-day, and from the neighbourhood around, without being invited, people came to help in the work, and to share in the liberal good cheer provided for the helpers.

"Bowden came to help cut wheat at the farm of one of the chief farmers in the parish, named B———. Cider had been flowing plentifully all day, and by supper time Bowden had become the worse for drink.

Instead, therefore, of quietly passing up his plate to receive a fresh supply of meat in the course of the supper, he flung it up the table, breaking three others.

"The mistress of the house, who presided at the supper, and who had rather a short temper, cried out, 'You witching old rogue, you've a broke three plates.'

"Upon this Bowden became violent and abusive, and the other men seized him and pitched him out of the kitchen; whereupon he went off in a rage.

"After he was gone, the B——'s talked the matter over, and became afraid that the witch would injure them; and their forebodings were soon verified.

"The first creatures to suffer were the poultry, of which they kept a vast quantity; and within a few days the fowls fell crippled, as if their backs were broken; they could not walk, and toppled over when they tried to stand; and the hens laid eggs with soft shells.

"Next a large number of the cattle began to die off in a mysterious manner, and with no apparent cause. Every night something or other would die, sometimes two or three things, sometimes only one cow, a sheep, horse or pig.

"At that time oxen were much used in agriculture; upon that farm four in a team. In the following February the ground was being harrowed on the B——'s farm by oxen, and one morning when the men came before daylight to feed the oxen in the 'shippen', they found the heavy 'drag' stuck on the top of the horns of one of the oxen, and the ox itself quite dead.

"A few days later, on coming again early in the morning to the same outhouse, they found in one of the yokes the necks of two oxen, the yoke being, of course, large enough only for one. Both the oxen were dead, the yoke being properly fastened about their necks.

"The next thing that happened was perhaps the most curious of all. Mr B—— the farmer had been to market at Crediton, and on his return jumped off his hackney and turned it loose into the stable, while he himself went into the house to send a lad out to attend to the horse.

"When the boy came out he could find no trace of it. He called his master, and several men and apprentice lads who lived in the house, but in spite of the most careful search, they could not find the horse that night. Next morning it was found three fields off in a quarry-pit; both the fore and hind legs on the near side were passed through one stirrup-iron above the fetlock, and it was quite dead.

"The smith was fetched to remove the stirrup, but was obliged to file it off. They then tried by every means to pass a single hoof through the other stirrup-iron, but it was impossible to do so. The smith was named William Parker, and he kept the stirrup-iron to the day of his death.

"Losses of the kind I have before mentioned went on for months. Mr B—— would not believe in witchcraft at first, and, although everyone persuaded him to do so, he would not consult the local white witch who lived at Barnstaple; but at last, when nearly the whole of his livestock had been swept away, he was induced by his wife and friends to try whether the white witch could undo the evil.

"On describing all that had happened, the white witch told him that by the time he got home again something else would be ill; this would die, but it would be the last thing he should lose.

"The first thing he was told on entering his house was that a very handsome and valuable calf was ill. He went down to the calves' house to see it, and as he opened the door, the calf gave a leap up to the beam, six feet high, and fell down dead.

"The white witch told Mr B—— to take the heart of the animal that should die up to the quarry where the horse had been found. There he was to make a fire and burn it; and this was to be done at night. At the same time something would burst out bleeding, and he was to save some of the blood and bring it to him.

"While the heart of the calf was being burnt at night in the quarry, two of Mr B——'s daughters were asleep together in the same bed. The younger awoke and found that her feet were quite wet. She struck a light and discovered that her sister's leg had burst out bleeding and that she was all but dead from exhaustion and loss of blood.

"A doctor was fetched, who stopped the bleeding; but the leg that had burst out bleeding was never sound afterwards. Some of the blood was sent to the white witch, and this was the end of the troubles at Bridge Farm."

From *Transactions of the Devonshire Association*, XIV, 1882 (witchcraft stories contributed by Paul Q. Karkeek. Sent to him by a clergyman whose grandfather had married the younger of the two daughters of the farmer mentioned in the story).
MOTIFS: G.265.4 [*Witches cause disease or death of animals*]; G.265.6 [*Witch causes animals to behave unnaturally*]; G.271.4.1(aa) [*Burning heart of bullock to break spell*] (Baughman).
¶ The white wizard would probably treat the blood of the victim in such a way as to affect the witch's blood.

THE WITCH OF AYTON

Gutch, *County Folk-Lore*, II, *North Riding of Yorkshire, etc.*, pp. 152–4.

A good many years ago there was an old witch lived in a tumble-down cottage near the waterfall [Ayton], and she was a mean old thing.

Very often nothing or anyone could please her. At that time there was a young fellow living in Newton, called Johnny Simpson, who was desperately in love with an Ayton lass called Mary Mudd, but Mary would have nothing to say to him, and in the end told him not to come bothering her any more. This grieved Johnny very much, but when he discovered that a young chap called Tom Smith had won Mary's heart, John's love turned into hate, and he determined to be revenged. To this end he sought the aid of the old witch, Nanny, to whom he told his woeful tale, begging her to work an evil spell on both Tom and Mary.

After much arguing, the old hag agreed, telling him to go to the churchyard and gather certain things. Then followed clear instructions as to what other proceedings he had to take, concluding with a reiterated command to wash in the old well, and to leave her besom by its side. After John had carefully carried out all her commands which were needful for him to work his evil spell upon the lovers, he broke faith, laughed at and ignored the witches [sic] final instructions, as to washing himself, and the disposal of her besom, setting off home fully satisfied with his night's evil work, and glorying in the fact that he had outwitted the old hag. But he speedily found out his mistake; before, behind, above, nay all about him, there came strange whisperings and flutterings of invisible wings, and by and by horrid faces shewed themselves to him; run or walk, it was all the same; there they were. And then you know when he got to the top of the rising ground, an owl sitting on the roof of one of the cottages, gave a fearful hoot; and then he was stopped by two night hags (there were three of them, but one remained seated, kicking her heels against the boulder upon which she rested.)

They told him they would have had no power to harm, or even detain him, had he been careful to carry out all Nan's commands. In the end they knocked him down, seized him by his hands and feet, and flew away with him to the top of Roseberry.

There they almost frightened the life out of him, as they bound Nan's besom between his legs, telling him to hurry away as quickly as ever he could, as they were going to hunt him with all the unearthly things such like could call to their aid. And they say throughout that night they hunted poor Johnny through the air, but they always headed him when he tried to cross the water, for witches cannot follow anyone over a running stream. After a terrible chase, he called to mind some words the witch had said, to the effect that he would be quite safe from harm so long as he had foothold of Ayton Bridge, so he turned in his flight, and made for it, but when he had only a few yards further to go, and right over the beck, of its own accord, the besom slipped from between his legs, when he fell head first into the water. Out of the beck he was rudely dragged, and then they made sad deed of him. They bit and scratched, and half-killed him; in the end, just as dawn was breaking, a cock crew, and at that, they every one flew away, leaving him more than half dead.

It may be mentioned a somewhat similar story is related of a bridge in Farndale (Blakeborough (2), pp. 7–10).

MOTIFS: W.126 [*Disobedience*]; F.401.5 [*Spires appear horrible*];G.269.10(*f*) [*Witch gives a man a beating for disregarding her instructions in using a spell against his sweetheart and another lover*] (Baughman); G.242.1 [*Witch flies through air on a broomstick*]; G.273.4 [*Witch powerless to cross stream*]; G.273.3 [*Witch powerless at cock-crow*].

¶ There is a Tam-o'-Shanter-like quality about this story, with the human hunted by the witch and the running stream as a refuge.

THE WITCH OF BERKELEY [summary]

William of Malmesbury, *Chronicle*, II, chap. 13, p. 230.

About the time of the Norman Conquest there lived a woman in the village of Berkeley who was a witch and augur, very gluttonous and luxurious, who led a life of riot and pleasure, although she was getting on in years. One day, as she was eating, her pet raven suddenly cried out loudly. At the sound the witch's knife dropped from her hand. "To-day my plough has reached its last furrow; there is nothing but grief before me from this day." No sooner had she spoken than a servant came running in with news of the death of her eldest son and all his family. This news struck her to the heart, and grief brought her to her death-bed.

When she knew that she had no hope of recovery she sent for her two surviving children, a monk and nun, both of great piety. When they had come she said to them: "My children, I have to confess to you that all my wealth has been gained by diabolical arts; all these years I have practised every wickedness, and have had no hope of salvation except in your piety. Even that has failed me now and I despair of my soul, but it may yet be that you can save my body from the Devil's clutches. Sew up my corpse in the skin of a stag, lay it on its back in a stone coffin and bind it with three great chains, curiously wrought. Let there be psalms sung for my soul for fifty nights, and masses said for fifty days. If I lie secure for three nights you may bury me on the fourth day."

With that she died, and her children did all they could to save her body from the Devil. On the first night, whilst the monks were singing their psalms, the bolted door of the church burst open, and a crowd of devils broke one of the chains. On the second night they broke another, but the third was more artfully made and resisted their efforts. On the third night, however, just before cock-crow, there was a tremendous rumbling like an earthquake, the foundations of the church shook, the door was shivered to splinters, and a great devil, more terrible than any of the rest, came up to the coffin. The monks' singing died on their lips, and their hair stood on end. The fiend called on the woman by name, and from the coffin she answered him: "I cannot come, I am chained."

"You shall be loosed," he said, and broke the massive chain like a piece of flax. He shattered the lid of the coffin with one thrust of his foot, and plucked out the woman. He led her through the door. A black charger was neighing outside, its back covered with iron hooks. He flung the woman on them and vanished with her from men's sight. But pitiable lamentations and cries for help were heard from the air for four miles.

MOTIFS: G.278.1 [*Marvellous manifestations at death of witch*]; G.275.1 [*Witch carried off by devil*]; G.303.7.1.1 [*Devil rides on black horse*].

¶ The same story in almost the same words is recorded in Ranulph's *Polychronicon*, translated by Trevisia, and also by Roger of Wendover, *Chronicle*, Bohn's Edition, I, p. 181.

See "Nancy Camel and the Devil", "The Round Square" (B, III), and other Devil tales.

THE WITCH OF BOROUGHBRIDGE [summary]

R. Blakeborough, *Wit, Character, Folk-Lore and Customs of the North Riding of Yorkshire*, p. 156.

At Kirby Hill, near Boroughbridge, a newly married couple met the witch Sally Carey near the Devil's Arrows. As they passed her, she shook her stick at them, and screamed, "You want a lad, but I'll make it a lass!" And a girl was born to them shortly afterwards. They had hoped for an heir, and earnestly trusted that their next child would be a son. But before its birth the young husband was thrown from his horse and killed.

Late one evening there was a knock at the door of the widow's house, and there stood the old witch, brandishing her stick, and yelling: "It shan't be a lad this time, neither!" The terrified girl fainted, and was long in recovering, but when she was strong enough her friends prevailed upon her to visit the wise man at Aldborough. He performed many rites, amongst which was the burning of a black cat and a black cock at midnight, behind sealed windows and doors, on a fire of rowan twigs. This was done in the presence of the widow, an unmarried friend (who later told the story) and a mother of seven sons; this was necessary for the working of the charm.

In time the baby was born; it was a boy, but it was crippled. The mother, in deep distress, again visited the wise man, who told her that if she would remain unmarried for seven years, her child would grow straight and well.

She promised, and carried it into effect; but the witch tried every way to cause her to break her word. She sent one handsome young man after another to her house on different pretexts, but the mother resisted them all, and her child grew up straight and well.

MOTIFS: M.411.12 [*Curse by witch*]; M.412.2 [*Curse given on wedding night*]; G.271.6 [*Exorcism of witch by charm worked by "white witch", "witch doctor", etc.*] (Baughman); T.291.1 [*Wife keeps vow never to wed after her husband's death*]; Q.83 [*Reward for marital fidelity*].

THE WITCH OF BRANDON CREEK

W. H. Barrett, *More Tales from the Fens*, p. 123.

Old Leah Erinkley was one of the witches that used to scare the folk round Brandon Creek. She was a gypsy and, after seventy years of wandering about the countryside, she and her husband, John, set up their caravan on a bit of waste ground beside the river-bank. John used to sit by the fire making clothes-pegs, while Leah tramped round the neighbourhood with a basket, selling them. These pegs, though, were really only an excuse for her to knock at people's doors and cadge a lot of this and that, because she was a first-rate beggar. She'd tell fortunes, too, for a bit of silver. Besides earning the money to buy food for the pair of them, she had to get the wood that John needed to make his pegs with. So there wasn't a post or rail within miles that she hadn't carried off, if she could lift it.

Although the river ran right beside their caravan, the couple never used the water except for cooking and brewing their black tea. During the first year or two of their stay, John used to play his fiddle on the bridge, while the boys and girls danced to it. Then he'd go round with his cap and get a few coppers to spend in the Ship.

Then the time came when John's feet, through his having spent most of his life sitting cross-legged by the fire, started going bad, and he had to lay up in the van. So Leah had to think up all the ways she could of getting money. One day she told a farmer's wife that John's legs had got so bad that she'd had to send him down the river to the workhouse, and no one ever saw him again. But twenty years later, when some men were deepening the dyke near where the caravan had been, they found his bones, wrapped in rotting canvas with bits of iron to keep him down in the mud. Leah had been dead herself for some years by then, so no one ever found out what really happened, though they guessed.

As she grew older, Leah got more and more bad-tempered, and her black eyes sank deeper and deeper into her head. The strongest people tried to keep out of her way, while the weak ones swore they'd been bewitched by her. Folks noticed, too, that even the fiercest yard-dogs would bristle up and slink into their kennels when she came near.

Now, in those days, everybody got their water from the river. It was the women's job to fetch it, and they had to fetch and carry it, some of them, for a mile, in buckets slung on yokes over their shoulders. Leah would stop them as they came along, and would peer into the water they carried and tell them she could see a lot of ill-luck reflected in it. But it would be all right, she'd say, if they gave her a silver sixpence. Of course, most of them did, and then Leah would say she'd driven the evil spirit away.

Well, if anybody did have any doubts as to whether the old girl was a witch or not, the day came when they knew for sure that she was. It happened this way. An old major, who'd been in the Indian Army, came down and settled in the manor house where his family had lived for years. He was a real peppery kind of chap and it wasn't long before he was like a little god in the village. He had quite a few servants living in the house, and if any of them had parents then these lived in tied cottages. If a skivvy left his service, unless it was to get married, then her parents had to leave their homes too.

Well, one day the major heard a great commotion going on at the kitchen door, and he found old Leah frightening his cook and the kitchen-maid out of their wits. So he seized the old woman by the neck with the crook of his big stick, dragged her into the yard, and hurled her into the swill tub. When she scrambled out, she pointed her finger at him and cursed every limb of his body. Then she told him that, as sure as the weathercock was on the steeple, he'd not be able to leave the house for six weeks, even though there wouldn't be a thing wrong with him.

Now, having spent so much of his life in India, the major found the Fen winds very cold and bitter. Only a few weeks before, he'd had a bad cold on his chest, and the doctor had told him he oughtn't to go out when the wind was in the north-east. So, to make sure, he'd got into the habit, every morning when he got up, of looking across at the weathercock on the church, to see which way the wind was blowing.

The morning after he'd thrown Leah out of the house, the major looked at the cock and saw it was looking full into the north-east; so he stayed indoors. The same thing happened the next day, and the next, until, after several days, he was fretting to go out.

On the sixth morning, when he saw that the cock hadn't moved, the major, in a flaming temper, fetched his gun, leaned out of the window and shot the bird. As the bullet hit it, the weathercock turned round then settled down again in the north-east. Well, do you know, it never moved for the next six weeks. The Rector was sent for, but he said there was nothing wrong with the weathercock. The servants went about in fear of their lives, as their master cursed and swore at them from dawn to dusk. Then, when they all swore they'd leave him, the major sent for a builder to bring a ladder and climb up the steeple. When the chap came to the church, the major made up his mind to risk things and to go over to the churchyard to watch that the builder did his work properly.

When he got to the gate, though, he saw Leah standing there. She spat at him, then looked up at the weathercock and shouted: "You can fly around again, now, like you used to. I've unpinned your wings. Now show this old fool where the wind is."

And, as she spoke, the weathercock swung round and faced south-east.

MOTIF: D.2142.0.1 [*Witch controls winds*].
¶ It is uncertain whether it was the wind or the weather-cock that was controlled by the witch in this story.

THE WITCH AND HER BUTTER-MILK

S. O. Addy, *Household Tales*, p. 35.

Once upon a time a farmer and his wife lived at a certain village in Nottinghamshire, and they had a son who got married, and brought a beautiful young wife to his father's house. Now, in the same village there lived an old woman who was said to be a witch, and the farmer and his wife used to give butter-milk to her.

One day when the old woman came for her butter-milk the beautiful young wife said:

"We've none to spare, so you must go without it." So the old woman went away without her butter-milk.

Soon afterwards the young wife began to churn, but the butter would not come, and she wondered why it did not. Whilst they were eating their dinner, the farmer said, "I wonder why old Sarah has not fetched her butter-milk today."

"Well," said the young wife, "an old woman has been here this morning for butter-milk, but I told her we had none to spare."

"Then you can put your churn away," said the farmer, "for you will churn no butter this week. But remember that you don't turn her away again without giving her butter-milk, for she has witched the cream."

MOTIF: D.2084.2 [*Butter magically kept from coming*].

THE WITCH OF CARTHORPE [summary]

R. Blakeborough, *Wit, Character, Folk-Lore and Customs of the North Riding of Yorkshire*, p. 153.

Dolly Ayre, the Carthorpe witch, once laid a spell on some cows belonging to a farmer known as "Old Tommy". Tommy went to consult the wise man, Sammy Banks of Mickly, and between them they mastered her, but not before one of the cows had wasted to death. All that was known of their counter-spells was that Tommy had to thrust something through the witch's latch-hole with a wicken stick—something very small, or it would never have gone through—and afterwards they burnt something at midnight which had a strange and vile smell.

But Dolly could be helpful to those who were good to her. Once a poor man was turned out of the farm on which he was a tenant. This man had once done a great service to Dolly, so when the newcomers arrived, for whom he was being turned out, they found written in blood-red letters, on every door and shutter, the words BAD LUCK; and underneath were more words, in a writing they could not understand. They moved in, however, and were putting their possessions in place when a small shelf on which they had put some pans suddenly fell down, and killed one of their children on the spot.

MOTIFS: G.271.6 [*Exorcism of witch by counter-charm worked by witch doctor*] (Baughman); G.272.2.1 [*Rowan wood protects against witches*]; G.265.8.1 [*Witch bewitches household articles*].

¶ The witch as a friend seems to have been more awkward than as an enemy.

THE WITCH OF FRADDAM AND THE ENCHANTER OF PENGERSWICK

Hunt, *Popular Romances of the West of England*, p. 326.

Again and again had the Lord of Pengerswick reversed the spells of the Witch of Fraddam, who was reported to be the most powerful weird woman in the west country. She had been thwarted so many times by this "white witch" that she resolved to destroy him by some magic more potent than anything yet heard of. It is said that she betook herself to Kynance Cove, and that there she raised the Devil by her incantations, and that she pledged her soul to him in return for the aid he promised. The enchanter's famous mare was to be seduced to drink from a tub of poisoned water placed by the roadside, the effect of which was to render her in the highest degree restive, and cause her to fling her rider.

The wounded Lord of Pengerswick was, in his agony, to be drenched by the old witch, with some hell-broth, brewed in the blackest night under the most evil aspects of the stars; by this he would be in her power for ever, and she might torment him as she pleased. The devil felt certain of securing the soul of the witch of Fraddam, but he was less certain of securing that of the enchanter. They say, indeed, that the sorcery which Pengerswick learnt in the East was so potent, that the devil feared him. However, as the proverb is, he held with the hounds and ran with the hare. The witch collected with the utmost care all the deadly things she could obtain, with which to brew her famous drink. In the darkest night, in the midst of the wildest storms, amidst the flashes of lightnings and the bellowings of the thunder, the witch was seen, riding on her black ram-cat over the moors and mountains in search of her poisons. At length all was complete—the horse-drink was boiled, the hell-broth was brewed. It was in March, about the time of the equinox; the night was dark, and the King of Storms was abroad. The witch planted her tub of drink in a dark lane, through which she knew the Lord of Pengerswick must pass, and near to it she sat, crooning over her crock of broth. The witch-woman had not long to wait; amidst the hurrying winds was heard the heavy tramp of the enchanter's mare, and soon she perceived the outline of a man and horse defined sharply against the line of lurid light which stretched along the western horizon. On they came; the witch was scarcely able to contain herself—her joy and her fears, struggling one with the other, almost overpowered her. On came the horse and her rider: they neared the tub of drink; the mare snorted loudly, and her eyes flashed fire as she looked at the black tub by the roadside.

Pengerswick bent him over the horse's neck, and whispered into her ear; she turns round, and flinging out her heels, with one kick she scattered all to the wild winds. The tub flew before the blow; it rushed against the crock, which it overturned, and, striking against the legs of the old Witch of Fraddam, she fell along with the tub, which assumed the shape of a coffin. Her terror was extreme: she who thought to have unhorsed the conjurer found herself in a carriage for which she did not bargain. The enchanter raised his voice, and gave utterance to some wild words in an unknown tongue, at which even his terrible mare trembled. A whirlwind arose, and the devil was in the midst of it. He took the coffin in which lay the terrified witch high into the air, and the crock followed them. The derisive laughter of Pengerswick and the savage neighing of the horse were heard above the roar of the winds. At length, with a satisfied tone, he exclaimed, "She is settled till the day of doom," gave the mare the spurs, and rode rapidly home.

The Witch of Fraddam still floats up and down, over the seas, around the coast, in her coffin, followed by the crock, which seems like a punt in attendance on a jolly-boat. She still works mischief, stirring up the winds with her ladle and broom till the waves swell into mountains, which heave off from their crests so much mist and foam that these wild wanderers of the winds can scarcely be seen through the mist. Woe to the mariner who sees the witch!

The Lord of Pengerswick alone had power over her. He had but to stand on his tower, and blow three blasts on his trumpet, to summon her to the shore, and compel her to peace.

MOTIFS: D.1719.1 [*Contest in magic*]; G.241.1.4 [*Witch rides on cat*]; G.275.1 [*Witch carried off by devil*].
¶ See "The Enchanter of Pengerswick".

THE WITCH OF GREAT AYTON [summary]

R. Blakeborough, *Wit, Character, Folk-Lore and Customs of the North Riding of Yorkshire*, p. 160.

It is probable that the following story, though told without names, relates to a witch known as "Au'd Nanny", who lived for many years, in the mid-eighteenth century, near the mill at the corner of the green at Great Ayton.

The grandmother of the old lady who told the story had once met Au'd Nanny. The grandmother's name was Mary Langstaff; she lived at Stokesley, and had a cousin, Martha Sokeld, living at Kildale. The two were greatly attached, and once when Martha fell ill she sent for Mary to help her. Mary set out as soon as she could make ready on the long walk to Kildale, and as she went she noticed an old woman hobbling along, and though she did not recognize her, she gradually became convinced that it was no other than the old witch. To avoid speaking to her, she stooped down and began to pick some flowers. But when the old woman came up to her, she called out: "No need to hang thy head down, Mary Langstaff; I know thee well. It wouldn't have cost thee much to pass the time of day with me; but I shan't forget this day. I'll pay thee out for it."

She banged on the ground three times with her stick, and disappeared.

Mary was wearing a bunch of wicken [mountain ash] berries at the time, which protected her from any immediate harm.

She arrived at her cousin's house to find her much better, so after three days she returned to Stokesley on a Monday afternoon. On the following Wednesday evening, to her great surprise, in walked Martha Sokeld, who said she had been very ill again, and feared she had not long to live.

She said that she had a great longing to see her sister at Northallerton, and begged Mary to let her rest for a while before going on the next day by the carrier's cart. In the meantime she asked Mary to fetch some things "from Hannah's" which she wished to take to her sister. She particularly impressed on her not to hurry back, so that she might have an uninterrupted sleep on the settle in her absence. Mary went, but she felt strangely uneasy, and did not stay away long. On reaching home, she moved very softly, and peered through a crack in the shutters to see if her cousin was asleep. To her horror, she saw her standing in front of a blazing fire, dropping things into a pot, and repeating over and over

> "Fire cum,
> Fire gan,
> Curling smeeak,
> Keep oot o't' pan.
> Here's a teead, theer's a frog,
> An' t' heart frev a crimson ask [newt];
> Here's a teeath fra' t'heead
> O' yan at's deead,
> 'At nivver gat thruff his task [committed suicide];
> Here's pricked i' blood a maiden's prayer
> 'At t'ee o' man maunt see;
> It's pricked reet thruff a yet warm mask [caul],
> Lapped aboot a breeght green ask,
> An' it's all foor him an' thee.
> > It boils, thoo'll drink,
> > He'll speeak, thoo'll think.
> > It boils, thoo'll see,
> > He'll speeak, thoo'll dee."

Mary felt certain that this was a spell against her and her sweetheart, Tom. She walked boldly in, and told the witch that she had heard and seen everything, and, taking hold of the Bible, she said, "You must do your worst; I hold by this." At once the witch turned the pan upside down on the fire, and shrieked; "Thou's 'scaped me this time, but I'll mell on thee yet!" And she disappeared.

Early next day a man rode over from Kildale with the news that Martha Sokeld was nowhere to be found. Three days later her dead body was discovered high up on the moor. It came to be believed that the witch had lured Martha up there, and by a spell had lured the life out of her, and then herself entered into her body to deceive Mary.

Mary, however, lived to be eighty-five, and brought up a large family, so it seemed that the witch had never been able to establish her power over Mary, nor her husband.

MOTIFS: G.262 [*Murderous witch*]; G.272.2.1 [*Rowan wood protects against witches*]; G.229.1 [*Soul of witch leaves the body*]; G.271.2.5 [*Bible used in exorcism of witch*].

THE WITCH HARE

Ruth L. Tongue, *Somerset Folklore*, pp. 71–2.

"No, I never heard of no ha'nting to Ellicombe Farm. Us lived to Ellicombe tew. There was the Ellicombe harnt, 'tis old tales, and the Ellicombe witch—but there, believe it or no 'tis all a sham.

"Well then, as I were going up whoame t'Ellicombe with the old pony, we did kip a pony for to drive t'Mine'd, and I seed a girt fat wold hare in behind a boosh—a fine one tew—and the two years of'n stuck right up above boosh; 'n I said, 'Yew bide theyur, my la-ady, 'n I'll have 'ee when I gets my gun.'

"So I goes down whoame'n gets my gun, 'twas a gude one tew, 'n I creeps up back, 'n there her two years was'n I seed her yed. 'Twadn' more'n 20 yards, 'n I lifs the gun'n lets vly! 'N her hops away so easy'n slow I lets 'n have't agen, but didn't make no difference, I couldn't shoot 'ee. I takes gun whoame, 'n I puts up playing card down hurchet [orchard], 60 yards, 'n I hits'n every time. Well, I telled a vuller 'bout'n 'n how I couldn't shoot'n, 'n her said, 'Nor yew won't never till 'ee puts zilver in yewer gun. 'Tis a witch hare, 'n us all knows'n yurabouts.' No, I couldn't shoot 'ee."

TYPE ML.3055. MOTIFS: G.211.2.7 [*Witch in form of hare*]; G.265.8.3.1.1 [*Gun bewitched so that it will not hit target*].
¶ See "The Bull-dog Pistol and the Hare".

WITCH AND HARE or THE WITCH HARE
[summary]

Hartland, *English Fairy and Folk-Tales*, p. 194.

An old witch, whenever she wanted money, would assume the form of a hare, and send her grandson to tell a certain huntsman who lived near by that he had seen a hare sitting in a particular spot. For this the boy always received sixpence; but after the same thing had happened a number of times, and the hare was never caught, one of the huntsmen began to suspect that this was no ordinary hare. A justice and a clergyman were consulted, and it was agreed that a neighbour of the witch should give warning the next time the old woman and her grandson were seen leaving the cottage together. As soon as the news arrived, the hounds were loosed, and the boy was heard to exclaim: "Run, Granny, run for your life!" Once again the hare got away; she ran into her cottage through a hole too small for the hounds to enter. All the huntsmen tried to break open the door, but until the parson and the justice arrived, they could do nothing. Their coming broke the spell, and the whole hunt burst into the cottage and up the stairs, where they found the old woman bleeding from many wounds, and still out of breath. She denied that she was the hare, but when the huntsmen said, "Call up the hounds. Let us see what they take her to be," both she and the boy fell on their knees and begged for mercy.

This was granted, but for the penalty of a whipping, and the two escaped for the time. But later the old woman was again brought to trial for causing a young woman to spit pins. Then the former tale was remembered, and she was at last burnt at the stake.

Mrs Bray, *The Borders of the Tamar and the Tavy*, II, p. 112.
TYPE ML.3055. MOTIFS: G.211.2.7.1 [*Witch as hare allows self to be coursed by dogs for pay*]; G.275.12 [*Witch in the form of an animal is injured or killed as a result of the injury done to the animal*]; G.275.3 [*Witch burned*].
¶ This ending to the tale marks it as a piece of folk-tradition rather than history. Burning was not a legal punishment for a witch in England, unless she was convicted of causing the death of her husband or master, which counted as petty treason.

THE WITCH OF MEMBURY

J. R. W. Coxhead, *Legends of Devon*, p. 157.

A most interesting and detailed account of the strange circumstances leading up to the terrible death of the Witch of Membury was given to Mr P. Q. Karkeek by an old nurse, who, when she was about eleven years of age in the service of the farmer mentioned in the tale, knew the witch well. The story, which appeared in the *Transactions of the Devonshire Association* XIV, pp. 387–90, is given below:

"About the year 1842 there lived at Membury, near Axminster, a well-to-do farmer named P——, with his wife and family. He had plenty of sheep, cattle and horses, and seemed to prosper. He had a brother who was rather 'gay'.

"Near the farmhouse, in a wood, on rather high ground, lived an old woman of very peculiar habits, called Hannah Henley, who was looked upon as a witch.

"Her hut had two rooms, which were kept wonderfully clean, and she always was a pattern of neatness and cleanliness. She generally wore short petticoats, with a large white apron, 'white as the driven snow', a plaid turnover, and a satin poke-bonnet. Cats she had in any number, and of all colours. I was in the service of Mr P—— and must have been at that time eleven years old.

"Old Hannah rather took a fancy to me, and used to invite me to come in and sit by her fire, and would often give me apple dumplings or crowdy pies, which she was famous in making. Her dumplings when cooked were much whiter than those made by other cooks.

"I had to bring the cows home to be milked, and often had to pass near the wood, so that Hannah could often see me, and when she did, would ask me in to sit a bit. I was not afraid of her, as were most of the other servants, and indeed my master and mistress.

"Hannah came to the house begging for everything: corn, bread, milk, flour, beer, and sometimes for money. For a long while she had whatever she asked for, but at last it became too great a tax, and she was refused. The 'gay' brother had been rather liberal to her, till one day he refused her money, and she at once turned to him and said, 'You'll not live long to use it yourself.' He died in great agony within three weeks.

"Owing to this, the farmer's wife took a dislike to Hannah, and sharply refused her when she begged. But she never asked like begging; she demanded.

"One day the youngest child was playing with a walnut, and because the nurse would not let him give it to Hannah, she stooped down and made the sign of a cross on the floor, and a circle round it, and then went away. In the night the child was taken very ill and died in four days; and while ill, the child would turn round and round and get dizzy.

"This seemed the beginning of trouble: the milk would not set, the butter could not be made, bread put to bake only ran about the oven, so these things had to be taken to another brother's house, and he was a butcher.

"Then, one day the mistress saw Hannah coming, and said to me: 'I'll not see her. You go and say I'm not at home.'

"I gave the message as I was told; but Hannah knew the truth, and said, 'Tell your missus that she shall not move out of the pantry now, even if she wishes.'

"This was true enough, for even her husband tried to get her to come out, but she could not move. This so enraged him against the old woman that he swore lustily, and followed her home with his gun in his hand. He had just loaded his gun and when he met the witch he threatened to shoot her; she dared him, and he was quite unable to fire.

"Another time she begged some barley from one of the men-servants, but he could not give it to her; and that night eight horses were taken ill. They beat themselves in their stable so badly that two had to be shot at once and four others died later on.

"Sheep died of uncertain diseases, sometimes eight or ten in a day. A horse that Mr P—— minded to sell had an eye destroyed, and what with one thing and another, he was nigh being ruined. So he determined to go and see a white witch who lived in Chard.

"This man came to stay in the house, and had the parlour to use. Of course, he worked only at night; by day he slept or walked on the hill where the witch lived, or on any high ground. He owned that he had never been so much troubled to put down a witch; that she was the strongest and 'runkest' he ever knew.

"The maidservants saw that the bed made for him was not used by night, and they wanted to know what he was doing; so one of them crept down to the parlour, and looked through the keyhole; she saw this man on his knees before his book, and sparks of fire flashing about the room.

"The next morning this maid told the mistress that she believed the parlour had been on fire, and was sharply reproved for her pains, and told not to meddle again, lest something dreadful should happen to her.

"The white witch went to the stable and saw the horses which were ailing; and then chose the largest crock, and had it filled with water, into which a large quantity of barley had been put, and then this had to be kept boiling all the time he was in the house.

"Again, he ordered six bullocks' hearts to be hung in the fireplace (one of those large ones, as in farm kitchens). Two in the centre were stuck with pins and the other four with new nails. These were slowly melted, and as they melted the witch's heart was to be melted too.

"Old Hannah came to the house day after day, begging for relief, and saying that since such a day she had no rest. She looked so miserable that the mistress felt sorry, and would have given her what she asked for, but the master would not let her; and the white witch said he felt that his work had been interfered with, and if the witch had been given what she had asked for, she would have gained double power, and all his skill been thrown away, and at an end.

"He had been in the house a month all but three days, and then he had a large number of nails driven into a butt. This was taken to the top of the hill, and set rolling till it came to the bottom.

"This was Thursday, and in the afternoon old Hannah came again to the house, saying she was dying, and begged for wine or spirits. The white witch then felt sure he had gained; and at four o'clock in the morning went towards the hut in the wood.

" This was Good Friday morning. He found the window was broken, and, looking about, he saw high above him, in a tree, the witch in a sheet, with a smutty kettle hanging by her side.

" There she was left for the bettermost folks to see, and also the servants. Then the tree was cut down, as she was too high to be got at; and as the tree fell, the witch fell into a gulley.

" She was 'laid out' on a 'kit', with just a sheet over her; and then was seen that her flesh was very much torn, as if by pins or nails; and inside the hut blood-marks were everywhere. This was all caused, so they said, by struggling with the Devil, who pulled her through the broken window.

"After her death a box on one side of her bed was opened, and in it money to a fair amount was found, with tea, sugar, bread and suchlike; while on the other side [were], two smaller boxes, containing toads of sizes.

"From Good Friday till the following Wednesday, the corpse was visited by scores of people from all parts; and then was buried at four cross-roads between Membury and Axminster; and afterwards horses used to shy when passing the grave.

" The white witch was paid one hundred pounds for his work.

"After a while they tried to kill old Hannah's cats, but they could not. Then the hut was burnt, and the cats all went away."

(For a reference to Hannah's house, see *Transactions of the Devonshire Association*, LX, p. 172. The date of the reference is 1865. Hannah died in 1841.)

MOTIFS: G.269.10 [*Witch punishes person who incurs her ill-will*]; G.269.10.1 [*Witch kills person as punishment*]; G.265.4.0.1 [*Witch punishes owner for injury or slight by killing his animals*]; G.271.6 [*Exorcism of witch by counter-charm worked by witch doctor*] (Baughman); G.271.4.1(a) [*Exorcism by burning or boiling animal heart stuck with pins. Usually this process brings the witch to the scene, because of the burning it sets up in her heart. She must promise to remove the spell before the ceremony is stopped. Sometimes she is allowed to die*] (Baughman); G.299.2 [*Witch is heard struggling with Devil*].

¶ See "The Witch of Ashreigney", "Nancy Camel".

THE WITCH AND THE PLOUGHMAN

S. O. Addy, *Household Tales*, pp. 44–5.

There was once a farmer who lived in Nottinghamshire, and kept many servants in his house. Near to his house there lived a witch, and the farmer often told his servants that if she asked them to give her anything they should never refuse. One day the farmer hired a ploughman, and said to him, "If the old witch up yonder ask thee for ought, thou must give it."

"I shall give the old lass nought," said the ploughman.

One day when he met the witch she asked him to give her something, and he would not. So the next day, when he began to plough, his horses would not go, but at last he coaxed her, and persuaded her to let them go.

Now this old witch lived by herself in a lonely cabin, and one day the ploughman said he would go and see her. So he knocked at the door of the cabin, and said, "Mother, I've come to take thee for a ride."

The witch said, "Wait till I have suckled my cubs and buckled my shoes, and then I will be with thee." So she suckled her cubs, and buckled her shoes, and followed him out. But as soon as the ploughman had mounted the horse she turned herself into a hare, and sprang with her claws upon the horse's back. The horse was very frightened, and jumped many feet, but the ploughman killed the hare on the spot.

MOTIFS: G.211.2.7 [*Witch as Hare*]; G.219.3 [*Witch has long nails*]; F.989.1.1 [*Horse's tremendous leap*]; G.275.8 [*Hero kills witch*].

¶ This is obviously a variant of "Blind Byard", for the Witch's chant is the same. See "Blind Byard", "Byard's Leap".

THE WITCH OF SEATON DELAVAL

F. Grice, *Folk-Tales of the North Country*, pp. 72–5.

Once upon a time a young lord was riding home in the darkness from Newcastle to Seaton Delaval, and his way led him past an old ruined chapel near Wallsend. He had ridden past the chapel many times without taking much notice of its fallen roof and broken windows; for it was dark and uninviting, and silent except for the hootings of an owl or two that had nested in the broken stairways, and the crying of an old goat that someone kept in the overgrown churchyard. But on this night the lord thought that he could see a strange light shining through the broken windows. He was puzzled to see a light where all was usually so dark, but he was late, so he rode on without giving much thought to it.

A short distance farther on he heard a strange noise. It was the noise of men hallooing in the meadows, and cracking their whips, and driving hares out of the fields.

"Why are you doing this?" he asked one.

"Why, sir," replied the cowherd, "to-night is May Day eve, and we have been told that on this night the witches meet. Sometimes they take the shape of hares and lie in our fields and hurt the cattle. So we drive them away with shouts and whips."

"Ah, yes," said the lord. "I had forgotten that to-morrow is May Day."

This meeting with the cowherds set him thinking again of the light he had seen in the old chapel, so he turned and galloped back. When he reached the chapel the light was still to be seen. It was a strange-coloured light, like the glowing of a fire that is fed with curious woods, and it aroused his curiosity more than ever.

"If I do not get home before dawn I must find out what mischief is brewing here," he said to himself, and dismounting he tied his horse to a gatepost and crept silently up to a window.

When he peeped through he saw an astonishing sight. On the floor of the church burned a fire with a pile of wood broken from the pews lying near it, and over it a black cauldron, fat and round. Twelve witches sat round the fire in a circle, all cross-legged and rocking from side to side, while a thirteenth stood over the pot, taking things from a sack and dropping them in one after another; and as she dropped each one in, she uttered a spell. "This is to make the young lambs swell and die.... This is to blight the blossom on the apple-trees.... This is to make the cowherds' bones ache and ache and ache."

As he watched her, the young lord's heart burned with anger.

"These are the bad women who hurt the herds' cattle and spoil their crops. But I'll send them packing," he said, and, leaping over the broken wall, he ran upon the witches and seized the chief witch round the waist. She screamed and tried to free herself, but he held on to her. Then he knocked over the cauldron, and as the contents poured on to the fire they hissed and clouds of evil-smelling steam arose. The church was in an uproar: the owls flew out of their hiding-places, the old goat ran round and round on its tether, and the witches fled shrieking. The chief witch scratched and kicked and screamed, but the young Lord Delaval held her in a tight grip and carried her to his horse and rode away.

The witch was cast into prison, and a few days later she was tried and sentenced to be burned for her misdeeds.

Many people came to her trial, and many told how she had put spells on their dogs and sheep; but when they saw the firewood being piled on the sands at Seaton their hearts began to melt, and they began to pity the old woman. For, although she had been a wicked witch, they were tender-hearted people, and did not like to see even a witch who had done them so much evil tied to a stake and burned.

"We must show some pity on the old woman," said one.

"Yes," said another. "Before she is to die we will grant her one wish." So turning to the witch they asked if she had any boon to ask before her death.

But the witch was more cunning than they thought. Although she had put on the looks of a good old woman to win their sympathy, at heart she was secretly thinking on ways of escaping her fate.

"Kind neighbours," she said, "I repent of all the harm I have ever done, and I have one little boon to ask before I die. All I ask is that you will give me two little wooden dishes, new ones that have never held water."

"That is a small request," said one of the women who were standing by. "I will run and get them."

When she returned the witch thanked her for the dishes. Then she laid them on the ground and put one foot in each dish. No sooner had she done this than she soared in the air like a lark rising from its nest, and as she soared she shook her fist at the people, and uttered curses on them.

"She has tricked us!" they all cried, except one man. He was the husband of the woman who had given the dishes.

"No, no," he said. "She has not tricked us yet. I knew that this witch was trying to outwit us, so I hurried to the house and hid one of the new dishes before my wife came. And in its place I put one that has been used a score of times. Look!"

And as he pointed upwards, suddenly one of the dishes fell from the witch's feet.

She dropped like a stone into the water and was seen no more.

MOTIFS: G.243 [*Witches' Sabbath*]; G.275.9 [*Fighting and wrestling with witch*]; G.275 [*Witch defeated*]; G.242.6 [*Witches use magic aids for flying*]; G.278 [*Death of witch*].

¶ It was a part of the seventeenth-century witch belief that a witch arrested and brought to trial lost her power to hurt. New vessels are generally insisted on in the recipes for charms. May Day Eve was one of the chief times for the meeting of witches.

THE WITCH IN THE STABLE

Jesse Salisbury, *A Glossary of the Words and Phrases of S.E. Worcestershire*, 1893.

A witch once entered a stable, and sat upon the manger, in the shape of a large black cat. The carter, seeing her, went and called a dog to drive her away, but the witch changed herself into a wheat straw, and laid herself across the horse's back.

Upon the carter's return to the stable, he could not see the cat, but seeing the wheat straw lying across the horse's back, he cut it through with his knife, causing it to bleed human blood. Alarmed at this, he ran out of the stable, and called his fellow-labourers, who, on going into the stable, found the dead body of an old woman, shockingly mutilated.

MOTIFS: G.211.1.7 [*Witch in form of cat*]; G.212.1 [*Witch in form of blade of straw*]; G.275.13 [*Rough treatment of object causes injury or death to witch*].

THE WITCH AND THE TOAD

Hunt, *Popular Romances of the West of England*, pp. 337–9.

An old woman called Alsey—usually Aunt Alsey—occupied a small cottage in Anthony, one of a row which belonged to a tradesman living in Dock—as Devonport was then designated to distinguish it from Plymouth. The old woman possessed a very violent temper, and this, more than anything else, fixed upon her the character of being a witch. Her landlord had frequently sought his rent, and as frequently he received nothing but abuse. He had, on the special occasion to which our narrative refers, crossed the Tamar and walked to Anthony, with the firm resolve of securing his rent, now long in arrear, and of turning the old termagant out of the cottage.

A violent scene ensued, and the vicious old woman, more than a match for a really kind-hearted and quiet man, remained the mistress of the situation. She seated herself in the door of her cottage, and cursed her landlord's wife, "the child she was carrying", and all belonging to him, with so devilish a spite that Mr —— owned he was fairly driven away in terror.

On returning home, he, of course, told his wife all the circumstances; and while they were discoursing on the subject—the whole story being attentively listened to by their daughter, then a young girl, who is my informant—a woman came into the shop requiring some articles which they sold.

"Sit still, father," said Mrs —— to her husband. " You must be tired. I will see to the shop."

So she went from the parlour into the shop, and, hearing the wants of her customer, proceeded to supply them, gossiping gaily, as was her wont, to interest the buyer.

Mrs —— was weighing one of the articles required, when something fell heavily from the ceiling of the shop, struck the beam out of her hand, and both—the falling body and the scales—came together with much noise on to the counter. At the same instant both women screamed—the shopkeeper calling also "Father! father!" meaning her husband thereby—with great energy.

Mr —— and his daughter were in the shop instantly, and there, on the counter they saw an enormous and most ugly toad sprawling amidst the chains of the scales.

The first action of the man was to run back to the parlour, seize the tongs, and return to the shop. He grasped the swollen toad with the tongs, the vicious creature spitting all the time, and, without a word, he went back and flung it behind the block of wood which was burning in the grate. The object of terror being removed, the wife, who was shortly to become the mother of another child, though usually a woman who had great command over her feelings, fainted.

This circumstance demanding all their attention, the toad was forgotten. The shock was a severe one; and although Mrs —— was restored in a little time to her senses, she again and again became faint. Those fits continuing, her medical attendant, Dr —— was sent for, and on his arrival he ordered that the patient should be immediately placed in bed, and the husband was informed that he must be prepared for a premature birth.

The anxiety occasioned by these circumstances, and the desire to afford every relief to his wife, so fully occupied Mr —— that for an hour or two he entirely forgot the cause of all this mischief; or, perhaps satisfying himself that the toad was burnt to ashes, he had no curiosity to look after it. He was, however, suddenly summoned from the bed-room, in which he was with his wife, by his daughter calling to him in a voice of terror—

"O father, the toad, the toad!".

Mr —— rushed downstairs, and he then discovered that the toad, though severely burnt, had escaped destruction. It must have crawled up over the log of wood, and from it have fallen down amongst the ashes. There it was now making useless struggles to escape, by climbing over the fender.

The tongs were again put in requisition, with the intention this time of carrying the reptile out of the house. Before, however, he had time to do so, a man from Anthony came hastily into the shop with the information that Aunt Alsey had fallen into the fire, as the people supposed, in a fit, and that she was nearly burnt to death. This man had been sent off with two commissions—one to fetch the doctor, and the other to bring Mr —— with him, as much of the cottage had been injured by fire, communicated to it by the old woman's dress.

In as short a time as possible the parish surgeon and Mr —— were at Anthony, and too truly they found the old woman most severely burnt —so seriously, indeed, there was no chance that one so aged could rally from the shock which her system must have received. However, a litter was carefully prepared, the old woman was placed in it, and carried to the workhouse. Every attention was given to her situation, but she never recovered perfect consciousness, and during the night she died.

The toad, which we left inside the fender in front of a blazing fire, was removed from a position so trying to any cold-blooded animal, by the servant, and thrown with a "hugh" and a shudder, upon one of the flower-beds in the small garden behind the house. There it lay the next morning, dead, and when examined by Mr ——, it was found that all the injuries sustained by the toad corresponded with those received by the poor old wretch, who had no doubt fallen a victim to passion.

As we have only to deal with the mysterious relation which existed between the witch and the toad, it is not necessary that we should attend further to the innocent victim of an old woman's vengeance, than to say that eventually a babe was born—that that babe grew to be a handsome man, was an officer in the navy, and, having married, went to sea, and perished, leaving a widow with an unborn child to lament his loss. Whether this was a result of the witch's curse, those who are more deeply skilled in witchcraft than I am may perhaps tell.

TYPE ML.3055. MOTIFS: G.211.6.1 [*Witch in form of toad*]; G.275.12(*f*) [*Injury to toad causes injury or death to witch*] (Baughman).

¶ Here again we have the tongs employed to deal with a magic creature. In this case, however, it is not of great significance, because many people considered a toad venomous.

See "The White Wizard of Preston Wynne".

THE WITCH OF TREVA

Hunt, *Popular Romances of the West of England*, pp. 335–6.

Once on a time, long ago, there lived at Treva, a hamlet in Zennor, a wonderful old lady deeply skilled in necromancy. Her charms, spells, and dark incantations made her the terror of the neighbourhood. However, this old lady failed to impress her husband with any belief in her supernatural powers, nor did he fail to proclaim his unbelief aloud.

One day this sceptic came home to dinner, and found, being exceedingly hungry, to his bitter disappointment, that not only was there no dinner to eat, but that there was no meat in the house. His rage was great, but all he could get from his wife was "I couldn't get meat out of the stones, could I?" It was in vain to give the reins to passion, the old woman told him, and he must know "that hard words buttered no parsnips". Well, at length he resolved to put his wife's powers to the proof, and he quietly but determinedly told her that he would be the death of her if she did not get him some dinner; but if in half an hour she gave him some good cooked meat, he would believe all she had boasted of her power, and be submissive to her for ever.

St Ives, the nearest market town, was five miles off; but nothing doubting, the witch put on her bonnet and cloak, and started. Her husband watched her from the cottage door, down the hill; and at the bottom of the hill he saw his wife quietly place herself on the ground and disappear. In her place a fine hare ran on at its full speed.

He was not a little startled, but he waited, and within the half-hour in walked his wife with "good flesh and taties all ready for aiting". There was no longer any doubt, and the poor husband lived in fear of the witch of Treva to the day of her death.

This event took place after a few years, and it is said the room was full of evil spirits, and that the old woman's shrieks were awful to hear. Howbeit, peace in the shape of pale-faced death came to her at last, and then a black cloud rested over the house when all the heavens were clear and blue.

She was borne to the grave by six aged men, carried, as is the custom, underhand.

When they were about halfway between the house and the church, a hare started from the roadside and leaped over the coffin. The terrified bearers let the corpse fall to the ground, and ran away. Another lot of men took up the coffin and proceeded.

They had not gone far when puss was suddenly seen seated on the coffin, and again the coffin was abandoned. After long consultation, and being persuaded by the parson to carry the old woman very quickly into the churchyard while he walked before, six others made the attempt, and, as the parson never ceased to repeat the Lord's Prayer, all went on quietly. Arrived at the church stile, they rested the corpse, the parson paused to commence the ordinary burial service, and there stood the hare, which, as soon as the clergyman began, "I am the resurrection and the life," uttered a diabolical howl, changed into a black, unshapen creature, and disappeared.

MOTIFS: G.211.2.7 [*Witch in form of hare*]; G.303.3.3.2.3 [*Devil in form of hare*]; G.303.16.2 [*Devil's power over one avoided by prayer*].

THE WITCHES OF BELVOIR

C. L. Billson, *County Folk-Lore*, I, Part 3, *Leicestershire and Rutland*, pp. 47–9.

On the 11th of March, 1618/19, two women, named Margaret and Philippa Flower, were burnt at Lincoln for the alleged crime of witch-craft. With their mother, Joan Flower, they had been confidential servants of the Earl and Countess of Rutland at Belvoir Castle. Dissatisfaction with their employers seems to have gradually seduced these three women into the practice of hidden arts in order to obtain revenge. According to their own confession, they had entered into communion with familiar spirits, by which they were assisted in their wicked designs. Joan Flower, the mother, had hers in the bodily form of a cat, which she called *Rutterkin*. They used to get the hair of a member of the family, and burn it; they would steal one of his gloves and plunge it in boiling water, or rub it on the back of Rutterkin, in order to effect bodily harm to its owner. They would also use frightful imprecations of wrath and malice towards the objects of their hatred. In these ways they were believed to have accomplished the death of Lord Rosse, the Earl of Rutland's son, besides inflicting frightful sicknesses upon other members of the family.

It was long before the Earl and Countess, who were an amiable couple, suspected any harm in these servants, although we are told that for some years there was a manifest change in the countenance of the mother, a diabolic expression being assumed. At length, at Christmas, 1618, the noble pair became convinced that they were the victims of a hellish plot, and the three women were apprehended, taken to Lincoln Gaol, and examined. The mother loudly protested innocence, and calling for bread and butter, wished it might choke her if she were guilty of the offences laid to her charge.

Immediately, taking a piece into her mouth, she fell down dead, probably, as we may allowably conjecture, overpowered by consciousness of the contrariety between these protestations and the guilty design which she had entertained in her mind.

Margaret Flower, on being examined, acknowledged that she had stolen the glove of the young heir of the family, and given it to her mother, who stroked Rutterkin with it, dipped it in hot water, and pricked it; whereupon Lord Rosse fell ill and suffered extremely. In order to prevent Lord and Lady Rutland from having any more children, they had taken some feathers from their bed, and a pair of gloves, which they boiled in water mingled with a little blood. In all these particulars, Philippa corroborated her sister.

Both women admitted that they had familiar spirits, which came and sucked them at various parts of their bodies; and they also described visions of devils in various forms which they had from time to time.

Associated with the Flowers in their horrible practices were three other women of the like grade in life—Anne Baker of Bottesford; Joan Willimot of Goodby; and Ellen Greene of Stathorne, all in the county of Leicester, whose confessions were much to the same purpose. Each had her own familiar spirits to assist in working out her malignant designs against her neighbours.

That of Joan Willimot was called *Pretty*. It had been blown into her mouth by her master, William Berry, in the form of a fairy, and immediately after came forth again and stood on the floor in the shape of a woman, to whom she forthwith promised that her soul should be enlisted in the infernal service.

On one occasion, at Joan Flower's house, she saw two spirits, one like an owl, the other like a rat, one of which sucked her under the ear.

This woman, however, protested that, for her part, she only employed her spirit in inquiring after the health of persons whom she had undertaken to cure. Greene confessed to having had a meeting with Willimot in the woods, when the latter called two spirits into their company, one like a kitten, the other like a mole, which, on her being left alone, mounted on her shoulders and sucked her under the ears, she had then sent them to bewitch a man and a woman who had reviled her, and who accordingly died within a fortnight. Anne Baker seems to have been more of a visionary than any of the rest. She once saw a hand and heard a voice from the air; she had been visited with a flash of fire—all of them ordinary occurrences in the annals of hallucination.

She also had a spirit, but, as she alleged, a beneficent one, in the form of a white dog.

A shortened account from the contemporary pamphlet printed in Nichols' *Leicestershire*.

MOTIFS: G.275.3 [*Witches burned*]; G.225 [*Witch's familiar spirit*]; G.225.0.1 [*Witch feeds animal familiar with her own blood*]; G.224.14(*b*) [*Witch has power over person if she gets any possession of the intended victim*] (Baughman); G.263.4 [*Witch causes sickness*]; D.2061.2.2 [*Murder by sympathetic magic*]; G.225.0.1(*b*) [*Familiars suck witches' ears*] (Baughman); H.232 [*Ordeal by bread and cheese*]; H.252 [*Act of truth*]; H.232.1.1* [*Suspected witch chokes on bread and cheese*] (Baughman).

¶ This is an account of an actual witch trial and a valuable testimony to the witch beliefs of the period. It has been included as a specimen, but is not so truly a folk-legend as most of the other tales. In an ordinary way, the statement that the witches were burned would be evidence of an intrusion of folk-legend into history, but in this case the deaths might be regarded as the murder of a master, and so liable to the penalties for petty treason. The witches were, however, hanged (Notestein, *Witchcraft in England*, p. 399).

THE WITCHES' BRIDLE

Campbell, *Popular Tales of the West Highlands*, II, pp. 69–71.

The Macgowans of Grayscroft in Tongland, and latterly of Bogra, had the power of witchcraft to a considerable extent, and it descended from one generation to another. At the time we refer to, Abraham Macgowan and his daughter Jenny resided at Grayscroft. Jenny had an unlimited power from Old Nick to act as she pleased.

The ploughmen at that time in their employ were Harry Dew and Davie Gordon, young men about twenty-two years of age; they had been there for the last twelve months; and conversing one day together, the following took place:

Harry: "Losh, man Davie, what makes ye sae drowsy, lazy, and sleepy-like the day, for I am verra sure ye work nae mair than I do;

ye eat the same and sleep the same as I do, and yet ye are so thin and wearied and hungry-like, I dinna ken ava what ails ye. Are ye weel eneugh, Davie?"

"I'm weel eneugh, Harry, but ut's a' ye ken about it; sleep a night or twa at the bedside, and maybe ye'll no be sae apt to ask me sic questions again, Harry."—"The bedside, Davie! What differ will that make? I hae nae mair objections to sleep there than at the wa'."

This being agreed to, they exchanged places. Nothing occurred to disturb either of them till the third night, although Harry kept watch: their bed was on the stable loft, when, about midnight, the stable door was opened cautiously, and someone was heard (by Harry only) coming up the ladder and to the bedside, with a quiet step. A bridle was held above the one next the bedside, and the words "Up horsey" whispered in his ear; in one moment Harry was transformed into a horse at the stable door. The saddle was got on with some kicking and plunging, but Jenny gets mounted, and off they set by the Elfcraigs, Auld Brig o' Tongland, the March Cleughs, and on till they reach the Auld Kirk o' Buittle. Harry was tied to the gate along with others. Meg o' Glencap was there on her dairy-maid, now a bonny mare, neat in all her proportions. "Tib" o' Criffle came on her auld ploughman, rather wind-broken. "Lizzy" frae the Bennan came on her cot-wife, limping with a swelled knee.

"Moll o' the Wood" came on a herd callant frae the "How o' Siddick". When all the horses were mustered, there was some snorting and kicking and neighing amongst them. Fairies, witches, brownies and all met in the kirk and had a blithe holiday, under the patronage of his Satanic Majesty, which continued till the crowing of the cock. Wearied with his gallop, Harry, when the charmed bridle was taken off, found himself in his own bed and in his own shape. Harry is determined to be revenged; he finds the charmed bridle in a hole in the kitchen in a week after; he tries it on Jenny, using the same words, when Jenny is transformed into the auld brown mare of the farm; he takes her to the neighbouring smithy, and gets her, after much ado, shod all round, when he returns and leaves her, after securing the wonderful bridle.

Next morning Harry is ordered to go for a doctor, as his mistress is taken ill. He goes into the house to ask for her; pulls the bedclothes off her, and discovers there was a horse-shoe on each hand and foot, when Harry says, "Jenny, my lass, that did ye." Jenny played many more similar tricks on her neighbour lads and lasses.

TYPE ML.3055. MOTIFS: D.535 [*Transformation to horse by putting on bridle*]; G.241.2.1 [*Witch transforms man to horse and rides him*]; G.243 [*Witches' Sabbath*]; G.211.1.1.2 [*Witch as horse shod with horse-shoes*]; G.275.12 [*Witch in form of an animal is injured as a result of the injuries done to the animal*].

THE WITCHES OF DELNABO

Douglas, *Scottish Fairy and Folk-Tales*, p. 185.

In the time of my grandmother, the farm of Delnabo was proportionally divided between three tenants. At first equally comfortable in their circumstances, it was in the course of some time remarked by all, and by none more forcibly than by one of the said three portioners, that, although superior in point of industry and talent to his two fellow portioners, one of the tenants was daily lapsing into poverty, while his two neighbours were daily improving in estate.

Amazed and grieved at the adverse fortune which thus attended his family, compared to the prosperous condition of his neighbours, the wife of the poor man was in the habit of expressing her astonishment at the circumstance, not only to her own particular friends, but likewise to the wives of her neighbours themselves.

On one of these occasions, the other two wives asked her what would she do to ameliorate her condition if it were in her power? She answered them she would do anything whatever. (Here the other wives thought they had got a gudgeon that would snap at any bait, and immediately resolved to make her their confidante.)

"Well, then," says one of the other two wives, "if you agree to keep our communications strictly secret, and implicitly obey our instructions, neither poverty nor want shall ever assail you more." This speech of the other wife immediately impressed the poor man's wife with a strong suspicion of their real character.

Dissembling all surprise at the circumstance, she promised to agree to all their conditions. She was then directed, when she went to bed that night, to carry along with her the floor broom, well known for its magical properties, which she was to leave by her husband's side in the course of the night, and which would represent her so exactly that the husband could not distinguish the difference in the morning. They at the same time enjoined her to discard all fears of detection, as their own husbands had been satisfied with those lovely substitutes (the brooms) for a great number of years. Matters being thus arranged, she was desired to join them at the hour of midnight, in order to accompany them to that scene which was to realize her future happiness.

Promising to attend to their instructions, the poor man's wife took leave of her neighbours, full of those sensations of horror which the discovery of such depravity was calculated to produce in a virtuous mind. Hastening home to her husband, she thought it no crime to break her promise to her wicked neighbours and, like a dutiful and prudent wife, to reveal to the husband of her bosom the whole particulars of their interview. The husband greatly commended his wife's fidelity, and immediately entered into a collusion with her, which displays no ordinary degree of ingenuity. It was agreed that the husband should exchange apparel with the wife, and that he should, in this disguise, accompany the wives to the place appointed, to see what cantrips they intended to perform.

He accordingly arrayed himself in his wife's habiliments, and, at the hour of midnight, joined the party at the place appointed. The "bride", as they called him, was most cordially received by the two Ladies of the Broom, who warmly congratulated the "bride" upon *her* good fortune, and the speedy consummation of *her* happiness. He was then presented with a fir torch, a broom, and a riddle, articles with which they themselves were furnished. They directed their course along the banks of the rolling Avon, until they reached Craic-pol-nain, or the Craig of the Bird's-pool. Here, in consequence of the steepness of the Craig, they found it convenient to pass to the other side of the river. This passage they effected without the use of the Navy, the river being fordable at the place.

They then came in sight of Pol-nain, and lo! what human eye ever witnessed such a scene before! The pool appeared as if actually enveloped in a flame of fire.

A hundred torches blazed aloft, reflecting their beams on the towering woods of Loynchork. And what ear ever heard such shrieks and yells as proceeded from the horrid crew engaged at their hellish orgies on Pol-nain? Those cries were, however, sweet music to the two wives of Delnabo. Every yell produced from them a burst of unrestrained pleasure, and away they frisked, leaving the amiable *bride* a considerable way behind. For the fact is that he was in no hurry to reach the scene, and when he did reach it it was with a determination to be only a spectator, and not a participator in the night's performance. On reaching the pool's side, he saw what was going on: he saw abundance of hags steering themselves to and fro in their riddles, by means of their oars (the brooms), hallooing and skirling [shrieking] worse than the bogles, and each holding in her left hand a torch of fir—whilst at other times they would swirl themselves into a row, and make profound obeisance to a large black ugly tyke [dog] perched on a lofty rock, and who was no doubt the "muckle thief" himself, and who was pleased to acknowledge most graciously those expressions of their loyalty and devotion by bowing, grinning, and clapping his paws. Having administered to the *bride* some preliminary instructions, the impatient wives desired him to remain by the pool's side until they should commune with his Satanic Highness on the subject of *her* inauguration, directing *her*, as they proceeded on their voyage across the pool, to speed them in their master's name. To this order of the black pair the *bride* was resolved to pay particular attention. As soon as they were embarked in their riddles, and had wriggled themselves, by means of their brooms, into a proper depth of water, "Go," says he, "in the name of the Best." A horrid yell from the witches announced their instant fate—the magic spell was now dissolved—crash went the riddles, and down sank the two witches, never more to rise, amidst the shrieks and lamentations of the Old Thief and all his infernal crew, whose combined power and policy could not save them from a watery end. All the torches were extinguished in an instant, and the affrighted company fled in different directions in such forms and similitudes as they thought most convenient for them to adopt; and the wily *bride* returned home at his leisure, enjoying himself vastly at the clever manner in which he had executed the instructions of his deceased friends. On arriving at his house, he dressed himself in his own clothes, and, without immediately satisfying his wife's curiosity at the result of his excursion, he yoked his cattle, and commenced his morning labours with as little concern as usual. His two neighbours, who were not even conscious of the absence of their wives (so ably substituted were they by the brooms), did the same.

Towards breakfast-time, however, the two neighbours were not a little astonished that they observed no signs of their wives having risen from bed—notwithstanding their customary earliness—and this surprise they expressed to the *late bride*, their neighbour. The latter archly remarked that he had great suspicions, in his own mind, of their *rising* even that day. "What mean you by that?" replied they. "We left our wives apparently in good health when we ourselves arose." "Find them now," was the reply—the *bride* setting up as merry a whistle as before. Running each to his bed, what was the astonishment of the husbands, when, instead of his wife, he only found an old broom? Their neighbour then told them that, if they chose to examine Pol-nain well, they would find both their dear doxies there. The grieving husbands accordingly proceeded thither, and with the necessary instruments, dragged their late worthy partners to dry land, and afterwards privately interred them. The shattered vessels and oars of those unfortunate navigators, whirling about the pool, satisfied their lords of the manner by which they came to their ends; and their names were no longer mentioned by their kindred in the land. It need hardly be added that the poor man gradually recovered his former opulence; and that in the course of a short time he was comparatively as rich as he was formerly poor.

TYPE ML.3050. MOTIFS: G.224.13.2* [*Initiation as witch*] (Baughman); D.2031 [*Magic illusion*]; G.243 [*Witches' Sabbath*]; G.243.1 [*Obeisance to devil at Witches' Sabbath*]; G.303.3.3.1.1(a) [*Devil in form of black dog*] (Baughman); G.224.1

[*Witch's charm opposite of Christian*]; G.241.4.3 [*Witch travels over water in a sieve or riddle*]; D.1783.4 [*Power over wizard obtained by reversing orders*].

¶ This is one of the best of the witch stories, embodying a number of witch beliefs. The Scottish witch-legends were more coherent, and less fragmentary than those to be found in England.

WITCHES AT HALLOWE'EN

W. H. Barrett, *More Tales from the Fens*, p. 133.

I reckon I was a lad of about seven or eight when, because Mother was expecting another little one to join our already crowded house, I was sent to stay with an old aunt in one of the loneliest parts of the Fens. She had a big family, this aunt, though most of them were grown up by then, except for a boy of fifteen and a girl of twelve.

Although there wasn't another house within a mile, that didn't bother them; the farm was run by the family, and for most of the year they went to bed when it got dark and got up at daybreak.

While I was there Hallowe'en came round. In the afternoon everyone was busy putting osier twigs in front of all the doors and windows, the pigsties, stables and cow-house.

Uncle killed one of his black hens and hung it on the chicken-house door after he'd pulled out two of its wing feathers and tied them on the yard-dog's collar; then he caught the cats and shut them up in the barn. From all the talk going on, I found out that this was the night when the witches went round the fen, meeting each other and then, at the chiming of midnight, coming to some spot they'd chosen and casting spells over all the folks and animals nearby. That was why the peeled osier rods were put at all the ways into the house because no witch dared cross over them, neither would they go near black chicken feathers.

As the evening went by we all sat round the big open hearth. Aunt didn't put peat on the fire that night because witches could smell peat smoke for miles away, she said; instead, huge logs of oak were blazing away. The candles had been blown out, so the only light we had came from the fire, as we sat and listened to Aunt's stories of what witches could get up to. After supper a plate of thick slices of ham and half of a loaf of bread were stood outside on the door-stone so that, if a witch called, she wouldn't have to go away hungry because, if she did, she might start casting her spells on us. Then I was given a glass of ginger wine while my aunt and uncle and the others drank a lot of home-made botanic beer. After a while Uncle stood up and said to me:

"Come along, it's time we were up and doing."

He told me it was the custom, this night, for the oldest man and the youngest boy in the house to go round the farm an hour before midnight; so we set off. It was very queer padding along behind Uncle as he carried the lantern. All the animals seemed restless, and Uncle said they were like that because they could see and hear things that we couldn't, and they all knew what was going on.

After we'd been round the farmyard we had to visit the bees. As we went into the orchard an owl swooped over us with a loud screech, just above Uncle's head. I was scared, but Uncle got a firm grip of the thick stick he was carrying and, when the owl turned to fly over us again, he caught it such a clout that it fell down to the ground, fluttered its wings a bit and then lay still. My uncle bent down, turned it over and said:

"Well, there's one old witch who won't go home tonight."

When we got to the bee-hive, we went close up and listened to the noise going on inside; it was just like the hum of a threshing tackle on a frosty morning.

"Bor," said Uncle, "they're all worked up because they're a lot wiser than we are"; then, after tapping the hive with his stick, he bent right down to the entrance and said:

"Well done, my old beauties. I got one just now and, by the sound of it, you've got another; push her outside when you've done with her."

When we were back indoors we all sat round the fire again while Uncle told my aunt and the others what had happened while we were out.

"It looks as though some of us will be tudded [bewitched] for sure before morning," said Aunt, "if we're not careful. There's nothing, after all, to stop one of those old witches coming down the chimney and casting a spell on us."

I saw everyone backing away from the fire, and I did so too. Then Aunt got up, went over to the cupboard in the corner and came back with a big brown-paper bag.

"Whatever any old hag turns herself into," she said, "I promise I'll make her cough before she gets to the hearth. This ought to make her sneeze a bit first," and she took a handful of flowers of sulphur out of the bag and threw them on the fire. Bright blue flames and yellow smoke roared up the chimney. Aunt did this several times, even though Uncle told her not to forget that the roof was thatch, and if we were burnt out it wasn't going to be any good blaming it on any witches; but she only told him to be quiet, she knew what she was doing. This started a lot of arguing; everybody joining in till it seemed to me that the witches had been forgotten and that I was in the middle of a good old family row. Anyway, Aunt got into such a temper that she threw the whole bag on to the fire and the yellow smoke came pouring out into the room worse than ever, making us all splutter and choke.

Uncle said that two could play at that game and he went over to the cupboard and fetched out a linen bag full of the black gunpowder he used in his muzzle-loader. He'd no sooner hurled it at the back of the fire than there was a hell of a bang and we were all smothered in soot from head to foot. Well, that cleared everybody's temper and when the smoke had cleared away a bit Uncle said: "Well, I'll be damned," because lying on Auntie's lap was a jackdaw just kicking out his last gasp. And just then the old grandfather clock struck midnight.

After that we all ate a lot of thick ham sandwiches and the others drank some more botanic beer and I had another glass of ginger wine. Then Uncle said to me: "Come on, bor. We've got to make another round."

It was still very dark when we got outside, but all the animals were quiet and settled down. When we got to the orchard we found the bees quiet, too, but on the flight board, believe it or not, was a dead mouse, still warm. Uncle picked it up then went back to fetch the owl which he'd killed the time we were out before. When we were back in the house he threw the owl, the mouse and the jackdaw on the fire and said:

"Three witches on one Hallowe'en isn't a bad bag. Now, all of you get up to bed and sleep well. You won't have to worry about any witches for another twelvemonth."

Now, if you want to know where all this happened, then just walk a couple of miles from Littleport till you come to Crouchmoor Drove. Go along the drove for three miles till you come to the place called Coldharbour, and by the side of the drove you'll see a corner of a field all grown up with wild plum and nettles. That's where the farm was where I spent that Hallowe'en, and that was over seventy years ago.

MOTIFS F.900.1.1 [*Wonders occur on Hallowe'en*]; G.272 [*Protection against witches*]; G.272.2 [*Magic herb protects against witch*]; G.211.4.4 [*Witch in form of owl*]; G.211.2.5 [*Witch in form of mouse*]; G.211.4.1 [*Witch in form of crow*]; G.275.12 [*Witch in the form of an animal is injured or killed as a result of the injury to the animal*].

¶ It is interesting to know that these ancient beliefs still had practical expression within living memory.

Curiously enough, the Motif Index does not mention Hallowe'en as the chief time of the meeting of witches, although ghosts and fairies are both mentioned as active at that time.

THE WITCH'S PURSE

Briggs and Tongue, *Folktales of England*, pp. 57–9.

When I was a little girl my mother had a new baby, and, of course, I was in the bedroom when this old lady came up in the bedroom, and was talking to my mother, and then the dog belonging to her began to howl.

My mother was very concerned, and she said, "Oh, do make that dog stop his noise. I hate to hear a dog howl."

Then the old lady said; "Let'en 'owl. Let 'en 'owl. He's 'owling arter that child." and 'er said: "Is anything the matter with that child?" "No, not that I know, except that it's going to die." And my mother was very concerned about it, and it did die—it died when it was height days old. And, of course, my mother was very concerned about it, and main frightened, and she wouldn't let anybody go anywhere near for days, for fear they'd tell her something to hurt this baby what was the matter.

They went to Charlbury, which is ever so far, about four or five miles, to fetch the doctor to see if there was anything the matter, and he said, "No, there's nothing the matter with it. No earthly reason why it should die." But it did die, and that's all I can tell you.

And some years after that, or some time after that, this old lady did die, and my mother went in to look after her from next door, and she said; "Rhoda, bring my purse off the table." And my mother said: "Why, do you want the purse for? You can't spend money. You aren't able to get up." "I wants my purse. You give it to me. I can't open it. You open it for me, and then I can manage." My mother opens this purse, and there was a quantity of sovereigns in it, my mother saw them quite plain, but she never counted them to know the quantity. And she says: "Oh, that's right. I shan't be here many more days." She counted 'em up. "My money'll last till then, and when that's gone," she says, "I shall go, because I'm not able to go to fetch any more." And she did die, and when the daughter that belonged to this poor lady, the daughter, my mother said to her: "You'd better take care of that purse. Because," she said, "your mother had it to look at. There's a lot of money in it. You take care of it," and the old lady said: "Let it alone. Leave it there!" And so they never moved it, and the daughter and my mother was there when she died. And when she died and they'd done different things to her, like what they has to do, one of them saying, "You'd better take care of that purse, and see that's safe," they opened the purse, and there was nothink in it; it was quite empty. The Devil had took her and the money together.

The story was more detailed and dramatic when she was not telling it on the tape. But the old witch's speeches were in more pronounced dialect, and some attempt at dramatic impersonation appeared in the story.

Mrs Falconer, aged eighty. She lived all her life in Leafield. Transcription from tape. Recorded 28 August 1962 by K. M. Briggs.
MOTIFS: B.733.2 [*Dog's howling ominous of death*]; M.341.1.2 [*Prophecy: early death*]; G.275.1 [*Devil carries off witch*].
¶ In this case it was the soul, not the body, of the witch that was thought to be carried off.

THE WITCHIE CLOCK

Shetland Folk-Book, II, p. 8.

A Yell man had for some years persistently poor crops although weather and other conditions were favourable; formerly they had almost uniformly been good.

He therefore suspected a neighbour woman, who was known "to say mair as her prayers", of doing him harm.

When he was sowing the corn-seed in voar he observed a large witchie clock [Beetle] being very active among his seed, he picked the beetle up and put it in his empty snuff-box.

In the evening the husband of the suspected woman came to inquire if anyone had seen his wife as it was now dagalien [the evening twilight] and she was not yet at home. But no one had seen her.

In the morning the man opened his snuff box and allowed the beetle its liberty. It was observed to take the direction of the suspected woman's house.

A little later he went to inquire and found that the woman had returned home that morning, stating that she had "willed" [strayed] during the dark hours.

MOTIF: G.211.5.3 [*Witch in form of beetle*].
¶ It is clear that this was a transformation, not an example of the witch travelling out of her body, otherwise she would have been at home in a trance.
See "The Soul as a Humble-Bee" (B, XII).

THE WITHYPOOL WITCH

Ruth L. Tongue, *Somerset Folklore*, p. 78.

A farmer who had lost some of his sheep and had seen a hare at the time of their deaths decided to consult the conjuror at Watercrow. He was told before he had spoken a word what his trouble was, and then shown the witch responsible. He promised he would deal with her. This hag had an ill name for halting wagons and scaring horses, but she now began to pine till "she was skin and bone hanged agin the wall." She became so feeble that many a time she was taken for dead. Then suddenly she would be gone, and they would find her "a-quat stark nekked in t'road or spinning around like a whirligig". Eventually she recovered, but remained quite harmless, more even than her old husband, who was a notable quiet soul, and prayed as hard as the neighbours for her death-bed.

MOTIFS: G.271.6 [*Exorcism of witch by counter-charm worked by witch-doctor*]; (Baughman); G.269.25 [*Witch causes person to spin around on bed-post*].

¶ The witch's antics would be supposed to be the effect of her charms being turned against her.

THE WIZARD OF LINCOLN

S. O. Addy, *Household Tales*, pp. 36–7.

At a farm in Lincolnshire there had once been a great robbery, and no-body could find out who the thief was. At last the farmer's wife said to her husband, "If you will send for the wizard of Lincoln, he will tell you."

So the farmer did as his wife had told him, and sent for the wizard, who came in the form of a blackbird. He flew into the crew-yard, and so frightened the cattle there that a man who was threshing wheat in the barn could hardly keep them out.

Then the blackbird spoke to the farmer, and said, "Shall I bring the thieves into thy house, or make their shadows appear on the wall?"

The farmer answered, "Do as thou thinkest right."

He had hardly spoken when one of the farmer's men servants, who had only that very moment begun his work in the fields, walked into the room, and at once passed out.

When he had gone, the blackbird said, "That is one of them."

Then he pointed to a shadow on the wall, and the farmer saw that it was the shadow of another of his servants.

"That is the other thief," said the blackbird, and flew away.

Soon after the two men were arrested, and the money which they had stolen was found.

MOTIFS: D.1817.0.1 [*Magic detection of theft*]; D.1817.0.1.4 [*Wizard shows shadow of thief*].

WRIGHTSON AND NATHAN AGAR AND OTHER STORIES

R. Blakeborough, *Wit, Character, Folk-Lore and Customs of the North Riding of Yorkshire*, p. 181.

Nathan Agar was a miserly old man who hid a stocking full of hoarded gold in the thatch of his house. At the age of sixty he had married a girl not nineteen, much against the advice of Wrightson, and to add to his store of money they kept a young man as lodger.

One day Nathan went to add another guinea to his stocking, and found it missing. In his distress, he went to Wrightson, who told him to lift one of the flagstones in front of his doorstep, and bury a certain leaf of the Bible under it. Then he was to watch and see who stumbled as he crossed the threshold. Nathan watched, and the first to stumble was the young lodger, but he was soon followed by Nathan's wife, who also stumbled. Nathan hurried off to Wrightson, who told him that his property was hidden in a certain place in the pig-sty, together with an old watch, which Nathan had not even missed. He persuaded Nathan to return home, give the guilty pair the guineas and send them off.

Once a man rode up in great haste to Wrightson's door to say that his mother was suffering from a terrible lump in her throat, and no one seemed to be able to help her. But before he even dismounted from his horse, Wrightson called out to him: "Bait thy horse, give it something to eat, and get back again. The lump has burst; she's all right now."

Old Willie Bradley of Great Ayton was the son of a quarryman who once had his tools stolen. He went to Wrightson, who immediately said, "Now then, thou's come about thy tools, but I can do nothing for thee. They've been taken across water. But I can tell thee where they be."

He took him into a darkened room, and told him to keep his eyes fixed on a looking-glass; if he took them off, something dreadful would happen. In terror, the quarryman did as he was bidden, but wished he had never troubled about the tools; however, soon he saw them quite plainly, lying among some bracken in a wood, in a place well known to him. Wrightson told him he must not touch them, but must bring him a live magpie. He tried by every means for a week, but could not find such a bird; and on returning to Wrightson, he was told, "Then I cannot work him any harm. Thou'll have to lose thy tools."

MOTIFS: T.237 [*Old man married to young unfaithful wife*]; D.1817.0.1 [*Magic detection of theft*]; D.1814.1 [*Advice from magician*]; D.1817.0.1.2 [*Wizard tells location of stolen property*]; G.273.4 [*Witch powerless to cross stream*].

¶ Wrightson confessed himself a witch when he said that he had no power across running water.

WRIGHTSON AND THE COWS [summary]

R. Blakeborough, *Wit, Character, Folk-Lore and Customs of the North Riding of Yorkshire*, p. 180.

Wrightson, the wise man of Stokesley, whose reputation stood high in the early part of the last century, was the seventh son of a seventh daughter, and the following story was told by an old man who had known him personally:

This old man's father had a friend named Scorer, who once bought some cattle at Northallerton fair. They were put in charge of an old drover, who brought them late that night to Stokesley, and put them, with another buyer's drove, into a field about quarter of a mile away from Scorer's land. In the morning two of Scorer's beasts were found to be missing, and the old drover was suspected of having sold them on the way home and pocketed the money. To prove this, the two purchasers agreed to visit Wrightson; but, having no experience of his powers, they decided to test them, by saying the horse was lost.

When they entered the house, Wrightson was in the scullery, and he called out to them that, if they were sharp enough to turn two cows into a horse, it was no use coming to him; for he had no power to turn a horse back into two cows. And no more would he say for a long time; but at last, still from the scullery, he shouted, "They're both in the beck, and have been there since yester night."

And there they found them, drowned, having missed the bridge in the darkness and fallen into the swollen water, which had carried them nearly a mile downstream.

MOTIFS: D.1810.0.2 [*Magic knowledge of magician*]; D.1814.1 [*Advice from magician*].

XIV MISCELLANEOUS LEGENDS

MISCELLANEOUS LEGENDS

The small mixed bag which follows is something on the lines of the "Unclassified Tales" at the end of the Aarne–Thompson Tale-type Index. It includes two modern legends, "The Foreign Hotel" and "The Stolen Corpse", which are generally believed by the tellers to be true, but which cannot be called either historical or supernatural. They can be compared, however, with "The Lady Restored to Life" as examples of the way in which legends can build themselves up.

"The Good Magpie" is a naturalistic version of a Supernatural Tale, though the conduct of the magpie might almost qualify it to be considered supernatural. It is a gruesome comment on the extreme poverty of the peasantry in the eighteenth and early nineteenth centuries. "The Widow's Son and the Old Man" (A, II) illustrates this poverty in the same way.

"The First Simnel Cake" is too trivial to belong to the Origin Myths, and is not quite in place among the Jocular Tales. "The Child and the Snake" has been listed as a narrative in the Tale-Type Index, but is really only a legend, and so slight in plot as hardly to count as a tale at all. It is, however, widely diffused, which means that there must be something in it which arouses interest. "Farmer Hewlett's Amends", again, is hardly a narrative, but it enshrines an unusual piece of folk-practice in the simulated birth which is supposed to give legal status to a son born out of wedlock.

"The Wooden Legs" is an interesting example of a folk-tale in reverse—a negative print of "Bluebeard", as it were. It is difficult to imagine it as anything but an invention. Perhaps the narrator felt it to be unconvincing, and so added the corroborative incident of someone beginning to tell the tale as an after-dinner story in the presence of its hero and heroine.

CHILD AND SNAKE

Hunt, *Popular Romances of the West of England*, p. 420.

A child who was in the habit of receiving its portion of bread and milk at the cottage door was found to be in the habit of sharing its food with one of the poisonous adders. The reptile came regularly every morning, and the child, pleased with the beauty of his companion, encouraged the visits. The babe and the adder were close friends.

Eventually this became known to the mother, and, finding it to be a matter of difficulty to keep the snake from the child whenever it was left alone—and she was frequently, being a labourer in the fields, compelled to leave her child to shift for itself—she adopted the precaution of binding an "ashen-twig" about its body.

The adder no longer came near the child; but from that day forward the child pined, and eventually died, as all around said, through grief at having lost the companion by whom it had been fascinated.

TYPE 285. MOTIF: B.765.18.1 [*Snake avoids white ash*].

¶ This little anecdote has been dignified with a type number because it is so widespread, and is recorded in the Grimm tales (no. 105). It is best known in this country in a literary form—Charles Lamb's "The Child and the Snake" in *Poems for Children*.

FARMER HEWLETT'S AMENDS

Ruth L. Tongue, *Somerset Folklore*, p. 148.

This was told to me by a bed-ridden old granny somewhere near Goathurst on the Quantocks. She was repeating the tale told by her mother, who as a girl of fourteen, was a witness, of this service. I do not know where the mother's family came from—it may have been another Western county, but for its interest I have included it. It is a verbatim report except where the dialect was so archaic that an interpreter was needed. Even so, I have tried to use phrases still to be heard in casual speech. The names and locality are slightly altered in order to protect any relatives.

"There was a farmer *Hewlett* up around as were highly thought of by all. When his time came he were terrible worrited 'bout Mr *George* as he'd done wrong by. Oh dear, 'twas a gurt shock 'twas! Mr George he'd a-handled varm and stock vor his vather come twenty year and there wadn't none as folks didn't set by like Mr George, Squire and all. Well, it did sim like he were going to lose all his labour, and farm would go to a cousin over to *Taunton*. But varmer he set his mind to do right by un, and his wold Missus as had been the friend to the whole parish she come out brave and she said she'd do as he wished. So poor Mr George he just done what his Dad want. I see them come to church, and me but a maid then. And Mr George he had a loving arm to his dear mother. Then she did up and say in front of all as her and Farmer wasn't a-wed when this dear son come along. Poor old soul! She called him her dear and there wadn't a dry eye to hear her old voice. And that gurt beardy man he do croopy on hands and knees and she do pull hem of her Sunday black over'n and Parson do say the words to right'n so he should a-get farm. Parson he was so quiet as death, but his looks they proper daunted any to miscall 'en, but there wadn' no rabblement, they was too well liked. Farmer died happy—but 'ee see, my dear—old sins do come up again like weeds after a shower."

MOTIFS: z.255 [*Hero born out of wedlock*]; z.100 [*Symbolism*]; T.670 [*Adoption of children*].

¶ This interesting survival, by which a grown man has a mock birth in order to prove himself born in wedlock, is so rare as to have no adequate motif.

THE FIRST SIMNEL CAKE [summary]

From Chambers' *Book of Days*.

An old couple living in Shropshire had a grown-up family, whose custom it was to return home every Easter. The old people's names were Simon and Nelly.

One year, Nelly, wishing to bake a cake for the family occasion, and having some of her Lenten unleavened dough still left, proposed to Simon to use it as the basis; and he suggested that the remains of their Christmas pudding might serve to fill in the inside. However, they failed to agree whether the resulting mixture would be better baked or boiled. So fiercely did they argue that Nelly threw her wooden stool at her husband, and followed it up with several blows from her broom, while he defended himself with a besom. But at last Nelly reasonably suggested that the cake should be first boiled, and then baked.

The stool was broken up and thrown on the fire to boil the great pot; the besom and broom were put into the oven for fuel. Eggs, which had been broken in the scuffle, were used to coat the outside of the cake after boiling, which gave it a shining gloss; and so was evolved the first Simnel cake.

¶ This is a trivial variant of A.1455 [*Origin of cooking*]. There is also a punning derivation for the name of Simnel cake. The ceremonial importance of the cake is shown even by this trivial tale.

THE FOREIGN HOTEL

Briggs and Tongue, *Folktales of England*, p. 98.

A lady and her daughter were travelling abroad, and arrived late at night, very tired after an exhausting journey, at the hotel where they had booked their rooms. The mother was particularly worn-out. They were put into adjoining rooms, and the daughter tumbled into bed and fell asleep at once. She slept long and heavily, and it was well on in the next day before she got up. She opened the door into her mother's room, and found it empty. And it was not the room into which they had gone the night before. The wallpaper was different, the furniture was different, and the bed was made up. She rang, and got no answer to her bell; she dressed and went downstairs.

"Can you tell me where my mother is?" she said to the woman at the reception desk.

"Your mother, mademoiselle?"

"Yes. The lady who arrived with me last night."

"But, mademoiselle, you came alone."

"We booked in; the night porter will remember; we wrote for two rooms!"

"Mademoiselle indeed wrote for two rooms, but she arrived alone."

And wherever she asked among the servants she got the same answer, until she began to think that she must be mad.

At last she went back to England and told her friends what had happened and one of them went to investigate. He went to the Consul and the police, and at last he found out the truth. The mother had been more than tired when she arrived that night, she had been in the invasion stages of cholera. No sooner had she gone to bed than she was taken violently ill; the doctor was sent for, she died, and the hotel-owners were filled with panic and decided to conceal all that had happened. The body was carried away, the furniture was taken out to be burnt, the wall was repapered, and all the staff were told to allow nothing to be guessed of what had happened. They knew that not a guest would be left to them if it was known that cholera had been in the house.

Yorkshire. K. M. Briggs from Agnes Hannam, 1915. Also heard by M. E. Luck (now Nash-Williams) at Warwick, c. 1926.

MOTIF: z.552*(a) [*The mysterious disappearance. A woman and her daughter take a room in a Paris hotel, etc.*] (Baughman).

¶ Alexander Northcott traced this legend in *While Rome Burns* (New York, 1934, pp. 87–94), and got as far back as a report in *The Detroit Free Press* in 1889. Baughman gives as a reference Foster, *Collier's Magazine*, 1 January 1949. There has also been an film "So Long at the Fair."

THE GOOD MAGPIE

S. O. Addy, *Household Tales*, p. 46.

There was once a gentleman who used to ride on horseback every day. One day he had occasion to call at a house by the roadside, where a woman and her little boy lived. Whilst he was talking to the woman, he saw that she was making the oven hot, and the little boy said to him, "Mother's holing the oven to put me in."

But the gentleman thought that the boy was only joking, so he took no heed and rode away. But he had not gone far before a magpie crossed his path, and kept flying in front of his horse, and would not go away. So at last he thought that the magpie wanted him to turn back. So he rode straight back to the house, and when he got there he found that the woman had gone, and that the poor little boy was roasting in the oven.

Nottinghamshire.
TYPE 781 (variant). MOTIFS: S.12 [*Cruel mother*]; G.72.1 [*Woman plans to eat her child*]; N.271.4 [*Birds point out the murder*]; B.450 [*Helpful bird*].
¶ This is a naturalistic and modified version of a widespread tale. Grimm, no. 141, is remotely allied to this tale. No. 141 has, however, a magical foundation, and the villainess is a stepmother, not a mother.

THE MAN WHO GOT INTO HIS CART

Ruth L. Tongue, *Somerset Folklore*, pp. 51–2. Buckland St Mary, South.

One May I met and stopped to talk to an elderly carter in a Quantock lane. After mutual admiration of the hill pony I rode, and his solid Shire mare, we went on to discuss their ways. Yes, they had both been difficult that day, and so, all unasked for, out came this tale: "'Tis May, you see." said the carter. "*Always 'troublesome' they are then*. I don't never trust'n, not even the old 'oss yur. I've worked she twenty years tew. My wife she have an old uncle over to they Blackdowns and they was carting stones to *mend their Church*. Uphill 'tis and a nasty piece of road—they was those days, all stones—and there was a bit of a bank down over. I'd a-walk any 'oss up there and down over but there was a carter, he did get intew the cart see—and *summat* give his 'osses a fright and he was killed outright. In May 'twas. There's a verse over at the church there. No; I don't like May. Never tell what a 'oss will take and do."

Quantock Hills, 1936.
MOTIF: C.755 [*Tabu: doing thing during certain time*].
¶ May is a curiously ambivalent month: May Day is the great festival of fertility, yet marriages in May have been considered unlucky since Roman times (Plutarch, *Romane Questions*, translated by Philemon Holland, no. 86). Animals born in May are also considered unlucky (*Somerset Folklore*, p. 51).

THE STOLEN CORPSE

Briggs and Tongue, *Folktales of England*, pp. 99–100.

I

This story was told me by my cousin, who had heard it from a friend in Leeds, about a couple whom he knew, who went for a camping holiday in Spain with their car. They had taken his stepmother with them, she slept in a different tent to the others. On the morning that they struck, they were very busy, and they didn't hear anything of her for a while, and then, when they went to her tent, they found she had died, and rigor had already set in. They were in a great state, and they didn't know what to do, but they decided to roll her up in the tent, and put her on top of the car, and go to the nearest town, and go to the consul and the police. So they did this, and went to the town, and then they felt very cold and miserable, and they hadn't had a proper breakfast. So they thought they'd get a cup of coffee to revive them before they went in search of the consul. So they parked the car, and went to a small café, and had their cup of coffee, and then came back to look for the car. But it wasn't there; it had gone. So they went home to England without the car or the stepmother. But the difficulty was, they couldn't prove her will.

II

Shortly after the end of the Second World War, when money for travel was very tight, a young bride and bridegroom were anxious to spend their honeymoon abroad, but couldn't afford it. The bride's godmother said: "I should like to go to Spain. Why not come as my guests, and bring your car? We can sit lightly to each other. You can go about as you like, and I'll sit in the sun and be quiet."

So it was arranged; and they had a very happy time; but the day before they left for home the godmother had a heart attack and died. The local doctor came, and was very helpful, and said he would make all funeral arrangements for them. The girl said: "She wanted to be cremated. I know she left it in her will."

"But she can't be cremated in Spain," said the doctor. "It's illegal."

"But it was her wish. She must be!" said the girl.

They were at a deadlock for some time, but at length the doctor suggested that they should smuggle the corpse across the border to France, where cremation was legal. The hotel was very ready to co-operate, as a death in the place was bad for trade. The corpse was dressed, wrapped in shawls, and carried down to the car after dark.

At the frontier there was a sleepy guard, who didn't look too curiously into the car when they were told that madame was asleep. The passports were all in order, and they got through without incident, but for all that it had been a nerve-racking experience, and they stopped in the first town where a café was open, locked the car and went to have a drink of coffee and a roll before making inquiries about the Consul. When they got back to the car-park, the car had been stolen with the corpse inside it. They had neither time nor money to stop in France, so they went straight home.

Kentish version

1 is recorded from Winifred E. Briggs in Burford, Oxfordshire, 3 November 1963. She heard it in Canada from a cousin who had heard it in Leeds, Yorkshire. It is by way of becoming an international migratory legend. Stewart Sanderson of Leeds University is making a collection of various versions of the tale, some of them dating back twenty years. It is, however, travelling, for Laurits Bødker of Copenhagen has seen it as a newspaper story told about Poland, and Bengt Holbek, also of the *Folkedigtning Institut* in Copenhagen, knew it in September 1963, having heard it from Gustav Henningsen—again about Spain—from a friend's friend. I have lately come across versions from Sussex and Kent. Richard M. Dorson heard an American variant in East Lansing, Michigan, 31 December 1963, localized in the South-West.

Other versions of the tale are rather different. A plausible one is about the German occupation of France in the Second World War. A young couple were staying with a grandmother who had a villa in the South of France. When the news of the German advance came, they prepared to escape, taking with them some particularly valuable Persian carpets, which they put in a roll on the top of the car. They were leaving early in the morning. In the night the grandmother died, and they would not leave her corpse to be insulted by the Germans, but rolled it up in the carpets. When they reached a port, they went to make enquiries about a boat, but when they got back to their locked car, they found the carpets had been stolen from the top, with the corpse inside (informant, Gerald Hardman, May 1964).

There are by now other and more extravagant variants.

THE TANTONY PIG*

Ruth L. Tongue, *Somerset Folklore*, pp. 56–7.

"There were a little nestle-tripe as were made a Tantony Pig, and everyone were that sorry for 'en that he grew twice so fast and fat with all he were gived to eat. There were a bell with a rope outzide clerk's cottage, and pig learned if he shook rope some'un 'ood come a-running to help, so when butcher time come along Tantony Pig he ups and daps along to rope and rings 'en hard for help. After that the town 'oodn't let 'en be bacon, so he runned round and eat up all their rubbidge for 'en grateful, and a wur a Tantony Pig all his days."

TYPE 207C. MOTIF: B.271.3 [*Animals ring bell and demand justice*].

¶ The best-known example of this story is "The Bell of Atri", given literary expression by Longfellow.

* A piglet rejected as unfit for the market was put under the protection of St Anthony, and fed on market scraps until it grew fat.

THE WOODEN LEGS

Augustus Hare, *In My Solitary Life*, pp. 109–11.

There was, and there still is, living in Cadogan Place, a lady of middle age who is clever, charming, amiable, even handsome, but who has the misfortune of having—a wooden leg. Daily, for many years, she was accustomed to amble every morning on her wooden leg down Cadogan Place and to take the air in the Park.

It was her principal enjoyment.

One day she discovered that in these walks she was constantly followed by a gentleman. When she turned, he turned: where she went, he went: it was most disagreeable. She determined to put an end to it by staying at home, and for some days she did not go out at all. But she missed her walks in the Park very much, and after a time she thought her follower must have forgotten all about her, and she went out as before. The same gentleman was waiting, he followed her, and at length suddenly came up to her in the Park and presented her with a letter.

He said that, as a stranger, he must apologise for speaking to her, but that he must implore her to take the letter, and read it when she got home: it was of great importance. She took the letter, and when she got home she read it, and found that it contained a violent declaration of love and a proposal of marriage.

She was perfectly furious. She desired her lawyer to enclose the letter to the writer, and say that she could not find words to describe her sense of his ungentlemanly conduct, especially cruel to one afflicted as she was with a wooden leg.

Several years elapsed, and the lady was paying a visit to some friends in the country, when the conversation frequently turned upon a friend of the house, who was described as one of the most charming, generous, and beneficent of mankind.

So delightful was the description that the lady was quite anxious to see the original, and was enchanted when she heard that he was likely to come to the house. But when he arrived, she recognised with consternation her admirer of the Park. He did not, however, recur to their former meeting, and after a time, when she knew him well, she grew to esteem him exceedingly, and at last, when he renewed his proposal after an intimate acquaintance, she accepted him and married him.

He took her to his country-house, and for six weeks they were entirely, uncloudedly happy. Then there came a day on which he announced that he was obliged to go up to London on business. His wife could not go with him, because the house in Cadogan Place was dismantled for the summer. "I should regret this more," he said, "but that where two lives are so completely, so entirely united as ours are there ought to be the most absolute confidence on either side. Therefore, while I am away, I shall leave you my keys. Open my desk, read all my journals and letters, make yourself mistress of my whole life. Above all," he said, "there is one cupboard in my dressing-room which contains certain memorials of my past peculiarly sacred to me which I should like you to make yourself acquainted with."

The wife heard with concern of her husband's intended absence, but she was considerably buoyed up under the idea of the three days in which they were to be separated by the thought of the very interesting time she would have. She saw her husband off from the door, and as soon as she heard the wheels of his carriage die away in the distance, she clattered away as fast as she could upon her wooden leg to the dressing-room, and in a minute she was down on all fours before the cupboard he had described.

She unlocked the cupboard. It contained two shelves. On each shelf was a long parcel sewn up in canvas. She felt a tremor of horror as she looked at them, she did not know why. She lifted down the first parcel, and it had a label on the outside. She trembled so she could scarcely read it. It was inscribed: "In memory of my dear wife, Elizabeth Anne, who died on the 24th of August, 1864".

With quivering fingers, she sought for a pair of scissors, and ripped open the canvas, and it contained—a wooden leg!

With indescribable horror, she lifted down the other parcel, of the same form and size. It also bore a label: "In memory of my dearest wife, Wilhelmine, who died on the 6th of March, 1869", and it contained —another wooden leg!

Instantly she rose from her knees. "It is evident," she said, "that I am married to a Bluebeard—a monster, who *collects* wooden legs. This is not the time for sentiment. This is the time for action." And she swept her jewels and some miniatures that she had into a handbag, and she clattered away on her own wooden leg, by the back shrubberies, to the high-road—and there she saw the butcher's cart passing, and she hailed it, and was driven by the butcher to the nearest station, where she just caught the next train to London, intending to make good her escape that night to France, and to leave no trace behind her.

But she had not consulted Bradshaw, and she found she had some hours to wait in London before the tidal train started. Then she could not resist employing them in going to reproach the people at whose house she had met her husband, and she told them what she had found. To her amazement, they were not the least surprised. "Yes," they said, "yes, we thought he ought to have told you: we do not wonder you were astonished. Yes, indeed, we knew dear Elizabeth Anne very well;

she was indeed a most delightful person, the most perfect of women and of wives; and when she was taken away, the whole light seemed blotted out of Arthur's life, the change was so very terrible. We thought he would never rally his spirits again; but then after two years he met dearest Wilhelmine, to whom he was first attracted by her having the same affliction which was characteristic of her predecessor. And Wilhelmine was perhaps even more a charming person than Elizabeth Anne, and made her husband's life uncloudedly happy. But she too, was alas! early snatched away, and then it was as if the whole world was cut from under Arthur's feet, until at last he met you, with the same peculiarity which was endeared to him by two lost and loved ones, and we believe that with you he has been more entirely, more uncloudedly happy than he was with either Wilhelmine or Elizabeth Anne."

And the wife was so charmed by what she heard that it gave quite a new aspect to affairs. She went home by the next train. She was there when her husband returned; and ever since they have lived perfectly happily between his house in the country and hers in Cadogan Place.

¶ Mrs de Bunsen (who told this story to A. H.) said that a cousin of hers was repeating this story when dining at the Balfours'. Suddenly he saw that his host and hostess were both telegraphing frantic signals to him, and by a great effort he turned it off. The lady of the wooden leg and her husband were both amongst the guests.

This story begins like a kind of echo of Type 312 (Bluebeard). It is indeed a kind of Bluebeard in reverse, in which the lady is given the keys of the hidden chamber, and expressly told to explore it. It is not surprising that so strange a predilection should have no motif attached to it.